# UNRAVELING ENVIRONMENTAL DISASTERS

# UNRAVELING ENVIRONMENTAL DISASTERS

DANIEL A. VALLERO, PhD,
*Duke University, Pratt School of Engineering, Durham, NC, USA*

TREVOR M. LETCHER, MSc(Natal), PhD(Natal), BEd(Natal), FRSC,
*Emeritus Professor, School of Chemistry, University of KwaZulu-Natal, Durban, South Africa*

Amsterdam • Boston • Heidelberg • London • New York • Oxford
ELSEVIER  Paris • San Diego • San Francisco • Sydney • Tokyo

Elsevier
225 Wyman Street, Waltham, MA 02451, USA
The Boulevard, Langford Lane, Kidlington, Oxford OX5 1GB, UK
Radarweg 29, PO Box 211, 1000 AE Amsterdam, The Netherlands

---

### Notice

No responsibility is assumed by the publisher for any injury and/or damage to persons or property as a matter of products liability, negligence or otherwise, or from any use or operation of any methods, products, instructions or ideas contained in the material herein. Because of rapid advances in the medical sciences, in particular, independent verification of diagnoses and drug dosages should be made

---

**Library of Congress Cataloging-in-Publication Data**
Vallero, Daniel A.
  Unraveling environmental disasters / Daniel Vallero, Trevor Letcher.
    p. cm.
  Includes bibliographical references and index.
  ISBN 978-0-12-397026-8
1. Environmental disasters.   I. Letcher, T. M. (Trevor M.)   II. Title.
  GE146.V45 2012
  363.7–dc23

2012019373

**British Library Cataloguing in Publication Data**
A catalogue record for this book is available from the British Library

ISBN: 978-0-12-397026-8

For information on all **Elsevier** publications
visit our web site at store.elsevier.com

Printed and bound in China

12  13  14  15    10  9  8  7  6  5  4  3  2  1

# Contents

# Preface

We often know a disaster when we see one, but there is little consensus on the precise meaning of a disaster. Indeed, there are many definitions of "disaster." Scientists generally loathe ambiguity in trying to explain physical phenomena. They try to be objective. To do so, they need a common naming technique. This taxonomy is a first step in describing and then characterizing phenomena. The next step is ontology, that is, how do all of these phenomena relate to each other?

When exploring the possibility of writing a book on environmental disasters, we asked a number of engineering and science leaders to provide their operational definition of a disaster. The definitions ranged in emphasis. Most agree that disasters are low-probability events with high-value consequences. Furthermore, problems become disasters when risks that are not properly managed result in significant physical damage to human life, ecosystems, and materials. Most engineering managers would also concur that substantial financial losses accompany most disasters. Certainly, there are also psychological and sociological aspects of a disaster.

Explaining a disaster calls for attention to the anthropogenic aspects of a disaster, i.e., a negative health or economic consequence as a result of human decisions. According to one respondent, this even includes so-called natural disasters. For example, "if humans avoided building on fault lines, the world would not experience earthquake-generated disasters." By extension, then, if humans avoided building on flood plains and other hydrologically inappropriate areas, flooding would not cause disasters. In other words, environmental phenomena occur within observable and expected ranges. The environment provides constraints and opportunities for disasters. It is the failure of the engineer, the construction manager, developer, planner, and other leaders who did not properly account for an environmental vulnerability. Whereas such a definition is harsh and strident, it is certainly a warning that the engineer be constantly aware of the first ethical canon of the profession, i.e., to hold paramount the safety, health, and welfare of the public. This includes avoiding, preparing for, and responding to any event that threatens public health or the environment, not just the disasters. It holds true also for the engineer when designing a chemical plant to build in safeguards and to alert the owners of the plant and possibly those living near the plant of potential dangers that operating the plant might pose (one of the glaring failures of the Bhopal, India, disaster, where allowing people to live near the hazard greatly and tragically exacerbated the consequences).

Most of the respondents focused on the damage wrought as the distinction between a disaster and a lesser problem. This includes both human-induced (e.g., oil spill, nuclear release, toxic substance subsurface leak) and natural events (e.g., volcanic eruption, earthquake, tsunami). In addition to severity, a disaster has temporal thresholds. That is, an environmental disaster is one that causes long-term damage to the ecosystem and/or human population. For problems that may affect large numbers of people, large geographic areas, and/or which are irreversible, precaution is in order. This is the basis for factors of safety in engineering design, buffers in zoning and land use planning, and consideration of worst case scenarios when making policy.

The spatial and temporal scale of an event influences its disaster classification.[1] For example, we used the term "long term." Obviously, an ecosystem that is not sufficiently elastic or resilient will experience irreversible and long-term harm more easily than a diverse and elastic system. If the system includes the only habitat of a threatened or endangered species, even an assault that is relatively localized may still cross the damage threshold to be deemed a disaster since the species may be lost forever.

The backgrounds of this book's two authors indicate large diversity of terminology and ontology, even among similar scientific disciplines, regarding complex phenomena like disasters. Letcher is a thermodynamicist. As such, he is concerned about the first principles of physics and chemistry, especially those related to the relationships between mass and energy within systems. Systems may range in scale from molecular to the universe. To Letcher, a disaster is merely the outcome of processes and mechanisms involving energy and substances. His explanation of a disaster is an exposition of events that led to an unpleasant outcome. The science that underpins these causal chains and the possible next steps can be explained and, hopefully, lead to scientifically sound steps that may reduce the likelihood of these outcomes in the future. The good news is that Letcher and his fellow scientists have improved understanding of these underpinning, first principles of physics. The bad news is that all science is fraught with uncertainty and variability. Even a "small" error or omission can lead to wrong and fateful decisions. And, although one scenario may be sufficiently explained, it will vary in profound and subtle ways from all other scenarios. Such variability is what keeps scientists awake at night.

Vallero's expertise is engineering and, in particular, environmental engineering. As such, he is interested in applying those same principles of interest to Letcher, but within the context of the environment. Environments consist of both living and nonliving components, i.e., biotic and abiotic, respectively. Thus, like Letcher, he is concerned with thermodynamic systems, especially how energy and mass flows and is transformed and how the organisms are affected by such energy and material flows. Again, the first principles of physics must be understood and applied to environmental phenomena. However, the system ranges usually fall between the habitat of a microbe (e.g., bacterium or virus) and the planet (effect of changes in the atmosphere on large ecosystems). As such, environmental scientists and engineers consider disasters to be collective outcomes of changes in these systems. This means the kinds of disasters that keep these folks up at night are those that are possible or even impending (e.g., some scientists fear biome shifts due to climate change leading to food crises).

## OUR FOCUS

This book is intended to consider why a disaster occurred from a scientific perspective. We conceived on this book when we coedited *Waste: A Handbook for Management* (ISBN: 978-0-12-381475-3), 2011. It has become apparent to us that much is omitted in the popular press when describing a disaster and its causes. Indeed, much is also missing in scientific writings, often because disasters are seen through the lenses of whatever scientific training we have received. Thus, we have endeavored to consider factors other than what we ordinarily might have (e.g., not only the thermodynamic aspects of a fire or explosion, but other contingencies that led up to that particular event). We have strived to look at these disasters in a systematic sense.

This could have been and in some ways is the second edition of Vallero's 2005 book, *Paradigms Lost: Learning from Environmental Mistakes, Mishaps and Misdeeds* (ISBN: 0750678887). It included explanations of environmental failures, including a number of the disasters in this book. However, the primary focus was on miscues that led to these failures.

*Unraveling Disasters* goes further. Certainly, we have included disasters that have occurred since 2005, notably Hurricane Katrina, Deepwater Horizon oil spill in the Gulf of Mexico, and the meltdown at Fukushima, Japan, following the earthquake and tsunami. We go beyond just describing the events and discuss where things went wrong. And, we look for lessons that need to be heeded so that we can make similar events rarer and, when they do occur, less devastating. The question is, "after reading this book, can one predict disasters?" If the explanations and lessons shared in this book are not heeded, then, unfortunately, it would indeed be possible to predict areas where and why these accidents happened. For example, lack of good housekeeping in a flour mill could lead to a dust explosion and unenforced safety procedures in a chemical factory producing toxic chemicals could result in a serious accident. More optimistically, however, we hope that some of the lessons learned will prevent and lessen

the effects of what would have been disasters.

We structured this book into 17 chapters, all interrelated, but which can be used independently: Failure, Science, Explosions, Plumes, Leaks, Spills, Fires, Climate, Nature, Minerals, Recalcitrance, Radiation, Invasions, Products, Unsustainability, Society, and Future. We include solutions and recommendations throughout, along with a summary in Chapter 17 of actions that could make a difference in responding to and preventing future environmental disasters. The book can be read from cover to cover or cherry-picked, choosing the chapter that concerns a particular reader the most.

The book is illustrated with images, graphs, tables and photographs that assist in interpreting the wealth of data related to public health and environmental and societal aspects of disasters. The International System of Units has been used throughout, but where appropriate, other units have been included in parentheses.

This book describes and discusses most of the important environmental disasters that have occurred over the past 50 years. Anyone involved in teaching or working in the main sciences of physics, chemistry, and biology or in the applied sciences, including engineering, design, planning, and homeland security should read the book to become acquainted with these very important issues.

Finally, we have written this book to be useful not only as a textbook and reference for environmental science and engineering courses and practitioners but also as a readable exposé for a wider audience. This can include students and faculty from other scientific and engineering departments (e.g., chemistry, biology, chemical engineering), especially those who consider failure and disasters. Moreover, the book is aimed at a worldwide audience. This is not a "First World" treatise on disasters but a reference book and set of guidelines for all, and that most certainly includes scientists, engineers, and interested people from the developing world, who are often at the center of these disasters and who have suffered greatly. It is also a book that should be read by law makers, parliamentarians, representatives, corporate decision makers, nongovernmental organization members, and others who drive policies and inform the public about what can be done to reduce accidents and to prevent disasters. We also hope that the book will interest other motivated readers from within and outside academia and the environmental professions.

We began this book as a conversation between two colleagues who are mutually interested in environmental disasters. The conversation that ensued caused us to be both frustrated and motivated. Our frustration stems from the amount of ignorance and avoidance of scientific credibility in many of the mistakes, mishaps, and misdeeds that have led to disasters. We were frustrated also by the willful neglect of sound science in key decisions about siting, hazards, and early warnings.

The conversation also motivated us to try to record and evaluate disasters scientifically and objectively. We hope we have been successful but are well aware that science is never entirely sufficient in failure analysis and is even more uncertain in predicting future events. We hope we have added a rung or two to the ladder of knowledge as it pertains to protecting future populations and ecosystems.

*Daniel Vallero and Trevor Letcher*

## Reference

1. Resnik DB, Vallero DA. Geoengineering: an idea whose time has come? *J Earth Sci Clim Change* 2011; S1:001 doi:10.4172/2157-7617.S1-001.

# 1

# Failure

A common feature of all environmental disasters is that they have a cause-effect component. Something happens and, as a result, harm follows. The "something" can be described an event, but more often as a series of events. A slight change in one of the steps in this series can be the difference between the *status quo* and a disaster. Such a series may occur immediately (e.g., someone forgetting to open a valve), or after some years (e.g., the corrosion of pipe), or may be the result of a series of events that occur over decades (buildup up of halocarbons in the stratosphere that destroy parts of the ozone layer).

The mass media and even the scientific communities often treat environmental disasters as "black swan events."[1] That is, even though we may observe a rare event, our scientific understanding argues that it does not exist. Obviously, the disasters occurred, so we need to characterize the events that led to them. Extending the metaphor, we as scientists cannot pretend that all swans are white, once we have observed a black swan. A solitary black swan or a unique disaster "undoes" the scientific underpinning that the disaster could not occur. That said, there must be a logic model that can be developed for every disaster and that model may be useful in predicting future disasters.

Some disasters result from mistakes, mishaps, or even misdeeds. Some are initiated from natural events; although as civilizations have developed, even natural events are affected greatly by human decisions and activities. For example, an earthquake or hurricane of equal magnitude would cause much less damage to the environment and human well-being 1000 years ago than today. There are exponentially more people, more structures, and more development in sensitive habitats now than then. This growth is commensurate with increased vulnerability.

Scientists and engineers apply established principles and concepts to solve problems (e.g., soil physics to build levees, chemistry to manufacture products, biology to adapt bacteria and fungi to treat wastes, and physics and biology to restore wetlands). We also use them as indicators of damage (e.g., physics to determine radiation dose, chemistry to measure water and air pollution, biology to assess habitat destruction using algal blooms, species diversity, and abundance of top predators and other so-called sentry species). Such scientific indicators can serve as our "canaries in the coal mine" to give us early warning about stresses to ecosystems and public health problems. Arguably most important, these physical, chemical, and biological indicators can be end points in themselves. We want just the right amount and types of electromagnetic radiation (e.g., visible light), but we want to prevent skin from exposure to other wavelengths (e.g., ultraviolet light). We want nitrogen and phosphorus for our crops, but must remove it from surface waters (eutrophication). We do not want to lose endangered species, but we want to eliminate pathogenic microbes.

Scientists strive to understand and add to the knowledge of nature.[2] Engineers have devoted entire lifetimes to ascertaining how a specific scientific or mathematical principle should be applied to a given event (e.g., why compound X evaporates more quickly, while compound Z under the same conditions remains on the surface). After we know why something does or does not occur, we can use it to prevent disasters (e.g., choosing the right materials and designing a ship hull correctly) as well as to respond to disasters after they occur. For example, compound X may not be as problematic in a spill as compound Z if the latter does not evaporate in a reasonable time, but compound X may be very dangerous if it is toxic and people nearby are breathing air that it has contaminated. Also, these factors drive the actions of first responders like the fire departments. The release of volatile compound X may call for an immediate evacuation of human beings; whereas a spill of compound Z may be a bigger problem for fish and wildlife (it stays in the ocean or lake and makes contact with plants and animals).

This is certainly one aspect of applying knowledge to protect human health and the environment, but is not nearly enough when it comes to disaster preparedness and response. Disaster characterization and prevention calls for extrapolation. Scientists develop and use models to go beyond limited measurements in time and space. They can also fill in the blanks between measurement locations (actually "interpolations"). So, they can assign values of important scientific features and extend the meaning. For example, if sound methods and appropriate statistics are applied appropriately, measuring the amount of crude oil on a small number of marine animals after a spill can be used to explain much about the extent of an oil spill's impact on whole populations of organisms being threatened or already harmed. Models can even predict how the environment will change with time (e.g., is the oil likely to be broken down by microbes and, if so, how fast?). Such prediction is often very complex and fraught with uncertainty. Missions of government agencies, such as the Office of Homeland Security, the U.S. Environmental Protection Agency, the Agency for Toxic Substances and Disease Registry, the National Institutes of Health, the Food and Drug Administration, and the U.S. Public Health Service, devote considerable effort in just getting the science right. Universities and research institutes are collectively adding to the knowledge base to improve the science and engineering that underpins the physical principles that underpin public health and environmental consequences from contaminants, whether these be intentional or by happenstance.

Beyond the physical sciences is the need to assess the "anthropogenic" factors that lead to a disaster. Scientists often use the term anthropogenic (*anthropo* denotes human and *genic* denotes origin) to distinguish human factors from natural or biological factors of an event, taking into account all of the factors that society imposes down to the things that drive an individual or group. For example, anthropogenic factors may include the factors that led to a ship captain's failure to control his ship properly. However, it must also include why the fail-safe mechanisms were not triggered. These failures are often driven by combinations of anthropogenic and physical factors, for example, a release valve may have rusted shut or the alarm's quartz mechanism failed because of a power outage, but there is also an arguably more important human failure in each. For example, one common theme in many disasters is that the safety procedures are often adequate in and of themselves, but the implementation of these procedures was insufficient. Often, failures have shown that the safety manuals and data sheets were properly written and available and contingency plans were adequate, but the workforce was not properly trained and inspectors failed in at least some crucial aspects of their jobs, leading to horrible consequences.

## EVENTS

Usually, the event itself or the environmental consequences of that event involve something hazardous being released into the environment (Figure 1.1). Such releases go by a number of names. In hazardous waste programs, such as the Leaking Underground Storage Tank program, contaminant intrusions into groundwater are called "leaks." In fact, underground tanks are often required to have leak detection systems and alarms. In solid waste programs, such as landfill regulations, the intrusion may go by the name "leachate." Landfills often are required to have leachate collection systems to protect adjacent aquifers and surface waters. Spills are generally liquid releases that occur suddenly, such as an oil spill. Air releases that occur suddenly are called leaks, such as chlorine ($Cl_2$) or natural gas leak. For clarity, this book considers such air releases to be "plumes."

Thus, predicting or deconstructing a disaster is an exercise in contingencies. One thing leads to another. Any outcome is the result of a series of interconnected events. The outcome can be good, such as improved food supply or better air quality. The outcome can be bad, such as that of a natural or anthropogenic disaster (see Figure 1.2).

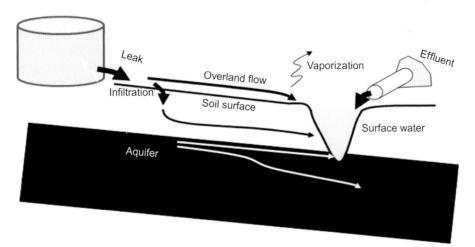

FIGURE 1.1   Contaminants from environmental releases may reach environmental compartments directly or indirectly. Pollutants from a leak may be direct to surface or ground water or indirect after flowing above or below the surface before reaching water or soil. They may even reach the atmosphere if they evaporate, and may subsequently contaminate surface and groundwater after deposition (e.g., from rain or on aerosols).

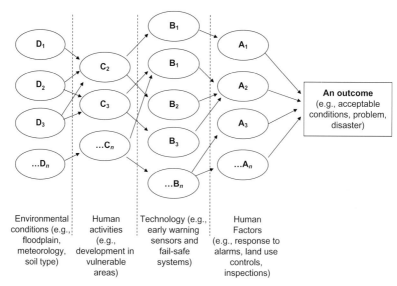

Environmental conditions (e.g., floodplain, meteorology, soil type) | Human activities (e.g., development in vulnerable areas) | Technology (e.g., early warning sensors and fail-safe systems) | Human Factors (e.g., response to alarms, land use controls, inspections)

FIGURE 1.2    Bayesian belief network showing interrelationships of events that may lead to a disaster. For example, if $D_1$ is a series of storm events that saturate soils, coupled with housing developments near floodplains and loss of water-bearing wetlands upstream, this could lead to a disaster. However, the disaster could be avoided, at least the likelihood of loss of life and property, with flood control systems and warning systems ($B_1$ and $B_2$). Further, if dikes and levees are properly inspected ($A_1$), the likelihood of disaster is lessened. Conversely, other contingencies of events would increase the likelihood and severity of a disaster [e.g., $D_3$ may be a 500-year storm; coupled with an additional human activity like additions of impervious pavement ($B_3$); coupled with failure of a dike ($C_3$); coupled with improper dike inspections ($D_4$)].

The general term for expected and unplanned environmental releases is just that, that is, "releases," such as those reported in the U.S. Environmental Protection Agency's Toxic Release Inventory (TRI).[3] This Web-based database contains data on releases of over 650 toxic chemicals from U.S. facilities. It also includes information on the way that these facilities manage those chemicals, for example, not merely treatment but also more proactive approaches like recycling and energy recover. The database is intended to inform local communities, by allowing them to prepare reports on the chemicals released in or near their communities (see Table 1.1).

## DISASTERS AS FAILURES

From a scientific and engineering perspective, disasters are failures, albeit very large ones. One thing fails. This failure leads to another failure. The failure cascade continues until it reaches catastrophic magnitude and extent. Some failures occur because of human error. Some because of human activities that make a system more vulnerable. Some failures occur in spite of valiant human interventions. Some are worsened by human ignorance. Some result

TABLE 1.1    Toxic Release Inventory Report for Los Angeles, CA, Zip Code (90222)

TRI on-site and off-site reported disposed of or otherwise released (in pounds), for all five facilities, for "facilities in all industries," for "all chemicals," "ZIP code 90222," in 2010. Note: 1 pound = 0.454 kg.

| Row # | Facility | TRIF ID | Total on-site disposal or other releases | Total off-site disposal or other releases | Total on- and off-site disposal or other releases |
|---|---|---|---|---|---|
| 1 | Cemex Compton Plant, 2722 N Alameda St, Compton, California 90222 (Los Angeles) | 90222CMXCN2722N | 0 | 10.9 | 10.9 |
| | Lead compounds | | 0 | 10.9 | 10.9 |
| 2 | DeMenno/Kerdoon Inc., 2000 N Alameda St, Compton, California 90222 (Los Angeles) | 90222DMNNK2000N | 176.59 | 64.25 | 240.84 |
| | 1,2,4-Trimethylbenzene | | 12.87 | | 12.87 |
| | Benzene | | 14.98 | 0.58 | 15.56 |
| | Cumene | | 1 | | 1 |
| | Ethylbenzene | | 13.73 | | 13.73 |
| | Ethylene glycol | | 10 | | 10 |
| | Lead | | 1.26 | 63.67 | 64.93 |
| | Naphthalene | | 2.42 | | 2.42 |
| | Toluene | | 62.64 | | 62.64 |
| | Xylene (mixed isomers) | | 57.69 | | 57.69 |
| 3 | Owens Corning Roofing & Asphalt LLC, 1505 N Tamarind Ave, Compton, California 90222 (Los Angeles) | 90224WNSCR1501N | 1.62 | 3.35 | 4.97 |
| | Benzo(g,h,i)perylene | | 0 | 0.5 | 0.5 |
| | Copper compounds | | | 0 | 0 |
| | Polycyclic aromatic compounds | | 1.62 | 2.85 | 4.47 |
| | Zinc compounds | | | 0 | 0 |
| 4 | S & K Plating Inc., 2727 N Compton Ave, Compton, California 90222 (Los Angeles) | 90222SKNDS2727N | 0 | | 0 |
| | Hydrochloric acid (1995 and after acid aerosols only) | | 0 | | 0 |

*Continued*

TABLE 1.1    Toxic Release Inventory Report for Los Angeles, CA, Zip Code (90222)—Cont'd

**TRI on-site and off-site reported disposed of or otherwise released (in pounds), for all five facilities, for "facilities in all industries," for "all chemicals," "ZIP code 90222," in 2010. Note: 1 pound = 0.454 kg.**

| Row # | Facility | TRIF ID | Total on-site disposal or other releases | Total off-site disposal or other releases | Total on- and off-site disposal or other releases |
|---|---|---|---|---|---|
| 5 | Thorock Metals Inc., 431 E Weber Ave, Compton, California 90222 (Los Angeles) | 90222THRCK431EW | 0 | 8 | 8 |
| | Copper | | 0 | 4 | 4 |
| | Lead | | 0 | 4 | 4 |
| | Total | 5 | 178.21 | 86.5 | 264.71 |

Reporting year (RY) 2010 is the most recent TRI data available. Facilities reporting to TRI were required to submit RY 2010 data to EPA by July 1, 2011. TRI Explorer is using the 2010 National Analysis data set (released to the public in October 2011). This data set includes revisions processed by EPA as of October 14, 2011 for the years 1988-2010. Revisions submitted to EPA after this time are not reflected in TRI Explorer reports.

Users of TRI information should be aware that TRI data reflect releases and other waste management activities of chemicals, not whether (or to what degree) the public has been exposed to those chemicals. Release estimates alone are not sufficient to determine exposure or to calculate potential adverse effects on human health and the environment. TRI data, in conjunction with other information, can be used as a starting point in evaluating exposures that may result from releases and other waste management activities which involve toxic chemicals. The determination of potential risk depends upon many factors, including the toxicity of the chemical, the fate of the chemical, and the amount and duration of human or other exposure to the chemical after it is released.

Off-site disposal or other releases include transfers sent to other TRI Facilities that reported the amount as on-site disposal or other release because not all states and/or not all industry sectors are included in this report.

For purposes of analysis, data reported as Range Code A are calculated using a value of 5 pounds (2.3 kg), Range Code B is calculated using a value of 250 pounds (114 kg) and Range Code C is calculated using a value of 750 pounds (340 kg).

The facility may have reported multiple NAICS codes to TRI in the current RY. See the facility profile report by clicking on the facility name to see a list of all NAICS codes submitted to TRI for the current reporting year.

*Source: U.S. Environmental Protection Agency. http://iaspub.epa.gov/triexplorer/release_fac?zipcode=90222&p_view=ZPFA&trilib=TRIQ1& sort=_VIEW_&sort_fmt=1&state=&city=&spc=&zipsrch=yes&chemical=All+chemicals&industry=ALL&year=2010&tab_rpt=1& fld=TRIID&fld=RELLBY&fld=TSFDSP; 2012 [accessed February 23, 2012].*

from hubris and lack of respect for the powers of nature. Some result from forces beyond the control of any engineering design, no matter the size and ingenuity.

Engineers and other scientists loathe failure. But, all designs fail at some point in time and under certain conditions. So what distinguishes failure from a design that has lasted through an acceptable life? And what distinguishes a disaster from any other failure? We will propose answers shortly. However, we cannot objectively and scientifically consider disasters without first defining our terms. In fact, one important rule of technical professions, particularly engineering and medicine, is that communications be clear.

## Reliability

Good engineering requires technical competence, of course. But, it also requires that the engineers be open and transparent. Every design must be scientifically sound and all assumptions clearly articulated. As such, engineers must be humble, since everything we design will fail. To help with this humility, the engineering profession incorporates a very important subdiscipline, reliability engineering. This field addresses the capacity of systems to perform within the defined constraints and conditions for a specific time period.

In most engineering applications, reliability is an expression of the extent to which a system will not fail prematurely. Reliability is the probability that something that is in operation at time 0 ($t_0$) will still be operating until the designed life (time $t = (t_t)$). As such, it is also a measure of the engineer's social accountability.

Unreliable systems range from simple nuisance, for example, needing to repaint your car, to catastrophic, for example, loss of life from a dam break. People using a product or living near a proposed facility want to know the systems will work and will not fail.

The probability of a failure per unit time is known as the "hazard" rate. Many engineers may recognize it as a "failure density," or $f(t)$. This is a function of the likelihood that an adverse outcome will occur, but note that it is not a function of the severity of the outcome. The $f(t)$ is not affected by whether the outcome is very severe (such as pancreatic cancer and loss of an entire species) or relatively benign (muscle soreness or minor leaf damage). The likelihood that something will fail at a given time interval can be found by integrating the hazard rate over a defined time interval:

$$P\{t_1 \leq T_f \leq t_2\} = \int_{t_1}^{t_2} f(t)\mathrm{d}t \qquad (1.1)$$

where $T_f$ = time of failure.

Thus, the reliability function $R(t)$, of a system at time $t$, is the cumulative probability that the system has not failed in the time interval from $t_0$ to $t_t$:

$$R(t) = P\{T_f \geq t\} = 1 - \int_0^t f(x)\mathrm{d}x \qquad (1.2)$$

Reliability can be improved by extending the time (increasing $t_t$), thereby making the system more resistant to failure. For example, proper engineering design of a landfill barrier can decrease the flow of contaminated water between the contents of the landfill and the surrounding aquifer, for example, a velocity of a few microns per decade. However, the barrier does not completely eliminate failure, that is, $R(t)=0$; it simply protracts the time before the failure occurs (increases $T_f$).

Equation (1.2) illustrates built-in vulnerabilities, such as unscientifically sound facility siting practices or the inclusion of inappropriate design criteria, for example, cheapest land. Such mistakes or malpractice shortens the time before a failure. Thus, reliability is also a term of efficiency. Failure to recognize these inefficiencies upfront leads to premature failures (e.g., loss of life, loss of property, law suits, and a public that has been ill-served).

Since risk is really the probability of failure (i.e., the probability that our system, process, or equipment will fail), risk and reliability are two sides of the same coin. The common graphical representation of engineering reliability is the so-called bathtub curve (Figure 1.3). The

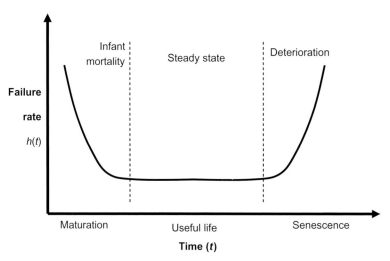

FIGURE 1.3    Prototypical reliability curve, that is, the bathtub distribution. The highest rates of failure, $h(t)$, occur during the early stages of adoption (infant mortality) and when the systems, processes, or equipment become obsolete or being to deteriorate. For well-designed systems, the steady-state period can be protracted, for example, decades. *Source: Vallero DA.* Paradigms lost: learning from environmental mistakes, mishaps, and misdeeds. *Burlington, MA: Butterworth-Heinemann; 2005.*

U-shape indicates that failure will more likely occur at the beginning (infant mortality) and near the end of the life of a system, process, or equipment. Actually, the curve indicates engineer's common proclivity to compartmentalize. We are tempted to believe that the process only begins after we are called on to design a solution. Indeed, failure can occur even before infancy. In fact, many problems in environmental justice occur during the planning and idea stage. A great idea may be shot down before it is born.

Engineers and scientists must properly communicate the meaning of reliability and any uncertainties. Full disclosure is simply an honest rendering of what is known and what is lacking for those listening to make informed decisions. Part of the uncertainty involves conveying the meaning; we must clearly communicate the potential risks. A word or phrase can be taken many ways. Engineers should liken themselves to physicians writing prescriptions. Be completely clear, otherwise confusion may result and lead to unintended, negative consequences.

That said, it important to keep in mind that the concept of safety is laden with value judgments. Thus, engineering decisions must rely on both sound science and quantifiable risk analysis.

## Failure Classification

Failure may occur in many forms and from many sources. A dam break or oil leak is an engineering failure, as is exposure to carcinogens in the air, water, and food. The former are examples more directly under the engineer's span of control, whereas the latter are indirect results of failures, that is, "second-order" engineering failures, if you will. A system that protects one group of people at the expense of another is a type of failure.

Failure varies in kind, degree, and extent. Human-induced or human-contributed disasters can result from mistakes, mishaps, and misdeeds. The terms all include the prefix "mis-" derived from Old English, "to miss." This type of failure applies to numerous ethical failures. However, the prefix "mis-" can connote that something is done "poorly," that is, a mistake. It may also mean that an act leads to an accident because the original expectations were overtaken by events, that is, a mishap. A mishap can occur as a result of not upholding the levels of technical competence called for by their field. Medical and engineering codes of ethics, for example, include tenets and principles related to competence, such as only working in one's area of competence or specialty. Finally, "mis-" can suggest that an act is immoral or ethically impermissible, that is, a misdeed. Interestingly, the theological derivation for the word "sin" (Greek: *hamartano*) means that when a person has missed the mark, that is, the goal of moral goodness and ethical uprightness, that person has sinned or has behaved immorally by failing to abide by an ethical principle, such as honesty and justice. Bioethical failures have come about by all three means. The lesson from Santayana is that we must learn from all of these past failures. Learning must be followed by new thinking and action, including the need to forsake what has not worked and shift toward what needs to be done.[4]

## TYPES OF FAILURE

Let us consider a few types familiar to engineers, particularly with regard to their likelihood of contributing to a disaster.

### Failure Type 1: Miscalculations

Sometimes scientists err due to their own miscalculations, such as when parentheses are not closed in computer code, leading to errors in predicting pharmacokinetic behavior of a drug. Some failures occur when engineers do not correctly estimate the corrosivity that occurs during sterilization of devices (e.g., not properly accounting for fatigue of materials resulting from high temperature and pressure of an autoclave). Such mistakes are completely avoidable if the physical sciences and mathematics are properly applied.

Disasters caused solely by miscalculations are rare, although there are instances where a miscalculation that was caught in the quality assurance/quality control (QA/QC) indeed prevented a failure, some potentially disastrous.[5] An illustrative engineering, but not an environmental engineering, case involved William LeMessurier, a renowned structural engineer. He was a principal designer of the Citicorp Tower in Manhattan, NY. The Citicorp tower was constructed using LeMessurier's diagonal-bracing design, that made the building unusually light for its size completed in 1977.[6] This technique also unfortunately increased the building's tendency to sway in the wind, which was addressed by installing a tuned-mass damper (including a 400-tonne concrete block floated on pressurized oil bearings) at the top to combat the expected slight swaying. During construction, without apprising LeMessurier, contractors thought that welding was too expensive and decided instead to bolt the braces. When he became aware of the change, however, LeMessurier thought that the change posed no safety hazard. He changed his mind over the next month when new data indicated that the switch from welded joints compounded another danger with potentially catastrophic consequences.

When LeMessurier recalculated the safety factor taking account of the quartering winds and the actual construction of the building, he discovered that the tower, which he had intended to withstand a 1000-year storm, was actually vulnerable to a 16-year storm. This meant that the tower could fail under meteorological conditions common in New York on average every 16 years. Thus, the miscalculation completely eliminated the factor of safety. The disaster was averted after LeMessurier notified Citicorp executives, among others. Soon after the recalculation, he oversaw the installation of metal chevrons welded over the bolted joints of the superstructure to restore the original factor of structural safety.

Miscalculation can be difficult to distinguish from negligence, given that in both, competence is an element of best practice. As humans, however, we all make arithmetic errors. Certainly, the authors have miscalculated far too frequently during our careers. The distinguishing features deeming the miscalculation as unacceptable are the degree of carelessness and the extent and severity of consequences.

Even a small miscalculation is unacceptable if it has the potential of either large-scale or long-lived negative consequences. At any scale, if the miscalculation leads to any loss of life or substantial destruction of property, it violates the first canon on the engineering profession to hold paramount the public's safety, health, and welfare, articulated by the National Society of Professional Engineers[7]:

Engineers, in the fulfillment of their professional duties, shall hold paramount the safety, health, and welfare of the public. To emphasize this professional responsibility, the engineering code includes this same statement as the engineer's first rule of practice.

## Failure Type 2: Extraordinary Natural Circumstances

Failure can occur when factors of safety are exceeded due to extraordinary natural occurrences. Engineers can, with fair accuracy, predict the probability of failure due to natural forces like wind loads and they design the structures for some maximum loading, but these natural forces can be exceeded. Engineers design for an acceptably low probability of failure—not for 100% safety and zero risk. However, tolerances and design specifications must be defined as explicitly as possible.

The tolerances and factors of safety have to match the consequences. A failure rate of 1% may be acceptable for a household compost pile, but it is grossly inadequate for bioreactor performance. And, the failure rate of devices may spike up dramatically during an extreme natural event (e.g., power surges during storms). Equipment failure is but one of the factors that lead to uncontrolled environmental releases. Conditional probabilities of failure should be known. That way, back-up systems can be established in the event of extreme natural events, like hurricanes, earthquakes, and tornados. If appropriate, contingency planning and design considerations are factored into operations, the engineer's device may still fail, but the failure would be considered reasonable under the extreme circumstances.

# Failure Type 3: Critical Path

No engineer can predict all of the possible failure modes of every structure or other engineered device, and unforeseen situations can occur. A classical, microbial case is the Holy Cross College football team hepatitis outbreak in 1969.[8] A confluence of events occurred that resulted in water becoming contaminated when hepatitis virus entered a drinking water system. Modeling such a series of events would probably only happen in scenarios with relatively high risks associated agents and conditions that had previously led to an adverse outcome.

In this case, a water pipe connecting the college football field with the town passed through a golf course. Children had opened a water spigot on the golf course, splashed around in the pool they created, and apparently discharged hepatitis virus into the water. A low pressure was created in the pipe when a house caught on fire and water was pumped out of the water pipes. This low pressure sucked the hepatitis-contaminated water into the water pipe. The next morning the Holy Cross football team drank water from the contaminated water line and many came down with hepatitis. The case is memorable because it was so highly unlikely—a combination of circumstances that were impossible to predict. Nevertheless, the job of engineers is to do just that, to try to predict the unpredictable and thereby to protect the health, safety, and welfare of the public.

This is an example of how engineers can fail, but may not be blamed for the failure, since such a set of factors had not previously led to an adverse action. If the public or their peers agree that the synergies, antagonisms, and conditional probabilities of the outcome could not reasonably be predicted, the engineer is likely to be forgiven. However, if a reasonable person deems that a competent engineer should have predicted the outcome, the engineer is to that extent accountable.

Indeed, there is always a need to consider risks by analogy, especially when related to complex, biological systems. Many complex situations are so dynamic and multifaceted that there is never an exact precedent for the events and outcomes for any real-world scenario. For example, every bioremediation project will differ from every other such project, but there are analogous situations related to previous projects that can be applied to a particular project. Are the same strains of microbes being used? Are the physical conditions, such as soil texture, and biological conditions, such as microbial ecology and plant root systems, ambient temperatures, and daily season variabilities, similar to those in previous studies? Are structurally similar compounds being degraded? Are the volumes of wastes and concentrations similar?

There are numerous examples of ignoring analogies to previous situations that led to adverse outcomes. The tragic industrial accident at Bhopal, India, illustrates this type of engineering failure (see Chapter 3). Perhaps the biggest air pollution disaster of all time occurred in Bhopal in 1984 when a toxic cloud drifted over the city from the Union Carbide pesticide plant. This gas leak killed many people and permanently injured about tens of thousands more. Failure is often described as an outcome when not applying the science correctly (e.g., a mathematical error and an incorrect extrapolation of a physical principle). Another type of failure results from misjudgments of human systems. Bhopal had both.

The pesticide manufacturing plant in Bhopal demonstrates the chain of events that can lead to failure.[9,10] In fact, if one were to chart the Bhopal incident as a Bayesian belief network (Figure 1.2), it is very nearly a worst case scenario.

The plant, up to its closing, had produced the insecticides Sevin and Cararyl since 1969, using the intermediate product methyl isocyanate (MIC) in its gas phase. The MIC was produced by the reaction:

$$\text{(1.3)}$$

This process was highly cost-effective, involving only a single reaction step. The schematic of MIC processing at the Bhopal plant is shown in Figure 1.4.

MIC is highly water reactive (see Table 1.2), that is, it reacts violently with water, generating a very strong exothermic reaction that produces carbon dioxide ($CO_2$). When MIC vaporizes, it becomes a highly toxic gas that, when concentrated, is highly caustic and burns tissues. This can lead to scalding of nasal and throat passages, blinding, and loss of limbs, as well as death.

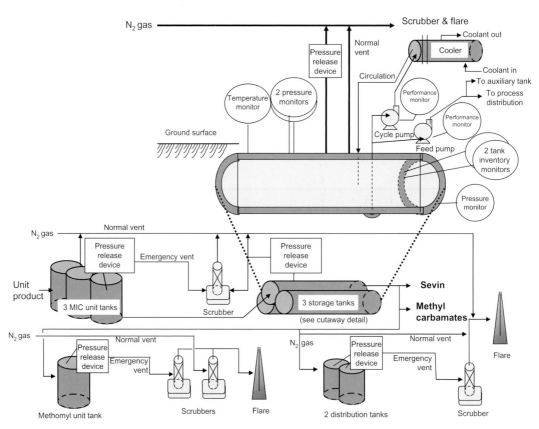

FIGURE 1.4    Schematic of methyl isocyanate processes at the Bhopal, India, plant (ca. 1984). *Source: Chem. Eng. News, February 11, 1985, 63(6), pp 27-33 by Ward Worthy.*

TABLE 1.2   Properties of Methyl Isocyanate (MIC)

| Common name | Isocyanic acid, methylester, and methyl carbylamine |
|---|---|
| Molecular mass | 57.1 |
| Properties | Melting point: $-45\,^{\circ}$C; boiling point: 43-45 $^{\circ}$C |
| | Volatile liquid |
| | Pungent odor |
| | Reacts violently with water and is highly flammable |
| | MIC vapor is denser than air and will collect and stay at low areas |
| | The vapor mixes well with air and explosive mixtures are formed |
| | May polymerize due to heating or under the influence of water and catalysts |
| | Decomposes on heating and produces toxic gases like hydrogen cyanide, nitrogen oxides, and carbon monoxide |
| Uses | Used in the production of synthetic rubber, adhesives, pesticides, and herbicide intermediates. It is also used for the conversion of aldoximes to nitriles |
| Side effects | MIC is extremely toxic by inhalation, ingestion, and skin absorption. Inhalation of MIC causes cough, dizziness, shortness of breath, sore throat, and unconsciousness. It is corrosive to the skin and eyes. Short-term exposures also lead to death or adverse effects like pulmonary edema (respiratory inflammation), bronchitis, bronchial pneumonia, and reproductive effects. The Occupational Safety and Health Administration's permissible exposure limit to MIC over a normal 8-h workday or a 40-h workweek is 0.05 mg m$^{-3}$ |

*Sources: U.S. Chemical Safety and Hazards Board. http://www.chemsafety.gov/lib/bhopal.0.1.htr; Chapman and Hall, Dictionary of organic chemistry, vol. 4, 5th ed. USA: Mack Printing Company; 1982; and Graham TW. Organic chemistry. 6th ed. Canada: John Wiley & Son, Inc.; 1996.*

On December 3, 1984, the Bhopal plant operators became concerned that a storage tank was showing signs of overheating and had begun to leak. The tank contained MIC. The leak rapidly increased in size, and within 1 h of the first leakage, the tank exploded and released approximately 80,000 lbs ($4 \times 10^4$ kg) of MIC into the atmosphere. The human exposure to MIC was widespread, with a half million people exposed. Nearly 3000 people died within the first few days after the exposure, 10,000 were permanently disabled. Ten years after the incident, thousands of death claims had been filed, along with 870,000 personal injury claims. However, only $90 million of the Union Carbide settlement agreement had been paid out.

The most basic physical science event tree begins with the water reactivity. That is, the combination of $H_2O$ and MIC resulted in a highly exothermic reaction. The rapid generation of the product of this reaction, $CO_2$, led to an explosive increase in pressure. The next step in the event tree was the release of 40 metric tons (tonnes) of MIC into the atmosphere. As of 2001, many victims had received compensation, averaging about $600 each, although some claims are still outstanding.

The Indian government had required that the plant be operated exclusively by Indian workers, so Union Carbide agreed to train them, including flying Indian workers to a sister plant in West Virginia for hands-on sessions. In addition, the company required that U.S.

engineering teams make periodic on-site inspections for safety and QC, but these ended in 1982, when the plant decided that these costs were too high. So, instead, the U.S. contingency was responsible only for budgetary and technical controls, but not safety. The last U.S. inspection in 1982 warned of many hazards, including a number that have since been implicated as contributing to the leak and release.

From 1982 to 1984, safety measures declined, attributed to high employee turnover, improper and inadequate training of new employees, and low technical savvy in the local workforce. On-the-job experiences were often substituted for reading and understanding safety manuals. (Remember, this was a pesticide plant.) In fact, workers would complain of typical acute symptoms of pesticide exposure, such as shortness of breath, chest pains, headaches, and vomiting, yet they would typically refuse to wear protective clothing and equipment. The refusal in part stemmed from the lack of air conditioning in this subtropical climate, where masks and gloves can be uncomfortable.

More lenient Indian standards than the U.S. safety standards, were generally applied at the plant after 1982. This likely contributed to overloaded MIC storage tanks (e.g., company manuals cite a maximum of 60% fill).

The release lasted about 2 h, after which the entire quantity of MIC had been released. The highly reactive MIC arguably could have reacted and become diluted beyond a certain safe distance. However, over the years, tens of thousands of squatters had taken up residence just outside of the plant property, hoping to find work or at least take advantage of the plant's water and electricity. The squatters were not notified of hazards and risks associated with the pesticide manufacturing operations, except by a local journalist who posted signs saying: "Poison Gas. Thousands of Workers and Millions of Citizens are in Danger."

This is a class instance of a "confluence of events" that led to a disaster. More than a few mistakes were made. The failure analysis found the following:

- The tank that initiated the disaster was 75% full of MIC at the outset.
- A standby overflow tank for the storage tank contained a large amount of MIC at the time of the incident.
- A required refrigeration unit for the tank was shut down 5 months prior to the incident, leading to a three- to fourfold increase in tank temperatures over expected temperatures.
- One report stated that a disgruntled employee unscrewed a pressure gauge and inserted a hose into the opening (knowing that it would do damage, but probably not nearly the scale of what occurred).
- A new employee was told by a supervisor to clean out connectors to the storage tanks, so the worker closed the valves properly, but did not insert safety discs to prevent the valves from leaking. In fact, the worker knew the valves were leaking, but they were the responsibility of the maintenance staff. Also the second-shift supervisor position had been eliminated.
- When the gauges started to show unsafe pressures, and even when the leaking gases started to sting mucous membranes of the workers, they found that evacuation exits were not available. There had been no emergency drills or evacuation plans.
- The primary fail-safe mechanism against leaks was a vent-gas scrubber, that is, normally, this release of MIC would have been sorbed and neutralized by sodium hydroxide (NaOH)

in the exhaust lines, but on the day of the disaster, the scrubbers were not working. (The scrubbers were deemed unnecessary, since they had never been needed before.)

- A flare tower to burn off any escaping gas that would bypass the scrubber was not operating because a section of conduit connecting the tower to the MIC storage tank was under repair.
- Workers attempted to mediate the release by spraying water 100 ft (31 m) high, but the release occurred at 120 ft (37 m).

Thus, according to the audit, many checks and balances were in place, but the cultural considerations were ignored or given low priority, such as, when the plant was sited, the need to recognize the differences in land use planning and buffer zones in India compared to Western nations, or the difference in training and oversight of personnel in safety programs.

In spite of a heightened awareness for years after the disaster, versions of the Bhopal incident have occurred and are likely to occur to smaller spatial extents and with, hopefully, more constrained impacts. For example, two freight trains collided in Graniteville, SC, just before 3:00 a.m. on January 6, 2005, resulting in the derailment of three tanker cars carrying $Cl_2$ gas and one tanker car carrying NaOH liquids. The highly toxic $Cl_2$ gas was released to the atmosphere. The wreck and gas release resulted in hundreds of injuries and eight deaths. Some of these events are the result of slightly different conditions not recognized as vulnerable or not considered similar to Bhopal. Others may have resulted or may result due to memory extinction. Even vary large and impactful disasters fade in memory with time. This is to be expected for the lay public, but is not acceptable to engineers.

Every engineer and environmental professional needs to recognize that much of their responsibility is affected by geopolitical realities and that we work in a global economy. This means that engineers must have a respect and appreciation for how cultures differ in their expectations of environmental quality. One cannot assume that a model that works in one setting will necessarily work in another without adjusting for differing expectations. Bhopal demonstrated the consequences of ignoring these realities. Chaos theory tells us that even very small variations in conditions can lead to dramatically different outcomes, some disastrous.

Dual use and bioterrorism fears can be seen as somewhat analogous to the lack of due diligence at Bhopal. For example, extra care is needed in using similar strains and species in genetically modified microbes (e.g., substantial differences and similarities in various strains of *Bacillus* spp.). The absence of a direct analogy does not preclude that even a slight change in conditions may elicit unexpected and unwanted outcomes (e.g., weapon-grade or resistant strains of bacteria and viruses).

Characterizing as many contingencies and possible outcomes in the critical path is an essential part of many biohazards. The Bhopal incident provides this lesson. For example, engineers working with bioreactors and genetically modified materials must consider all possible avenues of release. They must ensure that fail-safe mechanisms are in place and are operational. QA officers note that testing for an unlikely but potentially devastating event is difficult. Everyone in the decision chain must be "on board." The fact that no incidents have yet to occur (thankfully) means that no one really knows what will happen in such an event. That is why health and safety training is a critical part of the engineering process.

## Failure Type 4: Negligence

Engineers also have to protect the public from their members' own carelessness. The case of the woman trying to open a 2-l soda bottle by turning the aluminum cap the wrong way with a pipe wrench, and having the cap fly off into her eye, is a famous example of unpredictable ignorance. She sued for damages and won, with the jury agreeing that the design engineers should have foreseen such an occurrence. (The new plastic caps have interrupted threads that cannot be stripped by turning in the wrong direction.)

In the design of water treatment plants, engineers are taught to design the plants so that it is easy to do the right thing, and very difficult to do the wrong thing. Pipes are color-coded, valves that should not be opened or closed are locked, and walking distances to areas of high operator maintenance are minimized and protected. This is called making the treatment plant "operator proof." This is not a rap exclusively on operators. In fact, such standard operating procedures (SOPs) are crucial in any operation that involves repeated actions and a flow of activities. Hospitals, laboratories, factories, schools, and other institutions rely on SOPs. Examples include mismatched transplants due to mislabeled blood types and injuries due to improper warning labels on power equipment. When they are not followed, people's risks are increased. Biosystem engineers recognize that if something can be done incorrectly, sooner or later it will, and that it is their job to minimize such possibilities. That is, both risk and reliability are functions of time.

Risk is a function of time because it is a part of the exposure equation, that is, the more time one spends in contact with a substance, the greater is the exposure. In contrast, reliability is the extent to which something can be trusted. A system, process, or item is reliable so long as it performs the designed function under the specified conditions during a certain time period. In most engineering applications, reliability means that what we design will not fail prematurely. Or, stated more positively, reliability is the mathematical expression of success; that is, reliability is the probability that a system that is in operation at time 0 ($t_0$) will still be operating until the designed life (time $t=(t_t)$). As such, it is also a measure of the engineering accountability. People in neighborhoods near the facility want to know if it will work and will not fail. This is especially true for those facilities that may affect the environment, such as landfills and power plants. Likewise, when environmental cleanup is being proposed, people want to know how certain the engineers are that the cleanup will be successful.

As mentioned, time shows up again in the so-called *hazard rate*, that is, the probability of a failure per unit time. Hazard rate may be a familiar term in environmental risk assessments, but many engineers may recognize it as a *failure density*, or $f(t)$. This is a function of the likelihood that an adverse outcome will occur, but note that it is not a function of the severity of the outcome. The $f(t)$ is not affected by whether the outcome is very severe (such as pancreatic cancer and loss of an entire species) or relatively benign (muscle soreness or minor leaf damage). Recall that the likelihood that something will fail at a given time interval can be found by integrating the hazard rate over a defined time interval [Equation (1.1)] and that R(t) at time t is the cumulative probability that the system has not failed during time interval from $t_0$ to $t_t$ [Equation (1.2)].

Obsolescence, degradation and other failures over time remind us that engineers and planners must be humble, since everything we design will fail. We can improve reliability by extending the time (increasing $t_t$), thereby making the system more resistant to failure. For example, proper engineering design of a landfill barrier can decrease the flow of contaminated water between the contents of the landfill and the surrounding aquifer, for example, a velocity of a few microns per decade. However, the barrier does not completely eliminate failure, that is, $R(t) = 0$; it simply protracts the time before the failure occurs (increases $T_f$).

Hydraulics and hydrology provide very interesting case studies in the failure domains and ranges, particularly how absolute and universal measures of success and failure are almost impossible. For example, a levee or dam breach, such as the recent catastrophic failures in New Orleans during and in the wake of Hurricane Katrina, experienced failure when flow rates reached flows of cubic meters per second. Conversely, a hazardous waste landfill failure may be reached when flow across a barrier exceeds a few cubic centimeters per decade.

Thus, a disaster resulting from this type of failure is determined by temporal dimensions. If the outcome (e.g., polluting a drinking water supply) occurs in a day, it may well be deemed a disaster, but it the same level of pollution is reached in a decade, it may be deemed an environmental problem, but not a disaster. Of course, if this is one's only water supply, as soon as the problem is uncovered, it becomes a disaster to that person. In fact, it could be deemed worse than a sudden-onset disaster, since one realizes he or she has been exposed for a long time. This was the case for some of the infamous toxic disasters of the 1970s, notably the Love Canal incident.

Love Canal is an example of a cascade of failure. The eventual exposures of people to harmful remnant waste constituents resulted largely from a complicated series of events brought on by military, commercial, and civilian governmental decisions. The failures involved many public and private parties who shared the blame for the contamination of groundwater and exposure of humans to toxic substances. Some, possibly most, of these parties may have been ignorant of the possible chain of events that led to the chemical exposures and health effects in the neighborhoods surrounding the waste site. The decisions by governments, corporations, school boards, and individuals in totality led to a public health disaster. Some of these decisions were outright travesties and breaches of public trust. Others may have been innocently made in ignorance (or even benevolence, such as the attempt to build a school on donated land, which tragically led to the exposure of children to dangerous chemicals). But, the bottom line is that people were exposed to these substances. Cancer, reproductive toxicity, neurological disorders, and other health effects resulted from exposures, no matter the intent of the decision maker. As engineers, neither the public nor the attorneys and company shareholders accept ignorance as an excuse for designs and operations that lead to hazardous waste-related exposures and risks.

One particularly interesting event tree is that of the public school district's decisions on accepting the donation of land and building the school on the property (see Figure 1.5). As regulators and the scientific community learned more, a series of laws were passed and new court decisions and legal precedents established in the realm of toxic substances. Additional hazardous waste sites began to be identified, which continue to be listed on the EPA Website's National Priority Listing. They all occurred due to failures at various points along a critical path.

These failures resulted from unsound combinations of scientifically sound studies (risk assessment) and decisions on whether to pursue certain actions (risk management). Many of

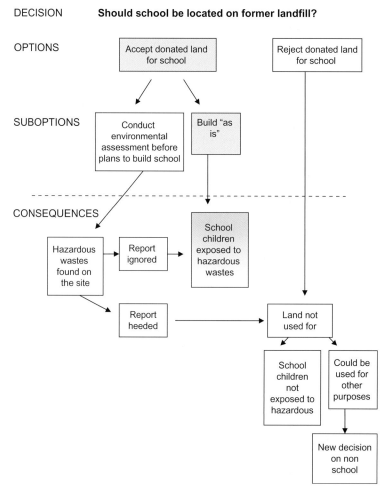

FIGURE 1.5    Event tree of school site decisions at Love Canal, NY. The gray boxes approximate the actual option, suboption, and consequence.

these disasters have been attributed in part to political and financial motivation, which were perceived to outweigh good science. This was a principal motivation for the National Academy of Science's recommendation that federal agencies separate the science (risk assessment) from the policy decisions (risk management). In fact, the final step of the risk assessment process was referred to as "characterization" to mean that "both quantitative and qualitative elements of risk analysis, and of the scientific uncertainties in it, should be fully captured by the risk manager."[11]

Whereas disclosure and labeling are absolutely necessary parts of reliability in engineering, they are wholly insufficient to prevent accidents. The Tylenol tampering incident occurred in spite of a product that, for its time, was well-labeled. A person tampered with the product, adding cyanide, which led to the deaths of seven people in Chicago in 1982. The company, Johnson & Johnson took some aggressive and expensive steps to counter what would have been the critical path. They eventually recalled 31 million bottles and pioneered innovations to tamper-resistant packaging. As a result after some large initial financial losses, the company completely recovered and avoided the business disaster many expected.[12]

Another example of a critical path failure occurred in the early 1970s, when jet-powered airliners were replacing propeller aircraft. The fueling system at airports was not altered, and the same trucks fueled both types of craft. The nozzle fittings for both types of fuels were therefore the same. A tragic accident occurred near Atlanta, where jet fuel was mistakenly loaded into a Martin 404 propeller craft. The engines failed on takeoff, resulting in fatalities. A similar accident occurred in 1974 in Botswana with a DC-4 and again near Fairbanks, Alaska, with a DC-6.[13] The fuel delivery systems had to be modified so that it was impossible to put jet fuel into a propeller-driven airplane and vice versa.

An example of how this can be done is the modification of the nozzles used in gasoline stations. The orifice in the unleaded gas tank is now too small to take the nozzles used for either leaded fuel or for diesel fuel. Drivers of diesel-engine cars can still mistakenly pump gasoline into their cars, however. By analogy, all engineers must recognize that no amount of signs or training could prevent such tragedies.

## Failure Type 5: Inaccurate Prediction of Contingencies

Every time something fails, whether a manufactured product (a medical implant) or a constructed facility (dam breaches), it is viewed as an engineering failure. Engineers historically have been called upon to predict the problems that can occur and to design so as to minimize these adverse outcomes, protecting people from design errors, natural forces, unforeseen events, and ignorance/carelessness.

For engineers, the concept of negligence (Failure Type 4) actually changed on September 11, 2001 with the attack on the United States by terrorists. The twenty-first century engineer is now expected to add a higher level of scrutiny and to be forward-thinking and proactive in designing ways to protect the health, safety, and welfare of the public from acts of intentional terrorism. It had not occurred to most engineers that they have a responsibility to protect people from those who would want to intentionally harm other people or to destroy public facilities intentionally. This is a totally new failure mode in engineering. Such failures can be considered to be "intentional accidents," or failures resulting from intentional actions.[14]

Engineers now find themselves in the position of having to address these "intentional accidents." Military engineers, of course, have had to design against such destructive actions since the days of moats and castles, but those were all structures built explicitly to withstand attack. Civilian engineers have never had to think in these terms, but are now asked to design structures for this contingency. Engineering and engineers have a new challenge—to prevent such "accidents" on civilian targets by terrorists bent on harm to the public.

## TYPES OF DISASTERS

Like anything else in science, a first step of studying disasters is to create a taxonomy. This allows scientists to apply various disciplines to increase the understanding of why disasters occur and how they may be prevented and how to ameliorate their effects.

### Sources of Disaster

A primary distinction among disasters is their source. The first classification is whether they are natural or anthropogenic. That is, do they occur naturally or are they principally the result of human actions and activities?

A few prominent sources of natural disaster are

1. Volcanic activity;
2. Severe meteorological[a] events, such as weather patterns leading to ship wrecks, plane crashes, and other disasters;
3. Epidemics, pandemics, and other health episodes (e.g., increased occurrence of birth defects or cancer from chemical releases or radiation; new strains of pathogens like the E. coli outbreak mentioned earlier or virulent strains of viruses like the influenza pandemic in the early part of the twentieth century); and
4. Planetary scale disasters, such as changes in the sun's activities like solar flares, could lead to changes in the earth's electromagnetic field.

Sources of anthropogenic disasters include

1. Large-scale releases of oil during exploration;
2. Mining accidents (e.g., loss of life due to cave-ins and collapses; loss of property and ecological damage due to release of slag and other mining residues);
3. Collapse of fish stocks and fish kills when streams receive large amounts of nutrients or toxins;
4. Fossil fuel combustion leading to $CO_2$ in the atmosphere;
5. Rain forest degradation from slash and burn activities and encroachment;
6. Structural failure, including dam, bridge, and infrastructural design and/or maintenance problems, as well as structural failures leading to chemical explosions, asbestos exposures, and radiation releases;
7. Direct environmental pollution such as particulates, ozone, hydrocarbons, and metal compounds in the air, large-scale releases of global greenhouse gases (e.g., chlorofluorocarbons, methane, $CO_2$) and water pollution of sea, rivers, and lakes;
8. Warfare and terrorism (such as the loss of life in the attack on the World Trade Center; environmental devastation due to the Kuwait oil fires, and H-bomb explosions over Nagasaki and Hiroshima); and

[a] Note that meteorology is distinguished from climatology. Some would consider meteorological events to be short lived (hours or days), such as tornadoes, hurricanes, and blizzards. Climatological events are often measured in time increments (decades or centuries), such as long-term warming and cooling cycles, where "disasters" like ice cap melting or shifting biomes occur gradually.

**9.** Well-intended but error-prone decisions at chemical and nuclear plants, at sea (Titanic disaster), in the air (plane crashes), misuse of pesticides and other chemicals, and improper use of antibiotics (e.g., in animal feeding operations, leading to resistant strains mentioned of pathogens).

Of course, most of these are interrelated. For example, a natural event such as a large storm may only have become a disaster due to human change, such as building levees upstream that increased the flow of water to the disaster area rather than flowing overland upstream.

## Disasters from a Societal Perspective

We recently polled some very smart people: engineers, scientists, policy makers, researchers, and educators regarding their definitions of a disaster. One common theme is that a disaster varies from some norm, not just which it is abnormal, but is outside the bounds of expectation. Scientists usually take care to describe a "norm." For example, a disaster is an event that occurs beyond so many standard deviations from the mean of similar events. In addition, the disaster must reach some level of adversity. For example, the loss of a single wetland due to a dam breakage may not be considered a disaster, whereas if that same dam breach destroys a town, it would be a disaster.

The forgoing example also indicates that disasters are subjective and value-laden. For example, if an endangered species' only habitat were that wetland lost in the breach, most ecologists and many people would deem that event to be a disaster. Thus, the process by which one decides on whether an adverse event is a disaster depends on societal values. That is, the same process under one condition can be a benefit, whereas the same process under a different condition is harmful. Interestingly, in this case, the release is not all that different from intentional activities, like applying pesticides (see Figure 1.6). The similarities between the events that may lead to an environmental disaster and those that may lead to a successful environmental treatment and cleanup may simply involve a slight change to one step in a long series. In fact, it is not the act of release (escape, if it is unintended) that renders the chain of events as deleterious or beneficial. Rather, it is the interrelationships and contingencies of the system in its entirety. Although the critical path seldom ends at the final steps shown in Figure 1.7, the process and its consequences will continue in time and space.

This goes beyond chemical disasters. For example, one of the major concerns about biotechnology is the possible release of genetically engineered organisms and attendant materials into the environment from biotechnological operations.[15] In the case of a deleterious effect in Figure 1.7A, additional impacts can ensue, such as if the released microbes change biodiversity, which in turn drifts into standing agricultural crops and damages the food supply. Or, if the deleterious effect of the microbial release is a virulent form of a bacterium, which not only causes a health effect from those who consume contaminated drinking water, but which may lead to cross-resistant pathogens, so that existing antibiotics become less effective in treating numerous other diseases.

Even a successful project, such as that shown in Figure 1.7B, can experience other unexpected events that occur after the specific success. For example, genetically modified bacteria have been widely and successfully used to degrade oil spills. If the bacteria, which have a

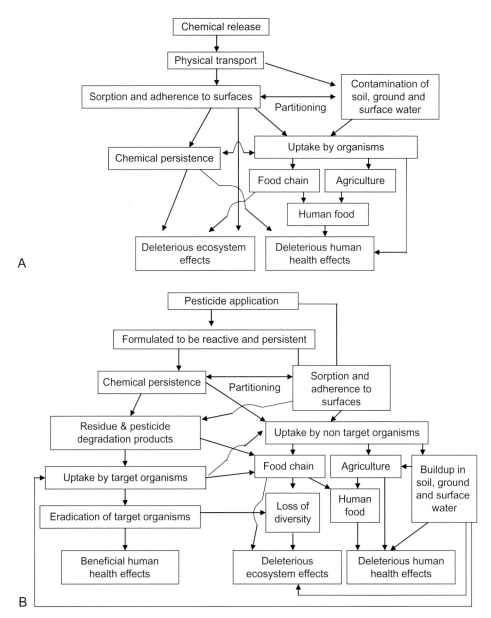

FIGURE 1.6    Critical paths of a chemical disaster scenario (A) versus a public health pesticide application scenario (B). In both scenarios, a chemical compound is released into the environment. The principal difference is that the effects in (A) are unwanted and deleterious, whereas the left side of (B) shows effects that are desired and beneficial, which can be eradication of a vector (e.g., mosquito) that carries disease (e.g., malaria). The same critical path can be applied to herbicides for weed control, rodenticides for rodents that carry disease, and fungicides for prevention of crop damage. The right side of (B) is quite similar to the chemical disaster scenario in (A); that is, the pesticide that would be useful in one scenario is simply a chemical contaminant in another. Examples include pesticide spills (e.g., in dicofol in Lake Apopka, Florida), or more subtle scenarios, such as the buildup of persistent pesticides in sediment for years or decades. *Source: Ref. 4.*

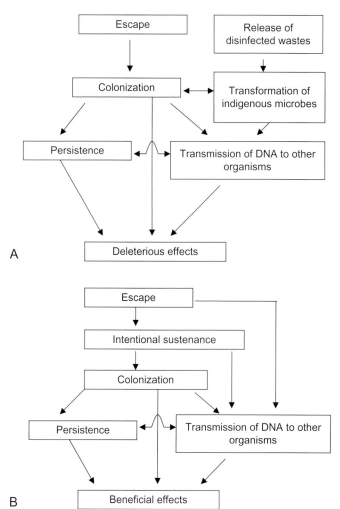

FIGURE 1.7 Critical paths of a microbial disaster scenario (A) versus a bioremediation success scenario (B). In both scenarios, a microbial population (either genetically modified or nongenetically modified) is released into the environment. The principal difference is that the effects in (A) are unwanted and deleterious, whereas the effects in (B) are desired and beneficial. *Source: Ref. 4.*

propensity to breakdown hydrocarbons, do not stop at the spill, but begin to degrade asphalt roads (i.e., the "bugs" do not distinguish between the preferred electron acceptors and donors in an oil spill or asphalt), this is a downstream, negative impact of a successful bioremediation effort (see Figure 1.8). Further, if the microbes do not follow the usual script, where the next generation are completely sterile, but are able to reproduce and become part of the formerly exclusively natural microbial species, the traits of the population may be altered in unknown ways.

The uncertainties and complexities also indicate that controlling and managing potential agents of disaster will often call for risk trade-offs. Every scenario has risks. Even the decision not to take any action has contravening risks. Let us consider a widespread and slow onset disaster, the exposure of millions of people to persistent organic pollutants (POPs). These

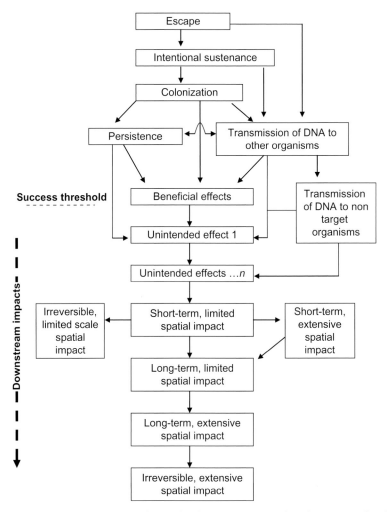

FIGURE 1.8   Same scenario as Figure 1.7A, but with subsequent or coincidental, unexpected and unremediated events, leading to downstream, environmental or public health impacts. *Source: Ref. 4.*

chemicals all had some valuable attribute demanded by society, such as disease control (1,1,1-trichloro-2,2-bis-(4-chlorophenyl)-ethane, best known as DDT), food supply (aldrin, dieldrin, hexachlorobenzene), and delivering electricity thousands of miles from power plants, enabling broadened access to rural areas (polychlorinated biphenyls, PCBs). Unfortunately, all of these benefits met with contravening risks.

Differences of opinion regarding the benefits of DDT, for example, centered around environmental and public health risks versus the commercial and agricultural need to kill crop-destroying and disease carrying insects. Even after bans in Canada and the United States, people may still be exposed by importing food that has been grown where these pesticides are not banned. In fact, Western nations may have continued to allow the pesticides be formulated at home, but would not allow their application and use. But in the long-run (short-term and long-term, extensive spatial impact boxes in Figure 1.8), the pesticide comes back in the important products treated with the domestically banned pesticide. This is known as the "circle of poisons." Later, the disputes had to do with fairness. Should more developed countries benefit from the use of pesticides they do not allow to be applied in their own country? And, even if they do not benefit, should there not be a universal ban against harmful chemicals?

Does this analogy hold for disasters? Indeed, it does. Consider Hurricane Katrina. Allowing the building of roads, homes, and other structures in a sensitive ecosystem provided localized benefits, but ignored the laws of nature. It was merely a matter of time, in the opinion of many earth scientists and hydrologists, before the Mississippi River reclaimed its flood plain. The complexity of the riverine system was not respected. The land use was treated as a series of simple, reductionist actions, rather than as a complex system.

Simply banning something does not necessarily solve a problem. Or, it may solve one problem (e.g., removing a harmful chemical from the marketplace) and exacerbate another (e.g., removing the same chemical from the market, but also removing the benefits it provides). This can be considered a "risks versus risk" conundrum. In other words, it is not simply a matter of taking an action, for example, banning worldwide use of DDT, which leads to many benefits, for example, less eggshell thinning of endangered birds and less cases of cancer. No, it sometimes comes down to trading off one risk for another. Since there are yet to be reliable substitutes for DDT in treating disease-bearing insects, policy makers must decide between ecological and wildlife risks and human disease risk. Also, since DDT has been linked to some chronic effects like cancer and endocrine disruption, how can these be balanced against expected increases in deaths from malaria and other diseases where DDT is part of the strategy for reducing outbreaks? Is it appropriate for economically developed nations to push for restrictions and bans on products that can cause major problems in the health of people living in developing countries? Some have even accused Western nations of "eco-imperialism" when they attempt to foist temperate climate solutions onto tropical, developing countries. That is, developed nations place a higher priority and export fixes based upon one set of values (anticancer, ecological) that are of lower priority and incongruent with another set of values of other cultures. Notably, developing nations may give primacy to acute diseases over chronic effects, for example, thousands of cases of malaria are more important to some than a few cases of cancer. Certainly, immediate threats to human life from vector-borne diseases are more important than threats to the bald eagle from a global reservoir of persistent pesticides.

Finding substitutes for chemicals that work well on target pests can be very difficult. This is the case for DDT. In fact, the chemicals that have been formulated to replace have either been found to be more dangers, for example, aldrin and dieldrin (which have also been subsequently banned) or much less effective in the developing world (e.g., pyrethroids). For example, spraying DDT in huts in tropical and subtropical environments, fewer mosquitoes are found compared to untreated huts. This likely has much to do with the persistence of DDT in mud structures compared to the higher chemical reactivity of pyrethroid pesticides.

The POPs provide abundant lessons about risk trade-offs. First, the engineer must ensure that recommendations are based upon sound science. While seemingly obvious, this lesson is seldom easy to put into practice. Sound science can be trumped by perceived risk, such as when a chemical with an ominous sounding name is uncovered in a community, leading the neighbors to call for its removal. However, the toxicity may belie the name. The chemical may have very low acute toxicity, has never been associated with cancer in any animal or human studies, and is not regulated by any agency. This hardly allays the neighbors' fears. The engineer's job is not done by declaring that removal of the chemical is not necessary, even though the declaration is absolutely right. The community deserves clear and understandable information before we can expect any capitulation.

Second, removal and remediation efforts are never entirely risk-free. To some extent, they always represent risk shifting in time and space. A spike in exposures is possible during the early stages of removal and treatment, as the chemical may have been in a place and in a form that made it less available until actions were taken. Due, in part, to this initial exposure, the concept of "natural attenuation" has recently gained greater acceptance within the environmental community. However, the engineer should expect some resistance from the local community when they are informed that the best solution is to do little or nothing but to allow nature (i.e., indigenous microbes) take its course (doing nothing could be interpreted as intellectual laziness!).

Third, the mathematics of benefits and costs is inexact. Finding the best engineering solution is seldom captured with a benefit/cost ratio. Opportunity costs and risks are associated with taking no action (e.g., the recent Hurricane Katrina disaster presents an opportunity to save valuable wetlands and to enhance a shoreline by *not developing and not rebuilding* major portions of the gulf region). The costs in time and money are not the only reasons for avoiding an environmental action. Constructing the new wetland or adding sand to the shoreline could inadvertently attract tourists and other users who could end up presenting new and greater threats to the community's environment.

Figures 1.5–1.7 illustrate the complexity of biological systems is complex. The interactions, modes of action, and mechanistic behaviors are incompletely and poorly understood. Much of what we know about biology at the subcellular level is more empirical and descriptive than foundational and predictive. Thus, there are so many uncertainties about these processes that even a seemingly small change ("tweaking") of any part of the genomic system can induce unexpected consequences.[16] Some have likened the need for a life cycle view and the need for humility under such uncertainty. It is much easier to view the consequences of a decision as an independent event. In fact, few decisions are independent. They are affected by and affect other components of a system. We shall consider this when we discuss life cycles in the next chapter.

## SYSTEMS ENGINEERING

Disasters result from a sequence and mix of events. Thus, understanding them requires a systematic view articulated by process engineering analyses, including articulation of the assumptions, needs, goals, and underpinning science that led to actions. Chemical engineers are familiar with process engineering, since the processes that most often cited are chemical plant design, operation, control, and optimization. However, this systematic mindset can be quite valuable to disasters. A scientific investigation must consider which actions that contributed to the prevention, mitigation, exacerbated, or caused a particular disaster. Likewise, proactive disaster prevention and planning must consider the potential of intended and unintended consequences, by-products, and ancillary costs and benefits.

## Seveso Plant Disaster

The event that is associated with a disaster is actually the consequence of many contributing events. This is demonstrated by the complexities of intertwined factors to the explosion of a chemical processing facility in Seveso, Italy.

Like Bhopal, the event in Seveso was a toxic cloud that threatened public safety.[b] It was indeed a harbinger of the toxic scares that paved the way for new environmental legislation around the world calling for programs to address toxic and hazardous substances. It was among the first industrial disasters that brought to the forefront the possibility of chemical exposure and risk to millions of people were living near industrial facilities. As a result, many countries promulgated so-called community right-to-know laws that have since emerged. However, from a systems engineering perspective, Seveso represents a teachable moment beyond the event itself in terms of complex and subtle cascades of contributing events, the need for indicators of exposures and risks, and how to apply these systems engineering lessons to future events (and even preventing them completely).

On July 10, 1976, an explosion at a 2,4,5-trichlorophenol (2,4,5-T) reactor at the Seveso Industrie Chimiche Meda Societa, Anonima (ICMSA) manufacturing plant resulted in the highest concentrations of the most toxic chlorinated dioxin (TCDD) levels known in human residential populations.[17] Up to 30 kg of TCDD was deposited over the surrounding area of approximately 18 km$^2$. To put this amount in perspective, scientists usually are worried about dioxin, and especially TCDD, if a gram or less is released in a year, whereas this explosion released 30,000 g of TCDD instantaneously.

The ICMSA was an Italian subsidiary of the Swiss company, Givaudan, which happened to be owned by another Swiss company, Hoffman-LaRoche.[18] A ruptured disc on a batch plant caused the explosion. The pesticide 2.4,5-T was formulated from 1,2,4,5-tetrachlorobenzene and caustic soda (NaOH), in the presence of ethylene glycol (see Figure 1.9). Normally, only a few molecules of dioxins form from trillions of molecules of the batch. In this instance, however, reactor temperatures rose beyond the tolerances, leading to a "runaway reaction," bursting the disc. As a result, it is likely that large amounts of hydrogen gas ($H_2$) formed, which propelled the six tons of fluid from the reactor into the lower atmosphere, from which it was deposited over the Seveso region.

As appalling as it was, Seveso was not really a worst case. Upon hearing the noise being made at the beginning of the release, a plant foreman opened a valve to release cooling waters onto the heating coils of the reactor. This action likely reduced the force of the exiting fluids.

The Seveso disaster can be seen as more than a chemical engineering disaster, but also as a human factors engineering failure and a public policy disaster. The Italian legislature had recently passed a law requiring the plant to shut down on weekends, notwithstanding the phase of the batch in the reactor at the time. This ostensibly could reduce the likelihood of

[b] As such, Seveso is a useful reminder to engineers to be ever mindful of the first canon of their profession, that is, to hold paramount the health, safety, and welfare of the public.

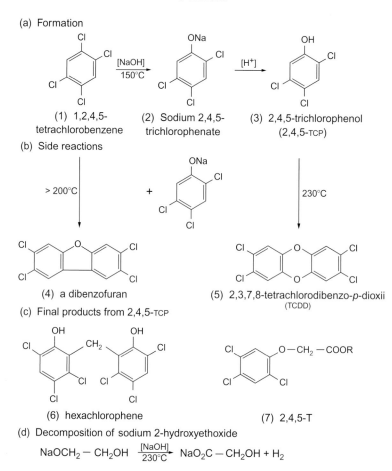

(a) Formation

(1) 1,2,4,5-tetrachlorobenzene

(2) Sodium 2,4,5-trichlorophenate

(3) 2,4,5-trichlorophenol (2,4,5-TCP)

(b) Side reactions

(4) a dibenzofuran

(5) 2,3,7,8-tetrachlorodibenzo-p-dioxii (TCDD)

(c) Final products from 2,4,5-TCP

(6) hexachlorophene

(7) 2,4,5-T

(d) Decomposition of sodium 2-hydroxyethoxide

$$NaOCH_2 - CH_2OH \xrightarrow[230°C]{[NaOH]} NaO_2C - CH_2OH + H_2$$

FIGURE 1.9 Reactions used in Seveso batch reactor to produce 2,4,5-T. *Source: Wilson DC. Lessons from Seveso. Chem Britain 1982;18(7):499-504.*

pollution by taking plants offline frequently, allowing for proper maintenance. On the weekend of the explosion, the plant was shut down after the formulation reaction, but before the complete removal of the ethylene glycol by distillation. This was the first time that the plant had been shut down at this stage. Based upon chemistry alone, the operator had no reason to fear anything would go awry. The mixture at the time of shutdown was 158 °C, but the theoretical temperature at which an exothermic reaction would be expected to occur was thought to be 230 °C. Subsequent studies have found that exothermic reactions of these reagents can begin at 180 °C, but these are very slow processes when below 230 °C. The temperature in fact rose, mainly due to a temperature gradient from the liquid to the steam phases. The reactor wall in contact with the liquid was much cooler than the wall in contact with the steam, with heat moving from the upper wall to the surface of the liquid. The stirrer was switched off so that the top few centimeters of liquid rose in temperature to about 190 °C, beginning the slow exothermic reaction. In 7 h, the runaway reaction commenced. The reactions may also have been catalyzed by chemicals in residue that had caked on the upper wall that, with the temperature increase, was released into the liquid in the reactor. Thus, the runaway reaction and explosion could have been prevented if the plant had not had to be prematurely shut down and if the plant operators had been better trained to consider contingencies beyond the "textbook" conditions.

A continuous, slight wind dispersed the contents over the region which included 11 towns and villages. The precipitate looked like snow. No official emergency action took place the day of the explosion. People with chemical burns checked themselves in local hospitals. The mayor of Seveso was only told of the incident the next day.

The response to the disaster and pending dioxin exposure was based on the potential risks involved. The contaminated area was divided into three zones based on the concentration of TCDD in the soil. The 211 families in Zone A, the most heavily contaminated area, were evacuated within 20 days of the explosion, and measures were taken to minimize exposure to residents in nearby zones. In a preliminary study, U.S. Centers for Disease Control and Prevention (CDC) tested blood serum samples from five residents of Zone A who suffered from the dioxin-related skin disease known as chloracne, as well as samples from four from Zone A without chloracne, and three from outside the contaminated area. All samples had been collected and stored shortly after the accident. Interestingly, TCDD was detected in only one sample from the unexposed group, but it was comparably high, that is, 137 part per trillion (ppt). The high elevated TCDD level was thought to be due to misclassification or sample contamination. In Zone A, serum TCDD levels ranged from 1772 to 10,439 ppt for persons without chloracne and from 828 to 56,000 ppt for persons with chloracne. The TCDD concentrations are the highest ever reported in humans. The CDC is presently evaluating several hundred historical blood samples taken from Seveso residents for TCDD. There are plans to determine half-life estimates and to evaluate serum TCDD levels for participants in the Seveso cancer registry.

As is often the case, scientific research has continued even after the sensational aspects of the disaster have waned. In fact, a recent study by Warner et al.[19] found a statistically significant, dose-response-increased risk for breast cancer incidence with individual serum TCDD level among women in the Seveso women; that is, a dose-response relationship of a twofold increase in the hazard rate associated with a 10-fold increase in serum TCDD. This result is an early warning because the Seveso cohort is relatively young, with a mean age at interview of less than 41 years. These findings are consistent with a 20-year follow-up study. No increased incidence of breast cancer had been observed in the Seveso population 10 and 15 years after the incident, but after 20 years, breast cancer mortality emerged among women who resided in heavily contaminated areas, and who were younger than 55 years at death [relative risk = 1.2, 95% confidence interval, 0.6-2.2]. However, this increase mortality was not found in women who lived longer than 55 years.

The findings are not significant statistically, but scary. For example, it is very difficult to characterize a population for even a year, let alone 20 years, because people move in and out of the area. Epidemiological studies are often limited by the size of the study group in comparison to the whole population of those exposed to a contaminant. In the Seveso case, the TCDD exposure estimates have been based on zone of residence, so the study is deficient in individual-level exposure data. There is also variability within the exposure area, for example, recent analyses of individual blood serum TCDD measurements for 601 Seveso women suggest a wide range of individual TCDD exposure within zones.[19]

Some argue that the public's response to the real risks from Seveso were overblown, considering no one died directly from the explosion and the immediate aftermath, although hundreds were burned by the NaOH exposure and hundreds other did develop skin irritations. This may true, but part of the response is the general response to the unknown, especially when the chemical of concern is TCDD, that has been established to cause cancer, neurological disorder, endocrine dysfunction and other chronic diseases. The medical follow-up

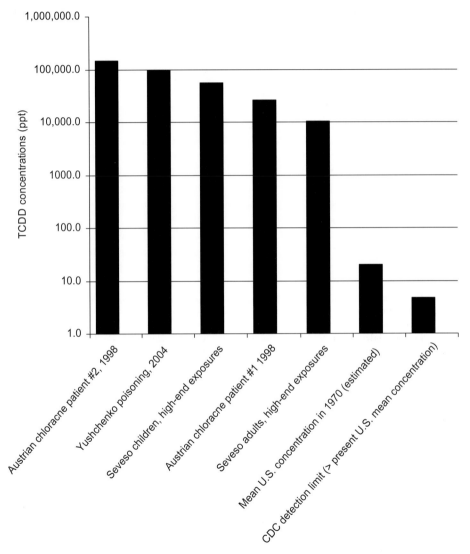

FIGURE 1.10  Tetrachlorodibenzo-*para*-dioxin blood serum concentrations from various exposure scenarios. *Sources: Center for Disease Control and Prevention; For the Seveso study, this link may be of use for citing: http://www. ncbi.nlm.nih.gov/pubmed/1826746 For the Austrian women, please refer to this study: http://www.ncbi.nlm.nih.gov/pubmed/ 11564625*

studies may indicate that the public response was plausible, given the latent connections to chronic diseases, like breast cancer.

The toxicity, especially the very steep cancer slope for TCDD, is met with some skepticism. Exposures at Seveso were high compared to general environmental exposures. However, some high profile cases, especially the recent suspected TCDD poisoning of the Ukrainian President Viktor Yushchenko in 2004 and the 1998 discovery of the highest blood levels of TCDD in two Austrian, have added to the controversy. In fact, both of these cases were precipitated by the adverse effects, especially chloracne. Usually, dioxins, PCBs, and other persistent, bioaccumulating toxicants are studied based on exposure, followed by investigations to see if any effects are present. This has been the case for Agent Orange, Seveso, Times Beach, and most other contamination instances. It is unusual to see such severe effects, but with the very high doses (see Figure 1.10) reported in the Yushchenko and Austrian cases, it would have come as a greater surprise not to have seen some adverse effect.

The Seveso disaster illustrates that the need to consider the likely consequences of failure early in the design process. Sufficient factors of safety are an engineering and an ethical imperative.

## References and Notes

1. Taleb NN. *The black swan.* 2nd ed. New York, NY: Penguin Books; 2010.
2. For example, see: Stokes DE. Pasteur's quadrant. Washington, DC: Brookings Institute Press; 1997 and Brooks H. "Basic and Applied Research," in Categories of Scientific Research, papers presented at a National Science Foundation Seminar, Washington, D.C., December 8, 1979, NSF 80-28, National Science Foundation, 1980.
3. U.S. Environmental Protection Agency. *Toxic release inventory.* http://www.epa.gov/tri/; 2012 [accessed February 23].
4. Vallero D. *Environmental biotechnology: a biosystems approach.* Burlington, MA: Elsevier Academic Press; 2009.
5. For example, Vallero made a 6 order of magnitude mistake in his book, *Environmental contamination.* In giving an example of units needed to calculate carbon monoxide concentrations, he had the wrong sign on an exponent, so instead of the value taken to the power of $+3$, it was taken to the power of $-3$. He thinks about this mistake frequently when doing calculations. It continues to be a lesson in humility.
6. National Academy of Engineering. *Part 3: the discovery of the change from welds to bolts. Online Ethics Center for Engineering 6/23/2006.* www.onlineethics.org/Topics/ProfPractice/Exemplars/BehavingWell/lemesindex/3.aspx; 2006 [accessed November 2, 2011].
7. National Society of Professional Engineers. *NSPE code of ethics for engineers.* Virginia: Alexandria; 2003. *http://www.nspe.org/ethics/eh1-code.asp* [accessed August 21, 2005].
8. Morse LJ, Bryan JA, Hurley JP, Murphy JF, O'Brien TF, Wacker TF. The Holy Cross Football Team hepatitis outbreak. *J Am Med Assoc* 1972;**219**:706–8.
9. Martin MW, Schinzinger R. *Ethics in engineering.* 3rd ed. New York, NY: McGraw-Hill; 1996.
10. Fledderman CB. *Engineering ethics.* Upper Saddle River, NJ: Prentice Hall; 1999.
11. National Research Council. *Science and decisions: advancing risk assessment.* Washington, DC: National Academies Press; 2009.
12. Jaques T. *Learning from past crises—do iconic cases help or hinder? Publ Relat J* 2009;**3**(1) http://www.prsa.org/SearchResults/download/6D-030103/0/Learning_from_Past_Crises_Do_Iconic_Cases_Help_or [accessed November 2, 2011].
13. Aviation Safety Network. http://aviation-safety.net/database/record.php?id=19740404-0; 2012 and http://aviation-safety.net/database/record.php?id=19760513-0; 2002 [accessed November 2, 2011].
14. Pfatteicher S. Learning from failure: terrorism and ethics in engineering education. *IEEE Technol Soc Mag* 2002;**21**(2) 8-12, 21.
15. This discussion is based on Ref. 4.

16. Picone C, Andresen D, Thomas D, Griffith D, et al. *Say no to GMOs! (Genetically Modified Organisms). Agenda.* University of Michigan Chapter of the New World Agriculture and Ecology Group; 1999 May/June 6-8.

17. Mocarelli P, Pocchiari F. Preliminary report: 2,3,7,8-tetrachlorodibenzo-p-dioxin exposure to humans—Seveso, Italy. *Morb Mortal Wkly Rep* 1988;37:733-736 and Di Domenico A, Silano V, Viviano G, Zappni G. Accidental release of 2,3,7,8-tetrachlorodibenzo-p-dioxin (TCDD) at Seveso, Italy: V. Environmental persistence of TCDD in soil. *Ecotoxicol Environ Saf* 1980;4:339-345.

18. Kletz T. *Learning from accidents.* 3rd ed. Oxford, UK: Gulf Professional Publishing; 2001.

19. Warner M, Eskenazi B, Mocarelli P, Gerthoux PM, Samuels S, Needham L, et al. Serum dioxin concentrations and breast cancer risk in the Seveso Women's Health Study. *Environ Health Perspect* 2002;**110**(7):625–8.

# Science

At their most basic level, every environmental disaster can be explained by the laws of motion and thermodynamics. The laws of motion describe the mechanics of how things move from one place to another. Thus, the winds and waves of a hurricane are explained by fluid mechanics. Possibly less obvious, even energy-related, phenomena, such as the destruction of the ozone layer and global climate change, must account for motion. For example, the ozone-destroying chlorine (Cl) atoms must find their way to the stratosphere and likewise, the greenhouse gases, like carbon dioxide ($CO_2$) and methane ($CH_4$), must leave their sources, move through the atmosphere and, ultimately, become mixed in the troposphere.

The loss of habitat due to changes in coastal development, for example, more impervious surfaces, changes the fluid dynamics so that there is less immediate infiltration and more run-off, as well as scouring of sand and other barriers as the ocean reclaims the coast line. Thus, fluid mechanics and other principles of motion are determinants in the extent and magnitude of environmental destruction.

In addition to motion, the laws of thermodynamics explain that energy and matter must be conserved, that is, every molecule and joule of energy must be accounted for in every system. Thus, the various vibrations and wavelengths of energy and the mass of greenhouse gases enter into arrangements that warm or cool various parts of the atmosphere and ocean. On a smaller scale, the solar energy of summer and fall is absorbed by earth, air, and water and is converted to mechanical energy manifested in a tornado or hurricane. Even more localized, the explosion of a tank is the result of temperature, pressure, and density relationships.

These laws are necessary, but cannot fully explain any of the disasters mentioned in this book. Indeed, all of the laws of physical sciences are not enough for disaster forensics. They must be combined with the principles of social sciences. Thus, the consideration of the interplay among science, engineering, and technology will begin our discussion of the science of disasters. The engineering component is where the social science perspectives will come into focus.

## SCIENTIFIC ADVANCEMENT

In Chapter 1, we considered disasters to be extreme failures. Scientific expression of success and failure often begins with the efficiency and effectiveness of a system. A disaster can result from combinations of inefficiency and ineffectiveness. Efficiency is a thermodynamics term.

Effectiveness is a management term. Recall that disasters involve both physical science and human factors. Efficiency is a measure as to how well a system is working in terms of the amount of mass and energy taken in versus the amount of mass or energy coming out. In contrast, effectiveness has to do with a particular set of values placed on that system and the extent to which the system performs with respect to providing those values.

Engineers are not restricted to deductive reasoning, so when an engineer determines whether a disaster is the result of a particular inefficiency or ineffectiveness that has led to a disaster, numerous methods can be used. For example, engineers base disaster assessments on previous experience and observation, that is, earlier successes and failures can serve as a baseline for acceptability of actions and decisions that have led up to a disaster. The challenge is choosing precedent cases that are sufficiently similar to the situation at hand. Scientists first generate rules based on observations (i.e., the laws of nature: chemistry, physics, biology, etc.) of the world around them and the way things work. Once they have this understanding, they may apply it by using the rules to create something, some technology designed to reach some end, from manufacturing insulin or making a crop more resistant to pests to degrading a toxic waste. According to the National Academy of Engineering:

> Technology is the outcome of engineering; it is rare that science translates directly to technology, just as it is not true that engineering is just applied science.[1]

Researchers are motivated by explaining the previously unexplained. This means they are never satisfied with the *status quo*. This is why they risk failure to advance science in such seemingly small doses. It was not that long ago, for example, that climatologists and meteorologists had little hope of predicting patterns in time and space in a manner much better than using primitive folklore and other methods. In fact, some of the folklore methods that worked well have been explained after scientific investigation. Thus, scientific investigation is fueled by curiosity, which leads to innovation. A particular challenge is why something works well in tightly controlled environments, like a laboratory, but not in the "real world."

In fact, the *status quo*, by definition, works against innovation. There is usually strong motivations, financial and technological, to become risk averse. The *status quo* is an easier route than one of shifting paradigms. The resistance may be the sheer difference between the concept of "normal" and "abnormal." Visualize the scientific mindset of the eighteenth century, it was not "normal" to expect that waste be treated before being released into a river. Actually such wastes may not have even been all that harmful, since the natural microbial population and the rest of the biological system could degrade the relatively dilute wastes efficiently. Also, most of the chemical compounds released to the river were not synthetic, so the microbes had already adapted capacities to biodegrade them. Thus, there was not a driving need to design a wastewater treatment plant like that in the twentieth century. However, the petrochemical revolution and industrial expansion took hold, and with it the observation that natural processes were no longer able to withstand the onslaught of chemical loading. Thus, the "normal" benchmark changed, so that the science and engineering of water quality had to advance.

Similar changes took place in the sciences that underpin disasters. Physics had to advance to explain the acoustics and wave behaviors that damaged structures. Biology had to change to explain agents of plagues and epidemics. Hydrology became a discipline to describe water flow and characteristics associated with storms and floods.

Scientific advancement ultimately leads to a paradigm shift, the term coined in the late twentieth century by Thomas S. Kuhn. He changed the meaning of the word "paradigm," extending the term to an accepted specific set of scientific practices. The scientific paradigm is made up, first, of what is to be observed and analyzed; second, the questions that arise; third, to whom such questions are to be asked; and lastly, how the results of the investigations into this scientific subject matter will be interpreted. The paradigm can be harmful if incorrect theories and information become accepted by the scientific and engineering communities. Excessive comfort with the *status quo*, that is, xenophobia, can be sometimes attributed to a community's well-organized protection against differences, a syndrome known as *groupthink*.[2]

As mentioned, innovations occur when a need or opportunity arises, or as the old saying goes, "necessity is the mother of invention." Environmental science advancement has followed a progression similar to other research advances since the mid-twentieth century. In 1944, Vannever Bush[3] observed that "basic research is performed without thought of practical ends." According to Bush, basic research is to contribute to "general knowledge and an understanding of nature and its laws." Seeing an inevitable conflict between research to increase understanding and research geared toward use, he held that "applied research invariably drives out pure."[4]

Today, Bush's "rugged individual approach" has been largely supplanted by teamwork. Certainly, individual creativity fuels many new technologies, but advancing and implementing many emerging technologies thrive on the synergies of a team. Here the emphasis has evolved toward a cooperative approach. For example, recent tsunamis have encouraged advances in early warning systems. Although the ideas for new systems may originate with individuals, bringing them to fruition will require synergies from many scientific and nonscientific disciplines. The view recognizes that, to be effective, groups of people must be both technically competent and able to collaborate to realize a common objective.[5]

Basic research seeks to broaden the understanding of the phenomena of a scientific field—it is guided by the quest to further knowledge. Disaster science has benefited, for example, from advances in remote sensing that was advanced by better understanding of particle-wave phenomena in basic physics research. In this vein, Louis Pasteur sought to understand germ theory (basic research), which led to his application of this knowledge to lower the spoilage rate of vinegar, beer, wine, and milk (applied research).[6]

The disparity between basic and applied research is captured in the "linear model" of the dynamic form of the postwar paradigm. It is important to keep in mind, though, that in the dynamic flow model, each of the successive stages depends upon the stage before it (Figure 2.1).

There is an interesting parallel between the advancement of science and the application of science. For example, does science always lead to engineering which subsequently drives the need for technology? This view may be the default, but is not the exclusive transition. Engineering has driven basic science (e.g., bioscience's "black boxes" that progressively, but never

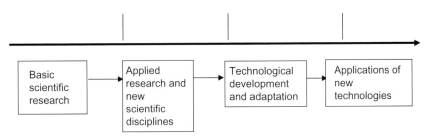

FIGURE 2.1 Progression from basic research to applied research to development of technologies.

completely, become understood by bioscience researchers). Technology has driven both science and engineering. A new device allows scientists to embark on whole new areas of research (e.g., the PCR in rDNA research) and engineers to conceive new designs (e.g., the DNA markers allow for enhanced bioremediation projects).

This simple, step-wise model of scientific advances has come to be called *technology transfer* as it describes the movement from basic science to technology. The first step in this process is basic research, which charts the course for practical application, eliminates dead ends, and enables the applied scientist and engineer to reach their goal quickly and economically. Then, applied research involves the elaboration and the application of what is known. Here, scientists convert the possible into the actual. The final stage in the technological sequence, i.e. development, is the stage where scientists systematically adapt research findings into useful materials, devices, systems, methods, and processes.[7]

The characterization of evolution from basic to applied science has been criticized for being too simple an account of the flow from science to technology. In particular, the *one-way* flow from scientific discovery to technological innovation does not seem to fit with twenty-first century science. The supposition that science exists entirely *outside* of technology is rather absurd in today's way of thinking. As mentioned, throughout history, a reverse flow is seen, a flow from technology to the advancement of science. The innovation of the calculus and the inventions of the microscope and telescope, and later examples of fractal dimensions and rDNA illustrate that science has progressively become more *technology derived*.[8] Biotechnology is a prime example of the technology advancing the science and vice versa. Disasters can occur when the underpinning science of such a technology is not fully understood, with hazards allowed to gestate.

The relationship between basic and applied sciences is not universally held within the science and engineering communities. Some agree that:

> The terms basic and applied are, in another sense, not opposites. Work directed toward applied goals can be highly fundamental in character in that it has an important impact on the conceptual structure or outlook of a field. Moreover, the fact that research is of such a nature that it can be applied does not mean that it is not also basic.[9]

Disaster preparedness and response must be based on sound science and requires a synthesis of the goals of understanding and use. Doing so depends on both theory and practice. The one-dimensional model of Figure 2.1 consists of a line with "basic research" on one end and "applied research" on the other (as though the two were polar opposites). Disaster science, then, calls for a balanced and strong commitment to *understanding* the theory (e.g. microbiological processes, fluid dynamics, thermodynamics) and to putting it into practice (e.g. controlling the effects of these processes). This would cover the entire line segment. Arguably, two points within a spectrum better represent Pasteur: one at the "basic research" end of the spectrum and another at the "applied research" end of the spectrum. This placement calls for a different model that reconciles the shortcomings of this one-dimensional model (see Figure 2.2).

This model can also be applied to the entities conducting scientific research and development. For example, a university might follow a flow similar to that in Figure 2.3. The science departments are concerned with knowledge-building, the engineering departments with applied knowledge to understand how to solve society's problems, and the university designer is interested in finding innovative ways to use this knowledge. For example, a civil engineer

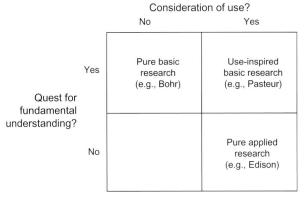

FIGURE 2.2 Research based on knowledge and utility considerations. *Adapted from Ref. 4.*

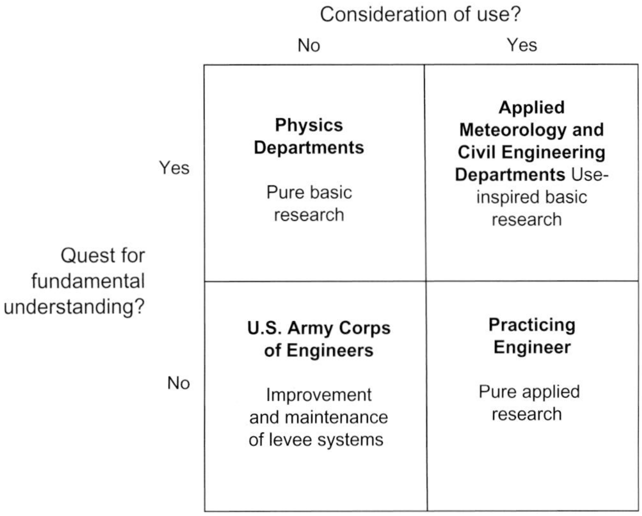

| | Consideration of use? | |
|---|---|---|
| | **No** | **Yes** |
| **Quest for fundamental understanding?** Yes | Pure basic research (e.g., Bohr) | Use-inspired basic research (e.g., Pasteur) |
| No | | Pure applied research (e.g., Edison) |

FIGURE 2.3 University research categorized according to knowledge and utility objectives.

| | Consideration of use? | |
|---|---|---|
| | **No** | **Yes** |
| **Quest for fundamental understanding?** Yes | **Physics Departments** Pure basic research | **Applied Meteorology and Civil Engineering Departments** Use-inspired basic research |
| No | **U.S. Army Corps of Engineers** Improvement and maintenance of levee systems | **Practicing Engineer** Pure applied research |

working for the U.S. Army Corps of Engineers is applying general scientific principles to upgrade levee designs, but may want to "figure out" better designs in terms of water retention and soil strength. The engineer is behaving much like Thomas Edison, who was most interested in utility and less interested in knowledge for knowledge's sake. In addition, the engineer must work closely with administrators and managers who purchase the systems. This is not to say that innovations do not come from the southwest box in Figure 2.3, because they clearly do. It simply means that their measures of success at many resource agencies call for major investments in operation and maintenance. In fact, the quadrants must all have feedback loops to one another.

This view can also apply to symbiotic relationships among institutions. Duke University is located at one of the points of Research Triangle in NC. The other two points are the University of North Carolina-Chapel Hill and North Carolina State University. All three schools have engineering programs, but their emphasis differs somewhat. Duke is recognized as a world leader in basic research, but its engineering school tends to place a greater emphasis on application of these sciences, for example, adaptive structures during an earthquake. To understand environmental systems, there is much collaboration between Duke's schools of engineering and environment. The School of Public Health houses the engineering programs at the University of North Carolina. As expected, this engineering research tends to focus on addressing and preventing environmental problems that would result from disasters, such as damage from confined animal feeding operations and nutrient loading of rivers. North Carolina State University is the first place that the State of North Carolina looks for designers, so the engineers graduating from NC State are ready to design as soon as they receive their diplomas. However, NC State also has an excellent engineering research program that applies the basic sciences to solve societal problems. All of this occurs within the scientific community of the Research Triangle, exemplified by Research Triangle Park (RTP), which includes centers supported by private and public entities that have a particular interest in mind. In this way, the RTP researchers are looking for new products and better processes. The RTP can be visualized as the "Edison" of the Triangle, although research in the other two quadrants is ongoing in the RTP labs. This can be visualized in an admittedly oversimplified way in Figure 2.4.

The degree to which a given body of research seeks to expand understanding is represented on the vertical access, and the degree to which the research is driven by considerations of use is represented on the horizontal axis. A body of research that is equally committed to potential utility and advancing fundamental understanding is represented as "use-inspired" research.[10]

During the last quarter of the twentieth century, advances and new environmental applications of science, engineering, along with their associated technologies began to coalesce into a whole new way to see the world, at least new to most of Western Civilization. Ancient cultures on all continents, including the Judeo-Christian belief systems, had warned that humans could destroy the resources bestowed upon us unless the view as stewards and caretakers of

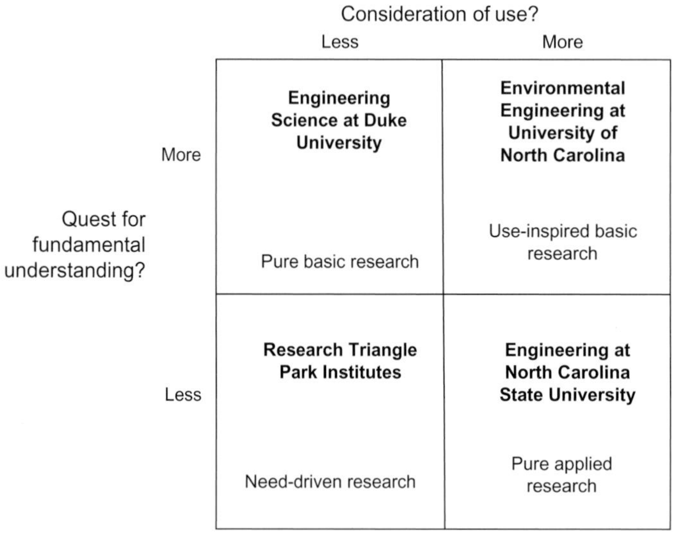

FIGURE 2.4 Differentiation of the knowledge and utility drivers in disaster-related research illustrated by institutions of the Research Triangle, NC.

the environment were taken seriously. Scientifically based progress was one of the major factors behind the exponential growth of threats to the environment. Environmental controls grew out of the same science, which is now part of a widely accepted environmental ethos. This ethos itself has evolved from the 1960s when environmental protection was mainly achieved through end-of-pipe strategy. Wastes have entered the environment and treated to some extent before being released. This, after-the-fact expectation is gradually being replace by one of sustainability.

Most practitioners and researchers see their work as beneficial and self-justified. In other words, their specific work is justified by the general societal need for better medicine, food, environmental quality, better products, and more efficient manufacturing. It should be noted that good science depends on both the ends and the means. If even important societal needs, such as advancing science, are sought through unethical means, as recent cases in cooking, trimming, and forging data can attest, such advancement is unacceptable. Some who have engaged in these unethical acts saw, or at least claimed to have seen, their deceptions as being necessary to advance science for an overall good. This is in opposition to sound science and public trust. Snow[11] put it this way:

> If we do not penalize false statements made in error, we open up the way, don't you see, for false statements by intention. And of course a false statement of fact, made deliberately, is the most serious crime a scientist can commit.

The societal demands for scientific advancement can be very compelling. That is why Snow likely saw the need to warn most scientists about a problem about which they would reflexively agree. After all, it all seems quite straightforward. Science is the explanation of the physical world, while engineering encompasses applications of science to achieve results. Thus, what we have learned about the environment by trial and error has incrementally grown into what is now standard practice of environmental science and engineering.

Trial-and-error learning certainly has advanced our understanding of disasters, but often at a great cost in terms of the loss of lives and diseases associated with mistakes, poorly informed decisions, and the lack of appreciation of environmental effects. That is why scientists must be careful to guard the public trust. Science and engineering are not popularity contests. That is one worrisome aspect of many public debates. Just because most scientists agree about something does not in itself mean that minority views are wrong. Similarly, the amount of funding, governmental support or media favor are not tantamount to good science.

Scientists can be recruited, sometimes unknowingly, as advocates for one cause or another. Many of these causes are worthwhile. Many studies are quite good and specifically directed toward a tightly defined research objective. However, research is seldom purely driven by objective, scientific need. Research priorities can be directed by both science and policy. For example, research proposals may be written to fit with what policy makers want, even if that means that the better and more relevant research would be in another area. In fact, recent discussions about scientific consensus related to climate change can be troubling. Seldom does the scientific community have complete consensus on anything except the basic principles (and even these are suspected in quantum mechanics and mathematics). Indeed, there is arguably *consensus* about many aspects of climate, such as the greenhouse effect and solar radiation. Not every aspect of climate change is at a consensus, that is, at this time there is no *unanimity* in any scientific discipline regarding many environmental disasters.

In disaster assessments, sometimes the only sure statement is that a factor makes a disaster either better or worse. For example, increased development along shorelines will likely worsen the impact of hurricanes. The exact amount of worsening is impossible to predict with complete precision. However, the fact that a greater number of vulnerable structures of economic value exist is unquestionable. Also, the decrease in buffering and changes in hydrology due to development will likely increase damage. The march toward credible science can be painstakingly slow so that recommendations on preventing disasters are often accompanied by large uncertainties and conservative factors of safety.

The foregoing discussion calls for a systematic view of benefits and risks. The good news is that popular culture has come to appreciate the systematic relationship between the sciences, engineering, and technologies. As evidence is the concept of "spaceship earth," that is, our planet consists of a finite life support system and that our air, water, food, soil, and ecosystems are not infinitely resilient in their ability to absorb humanity's willful disregard. It is also good news that scientific curiosity and the need to provide stronger evidence about hypotheses push researchers to revisit some previously neglected details that, in the long run, may well prevent future disasters.

## LAWS OF MOTION

The first law of motion states that every object in a state of uniform motion tends to remain in that state of motion unless an external force is applied to it. This is inertia, which must be understood when considering forces, with the most common external force that changes the state of uniform motion being friction. Thus, any design must see friction as the "enemy" if we want to keep things going (lubricants and smooth surfaces are needed to fight friction) and the essential "friend" if we want to change directions or stop things (e.g., brake shoes in an automobile).

The second law of motion describes the relationship between an object's mass $m$, its acceleration $a$, and the applied force:

$$F = ma \tag{2.1}$$

Acceleration and force are vectors, wherein the direction of the force vector is the same as the direction of the acceleration vector. With the second law, we can calculate unknowns from knowns. That is, if we know the mass of the structures and the applied force generated by the wind, we can calculate the acceleration of dislodged structures during a storm event.

The third law of motion tells us that for every action there is an equal and opposite reaction. Like the first law, this tells us that we can expect things to happen in response to what we do. If we apply a force, there will be an equal force in the opposite direction.

The laws of chemistry remind us that what we put into a reaction always leads to a specific product. Thus, science tells us that so long as we understand the variables and parameters of any system, the outcome is predictable. This is obviously not completely possible for disasters, but the more we know, the better our predictions and preparations will be. There are numerous ways to identify, characterize, and analyze conditions that have led to disasters and to determine why they led to health and environmental impacts. The key to any approach is that it accurately describes the events in an objective and comprehensive way in order to evaluate events, outcomes, and consequences.

# Fluid Properties

Since all disasters involve one or more fluids (notably air and water), fluid dynamics is a crucial part of any disaster assessment. For example, toxic plumes, like those in Bhopal and Seveso, indicate the role fluids play in disasters. Fluids are either liquid or gaseous. Every environmental disaster includes fluids at a number of scales, from molecular to global. The most common fluids are water and air. Fluid properties and dynamics determine the extent and severity of a disaster. For example, contaminant's fluid properties will determine how soluble it will be in water and blood, and how easily it moves through skin and lungs. A substance that is insoluble in water is often quite soluble in fats, meaning higher potential for skin penetration and that exposures will lead to buildup in lipids. If a chemical is easily absorbed, the hazard may be higher.

The fluid properties of an agent, whether chemical (methylisocyanate in Bhopal and/or dioxin in Seveso, respectively) or biological (e.g., bacteria, such as anthrax), determine where the contaminant is likely to be found in the environment after release (e.g., in the air as a vapor, sorbed to a particle, dissolved in water, or taken up by biota).

Physical transport is a function of the mechanics of fluids, but it is also a chemical process, such as when and under what conditions transport and chemical transformation processes become steady state or nearly steady state, for example, sequestration and storage in the environment. Thus, transport and transformation of contaminants and nutrients depend on the characteristics of environmental fluids.

A fluid is a collective term that includes all liquids and gases.[12] A liquid is matter that is composed of molecules that move freely among themselves without separating from each other. A gas is matter composed of molecules that move freely and are infinitely able to occupy the space in which they are contained. Engineers define a fluid as a substance that will deform continuously upon the application of a shear stress; that is, a stress in which the material on one side of a surface pushes on the material on the other side of the surface with a force parallel to the surface.

Fluids can be classified according to observable physical characteristics of flow fields. A continuum fluid mechanics classification is shown in Figure 2.5. Laminar flow is in layers,

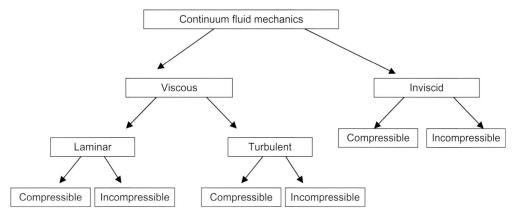

FIGURE 2.5    Classification of fluids based on continuum fluid mechanics. *Source: Research and Education Association. The essentials of fluid mechanics and dynamics I. Piscataway, NJ: REA; 1987.*

while turbulent flow has random movements of fluid particles in all directions. In incompressible flow, the variations in density are assumed to be constant, while the compressible flow has density variations, which must be included in flow calculations. Viscous flows must account for viscosity while inviscid flows assume viscosity is zero.

The time rate of change a fluid particle's position in space is the fluid velocity ($V$). This is a vector field quantity. Speed ($V$) is the magnitude of the vector velocity $V$ at some given point in the fluid, and average speed ($\bar{V}$) is the mean fluid speed through a control volume's surface. Therefore, velocity is a vector quantity (magnitude and direction), while speed is a scalar quantity (magnitude only). The standard units of velocity and speed are meters per second (m s$^{-1}$).

Velocity is important in determining pollution properties and mechanisms, such as mixing rates after an effluent is discharged to a stream, how rapidly an aquifer will become contaminated, and the ability of liners to slow the movement of leachate from a landfill toward the groundwater. The distinction between velocity and speed is seldom made, even in technical discussions. Surface water flow is known as *stream discharge*, $Q$, with units of volume per time. Although the appropriate units are m$^3$ s$^{-1}$, most stream discharge data in the United States are reported as number of cubic feet of water flowing past a point each second (cfs). Discharge is derived by measuring a stream's velocity at numerous points across the stream. Since heights (and volume of water) in a stream change with meteorological and other conditions, stream-stage/stream-discharge relationships are found by measuring stream discharge during different stream stages. The flow of a stream is estimated based upon many measurements. The mean of the flow measurements at all stage heights is reported as the estimated discharge. The calculation of discharge of the stream of width $w_s$ is the sum of the products of mean depth, mean width, and mean velocity[13]:

$$Q = \sum_{n=1}^{n} \frac{1}{2}(h_n + h_n - 1)(w_n + w_n - 1) \times \frac{1}{2}(v_n + v_n - 1)\frac{1}{2}(h_n + h_{n+1}) \qquad (2.2)$$

where $Q$ = discharge (m$^3$ s$^{-1}$)

$w_n = n^{th}$ distance from baseline or initial point of measurement (m)
$h_n = n^{th}$ water depth (m)
$v_n = n^{th}$ velocity (m s$^{-1}$) from velocity meter.

Another important fluid property is pressure, defined as a force per unit area ($p$):

$$p = \frac{F}{A} \qquad (2.3)$$

So, $p$ is a type of stress that is exerted uniformly in all directions. It is common to use pressure instead of force to describe the factors that influence the behavior of fluids. The standard unit of $p$ is the pascal (Pa), which is equal to 1 N m$^{-2}$. The preferred pressure unit in this book is the kilopascal (kPa), since the standard metric unit of pressure is the pascal, which is quite small. Thus, $Q$ is determined by not only the amount of water, but the characteristics of the stream. The same rainfall event in one stream regime may be disastrous, while in another completely uneventful.

Potential and kinetic energy discussions must consider the fluid acceleration due to gravity. In many ways, it seems that acceleration was a major reason for Isaac Newton's need to develop the calculus.[14] Known as the mathematics of change, calculus is the mathematical means of describing acceleration and addressed Newton's need to express mathematically his new law of motion. Acceleration is the time rate of change in the velocity of a fluid particle. In terms of calculus, it is a second derivative. That is, it is the derivative of the velocity function. And a derivative of a function is itself a function, giving its rate of change. This explains why the second derivative must be a function showing the rate of change of the rate of change, which is readily apparent from the units of acceleration: length per time per time ($m\ s^{-2}$).

The relationship between mass and volume is important in both environmental physics and chemistry and is a fundamental property of fluids. The density ($\rho$) of a fluid is defined as its mass per unit volume. Its metric units are $kg\ m^{-3}$. The density of an ideal gas is found using the specific gas constant and applying the ideal gas law:

$$\rho = p(RT)^{-1} \tag{2.4}$$

where $p$ = gas pressure
$\quad R$ = specific gas constant
$\quad T$ = absolute temperature.

The specific gas constant must be known to calculate gas density. For example, the $R$ for air is $287\ J\ kg^{-1}\ K^{-1}$. The specific gas constant for methane ($R_{CH_4}$) is $518\ J\ kg^{-1}\ K^{-1}$.

Scientists usually use the ideal gas equation for ideal gases and low pressure gases:

$$pV = nR'T \tag{2.5}$$

where $n$ is the number of moles and $R'$ is the gas constant, $R' = 8.315\ J\ K^{-1}\ mol^{-1}$.

Density is a very important fluid property for environmental situations. For example, a first responder must know the density of substances in an emergency situation. If a substance is burning, whether it is of greater or lesser density than water will be one of the factors on how to extinguish the fire. If the substance is less dense than water, the water will likely settle below the layer of water, making water a poor choice for fighting the fire. So, any flammable substance with a density less than water (see Table 2.1), such as benzene or acetone, will require fire-extinguishing substances other than water. For substances heavier than water, like carbon disulfide, water may be a good choice.

Another important comparison is that of pure water and seawater: some typical values are given in Table 2.1. The density difference between these two types of water can be a slowly unfolding disaster for the health of people living in coastal communities and for marine and estuarine ecosystems. Salt water contains a significantly greater mass of ions than does freshwater (see Table 2.2). The denser saline water can wedge beneath freshwaters and pollute surface waters and groundwater (see Figure 2.6). This phenomenon, known as "saltwater intrusion," can significantly alter an ecosystem's structure and function and threaten freshwater organisms. It can also pose a huge challenge to coastal communities who depend on aquifers for their water supply. Part of the problem and the solution to the problem can be found in dealing with the density differentials between fresh and saline waters.

The reciprocal of a substance's density is known as its specific volume ($\upsilon$). This is the volume occupied by a unit mass of a fluid. The units of $\upsilon$ are reciprocal density units ($m^3\ kg^{-1}$). Stated mathematically, this is:

$$\upsilon = \rho^{-1} \tag{2.6}$$

The weight of a fluid per its volume is known as specific weight ($\gamma$). Scientists and engineers sometimes use the term interchangeably with density. Geoscientists frequently refer to a

TABLE 2.1   Densities of Some Important Environmental Fluids

| Fluid | Density (kg m$^{-3}$) at 20 °C unless otherwise noted |
|---|---|
| Air at standard temperature and pressure (STP) = 0 °C and 101.3 kN m$^{-2}$ | 1.29 |
| Air at 21 °C | 1.20 |
| Ammonia | 602 |
| Diethyl ether | 740 |
| Ethanol | 790 |
| Acetone | 791 |
| Gasoline | 700 |
| Kerosene | 820 |
| Turpentine | 870 |
| Benzene | 879 |
| Pure water | 1000 |
| Seawater | 1025 |
| Carbon disulfide | 1274 |
| Chloroform | 1489 |
| Tetrachloromethane (carbon tetrachloride) | 1595 |
| Lead (Pb) | 11,340 |
| Mercury (Hg) | 13,600 |

TABLE 2.2   Composition of Freshwaters (River) and Marine Waters for Some Important Ions

| Composition | River water | Salt water |
|---|---|---|
| pH | 6-8 | 8 |
| $Ca^{2+}$ | $4 \times 10^{-5}$ M | $1 \times 10^{-2}$ M |
| $Cl^-$ | $2 \times 10^{-4}$ M | $6 \times 10^{-1}$ M |
| $HCO_3^-$ | $1 \times 10^{-4}$ M | $2 \times 10^{-3}$ M |
| $K^+$ | $6 \times 10^{-5}$ M | $1 \times 10^{-2}$ M |
| $Mg^{2+}$ | $2 \times 10^{-4}$ M | $5 \times 10^{-2}$ M |
| $Na^+$ | $4 \times 10^{-4}$ M | $5 \times 10^{-1}$ M |
| $SO_4^{2-}$ | $1 \times 10^{-4}$ M | $3 \times 10^{-2}$ M |

Sources: Hunter KA, Kim JP, Reid MR. Factors influencing the inorganic speciation of trace metal cations in freshwaters. Mar Freshw Res 1999;50:367-372 and Schwarzenbach RR, Gschwend PM, Imboden DM. Environmental organic chemistry. New York, NY: Wiley Interscience; 1993.

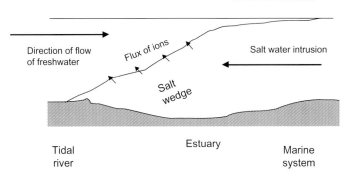

Direction of flow
of freshwater

Flux of ions

Salt
wedge

Salt water intrusion

Tidal
river

Estuary

Marine
system

FIGURE 2.6 Saltwater intrusion into a freshwater system. This denser saltwater submerges under the lighter freshwater system. The same phenomenon can occur in coastal aquifers. *Research and Education Association, 1987, The Essentials of Fluid Mechanics and Dynamics I, REA, Piscataway, NJ*

substance's specific weight. A substance's $\gamma$ is not an absolute fluid property because depends upon the fluid itself and the local gravitational force:

$$\gamma = gp \tag{2.7}$$

Specific weight units are the same as those for density; for example, $\text{kg m}^{-3}$.

The fractional change in a fluid's volume per unit change in pressure at constant temperature is the fluid's coefficient of compressibility. Any fluid can be compressed in response to the application of pressure ($p$). For example, water's compressibility at 1 atm is $4.9 \times 10^{-5} \text{ atm}^{-1}$. This compares to the lesser compressibility of mercury ($3.9 \times 10^{-6} \text{ atm}^{-1}$) and the greater compressibility of hydrogen ($1.6 \times 10^{-3} \text{ atm}^{-1}$). A fluid's bulk modulus, $E$, is a function of stress and strain on the fluid and is a description of its compressibility and is defined according to the fluid volume ($V$):

$$E = \frac{\text{stress}}{\text{strain}} = -\frac{dp}{dV/V_1} \tag{2.8}$$

$E$ is expressed in units of pressure (e.g., kPa water's $E = 2.2 \times 10^6$ kPa at 20 °C).

Surface tension effects occur at liquid surfaces (interfaces of liquid-liquid, liquid-gas, liquid-solid). Surface tension, $\sigma$, is the force in the liquid surface normal to a line of unit length drawn in the surface. Surface tension decreases with temperature and depends on the contact fluid. Surface tension is involved in capillary rise and drop. Water has a very high $\sigma$ value ($0.0728 \text{ N m}^{-1}$ at 20 °C). Of the environmental fluids, only mercury has a higher $\sigma$ (see Table 2.3). The high surface tension creates a type of skin on a free surface, which is how an object that is denser than water (e.g., a steel needle) can "float" on a still water surface. It is the reason insects can sit comfortably on water surfaces. Surface tension is somewhat dependent upon the gas that is in contact with the free surface. If not indicated, it is usually safe to assume that the gas is air.

Capillarity is a particularly important fluid property of groundwater flow and is important in determining the movement of contaminants above the water table. In fact, the zone immediately above the water table is called the *capillary fringe*. Regardless of how dense the arrangement of soil particles, void spaces (i.e., pore spaces) will exist between the particles. By definition, the pore spaces below the water table are filled exclusively with water. However, above the water table, the spaces are filled with a mixture of air and water.

TABLE 2.3    Surface Tension (Contact with Air) of Selected Environmental Fluids

| Fluid | Surface tension, $\sigma$ (N m$^{-1}$ at 20 °C) |
|---|---|
| Acetone | 0.0236 |
| Benzene | 0.0289 |
| Ethanol | 0.0236 |
| Glycerin | 0.0631 |
| Kerosene | 0.0260 |
| Mercury | 0.472 |
| $n$-Octane | 0.0270 |
| Tetrachloromethane | 0.0236 |
| Toluene | 0.0285 |
| Water | 0.0728 |

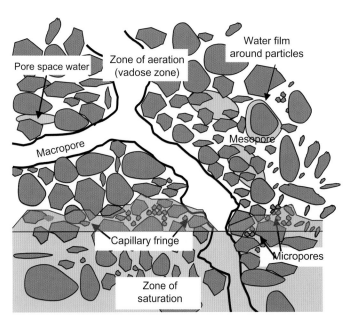

FIGURE 2.7    Capillarity fringe above the water table of an aquifer.

As shown in Figure 2.7, the spaces between unconsolidated material (e.g., gravel, sand, or clay) are interconnected, and behave like small conduits or pipes in their ability to distribute water. Depending on the grain size and density of packing, the conduits will vary in diameter, ranging from large pores (i.e., macropores) and medium pore sizes (i.e., mesopores), to extremely small pores (i.e., micropores).

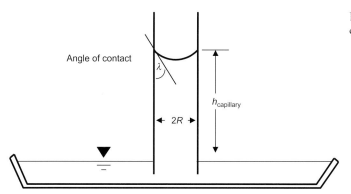

FIGURE 2.8   Rise of a fluid in a capillary.

Fluid pressures above the water table are negative with respect to atmospheric pressure, creating tension. Water rises for two reasons, its adhesion to a surface plus the cohesion of water molecules to one another. Higher relative surface tension causes a fluid to rise in a tube (or a pore) and this rise is indirectly proportional to the diameter of the tube. In other words, capillarity increases with decreasing diameter of a tube (e.g., tea will rise higher in a thin straw in your iced tea than a wider straw). The rise is limited by the weight of the fluid in the tube. The rise ($h_{capillary}$) of the fluid in a capillary is expressed as (Figure 2.8):

$$h_{capillary} = \frac{2\sigma \cos\lambda}{\rho_w g R} \tag{2.9}$$

where $\sigma =$ fluid surface tension (N m$^{-1}$)
  $\lambda =$ angle of meniscus (concavity of fluid) in capillary (degrees)
  $\rho_w =$ fluid density (kg m$^{-3}$)
  $g =$ gravitational acceleration (m s$^{-2}$)
  $R =$ radius of capillary (m).

The contact angle indicates whether cohesive or adhesive forces are dominant in the capillarity. When $\lambda$ values are greater than 90°, cohesive forces are dominant; when $\lambda < 90°$, adhesive forces dominate. Thus, $\lambda$ is dependent upon both the type of fluid and the surface to which it comes into contact. For example, water-glass, $\lambda = 0°$; ethanol-glass, $\lambda = 0°$; glycerin-glass, $\lambda = 19°$; kerosene-glass, $\lambda = 26°$; water-paraffin, $\lambda = 107°$; and mercury-glass, $\lambda = 140°$. The base of the capillary fringe of the soil is saturated without regard to pore size. In the vadose zone, however, the capillary rise of water will be highest in the micropores, where the relative surface tension and the effects of water cohesion are greatest.

Another property of environmental fluids is the mole fraction. If a composition of a fluid is made up of two or more substances (A, B, C, . . .), the mole fraction ($x_A, x_B, x_C, \ldots$) is number of moles of each substance divided by the total number of moles for the whole fluid:

$$x_A = \frac{n_A}{n_A + n_B + n_C + \cdots} \tag{2.10}$$

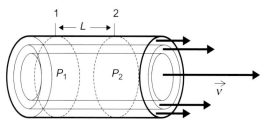

FIGURE 2.9 Viscous flow through a horizontal pipe. The highest velocity is at the center of the pipe. As the fluid approaches the pipe wall, the velocity approaches zero.

The mole fraction value is always between 0 and 1. The mole fraction may be converted to mole percent as:

$$x_{A\%} = x_A \times 100 \tag{2.11}$$

For gases, the mole fraction is the same as the volumetric fraction of each gas in a mixture of more than one gas.

The amount of resistance to flow when it is acted on by an external force, especially a pressure differential or gravity, is the fluid's viscosity. This is a crucial fluid property used in numerous green engineering applications, but particularly in air pollution plume characterization, sludge management, wastewater and drinking water treatment, and distribution systems.

Bernoulli's equation states that when a fluid is flowing in a long, horizontal pipe with constant cross-sectional area, the total pressure along the pipe must be constant. However, as the fluid moves in the pipe, there will be a pressure drop. A pressure difference is needed to push the fluid through the pipe to overcome the drag force exerted by the pipe walls on the layer of fluid that is making contact with the walls. Since the drag force exerted by each successive layer of the fluid on each adjacent layer that is moving at its own velocity, a pressure difference is needed (see Figure 2.9). The drag forces are known as viscous forces. Thus, the fluid velocity is not constant across the pipe's diameter, owing to the viscous forces. The greatest velocity is at the center (furthest away from the walls), and the lowest velocity is found at the walls. In fact, at the point of contact with walls, the fluid velocity is zero.

So, if $P_1$ is the pressure at point 1 and $P_2$ is the pressure at point 2, with the two points separated by distance $L$, the pressure drop ($\Delta P$) is proportional to the flow rate:

$$\Delta P = P_1 - P_2 \tag{2.12}$$

and,

$$\Delta P = P_1 - P_2 = I_v R \tag{2.13}$$

where $I_v$ is volume flow rate and $R$ is the proportionality constant representing the resistance to the flow. $R$ depends on the length ($L$) of pipe section, the pipe's radius, and the fluid's viscosity.

## LAWS OF CHEMISTRY AND THERMODYNAMICS

Changes in ecosystems are manifestations of the law of conservation of mass and of the laws of thermodynamics. The former states that the total mass remains constant during a chemical change or reaction or in any isolated process. We shall shortly apply it to material flow.

The first law of thermodynamics is also a law of energy conservation and can be expressed in the equation:

$$\Delta U = q + w \tag{2.14}$$

where $\Delta U$ is the change of internal energy of a system, $q$ is the heat that passes through the boundary into the system, and $w$ is the work done on the system. If the heat and work were lost by the system, the signs of $q$ and $w$ would be negative. This is a very important law which highlights the equivalence of heat and work and the fact that the internal energy of an isolated system is constant (conservation of energy).

If an electric motor produces $200$ kJ s$^{-1}$ of work by lifting a load and loses $50$ kJ s$^{-1}$ of heat to the surrounding air, then the change of internal energy of the motor per second is:

$$\Delta U = -2 - 15 = -17 \text{ kJ}.$$

The quantities $q$ and $w$ have negative signs as the system (motor) is losing work and heat to the surroundings.

The first law is, however, not the full story as it implies that heat can be completely converted into work. This we know by experience and observation is not possible—we cannot have perpetual motion. This we will discuss later in terms of the second law of thermodynamics.

The mass and energy coming in and going out across two-dimensional surfaces in these systems are known as *fluxes*. These fluxes are measured and yield energy balances within a region in space through which a fluid travels. This region, that is, the *control volume*, is where balances occur and can take many forms. With any control volume, the calculated mass balance is:

$$[\text{Quantity of mass per unit volume in a medium}] = [\text{total flux of mass}] \atop +[\text{rate of production or loss of mass per unit volume in a medium}] \tag{2.15}$$

This can be restated symbolically:

$$\frac{dM}{dt} = \frac{d(M_{in} - dM_{out})}{dt} \tag{2.16}$$

where $M$ = mass and $t$ = specified time interval.

If we are concerned about a specific chemical (e.g., environmental engineers worry about losing good ones, like oxygen, or forming bad ones, like the toxic dioxins), the equation needs a reaction term ($R$):

$$\frac{dM}{dt} = \frac{d(M_{in} - dM_{out} \pm R)}{dt} \tag{2.17}$$

Environmental systems are comprised of interrelationships among *abiotic* (nonliving) and *biotic* (living) components of the environment. Organisms live according to the transfer of mass and energy via the concept of "trophic state." Humans live within this interconnected network or web of life, so they are affected, positively or negatively, by the condition of these components. Disasters are major affronts to these finely balanced relationships.

There are many ways of expressing the second law but one that adds directly to the first law is: *that no process is possible in which heat absorbed from a reservoir can be completely converted into work*. In other words, NO perpetual motion! The second law introduces the concept of *spontaneous change* and in so doing introduces two vital properties in thermodynamics, namely *entropy (S)* and the *Gibbs energy (G)*. The Gibbs energy allows us to determine whether a process is spontaneous or not, which as we will see is a very important property in all sciences. The laws of thermodynamics are laws of observation, and so far have never been violated! Another way of expressing the second law is the entropy, $S$, of a system and its surroundings increases in the course of a spontaneous change:

$$\Delta S_{total} > 0 \tag{2.18}$$

This puts an end to any thought that perpetual motion is possible. The entropy can be considered as a measure of disorder. It is possible to actually calculate entropy values from theory and to determine it indirectly, but there is no way of measuring it like we can for heat ($q = m \cdot SH \cdot \Delta T$), where SH is the specific heat and $\Delta T$, the change of temperature or temperature (using a thermometer). Entropy values reflect its quantitative description as being a measure of disorder, and the standard entropy ($S_m^o$) of a solid such as a diamond (C), is very low, $2.4\,J\,K^{-1}\,mol^{-1}$ as it is a very ordered solid, while the value for $CO_2$ is large, $213.7\,J\,K^{-1}\,mol^{-1}$. This reflects the fact that gases are a very disordered state of matter.

As an example of the second law let us consider a gas at high pressure (say, in a cylinder) expanding into low pressure region (atmosphere). The gas changes from reasonably well ordered gas to a chaotic disordered gas and the entropy changes from a small value to a large value:

$$\Delta S = \Delta S_{final} - \Delta S_{initial} > 0 \tag{2.19}$$

The process as we know from experience is spontaneous and yes, the entropy is greater than zero.

Another way of expressing the second law is: in any spontaneous process, the change is always accompanied by a dispersal of energy into a more disordered state.

The bounce of a ball describes this perfectly. If we drop a ball from a height, it will bounce and bounce until it stops, that is, when it runs out of kinetic energy. But where has the energy gone? It has been dissipated and degraded into chaotic motions of floor molecules which have been heated by each bounce.

Thermodynamics has produced a very special equation to help us understand all of this and to predict whether a particular chemical reaction will be spontaneous or not:

$$\Delta_r G = \Delta_r H - T\Delta_r S \tag{2.20}$$

where subscript "$r$" refers to "reaction" or process and $H$ is the enthalpy which is simply the heat ($q$) at constant pressure. The process is spontaneous if $\Delta_r G < 0$, in other words if $\Delta_r G$ is negative. Alternatively, if $\Delta_r G$ is positive, the reaction does not go and is termed nonspontaneous.

Let us consider a simple reaction involved in the combustion of glucose at $37\,°C$ (body heat):

$$C_6H_{12}O_6 + 6O_2 = 6H_2O + 6CO_2$$

The enthalpy change for this reaction is $-2807.8\,kJ\,mol^{-1}$ and the entropy change is $182.4\,J\,K^{-1}\,mol^{-1}$.

So, the $\Delta_r G$ for this spontaneous reaction is:

$$\Delta_r G = [-2807.8 - (310.15 \times 182.4)/1000] \text{ kJ mol}^{-1} = -2864.4 \text{ kJ mol}^{-1}$$

This combustion or burning is thermodynamically the same as the biological process that takes place when we eat a mole (180.2 g) of glucose. This is the energy we use when we exercise. So if we only ate 18 g of glucose, our muscles would have at most 286 kJ of energy. Equating this to the energy involved in lifting a weight through a height $h$ ($E = mgh$), a 70 kg person could use this energy to climb 417 m.

In Chapter 8, we will consider potential climate change and the effects of increasing concentrations of $CO_2$ in the atmosphere. One way of stopping $CO_2$ from entering the atmosphere, you may say, is to use it in the manufacture of useful chemicals. Let us consider one possible useful reaction that of using $CO_2$ to produce ethanol, a possible liquid fuel for the future:

$$2CO_2(g) + 3H_2(g) = C_2H_5OH(l)$$

The way of determining the $\Delta_r G$ is simply by looking up the data in a table of thermodynamic properties—see Table 2.4. By using the $\Delta_f G$ (Gibbs energy of formation) for each compound or element in the reaction (the formation refers to the formation from its elements), the

$$\Delta_r G = \Delta_f G(\text{products}) - \Delta_f G(\text{reactants})$$
$$\Delta_r G = [-174.8 - 3(0) - 2(-394.4)]$$
$$= +614 \text{ kJ mol}^{-1} \tag{2.21}$$

The Gibbs energy is positive so the reaction is not spontaneous. What a pity!

One important lesson one learns here is that because the Gibbs energy of formation of $CO_2$ is so very large and negative, it will be virtually impossible to use it to make new chemicals. All is not lost, however, because it is possible to link (couple) reactions as is done in nature and get the $CO_2$ to make useful chemicals. This is being researched in many laboratories and $CO_2$

TABLE 2.4  Thermodynamic Data—Enthalpies and Gibbs Energies of Formation and Standard Entropy (at 298 K and 1 bar)

| Compound | $\Delta_f H$ (kJ mol$^{-1}$) | $\Delta_f G$ (kJ mol$^{-1}$) | $S^o m$ (kJ K$^{-1}$ mol$^{-1}$) |
|---|---|---|---|
| $CO_2$ | −393.5 | −394.4 | 213.7 |
| $CH_4$ (methane) | −74.8 | −50.7 | 186.3 |
| $C_2H_6$ (ethane) | −84.7 | −32.8 | 229.6 |
| $C_4H_{10}$ (butane) | −126.2 | −17.0 | 310.2 |
| $C_6H_6$ (benzene) | +49.0 | +124.3 | 173.3 |
| $CH_3OH$ (methanol) | −238.7 | −166.3 | 126.8 |
| $C_2H_5OH$ (ethanol) | −277.7 | −174.8 | 160.7 |
| $C_6H_{12}O_6$ (glucose) | −1268 | −910 | 212 |
| $H_2O$ | −285.8 | −237.1 | 69.9 |
| $H_2$ | 0 | 0 | 130.7 |

is being used in living processes involving algae to make hydrocarbon chemicals including diesel.

From data like those in Table 2.4, it is possible to determine whether any reaction you can possibly imagine will or will not happen spontaneously.

An interesting aspect of thermodynamics is that it is possible to determine properties from apparently unrelated properties. We have seen this in determining whether a reaction will go spontaneously or not from enthalpy data and from entropy data—apparently unrelated properties. There are many other such examples in thermodynamics and the Maxwell's relations are a particularly good set of examples. One of these relations is:

$$\left(\frac{dS}{dV}\right)_T = \left(\frac{dp}{dT}\right)_V \tag{2.22}$$

With this, one can determine the entropy change of a gas with respect to volume at constant temperature if you know the change of pressure with temperature at constant volume for the gas. The RHS of the equation is relatively easy to measure but RHS is impossible. The Maxwell relationship makes it possible to determine the LHS.

We have seen for chemical processes that the second law of thermodynamics can be used to show that the energy of a spontaneous process will be distributed in a way that minimizes the free energy of the process. The change in free energy associated with movement of the solute from one compartment to another is directly proportional to the difference in chemical potential between the compartments. In all energy exchanges in an isolated system, if no energy enters or leaves the system, the potential energy of the state will always be less than that of the initial state. This, as we have seen, is related to the entropy so that external energy is needed to keep things going—in a control volume, refrigerator, heat engine, waterfall, etc.

Physicists look to these laws to determine how mass and energy are distributed. Further, ecologists consider these distributions of mass and energy when investigating the complex interrelationships between and within the compartments of the food webs and chains, and consider humans to be among the consumers.[15] Food chains illustrate the complexity and vulnerability of environmental systems (see Figure 2.10). Species at a higher tropic level are predators of lower level species, so materials and energy flow downward. The transfer of mass and energy upwardly and downwardly between *levels of biological organization* can be measured and predicted, given certain initial and boundary conditions. However, the types and abundance of species and interaction rates vary in time and space. From a biotechnological standpoint, the introduction of modified species or changes in environmental conditions (e.g., introduction of nutrients and toxic byproducts) can change these trophic interrelationships.

The substance of all species consists mainly of molecular arrangements of the elements carbon, oxygen, hydrogen, and most contain nitrogen. These four biophile elements have an affinity for each other so as to form complex organic compounds. The smallest organisms, for example, the viruses, bacteria, and other microbes, are quite efficient in finding and using organic material as sources of energy and carbon, but for much of human history, the systems within microbes have been the agents of epidemics. However, the cause of the epidemics involves numerous interrelationships among the trophic states. For example, when habitats are changed to allow advantages to certain species (e.g., rats carrying plague microbes), the disaster cannot simply be attributed to the particular disease agent, but to the overall changes to the environment.

Trophic state

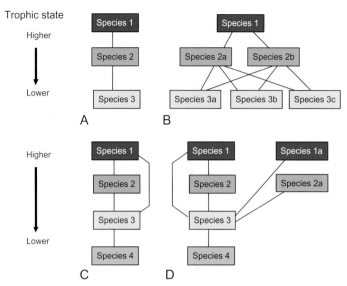

FIGURE 2.10 Energy and matter flow in environmental systems from higher trophic levels to lower trophic levels. Lines represent interrelationships among species. (A) Linear biosystem, (B) multilevel trophic biosystem, (C) omnivorous biosystem, and (D) multilevel biosystem with predation and omnivorous behaviors. An interference at any of these levels or changes in mass and energy flow can lead to disasters. *Source: Based on information from Ref. 15.*

Indeed, microbes are remarkably proficient in adapting to various hostile environments, which allow them to take advantage of environmental changes. Some produce spores; many have durable latency periods, all have the ability to reproduce in large numbers when environmental conditions become more favorable.

Such adaptive behaviors can also be displayed by larger organisms. For example, helminths (parasitic worms) are prevalent predominantly in tropical regions. There were 1.5 billion, 1.3 billion, and 1.1 billion people infected with *Ascaris*, hookworm, and *Trichuris*, respectively in 2002.[16] Helminths are responsible for much of the world's blindness, resulting from the disease schistosomiasis caused by *Schistosoma*. Most of the world's cases are in Africa (85%), where prevalence rates[a] can exceed 50% in local populations (see Figure 2.11). The larvae of the schistosomes hide and grow in freshwater snail hosts. Within the snail, they change into a sporocyst, which in turn produces thousands of new larvae (i.e., cercaria). Humans contact these larvae in water contaminated by infected snails, where the larvae penetrate the skin and reach the bloodstream, moving to the liver. In a few weeks, the helminth matures and mates. The female adult can live for 35 years, producing eggs daily.[17]

Schistosomiasis is an example of an endemic condition worsened by human activities, leading to a public health disaster. Large-scale water projects, like the Aswar Dam in Egypt, modified the aquatic habitat to provide ideal conditions for both the snails and the parasite. In fact, it would be rare for any large reservoir not to provide these ideal conditions:

> The incidence and extension of schistosomiasis and other waterborne diseases can be directly related to the proliferation of irrigation schemes, the stabilization of the aquatic biotope and subsequent ecological changes. By contrast, when agriculture depended primarily on seasonal rainfall, the relationship between snail host, schistosome parasite and human host was somewhat stabilized, and infection rates were low.[18]

---

[a] Prevalence is the number of cases at any given time and incidence is the number of new cases reported during a designated time period, often yearly.

FIGURE 2.11    Risk of contracting schistosomiasis. *Source: Ref. 16.*

This is an example of a change in the abundance of one species, which is not pathogenic, has led to environmental disasters attributed to another, pathogenic species. So, the flow of energy and mass to the snail has contributed to a disastrous outcome, large-scale blindness.

## SCIENCE IN THE PUBLIC EYE

Within 3 months between March and May of 2011, for example, the public looked to the scientific community for explanations of three very different, large-scale disasters: the failures and resulting releases of radiation in Japan; the devastation communities from tornadoes and floods in the United States; and the *Escherichia coli* outbreak across Europe.

These disasters share a number of commonalities. They resulted from a mix of natural and human-induced causes. They are actually large and complex chains of events and they involve interactions between people and the environment. They are manifestations of systems within systems.

The triggering mechanisms are quite different in these three disasters. An earthquake generated a devastating tsunami in Japan that, even without the impending nuclear plant destruction, would have been a disaster in terms of loss of human life and destruction of property. The events that led to the meltdown at the nuclear core of the power plant were combinations of natural and anthropogenic occurrences, such as pump failures due to loss of electricity, hydraulic problems due to lack of available water, and other factors that led to increasing heat due to continued fission occurring in the core material of the plant. This is truly an epic disaster and took nearly a year to get under control (with radiation disease and other effects for decades to come).

The Japanese nuclear disaster resulted from a complex of natural disasters, human error, and bad judgment. It points to the need for much greater vigilance and assurances that future safety levels will tightened. It also emphasizes the importance of science-based policy, such as siting nuclear reactors properly, avoiding recognized fault lines, and a safer system of controlling the uranium-containing rods. These features must be built into the design of the reactors so that they can be safely withdrawn in the case of an accident. Nuclear power is dangerous but will likely be the source of electricity for the foreseeable future for much of the world. Indeed, it does have the advantage of not producing carbon dioxide.

The tornadoes and floods also began with natural meteorological events (e.g., rains, snow melt, storm fronts), but were exacerbated by human activities. The population within certain types of building structures (especially modular and mobile homes) increases the risks to people during a severe storm event.

Tornadoes are fairly well understood by meteorologists and atmospheric scientists. When hot moist air at low altitudes meets cold dry air at higher altitudes water condenses. This together with an updraft (which is related to the density gradient of the air column, which relates to the rate of condensation of the water droplets) and wind shear (which imparts rotation) results in the formation of a tornado.

Since tornadoes result from severe atmospheric conditions, this leads the public to ask whether they are increasing due to global warming. Thermodynamically, the warmer the sea temperature, the greater will be the moisture content of the warm air and, other things being equal, the greater potential to form the amount of drops. However, this is counterbalanced by the lowering of the air density gradient due to warm air in the higher altitudes. So, one cannot say with total confidence that global warming and warmer seas result in a greater number and enhanced severity of tornadoes. Furthermore, the evidence does not yet show a relationship between global warming and tornadoes. The year 2011 saw over 500 deaths from about 1400 tornadoes (as of 5 June 2011). Mortality increases when tornadoes strike densely populated areas, so even if the tornado forces do not change, the mortality would increase. If indeed global climate change increases the frequency and intensity of storms and the population in vulnerable areas increases, then the disasters would be expected to increase even more.

Granted, the devastation in Missouri and Alabama included all types of structures. In Joplin, for example, large swaths of entire neighborhoods were completely devastated. However, the types and densities of structures play a role in the risks.

Tornadoes are atmospheric phenomena, whereas flooding is a hydrological phenomenon that involves air, water, and earth. Scientists calculate the risk of flooding using statistics based on hydrological conditions. Thus, a so-called 100-year flood is one that would be expected to occur once a century. But, this is based on geologic time, many thousands of years. So, communities may see two or three 100-year floods in a single season.

As in the case of tornadoes, human activities exacerbate the flooding potential. This is an example of trade-offs between various benefits and risks. For example, the United States has placed a premium on navigation throughout its history. As such, the U.S. Army Corps of Engineers has engaged in large-scale projects to make the waters of the United States more navigable, such as deepening channels in large stream systems, like the Missouri, Mississippi, and Ohio Rivers, and building large levee systems, along with locks and dams throughout the nation. As a result, most of the stream miles of large U.S. rivers have been modified.

Before the levees were put in place and the channeling of the Mississippi River, flooding was common and great swathes of land would periodically flood and the water soak away in the flood plains and natural wetlands. In modern times, excessive flood waters have no natural outlet and when the floods do come, low-lying cities and town get flooded. So, flooding is exacerbated by (a) the channeling of streams and (b) development in low-lying levels. Again, the public wants to know the extent to which global warming is increasing precipitation and the likelihood of flooding, due to warmer air and sea water, with greater evaporation and condensation rates.

Increased flooding is linked to other problems in the Mississippi delta region, for example, loss of soil and land surfaces due to erosion and wash-a-ways as well as nutrient (nitrogen and phosphorous) loss from farm runoff and deposition as the water enters the delta region.

In the last chapter, we will discuss solutions. However, it is important to note here that when it comes to storms and floods, the lowest technological solution may be best. That is, keeping people from moving into vulnerable areas and returning habitats to pre-channelized conditions would prevent loss of life and property. In addition, many engineered projects should mimic nature, such as the construction and rehabilitation of huge wetland areas in the larger river basins to act as a soak for the flood waters (on the order of the Everglades in Florida, which are themselves becoming highly stressed and less abundant).

Interestingly, flood control and navigation are both benefits often claimed for the same impoundment projects. The problem occurs when the trade-offs include losses to property, especially to those who do not benefit. This is the case when the government decided to flood large areas behind levees to protect downstream communities, like New Orleans. The farms and towns upstream had to suffer major losses to protect those living downstream.

The *E. coli* outbreak is an example of a disaster that begins incrementally, but grows precipitously. It is also an example of the need for early warning systems for life support systems. In this case, the food supply has become so interconnected that it is often difficult to track the entire life cycle of a food item. A recent outbreak was thought to have begun in northern Germany, but also has links to Spain. Interestingly, modern technology (e.g., DNA testing) has shown several unrelated strains of the pathogen. In addition, the virulence of the strains is almost without precedent, leading to hundreds of hemolytic uremic cases. It looks as though the 19 deaths and 2000 sick people have all had some connection with North Germany in the Lubeck region. The rare strain—enterohemorrhagic *E. coli*—appears to be a combination of two types of *E. coli* and seems to be more virulent and toxic producing than the usual *E. coli* strains that people have in their intestines. According to the U.S. Centers for Disease Control and Prevention, the stain is probably the same strain that killed a single Korean in the 1990s. The origin of this *E. coli* strain could lie in the ability of bacteria from humans and animals to trade genes. Human feces, animal contamination, and unwashed hands are most likely to be involved in the spread of the bacteria. And it looks as though it is also linked to some types of salad. Bean sprouts are the likely culprit. So far, there is no evidence in this case that the genetic manipulation of bacteria has played a role in the emergence of the virulent strains. It appears unlikely they have come from a laboratory where bacteria is studied or manipulated. The genome was relatively quickly sequenced by the Beijing Genomics Institute, so forensics seems to be increasing at a brisk pace. This may bode well for more rapid and reliable food surveillance.

These three recent disasters evoke a call for better certainty from the scientific community on phenomena without scientific unanimity or often even consensus. A number of contentious questions are being posed to the scientific community. Is nuclear power ever safe enough to be reliable? What is the role of anthropogenic climate change in these weather events? Does manipulation of natural systems by humans, for example, genetically modified organisms, have anything to do with the virulence of these newly identified pathogens? Do crowding and the lack of good land use planning play a role in exacerbating these disasters? The public demands answers to these other questions and steps to be taken to address environmental disasters in scientifically credible ways.

# References

1. National Academy of Engineering. *The engineer of 2020: visions of engineering in the new century.* Washington, DC: National Academy Press; 2004.
2. Janus I. *Groupthink: psychological studies of policy decisions and fiascoes.* 2nd ed. Boston, MA: Houghton Mifflin Company; 1982.
3. V. Bush was Franklin D. Roosevelt's director of the wartime Office of Scientific Research and Development. The section "Scientific Advancement" includes Bush's response when asked to consider the role of science in peacetime in V. Bush (1945). Science, the endless frontier; a report to the President on a program for postwar scientific research. Reprinted by the National Science Foundation, Washington, DC, 1990.
4. Stokes DE. *Pasteur's quadrant.* Washington, DC: The Brookings Institution; 1997.
5. Fernandez J. Understanding group dynamics. *Business Line. 2 December* 2002.
6. Stokes. 12.
7. Stokes. 10-11.
8. Stokes. 18-21.
9. Brooks H. Applied science and technological progress. *Science* 1967;**156**(3783):1706–12.
10. Stokes. 70–73.
11. Snow CP. *The search.* New York, NY: Charles Scribner's Sons; 1959.
12. Even solids can be fluids at a very large scale. For example, in plate tectonics and other expansive geological processes, solid rock will flow, albeit very slowly.
13. Lee C, Lin S. *Handbook of environmental engineering calculations.* New York, NY: McGraw-Hill; 1999.
14. Newton actually co-invented the calculus with Willhelm Leibniz in the seventeenth century. Both are credited with devising the symbolism and the system of rules for computing derivatives and integrals, but their notation and emphases differed. A debate rages on who did what first, but both of these giants had good reason to revise the language of science; that is, mathematics, to explain motion.
15. Grandel TE. On the concept of industrial ecology. *Annu Rev Energy Environ* 1996;**21**:69–98.
16. Centers for Disease Control and Prevention . *Infectious diseases related to travel.* [chapter 3]: *Travelers' health*; 2012 http://wwwnc.cdc.gov/travel/yellowbook/2012/chapter-3-infectious-diseases-related-to-travel/helminths-intestinal.htm [accessed 3 March 2012].
17. Goldsmith E, Hilyard N. Dams and disease. In: Goldsmith E, Hildyard N, editors. *The social and environmental effects of large dams: volume 1. Overview.* Cornwall: Wadebridge Ecological Centre, Worthyvale Manor Camelford; 1984. p. 220–31 [chapter 7].
18. Biswas AK. Environmental implications of water development for developing countries. In: Widstrand C, editor. *The social and ecological effects of water development in developing countries.* Oxford, UK: Pergamon; 1978.

# 3

# Explosions

Many disasters, including environmental disasters, are accompanied by violent explosions. Sometimes, this is the entirety of the disaster, with the loss of life and property, such as dust explosions. In other disasters, the explosion may be just the beginning of the harm. We shall begin with former in this chapter. We will mention a few important explosions here, but will continue to address the latter throughout the rest of this book, as explosions often begin or are part of many disasters. At first blush, the explosions in this chapter may not be considered to be "environmental disasters." However, they tend to occur in what are known as "microenvironments." In fact, much of a person's exposure to environmental contaminants occurs in these settings, e.g. the highest exposures to many gaseous pollutants often occur indoors. Explosions are the most extreme type of risks in microenvironments.

## DUST

Dust may seem to be a strange place to begin a discussion of explosions. After all, dust seems to be quite benign when compared to those chemical compounds that are notorious explosives, such as trinitrotoluene (TNT), as well as flammable substances that are also explosive, such as gasoline. Environmental scientists and engineers usually classify dust as particulate matter (PM), which is an important type of air pollutant. PM contributes to respiratory and other diseases. However, dust is also an explosion risk that can be just as explosive as TNT and maybe even more dangerous as it seems to be present everywhere. Dust explosion takes place when combustible dust particles suspended in air undergo rapid combustion in an enclosed space. The initial burning is initiated by a spark or heat source and this leads to the fire spreading throughout the cloud of suspended particles. Such explosions have been known to occur in grain storage silos, flour mills, icing sugar factories, dried milk factories, coal mines, and factories involved in the processing of metal, pharmaceuticals, pigments, plastics, rubber, wood, paper, food products, and chemicals. If the conflagration takes place in a confined area, the air pressure produced by the exploding dust can have a devastating effect and can destroy huge factories and storage facilities. Many processing plants involve some form of milling and grinding, and as a result, these explosions are a common occurrence in spite of warnings and safety measures.

The dust particles that make up the cloud must be of a combustible nature. Explosive dust is always composed of either a finely divided organic material or certain metals in

FIGURE 3.1   The aftermath of a dust explosion. *Photo credit: U.S Chemical Safety and Hazard Investigation Board (2006). Investigation Report: Combustible Dust Hazard Study, Report No. 2006-H-1.*

powder form. Noncombustible particles, such as tiny clay or sand particles, will not cause dust explosions. Materials that have been responsible for dust explosions include fiber-board sandings and saw residues; processed food products such as instant coffee, sugar, flour, milk powder, and custard powder; powdered metal filings (aluminum, magnesium, iron, titanium, etc.); wool; cotton; paper; powdered plastic (polyethylene, etc.); coal; sulfur; powdered carbon; and pharmaceuticals paracetamol, etc.).[1] Figure 3.1 shows the aftermath of a dust explosion in a factory.

Dust explosions occur in all countries of the world, and any person working in a factory, mine, or storage facility involved with or handling flammable dusts should be aware of the inherent dangers. Fortunately, only a few large explosions occur and these are usually well reported. Unfortunately, the many smaller accidents are either not reported or underreported so that a true picture of dust explosions is not seen. This does hamper the lessons to be learned and the drawing up of safety rules. Better reporting would make for a safer industry.[2]

The best documented dust explosions are from the Unites States. Over the past 40 years (1970-2010), there have been over 600 dust explosions in grain facilities across the United States, killing over 250 and injuring over 1000 people. In the decade between 1994 and 2004, there were 115 grain dust explosions in the United States killing 16 people and injuring 137. Of these, 58 were corn dust explosions in granaries or refineries, with only 8 in flour processing or storage plants.[3] The result of a wood dust explosion is shown in Figure 3.2.

One of the most important explosions was in Davenport, Iowa, where a flour mill dust explosion occurred in May 1975. Although only two deaths were recorded and seven people were injured, the explosion led to major changes in the safety rules at plants that were prone to dusty environments. These rules related to lubrication schedules for all the equipment, no smoking, oxygen suppression systems, and confinement systems to control possible explosions.[3]

Grain and flour silos and mills are not the only facilities that are plagued by dust explosions. On February 7, 2008, a sugar dust explosion at the Imperial Sugar refinery, Port Wentworth in Georgia took place, killing 14 people and injuring over 40. It was probably caused by static electricity igniting fine sugar dust that had become too dry.[4]

Other explosions include a pharmaceutical rubber manufacturing plant in North Carolina in January 2003, killing 6 and injuring 38, the combustible material was polyethylene powder; an acoustics insulation plant in Kentucky in February 2003, killing 7 and injuring 37; an aluminum casting facility in Indiana on October 29, 2003, killing one and seriously injuring

FIGURE 3.2    Aftermath of wood dust explosion. *Taken from http://www.hse.gov.uk/woodworking/fire.htm.*

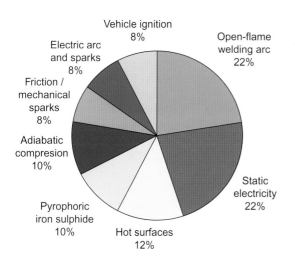

FIGURE 3.3    Causes of dust explosions. *Taken from http://www.firesandexplosions.ca/hazards/ignition_sources.php.*

six, the combustible material was finely divided aluminum; and in November 2011, an explosion destroyed part of a Kansas grain elevator, killing five and injuring two persons, the accident took place when unloading a bin into a rail car.[5] Grain elevators seem particularly susceptible to dust explosions, but no plant or factory or storage facility that involves fine dust is free from this danger. The causes of a number of dust explosions are summarized in Figure 3.3.

It has been reported that there are about two dust explosions in Europe every day. Of these, between 25% and 50% are in the food industry, followed closely by the wood and paper industries at 20-30% with the remainder distributed between the metal, chemical, and fuel industries. The initiator of many of these explosions appears to be due to mechanical friction, smoldering products, and hot surfaces giving rise to combustion followed by an explosion, but the root cause is very often due to human failure to implement safety rules and take all necessary precautions to ensure a safe plant.[6]

Examples of European dust explosions include a provender grinding mill in Glasgow, which exploded on November 10, 1911, killing five people including three children playing nearby. Two weeks after the Glasgow explosion, a similar type of mill exploded in Liverpool grain facility owned by J. Biddy and Sons, killing 39 with 101 injured; the official report concluded that a dust cloud ignited when a belt broke. Matches or an electrical fault was possibly to blame. The same company had a similar explosion in 1930, killing 11 and injuring 32. The combustible material in the storage facility was rice flour, sunflower seeds, and soya bean meal. Self-heating of sunflower seeds due to aerobic fermentation was the reported heating source.[6]

In Blaye in France, a grain terminal killed 11 people in 1997. Pieces of debris some weighing as much as 10 kg were found up to 140 m from the silo. In Metz, France in 1982, four 70 m tall barley silos were seriously damaged and four people killed when a blow torch set off a dust explosion.[7]

Wood dust from high-powered grinders and drying kilns make fiber and chip board factories very vulnerable; in 1989, an explosion in a fiber board factory spread through a plant at Hexham in the United Kingdom, killing one employee.

Aluminum powder is a notoriously explosive material and there have been many reports of explosions in factories that process aluminum by smelting, grinding, extruding, or casting the metal. On July 16, 1983, in Anglesey, Wales at the Aluminum Powder Co, an aluminum dust explosion resulted in injury to two men and an almost totally destroyed plant, which as a result was well publicized and documented.[8]

## The Science of Dust Explosions

A dust explosion can take place only if six necessary requirements are met:

1. The dust must be combustible—that is, it must react and burn in oxygen. The dust is the fuel or reductant in the explosive reaction.
2. The combustible dust must be in a finely divided form.
3. Oxygen must be present and this is usually in the form of atmospheric oxygen—this being the oxidant in the explosive reaction.
4. An ignition source must be present to ignite the dust particles.
5. There must be a sufficient concentration of the dust in the air. This is usually defined by the lower explosive limit (LEL).
6. The dust particles must be contained.

## Combustible Material

The combustible dust is usually an organic substance such as grain, flour, milk powder, wood, plastic, and powdered chemicals such as those found in the pharmaceutical industry but can also be a metal powder such as aluminum, titanium, magnesium, or iron.

Organic compounds can be represented by a carbohydrate. For example, the chemical formula for the simple carbohydrate, the sugar β-D-glucose, is $C_6H_{12}O_6$. When it reacts with oxygen, it forms carbon dioxide and water and releases heat:

$$C_6H_{12}O_6(s) + 6O_2(g) = 6CO_2(g) + 6H_2O(g), \quad \Delta H = -2538 \text{ kJ mol}^{-1} \tag{3.1}$$

The heat released (enthalpy) is 2538 kJ per 180.16 g of glucose.

For a metal such as aluminum (a very reactive metal), the combustion reaction is

$$Al + 3/2O_2(g) = 1/2Al_2O_3(s), \quad \Delta H = -1676 \text{ kJ mol}^{-1} \tag{3.2}$$

Again, the enthalpy is exothermic; this time with a value of 1676 kJ per 26.98 g of aluminum. This exothermic reaction is over four times more energetic than the glucose reaction if one considers the same mass of material. From this, one can see why finely divided aluminum is such a hazardous substance. The enthalpy for an iron reaction is about half that for aluminum reaction. Furthermore, 1 g of Al powder has the same explosive power (62 kJ g$^{-1}$) as 4 g of TNT (16 kJ g$^{-1}$).[9]

## Form

The rate of the reaction of combustible material with oxygen is strongly dependent on the surface area of the particles. To give some indication of how the surface changes with subdivision, we consider the following example:

Take a sphere of solid lump of mass 1 kg of carbohydrate material (say flour). If its density is 1 g cm$^{-3}$ (a value which is typical for flour), then the volume of this material would be 1000 cm$^3$ and the diameter of the sphere would be 12.4 cm with a surface area of 0.048 m$^2$. If we divided this sphere into $10^{11}$ equally sized spherical particles, the volume of each particle would be $10^{-8}$ cm$^3$ and the diameter of each particle would be 27 μm. This is about the diameter of a typical flour dust particle found in mills.[10] The total surface area of all these $10^{11}$ particles is 230 m$^2$. The division has increased the surface area by almost 5000-fold.

The subdivision and large surface area means that the energy barrier required to cause the combustible material to burn is much lower than if the material was in a bulky form.

To appreciate the significance of the subdivision and the tiny particles, let us consider the two processes—the burning of a lump of compressed flour and the conflagration that takes place with the same amount of flour in the form of dust.

If we can succeed in burning the lump of flour (striking a match at a corner), it will probably just smolder in the corner and slowly burn in the air. The heat of the reaction will be conducted away by the lump flour and some will heat up the surrounding air. Most of the oxygen molecules bombarding the lump will not have enough energy to start burning. It is only at the hot spot that some reaction will take place. But the process is slow and the heat is soon dissipated.

It should be useful to note that the total heat given out by the burning of the lump of, say, 180 g flour or sugar will be identical to that given out in the explosion with 180 g of flour or sugar dust. From Equation (3.1), this exothermic heat would be 2538 kJ. Although these figures are for sugar (a carbohydrate), the figures for flour (also a carbohydrate) will be of the same order.

When a dust particle in the air is heated to a sufficiently high temperature by a spark or by a hot source, it reacts according to Equation (3.1) and the heat of the reaction provides energy to the escaping gas molecules ($CO_2$ and $H_2O$) no heat is likely to be conducted away by the remaining flour as the fine particle would have a high probability of being totally consumed. The reaction with the oxygen is complete with the oxygen molecules attacking the fine particle from all sides. Thus, no flour remains. Calculations involving the LEL for flour

(100 g m$^3$ in air) show that only some of the oxygen is used to burn all the flour. The rest remains in the air. Getting back to the reaction, the heated gas molecules pass their energy onto other gas molecules and onto the flour particles, triggering a cascade of further reactions. These are fast reactions as the hot gas molecules move very rapidly. This also means that the reaction takes place too fast for the heat to escape to the walls or to the machinery and a dust explosion takes place.

The typical reaction, Equation (3.1), involves 6 molecules of $O_2$ reacting with 1 molecule of solid and producing 12 molecules of gas ($CO_2$ and $H_2O$). This doubling of the number of moles, and hence of the gas volume, together with the heat of the reaction causes the air to expand, and if contained, the pressure increases. It is this pressure that pushes back the walls and windows of the factory building and is the cause of explosions.

Dust particles are of course heavier than air and will eventually settle after the disturbance, which caused the dust cloud, has passed. This could be dust pouring out of a hole in a pipe or escaping from a grinding mill. These settled particles are in no danger of exploding but can cause a dangerous situation by smoldering if heated enough by a hot source. However, if the settled dust is disturbed and resuspended in the air and the dust concentration rises above the LEL, there is a danger of the dust exploding if a sufficiently energetic ignition source is present. Thus, conditions following a flour mill explosion represents two environmental risks. First, the smouldering fuel (in this instance, flour particles) continues to release pollutants. Second, the likelihood of a second explosion exists. Other fuels can exhibit the same risk. For example, these conditions, especially the first, occurred following the explosions in the World Trade Center disaster.

## Oxygen

Like any other combustion reaction, if there was no oxygen in the container (e.g. grain elevator, confined room or ship hull), there would be no possibility of a dust explosion taking place. It is of course possible to reduce the oxygen level, but that would require all workers to wear oxygen masks and this is not a serious proposition. The average concentration of molecular oxygen ($O_2$) in the air is about 20%, the second most abundant gas, with molecular nitrogen ($N_2$) making up most of the gas in the atmosphere.

## Ignition Source

The energy required to ignite a dust cloud depends on the type of material that the dust is made of, the moisture content of the dust, and the particle size of the dust. This energy can be as low as a static spark from discharging a bin of finely divided material into a truck or rail cars or as high as a hot flame from a burning log or a gas-fired boiler. Types of ignition sources include friction from overheated bearings, arching from machinery, gas flames, cigarettes, electrostatic discharges, hot surfaces, and fire from inadvertently burning solvents or sterilization chemicals used in the factory. In a recent brochure by the Bartec Company on Dust Explosion Protection, it was reported that mechanically produced sparks accounted for 30% of all initiators of dust explosion in Germany. Other ignition sources reported in the same article include heat caused by friction, static electric charges, smoldering fires, burning fires, hot surfaces, welding, and ignition.[11]

## Particle Concentration

The LEL of dust particles is between 50 and 100 g m$^{-3}$ with the upper explosive limit being of little value in this situation. A value below the LEL probably is insufficient to support dust explosion and a figure of 20% below the LEL is considered safe. The LEL value depends on properties such as the type of material, the moisture content, and the surface area of the particles. An Aeronautical Engineering Professor Bill Kauffman maintains that if one can see one's footprint in dust on the floor, or can write one's name on the wall, then there is enough dust to set off a conflagration. It is also said that if an observer in a dusty environment finds difficulty in distinguishing shapes from 60 cm, then there is a danger of a dust explosion.[12]

The dust explosion described above is known as a primary dust explosion. Most serious dust explosions are however secondary explosions. By this is meant the explosion that takes place as a result of accumulated dust being disturbed by the primary explosion. This often results in the major damage caused by dust explosions.

These accumulated piles of dust are found on high window ledges, on top of machinery, and in ceilings where they cannot easily be seen. A minor blast from a primary explosion dislodges these piles and this greatly increases the amount of suspended combustible material which then conflagrates causing a significant increase in pressure and hence damage. A smoldering pile of dust is a sufficient igniter of dust clouds.

## Containment

If the dust particles are not contained and confined on all sides of the container and if the dust is ignited, the result will be a fire ball or "flash fire" and the fire will be extinguished as soon as the dust fuel has been exhausted. The expanding gases will be vented and the damage will be minimal. If, however, the dust is ignited in a contained area, the resultant gas-air pressure from the rapidly expanding gases could reach 6 bar (six atmospheres), causing extensive damage to the occupants, the plant, and possibly the surrounding area. The increase in pressure is due to a greater than five-fold increase in the temperature (from 300 to 1700 K) and the increase in the number of moles of gas as combustion products ($CO_2$ and $H_2O$). This can be roughly calculated from the general gas equation:

$$PV = nRT \tag{3.3}$$

where $P$ is the pressure, $V$ is the volume of the contained space, $n$ is the number of moles of gas in the space after the reaction, and $T$ is the temperature.[13]

The high temperature of the explosive mixture of dust and oxygen is due to the heat of the reaction. The enthalpy heats up the gases in the factory ($N_2$, $O_2$, $CO_2$, and $H_2O$), and as the process is so fast, there is little time for the heat to be conducted away by machinery or walls, etc., and one can assume that the heat given out by the reaction is all transferred to the gases in the room and hence:

$$n_1 \Delta H = n_2 C_p \Delta T \tag{3.4}$$

where $n_1$ is the number of moles of reacting fuel (we will assume it is sugar and refer to Equation (3.1)), $n_2$ is number of moles of gas in the factory room before being the conflagration, $C_p$ is the molar heat capacity of the gases in the room, and $\Delta T$ is the rise in temperature.

Assuming a dust concentration of 100 g m$^{-3}$, the temperature of the air before the reaction is 300 K, and that $C_p$ for air containing a small percentage of $CO_2$ and $H_2O$ is 28 J K$^{-1}$ mol$^{-1}$, then using Equation (3.3) to calculate the number of gas moles in the room, followed by solving Equation (3.4) we get the result: $\Delta T = 1400$ K. This tells us that the temperature in the factory room rose from 300 to 1700 K.

The volume of the room is unimportant as it appears on both sides of Equation (3.4). We have made a few assumptions here. For example, we have assumed that the $C_p$ value is constant in this explosion and we have used the value at 1 bar. Also, we assume the explosion is too fast for any heat to be conducted to the walls or to the machinery and all the energy is transferred to all the gas molecules.

## Dust Explosion Lessons

Many lists of good housekeeping rules have been made around the world, especially after a serious dust explosion, but still explosions take place. A few rules have been recommended[14]:

- Introduce pressure relief vents.
- Ensure that settled dust is regularly cleaned away by using a fully earthed, centralized piped vacuum cleaning system.
- Ensure all machinery, lights and switches, and other electrical equipment are spark free and exclude obvious ignition sources.
- Keep the humidity at a reasonably high level.
- Keep all flames (e.g., from boilers) in separate areas from the dusty environments.
- Ensure all heating equipment is in good working order.
- Institute temperature monitors in areas where overheating can happen (bearings) and link these alarms.
- Take special precautions when welding or using dangerous equipment.
- Seal joints and leakage points around powder handling systems to prevent escape and accumulation of dust in the building and onto surrounding plant items.
- Maintain slight negative pressure on storage vessels such as bins and silos by use of extraction systems.
- Ensure that all personnel working in the dusty environment are aware of the safety rules and know how to implement them.
- Regularly check on bearings for lubrication. Note that each of these recommendations address one or more of the requirements for exposions, i.e. containment (pressure), fuel (high dust concentrations), and ignition (lights, switches, friction, welding equipment).

## AMMONIUM NITRATE

There have been a number of disasters due to ammonium nitrate explosions. For example, Texas City disaster of 1947 is reputed to be the deadliest industrial accident in the U.S. history killing at least 581 people and injuring nearly 8000 (see Figure 3.4).

Ammonium nitrate has been used for centuries in warfare, but is also a mainstay of commercial nitrogenous fertilizers. The explosive nature of ammonium nitrate is due to its

FIGURE 3.4    The 1947 Texas City ammonium nitrate explosion. *Courtesy of Special Collections, University of Houston Libraries. UH Digital Library*

decomposition into gaseous products (nitrogen, $H_2O$ vapor, and oxygen) and also due to the exothermic nature of the reaction. The decomposition reaction can be summarized as

$$NH_4NO_3 = N_2 + 2H_2O(g) + 0.5O_2$$
$$\Delta_r H^0 = -118.1 \, kJ \, mol^{-1} \quad and \quad \Delta_r G^0 = -273.3 \, kJ \, mol^{-1} \tag{3.5}$$

Ammonium nitrate however does not decompose spontaneously at room temperature in spite of the Gibbs function of reaction being negative. The temperature needs to be above 210 °C for the spontaneously decomposition reaction to take place. However, a serious jolt can initiate the decomposition reaction, even at room temperature. In the presence of certain impurities, the reaction is spontaneous at much lower temperatures. The effect of impurities can be judged from the following reaction with one such impurity, aluminum:

$$NH_4NO_3 + 2Al = N_2 + 2H_2O(g) + Al_2O_3 + 2H_2$$
$$\Delta_r H^0 = -1310.1 \, kJ \, mol^{-1} \quad and \quad \Delta_r G^0 = -1398.4 \, kJ \, mol^{-1} \tag{3.6}$$

Both the enthalpy and Gibbs function are very much more negative in Equation (3.6) than in Equation (3.5), indicating a very much greater heat of reaction and a more spontaneous reaction, with a low activation energy that needs only a relatively small jolt to set it off.[15] Once the decomposition reaction starts, the exothermic nature of reaction causes the temperature of the reaction to rise and this speeds up the reaction (reactions generally double in speed for every 10 °C rise in temperature). If the heat is not conducted away, the reaction rate increases, resulting in a run-a-way reaction, making it difficult to stop. With the increase in temperature, the gaseous products (nitrogen, water vapor, and oxygen in the case of reaction 1) rapidly expand and an explosion takes place, with the expanding gases pushing back anything in their way.

The biggest ammonium nitrate explosion that has taken place was the Texas City explosion on April 16, 1947. The cargo ship *Grandcamp* was in Texas City harbor being loaded when a fire was detected in the hold. There were 2600 tonnes of ammonium nitrate on board. The captain closed the hold and pumped in pressurized steam. One hour later, the ship exploded, killing several hundred people and setting fire to another vessel, the *High Flyer*, which was moored 250 m away. This ship contained 1050 tonnes of sulfur and 860 tonnes of ammonium nitrate. The *Grandcamp* explosion created a shockwave and knocked two small planes flying at 460 m (1500 ft) out of the sky. The *High Flyer* exploded the next day, after having burned for many hours.

Other ammonium nitrate industrial explosions have taken place at Morgan (now Sayreville), New Jersey 1918; Kriewald, Germany 1921; Oppau, Germany 1921; Brest, France 1947; Tessenderlo, Belgium 1942; Kansas City, Missouri 1988; Ryongchon, and North Korea, 2004. Most of these were caused by detonation, but a few were initiated by fires adjacent to piles of stored ammonium nitrate.

## PICRIC ACID AND TNT

Another very exothermic set of reactions are the detonation and oxidation reactions of picric acid (2,4,6-trinitrophenol or TNP; see Figure 3.5). Picric acid was used in warfare from the mid-nineteenth century and was superseded by TNT (a related chemical) during WW1.

The detonation or decomposition reaction of TNP is

$$C_6H_3N_3O_7 = 5.5CO + 1.5N_2 + 1.5H_2O + 0.5C, \quad \Delta_r H^0 = -2306.3 \text{ kJ mol}^{-1} \quad (3.7)$$

And the oxidation reaction of TNP is

$$C_6H_3N_3O_7 + O_2 = 2CO_2 + 1.5N_2 + 1.5H_2O, \quad \Delta_r H^0 = -2571.9 \text{ kJ mol}^{-1} \quad (3.8)$$

The reactions for TNT (see Figure 3.6) are similar in that they are very exothermic; they produce large quantities of gas (in this case $CO_2$ and $N_2$); and also requires a major bust of energy, a jolt

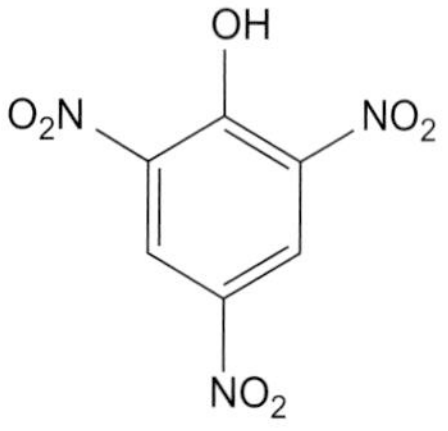

FIGURE 3.5   Picric acid.

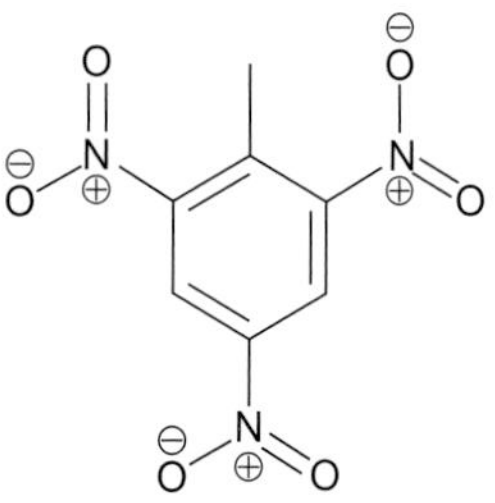

FIGURE 3.6   Trinitrotoluene.

or heat, to start the reaction. The TNT detonation reaction is a mixture of the following two reactions:

$$C_7H_5N_3O_6 \rightarrow 1.5N_2 + 2.5H_2O + 3.5CO + 3.5C \tag{3.9}$$

$$C_7H_5N_3O_6 \rightarrow 1.5N_2 + 2.5H_2 + 6CO + C \tag{3.10}$$

These reactions were responsible for the world's largest man-made accidental explosion which took place in the harbor at Halifax, Nova Scotia, on December 6, 1917.

The explosion flattened the city of Halifax and was due to the accidental collision of a Norwegian ship *SS Imo* with the French cargo ship, the *SS Mont-Blanc* in "the Narrows" section of the Halifax Harbor. The *Mont-Blanc* was an ammunitions vessel, containing 300 rounds of ammunition, 9 tonnes of gun cotton, 2100 tonnes of picric acid (TNP), and 1800 tonnes of TNT. Stacked on deck was a further 30 tonnes of fuel in drums. This was probably benzene. About 2000 people were killed by debris, fires, or collapsed buildings and it is estimated that over 9000 people were injured.[16]

The *Mont-Blanc* caught fire soon after the collision and this was probably due to the benzene which was also stored on board. This was followed by the gigantic explosion about half an hour later. All buildings and structures covering nearly 2 km$^2$ (500 acres) were obliterated. The explosion caused a tsunami in the harbor and a pressure wave of air from the expanding gases from the exploding TNP and TNT knocked down trees bent iron rails, flattened buildings, and fragments of the *Mont-Blanc* were found kilometers away. A black rain of carbon from the *Mont-Blanc* fell over the city after the blast (see Equation 3.9), covering the city debris with soot.

As in the case of the ammonium nitrate explosions, the force and strength of the explosion was due to the exothermic nature of the reactions which raised the temperature causing a the rapid acceleration of the reaction and the expanding hot gases which in this case were $CO_2$, $H_2O(g)$, $N_2$, and of course the surrounding air. It was the pressure waves from these expanding gases that were responsible for much of the destruction.

Unfortunately, the *Mont-Blanc* was not flying a red flag that would have indicated to all that she was carrying explosives and ammunition.[17]

## METHYL ISOCYANATE

The explosion and disaster at Bhopal will be discussed in detail in Chapter 4. In brief the explosion was related to the exothermic nature of the reaction between methyl isocyanate (MIC) and water. The MIC was used to make a pesticide called carbaryl in a one-step process with 1-naphthol. MIC is weakly soluble in water (6-10 parts per 100 parts), but it reacts exothermically with the water, producing carbon dioxide gas.

The MIC at Bhopal was kept in special storage tanks which ensured that the MIC did not come into contact with water. On December 2, 1984, workers were cleaning out pipes near to the MIC tanks. Whether one of the workers failed to keep the necessary valves shut or whether the valves failed or leaked, we will never know, but water entered one of the MIC tanks. To make matters worse, the tank was over 75% full which was in breach of the regulation that the MIC tanks should be only 50-60% full. The unfilled space was there to act as a buffer in case of an accident. The water leaking in slowly reacted with the MIC, causing the temperature and pressure to increase. Meanwhile, the workers had realized that MIC was leaking because their eyes were smarting. This was reported to the supervisor in the control room who checked the pressure in the tank and found it normal at 10 lbs per square in. (69 kPa). The normal range was 2-25 psi. An hour later, the pressure had shot up to 55 psi and the temperature was 25 °C. The refrigeration unit was not working as the coolant had been drained during a recent shutdown. Soon the pressure had reached 180 psi and the temperature 200° C and the concrete round the tank was cracking. In no time, the tank ruptured and the gas shot out of the tank into the atmosphere. The tank originally contained 36 tonnes of MIC (see Figure 3.7).

The problem in Bhopal was not that the reaction of MIC with water created a poisonous gas, but that the initial reaction heated the tank of MIC and produced $CO_2$ gas, which on heating expanded and ruptured the MIC tank, allowed MIC to escape into the air.

MIC is volatile, irritating to the nose and throat, and highly toxic. Although it is a liquid at room temperature, MIC has a low boiling point (39.5 °C) and has a high vapor pressure of 57.7 kPa at 25 °C.

The reaction of MIC with water produces methylamine and carbon dioxide,

$$CH_3NCO + H_2O = CH_3NH_2 + CO_2, \quad \Delta_r H^0 = -566.3 \text{ kJ mol}^{-1} \tag{3.11}$$

Methylamine and carbon dioxide are both gases at room temperature. The production of gas in the reaction raised the pressure in the container; the generation of heat from the exothermic reaction raised the pressure still further. This rise in pressure caused a rupture of the MIC vessel, releasing unreacted MIC into the atmosphere. The heat also made the MIC more volatile (the temperature in the MIC tank was far in excess of the boiling point of the MIC).

The plume of MIC vapor that enveloped the shanty town of Bhopal built around the chemical plant caused the deaths of over 2000 people soon after exposure. More people died later and over 200,000 were exposed to the MIC vapor.

FIGURE 3.7   Tanks photographed shortly after the Bhopal disaster. *Taken from http://sayiamgreen.com/blog/2009/10/the-worst-environmental-disasters-of-all-time/.*

The main causes of the disaster included:

- Storing the MIC in very large tanks and filling them beyond the recommended levels.
- Poor maintenance which was responsible for the failure of many safety systems.
- Safety systems being switched off to save money—including the MIC tank refrigeration system which could have reduced the rising temperature.
- The problem was made worse by the huge number of shacks in the near vicinity of the plant.[18]

Explosions can be disasters when they result in loss of life and property. Bhopal represents an environmental and human disaster with stages of effects. The explosion itself caused immediate damage and loss of life. This was followed by a short-term exposure scenario, where people were exposed to a toxic gas. The long-term effects continued as a result of this exposure, as chronic effects increased in the population months and years after the toxic cloud dissipated.

This is similar to other environmental disasters, such as the explosion of the oil rig in the Gulf of Mexico, wherein 11 people died immediately from the explosion. However, rather than the diseases in the human population, the subsequent long-term effects were mainly environmental (damage to coastal and aquatic habitats and wildlife insults).With regard to environmental disasters, they are usually one of the triggering events that lead to public health and environmental degradation. In Chapter 7, we will consider another form of triggering event, fires. However, before we do, we will address the way contaminants and harm move throughout the environment in the atmosphere, hydrosphere, and biosphere in Chapters 4-6.

## NATURAL EXPLOSIONS—VOLCANOES

Volcanoes can have an enormous effect on meteorology and climate, which, in turn, affects ecosystems. As explosions go, volcano eruptions are massive. The gases emitted from volcanoes are water vapor, carbon dioxide, sulfur dioxide ($SO_2$ high-temperature eruption), hydrogen sulfide ($H_2S$ -low-temperature eruption), nitrogen, argon, helium, neon, methane, carbon monoxide, and hydrogen. The composition does vary, but the most common gases are water vapor (usually more than 60%) and carbon dioxide (10-40%).

It is the particulate matter or ash that is perhaps the most important class of pollutants since it can alter weather patterns, even on a global scale. Figure 3.8 shows that after every large volcano eruption over the past 130 years, there has been a drop in global temperature over a period of a few years. This is due to the increase in albedo effect (higher reflection of the sun's energy) due to aerosol formation created by the vast amount of tiny particulate matter. It is the small airborne particulates of less than 10 μm that are the cause of respiratory problems because these particles can penetrate deep into the lungs. They represent something like 25-40% of all particulate matter blown out of volcanoes. The particulate matter is usually based on silica.[19,20] Note that sulfur is a component of volcanic releases, i.e. $SO_2$ at high temperatures and $H_2S$ at low temperatures). $SO_2$ is a cooling gas, which means that in addition to blocking incoming solar radiation, the presence $SO_2$ can lower temperatures even more.

The 2010 Eyjafjallökull volcano in Iceland caused 6 days of air travel interruption across western and northern Europe and the plume rose to a height of approximately 9 km (see Figure 3.9).

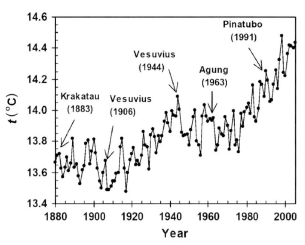

FIGURE 3.8 This graph shows the drop in temperature after each larger volcanic eruption. *From Dorman LI in Letcher TM. Climate change: observed impacts on planet earth. Oxford: Elsevier; 2009. p. 68. ISBN 978-0-444-53301-2.*

FIGURE 3.9 The 2010 Icelandic Volanic eruption. *Steve And Donna O'Meara/National Geographic Stock.*

Explosions are sometimes exclusively associated with loss of human life and property, but they have had large effects on ecosystems. As such, they represent an important type of environmental disaster. They remind us that perturbing ecosystems and human populations usually affects more than what is obvious at the outset. The explosion may be dramatic, but the subsequent series of events may extend the environmental disaster's effects, in both space and time.

## References

1. Zeeuwen P. Dust explosions: what are the risks?. In: *Paper presented at Euroforum Conference, Paris, France*; 1997.
2. U.S. Department of Labor. *Occupational Safety and Health Administration. Safety and Health Topics, Grain Handling.* www.osha.gov/SLTC/grainhandling/index.html; [accessed December 6, 2011].

3. U.S. Department of Labor. *Combustible dust in industry: preventing and mitigating the effects of fires and explosions. Occupational Safety and Health Administration. 31 July 2005.* www.osha.gov/dts/shib/shib073105.html; 2005 [accessed December 4, 2011].

4. Loller T. Huffington Post 14 November 2011. www.huffingtonpost.com/2011/11/14/dust-explosion-killing-factory-worker_n_1092664.html; 2011 [accessed December 1, 2011].

5. Deadly Kansas grain Elevator Explosion Deemed Accidental. Fox News, 18 November 2011.

6. Explosion Hazards, Limited. *The risks of explosion.* http://www.explosionhazards.co.uk/the-risks-of-explosion; 2011 [accessed March 4, 2012].

7. Ministry for National and Regional Development and the Environment. *Explosion of a grain silo—Blaye, France. Summary report.* www.ineris.fr/centredoc/**blaye**_report_va.pdf; 1998 [accessed March 4, 2012].

8. Explosion Hazards, Limited; 2011.

9. European Commission. *Recommendations from the Scientific Committee on Occupational Exposure Limits for Flour Dust.* SCOEL/SUM/123; http://ec.europa.eu/social/keyDocuments.jsp?policyArea=&type=0&country=0&year=0&advSearchKey=flour+dust&mode=advancedSubmit&langId=en; 2008 [accessed March 4, 2012].

10. Ministry for National and Regional Development and the Environment (1998) and European Commission (2008).

11. Bartec Safety Solutions and Technology . *Dust explosion protection.* www.bartec.de/homepage/eng/downloads/produkte/staubexschutz/Dust_ex.pdf; 2005 [accessed December 4, 2011].

12. European Commission; 2008.

13. The calculations in the section are based on: Weast RC. *CRC handbook of chemistry and physics.* Florida: CRC Press Boca Raton; 1981 and 1982; Atkins P. *Physical chemistry.* 6th ed. Oxford: Oxford University Press; 1998.

14. Health and Safety Executive. *Safe handling of combustible dusts: precautions against explosions HSG103.* Sudbury, Suffolk: Health and Safety Executive Books; 2003 ISBN 0 7176 0725 9.

15. Atkins P. *Physical chemistry.* 6th ed. Oxford: Oxford University Press; 1998 chapter 5.

16. White J. Exploding myths: the Halifax explosion in historical context. In: Ruffman Alan, Howell Colin D, editors. *Ground zero: a reassessment of the 1917 explosion in Halifax.* Halifax: Nimbus Publishing; 1994. p. 266.

17. http://www.en.wikipedia.org/wiki/List_of_the_largest_artificial_non-nuclear_explosions[accessed December 20, 2011].

18. http://www.bhopal.net/key-facts [accessed December 22, 2011].

19. Moore KR, Duffell H, Nicholl A, Searl A. Monitoring of airborne particulate matter during the eruption of Soufriere Hills Volcano, Montserrat. In: Druitt TH, Kokelaar BP, editors. *Memoirs.* London: Geological Society; 2002. p. 557–66.

20. Horwell CJ, Sparks RSJ, Brewer TS, Llewellin EW, Williamson BJ. Characterization of respirable volcanic ash from the Soufriere Hills volcano, Montserrat, with implications for human health hazards. *Bull Volcanol* 2003;**65**:346–62.

# Plumes

In Chapter 3, we described explosions. These are obviously important in terms of damage, but from an environmental perspective, they illustrate a sudden change that can shock a system. This shock can be the result of a large amount of energy and matter released. These releases may also precipitate fires and damage to structures, causing additional pollution. Whereas explosions are extreme events that may release large amounts of pollutants, they are rare in comparison to the myriad types of pollutant emissions that range from microscopic (methane released from an anaerobic bacterium) to localized (volatile organic compounds from idling motor vehicles) to regional (aerosols and oxides of sulfur and nitrogen from power plants) to global (volcanic eruptions).

Once matter is released from a source, it moves. The aggregation of matter is a plume. The plume is described with respect to its rate of movement, how rapidly it disperses or dilutes, and the concentration of pollutants. The components of the environment differ with respect to their vulnerability and damage when contacted by the plume. The plume must be considered from the physical, chemical, and biological perspectives. Ecosystems consist of both nonliving (abiotic) and living (biotic) components. The integrity of an ecosystem or a human population is determined by both. Thus, anything that enters has an impact, which may be beneficial, deleterious, or neutral. Abiotic and biotic agents, such as chemicals, heat, and microbes, enter the environment in various ways, intentionally (e.g., warfare agents) or unintentionally (e.g., failed containment).

## NOMENCLATURE

Usually, disasters are associated with unintentional releases to the environment. These releases have many names, including leaks, spills, emissions, effluent, pollution, contamination, seeps, leachate, and plumes.

A leak or spill may be the event that is most often associated with environmental disasters. Defining a leak or spill, like much environmental terminology, is not standardized. In fact, many terms are specifically defined in law and regulation, which varies by type of pollution. For example, an ongoing release of a contaminant into the air is often referred to as an "emission." Regulatory agencies keep track of such emissions, often depending on self-reporting by the entity doing the emitting. These data are collected and published as "emission inventories."

An emission may be direct, such as from a boiler unit connected directly to a stack from which gases and aerosols are emitted. Usually, such direct emissions are not allowed. That is, they must be controlled. Thus, engineers design pollution control equipment, such as cyclones, electrostatic precipitators, and scrubbers, to collect and treat pollutants before they are released. Thus, the concentrations of contaminants are much lower than if the emission were direct. Also, the conveyances may consist of air movers (e.g., fans), heat exchangers, ventilation equipment, and other devices and conduits, that exist in sequence before reaching the pollution control equipment. An emission is considered to be uncontrolled or improperly controlled if it leaks to the atmosphere before reaching the pollution control equipment, or if the equipment does not lower the concentrations of pollutants as required. The Bhopal and Seveso disasters are examples of the former, whereas poorly operating equipment is a much more common example of the latter.

A plume is a varying concentration of a substance after it is released into the environment. Usually, the plume is at a higher concentration near the source, owing to dispersion and dilution. This change in concentration with respect to distance is the concentration gradient:

$$\frac{dC}{dx},$$ (4.1)

where $C$ = contaminant concentration and $x$ = distance.

Plumes can range in size from very small (encompassing a building or two, such as those modeled in Figure 4.1) to urban scale (see modeled plumes in Figures 4.2 and 4.3) to almost global (see Figure 4.4). Chemical and biological agents can be transported long distances in high winds. For example, some of the invasive bacteria that threaten coral reef habitats may originate from Africa in the form of Saharan dust. Deserts commonly contain gravel and bedrock, along with some sand. The Sahara is the exception, with sand covering 20% of the spatial extent of the desert. This means that the Sahara often loses large amounts of dust by winds that advectively transport particles in plumes that can travel across the Atlantic Ocean; depositing dust along the way (see Figure 4.4). The smaller the dust particle, the longer it remains suspended, and the further it will travel. Saharan dust itself is an example of particle matter (PM), which causes health effects. In addition, PM contains toxic substances and carries disease-causing bacteria and fungi that have been associated with the destruction of coral reefs in the Caribbean Sea.

The extent and shape of plumes are determined by many factors, including the conditions of the atmosphere and the characteristics of the agents being carried. Assuming the most simple scenario (which is never the case in environmental science), the distribution of contaminants will be random. This is predicted using Gaussian dispersion algorithms (see Figure 4.5) to estimate drift over simple terrain (e.g., low roughness index and low relief). This approach assumes that the chemical contaminants and organisms or their materials (e.g., spores) will be dispersed randomly according to wind vectors. That is, standard deviations of particles (aerosols, microbes, spores, etc.,) in the $x$, $y$, and $z$ axes are calculated to determine the location of the plume carrying these particles. However, new atmospheric dispersion methods may be applied to more complex ecosystems characterized by vertical venting in forest areas, channeling down canyons, and both horizontal and vertical recirculations that may occur at local sites. In fact, some of the recent computational models that have been developed for air pollution in complex airsheds may be put to use in ecological risk assessments for disasters.

A

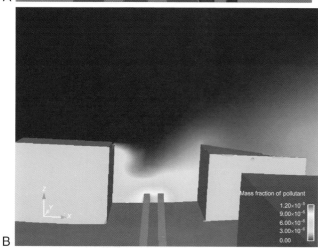

B

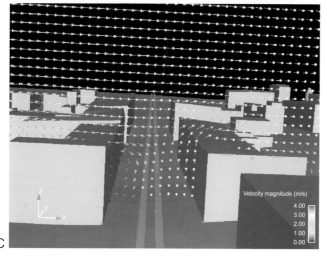

C

**FIGURE 4.1** Vertical slice view of a computation fluid dynamics model of roadway emissions represented as a source box along the roadway: (A) concentrations for street bounded by building on one side, (B) concentrations for street canyon, and (C) wind vectors for street canyon. *Photos used with permission from: U.S. Environmental Protection Agency. North Carolina: Research Triangle Park.*

FIGURE 4.2    Example of a simulated plume of neutrally buoyant smoke released from the World Trade Center; using a physical wind-tunnel model, flow from left to right isdisplayed; natural light is illuminating the smoke and a vertical laser sheet is additionally illuminating the plume near the centerline of source. Vertical laser sheet is additionally illuminating the plume near the centerline of source. *Photo used with permission from: U.S. Environmental Protection Agency. Perry S, Heath D. Fluid modeling facility. North Carolina: Research Triangle Park; 2006.*

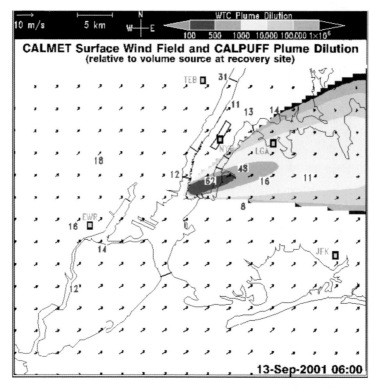

FIGURE 4.3    Plume simulated with CALPUFF model showing the averaged-hourly particulate concentration $\leq 2.4\ \mu m$ ($PM_{2.5}$) dilution of a volume source at the World Trade Center, New York City. *Photo used with permission from: Alan Huber and U.S. Environmental Protection Agency.*

FIGURE 4.4 Plumes exiting from Africa's west coast on January 22, 2008. The plumes transport dust from the Sahara Desert across the Atlantic Ocean. The dust in the plumes contains bacteria, fungi, and their spores that have been associated with coral reef destruction. In this photo, the dust stayed airborne over the Atlantic Ocean for several days in mid-January 2008, before the National Air and Space Agency's Aqua satellite captured this image using Moderate Resolution Imaging Spectroradiometer (MODIS).

## EARLY AIR QUALITY DISASTERS

### Donora

In 1948, the United States experienced its first major air pollution catastrophe in Donora, Pennsylvania. Contaminant releases from a number of industries, including a sulfuric acid plant, a steel mill, and a zinc production plant, became trapped in a valley by a temperature inversion and produced an unbreathable mixture of fog and pollution. Six-thousand suffered illnesses ranging from sore throats to nausea. There were 20 deaths in 3 days. Sulfur dioxide ($SO_2$) was estimated to reach levels as high as 5500 $\mu g\ m^{-3}$.

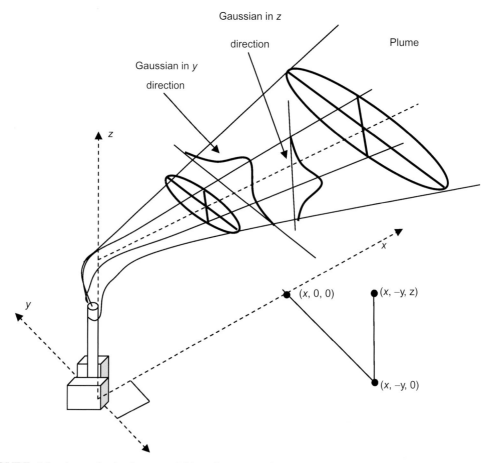

FIGURE 4.5 Atmospheric plume model based upon random (Gaussian) distributions in the horizontal and vertical directions. This is usually an oversimplified plume characterization, since the plume is always permutated by variable terrain, winds, and other physical phenomena.

This particular form of sulfur is highly toxic, whereas many other compounds of sulfur are essential components of biological systems. In the wrong place at the wrong time, these same compounds are hazardous to health, welfare, and the environment. A common feature of many air pollution episodes is the thermal inversion. In the air, meteorology helps to determine the opportunities to control the atmospheric transport of contaminants. For example, industries are often located near each other, concentrating the release and mixing of pollutants. Cities and industrial centers have often been located near water bodies. This means they are inordinately common in river valleys and other depressions. Locating emission sources in this topography increases the likelihood of occurrences of ground-based inversions, elevated inversions, valley winds, shore breezes, and city heat islands (see Figure 4.6). When this happens, as it did in Donora, the air stagnates to a point where pollutants become locked into air masses and the rates of exchanges to atmosphere decrease. As a result, the concentrations of the pollutants can quickly pose substantial risks to public health and the environment.

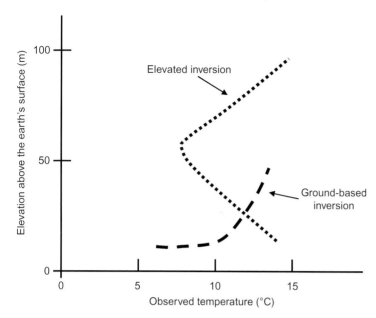

FIGURE 4.6 Two types of thermal inversions that contribute to air pollution.

## Poza Rica

Poza Rica, Mexico, was a town of 15,000 people on the Gulf of Mexico with a substantial petrochemical center in the 1940s (see Table 4.1). The disaster originated from an accident at one of the local factories which recovers sulfur from natural gas. The resultant release of hydrogen sulfide ($H_2S$) into the ambient air lasted less than one-half hour. However, the dispersal of the gas under a shallow inversion with foggy and calm conditions killed 22 people and hospitalized 320.

Note that this form of sulfur, i.e. reduced, is different from the $SO_2$ in the Donora disaster. Hydrogen sulfide ($H_2S$), a colorless gas which, is often produced as an unintended byproduct of combustion, desulfurization processes, and chemical operations. Table 4.2 provides the

TABLE 4.1 Crude Oil Production by Field

| Field | Share of national petroleum production | | |
| --- | --- | --- | --- |
| | 1940 | 1945 | 1949 |
| Poza Rica | 65% | 53% | 59% |
| Pánuco-Ebano | 14% | 12% | 17% |
| Faja de Oro (Golden Lane) | 9% | 23% | 13% |
| Isthmus de Tehuantepec | 13% | 12% | 11% |
| Reynosa | 0% | 0% | 0%[a] |

[a]Less than 1%.

Source: Watkins T. San Jose State University: http://www2.sjsu.edu/faculty/watkins/watkins.htm [accessed 19 April 2005].

TABLE 4.2  Physicochemical Properties of Hydrogen Sulfide ($H_2S$)

- Molecular weight: 34.08 g mol$^{-1}$

- Melting point: $-86\,°C$
- Latent heat of fusion (1.013 bar at triple point): 69.75 kJ kg$^{-1}$

- Liquid density (1.013 bar at boiling point): 914.9 kg m$^{-3}$
- Liquid/gas equivalent (1.013 bar and 15 °C (59 °F)): 638 vol vol$^{-1}$
- Boiling point (1.013 bar): $-60.2\,°C$
- Latent heat of vaporization (1.013 bar at boiling point): 547.58 kJ kg$^{-1}$
- Vapor pressure (at 21 °C or 70 °F): 18.2 bar

- Critical temperature: 100 °C
- Critical pressure: 89.37 bar

- Gas density (1.013 bar at boiling point): 1.93 kg m$^{-3}$
- Gas density (1.013 bar and 15 °C (59 °F)): 1.45 kg m$^{-3}$
- Compressibility factor (Z) (1.013 bar and 15 °C (59 °F)): 0.9915
- Specific gravity (air=1) (1.013 bar and 15 °C (59 °F)): 1.189
- Specific volume (1.013 bar and 21 °C (70 °F)): 0.699 m$^3$ kg$^{-1}$
- Heat capacity at constant pressure (Cp) [1 bar and 25 °C (77 °F)]: 0.034 kJ (mol K)$^{-1}$
- Viscosity [1.013 bar and 0 °C (32 °F)]: 0.0001179 poise
- Thermal conductivity (1.013 bar and 0 °C (32 °F)): 12.98 mW (m K)$^{-1}$

- Solubility in water (1.013 bar and 0 °C (32 °F)): 4.67 vol vol$^{-1}$
- Autoignition temperature: 270 °C

*Source: Air Liquide: http://www.airliquide.com/en/business/products/gases/gasdata/index.asp?GasID=59 [accessed 20 April 2005].*

physicochemical properties of the compound. It does have industrial uses, such as a reagent and as an intermediate in the preparation of other reduced sulfur compounds. Other principal sources of $H_2S$ include geothermal power plants (due to the reduction of sulfur in makeup water), petroleum refining (reduction of sulfur in the crude oil), and gas releases from sewers (when plants go anaerobic or when pockets of anoxic conditions exist in the plants or in the sewer lines).

In 1969, California set an ambient air quality standard for $H_2S$ of 0.03 ppm (42 µg m$^{-3}$), averaged over a period of 1 h and not to be equaled or exceeded, to protect against the substance's nuisance odor, i.e., the "rotten egg smell."[1] As new studies began to link $H_2S$ exposures to health effects, the acceptable air levels dropped further. Based on a study demonstrating nasal histological changes in mice, the State of California lowered the acceptable concentration to 8 ppb (10 µg m$^{-3}$) as the chronic Reference Exposure Level for use in evaluating long-term emissions from facilities in high emission areas.[2] The United States does not currently classify $H_2S$ as either a criteria air pollutant or a Hazardous Air Pollutant. The U.S. Environmental Protection agency has issued safety levels, known as reference concentrations (RfCs), and for $H_2S$, for long-term (chronic) effects it is 0.001 mg m$^{-3}$ (1 µg m$^{-3}$).[3] The RfC is an estimate of a daily inhalation exposure of the human population that is likely to be without an appreciable risk of adverse effects during a person's expected lifetime (see Chapter 5 for more details on how the RfC is developed). Exposure to $H_2S$ concentrations of 250 ppm irritates mucous membranes and can lead to conjunctivitis, photophobia, lacrimation, corneal opacity, rhinitis, bronchitis, cyanosis,

TABLE 4.3 Predicted Effects of Exposure to Ambient Concentrations of Hydrogen Sulfide ($H_2S$)

| $H_2S$ (ppb) | % Able to detect odor[a] | Perceived odor intensity[b] (ratio) | Median odor units[c] | % Annoyed by odor[d] |
|---|---|---|---|---|
| 200 | 99 | 2.31 | 25 | 88 |
| 100 | 96 | 1.93 | 12 | 75 |
| 50 | 91 | 1.61 | 6.2 | 56 |
| 40 | 88 | 1.52 | 5.0 | 50 |
| 35 | 87 | 1.47 | 4.4 | 47 |
| 30 | 83 | 1.41 | 3.7 | 40 |
| 25 | 80 | 1.34 | 3.1 | 37 |
| 20 | 74 | 1.27 | 2.5 | 31 |
| 15 | 69 | 1.18 | 1.9 | 22 |
| 10 | 56 | 1.06 | 1.2 | 17 |
| 8 | 50 | 1.00 | 1.00 | 11 |
| 6 | 42 | 0.93 | 0.75 | 8 |
| 4 | 30 | 0.83 | 0.50 | 5 |
| 2 | 14 | 0.70 | 0.25 | 2 |
| 1 | 6 | 0.58 | 0.12 | 1 |
| 0.5 | 2 | 0.49 | 0.06 | 0 |

[a]Based on mean odor detection threshold of 8.0 ppb and standard deviation ±2.0 binary step.
[b]Based on intensity exponent of 0.26.
[c]$H_2S$ concentration divided by mean odor detection threshold of 8 ppb.
[d]Based on assumption that the mean annoyance threshold is 5× the mean odor detection threshold, and standard deviation ±2.0 binary steps.
Sources: California Air Resources Board. Hydrogen sulfide: evaluation of current California air quality standards with respect to protection of children. Sacramento, CA, 2000; Amoore JE. The perception of hydrogen sulfide odor in relation to setting an ambient standard. Berkeley, CA: Olfacto-Labs; 1985 [prepared for the California Air Resources Board].

and acute lung injury. Concentrations between 250 and 500 ppm can induce headache, nausea, vomiting, diarrhea, vertigo, amnesia, dizziness, apnea, palpitations, tachycardia, hypotension, muscle cramps, weakness, disorientation, and coma. Higher levels, >700 ppm, may cause abrupt physical collapse, respiratory paralysis, asphyxial seizures, and death.[4]

Hydrogen sulfide is one of only a relatively few compounds whose detection is directly related to olfactory sensitivity. The greater the concentration, the more likely people can identify $H_2S$ (see Table 4.3), although the sense of smell is paralyzed (known as "extinction") at airborne concentrations >150 ppm (or as low as 50 ppm). Perceiving the presence of a pollutant is not often the case in environmental pollution, where many very toxic compounds are imperceptible even at dangerously high concentrations. That is to say, pollutants are all too often odorless, tasteless and colorless at concentrations that can cause disease and environmental damage.

Environmentally, $H_2S$ reverts chemically to elemental sulfur in surface waters. In soil and sediment, microbes mediate oxidation-reduction reactions that oxidize hydrogen sulfide to elemental sulfur. Bacterium genera *Beggiatoa*, *Thioploca*, and *Thiotrix* exist in transition zones between aerobic and anaerobic conditions where both molecular oxygen and $H_2S$ are present. A few photosynthetic bacteria also oxidize hydrogen sulfide to elemental sulfur. Purple sulfur bacteria (*Chlorobiaceae* and *Chromatiaceae*), which are phototropic aerobes, can live in high $H_2S$ water. The interactions of these organisms with their environments are key components of the global sulfur cycle. Due to its abiotic and biological reactions, $H_2S$ does not bioaccumulate.[4]

## London, England

Known infamously as "the London Fog," from December 5 to 8, 1952, London experienced the worst ambient air pollution disaster ever reported. The meteorological conditions were ideal for a pollution event. Anticyclonic or high pressure weather with stagnating continental polar air masses trapped under subsidence inversions produced a shallow mixing layer with an almost complete absence of vertical and horizontal air motion. Fireplaces and industries supplied the hygroscopic condensation nuclei into the air to form dense fog. The daily temperatures were below the average. With such adverse conditions, the concentrations of pollutants reached high values.

The elderly are often more sensitive to the effects of air pollutants than is the general population, i.e., they are considered to be a "sensitive subpopulation." This was the case in the London fog incident. Deaths from bronchitis in the elderly increased by a factor of 10, influenza by 7, pneumonia by 5, tuberculosis by 4.5, other respiratory diseases by 6, heart diseases by 3, and lung cancer by 2. When a change in weather finally cleared the fog, 4000 Londoners had perished in their "pea soup."

Subsequent air pollution episodes with comparably elevated pollution occurred in 1957-1958 and again in 1962-1963. But the 1952 incident showed much greater mortality and morbidity.

## New York City

New York City experienced air pollution-related deaths in 1953, 1962-1963, and 1966, beyond what epidemiologists would have expected. New York had very high $SO_2$ atmospheric concentrations through much of the twentieth century, but its local meteorology often helped the city avert air pollution disasters. However, when these conditions change, as they did in December 1962, which experienced calm winds and the occurrence of shallow inversions, then the $SO_2$ and aerosol concentrations peaked. Total deaths increased to 269, which was in excess (more than three standard deviations greater than the mean!) beyond the expected mortality for that week.

These episodes reinforced the need to address air pollution, mainly in urban areas. The Clean Air Act of 1970 greatly increased the requirements of pollution control technologies and compliance with air quality standards in the United States. In fact, this was one of the major environmental successes of the twentieth century. This law authorized the U.S.

TABLE 4.4    Percentage Decrease in Ambient Concentrations of National Ambient Air Quality Standard Pollutants from 1985 Through 1994

| Pollutant | Decrease in concentration (%) |
|---|---|
| CO | 28 |
| Lead | 86 |
| $NO_2$ | 9 |
| Ozone | 12 |
| $PM_{10}$ | 20 |
| $SO_2$ | 25 |

*Source: Code of Federal Regulations, Part 40; CFR 1507.3.*

Environmental Protection Agency (EPA) to establish National Ambient Air Quality Standards (NAAQS) to protect public health and the environment from the "conventional" pollutants (contrasted with "toxic" pollutants that would be addressed to a much greater extent later with the 1990 amendments). These pollutants were carbon monoxide, particulate matter (PM), oxides of nitrogen, oxides of sulfur, and photochemical oxidant smog or ozone. The metal lead (Pb) was later added as the sixth NAAQS pollutant.

The original goal was to set and to achieve NAAQS in every state by 1975. These new standards were combined with charging the 50 states to develop state implementation plans to address industrial sources in the state. The ambient atmospheric concentrations are measured at over 4000 monitoring sites across the United States. The ambient levels have continuously decreased, as shown in Table 4.4. About the same time, other countries passed similar laws and regulations to address these conventional air pollutants.

# TOXIC PLUMES

## Bhopal

As mentioned in Chapter 3 in our discussion of the methyl isocyanate (MIC) explosion, arguably the worst chemical plume disaster occurred in Bhopal in 1984 when a toxic cloud from the Union Carbide pesticide plant came into contact with thousands of people. This contamination killed many people and permanently injured about tens of thousands more. As discussed in Chapter 1, a failure is often described as an outcome when not applying the science correctly (e.g., a mathematical error and an incorrect extrapolation of a physical principle). Another type of failure results from misjudgments of human systems. Bhopal had both.

The pesticide manufacturing plant (see Figure 1.4) in Bhopal demonstrates that even unlikely events can occur and lead to disaster.[5,6] The plant, up to its closing, had produced the insecticides Sevin and Carbaryl since 1969, using MIC as an intermediate product in its gas phase. The MIC was produced by the reaction

$$(4.2)$$

This process was highly cost effective, involving only a single reaction step. The schematic of MIC processing at the Bhopal plant is shown in Equation (4.2).

The MIC is highly water reactive (see Table 4.5); i.e., it reacts violently with water, generating a very strong exothermic reaction that produces carbon dioxide. When MIC vaporizes, it becomes a highly toxic gas that, when concentrated, is highly caustic and burns tissues. This can lead to scalding of nasal and throat passages, blinding, and loss of limbs, as well as death.

On December 3, 1984, the Bhopal plant operators became concerned that a storage tank was showing signs of overheating and had begun to leak. The tank contained MIC. The leak rapidly increased in size and within 1 h of the first leakage, the tank exploded and released approximately $4 \times 10^4$ kg (80,000 lbs) of MIC into the atmosphere. The human exposure to MIC was widespread, with a half million people exposed. Nearly 3000 people died within the first

TABLE 4.5   Properties of Methyl Isocyanate (MIC)

| Common name | Isocyanic acid, methylester, and methyl carbylamine |
|---|---|
| Molecular mass | 57.1 |
| Properties | Melting point: $-45\,^{\circ}$C; boiling point: 43-45 $^{\circ}$C |
|  | Volatile liquid |
|  | Pungent odor |
|  | Reacts violently with water and is highly flammable |
|  | MIC vapor is denser than air and will collect and stay at low areas |
|  | The vapor mixes well with air and explosive mixtures are formed |
|  | May polymerize due to heating or under the influence of water and catalysts |
|  | Decomposes on heating and produces toxic gases such as hydrogen cyanide, nitrogen oxides, and carbon monoxide |
| Uses | Used in the production of synthetic rubber, adhesives, pesticides, and herbicide Intermediates. It is also used for the conversion of aldoximes to nitriles |
| Side effects | MIC is extremely toxic by inhalation, ingestion, and skin absorption. Inhalation of MIC causes cough, dizziness, shortness of breath, sore throat, and unconsciousness. It is corrosive to the skin and eyes. Short-term exposures also lead to death or adverse effects like pulmonary edema (respiratory inflammation), bronchitis, bronchial pneumonia, and reproductive effects. The Occupational Safety and Health Administration's permissible exposure limit to MIC over a normal 8-h workday or a 40-h workweek is 0.05 mg m$^{-3}$ |

Sources: US Chemical Safety and Hazards Board. http://www.chemsafety.gov/lib/bhopal.0.1.htr; Chapman and Hall. Dictionary of organic chemistry. vol. 4, 5th ed. USA: Mack Printing Company; 1982; Graham TW. Organic chemistry. 6th ed. Canada: John Wiley & Son, Inc.; 1996.

few days after the exposure, and 10,000 were permanently disabled. Ten years after the incident, thousands of death claims had been filed, along with 870,000 personal injury claims. However, only $90 million of the Union Carbide settlement agreement had been paid out.

The most basic physical science event tree begins with the water reactivity. That is, the combination of $H_2O$ and MIC resulted in a highly exothermic reaction. The rapid generation of the product of this reaction, carbon dioxide ($CO_2$), led to an explosive increase in pressure. The next step in the event tree was the release of 40 tonnes of MIC into the atmosphere. As of 2001, many victims had received compensation, averaging about $600 each, although some claims are still outstanding.

The Indian government had required that the plant be operated exclusively by Indian workers, so Union Carbide agreed to train them, including flying Indian workers to a sister plant in West Virginia for hands-on sessions. In addition, the company required that U.S. engineering teams make periodic on-site inspections for safety and quality control, but these ended in 1982, when the plant decided that these costs were too high. So, instead, the U.S. contingency was responsible only for budgetary and technical controls, but not safety. The last U.S. inspection in 1982 warned of many hazards, including a number that have since been implicated as contributing to the leak and release.

As is too often the case, safety and environmental actions may be quite good at first, but disintegrate rapidly unless they are continuously reinforced. From 1982 to 1984, safety measures declined, attributed to high employee turnover, improper and inadequate training of new employees, and low technical savvy in the local workforce. On-the-job experiences were often substituted for reading and understanding safety manuals (remember, this was a pesticide plant.) In fact, workers would complain of typical acute symptoms of pesticide exposure, such as shortness of breath, chest pains, headaches, and vomiting, yet they would typically refuse to wear protective clothing and equipment. The refusal in part stemmed from the lack of air conditioning in this subtropical climate, where masks and gloves can be uncomfortable.

More lenient Indian standards, rather than the U.S. safety standards were generally applied at the plant after 1982. This likely contributed to overloaded MIC storage tanks (e.g., company manuals cite a maximum of 60% fill).

The release lasted about 2 hours, by which time the entire quantity of MIC had been released. The highly reactive MIC arguably could have reacted and become diluted beyond a certain safe distance. However, over the years, tens of thousands of squatters had taken up residence just outside of the plant property, hoping to find work or at least take advantage of the plant's water and electricity. The squatters were not notified of hazards and risks associated with the pesticide manufacturing operations, except by a local journalist who posted signs saying: "Poison Gas. Thousands of Workers and Millions of Citizens are in Danger."

This is a classic instance of a "confluence of events" that led to a disaster. More than a few mistakes were made. The failure analysis found the following:

- The tank that initiated the disaster was 75% full of MIC at the outset.
- A standby overflow tank for the storage tank contained a large amount of MIC at the time of the incident.
- A required refrigeration unit for the tank was shut down 5 months prior to the incident, leading to a three- to fourfold increase in tank temperatures over expected temperatures.

- One report stated that a disgruntled employee unscrewed a pressure gauge and inserted a hose into the opening (knowing that it would do damage, but probably not nearly the scale of what occurred).
- A new employee was told by a supervisor to clean out connectors to the storage tanks, so the worker closed the valves properly, but did not insert safety discs to prevent the valves from leaking. In fact, the worker knew the valves *were* leaking, but they were the responsibility of the maintenance staff. Also the second-shift supervisor position had been eliminated.
- When the gauges started to show unsafe pressures, and even when the leaking gases started to sting mucous membranes of the workers, they found that evacuation exits were not available. There had been no emergency drills or evacuation plans.
- The primary fail-safe mechanism against leaks was a vent-gas scrubber, i.e., normally, this release of MIC would have been sorbed and neutralized by sodium hydroxide (NaOH) in the exhaust lines, but on the day of the disaster, the scrubbers were not working. (The scrubbers were deemed unnecessary, since they had never been needed before.)
- A flare tower to burn off any escaping gas that would bypass the scrubber was not operating because a section of conduit connecting the tower to the MIC storage tank was under repair.
- Workers attempted to mediate the release by spraying water 100 ft (31 m) high, but the release occurred at 120 ft (37 m).

Scientists and engineers tend to focus on the physical aspects of any system. However, Bhopal demonstrates that the most vulnerable aspects of a system and the major contributing factors to a disaster are often the human factors. As evidence, according to the audit, many checks and balances were in place, but the cultural considerations were ignored or given low priority, such as, when the plant was sited, the need to recognize the differences in land use planning and buffer zones in India compared to Western nations, or the difference in training and oversight of personnel in safety programs.

Another sad reality is that even dramatic failures like Bhopal fade in memory or are not applied to similar, vulnerable situations. In spite of a heightened awareness for years after the disaster, versions of the Bhopal incident have occurred and are likely to occur to smaller spatial extents and with, hopefully, more constrained impacts. For example, two freight trains collided in Graniteville, SC, just before 3:00 a.m. on January 6, 2005, resulting in the derailment of three tanker cars carrying chlorine ($Cl_2$) gas and one tanker car carrying sodium hydroxide (NaOH) liquids. The highly toxic $Cl_2$ gas was released to the atmosphere. The wreck and gas release resulted in hundreds of injuries and eight deaths. Some of these events are the result of slightly different conditions not recognized as vulnerable or not considered similar to Bhopal. Others may have resulted or may result due to memory extinction. Even early large and impactful disasters fade in memory with time. This is to be expected for the lay public but is not acceptable for plant managers and engineers.

Bhopal illustrates that disasters can be affected by geopolitical realities and the global economy. In this case, cultural differences between the United States and India were not properly considered when transposing U.S. plant designs onto an Indian physical and cultural landscape. Even within the same country or state, it is dangerous to assume that a model that works in one setting will necessarily work in another without adjusting for differing expectations. Chaos theory tells us that even very small variations in conditions can lead to dramatically different outcomes. The earlier these perturbations appear in the event tree, the more profound the changes can be. In Bhopal, the outcome differences were disastrous.

Characterizing as many contingencies and possible outcomes in the critical path is an essential part of many hazards. The Bhopal incident provides this lesson. For example, engineers working with emerging or even well-established technologies must consider all possible avenues of hazard. This calls for ensuring that fail-safe mechanisms are in place *and* are operational. Quality assurance officers note that testing for an unlikely but potentially devastating event is difficult. Everyone in the decision chain must be "on board." The fact that no incidents have yet to occur (thankfully) means that no one really knows what will happen in such an event. That is why health and safety training is a critical part of the engineering process. Medicine has provided lessons to environmental science. For example, a recent case of transplanting a heart of a different blood type into a patient resulted in her death. The process for classifying the blood had been taken for granted by the surgeon. He had done everything correctly *except* ensuring the blood match. Thus, this single factor led to a horrible failure. Environmental systems, like the human body, are highly complex and vulnerable to seemingly small factors.

## Seveso

Like Bhopal, the event in Seveso, Italy, began with an explosion that produced a toxic cloud that threatened public safety.[a] Actually, the exposures were similar, but the outcomes were different. In Bhopal, the most devastating hazard was acute, with a rapid onset, whereas the threat from Seveso was chronic, with potential health problems expected over years and decades.

The explosion at the chemical processing facility resulted from complexities of intertwined factors and events. Indeed, a surprisingly small number of mistakes led to the disaster. The lesson is that seemingly inconsequential events in the right combination lead to substantial problems. Indeed, Seveso was to become a harbinger of the toxic scares that paved the way for new environmental legislation around the world calling for programs to address toxic and hazardous substances. The Seveso explosion was among the first industrial disasters to illustrate the potential of chemical exposures to millions of people who live near industrial facilities. In its wake, many countries promulgated so-called community right-to-know laws that have since emerged. However, from a systems engineering perspective, Seveso represents a teachable moment beyond the event itself in terms of complex and subtle cascades of contributing events, the need for indicators of exposures and risks, and how to apply these systems solutions to future events (and even preventing them completely).

The event that is associated with a disaster is actually the consequence of many contributing events. On July 10, 1976, an explosion at a 2,4,5-trichlorophenol (2,4,5-T) reactor at the Seveso Industrie Chemiche Meda Societa, Anonima (ICMSA) manufacturing plant resulted in the highest concentrations of the most toxic chlorinated dioxin (TCDD) levels known in human residential populations.[7] Up to 30 kg of TCDD were deposited over the surrounding area of approximately 18 km$^2$. To put this amount in perspective, scientists usually are

---

[a] As such, Seveso is a useful reminder to engineers to be ever mindful of the first canon of their profession, i.e. to hold paramount the health, safety, and welfare of the public.

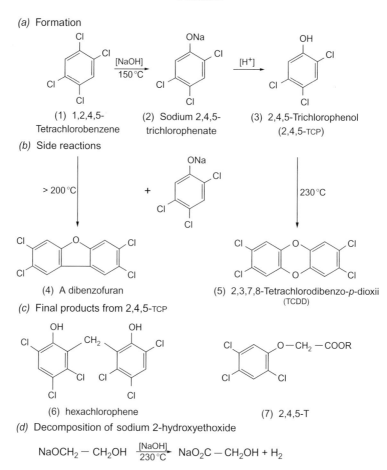

FIGURE 4.7    Reactions used in Severo batch reactor to produce 2,4,5-T. *Source: Wilson DC. Lessons from Seveso. Chem Brit 1982;18:499-504.*

worried about dioxin, and especially TCDD, if a gram or less is released in a year, whereas this explosion released 30,000 g of TCDD instantaneously.

The ICMSA was an Italian subsidiary of the Swiss company, Givaudan, which happened to be owned by another Swiss company, Hoffman-LaRoche.[8] A ruptured disc on a batch plant caused the explosion. The pesticide 2,4,5-T was formulated from 1,2,4,5-tetrachlorobenzene and caustic soda (NaOH), in the presence of ethylene glycol (see Figure 4.7). Normally, only a few molecules of dioxins form from trillions of molecules of the batch. In this instance, however, reactor temperatures rose beyond the tolerances, leading to a "runaway reaction," bursting the disc. As a result, it is likely that large amounts of hydrogen gas ($H_2$) formed, which propelled the 6 tons of fluid from the reactor into the lower atmosphere, from which it was deposited over the Seveso region.

As appalling as it was, Seveso was not really a worst case. Upon hearing the noise being made at the beginning of the release, a plant foreman opened a valve to release cooling waters onto the heating coils of the reactor. This action likely reduced the force of the exiting fluids.

The Seveso disaster can be seen not only as more than a chemical engineering disaster but also as a human factor engineering failure and a public policy disaster. The Italian legislature had recently passed a law requiring the plant to shut down on weekends, without consideration of the extent to which a batch was complete or not. This ostensibly could reduce the likelihood of pollution, but on the weekend of the explosion, the plant was shut down after the formulation reaction, but before the complete removal of the ethylene glycol by distillation. This was the first time that the plant was shut down at this stage. Based upon chemistry alone, the operator had no reason to fear anything would go awry. The mixture at the time of shutdown was 158 °C, but the theoretical temperature at which an exothermic reaction would be expected to occur was thought to be 230 °C. Subsequent studies have found that exothermic reactions of these reagents can begin at 180 °C, but these are very slow processes. The temperature in fact rose, mainly due to a temperature gradient from the liquid to the steam phase. The reactor wall in contact with the liquid was much cooler than the wall in contact with the steam, with heat moving from the upper wall to the surface of the liquid. The stirrer was switched off so that the top few centimeters of liquid rose in temperature to about 190 °C, beginning the slow exothermic reaction. After 7 h the runaway reaction commenced. The reactions may also have been catalyzed by chemicals in the residue that had caked on the upper wall that, with the temperature increase, was released into the liquid in the reactor. Thus, the runaway reaction and explosion could have been prevented if the plant had not been prematurely shut down and if the plant operators had been better trained to consider contingencies beyond the "textbook" conditions.

A continuous, slight wind dispersed the contents over the region which included 11 towns and villages. The precipitate looked like snow. No official emergency action took place on the day of the explosion. People with chemical burns checked themselves into local hospitals. The mayor of Seveso was only told of the incident the next day.

The response to the disaster and pending dioxin exposure was based on the potential risks involved. The contaminated area was divided into three zones based on the concentration of TCDD in the soil. The 211 families in Zone A, the most heavily contaminated area, were evacuated within 20 days of the explosion and measures were taken to minimize exposure to residents in nearby zones. In a preliminary study, U.S. Center for Disease Control and Prevention (CDC) tested blood serum samples from five residents of Zone A who suffered from the dioxin-related skin disease known as chloracne, as well as samples from four from Zone A without chloracne, and three from outside the contaminated area. All samples had been collected and stored shortly after the accident. Interestingly, TCDD was detected in only one sample from the unexposed group, but it was comparably high, i.e., 137 part per trillion (ppt). The high elevated TCDD level was thought to be due to misclassification or sample contamination. In Zone A, serum TCDD levels ranged from 1772 to 10,439 ppt for persons without chloracne and from 828 to 56,000 ppt for persons with chloracne. The TCDD concentrations are the highest ever reported in humans. The CDC is presently evaluating several hundred historical blood samples taken from Seveso residents for TCDD. There are plans to determine half-life estimates and to evaluate serum TCDD levels for participants in the Seveso cancer registry.

As in the case of the snail darter controversy, scientific research has continued even after the sensational aspects of the disaster have waned. In fact, a recent study by Warner et al.[9] found a statistically significant, dose-response-increased risk for breast cancer incidence with individual serum TCDD level among women in the Seveso women, i.e., a dose-response relationship of a twofold increase in the hazard rate associated with a 10-fold increase in serum TCDD. This result is an early warning because the Seveso cohort is relatively young, with a mean age at interview of <41 years. These findings are consistent with a 20-year follow-up study that showed that even though no increased incidence of breast cancer had been observed in the Seveso population 10 and 15 years after the incident, after 20 years breast cancer mortality emerged among women who resided in heavily contaminated areas, and who were younger than 55 years at death (relative risk = 1.2, 95% confidence interval, 0.6-2.2), but not in those who were older.

The findings are not significant statistically, but scary. For example, it is very difficult to characterize a population for even a year, let alone 20 years, because people move in and out of the area. Epidemiological studies are often limited by the size of the study group in comparison to the whole population of those exposed to a contaminant. In the Seveso case, the TCDD exposure estimates have been based on the zone of residence, so the study is deficient in individual-level exposure data. There is also variability within the exposure area, for example, recent analyses of individual blood serum TCDD measurements for 601 Seveso women suggest a wide range of individual TCDD exposure within zones.[9]

Some argue that the public's response to the real risks from Seveso were overblown, considering no one died directly from the explosion and the immediate aftermath, although hundreds were burned by the NaOH exposure and hundreds other did develop skin irritations. This may be true, but part of the response is the general response to the unknown, especially when the chemical of concern is TCDD, that has been established to cause cancer, neurological disorder, endocrine dysfunction, and other chronic diseases. The medical follow-up studies may indicate that the public response was plausible, given the latent connections to chronic diseases, like breast cancer.

The toxicity, especially the very steep cancer slope for TCDD, is met with some skepticism. Exposures at Seveso were high compared to general environmental exposures. However, some high profile cases, especially the recent suspected TCDD poisoning of the Ukrainian President Viktor Yushchenko in 2004 and the 1998 discovery of the highest blood levels of TCDD in two Austrians have added to the controversy. In fact, both these cases were precipitated by the adverse effects, especially chloracne. Usually, dioxins, PCBs, and other persistent, bioaccumulating toxicants are studied based on exposure, followed by investigations to see if any effects are present. This has been the case for Agent Orange, Seveso, Times Beach, and most other contamination instances. It is unusual to see such severe effects, but with the very high doses (see Figure 4.8) reported in the Yushchenko and Austrian cases, it would have come as a greater surprise not to have seen some adverse effect.

The Seveso disaster illustrates the need to consider the likely consequences of failure early in the design process. Sufficient factors of safety are an engineering and an ethical imperative.

## PLUME CHARACTERIZATION

The fluid properties discussed in Chapter 2 are important for plume characterization, including density and vapor pressure. For example, a highly dense substance is likely to gather near the ground surface, which, if explosive or flammable, presents a major hazard to health and safety. Likewise, substances with high vapor pressures are more likely to stay aloft, as they will be more likely to remain in the vapor phase compared to lower vapor pressure compounds.

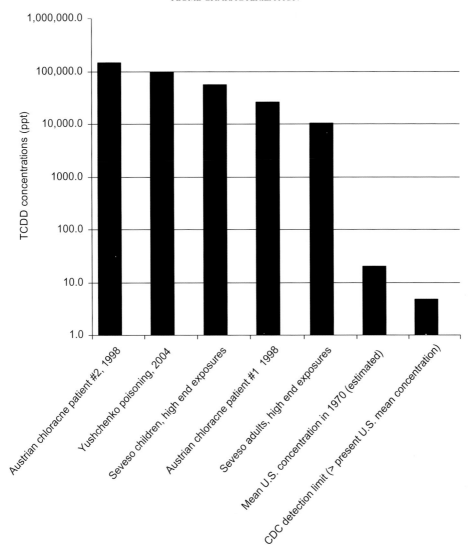

FIGURE 4.8 Tetrachlorodibenzo-*para*-dioxin blood serum concentrations from various exposure scenarios. *Sources: Center for Disease Control and Prevention; For the Seveso study, this link may be of use for citing: http://www. ncbi.nlm.nih.gov/pubmed/1826746 For the Austrian women, please refer to this study: http://www.ncbi.nlm.nih.gov/pubmed/ 11564625*

Vapor pressure is the pressure exerted by a vapor in a confined space. Similarly, vaporization is the change of a liquid or solid to the vapor phase. So, if a substance vaporizes, it can enter a plume. Thus, a principal means of a substance being released as a plume is volatilization, which is a function of the concentration of a contaminant in solution and the contaminants partial pressure. Henry's law states that the concentration of a dissolved gas is directly proportional to the partial pressure of that gas above the solution:

$$p_a = K_H[c], \tag{4.3}$$

where $K_H$, Henry's law constant; $p_a$, partial pressure of the gas; [c], molar concentration of the gas or

$$p_A = K_H C_W, \tag{4.4}$$

where $C_W$ is the concentration of gas in water.

This means that, for any chemical contaminant, a proportionality can be established between solubility and vapor pressure. Henry's law is an expression of this proportionality between the concentration of a dissolved contaminant and its partial pressure in the headspace (including the open atmosphere) at equilibrium. A dimensionless version of the partitioning is similar to that of sorption, except that instead of the partitioning between solid and water phases, it is between the air and water phases ($K_{AW}$):

$$K_{AW} = \frac{C_A}{C_W}, \tag{4.5}$$

where $C_A$ is the concentration of gas A in the air.

The relationship between the air/water partition coefficient and Henry's law constant for a substance is

$$K_{AW} = \frac{K_H}{RT}, \tag{4.6}$$

where $R$ is the gas constant ($8.21 \times 10^{-2}$ L atm mol$^{-1}$ K$^{-1}$) and $T$ is the temperature (K).

Henry's law relationships work well for most environmental conditions. It represents a limiting factor for systems where a substance's partial pressure is approaching zero. At very high partial pressures (e.g., 30 pascals—high by ambient atmospheric standards) or at very high contaminant concentrations (e.g., >1000 ppm), Henry's law assumptions cannot be met. Such vapor pressures and concentrations are seldom seen in ambient environmental situations, but may be seen in industrial and other source situations. Thus, in modeling and estimating the tendency for a substance's release in vapor form, Henry's law is a good metric and is often used in compartmental transport models to indicate the fugacity from the water to the atmosphere.

The other major physical phase whereby a substance may enter a plume is aerosolization. In the environmental sciences, the use of the term "phase" is nuanced from that of physics. In atmospheric sciences, the most important phase distribution is that of *vapor* versus *particulate* phase. The distinction between gases and vapors has to do with the physical phase that a substance would be under environmental conditions, e.g., at standard temperature and pressure. Particulate matter (PM) is an expression of all particles, whether liquid or solid. An aerosol is a liquid or solid particle that is suspended in a gas; in environmental sciences, this gas is usually air, but in reactors, stacks and other nonambient conditions, this can be various flue gases. Standard atmospheric conditions can be defined as 1 atm pressure (760 mmHg) and 25° (298.15 K).[10]

As mentioned, PM is problematic in itself, but is also an important vector for pollutant transport (e.g., moved by advection, or dissolved in or sorbed to aerosols). As mentioned, in the United States, the Clean Air Act established the ambient standard (NAAQS) for PM. In 1971, the U.S. EPA required measurements of total suspended particulates (TSP) as measured by a high volume sampler, i.e., a device that collected a large range of sizes of particles (aerodynamic diameters up to 50 μm). Smaller particles are more likely to be inhaled than larger particles, so in 1987 the U.S. EPA changed the standard for PM from TSP to $PM_{10}$, i.e., particle matter $\leq 10$ μm diameters.[11] The NAAQS for $PM_{10}$ became a 24-h average of 150 μg m$^{-3}$ (not to exceed this level more than once per year), and an annual average of 50 μg m$^{-3}$ arithmetic mean. However, subsequent research showed the need to protect people breathing even smaller PM in air, since most of the particles that penetrate deeply into the air-blood exchange regions of the lung are very small. Thus, in 1997, the U.S. EPA added a new fine particle (diameters $\leq 2.5$), known as $PM_{2.5}$.[12]

Aerosols are collected using equipment that separates out the size fraction of concern. Filtration is an important technology in every aspect of environmental engineering, i.e., air pollution, waste water treatment, drinking water, and even hazardous waste and sediment cleanup. Basically, filtration consists of four mechanical processes: (1) Diffusion, (2) interception, (3) inertial impaction, and (4) electrostatics (see Figure 4.9).

Diffusion is important only for very small particles ($\leq 0.1$ μm diameter) because the Brownian motion allows them to move in a "random walk" away from the air stream. Interception works mainly for particles with diameters between 0.1 and 1 μm. The particle does not leave the air stream but comes into contact with the filter medium (e.g., a strand of fiberglass). Inertial impaction collects particles that are sufficiently large to leave the air stream by inertia (diameters $\geq 1$ μm). Electrostatics consist of electrical interactions between the atoms in the filter and those in the particle at the point of contact (Van der Waal's forces), as well as electrostatic attraction (charge differences between particle and filter medium). Other important factors affecting filtration efficiencies include the thickness and pore diameter or the filter, the uniformity of particle diameters and pore sizes, the solid volume fraction, the rate of particle loading onto the filter (e.g., affecting particle "bounce"), the particle phase (liquid or solid), capillarity and surface tension (if either the particle or the filter media are coated with a liquid), and characteristics of air or other carrier gases, such as velocity, temperature, pressure, and viscosity.

Thus, aerosol measurement is an expression of the mass of each particle size of particle. Figure 4.10 shows an inlet of the $PM_{2.5}$ sampler that is designed to extract ambient aerosols

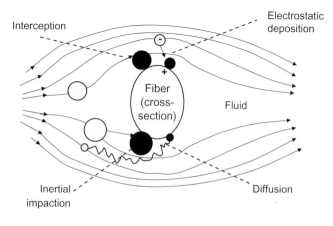

FIGURE 4.9 Mechanical processes involved in collecting particulate matter. *Source: Vallero DA. Fundamentals of air pollution. 4th ed. Burlington, MA: Elsevier Academic Press; 2008; adapted from: Rubow KL. "Filtration: fundamentals and applications" in aerosol and particle measurement short course. Minneapolis, MN: University of Minnesota; 2004. August 16-18.*

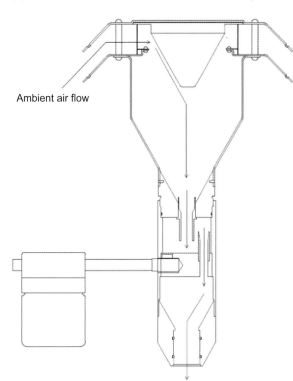

Ambient air flow

Flow to WINS impactor

FIGURE 4.10    Flow of air through a sampler inlet head used to collect particulate matter with aerodynamic diameters <2.5 μm (PM$_{2.5}$). WINS, well impactor 96, i.e., the design of the particle impactor specified by the U.S. EPA for reference method samplers for PM$_{2.5}$. *Source: U.S. Environmental Protection Agency.* Quality assurance guidance document 2.12. Monitoring PM$_{2.5}$ in ambient air using designated reference or class I equivalent methods. *North Carolina: Research Triangle Park; 1998.*

from the surrounding airstream, remove particles with aerodynamic diameters $>10\,\mu m$, and move the remaining smaller particles to the next stage. Figure 4.11 illustrates the impactor and filter assembly for removing those particles $<10\,\mu m$ but $>2.5\,\mu m$ in diameter but allows particles of $2.5\,\mu m$ in diameter to pass and be collected on a filter surface. Particles $<10\,\mu m$ but $<2.5\,\mu m$ are removed downstream from the inlet by a single-stage, single-flow, single-jet impactor assembly. Aerosols are collected on filters which are weighed before and after sampling. This system uses 37 mm diameter glass filters immersed in low-volatility, low-viscosity diffusion oil. The oil is added to reduce the impact of "bounce," i.e., particles hit the filter and are not reliably collected.[12]

# NUCLEAR FALLOUT PLUMES

We shall consider radiation disasters in detail in Chapter 12, but it is important to point out that these disasters change from being localized problems to regional or even global concerns when their contaminants are spread via plumes.

From aerosol inlet

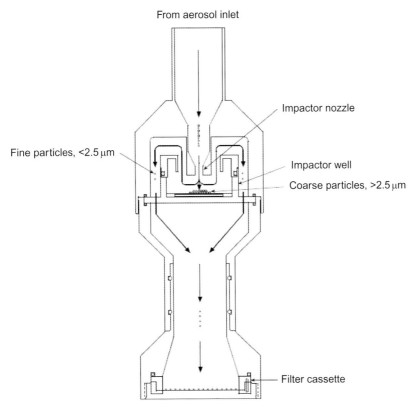

FIGURE 4.11   Flow of air through an impactor well and filter holder used to collect particulate matter with aerodynamic diameters <2.5 μm (PM$_{2.5}$). *Source: U.S. Environmental Protection Agency. Quality assurance guidance document*

## Chernobyl

The heat energy from a nuclear reactor is based on splitting $^{235}$U atoms into smaller atoms which are invariably radioactive. A typical reaction is

$$^{235}_{92}\text{U} +^{1}_{0}\text{n} =^{142}_{56}\text{Ba} +^{92}_{36}\text{Kr} +^{2}_{0}\text{n} + \gamma. \tag{4.7}$$

Other related reactions split the atoms slightly differently and produces isotopes such as $^{131}$I, $^{93}$Y, $^{140}$Cs, $^{92}$Rb, $^{137}$Cs, $^{103}$Ru, and $^{90}$Sr. When the reactor at Chernobyl exploded on Friday, April 25, 1986 and burned for 3 weeks, these radioactive isotopes and also small pieces of fuel were lifted into the air and carried by the winds and dropped in many places in Russia and Europe. The settling of the particles was accelerated by falling rain. Some of the falling particles were inhaled or ingested by humans. The real danger of ingesting radioactive isotopes lies in possible mutations of dexoyribonucleic acid (DNA) material caused by ionization and bombardment. These mutations can often lead to cancer. It is estimated that between 30,000 and 60,000 people will eventually succumb to cancer as a result of this fallout. The damage done to humans by the radioactive nuclide is due to the emission of gamma radiation (ionizing radiation which is very dangerous to living cells), beta radiation (electron emissions which does penetrate human skin to a small extent), and alpha radiation (helium nuclei and charged, which is not as dangerous as beta radiation).

It has been estimated that the amount of radioactive material released at Chernobyl was 400 times than produced by the Hiroshima bomb. However, the Chernobyl disaster released only 1/100 to 1/1000 of the total amount of radioactivity released by nuclear weapons testing during the 1950s and 1960s. About 100,000 km$^2$ of land was contaminated as a result of the Chernobyl fallout. The worst hit regions being in the old Soviet Union countries of Belarus, Ukraine, and Russia. The levels in Europe were lower than those experienced in the old Soviet Union. The Iberian Peninsula seems to have escaped most of the fallout.[13]

In any nuclear disaster, the size of the plume, its shape, and the radioactive material it is carrying depend on the temperature of the nuclear explosion and subsequent fires. The ejected radioactive particles rise with the heat of the flames and the height to which each isotope reaches depends on its mass, the temperature of the fire, and the velocity of the hot gases rising out of the fire. In the case of Chernobyl, the fire was burning graphite and, together with the heat of the molten fuel rods, sent the radioactive debris high into the air. The volatile elements, in particular, the radioactive iodine and cesium, went high into the atmosphere and were then taken by the winds over Europe where they settled with the help of rain. The less volatile material such as the strontium and bits of zirconium and uranium oxide fuel was deposited within a 30-km mile radius of the disaster. The plume probably traveled at a height of a couple of thousand meters but was at the mercy of the winds and the degree of atmospheric turbulence.

The fission products of uranium nuclear reactions are particularly dangerous to humans (very much more dangerous that plutonium reactors) because three of the fallout isotopes are radioactive iodine and cesium and strontium. These elements are readily absorbed by the body. Iodine is taken up by the thyroid; cesium because of its sodium like properties is taken by the body and muscles in particular; and strontium, with its calcium-like properties, is taken up by the bones.

When measuring radioactive activity, the unit "bequerel" (Bq) is used, which has units of s$^{-1}$. It relates to the counts per second of radioactive disintegration. It is a very small unit and prefixes such as peta (P implying $10^{15}$) or tera (T implying $10^{12}$) are used. To put it in context, the average human body has 4400 Bq from decaying $^{40}$K in our bodies. This isotope is a naturally occurring isotope of potassium and has a half-life of about $10^9$ years.

The radioisotopes in the Chernobyl disaster plume were partly determined by their volatility. All of the noble gases such as krypton and xenon were released from the reactor immediately after the first explosions. Fifty-five percent of the radioactive iodine in the reactor, containing about 1760 PBq or 400 kg of $^{131}$I was released, as a mixture of vapor and solid particles. The $^{137}$Cs (85 PBq) isotope was released in aerosol form. It was also estimated that $3.5 \pm 0.5\%$ of the fuel material of the reactor was released into the atmosphere, amounting to 6 tons of uranium fuel. The total release of all radioactive isotopes into the plume was estimated at 5200 PBq.[14,15]

The released particles were small and could be divided into two types: fine particles with diameters of 0.3–1.5 μm usually transported in aerosol form and coarse particles, with diameters up to 10 μm. Most of the nonvolatile materials in the plume were in this latter group and included zirconium from the fuel pellet housing and even uranium oxide fuel.

Radioactive half-life ($t_{1/2}$) is of paramount importance in any nuclear fallout. Some of the isotopes from the Chernobyl plume (together with their half lives) are $^{131}$I (8 days), $^{144}$Ce

(300 days), $^{95}$Zr (65 days), $^{137}$Cs (30 years), $^{103}$Ru (40 days), and $^{90}$Sr (28 years). It is the long half-life material that presents the protracted and continuous risk to humans. Chronic risks are particularly important for strontium, cesium, and to a lesser extent, iodine, because they are so readily absorbed by the body.

In much the same way that large volcanic eruptions are eventually transported globally; the spread of radioactive debris into the atmosphere from the Chernobyl accident was eventually detected all over the world.

The plume from the burning graphite initially traveled in a northwest direction toward Sweden, Finland, and Eastern Europe, exposing the public, especially in parts of Poland to the radiation exposures which were as high as 10 μSv h$^{-1}$. The radiation activity held this strength for 10 days, while the Chernobyl fire continued and slowly decreased to background levels after 3 weeks. The most serious concern related to the contamination of grain and dairy products from fallout as this could result in human contamination through ingestion of the wheat or milk. A person exposed to the dose of 10 μSv h$^{-1}$ over 10 days would end up with an exposure of twice the annual acceptable maximum dose, which is 1 mSv y$^{-1}$. To put it in perspective, some parts of the world have high natural background levels of radioactivity, where people are exposed continuously to 50 mSv y$^{-1}$. In comparison, the criterion for relocation after the Chernobyl accident was a *lifetime* exposure of 350 mSv.[16]

## Fukushima Plume

The plume from the Fukushima nuclear disaster did not have the initial energy that the Chernobyl plume had and the heavy elements appeared to stay in the reactor, while the volatiles, especially $^{131}$I, traveled with the plume (see Figure 4.12). Iodine from Fukushima was even detected in Scotland a few days after the disaster. The initial winds blew toward the east (toward the United States), but after 2 days, the wind swung round and blew toward the southwest for a day and then returned to blow to the east. One reason for the small exclusion zone of only 20 km in the case of Fukushima was as a result of the low energy of the explosion. Relatively little heavy material was ejected from the reactor. As in most nuclear disasters, it was $^{131}$I and $^{137}$Cs that was emitted into the plume and traveled with the winds. The detectors in Sacramento in California detected radioactive iodine, but by the time the plume reached the U.S. west coast, the level of radioactivity was very low and not dangerous. This occurred when the winds blew toward the southwest that dangerous levels in Japan were experienced. It so happened that a large number of evacuees had decamped to an area southwest of Fukushima, and levels there, 2 days after the accident were apparently higher than at the boundary of the accident site. The heavier cesium in the plume was deposited in a line southwest of Fukushima. It has been reported that 8% of the Japanese land has now been contaminated with cesium-137 (half-life in 30 years).[17]

## Radiation Dose

People are exposed to radiation after a disaster as a result of the increased concentrations of radioiodine and similar radionuclides in the thyroid gland, or as a whole-body dose caused largely by external irradiation. The latter is usually in the form of radioactive cesium. Health

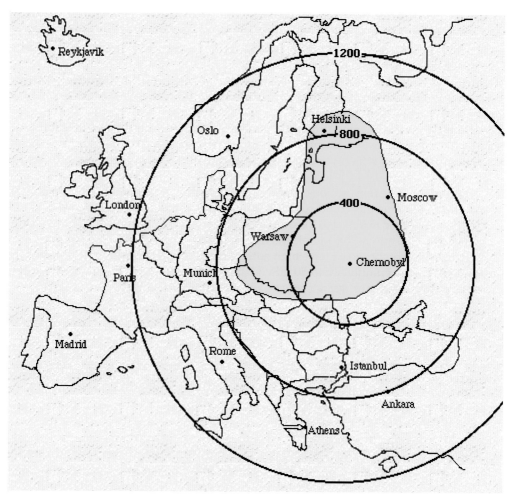

FIGURE 4.12     The main path of the Chernobyl plume. *Source: Penn State Nuclear Engineering Students (2012). Chernobyl: An Update; http://users.owt.com/smsrpm/Chernobyl/glbrad.html.l; accessed on March 4, 2012.*

scientists consider an absorbed dose to the whole body to be about 20 times more harmful than the same dose to the thyroid.[18]

About 600,000 people participated in cleanup and mitigation activities with the 30-km zones surrounding the Chernobyl reactor. As is commonly the case, the most highly exposed were the responders, e.g., firemen and the power plant personnel, during the first days of the accident. External irradiation from the fuel fragments and radioactive particles deposited on various surfaces was the largest source of exposure. Over 100,000 people were evacuated during the first days following the accident, mainly from the 30-km zone surrounding the reactor. Before the evacuation, these people were exposed to external irradiation from radioactive materials transported by the plume and deposited onto the ground surface. They also received internal irradiation essentially by inhaling radioactive materials in the plume.

Similarly, the radioactive material transported from the reactor breech and fire at the Fukushima plant increased the dose to the population.

Atmospheric transport is a part of many environmental disasters. Characterizing the plumes has been an important part of the response to major disasters, such as those in Bhopal, Seveso, Chernobyl, and Japan.

The extent of the plumes show that environmental disasters can grow in time and space. What may begin as a localized problem can become threats to greater numbers of people and ecosystems. We will consider other transport mechanisms in the next chapters.

## References and Notes

1. California State Department of Public Health. *Recommended Ambient Air Quality Standards.* (Statewide standards applicable to all California Air Basins), HS-3; 1969.
2. Canadian Office of Environmental Health Hazard Assessment. *Air Toxics Hot Spots Program Risk Assessment Guidelines, Part III.* Technical Support Document for the Determination of Noncancer Chronic Reference Exposure Levels. Available on-line athttp://www.oehha.ca.gov; 2000.
3. U.S. Environmental Protection Agency. *Integrated Risk Information System (IRIS) database: reference concentration (RfC) for hydrogen sulfide;* Available on-line at http://www.epa.gov/ngispgm3/iris/subst/index.html; 1999.
4. Air Products, Inc. *Material Safety Data Sheet for Hydrogen Sulfide.* http://avogadro.chem.iastate.edu/MSDS/hydrogen_sulfide.pdf; 2005 [accessed 20 April 2005].
5. Martin MW, Schinzinger R. *Ethics in engineering.* 3rd ed. New York: McGraw-Hill; 1996.
6. Fledderman CB. *Engineering ethics.* Upper Saddle River, NJ: Prentice Hall; 1999.
7. Mocarelli P, Pocchiari F. Preliminary report: 2,3,7,8-tetrachlorodibenzo-p-dioxin exposure to humans—Seveso, Italy. *Morb Mortal Wkly Rep* 1988;**37**:733–6; Di Domenico A, Silano V, Viviano G, Zappni G. Accidental release of 2,3,7,8-tetrachlorodibenzo-p-dioxin (TCDD) at Seveso, Italy: V. Environmental persistence of TCDD in soil. *Ecotoxicol Environ Saf* 1980;**4**:339–45.
8. Kletz T. *Learning from accidents.* 3rd ed. Oxford, UK: Gulf Professional Publishing; 2001.
9. Warner M, Eskenazi B, Mocarelli P, Gerthoux PM, Samuels S, Needham L, et al. Serum dioxin concentrations and breast cancer risk in the Seveso Women's Health Study. *Environ Health Perspect* 2002;**110**(7):625–8.
10. U.S. Environmental Protection Agency. *Quality assurance guidance document 2.12. monitoring $PM_{2.5}$ in ambient air using designated reference or class I equivalent methods.* North Carolina: Research Triangle Park; 1998.
11. The diameter most often used for airborne particle measurements is the "aerodynamic diameter." The aerodynamic diameter ($D_{pa}$) for all particles $>0.5$ μm can be approximated as the product of the Stokes particle diameter ($D_{ps}$) and the square root of the particle density ($\rho_p$):

$$D_{pa} = D_{ps}\sqrt{\rho_p}. \qquad (4.8)$$

If the units of the diameters are in μm, the units of density are g cm$^{-3}$.
The Stokes diameter $D_{ps}$ is the diameter of a sphere with the same density and settling velocity as the particle. The Stokes diameter is derived from the aerodynamic drag force caused by the difference in velocity of the particle and the surrounding fluid. Thus, for smooth, spherical particles, the Stokes diameter is identical to the physical or actual diameter.
12. For information regarding particle matter (PM) health effects and inhalable, thoracic and respirable PM mass fractions see:U.S. Environmental Protection Agency. *Air Quality Criteria for Particulate Matter. Technical Report No.EPA/600/P-95/001aF,* Washington, DC.
13. Marples DR. *Chernobyl: the decade of despair.* Bulletin of the Atomic Scientists; 1996 p. 20.
14. Gudiksen PH, Harvey TF, Lange R. Chernobyl source term, atmospheric dispersion, and dose estimation. *Health Phys* 1989;**57**(5):697–706.

15. Asahi Shimbum. *Fukushima radioactive water could overflow soon.* http://www.asahi.com/english/TKY201106040157.html; 2011 [accessed 27 February 2012].

16. Our Food—Database of Food and Related Sciences. *Radioactivity and food.* http://www.ourfood.com/Radioactivity_Food.html; 2012 [accessed 4 March 2012].

17. New Scientist. *Special report: the fallout from Fukushima.* http://www.newscientist.com/special/fukushima-crisis; 2011 [accessed 27 February 2012].

18. Nuclear Energy Agency. *Dose estimates. Chernobylâ ten years on: radiological and health impact. Committee on Radiation Protection and Public Health.* Organization for Economic Co-operation and Development; 1995.

# 5

# Leaks

Two environmental scientific disciplines address plumes in different parts of the environment. As we discussed in Chapter 4, the atmospheric sciences address the dispersion and movement of vapors and aerosols after their release to the atmosphere. Similarly, hydrogeologists are interested in how a plume moves beneath the Earth's surface. We will distinguish these hydrogeological plumes from atmospheric plumes in this chapter, by referring to them as leaks. Thus, we will now consider environmental or potential disasters from the perspective of groundwater contamination.

## SURREPTITIOUS DISASTERS

The onset of a toxic disaster can be immediate, like the toxic plume in Bhopal, India (see Chapter 3). Other toxic disasters can take years or decades before they become problems or, as is often the case, before the problems are recognized. Since most toxic contaminants are odorless, tasteless and colorless at levels that can present health risks, decades can pass before even sophisticated equipment can detect them. That is, they are more than ticking time bombs; they have already detonated and have slowly and continuously released imperceptible, but very harmful chemicals. The continuous contamination threatens public health with chronic diseases, such as cancer and neurological ailments.

In many underground disasters, not only does the release continue, but the rate of contamination may very well increase as vessels corrode and the toxic compounds percolate underground, reach the atmosphere, contaminate groundwater, and otherwise come into contact with humans and other creatures.

Until relatively recently, public concern about pollution was predominantly about acute and readily identifiable hazards. Laws were passed to deal with these high-profile episodes, like the mortality resulting from inversion-related air pollution in the 1950s and 1960s in valley cities, such as those discussed in Chapter 3. Thus, the second half of the twentieth century saw the passage of new air, water, and open dump laws in North America and Western Europe. With court rulings supporting the public outcry, environmental protection regulations began to address more vigorously the so-called traditional pollutants, viewing them less as nuisances and more as health hazards. Surreptitious pollutants were not the focus of public health and environmental agencies until the late 1970s, when Love Canal and a few other prominent toxic waste disasters caused the public to become keenly aware of toxic pollutants and hazardous substances. Such new problems associated with metals and exotic chemical made front page news.

Some of the awareness can be attributed to scientific advances, such as improving public health analytical methods and epidemiological studies, especially those linking lifestyles and environmental factors to cancer. Epidemiologists began to distinguish "nature" from "nurture" in the search for causes of cancers, for example. The former was considered under the realm of genetics research and the latter under a broad grouping of so-called "environmental" factors, including pollution, but also diet and habits, like smoking.

Outrage and frustration over the toxic substances found at Love Canal in New York, Times Beach, Missouri, and the Valley of the Drum in Kentucky were the impetus behind numerous environmental laws, notably the 1980 Comprehensive Environmental Response, Compensation, and Liability Act (CERCLA), better known as "Superfund." These toxic disasters changed the whole legal arsenal against environmental problems. As mentioned, much of the previous legal precedence for environmental jurisprudence had been more on the order of nuisance laws or to protect against a small number of conventional air and water pollutants, such as sulfur dioxide and pathogens, respectively. This increased recognition of public health risks associated with toxic substances called for more aggressive and scientifically based responses.

## POLLUTANT TRANSPORT IN GROUNDWATER

Groundwater contamination is important in disaster scenarios, as aquifers may continue to be contaminated long after the event, such as tanks containing hazardous materials, such as gasoline, agricultural chemicals (Figure 5.1), or industrial solvents, that have been cracked. Groundwater is also contaminated when active, engineered systems fail, such as when pumping stations fail due to loss of electricity (Figure 5.2); or otherwise, and have been compromised by allowing their contents to reach the groundwater and threaten the quality of drinking water supplies or even find their way into residences.

After release, substances can find their way to subsurface environments as they move with the flow of water through porous material. This is known as advective transport, i.e. the same process as when air pollutants are carried along by a plume moving through the atmosphere (See Chapter 3). Pollutants are carried in either solutions or suspensions. In solution transport, contaminating compounds become dissolved in surface or soil water and seep into the soil. As they come into contact with clay, silt, soil, and other underground materials, they may be sorbed to subsurface particles, some of which may be suspended and carried with soil water. They may also evaporate, particularly if they have high vapor pressures and remain on or near the surface. Underground water reservoirs, i.e., aquifers, become contaminated when pollutants remain either dissolved or suspended and move with the groundwater plume (see Figure 5.3). The physical phase of these compounds ultimately depends upon both properties of the molecules themselves and the conditions in which they exist, including the hydrogeologic characteristics of the soil and aquifer.

FIGURE 5.1 Aerial of farm structures flooded by the Mississippi River at La Grange, Missouri on June 20, 2008. Photo by J. Augustino. *Source: Federal Emergency Management Administration, 2011.*

FIGURE 5.2 Electric powered water pumps are in danger of submergence and shutdown the rising Mississippi River in Vicksburg, Mississippi on May 6, 2011. Photo by H. Greenblatt. *Source: Federal Emergency Management Administration, 2011.*

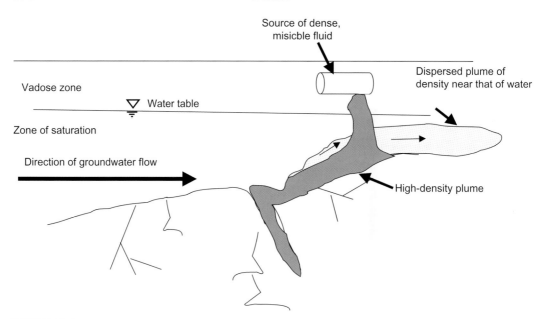

FIGURE 5.3   Hypothetical plume of dense, highly hydrophilic fluid. *Based on information provided by: Sara MN. Groundwater monitoring system design. In: Nielsen DM, editor.* Practical handbook of ground-water monitoring. *Chelsea, MI: Lewis Publishers; 1991.*

Groundwater usually moves by flowing through porous media, e.g. gravel, sand and silt.* Water stands in a well at a particular level, known as hydraulic head ($h$). Groundwater flows in the direction of decreasing head (see Figure 5.4). The change in head measurement is the hydraulic gradient ($dh/dx$). The units are length per length (e.g., $m\ m^{-1}$).

The capability of a medium to transmit a fluid, especially water, is known as hydraulic conductivity ($K$). The various layers (strata) under the earth's surface may be consolidated (not broken up), such as limestone or other rock layers. These layers may also consist of un-consolidated materials, such as soil, sand, or gravel. Darcy's Law is an empirically derived equation for the flow of fluids through a cross section of porous media ($A$). It states that the specific discharge, $Q$, is directly proportional to the $K$ and hydraulic gradient:

$$\text{Darcy's law}: Q = -KA\ dh/dx \tag{5.1}$$

The law assumes that flow is laminar and that inertia can be neglected. Thus, if $K = 0.5\ m\ s^{-1}$, $dh/dx = 0.0085\ m\ m^{-1}$, and $A = 500\ m^2$, then $Q = 2.125\ m^3\ s^{-1}$. Thus, if a leak has produced a plume, the aquifer is being contaminated at a rate of $2.125\ m^3\ s^{-1}$ (see Figure 5.5).

*The major exception is Karst topography, which has caves formed from eroded massive limestone and dolomite formations. The carbonate compounds in these sedimentary rocks dissolve over time along cracks that expand to caves in which water flows as underground streams. Since people have actually seen these impressive systems, they often incorrectly assume that this is how most groundwater moves. Indeed, most follow Darcy's Law.

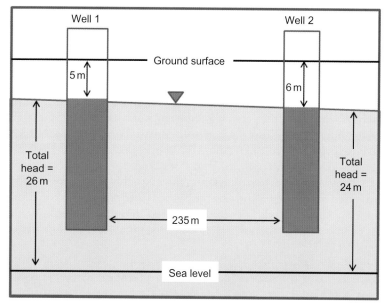

FIGURE 5.4    Hydraulic gradient between two wells. The difference in head is 2 m over 235 m, so the hydraulic gradient $= \frac{26m - 24m}{235m} = 0.0085$ m m$^{-1}$. *Adapted from: North Carolina Department of Enviroment and Natural Resources. Basic hydrogeology. http://www.ncwater.org/Education_and_Technical_Assistance/Ground_Water/Hydrogeology/; 2012 [accessed February 24, 2012].*

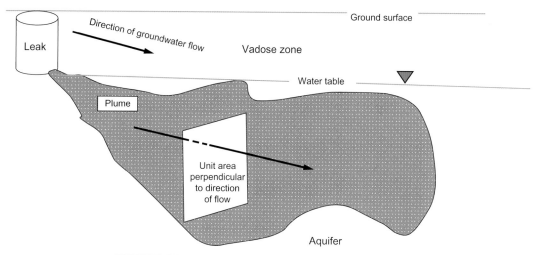

FIGURE 5.5    Contamination of an aquifer from a leaking tank.

## Solubility

As mentioned, before a contaminant can be carried by a fluid, it must be either dissolved or suspended in that fluid. The measure of the amount of chemical that can dissolve in a liquid, i.e., solubility, is commonly expressed in units of mass of solute (that which is dissolved) in the volume of solvent (that which dissolves). Usually, unless otherwise specified, the term "solubility," applies to the measure of the amount of the solute in water, i.e., aqueous solubility. Publications of the hazards or other characteristics of a substance, e.g., a material safety data sheet, will often list other solubilities, such as solubility in benzene, methanol, or hexane. Solubility may also be expressed in mass per mass or volume per volume, represented as parts per million (ppm), parts per billion (ppb), or parts per trillion (ppt). Occasionally, solubility is expressed as a percent or in parts per thousand; however, this is uncommon for contaminants and is usually reserved for nutrients and essential gases (e.g., percent carbon dioxide in water or ppt water vapor in the air). Solubility is often expressed in units of moles per liter or as a mole fraction, $x_A$ as in Table 5.1. Mole fraction is defined as the moles of the solute divided by the total moles in the solution.

Solubility is defined as the concentration of a dissolved solute in a solvent in equilibrium with undissolved solute at a fixed temperature and pressure. Knowledge of this is vitally important to environmental disasters (e.g., methyl mercury chloride uptake in aquatic organisms and fish). The solubility of gases in water (Table 5.1) gives an indication of the wide range of solubilities that do exist.[1,2]

TABLE 5.1   Solubility of Gas (A) in Water (B)

| Gas | Mole fraction, $x_A \times 10^{5a}$ | Ideal solubility, $x_A \times 10^5$ |
|---|---|---|
| He | 0.71 | – |
| Ar | 2.53 | – |
| $H_2$ | 1.41 | – |
| $N_2$ | 1.18 | – |
| $O_2$ | 2.30 | – |
| $CH_4$ | 2.55 | – |
| $C_3H_8$ | 6.99 | 11,600 |
| $SF_6$ | 0.44 | 4000 |
| $C_2F_6$ | 0.10 | – |
| $CO_2$ | 61 | 1780 |
| $CH_3F$ | 106.2 | 3000 |
| $SO_2$ | 2460 | 2500 |
| HCl | 25,900 | 2000 |

[a] At 25 °C and 101,325 Pa (1 atm).

Sources: Letcher TM, Battino R. An introduction to the understanding of solubility. J Chem Ed 2001;78:103–11; IUPAC. The Solubility Data Series, The Solubility Data Commission (volume 8). ResearchTriangle Park, NC; 1980.

The solubilities range over five orders of magnitude, from a low of one molecule of $C_2F_6$ in 1 million water molecules to 35 molecules of HCl in 100 molecules of water.

Thermodynamicists have a simple way of understanding solubility by first defining an ideal solubility; solute-solvent systems that obey Raoult's law. Ideal solubility implies that the interactions of the solute molecules, A, with the solute molecules, B, are the same as the A-A and B-B interactions. The ideal solubility for a solute, A, at a temperature $T$ and at a partial pressure of $p$ (1.0 atm) is given by[3]:

$$B\text{-}B \gg A\text{-}B < \text{ or } = A\text{-}A \tag{5.2}$$

where $p_A^*$ is the vapor pressure of the solute at temperature $T$.

The calculated ideal solubilities for some solutes in water are given in Table 5.1.

To understand the data in Table 5.1, we must appreciate that the $H_2O$ molecules are strongly associated; in this table, this relates to strong B-B interactions. By comparison, the molecules of nonpolar solutes are weakly associated and $B\text{-}B \gg A\text{-}B \ll A\text{-}A$. For those substances ($C_3H_8$, $SF_6$), the solute-solvent association is so weak that the experimental solubility is very much lower than the ideal solubility. For HCl, however, it is clear that something else is taking place. There are strong interactions between the polar HCl and the $H_2O$ taking place and the solubility is large, larger than either B-B or A-A interactions, and the result is a very high solubility for HCl.

Water is a very special case because of its strong self-association through hydrogen bonding. One can expect much higher discrepancies between experimental and ideal solubilities for water systems than for most other systems.

Another set of data which will support our conclusions relates to $CO_2$ in a variety of solvents, including water. The data are given in Table 5.2 and refer to 20 °C.[4]

The range here, apart from the value for water, is small compared to the values in Table 5.1. Furthermore, the ideal solubility of $CO_2$ is reasonable close to the experimental values, and

TABLE 5.2　Solubility of $CO_2$ in Liquids

| Solvent | Mole fraction, $X_{CO_2} \times 10^{2a}$ |
| --- | --- |
| Amyl acetate | 2.70 |
| Pyridine | 1.29 |
| Ethylene chloride | 1.25 |
| Chloroform | 1.23 |
| Toluene | 1.07 |
| Carbon tetrachloride | 1.00 |
| Ethyl alcohol | 0.70 |
| Carbon disulphide | 0.22 |
| Water | 0.061 |
| Ideal solubility | 1.78 |

[a] At 20 °C and 101,325 Pa (1 atm).

Source: Denbigh KG. Principles of Chemical Equilibria. Cambridge: Cambridge University Press; 1981 [chapter 4].

we assume that the strengths of the associations are all similar, i.e., A-A = A-B = B-B, a situation brought about by the nonpolar nature of both the $CO_2$ and the solvents.

However, the result for $CO_2$ in *water* poses a different picture. With very strong hydrogen bonds between the $H_2O$ molecules and relatively weak $CO_2$-$H_2O$ and $CO_2$-$CO_2$ associations, the solubility of $CO_2$ is less than the ideal.

So, generally, nonpolar compounds, such as hydrocarbons, will always have low solubility in water, whereas ionic compounds such as HCl will have a very high solubility in water. The old adage of "like" dissolves "like" is very much applicable, and by "like," we mean the structure and polar nature of the molecules.

Thermodynamicists have also derived an equation for the ideal solubility of solids in liquids:

$$\ln x_A = -[\Delta H_{fusion,A}(T_m)/RT][1 - T/T_m] \tag{5.3}$$

where $x_A$ is the solubility mole fraction of the solute at temperature $T$; $T_m$ is the melting temperature of the solute, and $\Delta H_{fusion,A}$ is the enthalpy of fusion (melting) of the solute at $T_m$. This implies that the solute will have the same solubility in all solvents as the solvent properties do not appear in the equation.

By way of example, the solubility of naphthalene in various solvents at 20 °C is given in Table 5.3.[4]

Another set of solubility data, this time of aromatic compounds dissolving in benzene, will support our understanding of the idea of "like" dissolving "like" (see Table 5.4).

The solutes are all aromatic in nature and so is the solvent benzene, so we would expect a reasonably close agreement between experimental and ideal values and that is what we get. Finally, let us take a look at an ionic compound NaCl in organic liquids and in water. The data set is given in Table 5.5.[5]

The solubility of NaCl is reasonably ideal in the organic solvents implying that the NaCl does not appear to dissociate. In water, however, the difference between experimental and ideal is greater than three orders of magnitude. Here, the NaCl dissociates into ions, and each ion forms strong associations with the polar water molecules, a process called hydration. This gives NaCl a much bigger solubility than predicted from the simple ideal model.

TABLE 5.3    Solubility of Naphthalene in Various Organic Solvents at 20 °C

| Solvent | Solubility mole fraction, $x_A$ |
|---|---|
| Chlorobenzene | 0.256 |
| Benzene | 0.241 |
| Toluene | 0.224 |
| Carbon tetrachloride | 0.205 |
| Hexane | 0.090 |
| Ideal solubility[a] | 0.273 |

[a] *The ideal solubility was determined from Equation (5.3) using $\Delta H_{fusion,A}$ and the $T_m$ for naphthalene as 18.58 kJ mol$^{-1}$ and 353.20 K, respectively. The agreement between the experimental and ideal values is good considering the simple nature of the ideal model which again is based on the idea that A-A, B-B, and A-B interactions are all the same.*
*Source: Denbigh KG. Principles of Chemical Equilibria. Cambridge: Cambridge University Press; 1981 [chapter 4].*

TABLE 5.4 Solubility of Aromatic Solids in Benzene at 25 °C

| Solute, A | $\Delta H_{fusion,A}$ (kJ mol$^{-1}$) | $T_m$ (K) | $x_A$ Ideal | $x_A$ Experimental |
|---|---|---|---|---|
| Biphenyl | 16.8 | 299.2 | 0.39 | 0.39 |
| Naphthalene | 19.1 | 353.4 | 0.30 | 0.24 |
| Phenanthrene | 16.5 | 373 | 0.25 | 0.19 |
| Anthracene | 28.8 | 490 | 0.011 | 0.0063 |

*Source: Letcher TM, Battino R. An introduction to the understanding of solubility. J Chem Ed 2001;78:103–11.*

TABLE 5.5 Solubility of NaCl in Various Solvents at 25 °C

| Solvent | Solubility mole fraction, $x_A$ |
|---|---|
| Methanol | $7.6 \times 10^{-3}$ |
| Ethanol | $5.0 \times 10^{-4}$ |
| Propanol | $1.6 \times 10^{-4}$ |
| Acetone | $0.41 \times 10^{-6}$ |
| Water | 0.10 |
| Ideal solubility[a] | $2.68 \times 10^{-4}$ |

[a] *The ideal solubility was determined from the $\Delta H_{fusion,NaCl}$ and $T_m$ for NaCl which was 28.2 kJ mol$^{-1}$ and 1074 K, respectively.*
*Source: Burgess J. Metal Ions in Solution. New York: Ellis Horwood; 1978. ISBN 0-85312-027-7.*

## Liquid in Liquid Solubility

We have not discussed the effects that take place when a liquid is mixed with another liquid giving rise to a solution or showing partial miscibility. However, from a qualitative point of view, the same idea of "like" dissolve "like" can be used to give some understanding to the processes involved. For example, water (very polar) will not dissolve in petrol (nonpolar), hexane (nonpolar) will mix in all proportions with octane (nonpolar), and octanol (weakly polar) will only partially mix with water (very polar).

These concepts and the basic idea of "like" dissolves "like" are important in environmental issues and can have a major input in understanding disasters such as the methylmercury disasters of Minamata and Iraq. The low solubility of the methylmercury chloride in water coupled with the relatively high solubility in lipid material and fatty tissues led to an understanding of why that particular mercury compound was so toxic. The disaster at Bhopal also involved solubilities as the water (very polar) that poured into the methylisocyanate (nonpolar) tank on that fateful day did not dissolve very much and the reaction that took place was largely at the interface of the two liquids. When the tank finally ruptured, it filled the air with largely unreacted and highly toxic methylisocyanate.

TABLE 5.6   Solubility of Tetrachlorodibenzo-*para*-dioxin in Water and Organic Solvents

| Solvent | Solubility (mg L$^{-1}$) | References |
|---|---|---|
| Water | $1.93 \times 10^{-5}$ | Podoll, R.T., Jaber, H.M. and Mill, T. *Environ Sci Technol.* 1986;20:490-2 |
| Water | $6.90 \times 10^{-4}$ (25 °C) | Fiedler, H. and Schramm, K.W. *Chemosphere.* 1990;20:1597-1602 |
| Methanol | 10 | International Agency for Research on Cancer[6] (IARC) |
| Lard oil | 40 | IARC |
| *n*-Octanol | 50 | IARC |
| Acetone | 110 | IARC |
| Chloroform | 370 | IARC |
| Benzene | 570 | IARC |
| Chlorobenzene | 720 | IARC |
| Orthochlorobenzene | 1400 | IARC |

Understanding the principles of solubility helps us appreciate why swallowing a small volume of mercury metal, which is relatively insoluble in aqueous and in lipid material, is not particularly toxic, but ingesting methylmercury chloride is highly toxic.

The diversity of solubilities in various solvents is a fairly reliable indication of where one is likely to find the compound in the environment. For example, the various solubilities of the most toxic form of dioxin, 2,3,7,8-dibenzo-*para*-dioxin (TCDD), are provided in Table 5.6. Dioxins appear to have a much greater affinity for sediment, organic particles, and the organic fraction of soils. The low water solubility indicates that dissolved TCDD in a water column should be in extremely low concentrations. However, other processes, such as cosolvation (wherein the dioxin dissolves in something else like benzene that itself has much higher aqueous solubility) will change the behavior of a contaminant. This is a good example of the need to consider contamination from a systematic perspective.

If a compound has a high aqueous solubility, i.e., it is easily dissolved in water under normal environmental conditions of temperature and pressure, it is *hydrophilic*. If, conversely, a substance is not easily dissolved in water under these conditions, it is said to be *hydrophobic*. As many contaminants are organic (i.e., consist of molecules containing carbon-to-carbon bonds and/or carbon-to-hydrogen bonds), the solubility can be further differentiated as to whether under normal environmental conditions of temperature and pressure, the substance is easily dissolved in organic solvents. If so, the substance is said to be *lipophilic* (i.e., readily dissolved in lipids). If, conversely, a substance is not easily dissolved in organic solvents under these conditions, it is said to be *lipophobic*.

This affinity for either water or lipids underpins an important indicator of environmental partitioning: i.e., the octanol-water partition coefficient ($K_{ow}$). The $K_{ow}$ is the ratio of a substance's concentration in octanol ($C_7H_{13}CH_2OH$) to the substance's concentration in water at equilibrium (i.e., the reactions have all reached their final expected chemical composition in

TABLE 5.7    Solubility, Octanol-Water Partitioning Coefficient, and Density Values for Some Environmental
            Pollutants

| Chemical | Water solubility (mg L$^{-1}$) | $K_{ow}$ | Density (kg m$^{-3}$) |
|---|---|---|---|
| Atrazine | 33 | 724 | |
| Benzene | 1780 | 135 | 879 |
| Chlorobenzene | 472 | 832 | 1110 |
| Cyclohexane | 60 | 2754 | 780 |
| 1,1-Dichloroethane | 4960 | 62 | 1180 |
| 1,2-Dichloroethane | 8426 | 30 | 1240 |
| Ethanol | Completely miscible | 0.49 | 790 |
| Toluene | 515 | 490 | 870 |
| Vinyl chloride | 2790 | 4 | 910 |
| Tetrachlorodibenzo-*para*-dioxin (TCDD) | $1.9 \times 10^{-4}$ | $6.3 \times 10^{6}$ | |

*Source: Hemond HF, Fechner-Levy EJ.* Chemical fate and transport in the environment, *San Diego, CA: Academic Press; 2000; TCDD data from the NTP Chemical Repository, National Environmental Health Sciences Institute, 2003; and U.S. Environmental Protection Agency, 2003, Technical Fact sheet on Dioxin (2,3,7,8-TCDD).*

a control volume of the fluid). Octanol is a surrogate for lipophilic solvents, in general, because it has degrees of affinity for both water and organic compounds, that is, octanol is *amphibilic*. As the ratio forming the $K_{ow}$ is [$C_7H_{13}CH_2OH$]:[$H_2O$], then the larger the $K_{ow}$ value, the more lipophilic the substance is. Values for solubility in water and $K_{ow}$ values of some important environmental compounds, along with their densities, are shown in Table 5.7.

Table 5.7 elucidates some additional aspects of solubility and organic/aqueous phase distribution. Water solubility is generally inversely related to $K_{ow}$, as the more hydrophobic the compound, the greater its affinity for the octanol compared to the water. However, the inverse relationship is not universal as organic compounds have a wide range of aqueous solubilites. Indeed, organic compounds can have affinities for neither, either, or both the organic and the aqueous phases. Most compounds are not completely associated with either phase, i.e., they have some amount of amphibilicity. In fact, the fluid representing the organic component, octanol, is actually amphibilic, as it contains the very polar hydroxyl group ($OH^-$) like all alcohols.

Seemingly minor structural attributes of a molecule can make quite a difference in phase partitioning and in density. Even the isomers (i.e., same chemical composition with a different arrangement) vary in their $K_{ow}$ values and densities (note the "1,1" versus "1,2" arrangements of chlorine atoms on 1,1-dichloroethane, and 1,2-dichloroethane, causes the former to have a slightly decreased density but twice the $K_{ow}$ value than the latter. The location of the chlorine atoms alone accounts for a significant difference in water solubility in the two compounds.

The relationship between density and organic/aqueous phase partitioning is very important to pollutant transport, as shown in Figure 5.6. The transport of the nonaqueous phase liquids (NAPLs) through the vadose zone assumes that the NAPLs have extremely high $K_{ow}$ values and extremely low water solubility. That is, they have a greater affinity for lipids

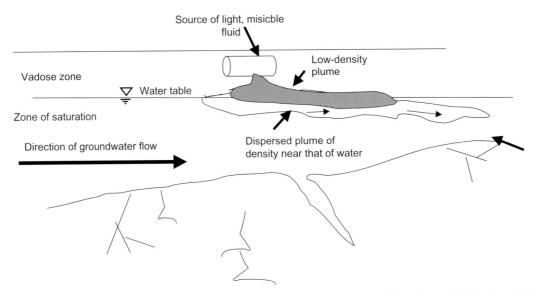

FIGURE 5.6   Hypothetical plume of light, highly hydrophilic fluid. *Based on information provided by: Sara MN. Groundwater monitoring system design. In: Nielsen DM, editor.* Practical handbook of ground-water monitoring. *Chelsea, MI: Lewis Publishers; 1991.*

than for water. As the aqueous solubility of a substance increases, its flow will increasingly follow the water flow lines.

When a dense, miscible fluid seeps into the zone of saturation, the contaminants move downward if their densities are greater than that of the water. When these contaminants reach the bottom of the aquifer, the shape dictates their continued movement and slope of the underlying bedrock or other relatively impervious layer, which will likely be in a direction other than the flow of the groundwater in the aquifer. Solution and dispersion near the boundaries of the plume will have a secondary plume that will generally follow the general direction of groundwater flow. The physics of system indicates that estimating the direction of the plume will entail more than the fluid densities and must include solubility and phase partitioning. So, monitoring wells will need to be installed upstream and downstream from the source.

If a source consists entirely of a light, hydrophilic fluid, the plume may be characterized as shown in Figure 5.6. Low-density organic fluids, however, often are highly volatile, i.e., their vapor pressures are sufficiently high to change phases from liquid to gas. So, let us now consider another physicochemical property of environmental fluids, vapor pressure, which must be considered along with density and solubility.

An important process in plume migration is that of *cosolvation*, the process where a substance is first dissolved in one solvent and then the new solution is mixed with another solvent. As mentioned, with increasing aqueous solubility, a pollutant will travel along the flow lines of the ground- or surface water. However, even a substance with low aqueous solubility can follow the flow under certain conditions. Even a *hydrophobic* compound like a chlorinated benzene (called a dense nonaqueous phase liquid, DNAPL), which has very low solubility in pure water, can migrate into and within water bodies if it is first dissolved in an alcohol or an organic solvent (e.g., toluene). So, a DNAPL will travel downward because its *density* is less than that of water and is transported in the DNAPL which has undergone cosolvation with the water. Likewise, the ordinarily lipophilic compound can be transported in the vadose zone or upper part of the zone of saturation where it undergoes cosolvation with water and a light nonaqueous phase liquid (LNAPL), e.g., toluene.

## Suspension and Sorption

Even if a contaminant is not in solution, it can still be transported as a suspension. Fine particles can be held in suspension if the water flow has sufficient energy. When the energy falls below a certain level, the suspended particles will settle. Many suspended contaminants in groundwater are small colloidal particles, i.e., so small that Brownian motion provides enough energy to keep them from settling.

When a contaminant enters soil, some of the chemical remains in soil solution and some is adsorbed onto the surfaces of the soil particles. Sometimes this sorption is strong due to cations adsorbing to the negatively charged soil particles. In other cases, the attraction is weak. Sorption of chemicals onto solid surfaces needs to be understood because in this way solids can hold onto contaminants, not allowing them to move freely with the pore water or the soil solution. Therefore, sorption slows that rate at which substances move downwardly through the soil profile.

Compounds eventually establish a balance between the mass on the solid surfaces and the mass that is in solution. Molecules will migrate from one phase to another to maintain this balance. The properties of both the chemical and the soil (or other matrix) will determine how and at what rates the molecules partition into the solid and liquid phases. These physicochemical relationships, known as *sorption isotherms*, are found experimentally.

Other properties are important in groundwater contamination, including those discussed in Chapter 2. Notably, density, capillarity, and surface tension are among the fluid properties that can greatly affect the rate of contaminant movement into an aquifer, as well as which part of an aquifer will be most contaminated (e.g., strong surface tension could increase sorption onto soil particles).

## LOVE CANAL

The seminal and arguably the most infamous case, relating to leaks is the contamination in and around Love Canal, New York. The beneficent beginnings of the case belie its infamy. In the nineteenth century, William T. Love foresaw an opportunity for electricity generation from Niagara Falls and the potential for industrial development. To achieve this, Love planned to build a canal that would also allow ships to pass around the Niagara Falls and travel between the two great lakes: Erie and Ontario. The project started in the 1890s, but soon floundered due to inadequate financing and also due to the development of alternating current which made it unnecessary for industries to locate near a source of power production. Hooker Chemical Company purchased the land adjacent to the Canal in the early 1990s and constructed a production facility. In 1942, Hooker Chemical began disposal of its industrial waste in the Canal. This was war time in the United States, and there was little concern for possible environmental consequences. Hooker Chemical (which later became Occidental Chemical Corporation) disposed of over 21,000 tons of chemical wastes including halogenated pesticides, chlorobenzenes, and other hazardous materials into the old Love Canal. The disposal continued until 1952 at which time the company covered the site with soil and deeded it to the City of Niagara Falls which wanted to use it for a public park. In the transfer of the deed, Hooker specifically stated that the site was used for the burial of hazardous materials and warned the City that fact should govern future decisions on the use of the land. Everything Hooker Chemical did during those years was legal and aboveboard.

About this time, the Niagara Falls Board of Education was looking around for a place to construct a new elementary school and the old Love Canal seemed like a perfect spot. This area was a growing suburb with densely packed single-family residences on streets paralleling the old canal. A school on this site seemed like a perfect solution and so it was built.

In the 1960s, the first complaints began and intensified during the early 1970s. The groundwater table rose during those years and brought to the surface some of the buried chemicals. Children in the school playground were seen playing with strange 55-gallon drums that popped out of the ground. The contaminated liquids started to ooze into the basements of the nearby residents, causing odor and health problems. More importantly, perhaps, the contaminated liquid was found to have entered the storm sewers and was being discharged upstream of the water intake for the Niagara Falls water treatment plant.

The situation officially could be recognized as a "disaster" when, in 1978, President Jimmy Carter declared an environmental emergency. This designation required that 950 families be evacuated from an area of 10 square blocks around the canal. In addition to the logistics of relocating and calming the people affected, the disaster response presented a difficult engineering problem. Excavating the waste would have been dangerous work and would probably have caused the death of some of the workers. Digging up the waste would also have exposed it to the atmosphere resulting in uncontrolled toxic air emissions. Finally, there was the question as to what would be done with the waste. As it was all mixed up, no single solution such as incineration would have been appropriate. The U.S. Environmental Protection Agency (EPA) finally decided that the only thing to do with this dump was to isolate it and continue to monitor and treat the groundwater. The contaminated soil on the school site was excavated, detoxified, and stabilized and the building itself was razed. All of the sewers were cleaned, removing 62,000 tons of sediment that had to be treated and removed to a remote site. The EPA has removed the site from its National Priority Listing (NPL), i.e., the worst of the worst hazardous waste sites.[7]

Costs were unprecedented. Occidental Chemical paid $129 million and continues to pay for oversight and monitoring. Total disaster response costs may have exceeded $250 million, with the difference being paid by the Federal Emergency Management Agency and by the U.S. Army, which was found to have contributed waste to the canal.

The Love Canal story galvanized the American public into understanding the problems of hazardous waste and was the impetus for the passage of several significant pieces of legislation, such as the Resource Conservation and Recovery Act, the CERCLA, and the Toxic Substances Control Act. In particular, a new approach to assessing and addressing these problems had evolved.

# CHESTER

In 1978, a fire in Chester, Pennsylvania, ushered in a new era of emergency response in the U.S. Firefighters and other first responders[8] were not ready for what they found, i.e., large quantities of illegally stored chemicals, among them highly flammable, extremely toxic, and highly volatile materials. This is a potentially deadly combination of physical and chemical factors.

Volatile organic compounds (VOCs) have relatively high vapor pressures (greater than 0.01 kilopascals). Other chemical factors such as halogenation and sorption affect vapor pressure. Substituting halogens, for example, lowers vapor pressure. Thus, many chlorinated compounds are considered less volatile, i.e., semivolatile organic compounds (SVOCs). A particularly toxic group of SVOCs, the polychlorinated biphenyls (PCBs), were stored at Chester. SVOCs present special challenges during disasters. They are potential air pollutants from storage tanks, presenting problems to first responders. Volatile compounds that are also flammable were central to the disaster at Chester. The fire and explosion hazards were greater if the substances were merely flammable, but less volatile.

The intense fire destroyed one building and caused extensive damage to two others used for stockpiling drummed wastes. Forty-seven firefighters were hospitalized. In the fire's aftermath, there remained a controversial three-acre site, located on the west bank of the Delaware River and in a light industrial area. Homes were within 300 m from the site. From the 1950s to the 1970s, the site was used as a rubber recycling facility, and then it was converted to an illegal industrial waste storage and disposal facility until 1978. Numerous 55-gallon (200 L) drums were stored on the site or dumped their contents either directly onto the ground or into trenches, severely contaminating soil and groundwater. Wastes included toxic chemicals and PCBs, as well as acids and cyanide salts. Burned building debris, exploded drums, tires, shredded rubber, and contaminated earth littered the property. About 150,000 gallons (570,000 L) of waste materials remained on site after the fire. Most of the wastes were in 55-gallon drums stored in the fire-damaged buildings. Because of the dumping of contaminants and the fire, the groundwater and soil were contaminated with heavy metals including arsenic, chromium, mercury, and lead; PCBs; plastic resins; and VOCs from past disposal activities. In addition to the public health menace, the fire and latent effects of the stored contaminants took place in an ecologically sensitive area, including nearby wetlands and other habitats for wildlife and marine animals. Several cleanup actions were conducted until it was ultimately removed from the Superfund list of most hazardous sites. Currently, with EPA and state approval, the site is undergoing construction to provide parking for the City of Chester's adjacent Barry Bridge Park redevelopment.

## TIMES BEACH

The disaster at Times Beach, like Love Canal, was slow and cumulative in forming, but with pronounced and long-term impacts. The town of Times Beach was a popular resort community along the Meramec River, about 17 miles (27 km) west of St. Louis. With few resources, the roads in the town were not paved and dust on the roads was controlled by spraying oil. For 2 years, 1972 and 1973, the contract for the road spraying went to a waste oil hauler named Russell Bliss. The roads were paved in 1973 and the spraying ceased.

Bliss obtained his waste oil from the Northeastern Pharmaceutical and Chemical Company in Verona, Missouri, which manufactured hexachlorophene, a bactericidal chemical. In the production of hexachlorophene, considerable quantities of dioxin-laden waste had to be removed and disposed of. A significant amount of the dioxin was contained in the "still bottoms" of chemical reactors, and the company found that having it burned in a chemical incinerator was expensive. The company was taken over by Syntex Agribusiness in 1972, and the new company decided to contract with Russell Bliss to haul away the still bottom waste without telling Bliss what was in the oily substance. Bliss mixed it with other waste oils and this is what he used to oil the roads in Times Beach, unaware that the oil contained high concentration of dioxin (greater than 2000 ppm), including the most toxic congener, 2,3,7,8-dibenzo-*para*-dioxin (TCDD).

Bliss also had an oil spraying business where he oiled roads and sprayed oil to control dust, especially in horse arenas. He used the dioxin-laden oil to spray the roads and horse runs in nearby farms. In fact, it was the death of horses at these farms that first alerted the Center for Disease Control to sample the soil at the farms. They found the dioxin but did not make the connection with Bliss. Finally in 1979, the U.S. EPA became aware of the problem when a former employee of the company told them about the sloppy practices in handling the dioxin-laden waste. The EPA converged on Times Beach in "moonsuits" and panic set in among the populace. The situation was not helped by the message from the EPA to the residence of the town. "If you are in town it is advisable for you to leave and if you are out of town do not go back." In February 1983, on the basis of an advisory from the Centers for Disease Control, the EPA permanently relocated all of the residents and businesses at a cost of $33 million. Times Beach was by no means the only problem stemming from the contaminated waste oil. Twenty-seven other sites in Missouri were also contaminated with dioxins.

The acute toxicity concern with dioxin, however, may have been overstated. As a previous accident in Seveso, Italy, had shown, dioxin is not nearly as acutely toxic to humans as originally feared, causing some to conclude that it is unlikely that the reported damage to human health in Times Beach was anywhere near the catastrophe originally anticipated. Even some U.S. EPA officials later admitted that the evacuation and bulldozing of the community was probably unnecessary. But given the knowledge of dioxin toxicity in 1979, the decision to detoxify the site was not unreasonable. Indeed, the long-term, chronic effects from dioxin exposure may well be the biggest concern. As evidence, the carcinogenicity of TCDD was later better established and found to be very high (slope factors $> 10^5$ for inhalation, ingestion, and dermal routes).

After all residents had been evacuated from Times Beach, the houses were razed. The Superfund site was eventually decontaminated at a cost of over $200 million. Cleaning the Times Beach Superfund site was the result of an enormous effort, including the installation of a temporary incinerator to burn the contaminated soil and the erection of a 15-ft (4.6 m) high barrier around the incinerator to protect from regular flooding by the Meramec River. A consent decree between the United States, the State of Missouri, and the Syntex Agribusiness, the company that assumed responsibility of the site's cleanup, required the implementation of the EPA Record of Decision (ROD), which was issued on September 29, 1988. This decision called for incineration at Times Beach of dioxin-contaminated soils from 28 sites, including Times Beach, in eastern Missouri. Times Beach has been as ghost town since 1983, when it was purchased by the State of Missouri, using Superfund monies. By the end of 1997, cleanup of the site was completed by EPA and Syntex Agribusiness. More than 244 000 tonnes of dioxin-contaminated soil from the site and 27 nearby areas had been cleaned. The federal government and the State of Missouri worked closely with Syntex during cleanup to ensure that the restoration made the site suitable for productive use. In 1999, a new 500-acre (203 ha) State park commemorating the famous Route 66 opened on what was once one of the most recognized sites in the country. Thousands of visitors now enjoy the scenic riverside area in Missouri once known as Times Beach. So, perhaps the policy makers were correct in their precautions. Quite a few lessons were learned, including remediation techniques, contaminant destruction (e.g. incineration), and post clean-up use. One may argue that this was one of the first efforts at looking at the hazardous waste problem from a life cycle perspective, considering possible uses after cleanup. In this way, Times Beach set the stage for the many brownfield projects throughout the U.S.

## VALLEY OF THE DRUMS

Two of the most important and policy-changing events occurred in the year 1967: the Torrey Canyon supertanker oil spill (see Chapter 6) and the identification of an uncontrolled hazardous waste dump (Figure 5.7) that came to be known as the infamous Valley of the Drums site.

The A.L. Taylor hazardous waste site, covering 13 acres (5.3 ha) in Brooks, Kentucky, 12 miles(19 km) south of Louisville, served as a refuse dump, drum recycling center, and chemical dump from 1967 to 1977. The chemical wastes were largely from the paint and coating industries of Louisville. During that time, over 100,000 drums of waste were delivered illegally to the site. About a fourth of the drums were buried and the rest were directly discharging their hazardous contents into pits and trenches. The hydrology of the site allowed for the wastes to move into a nearby creek by storm water runoff. This situation led to a large slug of contaminants reaching the creek in 1979 during a snow melt, precipitating an emergency response action by the U.S. EPA. The subsequent EPA sampling and analysis of the soil and water indicated the presence of elevated concentrations of heavy metals, PCBs, and 140 other chemical contaminants. The EPA required the remediation of the site in 1986 and 1987 in order to reduce exposures and to stem subsequent pollution to the creek and the surrounding environment.

FIGURE 5.7    The hazardous waste site known as the Valley of the Drums was among the earliest and most severe hazardous waste sites in terms of sheer quantity of illegally disposed contaminants. Discovery of this site helped to motivate the U.S. Congress to pass the Superfund law. *Photo credit: U.S. Environmental Protection Agency; http://www. epa.gov/history/topics/drums/01.html [accessed January 4, 2012].*

# STRINGFELLOW ACID PITS

In southern California, near Glen Avon, 5 miles (8 km) northwest of Riverside, the String-fellow Quarry Company managed a state-approved hazardous waste disposal facility during 1956 and 1972 (see Figure 5.8). The Stringfellow Quarry Company disposed 120 million liters of industrial wastes into an unlined evaporation pond. The contaminants came from

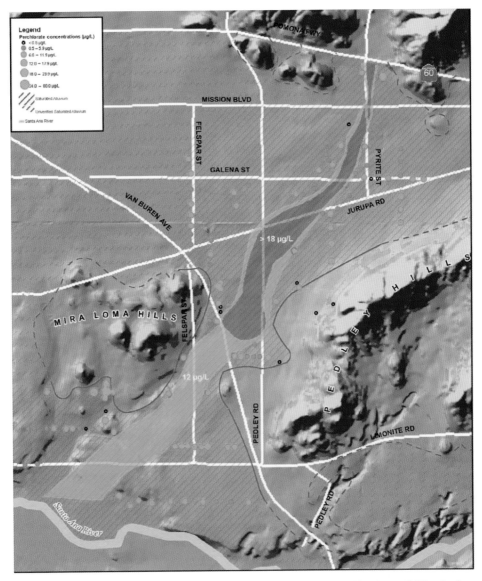

FIGURE 5.8   Site map and perchlorate concentrations at the Stringfellow site, Glen Avon, California. *Source: U.S. Environmental Protection Agency. Stringfellow Superfund Site Perchlorate RI/FS Update, Fact Sheet, October 2006; http:// yosemite.epa.gov/r9/sfund/r9sfdocw.nsf/3dc283e6c5d6056f88257426007417a2/ebd8b62494cedd7d882575fd007924b6/$FILE/ Revised%20fact%20sheet%20text.pdf; 2006 [accessed January 4, 2012].*

production of metal finishing, electroplating, and the formulation of the pesticide DDT (dichlorodiphenyltrichloroethane) or 1,1,1 trichloro-2,2-di(1-chlorophenyl)ethane. Due to the pond being unlined, the waste leached into the underlying groundwater table and developed a 2 miles (3 km) contaminated plume downstream. The Stringfellow Quarry Company voluntarily closed the site, and the California Regional Water Quality Control Board declared the property a problem area. A policy was adopted to contain waste and keep any further migration of waste to a minimum. Between 1975 and 1980, 2 million liters of liquid waste and DDT contaminants were recovered. In 1980, the EPA recovered another $3.8 \times 10^7$ L (10 million gallons) of hazardous waste from the groundwater. The disposal facility was claimed as California's worst environmental hazards in 1983. Since 1983, the EPA required further concentrated effort to be taken at the site on four different occasions. About three quarters of a billion dollars has been spent for remedial action to date.

The groundwater at the site was found to contain various VOCs and heavy metals, including cadmium, nickel, chromium, and manganese. The soil had been contaminated with pesticides, PCBs, sulfates, and heavy metals, all putting the nearby populations at risk, so steps were immediately taken to reduce exposure. For example, the original disposal area is now covered by a clay cap, fenced, and guarded by security services. No one is currently drinking water affected by the contaminant plume.

The earliest response actions at the site, taken between 1980 and 1984, included the installation of three groundwater extraction wells, a subsurface barrier structure, and an on-site surface water drainage system with gunite[9] channels was built. All liquid wastes at the surface of the site were removed to a federally approved hazardous waste disposal facility. With the exception of 760 m$^3$ (1000 cubic yards) of DDT-contaminated soil, which were taken to a Federally approved facility, contaminated soils from the site were used to fill waste ponds. The surface was graded, covered with clean soil, and seeded. In 1984, the State of California completed initial cleanup measures including fencing the site, maintaining the existing soil cap, controlling erosion, and disposing of the leachate extracted above and below the on-site clay barrier dam. In 1989, residences that had been receiving bottled water from the State were connected to the Jurupa Community Services District.

Numerous actions have been put in place to remedy the site. In 1984, the EPA selected a remedy for interim treatment of contaminated groundwater. The remedy featured installing a pretreatment system (Figure 5.9) consisting of lime ($CaCO_3$) precipitation for removing heavy

FIGURE 5.9 Worker standing on surface drainage gutter and drain inlet basin in the southern part of Zone 1, facing northeast. 25 K at Stringfellow site. *Photo credit: U.S. Environmental Protection Agency. http://yosemite.epa.gov/ r9/sfund/r9sfdocw.nsf/3dc283e6c5d6056f8825742 6007417a2/701f424f17ca525d8825700700754b3b! OpenDocument [accessed January 4, 2012].*

metals and granular activated carbon treatment for removing VOCs. The treated ground-water is discharged to an industrial sewer line, which ultimately discharges to a publicly owned treatment works system. Additional interceptor and monitoring wells were installed to extract contaminated groundwater downgradient of the site. The State completed installa-tion of the pretreatment plant in 1985. As of March 1996, nearly 128 million gallons (485 million liters) of groundwater had been extracted from the aquifer and treated (i.e., known as "pump and treat"). This treatment system will operate until established cleanup levels have been met.

In 1987, the EPA selected a remedy to (1) capture and treat groundwater in the lower canyon area of the site with a groundwater barrier system, (2) install a peripheral channel to divert clean surface water runoff from upgradient areas, (3) extend the existing gunite channels southward to discharge surface water into Pyrite Creek, and (4) reconstruct the Pyrite Creek Channel. The potentially responsible parties (PRPs) installed the groundwater barrier system and reconstructed the Pyrite Creek Channel. The State of California designed the system and com-pleted construction of the northern channels in 1990. A groundwater extraction system was installed in the community to treat contaminated groundwater that migrated downgradient to the area, possibly followed by reinjection of the treated water. The PRPs have installed an initial community wells extraction system, in an attempt to control the hydraulic conditions of the plume of contaminated groundwater. Further work was begun in September 1997 to install an additional extraction well in order to put the remaining portions of the plume under hydraulic control. In addition, remediation included dewatering of the on-site groundwater, a more aggressive effort to remove water from the water table, as an interim source control measure.

Overall, the liquid waste removal, the connection of affected residences to an alternate water supply, and the installation of a groundwater capture and treatment system have reduced the potential for exposure to contaminated materials at the Stringfellow site while the remaining cleanup activities continue to this day.

## TAR CREEK

In 1901, lead and zinc ores were first discovered in the Picher field in Ottawa County, Oklahoma, and Cherokee County, Kansas. Mining began shortly thereafter. Over time, the contamination occurred due to mining activities at the lead-zinc (Pb-Zn) subregions which comprise the tri-state mining region of Oklahoma, Kansas, and Missouri. Picher field encom-passes 6 square miles. Surface features are characterized by numerous large tailing piles con-sisting primarily of limestone and chert (metamorphosed limestone). Numerous collapsed structures and mine shaft cave-ins are also present. The Ozark Plateau, where Picher field is located, is a broad, low-structured dome laying mainly in southern Missouri and northern Arkansas, although the main mining area is within the central lowland province.[10]

Elm creek, on the western edge of the field, and Tar Creek and its main tributary, Lytle creek, are the principal streams. A short distance east of the mining field is the spring river, which is the major south-flowing tributary of the Neosho. The principal communities within the Picher field are Miami, Picher, Cardin, Quapaw, and Commerce. These and other com-munities receive their drinking water from the Rubidoux aquifer, which is approximately 330 m (1100 ft) from the surface.

Large-scale mining activities ended in the mid-1960s and pumps were removed from the mines. By 1979, the majority of the underground mine workings were completely flooded and acid mine water began to discharge via abandoned or partially plugged mine shaft openings and boreholes. For some time, highly mineralized acid mine discharges from flooded underground lead-zinc mines have reached the Tar Creek watershed. The Oklahoma Water Resources Board (OWRB) in cooperation with the Tar Creek task force investigated the problem initially in 1980 and 1981.

In October 1981, Tar Creek was listed among the sites on the National Priorities List under the CERCLA. It was the largest Superfund site ever listed by the EPA, with millions of cubic yards of mining tailings, much of which is contaminated with lead (Pb), cadmium (Cd), and zinc (Zn).

The Picher field is among several mines in the region to experience continuous inflow of groundwater during mining. This required large-scale pumping, but when the mining stopped, so did the pumping, allowing the inflow of water to return. The pyrite-rich waste piles were oxidized by exposure to the oxygen-rich atmosphere while mining was occurring. Oxidized sulfides have high aqueous solubility, so they readily dissolved into the surrounding groundwater. In turn, the water became acidic and reacted with the surrounding rock. This caused many of the metals present to dissolve, resulting in water with high concentrations of zinc, lead, and cadmium (see Table 5.8). Note that the bottom concentrations are much higher for the four metals listed, meaning that the aquifer is more contaminated than the topsoil. In addition, the tailings do not readily support vegetation[11] so that fine particles are readily removed and carried by wind (Figure 5.10).

The chemical form of these and other metals determines their toxicity to humans and other organisms. It also determines where a metal is likely to concentrate in the environment (see Figure 5.11). In groundwater, the lower pH and elevated metals in solution threaten water supplies that use these aquifers.

Lead-contaminated soils and chat piles are the source of exposure of toxic substances (principally Pb, Cd, and Zn) to the population, especially to young children, who are quite susceptible to the neurological effects of Pb. Residents were found to have abnormally high blood lead levels. Kidney disease also appeared to be elevated. The percentage of children with elevated blood lead levels remains well above state and national averages. In Spring of 2006, the EPA decided that the site would be closed and all residents relocated. A total of 83 abandoned wells have allowed infiltration of acidic water, leading to contamination of public drinking water supplies. These have been plugged and surface waters diverted.[12]

TABLE 5.8   Example of Groundwater Surface and Bottom of the Admiralty No. 4 Mine Shaft at Picher Field, Oklahoma

| Parameter | Surface concentration | Bottom concentration | U.S. drinking water standard |
|---|---|---|---|
| pH | 5.8 | 5.4 | 6.5-8.5 |
| Cadmium ($\mu g\ L^{-1}$) | 2 | 82 | 10 |
| Iron ($\mu g\ L^{-1}$) | 72,000 | 277,000 | 300 |
| Lead ($\mu g\ L^{-1}$) | 20 | 80 | 50 |
| Zinc ($\mu g\ L^{-1}$) | 60,000 | 331,000 | 5000 |

*Source: U.S. Environmental Protection Agency. EPA Superfund Record of Decision: Tar Creek (Ottawa County); 1984. EPA ID: OKD980629844-OU 01. Report No. EPA/ROD/R06-84/004.*

FIGURE 5.10   Tailings at Picher Field, Tar Creek, Oklahoma. *Source: U.S. Geological Survey. Oklahoma Water Science Center. http://ok.water. usgs.gov/projects/tarcreek; 2012 [accessed March 5, 2012].*

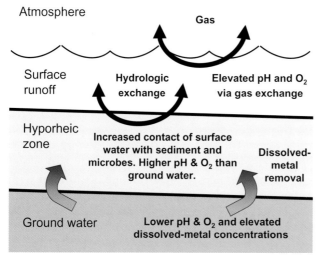

FIGURE 5.11   Exchanges and reactions that can occur in groundwater, sediment, and surface water. Some of the stream water moves into and out of the sediment and in shallow groundwater (i.e., the hyporheic zone). The process can increase the mobility of dissolved metallic compounds. *Source: U.S. Geological Survey and Vallero DA.* Environmental contaminants: assessment and control. *Burlington, MA: Academic Press, Elsevier Sciences; 2004.*

# LESSONS LEARNED[13]

The world is very different now, to what it was in the 1970s. This is quite true for toxic and hazardous substances. Expectations for a clean environment go beyond the obvious air and water pollution. Groundwater is rightfully seen to be a precious resource. Now, a more vigilant and technologically sound approach is in place.

International and domestic agencies have established sets of steps to determine the potential for the release of contaminants from a hazardous waste site. In the United States, the steps shown in Figure 5.12 comprise the "Superfund Cleanup Process," because they have been developed as regulations under the CERCLA, more popularly known as "Superfund." The first step in this cleanup process is a Preliminary Assessment/Site Inspection, from which the site is ranked in the Agency's Hazard Ranking System (HRS). The HRS is a process that screens the threats of each site to

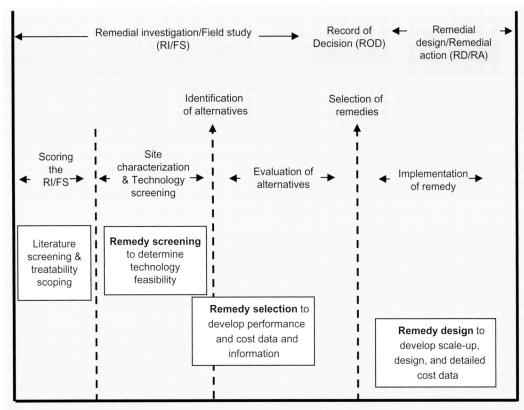

FIGURE 5.12    Steps in a contaminated site cleanup, as mandated by Superfund. *Source: U.S. Environmental Protection Agency. Guide for Conducting Treatability Studies under CERCLA: Thermal Desorption; 1992. EPA/ 540/R-92/074 B.*

determine if the site should be listed on the NPL, which is the list of most serious sites identified for possible long-term cleanup, and what the rank of a listed site should be. Following the initial investigation, a formal remedial investigation/feasibility study (RI/FS) is conducted to assess the nature and the extent of contamination. The next formal step is the ROD, which describes the various possible alternatives for cleanup to be used at an NPL site. Next, a remedial design/remedial action (RD/RA) plan is prepared and implemented. RD/RA specifies which remedies will be undertaken at the site and lays out all plans for meeting cleanup standards for all environmental media. The Construction Completion step identifies the activities that were completed to achieve cleanup. After completion of all actions identified in the RD/RA, a program for Operation and Maintenance is carried out to ensure that all actions are as effective as expected and that the measures are operating properly and according to the plan. Finally, after cleanup and demonstrated success, the site may be deleted from the NPL.

Certainly, every site is unique, but it is possible and preferable to undertake consistent steps when encountering hazardous wastes. First, the location of the site and boundaries should be clearly specified, including the formal address and geodetic coordinates. The history of the site, including present and all past owners and operators, should be documented. The search for this background information should include both formal (e.g., public records) and informal documentation (e.g., newspapers and discussions with neighborhood groups[14]). The main or most recent businesses that have operated on the site, as well as any ancillary or previous interests, should be documented and investigated. For example, in the infamous Times Beach, MO dioxin contamination incident, the operator's main business was an oiling operation to control dust and to pave roads. Regrettably, the operator also ran an ancillary waste oil hauling and disposal business. The operator "creatively" merged these two businesses, i.e., spraying waste oil that had been contaminated with dioxins, which led to the widespread problem and numerous Superfund sites in Missouri, including the relocation of the entire town of Times Beach.

The investigation at this point should include *all* past and present owners and operators. Any decisions regarding *de minimis* interests will be made at a later time (by the government agencies and attorneys). At this point, one should be searching for every PRP. A particularly important part of this review is to document all sales of the property or any parts of the property. Also, all commercial, manufacturing, and transportation concerns should be known, as these may indicate the types of wastes that have been generated or handled at the site. Even an interest of short duration can be very important, if this interest produced highly persistent and toxic substances that may still be on-site or that may have migrated off-site. The investigation should also determine whether any attempts were made to dispose of wastes from operations, either on-site or, through manifest reports, whether any wastes were shipped off-site. A detailed account should be given of all waste reporting, including air emission and water discharge permits, voluntary audits that include tests like the toxicity characteristic leaching procedure (TCLP), and compare these results to benchmark levels, especially to determine if any of the concentrations of contaminants exceed the U.S. EPA hazardous waste limit (40 CFR 261). For example, the TLCP limit for lead (Pb) is 5 mg L$^{-1}$. Any exceedances of this federal limit in the soil or sand on the site must be reported.

Initial monitoring and chemical testing should be conducted to target those contaminants that may have resulted from. A more general surveillance is also needed to identify a broader suite of contaminants. This is particularly important in soil and groundwater, as their rates of migration ($Q$) are quite slow compared to the rates usually found in air and surface water transport. Thus, the likelihood of encountering remnant compounds is greater in soil and groundwater. Also, in addition to parent chemical compounds, chemical degradation products should also be targeted, since decades may have passed since the waste was buried, spilled, or released into the environment.

An important part of the preliminary investigation is the identification of possible exposures, both human and environmental. For example, the investigation should document the proximity of the site to schools, parks, water supplies, residential neighborhoods, shopping areas, and businesses.

One means of efficiently implementing a hazardous waste remedial plan is for the present owners (and past owners, for that matter) to work voluntarily with government health and environmental agencies. States often have voluntary action programs that can be an effective means of expediting the process, which allows companies to participate in, and even lead, the RI/FS consistent with a state-approved work plan (which can be drafted by their consulting engineer).

The FS delineates potential remedial alternatives, comparing the cost-effectiveness to assess each alternative approach's ability to mitigate potential risks associated with the contamination. The FS also includes a field study to retrieve and chemically analyze (at a state-approved laboratory) water and soil samples from all environmental media on the site. Soil and vadose zone contamination will

FIGURE 5.13 Environmental specialists carefully dispose of chemicals released at Cameron, Louisiana by Hurricane Rita on November 10, 2005. This operation included both removal and remedial actions exposed to any hazards. Photo by M. Nauman. *Source: Federal Emergency Management Administration, 2011.*

likely require that test pits be excavated to determine the type and extent of contamination. Samples from the pit are collected for laboratory analysis to determine general chemical composition (e.g., a so-called total analyte list) and TCLP levels (that indicate leaching, i.e., the rate of movement of the contaminants).

An iterative approach may be appropriate as the data are derived. For example, if the results from the screening (e.g., total analytical tests) and the leaching tests indicate the site's main problem is with one or just a few contaminants, then a more focused approach to cleanup may be in order. Also, if preliminary investigation indicated that for most of the site's history a metal foundry was in operation, then the first focus should be on metals. If no other contaminants are identified in the subsequent investigation, a remedial action that best contains metals may be in order. If a clay layer is identified at the site from test pit activities and extends laterally beneath the foundry's more porous overburden material, the clay layer should be sampled to see if any screening levels have been exceeded. If groundwater has not been found beneath the metal-laden material, an appropriate interim action removal may be appropriate (see Figure 5.13), followed by a metal treatment process for any soil or environmental media laden with metal wastes. For example, metal-laden waste has recently been treated by applying a buffered phosphate and stabilizing chemicals to inhibit Pb leaching and migration.

During and after remediation, water and soil environmental performance standards must be met confirmed by sampling and analysis, i.e., poststabilization sampling and TCLP analytical methods to assess contaminant leaching (e.g., to ensure that concentrations of heavy metals and organics do not violate the federal standards, e.g., Pb concentrations $< 5$ mg L$^{-1}$). Confirmation samples must be analyzed to verify complete removal of contaminated soil and media in the lateral and vertical extent within the site.

The remediation steps should be clearly delineated in the final plan for remedial action, such as the total surface area of the site to be cleaned up and the total volume of waste to be decontaminated. At a minimum, an Remedial Action is evaluated on the basis of the current and proposed land use around the site; applicable local, state, and federal laws and regulations; and a risk assessment specifically addressing the hazards and possible exposures at or near the site. Any proposed plan should summarize the environmental assessment and the potential risks to public health and the environment posed by the site. The plan should clearly delineate all remedial alternatives that have been considered. It should also include data and information on the background and history of the property, the results of the previous investigations, and the objectives of the remedial actions. As this is an official document, the State environmental agency must abide by federal and state requirements for public notice, as well as to provide a sufficient public comment period (about 20 days).

The final plan must address all comments. The Final Plan of Remedial Action must clearly designate the selected Remedial Action, which will include the target cleanup values for the contaminants, as well as all monitoring that will be undertaken during and after the remediation. It must include both quantitative (e.g., are to mitigate risks posed by metal-laden material with total $[Pb] > 1000$ mg kg$^{-1}$ and TCLP $[Pb] \geq 5.0$ mg l$^{-1}$) and qualitative objectives (e.g., control measures and management to ensure limited exposures during cleanup). The plan should also include a discussion on planned and potential uses of the site following remediation (e.g., will it be zoned for industrial use or changed to another land use). The plan should distinguish between interim and final actions, as well as interim and final cleanup standards. The Proposed Plan and the Final Plan then constitute the "Remedial Decision Record".

The ultimate goal of the remediation is to ensure that all hazardous material on the site has either been removed or rendered nonhazardous through treatment and stabilization. The nonhazardous, stabilized material can then be properly disposed of, for example, in nonhazardous waste landfill.

## THE MARCH CONTINUES

There are hundreds of hazardous waste sites that could be described here. It suffices to say that the aggregate effect of the sites being found and needing cleanup throughout the world brought about a new paradigm in environmental protection. We will continue our discussion of water-related disasters in the next chapters but will redirect our focus from under the ground to surface waters.

## References and Notes

1. Letcher TM, Battino R. An introduction to the understanding of solubility. *J Chem Ed* 2001;**78**:103–11.
2. IUPAC. *The Solubility Data Series. The Solubility Data Commission (volume 8)*. ResearchTriangle Park, NC; 1980.
3. Atkins PW. *Physical chemistry*. 7th ed. Oxford: Oxford University Press; 2003 [chapters 4,7].
4. Denbigh KG. *Principles of chemical equilibria*. Cambridge: Cambridge University Press; 1981 [chapter 4].
5. Burgess J. *Metal ions in solution*. New York: Ellis Horwood; 1978 ISBN 0-85312-027-7.
6. *Reference for all of the organic solvents: International Agency for Research on Cancer. Monographs on The Evaluation of The Carcinogenic Risk of Chemicals To Man: 1972-Present*. Geneva, Switzerland: World Health Organization; 1977.
7. U.S. Environmental Protection Agency. *Superfund Information Systems*. http://cfpub.epa.gov/supercpad/cursites/csitinfo.cfm?id=0201290#CleanupImpact; 2012 [accessed on January 4, 2012].
8. As the name implies, first responders are the teams who first arrive on the scene of an emergency. They include firefighters, HAZMAT teams, police, and medical personnel. These people are particularly vulnerable to exposures. Often, the contents of items and areas needing response are not well known, so the wrong treatment or

response can be dangerous, such as spraying water on low density or water-reactive substances. Other vulnerabilities include the frenetic nature of an emergency response. For example, the first responders to the World Trade Center attacks on September 11, 2001, the first responders had incompatible radios and, since cell phone networks collapsed, they were not able to communicate well with each other. This undoubtedly led to a number of deaths. The vulnerability has been articulated well by Captain Larry R. Collins, a 24-year member of the Los Angeles County Fire Department (*Frontline First Responder*, April 5, 2003): A truly accurate assessment of the stability of damaged structures often requires the skill, experience, training, and knowledge of a certified structural engineer who is prepared to perform a risk analysis and make certain calculations about the weight of the material, the status of key structural members, how the loads have been redistributed after the event, and the need for stabilization or evacuation. Unfortunately, first responders typically do not have those capabilities, and when lives are hanging in the balance, they do not have the luxury of time to wait for a structural engineer. Someone needs to make immediate decisions about firefighting, search and rescue, and other emergency operations.

9. Gunite is a patented construction material composed of cement, sand, or crushed slag and water mixed pneumatically. Often used in the construction of swimming pools, it provides a waterproof lining.

10. U.S. Environmental Protection Agency. *EPA Superfund Record of Decision: Tar Creek (Ottawa County)*. 1984. EPA ID: OKD980629844-OU 01. Report No. EPA/ROD/R06-84/004.

11. U.S. Geological Survey. *Oklahoma Water Science Center*. http://ok.water.usgs.gov/projects/tarcreek; 2012 [accessed March 5, 2012].

12. U.S. Environmental Protection Agency. *Tar Creek (Ottawa County), Oklahoma Superfund Site Update*. http://www.epa.gov/region6/6sf/pdffiles/0601269.pdf; 2012 [accessed March 5, 2012].

13. Vallero DA. *Paradigms lost: learning from environmental mistakes, mishaps and misdeeds*. Amsterdam, NV: Butterworth-Heinemann; 2005.

14. Many community resources are available, from formal public meetings held by governmental authorities to informal groups, such as homeowner association meetings, neighborhood "watch," and crime prevention group meetings. Any research-related activities should adhere to federal and other governmental regulations regarding privacy, intrusion, and human subject considerations. Privacy rules have been written according to the Privacy Act and the Paperwork Reduction Act (e.g., the Office of Management and Budget limits the type and amount of information that U.S. agencies may collect in what is referred to as an Information Collection Budget). Regarding any research that affects human subjects, at a minimum, should have prior approval for informed consent of participants and thoughtful consideration of the need for an institutional review board (IRB) approval.

CHAPTER

6

# Spills

An effluent is a direct release of a liquid waste from a defined point (e.g., outfall structure). Throughout most of the history of sanitary engineering, which eventually evolved into present-day environmental engineering, most effluents of concern were those that: caused diseases (i.e., coliform bacteria); decreased dissolved oxygen ($O_2$); and dissolved or suspended solids. These continue to be important. However, numerous so-called toxic effluents are now measured and controlled.

Problems from systems designed to collect and treat wastes result from effluent that has not been properly treated. Sometimes this is the result of toxic wastes entering a treatment facility for which it has not been designed. For example, some such influents are so toxic that they kill the beneficial bacteria in the treatment plant. Other problems can occur when a system becomes overloaded, albeit with the wastes for which it was designed. This was a common occurrence some decades ago, when many treatment plants received wastes from combined sewers, that is, sewage and stormwater were collected and somewhere along the way they became combined and reached a treatment plant or the combined sewage bypassed the plant completely. These were "disasters" for large and small communities that have become quite rare in recent years.

A spill has some of these same characteristics, although by definition it is an unintended release. Usually, a spill comes from a central location, even though the location is not where or when substances had been designed to be released. For example, a cargo ship is not designed to release its contents into open water, and it was designed only to release them through valves connected to some receiving point at a port. So, a spill is a function of space and time. If either is violated, the release is a spill. For example, if the contents are emptied from the release valve, but the release is into the water or onto the ground near the receiving point at the port, it is indeed a spill.

When engineers speak of an effluent being "discharged," they usually are referring to waste that is released directly into surface waters. In fact, this is consistent with the $Q$ term introduced in Chapter 5. Thus, the discharge includes the flow of the effluent, which is mostly water. Even highly polluted waters generally consist of a small percent of the mass or volume of pollutant compared to the water. However, it is this small percentage that distinguishes acceptable water quality from polluted water.

Regulatory agencies around the world require that these discharges be treated to meet certain standards, many of which are health based. That is, protection of public health prescribes the framework by which many nations regulate water pollution; the entity releasing the effluent reports the type and quantity of the released pollutant. The regulatory concept is similar to that of tax oversight by the Internal Revenue Service, with facilities randomly audited to ensure that the reported information is sufficiently precise and accurate and, if not, the facility is subject to civil and criminal penalties. In fact, reports by the Inspector General of the U.S. EPA often include discovered felonious reporting violations by effluent permit holders. For example, a Greek shipping Company, Ilios Shipping Company S.A., recently pleaded guilty in U.S. Federal Court in New Orleans for violating the Act to Prevent Pollution from Ships, as well as obstruction of justice. The plea agreement states that, from April 2009 until April 2011, the 36,573 bulk carrier ships that hauled grain routinely discharged oily bilge waste and sludge directly into the sea without the use of required pollution prevention equipment. The violations were exacerbated by falsifying records in the vessel's oil log book, including destruction of computer records and lying to the U.S. Coast Guard.[1]

Other, less predictable releases go by a number of names. In hazardous waste programs, such as the Leaking Underground Storage Tank (LUST) program mentioned in chapter 5, such contaminant intrusions into groundwater are called "leaks." In fact, new underground tanks are often required to have leak detection systems and alarms. In solid waste programs, such as landfill regulations, the intrusion may go by the name "leachate." Landfills often are required to have leachate collection systems to protect adjacent aquifers and surface waters. Spills are generally liquid releases that occur suddenly, such as an oil spill. Air releases that occur suddenly are called leaks, such as chlorine or natural gas leak. The general term for expected and unplanned environmental releases is just that, that is, "releases," such as those reported in the U.S. Environmental Protection Agency's Toxic Release Inventory.

In this chapter, our focus will be direct releases to surface waters. The disasters caused by these releases are often the most well known and frequently reported by the news media. There is no consistent metric for determining which is the worst, but they usually involve imminent threats to sea life and destruction of coastal and open water habitats.

## DISASTROUS RELEASES

When newspapers report leaks and spills, people are most concerned about their likelihood of being exposed and risks to their personal and family's health. Next, they may be concerned about their well-being, such as whether their employment is threatened; for example, fishing is a major employing industry in coastal communities. Often, concerns about ecosystem damage are driven by governmental agencies (e.g., U.S. Coast Guard, National Oceanic and Atmospheric Agency, EPA, and the European Maritime Safety Agency) and advocacy groups, known as Nongovernmental Organizations, such as Greenpeace, Sierra Club, and Nature Conservancy. The initial concern focuses on what has been released and what damage has already been caused, but this quickly moves to concerns about potential threats and the possible harm it may cause to sensitive habitats and organisms. Indeed, the damage will vary by what is released and where the release occurs.

Notorious examples of liquid spills include oil from the wrecked Exxon Valdes off the Alaskan coast and the massive release of crude oil from the breach of the Deepwater Horizon piping in the Gulf of Mexico. These are all examples of immediate releases of a contaminant. In the case of the Exxon Valdez, the release itself was from a single vessel (i.e., a ship's hull or a tank). This is similar to the toxic air plumes discussed in Chapter 4. In the case of the

Deepwater Horizon spill, the release continued for months, which is similar to the leaks discussed in Chapter 5, albeit with a greater emphasis in the long-term on ecosystems compared to public health associated with most hazardous wastes sites.

The extent and duration of a leak or spill is determined by the available volume of a substance. Once the ship hull or tank is emptied, the spill itself ends, but the damage it causes can endure for decades. If the source is vast, such as the oil in rock strata under the Gulf of Mexico, the spill will end only after the pressure differential between the strata and the surface reaches equilibrium, or until the available substance is depleted. Thus, the properties of the fluid and the characteristics of the environment determine the amount and rate of a contaminant that is released in a disaster.

## OIL SPILLS

There have been numerous oil spills since crude oil and oil products began to be shipped over large distances (see Table 6.1). The largest spill at sea in terms of amount of release occurred in 1979 when the Atlantic Empress spill 287,000 tonnes of crude oil near Tobago in the West Indies. Oil spills result from many causes. Actually, the Exxon Valdez was the most notorious spill prior to the Deepwater Horizon spill in the Gulf of Mexico. However, the Valdez stands at in 35th position in terms of weight (37,000 tonnes). This illustrates that the amount spilled is only part of the criteria used to determine disaster status of an event.

TABLE 6.1  Major Oil Spills Since 1967, Ranked by Weight of Product Spilled

| Position | Ship name | Year | Location | Spill size tonnes |
|---|---|---|---|---|
| 1 | Atlantic Empress | 1979 | Off Tobago, West Indies | 287,000 |
| 2 | ABT Summer | 1991 | 700 Nautical miles off Angola | 260,000 |
| 3 | Castillo de Bellver | 1983 | Off Saldanha Bay, South Africa | 252,000 |
| 4 | Amoco Cadiz | 1978 | Off Brittany, France | 223,000 |
| 5 | Haven | 1991 | Genoa, Italy | 144,000 |
| 6 | Odyssey | 1988 | 700 Nautical miles off Nova Scotia, Canada | 132,000 |
| 7 | Torrey Canyon | 1967 | Scilly Isles, UK | 119,000 |
| 8 | Sea Star | 1972 | Gulf of Oman | 115,000 |
| 9 | Irenes Serenade | 1980 | Navarino Bay, Greece | 100,000 |
| 10 | Urquiola | 1976 | La Coruna, Spain | 100,000 |
| 11 | Hawaiian Patriot | 1977 | 300 Nautical miles off Honolulu | 95,000 |
| 12 | Independenta | 1979 | Bosphorus, Turkey | 95,000 |
| 13 | Jakob Maersk | 1975 | Oporto, Portugal | 88,000 |
| 14 | Braer | 1993 | Shetland Islands, UK | 85,000 |
| 15 | Khark 5 | 1989 | 120 Nautical miles off Atlantic coast of Morocco | 80,000 |

*Continued*

TABLE 6.1    Major Oil Spills Since 1967, Ranked by Weight of Product Spilled—Cont'd

| Position | Ship name | Year | Location | Spill size tonnes |
|----------|-----------|------|----------|-------------------|
| 16 | Aegean Sea | 1992 | La Coruna, Spain | 74,000 |
| 17 | Sea Empress | 1996 | Milford Haven, UK | 72,000 |
| 18 | Nova | 1985 | Off Kharg Island, Gulf of Iran | 70,000 |
| 19 | Katina P | 1992 | Off Maputo, Mozambique | 66,700 |
| 20 | Prestige | 2002 | Off Galicia, Spain | 63,000 |
| 35 | Exxon Valdez | 1989 | Prince William Sound, Alaska, USA | 37,000 |

*Source: International Tanker Oil Owners Pollution Federation, Limited. Statistics. http://www.itopf.com/information-services/data-and-statistics/statistics; 2012 [accessed March 14, 2012].*

TABLE 6.2    Incidence of Spills 7-700 tonnes by Operation at Time of Incident and Primary Cause of Spill, 1970-2011

| | Operations | | | |
|---|---|---|---|---|
| | Loading/discharging | Bunkering | Other operations | Unknown |
| **CAUSES** | | | | |
| Collisions | 4 | 0 | 32 | 308 |
| Groundings | 0 | 0 | 16 | 253 |
| Hull failures | 36 | 4 | 10 | 50 |
| Equipment failures | 141 | 6 | 17 | 38 |
| Fires/explosions | 8 | 0 | 13 | 26 |
| Other/unknown | 199 | 23 | 48 | 110 |
| Total | 388 | 33 | 136 | 785 |

*Source: International Tanker Oil Owners Pollution Federation, Limited. Statistics. http://www.itopf.com/information-services/data-and-statistics/statistics; 2012 [accessed March 14, 2012].*

In the case of the Valdez, much of the problem had to do with where the spill occurred and sensitivity of the habitat.

The causes of spills vary widely, but there appears to be a difference between very large and smaller spills. Equipment and hull failures account for nearly half (46%) of all spills. The difference seems to lie in where the spills occur (see Tables 6.2 and 6.3). Most large spills occur in open water, whereas for the smaller spills (less than 7 tonnes) where the cause is known, most occur in the port, for example, loading and discharging the fluid.[2]

## Deepwater Horizon

The Deepwater Horizon was a dynamically positioned, semi-submersible offshore oil drilling rig, designed to drill in ultra-deep waters (Figure 6.1). Dynamic positioning means that the vessel is kept in place using computerized thrusters and propellers. By April 14, 2010,

TABLE 6.3  Incidence of Spills >7 tonnes by Operation at time of Incident and Primary Cause of Spill, 1970-2011

| | Operations | | | | | | |
|---|---|---|---|---|---|---|---|
| | At anchor (inland/ restricted) | At anchor (open water) | Underway (inland/ restricted) | Underway (open water) | Loading/ discharging | Bunkering | Other operations/ unknown |
| **CAUSES** | | | | | | | |
| Allisions/ collisions | 6 | 5 | 33 | 65 | 1 | 0 | 24 |
| Groundings | 4 | 2 | 45 | 66 | 2 | 0 | 29 |
| Hull failures | 0 | 1 | 0 | 50 | 0 | 0 | 8 |
| Equipment failures | 0 | 0 | 0 | 7 | 11 | 0 | 1 |
| Fires/ explosions | 1 | 1 | 3 | 25 | 14 | 1 | 9 |
| Other/ unknown | 2 | 0 | 1 | 12 | 13 | 0 | 12 |
| Total | 13 | 9 | 82 | 225 | 41 | 1 | 83 |

*Source: International Tanker Oil Owners Pollution Federation, Limited.* Statistics. *http://www.itopf.com/information-services/data-and-statistics/statistics; 2012 [accessed March 14, 2012].*

FIGURE 6.1  Deepwater Horizon drilling rig in flames. U.S. Environmental Protection Agency photo.

BP Exploration & Production Inc. (BP) had nearly completed the exploratory phase of the Macondo well, with two well operations tasks remaining: running the well casing and preparing the well to be temporarily abandoned. The Deepwater Horizon was scheduled to depart the well once these tasks were completed. By this time, BP had verified the existence of a hydrocarbon reservoir but did not plan to immediately produce it; a different rig would commence completion operations for the operator at a later date.[3]

BP had cut the total depth of the well short of the original target depth because the margin between pore pressure (the pressure at which hydrocarbons push into the wellbore) and the formation fracture pressure (the pressure required to fracture the rock at a given depth) became increasingly narrow with depth, restricting the window for safe drilling.

Originally, for the Macondo well, BP was to use a long-string casing, but circulation problems led to BP's considering a liner to lower the down-hole pressure that installation and cementing would exert. However, in spite of these expected pressure reductions, BP engineers decided to keep the original design of a long-string production casing. That is, they would use a single length of 9-7/8-in. $\times$ 7-in. (250 mm by 180 mm) casing extending from the sub-sea to 4035 m (13,237 ft) below the seabed—a total depth of 5579 m (18,304 ft).

In the early morning of April 18, 2010, the Deepwater Horizon drill crew began lowering the long-string production casing. Six centralizers had already been installed on the lower 7-in. (180 mm) interval of the production casing string, which was significantly less than called for by cementing models. Such models recommended larger numbers of centralizers in order to reduce the reasonable risk of cement channeling and subsequent gas flow. The drill crew completed running the production casing on April 19, 2010. Casing is typically installed with two sets of cementing check valves: the float shoe, located on the very bottom of the casing string, and the float collar, usually installed from two to six casing joints above the bottom. BP's production casing design for the Macondo well called for only one cementing check device, consisting a double valve and an auto-fill float collar.

Lowering the casing string into the well with the float equipment installed pushes drilling fluid ahead of it and can create surge pressures that can fracture the formation, leading to loss of drilling fluids and damage of the hydrocarbon production zones. To reduce surge pressure and protect the formation, BP incorporated a surge reduction system including an auto-fill type of float collar and reamer shoe. The float collar used at Macondo contained two flapper check valves that are held open during installation by an auto-fill tube. While open, these valves allow mud to pass through the float collar and up into the casing. Before cementing, the float collar is "converted" or closed. Specifically, the auto-fill tube is forced out of the float collar so that the flapper valves close and prevent mud and cement slurry from flowing back up into the casing.

Applying pressure to a ball that is preinstalled at the base of the auto-fill tube will convert the float collar. Differential pressure between the top and bottom of the ball is created by two small ports on the sides of the tube that allow circulation of drilling fluid through the tube. BP's procedure to convert the float collar called for slowly increasing fluid circulation rates to 13-22 L s$^{-1}$ [5-8 barrels per minute (bpm)] and applying 3.5-4.8 MPa [500-700 pounds per square inch (psi)] of differential pressure, consistent with manufacturer guidelines. However, BP deviated from its planned procedures during the conversion.

The window for safe drilling between the fracture gradient and the pore-pressure gradient decreased as the drilling became deeper. It became increasingly difficult to keep the right amount of equivalent circulating density so that perturbances and fluid losses increased. As this safety window narrowed, BP began to change plans by reducing the well's target depth, considering changes in well casings, reducing the circulating rate below the parameters specified to convert the float collar, decreasing the density of cement with nitrogen foam, using less cement, and ceasing to conduct complete bottoms-up cementing. While these actions may have protected the formation and allowed operations to continue, they contributed to the disastrous spill.

In addition, the initial displacement was not properly planned and executed. A negative pressure test was needed to make certain that the cement would stop flowing from the oil reservoir into the well after seawater replaced the drilling mud. The test should have been a red flag of trouble ahead; that is, the pressure readings on the drill pipe were abnormal. This should have been a warning that the cement barrier was not working. Pressure was bypassing the cement and float equipment so that the well was still connected to the oil formation. At the very least, this was a miscalculation, since the negative pressure test results were misinterpreted. The failure was compounded when BP decided to go ahead with the final displacement.

The BP oil spill flowed into the Gulf for 3 months and is the largest oil spill disaster in the history of the oil industry. The explosion on the rig killed 11 men and injured 17. The oil poured out of a leak on the seafloor bottom. It released 780,000 m$^3$ (4.9 million barrels) of oil into the Gulf of Mexico, and about 500 miles off Louisiana, Mississippi, Florida, and Alabama coastline were contaminated. The spill affected every type of flora and fauna in the area, whales and dolphins died at twice their normal rate, wetland grass and flora died and fishing came to a halt, and an underwater plume, not visible on the surface, killed seafloor flora and fauna; BP admitted that it made mistakes and soon after the accident set up a $20 billion fund to compensate victims of the oil spill. Every effort was made to reduce the impact of the oil and to collect as much as possible. Skimmers were used, detergents sprayed on the oil, and controlled burning took place. About 30–40% of the spilled crude remains in the Gulf, depending on the amount of biodegradation that has occurred.[4]

## The Exxon Valdez

Until the recent spill in the Gulf of Mexico, the Exxon Valdez oil spill was emblematic of the pending disasters associated with the modern-day dependence on crude oil. The Valdez disaster changed the consciousness of the vulnerability of sensitive coastal habitats and littoral ecosystems. It accentuated the importance of the anthropogenic aspects of disasters (e.g., human error, poor judgment, lack of leadership, and inadequate accountability) as well as the need for measures to prevent and respond to accidents.

The standard operating procedures of the Exxon Valdez tanker's regular mission was not unusual. It loaded oil from the trans-Alaska pipeline from the Valdez terminal and delivered it to West Coast states (see Figure 6.2). On the day of the wreckage, oil was loaded onto the Exxon Valdez for shipment to Los Angeles/Long Beach, California. Shortly after leaving the Port of Valdez, on March 24, 1989, the tanker grounded on Bligh Reef, Alaska, releasing more than 40 million liters of oil into Prince William Sound (see Figure 6.3).

Human error and chain of command were important factors. At the time that the vessel ran aground on the reef, the Captain of the ship, Joe Hazelwood was not at the wheel because he

FIGURE 6.2 Valdez, Alaska oil transport terminal. *Photo credit: National Oceanic and Atmospheric Administration.*

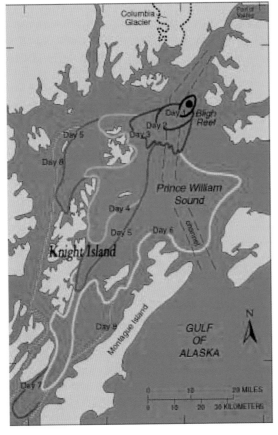

FIGURE 6.3 The Exxon Valdez ran aground on Bligh Reef on March 24, 1989. The map shows the expansion of oil front from Day 1 to Day 8. Map credit: U.S. Geological Survey from 1 to 8 days after the spill. Map credit: U.S. Geological Survey; *source: National Oceanic and Atmospheric Administration.* Prince William's oily mess: a tale of recovery. *http://oceanservice.noaa.gov/education/stories/oilymess/oily07_time.html; 2012 [accessed March 6, 2012].*

was in his bunk sleeping in an alcoholic stupor. As a result, the third mate was in charge at the helm. Many other factors contributed to the wreck and the resulting environmental disaster. The tanker had a state-of-the-science radar system, but it was not functioning when the wreck occurred. The company was aware of the broken radar system, but had not replaced it for a year. Had the third mate been able to use this radar system, he should have been able to avoid the reef.

Lack of preparedness meant that containment was ineffective. After the ship ran aground, the response was too late and insufficient. A letter written to the Exxon executives meeting several months before the spill declared that not enough oil containment equipment, which was required by law, was available to control a spill that had occurred in the middle of Prince William Sound. Instead, the Exxon executives hoped to disperse the oil with the remaining residue drifting out to sea. In addition, early indications of shipping vulnerabilities were ignored. Shipping and oil managers did not pay sufficient heed to several smaller oil spills in Prince William Sound, either because they were not disclosed or were concealed. There were even indications of fraudulent testing, for example, replacing sound water with clean water during testing. This would have meant that governmental authorities were not notified of the lack of containment equipment at the Alaskan port. Figure 6.4 shows a possible decision tree for the disaster that illustrates that eliminating two contributing factors, that is, poor maintenance and an impaired captain, the likelihood of a massive oil spill may well have been avoided.

The Exxon Valdez spill was the sixth largest oil spill in terms of released volume, but the toll on wildlife from the spill was quite possibly the worst of all oil spills prior to the Deepwater Horizon incident. An estimated 250,000 seabirds, 2800 sea otters, 300 harbor seals, 250 bald eagles, and as many as 22 killer whales were killed as a direct result of the spill. Large but unknown numbers of important fish species, especially salmon and herring, were lost. The persistence is also unprecedented. Ten years after the spill, only two animal species, bald eagles and river otters, had completely recovered from the spill.

Indeed, the Valdez experience was a testament to environmental response. After the ship ran aground and the leakage of large volumes of oil was apparent, oil was transferred from to another tanker, the Exxon Baton Rouge. This kept most of the oil originally carried in the Valdez from spilling into Prince William Sound. About 20% of oil carried by the Valdez oil was spilled, but over 160 million liters was transferred to the Baton Rouge. Other protective measures included shielding sensitive habitats, such as fish spawning areas, from the encroaching oil slick.

Cleanup operations included skimming oil from the water surface using boats to tow booms. Oil is collected within the boom, while a small skimmer at the apex of the boom is removing the oil from the water surface. The skimmed oil pumped the barge behind the skimmer.

Unfortunately, the spill also indicated the difficulty and persistence of contaminants released into the environment. After a decade, 14% of the oil was recovered, 20% volatilized and was degraded by sunlight, 13% settled in subtidal sediment, and 50% was broken down by microbes or photolyzed in the water. The rest remained on the beaches and dispersed in water, with as much as 2% persisting on the beaches.

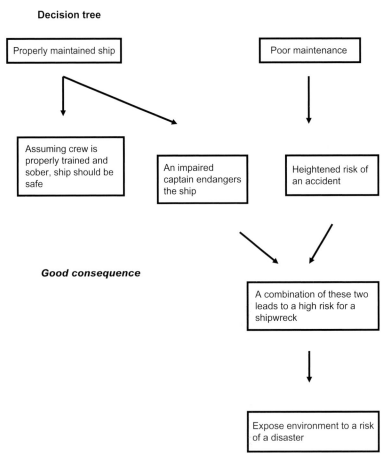

**Decision tree**

FIGURE 6.4    Simple decision tree showing the difference in consequences had two contributing factors been ignored. *Source: Vallero DA. Environmental contaminants: assessment and control. ISBN: 0127100571. Burlington, MA: Elsevier Academic Press; 2004.*

## Torrey Canyon Tanker Spill

Torrey Canyon oil spill is one of the most important spills since it was the first major tanker spill and because it released a large amount, that is, 108,000 tonnes (119,000 tons), of crude oil. On March 18, 1967, the Liberian oil tanker Torrey Canyon, operated by a subsidiary of the Union Oil Company of California, ran aground between the Scilly Isles and the British coast (see Figure 6.5). The accident was precipitated by a navigational error causing the tanker to strike Pollard's Rock in the Seven Stones reef between the Scilly Isles and Land's End, England.

Valiant response efforts ensued, using dispersants and other available recovery means available. Since the Torrey Canyon was the first major supertanker spill, no comprehensive plans were in place. Attempts to refloat the tanker were unsuccessful. A member of a Dutch salvage team was killed. Attempts to sink the wrecked ship and to combust slick to reduce the

FIGURE 6.5 Torrey Canyon tanker run aground at Scilly Isles and the British coast. *Source and photo credit: National Oceanic and Atmospheric Administration.*

leakage even included bombing by Royal Navy. Also attempting to burn the slick, the Royal Air Force dropped gasoline and napalm. However, in spite of these efforts, oil slicks drifted in the English Channel, making their way to French and British shorelines. Remnants of damage from the spill have persisted, including the lag in recovery in the diversity of bird populations, even after noble efforts to save them.

The accident raised the awareness of Europeans to the risks associated with tankers and was a call to arms for new emergency response and water pollution prevention programs. Most notably, the UK government immediately formed the Coastguard Agency's Marine Pollution Control Unit to provide a command and control structure for decision making and response following a shipping incident that causes, or threatens to cause, pollution in UK waters. The spill also subsequently led to a comprehensive National Contingency Plan (NCP) in the UK and internationally.[5] The NCP categorizes spills into an internationally adopted Tier system:

Tier 1: A small operational spill employing local resources during any cleanup.
Tier 2: A medium-sized spill requiring regional assistance and resources.
Tier 3: A large spill requiring national assistance and resources. The NCP will be activated. (If the Torrey Canyon spill were to have occurred today, it would call for a Tier 3 response.)

A new procedure was required, that is, "load on top" which reduced oil losses and helped prevent water pollution. The system collects washings resulting from tank cleaning by pumping them into a special tank. During the voyage back to the loading terminal, the oil and water separate. The water at the bottom of the tank is pumped overboard and at the terminal oil is pumped on to the oil left in the tank.

The spill led to a number of changes in international shipping conventions, with a number of important amendments to the International Convention for the Prevention of Pollution of the Sea by Oil, 1954 (OILPOL 1954).[6] In 1971, the size of cargo tanks was limited in all tankers ordered after 1972 so that in the event of a future spill, a limited and more manageable amount of oil would be leaked. In 1973, oil and other potentially hazardous cargo shippings were expanded and improved. The new provision specified requirements for continuous monitoring of oily water discharges and included the requirement for governments to provide shore reception and treatment facilities at oil terminals and ports. It also established a number of special areas in which more stringent discharge standards were applicable, including the Mediterranean, Red Sea and Gulf, and Baltic Seas. These special areas would be implemented when the littoral states concerned had provided adequate reception facilities for dirty ballast and other oily residues.

In the United States, the national oil spill response strategy is based on the National Oil and Hazardous Substances Pollution Contingency Plan (NCP).[7] The first NCP was issued in 1968, in part as a response to Torrey Canyon. The U.S. NCP provides the institutional framework to

Define responsibilities of federal, state, and local governments;
Describe resources available for response;
Establish a hierarchy of response teams;
Specify a command structure to oversee spill response;
Require federal, regional, and area contingency plans;
Summarize state and local emergency planning requirements, as well as response priorities, phases, and procedures; and
Provide procedures for the use of chemicals (e.g., dispersants, shoreline cleaning agents) in removing spilled hazardous materials.

This general framework has been retained and periodically revised over the past 30 years.

## DISCUSSION BOX: CHEMICAL DISPERSANTS

Chemical dispersants were one of the areas of controversy in the Deepwater Horizon spill response. Before deciding on the benefits and risks of the chemicals used, there needs to be an understanding of its structure and actions in the environment.

### Detergents and Surfactants

Detergents are very much in the news when a new oil spill has to be cleaned up. They have the property to break up oil spills into tiny separate globules and in that way allow the oil to be dispersed. This action of detergents is based on the property of surfactants which are surface active agents and in dilute aqueous solution, the surfactant molecules tend to form layers on the surface of the water. Surfactant molecules are characterized by long chain non-polar chains attached to a polar head. For example, sodium lauryl sulphate:

$$CH_3(CH_2)_{11} - OSO_3^- Na^+$$

In the dilute aqueous solution, these surfactant molecules line up on the surface with their polar heads in the water and the non-polar tails in the air.

In more concentrated solutions, surfactants form micelles. These are clusters of surfactant molecules in which the polar heads point outwards, towards the water and the hydrocarbon tails all point inwards with the cluster taking on a spherical shape.

These surfactant molecules can act as cleaning agents and they do this by using the non-polar tails to wrap around oil droplets or grease dirt (these are invariably hydrocarbons) forming micelle-like structures. The charged polar heads surrounding the micelle, keep the micelle encapsulated oil or grease in suspension, which can then be washed away.

Modern day surfactants, such as the example given above, have replaced soap which is also a surfactant. Soap,which is calcium stearate, has the formulae:

$$[CH_3(CH_2)_{16} - COO^-]_2 Ca^{2+}$$

Soap also has the property of micelle formation, but unfortunately in hard water (containing $Ca^{2+}$ and $Mg^{2+}$ ions) the added calcium ions cause the calcium stearate to precipitate and form a scum. If the soap is used to wash clothes in hard water, the scum gets into the material and white clothes will begin to look grey and drab after a few washes. Today, soap has been replaced by detergents which are a mixture of a number of components: a surfactant (for example sodium lauryl sulfate); a foam reducer; a filler (used to generate bulk); a bleach and a brightener (which is another name for a water softener). These brighteners are usually polyphosphates such as sodium triphosphate. These compounds complex with the $Ca^{2-}$ and $Mg^{2-}$ ions of the hard water, forming soluble complexes and thus do not form scums.

## Eutrophication

There is a serious problem with the phosphate component of detergents; it contributes to the eutrophication of rivers and lakes. This is the green "bloom" caused by a rapid growth in phytoplankton that sometimes occurs as a result of an increase in the levels of nutrients. This over-fertilization also causes plants and other algae in rivers and lakes to multiply and grow rapidly. The end result is the depletion of oxygen in the water and the death of fish and aquatic life.

Eutrophication was recognized as a problem in European and North American lakes and reservoirs in the mid-20th century as a result of the inclusion of phosphates in detergents. Surveys have shown that half the lakes in Asia, Europe and North America have serious eutrophication problems.

In many parts of the world (for example in the European Union and in many states in the US), in an attempt to reduce the effects of eutrophication, phosphates are no longer allowed to be components of laundry detergents.

The reason why phosphates in rivers and lakes are considered to be the main contributory factor in eutrophication is that plants and algae need three main types of atoms to grow – carbon, nitrogen and phosphorus. The C is extracted from $CO_2$ in the air, N is 'fixed' from the $N_2$ in the air and usually the P comes from natural sources. If P is not available in large concentrations, no bloom takes place. Increasing this to higher levels results in the plants and algae multipling very rapidly.

## Oil Spills

As mentioned, detergents are used to clean up oil spills. In particular, they are used to disperse oil slicks. Thus, in these uses, they are usually called dispersants; however, the action is the same – they act as surfactants and solubilize the oil into small separate globules.

Oil spills at sea and especially along coastal waters have caused untold ecological damage. Oil penetrates into the feathers of birds and fur of mammals, making them less buoyant, and diminishing their insulating ability. Furthermore, animals rely on scent to find their young or their mothers and the oil either dissolves the scent chemicals or masks the scent, resulting in rejected, starved and abandoned young which are left to die. Oil contamination also impairs a bird's ability to fly and hence forage for food. When a bird preens itself after being covered in oil its digestive tract and other functions of the bird become damaged and the bird dies. Attempts to salvage oil coated birds have not been very successful.

The various methods used to clean up oil spills include: controlled burning; skimming; adding adsorbants to absorb the oil; sucking the oil from the water surface followed by centrifugal separation; and the addition of dispersants which act as surfactants. The method used depends on many factors such as: the type of oil spilled; the spill environment (rocky shoreline, beach or deep sea); and the temperature of the water (as this influences the rate of evaporation and of the biodegradation processes).

Dispersants provide a number of benefits to cleanup. They remove the sheen from the water and aesthetically improve the water surface. In dispersing the oil through the formation and action of micelles (see Figure 6.6), the oil is broken down into smaller globules which can be scattered more

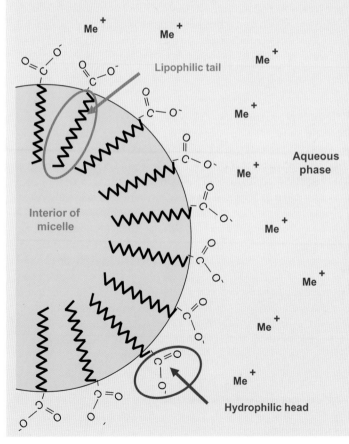

FIGURE 6.6  Structure of micelle in an aqueous solution forming an aggregate with the hydrophilic heads in contact with surrounding water and its dissociated substances (e.g. metal cations, $Me^+$, such as $Na^+$), and sequestering the lipophilic tails in the micelle's interior. For example, the nonpolar chains of the fatty acids become oriented toward the interior of the micelle, and the polar carboxylate groups keep the micelles in colloidal suspension in water. This allows otherwise nonpolar substances, e.g. halogenated hydrocarbons, to be suspended and dispersed within the aqueous phase. *Source: D.A. Vallero (2010). Environmental Biotechnnology: A Biosystems Approach. Elsevier Academic Press. Burlington, MA.*

widely. Unfortunately, these small globules can infiltrated crevices in rocks and corals and can remain there for many years before the slow natural biological processes can break down the oil through oil-consuming bacteria. Furthermore, the effect of these tiny globules on sea life (animal and plant) is not completely understood, so adding large amounts of dispersants to oil slicks is a risky business and we do not know just how damaging these chemicals in the dispersants are to the local ecology. As a result the EPA has made the statement:

"Dispersants are generally less toxic than oil. When considering the use of a dispersant in the deep ocean, the US federal government weighs the effectiveness of the dispersant in breaking down the oil at such depths, the benefits of preventing the oil from rising to the surface and eventually hitting the shore where it is likely to do significant damage to birds, wetlands and aquatic life, and the long term impacts of the dispersant mixed with oil in deeper waters. We have a monitoring and sampling plan in place to track the movement of the oil and we reserve the right to stop the use of these dispersants at any time based on the results." (see http://www.epa.gov/bpspill/disper sants.html.)

The surfactant used in the Deepwater Horizon oil spill was "Tween-80" (polyoxyethylene sorbitan monooleate). This was sprayed onto the oil slick with the aim of isolating small droplets of oil thus making it easier for the microbes to digest them. However, some scientists say that, rather than helping the situation, the surfactant managed only to disperse and sink the oil below the surface and out of sight. Naturally occurring oil-consuming microbes have evolved on the bottom of the ocean, where they have adapted to live in areas where oil seeps naturally from the ocean floor.

Tween-80 is a non-ionic surfactant which behaves in a similar way to the ionic surfactants discussed above. It is also composed of a lipophilic (oil-like and oil- loving) long hydrocarbon tail and a hydrophilic (water loving, i.e. high aqueous solubility) head. In this case the head is not ionic but composed of an organic component containing many hydroxyl (OH) groups that give it a polar property which is attracted to the OH group in water.

The jury, however, is still out on whether the use of this surfactant and also other surfactants and dispersants are acceptable from an overall ecological aspect. Questions remain on the risk tradeoffs. These include comparisons of the toxicity of the spilled substance with that of the dispersing agent, whether the dispersion is simply a means of hiding the spill through dilution, and whether harmful mixtures may result from complexes formed among dispersants and spilled materials.

## Santa Barbara Oil Spill

On January 29, 1969, a Union Oil Company oil drilling platform 10 km off the Santa Barbara coast suffered a blowout. The problem resulted when riggers were pulling up pipe that had been dropped about 1000 m below the ocean floor in effort to replace a broken drill bit. The failure occurred because an insufficient amount of "mud" was available to control pressure, leading to a natural gas blowout. After a successful capping, pressure increased to a point where the expansion of the capped material created five fissures in an ocean floor fault, allowing gas and oil to reach the surface.[8]

The cause of the spill was a rupture in Union Oil's Platform A due to an inadequate protective casing. The U.S. Geological Survey had given approval to operate the platform using casings that did not meet federal and California standards. Investigators would later determine that more steel pipe sleeve inside the drilling hole would have prevented the rupture.

Because the oil rig was beyond California's 3-mile coastal zone, the rig did not have to comply with state standards. At the time, California drilling regulations were far more rigid those implied by the federal government.

For 11 days, oil workers struggled to cap the rupture. During that time, 800,000 L of crude oil surfaced and spread into an 800-square-mile slick by winds and the ocean swells. Tides carried the thick tar into beaches from Rincon Point to Goleta, damaging about 50 km of coastline. The slick also moved south, tarring Frenchy's Cove of Anacapa Island and beaches on the Santa Cruz, Santa Rosa, and San Miguel Islands.

The spill caused massive ecological and sea-life damage. The thick oil clogged the blowholes of the dolphins, leading to lung hemorrhages. Terrestrial fauna that ingested the oil were acutely poisoned. Gray whales for months after altered their migratory routes to avoid the polluted channel. Shorebirds that feed on sand creatures fled. However, diving birds dependent on nourishment from the ocean water were soaked with tar in the feeding process. Less than 30% of the tarred birds treated by the wildlife response effort survived. Many other birds simply died on the beaches in search of sustenance. Even the cleanup was hazardous to wildlife. For example, detergents used to disperse the oil slick can be toxic to birds, because it removes the natural waterproofing depended on by seabirds to stay afloat. A total of nearly 4000 birds were estimated to have died because of contact with oil.

The leak was not under control until 11.5 days after the spill began. Cleanup consisted of pumping chemical mud down the 1000 m shaft at a rate of 1500 barrels per hour and capping it with a cement plug. Some gas continued to escape and another leak occurred in the following weeks later, and residual oil was released for months after the spill. Skimmers scooped up oil from the surface of the ocean. In the air, planes dumped detergents on the tar covered ocean in an attempt to break up the slick. On the beaches and harbors, straw was spread on oily patches of water and sand. The straw soaked up the black mess and was then raked up. Rocks were steamed cleaned, cooking marine life like limpets and mussels that attach themselves to coastal rocks.

The next spring, the first Earth Day was celebrated. The Santa Barbara spill was certainly a topic of discussion and a significant impetus to the environmental movement.

## Prestige Oil Spill[9]

In 2002, the Prestige was a 26-year-old tanker 2 years from retirement. The ship had a single hull, and was such a large risk that no major oil companies would hire her, and she was not allowed near ports in the United States. In 2000, she was dry docked in China where workers reinforced her hull. Following this work, engineers from the American Bureau of Shipping certified that the vessel was sea worthy.

The Prestige left St. Petersburg, Russia on October 30, 2002, fully loaded with fuel oil, proceeding southerly along the coast toward Spain. Off the Spanish coast, the tanker encountered a storm with large waves. Because such large ships are built to withstand dangerous storms, the captain saw no need to take precautions. On the fourth day of the storm, the size of the waves continued to grow and the captain decided to slow the ship and ride out the storm. The waves approached the ship from the right hand side of the vessel and broke over the deck. One particularly large wave approached the vessel and as it broke over the deck, the officers on board heard a large explosion. After the water cleared the deck, the captain noticed that some of the cargo lids had broken loose and some oil was flowing from the tanks into the ocean. In addition, there was a large hole in the starboard side of the ship. Eventually, the ship began to list and the Spanish Coast Guard helped to evacuate all but the captain and the chief officer and chief engineer. At this point, the captain flooded the ballast tanks on the side opposite of the list in order to level the tanker.

The engines shut off and a Spanish tugboat attempted to fasten a line in order to keep the oil tanker from drifting onto the Spanish coast, but all attempts were unsuccessful. It was rumored that the tugboat took so long to get to the oil tanker because the company that owned the oil tanker was haggling over the price of the assistance from the Spanish tugboat. Therefore, Seragin Diaz Requiero, the head port authority of the Spanish town La Coruna, was airlifted onto the tanker in order to get the engines started. While Requiero was trying to get the engines restarted, he claims that most of the problems that prevented the engine from starting were the result of poor maintenance and maybe even sabotage. From his time on the boat, Seragin claims that Captain Mangouras was trying to prevent the engines from being restarted because he wanted to beach the boat on the coast of Spain. If the boat were beached, there would be a large oil spill, but the company that owned the boat would collect insurance money. Eventually, Seragin Requiero restarted the engines and directed the boat away from the coast. Neither the Spanish Government nor the Portuguese would allow the tanker refuge in its ports for fear of a major environmental disaster. Unfortunately, the boat broke up and sank several days later. Captain Mangouras was extradited to Spain, charged with sabotage, and placed under a $3.2 million bail.

## NIGER RIVER DELTA OIL SPILLS

We have detailed the Deep water Horizon disaster in the Gulf of Mexico and have ignored the tragic oil spill disasters that have taken place in the Nigerian delta region. It has been reported that there were more than 7000 spills between 1970 and 2000, and there are 2000 official major spillages sites, many going back decades, with thousands of smaller ones still waiting to be cleared up. More oil is spilled from the delta's network of terminals, pipes, pumping stations, and oil platforms every year than has been lost in the Gulf. The causes are due to malfunctioning equipment, corroding 40-year-old pipes and also sabotage. There are many legal cases being filed against the oil companies. In the meanwhile ten of thousands of Nigerians have lost their livelihood which includes fishing, and it is estimated that it will take 30 years to clean up the area (see Figures 6.7 and 6.8). There are over 600 oil wells in the Niger delta region which supply 40% of the U.S. crude oil imports.[10]

## OTHER SPILLS

Of all contaminant releases, oil spills represent some of the most prominent environmental disasters in terms of amount of pollution released, area impacted, and damage to ecosystems. In fact, oil leaks continuously, but usually the impacts are localized and less severe than the high-profile spills. However, any substance that is transported is at risk of being spilled. For example, when dikes and dams fail, such as what happened in 2000, when a dam wall gave

FIGURE 6.7    The impact of an oil spill near Ikarama in the Niger delta. *Photograph: Amnesty International. The impact of an oil spill near Ikarama in the Niger delta. Photograph (c) Amnesty International UK*

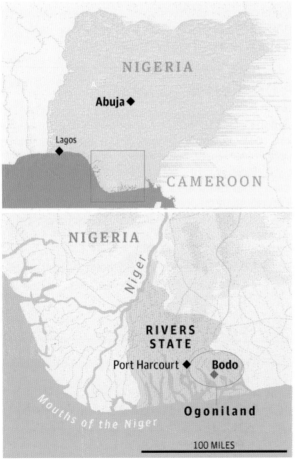

FIGURE 6.8 Map: Ogoniland in Nigeria. Photograph: Guardian Newspaper *www.guardian.co.uk/environment/2011/aug/03/shell-liability-oil-spills-nigeria.*

way and released massive concentrations of cyanide from reclaimed failings from mining operations in Baia Mare, Romania. The Tisa River was polluted by 10,000 m$^3$ of waste that reached the Danube River and traveled all the way to the Black Sea. Massive fish kills resulted. We shall address mining disasters in greater detail in Chapter 10.

## Indirect Harm

The damage from toxic substances like cyanide is direct and obvious. However, the spilled material may not be the direct cause of environmental damage, such as a fish kill. In fact, some seemingly benign matter may be released, such as corn starch, that triggers growth of microbes in the water that use up the dissolved oxygen available to the fish. Ecosystems are complex in term of the damage caused from such as release. For example, the adult fish and even young fish (i.e., young-of-the-year) may be relatively unfazed, but the larvae could be devastated by even a relatively small change in dissolved oxygen concentrations (see Figure 6.9). This means that future fish populations could be drastically reduced and, if the fish are threatened or endangered, the risk of extinction is real.

Biochemical oxygen demand (BOD) reflects this demand for dissolved oxygen. Five-day BOD (BOD5) is simply the measured DO at the beginning time, i.e., the initial DO ($D_1$),

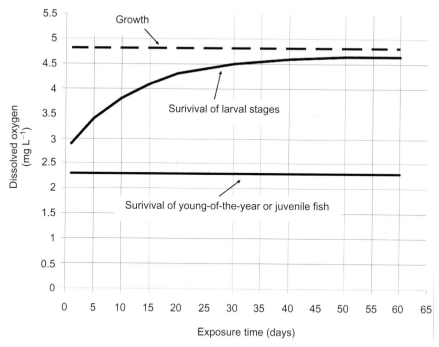

FIGURE 6.9   Dissolved oxygen (O$_2$) criteria for persistent exposure for a fish population. Shown are the lower bound limits on protective O$_2$ concentrations. The chronic growth limit may be violated for a specific number of days provided the chronic larval recruitment limit is not violated. *Source: U.S. Environmental Protection Agency. Ambient aquatic life water quality criteria for dissolved oxygen (saltwater): Cape Cod to Cape Hatteras. Report No. EPA-822-R-00-012. Washington, DC; 2000.*

measured immediately after it is taken from the source) minus the DO of the same water measured exactly 5 days after $D_1$, that is, $D_5$:

$$BOD = \frac{D_1 - D_5}{P} \qquad (6.1)$$

where $P$ = decimal volumetric fraction of water utilized and D units are in mg L$^{-1}$.

Thus, the microbial population in this water is demanding 100 mg L$^{-1}$ dissolved oxygen over the 5-day period. So, if a conventional municipal wastewater treatment system is achieving 95% treatment efficiency, the effluent discharged from this plant would be 5 mg L$^{-1}$.

Since available carbon is a limiting factor, the carbonaceous BOD reaches a plateau, that is, the ultimate carbonaceous BOD (see Figure 6.10). However, carbonaceous compounds are not the only substances demanding oxygen. Microbial populations will continue to demand $O_2$ from the water to degrade other compounds, especially nitrogenous compounds, which accounts for the bump in the BOD curve. Thus, in addition to serving as an indication of the amount of molecular oxygen needed for biological treatment of the organic matter, BOD also provides a guide to sizing a treatment process, assigning its efficiency, and giving operators and regulators information about whether the facility is meeting its design criteria and is complying with pollution control permits.

As mentioned, spilled substances with high BOD concentrations may diminish dissolved oxygen to levels lethal to some fish and many aquatic insects. As the water body re-aerates as a result of mixing with the atmosphere and by algal photosynthesis, $O_2$ is added to the water, the oxygen levels will slowly increase downstream. The drop and rise in DO concentrations downstream from a source of BOD is known as the DO sag curve, because the concentration of dissolved oxygen "sags" as the microbes deplete it. So, the falling $O_2$ concentrations fall with both time and distance from the point where the high BOD substances enter the water (see Figure 6.11).

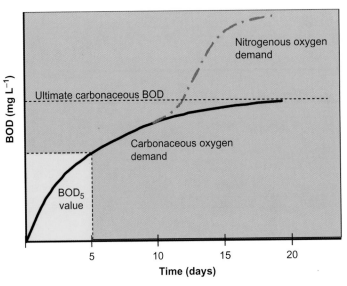

FIGURE 6.10  Biochemical oxygen demand (BOD) curve showing ultimate carbonaceous BOD and nitrogenous BOD. *Adapted from: Gerba CP, Pepper IL. Wastewater treatment and biosolids reuse. In: Maier RM, Pepper IL, Gerba CP. Environmental microbiology. 2nd ed. Burlington, MA: Elsevier Academic Press; 2009.*

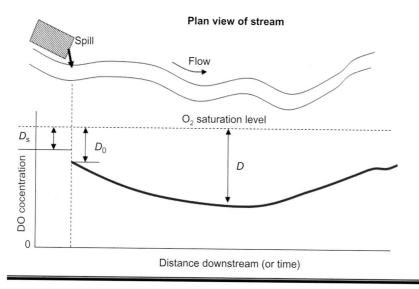

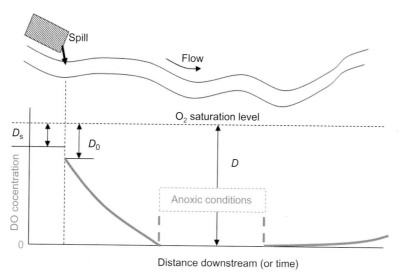

FIGURE 6.11   Dissolved oxygen sag curve downstream from a spill of an oxygen-depleting contaminant source. The concentration of dissolved oxygen in Curve A remains above 0, so although the available oxygen is reduced, the system remains aerobic. Curve B sags where dissolved oxygen falls to 0, and anaerobic conditions result and continue until the DO concentrations begin to increase. $D_S$ is the background oxygen deficit before the pollutants enter the stream. $D_0$ is the oxygen deficit after the pollutant is mixed. $D$ is the deficit for contaminant A which may be measured at any point downstream. This indicates both distance and time of microbial exposure to the source. For example, if the stream's average velocity is 5 km h$^{-1}$, $D$ measured 10 km downstream also represents 2 h of microbial activity to degrade the pollutant.

## PARTITIONING IN THE ENVIRONMENT

Thus far, we have introduced a number of concepts related to how substances move and change after they have been released; notably solubility and volatilization. When substances, like oil and other chemicals, are spilled, their disposition in the environment is determined by their inherent properties and the conditions of the environment into which they have been spilled. The interconnectedness between physical, chemical, and biological processes affects the fate and transport of substances as move among environmental compartments (e.g., soil, sediment, air, or water). The type of compartment where they reside and the physicochemical properties determine the ultimate fate of these substances. The inherent properties of the substance are influenced and changed by the extrinsic properties of the media. Environmental fate of a spilled substance, for example, is determined by numerous processes, including both abiotic and biotic media; abiotic media include air, water, and the nonliving parts of soil and sediment. Biotic media include all levels of biological organization, from subcellular and cellular matter in organisms to communities within biomes. Table 6.4 summaries a number of the processes that influence the fate of spilled substances.

Some of the most important equilibrium coefficients that influence the fate of a substance after it is released are the coefficients of sorption (distribution coefficient, $K_D$, or solid-water partition coefficient, $K_p$), dissolution or solubility, air-water partitioning (the Henry's law ($K_H$) constant), and organic carbon-water ($K_{oc}$).

The environment is subdivided into finite compartments, but there is much traversing by mass and energy among these compartments. As we discussed in Chapter 2, the mass of the contaminant entering and the mass leaving a control volume must be balanced by what remains within the control volume, according to the laws of thermodynamics. In a similar way, each environmental compartment may be a gainer or loser of the contaminant mass, but the overall mass must balance. The generally inclusive term for these compartmental changes is known by the thermodynamic term *fugacity*, that is, the chemical compound's "fleeing potential." Thus, a chemical compound's fugacity is the propensity of that chemical to escape from one type of environmental compartment and join another. The fate of a chemical may be modeled by combining the partitioning taking place within and between environmental compartments.[11]

Fugacity can tells us something about a substance's likely fate. Based solely on a compound's inherent properties, we can expect that chemical to have an affinity for particular environmental locations in air, water, soil, sediment, and biota (see Figure 6.12). However, this is a gross oversimplification. For example, even within a single compartment, a compound may exist in various phases (e.g., dissolved in water and sorbed to a particle in the solid phase). The physical interactions of a contaminant at the interface between each compartment are a determining factor in the fate of the pollutant. Within a compartment, a contaminant may remain unchanged (at least during the designated study period), or it may move physically, or it may be transformed chemically into another substance. Actually, in many cases, all three mechanisms will take place. A mass fraction will remain unmoved and unchanged. Another fraction remains unchanged but is transported to a different compartment. Another fraction becomes chemically transformed with all remaining products staying in the compartment where they were generated. And, a fraction of the original contaminant is transformed and then moved to another compartment. So, upon release from a source, the contaminant moves as a result of thermodynamic forces. We were introduced

TABLE 6.4 Processes Influencing the Disposition of Substances and Fate of Chemical Compounds After Release into the Environment

| Process | Description | Physical phases involved | Major mechanisms at work | Outcome of process | Factors included in process |
|---|---|---|---|---|---|
| Advection | Transport by turbulent flow; mass transfer | Aqueous, gas | Mechanical | Transport due to mass transfer | Concentration gradients, porosity, permeability, hydraulic conductivity, circuitousness or tortuosity of flow paths |
| Dispersion | Transport from source | Aqueous, gas | Mechanical | Concentration gradient-driven | Concentration gradients, porosity, permeability, hydraulic conductivity, circuitousness or tortuosity of flow paths |
| Molecular diffusion | Fick's Law (concentration gradient) | Aqueous, gas, solid | Mechanical | Concentration gradient-driven transport | Concentration gradients |
| Liquid separation | Various fluids of different densities and viscosities are separated within a system | Aqueous | Mechanical | Recalcitrance to due formation of separate gas and liquid phases (e.g., gasoline in water separates among benzene, toluene, and xylene) | Polarity, solubility, $K_d$, $K_{ow}$, $K_{oc}$, coefficient of viscosity, density |
| Density stratification | Distinct layers of differing densities and viscosities | Aqueous | Physical/chemical | Recalcitrance or increased mobility in transport of lighter fluids (e.g., LNAPLs) that float at water table in groundwater, or at atmospheric pressure in surface water | Density (specific gravity) |

*Continued*

TABLE 6.4    Processes Influencing the Disposition of Substances and Fate of Chemical Compounds After Release into the Environment—Cont'd

| Process | Description | Physical phases involved | Major mechanisms at work | Outcome of process | Factors included in process |
|---|---|---|---|---|---|
| Migration along flow paths | Faster through large holes and conduits, for example, path between sand particles in an aquifer | Aqueous, gas | Mechanical | Increased mobility through fractures | Porosity, flow path diameters |
| Sedimentation | Heavier compounds settle first | Solid | Chemical, physical, mechanical, varying amount of biological | Recalcitrance due to deposition of denser compounds | Mass, density, viscosity, fluid velocity, turbulence ($R_N$) |
| Filtration | Retention in mesh | Solid | Chemical, physical, mechanical, varying amount of biological mechanisms | Recalcitrance due to sequestration, destruction, and mechanical trapping of compounds in soil micropores | Surface charge, soil, particle size, sorption, polarity |
| Volatilization | Phase partitioning to vapor | Aqueous, gas | Physical | Increased mobility as vapor phase of contaminant migrates to soil gas phase and atmosphere | $P^0$, concentration of contaminant, solubility, temperature |
| Dissolution | Cosolvation, attraction of water molecule shell | Aqueous | Chemical | Various outcomes due to formation of hydrated compounds (with varying solubilities, depending on the species) | Solubility, pH, temperature, ionic strength, activity |

| Term | Definition | Phase | Mechanism | Relevance | Factors |
|---|---|---|---|---|---|
| Fugacity | Escape from one type of environmental compartment to another | All phases | Physical, but influenced by chemical and biological | Fleeing potential | All partitioning conditions affect fugacity |
| Absorption | Retention on solid surface | Solid | Chemical, physical, mechanical, varying amount of biological mechanisms | Partitioning of lipophilic compounds into soil organic matter | Polarity, surface charge, Van der Waals attraction, electrostatics, ion exchange, solubility, $K_d$, $K_{ow}$, $K_{oc}$ coefficient of viscosity, density |
| Adsorption | Retention on solid surface | Solid | Chemical, physical, varying amount of biological mechanism | Recalcitrance due to ion exchanges and charge separations | Polarity, surface charge, Van der Waals attraction, electrostatics, ion exchange, solubility, $K_d$, $K_{ow}$, $K_{oc}$ coefficient of viscosity, density |
| Chemisorption | Retention on surface wherein strength of interaction is stronger than solely physical adsorption, resembling chemical bonding | Solid | Chemical and biochemical in addition to the physical mechanisms | Recalcitrance due to ion exchanges and charge separations | Polarity, surface charge, Van der Waals attraction, electrostatics, ion exchange, solubility, $K_d$, $K_{ow}$, $K_{oc}$ coefficient of viscosity, density, presence of biofilm |
| Ion exchange | Cations attracted to negatively charged particle surfaces or anions are attracted to positively charged particle surfaces, causing ions on the particle surfaces to be displaced | Solid | Chemical and biochemical in addition to the physical mechanisms | Recalcitrance due to ion exchanges and charge separations | Polarity, surface charge, Van der Waals attraction, electrostatics, ion exchange, solubility, $K_d$, $K_{ow}$, $K_{oc}$ coefficient of viscosity, density, presence of biofilm |
| Complexation | Reactions with matrix (e.g., soil compounds like humic acid) that form covalent bonds | Solid | Chemical, varying amount of biological | Recalcitrance and transformation due to reactions with soil organic compounds to | Available oxidants/reductants, soil organic matter content, pH, chemical interfaces, |

*Continued*

TABLE 6.4   Processes Influencing the Disposition of Substances and Fate of Chemical Compounds After Release into the Environment—Cont'd

| Process | Description | Physical phases involved | Major mechanisms at work | Outcome of process | Factors included in process |
|---|---|---|---|---|---|
| | | | | form residues (bound complexes) | available $O_2$, electrical interfaces, temperature |
| Oxidation/reduction | Electron loss and gain | All | Chemical, physical, varying amount of biological | Destruction or transformation due to mineralization of simple carbohydrates to $CO_2$ and water from respiration of organisms | Available oxidants/reductants, soil organic matter content, pH, chemical interfaces, available $O_2$, electrical interfaces, temperature |
| Ionization | Complete cosolvation leading to separation of compound into cations and anions | Aqueous | Chemical | Dissolution of salts into ions | Solubility, pH, temperature, ionic strength, activity |
| Hydrolysis | Reaction of water molecules with contaminants | Aqueous | Chemical | Various outcomes due to formation of hydroxides (e.g., aluminum hydroxide) with varying solubilities, depending on the species | Solubility, pH, temperature, ionic strength, activity |
| Photolysis | Reaction catalyzed by electromagnetic energy (sunlight) | Gas (major phase) | Chemical, physical | Photo-oxidation of compounds with hydroxyl radical upon release to the atmosphere | Free radical concentration, wavelength, and intensity of EM radiation |
| Bioavailability | Fraction of the total mass of a compound present in a compartment that has the potential of being absorbed by the organism | All phases | Biological and chemical | Uptake, absorption, distribution, metabolism, and elimination | *Bioaccumulation* is the process of uptake into an organism from the abiotic compartments. *Bioconcentration* is the concentration of the pollutant within an organism above levels found in the compartment in which the organism lives |

| Term | Definition | Type | Outcome | Factors |
|---|---|---|---|---|
| Biodegradation | Microbially mediated, enzymatically catalyzed reactions | Aqueous, solid | Chemical, biological | Various outcomes, including destruction and formation of daughter compounds (degradation products) intracellularly and extracellularly | Microbial population (count and diversity), pH, temperature, soil moisture, acclimation potential of available microbes, nutrients, appropriate enzymes in microbes, available and correct electron acceptors (i.e., oxygen for aerobes, others for anaerobes) |
| Cometabolism | Other organic compounds metabolized concurrently by microbes that are degrading principal energy source | Aqueous, but wherever biofilm comes into contact with organic compounds | Biochemical | Coincidental degradation of organic compounds | Enhanced microbial activity, presence of a good energy source (i.e., successful acclimation) and production of enzymes in metabolic pathways |
| Activation | Metabolic, detoxification process that renders a compound more toxic | Aqueous, gas, solid, tissue | Biochemical | Phase 1 or 2 metabolism, for example, oxidation may from epoxides on aromatics | |
| Cellular respiration | Conversion of nutrients' biochemical energy into adenosine triphosphate, with release of waste products | Catabolic reactions, oxidation of one molecule and reduction of another | Biochemical | Microbial respiration, along with metabolism, degrades organic compounds | Aerobic respiration involves oxygen as final electron acceptor, whereas anaerobic respiration has another final electron acceptor |
| Fermentation | Cellular energy derived from oxidation of organic compounds | Endogenous electron acceptor, that is, usually an organic compound. Differs from cellular respiration where electrons are donated to an exogenous electron acceptor (e.g., O$_2$) via an electron transport chain | Biochemical | Organic compounds degraded to alcohols and organic acids, ultimately to methane and water | Often an anaerobic process |

Continued

**TABLE 6.4** Processes Influencing the Disposition of Substances and Fate of Chemical Compounds After Release into the Environment—Cont'd

| Process | Description | Physical phases involved | Major mechanisms at work | Outcome of process | Factors included in process |
|---|---|---|---|---|---|
| Enzymatic catalysis | Cell produces biomolecules (i.e., complex proteins) that speed up biochemical reactions | Enzyme's reactive site binds substrates by noncovalent interactions | Biological (intracellular in single-celled and multi-celled organisms) | Catalyzed reaction follows three steps: substrate fixation, reaction, and desorption of the product | Noncovalent bonding includes hydrogen bonds, dipole–dipole interactions, van der Waals or dispersion forces, π stacking interactions, hydrophobic effect |
| Metal catalysis | Reactions speed up in the presence of certain metallic compounds (e.g., noble metal oxides in the degradation of nitric acid) | Aqueous, gas, solid, and biotic | Chemical (especially reduction and oxidation) | Same chemical reaction, but faster | Chemical form of metal, pH, temperature |
| Pharmacokinetics/ toxicokinetics | Rates at which uptaken substances are absorbed, distributed, metabolized, and eliminated | Absorption, distribution, metabolism, and elimination of a substance by the body, as affected by uptake, distribution, binding, elimination, and biotransformation | Biochemical | Mass balance of substance after uptake | Available detoxification and enzymatic processes in cells |
| Pharmacodynamics/ toxicodynamics | Effects and modes of action of chemicals in an organism | Uptake, movement, binding, and interactions of molecules at their site of action | Biochemical | Fate of compound or its degradates | Affinities of compounds to various tissues |

Source: Vallero DA. Environmental biotechnology: a biosystems approach. Amsterdam, NV: Elsevier Academic Press; 2010.

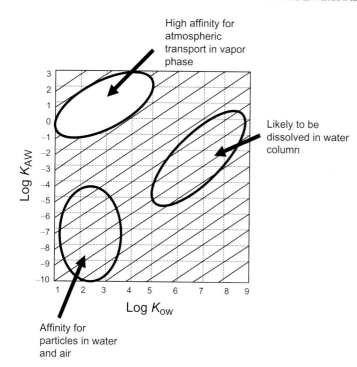

High affinity for
atmospheric
transport in vapor
phase

Likely to be
dissolved in water
column

Affinity for
particles in water
and air

FIGURE 6.12  Relationship between air-water partitioning and octanol-water partitioning and expected affinity of classes of contaminants for certain environmental compartments. *Adapted from: van de Meent D, McKone T, Parkerton T, Matthies M, Scheringer M, Wania F, et al. Persistence and transport potential of chemicals in a multimedia environment. In:* Proceedings of the SETAC Pellston workshop on criteria for persistence and long-range transport of chemicals in the environment, *14-19 July 1998, Fairmont Hot Springs, British Columbia, Canada. Pensacola, FL: Society of Environmental Toxicology and Chemistry; 1999.*

to fugacity principles in our discussion of the fluid properties $K_{ow}$ and vapor pressure and the partial pressure of gases.

Fugacity requires that at least two phases be in contact with the contaminant. For example, recall that the $K_{ow}$ value is an indication of a compound's likelihood to exist in the organic versus aqueous phase. This means that if a substance is dissolved in water and the water comes into contact with another substance, for example, octanol, the substance will have a tendency to move from the water to the octanol. Its octanol-water partitioning coefficient reflects just how much of the substance will move until the aqueous and organic solvents (phases) will reach equilibrium. So, for example, in a spill of equal amounts of the polychlorinated biphenyl, decachlorobiphenyl (log $K_{ow}$ of 8.23), and the pesticide chlordane (log $K_{ow}$ of 2.78), the PCB has much greater affinity for the organic phases than does the chlordane (more than five orders of magnitude). This does not mean than a great amount of either of the compounds is likely to stay in the water column, since they are both hydrophobic, but it does mean that they will vary in the time and mass of each contaminant moving between phases. The rate (kinetics) is different, so the time it takes for the PCB and chlordane to reach equilibrium will be different. This can be visualized by plotting the concentration of each compound with time (see Figure 6.13). When the concentrations plateau, the compounds are at equilibrium with their phase.

When phases contact one another, a contaminant will escape from one to another until the contaminant reaches equilibrium among the phases that are in contact with one another. The kinetics of the process determines the time it takes for equilibrium to be achieved.

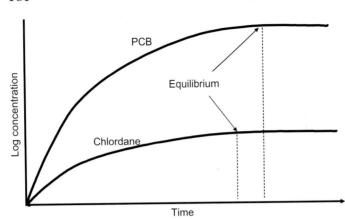

FIGURE 6.13 Bioreactor relative concentrations of a polychlorinated biphenyl (PCB) and chlordane in octanol with time. *Source: Vallero DA. Environmental biotechnology: a biosystems approach. Burlington, MA: Elsevier Academic Press; 2009.*

After it is spilled, a contaminant may attach to or permeate into surfaces of solid phase particles, that is, they become sorbed. Sorption is the process in which a chemical compound becomes associated, physically or chemically, with a solid substance, that is, the sorbant. Sorption is arguably the most important transfer process that determines how bioavailable or toxic compound will be in surface waters. This chemical transfer from a liquid (e.g., seawater) to solid (suspended solids in the water)[12] of a chemical, A, is expressed as:

$$A_{(solution)} + solid = A\text{--}solid \tag{6.2}$$

The interaction of the chemical being sorbed with the surface of a solid surface can be complex, depending on both the properties of the chemical and the water. In fact, this is the principle behind the use of dispersants after oil spills. The dispersant can be a surfactant, that is, a substance that lowers the surface tension. An oil dispersant reduces the interfacial tension between oil and water, that is, the oil and water cannot mix uniformly. This also helps to prevent the oil from sorbing to particles and from coagulating into a mass; hence the term, dispersant.

Other fluids are often of such small concentrations that they do not determine the ultimate solid-liquid partitioning. While it is often acceptable to consider "net" sorption, let us consider briefly the four basic types or mechanisms of sorption:

1. *Adsorption* is the process wherein the chemical in solution attaches to a solid surface, which is a common sorption process in clay and organic constituents in soils. This simple adsorption mechanism can occur on clay particles where little carbon is available, such as in groundwater.
2. *Absorption* is the process that often occurs in porous materials so that the solute can diffuse into the particle and be sorbed onto the inside surfaces of the particle. This commonly results from short-range electrostatic interactions between the surface and the contaminant.
3. *Chemisorption* is the process of integrating a chemical into porous materials surface via chemical reaction. In soil, this is usually the result a covalent reaction between a mineral surface and the contaminant.

4. *Ion exchange* is the process by which positively charged ions (cations) are attracted to negatively charged particle surfaces or negatively charged ions (anions) are attracted to positively charged particle surfaces, causing ions on the particle surfaces to be displaced. Particles undergoing ion exchange can include soils, sediment, airborne particulate matter, or even biota, such as pollen particles. Cation exchange has been characterized as being the second most important chemical process on earth, after photosynthesis. This is because the cation exchange capacity, and to a lesser degree anion exchange capacity in tropical soils, is the means by which nutrients are made available to plant roots. Without this process, the atmospheric nutrients and the minerals in the soil would not come together to provide for the abundant plant life on planet Earth.[13]

These four types of sorption are a mix of physics and chemistry. The first two are predominantly controlled by physical factors, and the second two are combinations of chemical reactions and physical processes. We will spend a bit more time covering these specific types of sorption when we consider the surface effects of soils. Generally, sorption reactions affect three processes[14] in aquatic systems:

1. The chemical contaminant's transport in water due to distributions between the aqueous phase and particles;
2. The aggregation and transport of the contaminant as a result of electrostatic properties of suspended solids; and
3. Surface reactions such as dissociation, surface-catalysis, and precipitation of the chemical contaminant.

## LESSONS LEARNED

The lessons from the spills and sudden releases of contaminants to waterways are legion. But, two are particularly relevant, that is, economies that depend on crude oil are particularly vulnerable to extensive environmental problems; and environmental policies must be proactive and highly adaptive to looming threats.

Dependence on fossil fuels is the underlying problem. Until we become significantly less dependent, however, aggressive risk reduction and ecological protection steps will need to be pursued.

Every vehicle travelling by land, water, or air is at risk of spilling its contents as are the tanks and pipelines throughout the world. Thus, a paramount lesson to be learned from this spillage is the need to replace chemicals that must be transported with more benign substances that meet the same societal objectives. In other words, there is a great need for safe substitutes and other life cycle considerations, including Design for the Environment, Design for Disassembly, and Design for Recycling.[15] Life cycle perspectives call for some improved technology-based approaches as well as better quality-based approaches, such as leveling out the pollutant loadings and using less expensive technologies to remove the first large bulk of pollutants, followed by higher operation and maintenance technologies to ensure that releases do not increase over the life of a vehicle or pipeline. The net effect can be a greater reduction of pollutant emissions and effluents. So, before building a cargo vessel or pipeline, engineers should conduct a thorough life-cycle analysis, prioritizing potential problems in terms of both severity and likelihood, and matching the technologies and operations to address them.

# References and Notes

1. U.S. Department of Justice. *Press Release: Greek shipping company, master and chief engineer of m/v Agios Emilianos convicted for intentional cover-up of oil pollution and obstruction of justice.* December 13, 2011.
2. International Tanker Oil Owners Pollution Federation, Limited. *Statistics.* http://www.itopf.com/information-services/data-and-statistics/statistics; 2012 [accessed March 14, 2012].
3. The source for this summary of events is: Transocean, Inc. Macondo well incident. *Transocean investigation report*, vol. I; June 2011.
4. National Oceanic and Atmospheric Administration. *NOAA Deepwater Horizon/BP Oil Spill Archive.* http://response.restoration.noaa.gov/deepwaterhorizon; 2012 [accessed March 14, 2012].
5. Maritime and Coast Guard Agency (UK). *Safer Lives, Safer Ships, Cleaner Seas.* http://www.mcga.gov.uk/c4mca/mcga-environmental/mcga-dops_cp_environmental-counter-pollution.htm; 2005 [accessed April 16, 2005].
6. The potential for oil to pollute the marine environment was recognized by the International Convention for the Prevention of Pollution of the Sea by Oil, 1954 (OILPOL 1954). The Conference adopting the Convention was organized by the UK government, and the Convention provided for certain functions to be undertaken by IMO when it came into being. In fact, the Convention establishing IMO entered into force in 1958 just a few months before the OILPOL convention entered into force, so IMO effectively managed OILPOL from the start, initially through its Maritime Safety Committee.
   The OILPOL Convention recognized that most oil pollution resulted from routine shipboard operations such as the cleaning of cargo tanks. In the 1950s, the normal practice was simply to wash the tanks out with water and then pump the resulting mixture of oil and water into the sea.
7. U.S. Environmental Protection Agency. National oil and hazardous substances pollution contingency plan: Final Rule 40 CFR Part 300. *Fed Regist* 1993;**59**(178):47384–495.
8. Source: Santa Barbara Wildlife Care Network. http://www.sbwcn.org/spill.shtml; 2005 [accessed April 15, 2005].
9. The research for this case was conducted in April of 2005 by Chris Sundberg, a Duke University student, as part of his requirements for EGR 108S, Ethics in Professions, an undergraduate engineering course.
10. Vidal J. *Shell accepts liability for two oil spills in Nigeria.* www.guardian.co.uk/environment/2011/aug/03/shell-liability-oil-spills-nigeria; 2011 [accessed March 14, 2012].
11. Fugacity models are valuable in predicting the movement and fate of environmental contaminants within and among compartments. This discussion is based on work by one of the pioneers in this area, Don MacKay and his colleagues at the University of Toronto. See, for example, MacKay D, Paterson S. Evaluating the fate of organic chemicals: a level III fugacity model. *Environ Sci Technol* 1991;25:427-436.
12. Lyman W. Transport and transformation processes. [Chapter 15] In: Rand G, editor. *Fundamentals of aquatic toxicology: effects, environmental fate, and risk assessment.* 2nd ed. Washington, DC: Taylor & Francis; 1995.
13. Professor Daniel Richter of Duke University's Nicholas School of the Environment has waxed eloquently on this subject.
14. See Westfall J. Adsorption mechanisms in aquatic surface chemistry. In: Stumm W, editor. *Aquatic Surface Chemistry.* New York, NY: Wiley-Interscience; 1987. p. 83–110.
15. Billatos SB. *Green technology and design for the environment.* Washington, DC: Taylor & Francis; 1997 and Allada V. Preparing engineering students to meet the ecological challenges through sustainable product design. *Proceedings of the 2000 international conference on engineering education*, Taipei, Taiwan; 2000.

# Fires

Fire is often associated with disasters. The environmental effects of fire can be direct, such as when people are directly harmed by the heat and fumes of a fire or when wildlife is destroyed and property lost due to uncontrolled fires, such as range and forest fires. Fires seriously harm the environment in many ways. Toxic gases emitted from fires include the products of incomplete combustion such as carbon monoxide (CO), oxides of nitrogen ($NO_x$), sulfur dioxide ($SO_2$), dioxins, furans, and polycyclic aromatic compounds (notably benzo(a)pyrene). In addition, fires release pollutants in solid and liquid phases, i.e., aerosols.

From a health perspective, particulate matter (PM) includes some of the most dangerous substances (soot, tar, etc.). This type of pollutant is formed in fires that have insufficient oxygen, which refers to most uncontrolled fires. As mentioned in Chapter 4, the only way that a simple fire can obtain oxygen is by diffusion. In the air, this a reasonably slow process that is particularly slow compared to a raging fire. Also, industrial fires often involve the conflagration of some organic compound (pharmaceuticals, pesticides, tires, clothing, etc.), and the products of burning are often toxic (known as products of incomplete combustion, or PICs).

Indeed, fires evoke more than air pollution, such as when the Sandoz factory in Basel, Switzerland, burnt down on November 1, 1986, with the hazardous chemicals washed into the river Rhine, killing untold numbers of fish and ruined the drinking water of many. Taken cumulatively, fires contribute enormous pollutants to the atmosphere. It has been estimated that if all uncontrolled fires (especially burning coal in mines and deposits) were extinguished, the total $CO_2$ in the atmosphere could be reduced by 2-3%. One of the worst underground fires in the United States exists in the Centralia mine in Pennsylvania. It has been burning since May 1962. Tire fires are also a problem and are discussed in this chapter.

## FIRE DISASTER THERMODYNAMICS

Fires can be considered as an oxidation-reduction (redox) reaction and are accompanied by the production of heat and light. The two chemical requirements are an oxidizing agent and a reducing agent. The oxidizing agent is usually the oxygen in the air but can be chemicals such as nitrates, chlorates and peroxides. From a plant management perspective, these chemicals and any oxidizing agent must never be stored next to combustible materials. The reducing agent or fuel can be wood, grass, trees if outside or paper or some organic polymer

163

such as a textile material, terylene or nylon, or can be flammable liquids such as gasoline or flammable vapors such as propane.

All fires require an initial input of heat for the fuel to reach a temperature before the fire can be self-sustaining. This temperature is the autoignition temperature. The initial heat input can be a lighted match, an electrical heater involving a hot wire, or a burning piece of wood. The first part of the burning process often involves vaporizing the chemicals in the solid or liquid fuel. If the fuel is wood, it involves heating the wood to release the volatile, combustible vapors such as turpentine or other hydrocarbons to the temperature at which the vapors of the material start burning. This input of energy is called the activation energy. This first part of the burning process is said to be endothermic, implying that heat must be put in for the process to take place. The second part of the process involves the redox reaction and the formation of products such as water and $CO_2$ and can only take place once the autoignition temperature has been reached. This process is the burning process and is exothermic, implying that heat is given out. For the combustion of cellulosic material, the reaction can be summarized as

$$(CH_2O)_n + nO_2 = nCO_2 + nH_2O, \quad \text{where } n = 6 \tag{7.1}$$

For a related reaction involving a pure compound, $C_6H_{12}O_6$, glucose, the reaction is

$$C_6H_{12}O_6 + 6O_2 = 6CO_2 + 6H_2O, \quad \Delta H^\circ = -2805 \text{ kJ mol}^{-1} \tag{7.2}$$

This exothermic heat is equivalent to $-15.6 \text{ kJ g}^{-1}$.

It is this exothermic heat that sustains a fire once it is lit. If the heat is removed by the presence of a large chunk of metal or some other body that can conduct this heat away, the fire will be extinguished.

A good example of the autoignition temperature is related to the temperature at which paper will burn spontaneously. If the air in contact with paper is heated to about 233 °C (or 451 °F), the paper will spontaneously burst into flames. This idea was made the title of a book (by Ray Bradbury) and a film "Fahrenheit 451" which involved the burning of books. The autoignition temperature is the lowest temperature at which a solid, liquid, or vapor will spontaneously ignite without the presence of an additional heat source (flame, spark, or hot source) and Table 7.1 lists the autoignition temperatures of a number of useful chemicals.

If there is not enough available oxygen or fuel to maintain the burning process, the fire will be extinguished. The oxygen in an open fire is controlled by diffusion and convection. Diffusion is a fairly slow process and a fire can be stifled by piling up planks over the fire, thus reducing the diffusion of air into the fire. In a fireplace, the chimney creates a draught forcing the hot gases from a fire up the chimney, creating a low pressure in the region of the fire which draws in fresh air. A candle is also fed by the same process. The hot gases, being less dense, rise from the candle flame, creating a low pressure and forcing in fresh air to feed the burning flame. This process is called convection and is a way of boosting the natural diffusion process. In a zero-gravity situation, where density gradients do not result in air movement, it is impossible to sustain a lighted candle. So no birthday candles in your spacecraft when you fly to the moon. In an industrial furnace, the flow of air is controlled by powerful blowers which force air and oxygen into the fuel burning region.

The convection and diffusion processes can be seen at work in forest fires with the burning fire of wood and sticks and leaves near the ground with another fire up in the tops of the trees, and no fire in between. The explanation is that the heat of the ground fire vaporizes and heats

TABLE 7.1   Autoignition Temperatures for a Number of Chemicals and Materials

| Chemicals or materials | Autoignition temperature (°C) |
| --- | --- |
| Acetone | 465 |
| Benzene | 560 |
| Butane | 420 |
| Carbon | 700 |
| Dry wood | 480 |
| Charcoal | 349 |
| Coal | 400 |
| Ethanol | 365 |
| Kerosene | 295 |
| Methane | 580 |
| Butane | 405 |
| Heptane | 215 |

Source: The Engineering ToolBox. www.engineeringtoolbox.com/fuels-ignition-temperatures-d_171.html; 2012 [accessed March 9, 2012].

up the volatile oils in the leaves and wood of the trees and as a result these hot vapors rise. When the hot vapors reach the top of the trees, they meet fresh oxygen and begin to burn, taking in the top leaves and top branches. The fire on the ground uses up all available oxygen and only when the hot vapors reach the tree tops and a fresh supply of air, do they burst into flame. Further, the ground fire is seen to burn fiercely at the perimeter of the fire where fresh air can be found and diffusion and convection can play their part.

Heat can be transferred in three ways: conduction, convection, and radiation and all have a place in understanding how fires spread. In conduction, the heat conducted by any hot body to a colder body (where the body can be a solid, liquid, or gas) is dependent on the difference in temperature between the hot body and the cold body; the hotter a body, the greater will be the transfer of heat. It is done by a transfer involving the molecules of the bodies concerned. The fast vibrating or moving molecules in the hot body will transfer heat to the slower vibrating or moving molecules in the cold body. This process will go on until the two bodies are at the same temperature with all molecules having the same energy. Fires spread by conduction with burning pieces of material passing the heat to adjacent pieces of material and setting them alight.

We have seen convection at work. It is dependent on the difference in density between the hot rising vapors and gases and the density of the air around the fire. In a gravitational field, less dense material rises in a sea of high dense material. This type of heat transfer involves a transfer of matter—a movement of molecules. Fire cannot be sustained without convection as seen with the candle in a zero-gravity situation.

Radiation is perhaps the most important heat transfer mode in fires. This is the heat transferred from a hot flame to combustible material. This heat is largely responsible for the spreading of a fire. The transfer is done by electromagnetic radiation in the visible and infrared regions, and this radiation heat is the same type of heat as the heat we receive from the sun and does not involve a transfer of molecules. All bodies with a temperature above absolute zero (0 K) emit radiation. If a body is in thermal equilibrium, it will absorb and radiate heat at the same rate. The hotter a body of flame, the greater will be the radiation.

The speed at which a fire spreads depends largely on the material (fuel) being burned and the amount of oxygen that can get to the front of the fire. The hotter the flames and the larger the flames, the greater will be the transfer of radiant heat to the adjacent material and the quicker will the fresh unburned fuel material begin to burn. A wind will always increase the rate of burning of a fire simply by forcing more oxygen into the fire. This gives some idea of the control that diffusion has on the rate at which a fire can burn. Diffusion is a vital parameter in understanding the spreading of a fire. In a house fire, closing all the doors and windows will help to stifle a fire. Opening a door after a fire has been partially extinguished will cause the fire start up again. Throwing sand on a burning wood fire does three things: it separates the oxidant (air) from the fuel and the fire is extinguished, it reduces the temperature of the hot burning wood by absorbing some of the heat, and thirdly, it acts as a barrier in reducing the diffusion of air to the fire.

Fires involving burning vapors of organic liquids can be very serious and can involve explosions. The worst kinds are the boiling liquid expanding vapor explosions (BLEVEs). A BLEVE occurs when a closed container of flammable liquid (often propane) is heated. It can be caused by an external source, such as a burning fire or a burning vehicle adjacent to the liquid in the container, drum, cylinder, or tank. The internal pressure builds up more rapidly than it can be vented and the containment fails, and an explosion takes place. With the ignition source already present, the rapidly expanding cloud of hot vapor ignites. At a minimum, the ignition will lead to a deflagration. Or, if conditions are right, the fuel/air mix will detonate, resulting in a fireball explosion. These BLEVEs often happen when tankers carrying inflammable and volatile liquids overturn.

The reaction and the enthalpy (heat) of a typical BLEVE are given by

$$C_3H_8 + 5O_2 = 3CO_2 + 4H_2O, \quad \Delta H = -2220 \text{ kJ mol}^{-1} \tag{7.3}$$

In order to extinguish a fire, one of the basic requirements—heat, or oxidant, or fuel—must be completely removed. This can be done by cutting off the fuel supply and separating the fuel from the air (starvation and smothering) or by lowering the temperature of the fire to below the ignition point (cooling). There are five main types of fire extinguishers: water, foam, carbon dioxide, Halon 1211, and dry powder. The choice of extinguisher depends on the type of fuel and whether there is danger from live electrical equipment. Fires can be divided into the five classes as given below; this classification makes it easy to define which type of extinguisher to use:

Class A: involving organic solids such as wood, paper, textiles, hay, grain, plastics, sugar, coal, etc.
Class B: involving flammable liquids such as gasoline, oils, fats, kerosene, turpentine, wax, varnish, paints, alcohols, acetone, organic solvents, etc.
Class C: involving flammable gases such as CNG (methane), propane, butane (LPG), hydrogen.

Class D: involving combustible metals such as sodium, magnesium, lithium, aluminum, etc.
Class E: involving fires which are in areas where there is electricity.

Class A fires can be extinguished using water, foam, dry powder; B fires require dry powder, foam, $CO_2$, or Halon; C and E require dry powder, $CO_2$, or Halon; and D requires special dry powders or sand.
The types of extinguishers and their properties are given below.

## Water

The purpose of adding water to a fire is to reduce the fire temperature to below the ignition point. The cooling action of water is mainly due to its heat of vaporization. The heat of the fire is taken up by first of all heating the cool water from an ambient temperature to 100 °C and then evaporating the water, turning it into steam. The molar heat of vaporization, $\Delta_{vap}H$ ($H_2O$,l), is 42 kJ mol$^{-1}$ or 2.3 kJ g$^{-1}$, and its molar heat capacity, $C_{p,m}$, is 75 J K$^{-1}$ mol$^{-1}$ or 4.2 J K$^{-1}$ g$^{-1}$. From these data, we can calculate that the heat lost by the fire in raising the temperature of the water from 25 to 100 °C is only 0.32 kJ g$^{-1}$, while the heat required to vaporize the water is seven times greater at 2.3 kJ g$^{-1}$. So 1.0 g of water will absorb 2.6 kJ. We have seen that the enthalpy of combustion of glucose, a typical building block of cellulose, is 15.6 kJ g$^{-1}$. This implies that it will take 7 g of water to remove the heat from 1 g of wood or other cellulosic material, in other words, 7 L of water for a kilogram of wood.

Water cannot be used in organic chemical fires, such as gasoline fires, because of the difference in densities between water (density: 1.0 g cm$^{-3}$) and gasoline (density: 0.74 g cm$^{-3}$). Pouring water onto burning gasoline will result in the water sinking down below the gasoline and the fire will continue to burn on the gasoline surface.

## Foams

A foam is simply air-filled bubbles, made of water stabilized with a surfactant. It has a lower density than oil and gasoline and hence can be used to extinguish oil or gasoline fires by simply acting as a blanket and separating the fuel from the air.
A foam is made by first compressing a mass of water containing a surfactant with nitrogen, and when required for fire extinguishing, the pressure is released and the foam which forms can then be sprayed onto the flames of a class A or B fire.

## Carbon Dioxide

Carbon dioxide is a gas at room temperature, and it has a density which is greater than that of air. It extinguishes fires by smothering it. Another important property of $CO_2$ is that it is relatively inert and cannot be further oxidized. Carbon dioxide has a triple point (the pressure and temperature where gas, liquid, and solid forms coexist) of 5.17 bar and $-57$ °C; at 25 °C and 1 bar, it sublimes from solid to gas form. At a pressure above 67 bar (atmospheres), it can be liquefied and as a result makes an ideal fire-fighting chemical as it can be rapidly pumped onto a fire by simply opening the valve of a pressurized canister of $CO_2$. Its vapor density of 1.8 g L$^{-1}$ is greater than that of air which is 1.2 g L$^{-1}$ at 1 bar and 25 °C.

## BCF (Halon 1211)

BCF or Halon 1211 is $CF_2ClBr$; the numbers refer to the numbers of bromine, fluorine, and chlorine atoms in the molecule. It has a boiling point of $-4\,°C$, and thus it is easily liquefied by pressure at room temperature and has a vapor pressure of 2.4 bar at 25 °C and its vapor density is $6.7\,g\,L^{-1}$ at 1 bar and 25 °C. If pressurized at 2.4 bar, on opening the valve, the BCF comes out from its container with much less pressure than $CO_2$ and is not so likely to disperse a fire. Smothering is not the only way in which BCF works. It also acts as scavengers of free radicals in a flame and terminates the propagation of chain reactions and thus acts as an antioxidant. As a result, it is suitable for all classes of fire.

## Dry Powders

Sand is a cheap and useful extinguisher of fires. It acts as a smothering agent separating the fuel from the air. In addition to sand, sodium bicarbonate ($NaHCO_3$) is used as a dry chemical for class A, B, and C fires. Sodium bicarbonate acts in a very different way to sand. It decomposes at 270 °C according to the reaction

$$2NaHCO_3 = H_2O + CO_2 + Na_2CO_3, \quad \Delta_r H° = 91\,kJ\,mol^{-1}. \tag{7.4}$$

It acts in a number of ways; the decomposition products are water (a good fire-fighting chemical), $CO_2$ (which smothers the fire), and sodium carbonate powder which also acts as an inert smothering agent. Further, the reaction is endothermic, so it absorbs heat from the fire and this helps in reducing the temperature. In a fire extinguisher, the powder is driven out of its container by either nitrogen or $CO_2$ under pressure.

The foregoing thermodynamic factors influence not only the extent and duration of a fire disaster but also the type of damage. For example, the choice of fire extinguishing materials can affect the types of emissions released from the fire. This could entail a trade-off between fire control and emissions that could impact health and environmental quality. We shall now consider some notorious fires that have had disastrous effects on the environment.

## KUWAIT OIL FIRES

In January and February of 1991, the Iraqi retreating army set fire to 700 Kuwaiti oil wells as part of a scorched earth policy. The amount of oil that burnt was staggering, and it was recorded that at the height of the burning, $950,000\,m^3$ (6 million barrels) were lost each day. The last of the fires was extinguished some 10 months later in November 1991. One of the reasons why the fires were not put out earlier was that land mines had been put in place in the area around the burning wells. The smoke from the fires cut out much of the sun in the Persian Gulf region and rose to over 3000 m (10,000 ft). These Kuwait oil fires dominated the weather patterns in the Gulf area for much of 1991, and carbon fallout was a regular occurrence. The heat of the fire heated the surrounding air making it less dense, creating a powerful draught. The reaction and enthalpy from the fire (assuming that it was burning octane) can be summarized as:

$$C_8H_{18} + 12.5O_2 = 8CO_2 + 9H_2O, \quad \Delta H = -5471\,kJ\,mol^{-1} \tag{7.5}$$

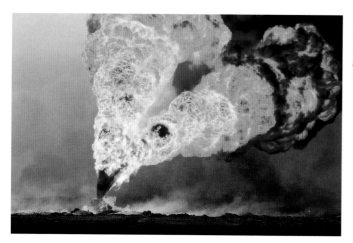

FIGURE 7.1 Kuwait oil fires as a result of the Gulf war of 1991. *Image Source Page: http://www.evidence.org.kw/photos.php?page=0001_Oil-Well-Fire - photogragher of this photo: Adel Alyousifi*

The hotter the fire, the faster the column of light air rises. The hot air also creates a region of low pressure which drives in more air and increases the rate of burning. In spite of this, these fires were apparently starved of oxygen as the plumes were very black in color due to soot (carbon particles), and this in turn is a result of unburned fuel (see Figure 7.1). The smoke plume did not, however, seriously affect the rest of the world. This might have been due to lack of wind or that the soot particles were heavy enough to gravitate to earth soon after forming. It was estimated that over 3000 tonnes of soot was pumped into the atmosphere everyday, and the carbon dioxide emitted from the fires was estimated to be about 2% of the global emission. It was a major disaster and respiratory problems were rife in the Gulf area. Apart from the fires and the atmospheric pollution, unburned oil formed hundreds of oil lakes which contaminated 40 million tonnes of sand and earth. This oil was covered with soot, and it has been estimated that it covers 5% of the land in Kuwait. The oil from these wells has been sinking into the sands with unknown consequences for Kuwait's precious ground water resources. The many problems that this Gulf war has precipitated will take decades to clear.

## RELEASE OF RADIOACTIVE MATERIAL

In the nuclear disaster at Chernobyl, the intense heat of the graphite fire from just one reactor created a massive column of rising hot air which took with it debris and radioactive fallout from the reactor. The strength of the updraft is a function of the temperature of the fire, and by all accounts, the Chernobyl fire was intense. The plume rose very high and 100 different isotopes were spewed high into the atmosphere where they were then carried horizontally across parts of Europe. Most of the isotopes were sufficiently short lived to be of no danger. But the isotopes iodine-131, strontium-90, and caesium-137, with half-lives of 8 days, 29 years, and 30 years, respectively, are dangerous and the latter two are still in the area today. An area of 150,000 km$^2$ in Belarus, Russia, and the Ukraine was the worst affected. The fallout extended for 500 km in a northerly direction. More details on this disaster are given in Chapter 12. As can be seen, it is fire from the nuclear explosion that created the energy to carry the radiation far and wide.

Part of the heat of the Chernobyl disaster was the burning graphite fire

$$C + O_2 = CO_2, \quad \Delta H = -394.4 \text{ kJ mol}^{-1} \tag{7.6}$$

The Fukushima nuclear disaster was arguably not as serious as that in Chernobyl in spite of the large amount of radioactive fuel that was stored at the site or was being used in the reactor. All in all, three reactors exploded at Fukushima but the resultant fires were small and the plumes were not anywhere as energetic as the one at Chernobyl. Thus, the extent and intensity of the fire during a nuclear disaster has a substantial impact on the amount of nuclear material released. As a result, in the Japanese tsunami aftermath the amount of radioactive material carried in the hot columns from the hydrogen explosions (see Chapter 12 for more details) was largely limited to iodine-131.

## INDONESIAN WILDFIRES

Wildfires can devastate human settlements. For example, hundreds of homes have been destroyed and thousands of hectares charred in recent wildfires in the American West and Rocky Mountain regions in the Spring and Summer of 2012. Some wildfires can alter entire ecosystems. In 1997, massive wildfires overran huge tracts of forests in Indonesian Borneo and the rate of $CO_2$ entering the atmosphere increased from an average of 3.2 to 6.0 Gt year$^{-1}$. Once the trees had been burnt and the land drained, the peatlands became susceptible to smoldering and burning. These ancient peat bogs can be over 20 m deep and supported the forest growth. Satellite studies before and after the fires showed that over 700,000 ha had been burnt. Between 0.81 and 2.57 Gt of carbon was released into the atmosphere. This is equal to between 13% and 40% of the annual carbon emissions caused by burning fossil fuels around the world. It was the largest increase in atmospheric $CO_2$ since records began in 1957. More than 20 million people were exposed to high levels of pollutants in the air. It had a catastrophic effect on the

FIGURE 7.2   Indonesian Borneo wildfires, 1997. *Image from* http://www.ens-newswire.com/ens/nov2002/2002-11-08-06.asp.

biodiversity of the area. For example, the orangutan population of Indonesian Borneo was reduced by half. The conclusion on analyzing these wildfires is that catastrophic events in small areas of the world can have a massive global impact (see Figure 7.2). If we are to slow global warming, such unsustainable destruction must also be reduced.[1] These fires seemed to have burnt with very smoky flames indicating unburned fuel (cellulose and carbon). This was probably due to insufficient oxygen or the low temperature of the burning fire. The equation for the burning of cellulosic material assuming a sufficient supply of oxygen is given by Equation (7.1).

## WORLD TRADE CENTER FIRE

In the World Trade Center, the fires were initially started from the ejected fuel from the planes that crashed into the Twin Towers. With the enormous friction of the metal plane striking the concrete towers, there would have been enough heat to set the fuel alight so long as there was enough oxygen. With a plentiful supply of oxygen, the hydrocarbons should have burnt to $CO_2$ as

$$C_{12}H_{26} + 18.5O_2 = 12CO_2 + 13H_2O, \quad \Delta H = -6730 \text{ kJ mol}^{-1}. \tag{7.7}$$

But in a fire in a building, there is always a shortage of oxygen because of the restriction on the amount of incoming air (few windows), unless there is a strong wind bringing in fresh supplies. Remember fires need heat to start the fire, fuel to burn, and oxygen to react with the fuel. This lack of $O_2$ in the confines of the building would have resulted in only a partially oxidized fuel and the reaction could be written as

$$C_{12}H_{26} + 12.5O_2 = 6C + 6CO_2 + 13H_2O, \quad \Delta H = -6730 \text{ kJ mol}^{-1}. \tag{7.8}$$

The black color of the billowing smoke plumes that poured out of the Twin Towers was due to this carbon and is a result of partially burnt fuel. In the WTC, the flammable material would have been carpets, curtains, paper, and soft furniture and even partitioning walls made of fiber board. All of this would burn once it was hot enough but again due to the lack of oxygen would have burnt with an exceedingly black carbonized smoke.

Fires often accompany disasters, as was seen in the 2001 World Trade Center and the 2011 Japanese earthquake disasters. The initial fire at the 9/11 World Trade Center was due to the burning of the jet fuel, much of which was kerosene; this lasted only a short time, in spite of the huge volume of kerosene carried by the planes. However, the fires raged in the building for weeks afterward and it was not until December 19 that the NYC fire marshal declared the fires extinguished. The light construction and hollow nature of the structures allowed the jet fuel to penetrate far inside the towers, igniting many fires simultaneously (see Figure 7.3). The fires were hot enough to soften and weaken the steel lattice reinforcing columns which caused floors to sag, pulling perimeter columns inward and reducing their ability to support the mass of the building above.[2,3]

The temperature appears to have reached between 800 and 1000 °C and over 10,000 tonnes of aluminum melted in the process. The melting point of Al is only 660 °C.[4,5]

The fires continued to flare up and burn long into the cleanup stage. The removal of steel beams and debris from the top of the pile allowed oxygen to reach the fires smoldering below, and as a result, the flames often flared up, hampering workers on site.

FIGURE 7.3 The collapse of the World Trade Center seen from Williamsburg, Brooklyn. *Picture from: http://www. en.wikipedia.org/wiki/Collapse_of_the_World_ Trade_Center The North Tower as seen from a NYC Police helicopter. http://www.epa.gov/ wtc/pictures.html*

About the time the WTC buildings were opened (1973), there was a scare related to the use of asbestos as an insulating medium and as a fire retarder in buildings. As a result, much of the asbestos that was in the buildings originally were subsequently removed so the asbestos problem was not as serious as it might have been. It is doubtful whether any fire retardation measures could have reduced the fires in the WTC; the building was never designed to withstand such an act of terrorism.

This was not the first fire in the WTC: On February 13, 1975, a fire broke out on the 11th floor of the North Tower. Fire spread through the core to the 9th and 14th floors by igniting the insulation of telephone cables in a utility shaft that ran vertically between floors. Areas at the furthest extent of the fire were extinguished almost immediately and the original fire was put out in a few hours. Most of the damage was concentrated on the 11th floor, fueled by cabinets filled with paper, alcohol-based fluid for office machines, and other office equipment. Fireproofing protected the steel and there was no structural damage to the tower. Other than the damage caused by the fire, a few floors below suffered water damage from the extinguishing of the fires above. At that time, the World Trade Center had no fire sprinkler system.[6–9]

All fires contain some dangerous substances. CO is a typical pollutant and is a result of incomplete combustion. This forms when there is insufficient oxygen in the fire. It was reported that the following pollutants were found at the WTC site: lead, cadmium, PCBs, asbestos, and dioxin-like compounds. However, the fire was high enough for most of the airborne pollutants to be carried away from the scene.

## THE JAPANESE EARTHQUAKE AND TSUNAMI

The previously mentioned Japanese earthquake of 8.9 magnitude and resultant tsunami of March 2011 sparked at least 80 fires in cities and towns along the coast (see Figure 7.4). The quake was the most powerful since Japan started keeping records 140 years ago.

FIGURE 7.4    Fires in Japan after the massive earthquake on March 11, 2011. *Picture from http://www.bbc.co.uk/news/world-asia-pacific-12719705.*

The heat of this reaction came from the uranium-235 fission reaction

$$^{235}U + {}^{1}n = {}^{142}Ba + {}^{92}Kr + 2n + \gamma, \quad \Delta H = -3.1 \times 10^{11}\,J\,mol^{-1} \tag{7.9}$$

This is nearly one million times more heat per mole than we saw with the kerosene reaction (Equation 7.7). When the cooling system of the reactors failed this nuclear reaction continued pumping out heat and this finally led to the explosions.

Houses in Japan are mostly built from wood as this material offers some degree of flexibility and is reputed to be the safest material in an earthquake-prone region. When the big earthquake struck Japan's NW coast, in March 2011, the result was widespread fires. The energy and heat to start the fires was readily available from broken power lines causing sparking and together with leaking gas from severed gas mains and pipes, the initial fuel was available for explosions and for burning. Furthermore, the heat from the friction caused by the massive movements of buildings, cars, trees, houses, and machinery precipitated by the earth ripping quakes was enough to set fire to all available fuel which included the material from which the houses were built, and widespread fire was inevitable. The more dense the housing, the greater was the conflagration. The same is true for all earthquake-type fires in earthquake-prone countries.

## OTHER MAJOR FIRES

The fires that broke out after Katrina were probably started by severed gas mains which together with downed power lines created the initial heat and sparks for the fires to start. The fires would have initially been contained in areas where there was fuel to burn—wood, gas, trees, and wooden houses. But with the hurricane force winds fanning flames (increasing the rate at which oxygen reached the hot fuel) and indeed carrying burning pieces, the fires soon spread.

Fire is ubiquitous in the dried rural parts of the world (Africa, Australia, dried parts of the United States, and China) and they are a regular occurrence. These fire usually burn vegetation. It is, however, the fires that consume coal and tires that are the most polluting.

## TIRE FIRES

The transportation sector is a major contributor to air, water and soil pollution. Fossil fuels are extracted, processed, stored and transported; with spills and leaks inevitable by-products. Vehicles release pollutants from exhaust during their useful lives. They continue to pollute for decades as their remnants end up in junkyards and landfills.

One particularly vexing remnant is the tire. Tires are a ubiquitous product of the era of motor transport. They often end up in massive piles. Although, they are not easily set alight, huge piles of burning tires are not uncommon in our society. Such fires produce a lot of smoke (uncombusted and incompletely combusted material) and produce a host of toxic gases such as CO, sulfur dioxide, and PM made up of soot (carbon) and aromatic compounds following the breakdown of butadiene, a major component of tires. There have been some notable tire fires worldwide: notably, on August 21, 1999 in Sycamore, Ohio, an estimated 25 million burned for 30 h and caused significant environmental damage. The fire was extinguished by covering it with dirt; in 1989 in Powys, Wales a fire involving about 10 million tires burnt for at least 15 years.

## COAL MINE FIRES

A coal mine fire is a smoldering fire, often underground or in a deposit above ground. They smolder because of the lack of sufficient oxygen. They are a serious problem from many aspects: economic (burning a vital commodity), environmental (emitting vast amounts of greenhouse gases [notably $CH_4$ and $CO_2$] and bioaccumulating compounds [e.g., mercury]), dangerous (result in subsidences), and toxic (oxides of sulfur, CO, and aerosols). They are very difficult to extinguish, especially the underground fires. Internationally, there are probably many hundreds of coal fires presently burning, and countries such as Australia, Canada, China, Germany, India, Indonesia, New Zealand, Norway, South Africa, and the United States have documented details of ongoing fires. It has been estimated that these fires contribute to at least 3% of the world's annual emissions. Coal fires are also discussed in Chapters 3 and 8.

## INDIRECT EFFECT: FORMATION OF TOXIC SUBSTANCES

Fire is actually just a very fast type of oxidation known as combustion. The manner in which substances form during combustion is dependent on a number of factors, including temperature, presence of precursor compounds, and the available sites for sorption. For example, complete or efficient combustion (thermal oxidation)

$$(CH)_x + O_2 \rightarrow CO_2 + H_2O \tag{7.10}$$

Combustion is actually the combination of $O_2$ in the presence of heat (as in burning fuel), producing $CO_2$ and $H_2O$ during complete combustion of organic compounds, such as the combustion of octane

$$C_8H_{18}(l) + 17O_2(g) \rightarrow 8CO_2(g) + 9H_2O(g) \tag{7.11}$$

Combustion may also result in the production of molecular nitrogen ($N_2$) when nitrogen-containing organics are burned, such as in the combustion of methylamine

$$4CH_3NH_2(l) + 9O_2(g) \rightarrow 4CO_2(g) + 10H_2O(g) + 2N_2(g) \tag{7.12}$$

In addition, fires change the chemical species of stored substances, often making them more hazardous and products of incomplete combustion, such as polycyclic aromatic hydrocarbons (PAHs), dioxins, furans, and CO. Analysis of environmental pollutants is dependent on the species. Some of the methods employed are listed in Table 7.2. A typical HPLC trace is shown in Figure 7.5.

TABLE 7.2    Analytical Methods Used to Determine the Presence and to Quantify Concentrations of Substances in the Environment

| Method | Description | Applications |
|---|---|---|
| A: Inorganic species | | |
| 1. Atomic absorption spectroscopy (AAS) | A solution containing the element to be analyzed is sucked into a flame or placed in a pyrolytic carbon furnace. At ca. 1000 °C, energy is absorbed at characteristic frequencies. Comparison with standard solutions gives the concentration of the species | A whole variety of elements can be analyzed, e.g., arsenic, cadmium, chromium, lead, mercury, selenium, vanadium, and zinc. The correct preparation of the sample and correction for background interference are important. The technique is widely used in South Africa and is relatively cheap |
| 2. Atomic emission spectroscopy (AES) | The technique uses similar principles to AAS, except a plasma is used to heat the sample to ca. 2500 °C, and the emission of energy is monitored | Similar elements can be analyzed to AAS but usually with greater sensitivity and less interferences. It can also be more readily adapted for sequential analysis of many species in the same sample. The instrument can cost up to 10 times those used for AAS |
| 3. X-ray fluorescence spectroscopy (XRF) | Measurement of the secondary X-rays or fluorescent radiation emitted after bombarding a target material with primary X-rays gives quantitative information on the composition of the material | The rapid analysis of elements from sodium to uranium can be done routinely from 0.1% and above. Lighter elements down to boron can be determined with the appropriate attachments. It is widely used for the rapid elemental analysis of solid wastes, e.g., ash |
| 4. Ion chromatography | Separation of positive ions (cations) or negative ions (anions) is achieved by passing a solution through special cation- or anion-exchange resins. The ions can be detected by conductivity after chemical suppression or by using special eluents and with UV/visible and electrochemical detectors | The rapid multicomponent analysis of anions, e.g., fluoride, chloride, nitrate, nitrite, and sulphate, or cations, e.g., sodium, potassium, calcium, and magnesium, can be achieved. Heavy metal ions such as iron, cobalt, and nickel and their complex ions plus species such as arsenate and fatty acid anions can also be analyzed |

*Continued*

TABLE 7.2    Analytical Methods Used to Determine the Presence and to Quantify Concentrations of Substances in the Environment—Cont'd

| Method | Description | Applications |
|---|---|---|
| 5. Wet methods | Traditional analytical techniques such as titrimetric, gravimetric, and colorimetric analyses | Methods exist for the analysis of many elements and their compounds. These methods can be accomplished by relatively unskilled personnel and are well suited to ad hoc analyses without the need for expensive equipment |
| B: Organic species | | |
| 6. Organic indicator analysis | Chemical oxygen demand (COD): Total organic carbon is measured by oxidation with chromic acid | All methods are widely used and give a gross measure of the organic content. The results must be interpreted with caution. The tests should be compared to each other for a better understanding of the nature of the organic content |
| | Biological oxygen demand (BOD): Total biodegradable carbon and sometimes the oxidizable nitrogen | |
| | Total organic carbon (TOC): Total carbon including inorganic carbon dioxide, bicarbonate, and carbonate measured as carbon dioxide | |
| | Dissolved organic carbon (DOC): Similar to TOC | |
| | Total organic halogen (TOX): All organic halogen compounds are converted to chloride, bromide, and iodide and analyzed by conventional methods | |
| | Permanganate value (PV): Similar to COD, except that permanganate is used under less rigorous conditions | |
| 7. Gas chromatography (GC) | The organic components of a waste are split into their individual components by vaporizing and passing the resulting gas through a column of material which has a different affinity for each compound. They are detected as they come off the column and identified by comparison with a standard or by a mass spectrometer or mass selective detector | The procedure can only be applied to those species which are volatile. Thousands of compounds can be analyzed including aromatics, solvents, halogenated compounds including PCBs and dioxins, organic acids and bases, and aliphatic compounds |
| 8. High-performance liquid chromatography (HPLC) | The principles are similar to IC and GC with the organic being in the liquid phase and being a neutral species. Detection of the individual components by UV/visible spectroscopy, fluorescence, and electrochemical means | A technique that lacks the general versatility of GC but is finding increasing application in the analysis of many organic compounds including polynuclear aromatic hydrocarbons and large molecules |

Source: South African Department of Water Affairs and Forestry. Waste management series. http://www.dwaf.gov.za/dir_wqm/docs/Pol_Hazardous.pdf; 2005 [accessed April 17, 2005].

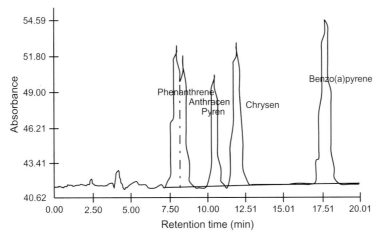

**FIGURE 7.5** Chromatogram of five polycyclic aromatic hydrocarbons (PAHs), determined using reverse-phase high-performance liquid chromatography, a 25-cm × 4.6-mm inside diameter stainless steel column packed with 6-μm DuPont Zorbax ODS sorbent. The mobile phase was 85% acetonitrile and 15% water mixture (by volume). The detection wavelength was in the ultraviolet range (254 nm). Analyte injection volume = 10 μL, with a retention time (RT) range of 7-18 min. *Source: U.S. Occupational Safety and Health Administration.* Sampling and analytical methods, coal tar pitch volatiles (CTPV), coke oven emissions (COE), and selected polynuclear aromatic hydrocarbons (PAHs); 2005.

Products of incomplete combustion can be either well-known and all too common, such as CO, or exotic and complex, such as the dioxins. Chlorinated dioxins have 75 different forms and there are 135 different chlorinated furans, depending on the number and arrangement of chlorine atoms on the molecules. The compounds can be separated into groups that have the same number of chlorine atoms attached to the furan or dioxin ring. Each form varies in its chemical, physical, and toxicological characteristics (see Figure 7.6).

Disasters involving dioxins are of two types: those released during a fire, such as the World Trade Center fires, or from dioxin-laden substances, such as the wastes buried in Love Canal or the oils sprayed in Times Beach. Dioxins form during combustion processes and are not intentionally synthesized for any other reason than for scientific investigation, e.g., to make analytical standards for testing. The most toxic form is the 2,3,7,8-tetrachlorodibenzo-*p*-dioxin (TCDD) isomer. Other isomers with the 2,3,7,8 configuration are also considered to have higher toxicity than the dioxins and furans with different chlorine atom arrangements. Incinerators of chlorinated wastes represent the most common environmental sources of dioxins, accounting for about 95% of the volume. The emission of dioxins and furans from combustion processes may follow three general formation pathways. The first occurs when the fuel material already contains dioxins and/or furans and a fraction of these compounds survives thermal breakdown mechanisms and volatilizes. This is not considered to account for a large volume of dioxin released to the environment, but it may account for the production of dioxin-like, coplanar polychlorinated biphenyls (PCBs).

Dioxins can also be formed from the thermal breakdown and molecular rearrangement of precursor compounds, such as the chlorinated benzenes, chlorinated phenols (such as pentachlorophenol (PCP)), and PCBs, which are chlorinated aromatic compounds with structural

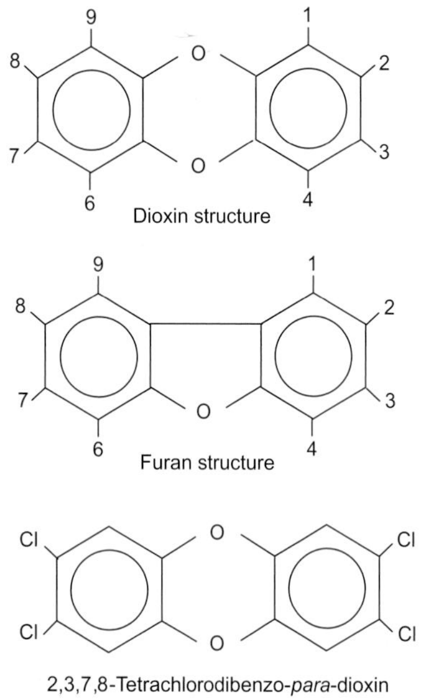

FIGURE 7.6 Molecular structures of dioxins and furans. Bottom structure is of the most toxic dioxin congener, tetrachlorodibenzo-*para*-dioxin (TCDD), formed by the substitution of chlorine for hydrogen atoms at positions 2, 3, 7, and 8 on the molecule.

resemblances to the chlorinated dioxin and furan molecules. Dioxins appear to form after the precursor has condensed and adsorbed onto the surface of particles, such as fly ash. This is a heterogeneous process, i.e., the reaction occurs in more than one physical phase (in this case, in the solid and gas phases). The active sorption sites on the particles allow for the chemical reactions, which are catalyzed by the presence of inorganic chloride compounds and ions sorbed to the particle surface. The process occurs within the temperature range 250-450 °C, so most of the dioxin formation under the precursor mechanism occurs away from the high temperature of the fire, where the gases and smoke derived from combustion of the organic materials have cooled.

Dioxins can also form from simpler compounds that contain the elements comprising the dioxin molecule. This is known as *de novo* formation. Generally, these reactions can involve numerous halogenated compounds such as polyvinylchloride as well as nonhalogenated organic compounds such as petroleum products, nonchlorinated plastics (polystyrene), cellulose, and lignin (wood), which are common building materials and which were likely present in the Chester fire. Other substances, e.g., coal and inorganic compounds such as particulate carbon, and hydrogen chloride gas can provide the necessary chemical compositions for dioxin formation under the right conditions. Whatever *de novo* compounds are involved, however, the process needs a chlorine donor (a molecule that "donates" a chlorine atom to the precursor molecule). This leads to the formation and chlorination of a chemical intermediate that is a precursor. The reaction steps after this precursor is formed can be identical to the precursor mechanism discussed in the previous paragraph.

*De novo* formation of dioxins and furans may involve even more fundamental substances than those moieties mentioned above. For example, dioxins may be generated[10] by heating of carbon particles absorbed with mixtures of magnesium-aluminum silicate complexes when the catalyst copper chloride ($CuCl_2$) is present (see Table 7.3 and Figure 7.7). The *de novo* formation of chlorinated dioxins and furans from the oxidation of carbonaceous particles seems to occur at around 300 °C. Other chlorinated benzenes, chlorinated biphenyls, and chlorinated naphthalene compounds are also generated by this type of mechanism.

TABLE 7.3   *De Novo* Formation of Chlorinated Dioxins and Furans After Heating Mg-Al Silicate, 4% Charcoal, 7% Cl, 1% $CuCl_2 \cdot H_2O$ at 300 °C

| | Concentrations (ng g$^{-1}$) | | | | |
| | Reaction time (h) | | | | |
| Compound | 0.25 | 0.5 | 1 | 2 | 4 |
|---|---|---|---|---|---|
| Tetrachlorodioxin | 2 | 4 | 14 | 30 | 100 |
| Pentachlorodioxin | 110 | 120 | 250 | 490 | 820 |
| Hexachlorodioxin | 730 | 780 | 1600 | 2200 | 3800 |
| Heptachlorodioxin | 1700 | 1840 | 3500 | 4100 | 6300 |
| Octachlorodioxin | 800 | 1000 | 2000 | 2250 | 6000 |
| Total chlorinated dioxins | 3342 | 3744 | 7364 | 9070 | 17,020 |
| Tetrachlorofuran | 240 | 280 | 670 | 1170 | 1960 |
| Pentachlorofuran | 1360 | 1670 | 3720 | 5550 | 8300 |
| Hexachlorofuran | 2500 | 3350 | 6240 | 8900 | 14,000 |
| Heptachlorofuran | 3000 | 3600 | 5500 | 6700 | 9800 |
| Octachlorofuran | 1260 | 1450 | 1840 | 1840 | 4330 |
| Total chlorinated furans | 8360 | 10,350 | 17,970 | 24,160 | 38,390 |

*Source: Stieglitz L, Zwick G, Beck J, Bautz H, Roth W. Chemosphere 1989;19:283.*

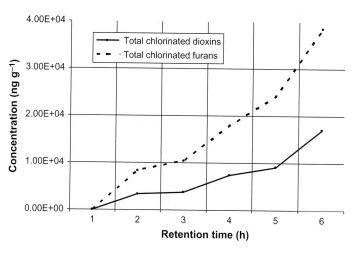

FIGURE 7.7   *De novo* formation of chlorinated dioxins and furans after heating Mg-Al silicate, 4% charcoal, 7% Cl, 1% $CuCl_2 \cdot H_2O$ at 300 °C. *Source: Stieglitz L, Zwick G, Beck J, Bautz H, Roth W.* Chemosphere *1989;19:283.*

The presence of dioxins must always be considered during and after a fire. Also, since dioxin and dioxin-like compounds are lipophilic (fat soluble) and persistent,[11] they accumulate in soils, sediments, and organic matter and can persist in solid and hazardous waste disposal sites.[12] These compounds are semivolatile, so they may migrate away from these sites and be transported in the atmosphere either as aerosols (solid and liquid phases) or as gases (the portion of the compound that volatilizes). Therefore, great care must be taken during any hazardous waste removal and remediation efforts not to unwittingly cause releases from soil and sediments via volatilization or via perturbations, such as an environmental cleanup after a fire, a leaking tank, or drum removal operations.

## INDIRECT IMPACT: TRANSPORT

In addition to the formation of toxic substances, fire can play a large role in freeing and releasing toxic substances. Fires are often associated with exposures to asbestos, lead (Pb), and other toxic components of the burning structure. For example, asbestos was released from the World Trade Center as the structures fell and disintegrated but could also have been released by the fires and carried in the smoke plumes. The asbestos was not formed thermally, but the fire served to loosen the fibers after the combustible materials were destroyed.

Another group of chemicals that can be produced by fires and transported long distances are the persistent organic pollutants (see Chapter 11). For example, dioxins are released into the air by intentional and unintentional combustion, including commercial, municipal, or medical waste incineration, fuel burning, and garbage burning. Dioxins have also been detected at low concentrations in cigarette smoke, home-heating systems, and exhaust gases from cars. These compounds are produced from the combustion of substances that contain chlorine, e.g., plastics, wood treated with PCP, pesticide treated waste producing dioxins, as well as from forest fires and volcanic eruptions.[13]

Fires have been the part of many environmental disasters in terms of direct destruction and the release of toxic substances. Some fires have been so intense and extensive that they have been environmental disasters in and of themselves. Many fires are triggering agents to other environmental and public health disasters. Thus, fire prevention and management are necessary components of any disaster contingency plan, as well as part of any emergency response program.

## References and Notes

1. Page SE, Siegert F, Rieley JO, Boehm H-DV, Jaya A, Limin S. The amount of carbon released from peat and forest fires in Indonesia during 1997. *Nature* 2002;**420**:61–5.
2. http://www.en.wikipedia.org/wiki/Collapse_of_the_World_Trade_Center [accessed December 1, 2011].
3. National Construction Safety Team. *Executive summary. Final report on the collapse of the World Trade Center Towers.* NIST; 2005 September.
4. Gross JL, McAllister TP. *Structural fire response and probable collapse sequence of the World Trade Center Towers. Federal building and fire safety investigation of the World Trade Center Disaster NIST NCSTAR 1—6.* National Institute of Standards and Technology; *http://wtc.nist.gov/NCSTAR1/PDF/NCSTAR%201-6.pdf*; 2004 [accessed December 1, 2011].

5. Wilkinson T. *World Trade Center—some engineering aspects.* http://www.civil.usyd.edu.au/wtc.shtml; 2006 [accessed December 1, 2011].

6. Trade Centre Hit by 6-Floor Fire. *The New York Times* 1975; February 14.

7. Trade Centre Hit by 6—Floor Fire. http://www.nytimes.com/1975/02/14/nyregion/14WTC.html; 2008 [retrieved February 15, 2012].

8. The Emergency Response Operations. *Federal building and fire safety investigation of the World Trade Center Disaster.* NIST; 2005 October.

9. National Institute of Standards and Testing. *World Trade Center Disaster.* http://wtc.nist.gov/pubs/NISTNCSTAR1-8.pdf; 2011 [Retrieved 15 February 2012].

10. Stieglitz L, Zwick G, Beck J, Bautz H, Roth W. Carbonaceous particles in fly ash: a source for the de nova synthesis of organochloro compounds. *Chemosphere* 1989;**19**:283–90.

11. Hites R. *Atmospheric transport and deposition of polychlorinated dibenzo-p-dioxins and dibenzofurans.* Research Triangle Park, NC; 1991. EPA/600/3-91/002.

12. Koester C, Hites R. Wet and dry deposition of chlorinated dioxins and furans. *Environ Sci Technol* 1992;**26**:1375–82.

13. Minnesota Department of Health. *Facts about dioxins.* http://www.health.state.mn.us/divs/eh/risk/chemhazards/dioxins.html; 2006 [accessed on March 9, 2012].

# CHAPTER

# 8

# Climate

Our planet Earth is amazingly balanced in its ability to support life. It is the right distance from our major energy source, the sun. It is tipped at 23.5°, giving us our seasonal changes; it revolves around the sun in 1 year. And, it has a wonderful balance of water and air in the right concentrations and in the right places with respect to whether an organism is terrestrial like us humans or aquatic like the plankton or blue whales. Life on earth survives within this narrow range of temperature, pressure, solar radiation, concentration of atmospheric gases, and concentrations of elements in the water and soils. Any significant changes to these conditions will result in disaster. Thus, any perceived change to the atmosphere is met with widespread fear.

## GLOBAL CLIMATE CHANGE

The earth in is dynamic equilibrium as it continually absorbs and emits electromagnetic radiation. The sun and the earth are both black body radiation emitters, i.e., they emit electromagnetic radiation as opaque and nonreflective bodies. The radiation from these bodies is based on the Stefan's and Wein's laws which state that the total energy emitted per unit time, integrated over all wavelengths is proportion to the fourth power of the Kelvin temperature, $(T/K)^4$, and that the maximum wavelength ($\lambda_{max}$) varies inversely with the Kelvin temperature, that is, $\lambda_{max} \propto (T/K)^{-1}$. As a result, the sun emits UV/visible radiation with a peak at 500 nm which is based on the sun's surface temperature ($T_{sun}$) = 5780 K. The earth's average temperature ($T$) = 290 K, and its black body emission curve peaks at about 10,000 nm, which is 20 time longer than the sun's peak radiation. The radiation from the earth is in the range of about 4000-25,000 nm ($4 \times 10^{-6}$-$25 \times 10^{-6}$ m) and is in the infrared (IR) region of the electromagnetic spectrum. Figure 8.1 shows the IR emission spectrum with the adsorption bands at 12 and 17 µm, at 9.6 µm, and at $\lambda < 8$ µm for $CO_2$, ozone ($O_3$), and $H_2O$, respectively. These three gases are the primary greenhouse gases (GHGs). The absorption of the IR energy by the CO, OO, and HO bonds of the three GHG molecules in effect retains heat which would otherwise disappear into space, and it is this retention of heat that warms the planet. This figure is a wonderful physical demonstration of the adsorption of IR by the small amount of $CO_2$ in the atmosphere.

In the 1970s, we recall the concern among earth scientists about global cooling. This is a legitimate concern, since large amounts of sulfates and particulate matter (which with the

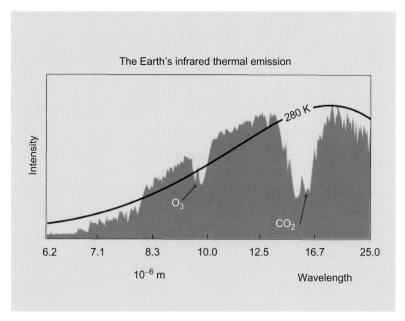

The Earth's infrared thermal emission

FIGURE 8.1    The Earth's infrared thermal emission spectrum. *Taken from: http://physicsforums.com/showthread.php? t=243619.*

water vapor in the air formed aerosols) were and still are being released into the atmosphere, mainly from the combustion of fossil fuels. Indeed, the particles and gases absorb certain wavelengths of incoming solar radiation, so modelers were predicting a cooling effect[1] on top of the GHG global warming. The cooling effect was in fact reducing some of global warming. Since the 1980s, many scientists have accepted that human activities play a significant role in warming of the planet (Union of Concerned Scientists, 2011). Global surface temperatures increased 0.74 °C between 1906 and 2005. Eleven of the 12 years between 1993 and 2006 had the highest recorded surface temperatures since 1850.[2] The years 2005 and 2010 were the hottest on record (National Oceanic and Atmospheric Administration, 2011). Sea levels have risen about 1.8 mm per year since 1961, and 3.1 mm per year since 1993, due to melting ice from polar ice sheets and glaciers. The production of GHGs, chiefly carbon dioxide ($CO_2$) and methane ($CH_4$), is largely responsible for the increase in global temperatures. GHGs warm the Earth by preventing solar radiation from being reflected into outer space. Increased concentrations of GHGs in the atmosphere are associated with global warming. Anthropogenic GHGs, which have risen steadily since 1750, increased 70% from 1970 to 2004. Numerous human activities, including transportation, manufacturing, urban development, indoor heating, electric power generation, cement manufacture, and agriculture, produce GHGs.

If no actions are taken to stabilize or reduce emissions of anthropogenic GHGs, global temperatures and sea levels may continue to rise. According to various estimates, average global temperatures can be expected to rise between 1.1 and 6.4 °C in the next century, and sea levels will rise between 0.18 and 0.59 m, unless steps are taken to stabilize GHG emissions. Global temperatures and sea levels will continue to rise even if GHG emissions remain at current levels, due to time lags between GHG levels and geological and biological responses, such as removal of $CO_2$ from the air by plants.

Much of the debate within the scientific community has involved two aspects of climate change. First, how much of the observed and projected mean global temperature increase is the result of human activities (anthropogenic sources of GHGs)? Second, how certain are we in estimating future global climate? We acknowledge this debate and are not ignoring recent controversies regarding the data and models being used. In fact, global climate change is similar to other modeling efforts in that accuracy of prediction depends on the quality and representativeness of the data and the algorithms. Errors in assumptions and improper weighting of variables will lead to incorrect predictions. Thus, policy makers are looking to engineers and scientists to evaluate the state of the science for predicting future climate. Unfortunately, climate is a function of many variables, and the contribution of each variable is not known with very much precision. Only more data over longer time spells will help in defining the role of each variable.

Presently, environmental and health policies are made from two perspectives: evidence-based risk assessments and precaution. Risk assessments require information on both the hazard and the likelihood of exposure to that hazard. Thus, if this information is scarce or unreliable, the risk assessment is useless at best and dangerous at worst, since it either underestimates or overestimates the risk. For problems that may affect large numbers of people, large geographic areas, and/or which are irreversible, precaution is in order. This is the basis for factors of safety in engineering design. Therefore, precaution applies to estimates of global climate change (see Figure 8.2).

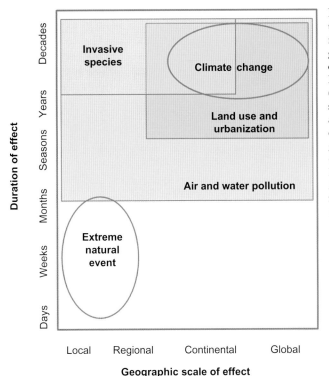

FIGURE 8.2    The response to stressors has temporal and spatial dependencies. Near-field stressors can result from a spill or emergency situation. At the other extreme, global climate change can result from chronic releases of greenhouse gases with expansive (planetary) impacts in direct proportion to significant changes in global climate (temperature increases in the troposphere and oceans, shifting biomes, sea level rise, and migratory patterns). *Resnik DB, Vallero DA. Geoengineering: an idea whose time has come? Earth Sci Clim Change S1:001. doi:10.4172/2157-7617.S1-001;* based on drawing by Betsy Smith, US Environmental Protection Agency (used with permission).

# GREENHOUSE GASES

Predicting whether climate change will become a disaster depends on sufficiently precise and accurate answers to two questions. First, are changes in climate occurring at rate different from the expected norms? Second, if changes are occurring to what extent are these changes the result of human activities? Pollution releases are indeed indicators of human activities. Some pollutants are the same as those released from natural sources, but due to human activities, these are found in higher quantities or in different places than would be released by natural systems. For example, forests release formaldehyde, but at much lower concentrations than certain manufacturing facilities or even from furniture and other household items. Other pollutants would not be produced by natural systems, such as many of the toxic organic compounds, like polychlorinated biphenyls (PCBs).

GHGs fall into both categories. In fact, the two principal GHGs, carbon dioxide ($CO_2$) and methane ($CH_4$), are naturally produced gases. Indeed, $CO_2$ is not only the product of photosynthesis and respiration (natural) but also the product of combustion (natural and anthropogenic). Likewise, $CH_4$ is a product of microbial degradation, which is part of the decomposition components of food webs and volcanic emissions (natural) as well as released from livestock and other feeding operations and manufacturing facilities (anthropogenic). Other GHGs are entirely anthropogenic, such as the chlorofluorocarbons (CFCs).

Based on atmospheric measurements, there indeed has been a continuous increase in the concentration of atmospheric $CO_2$ in recent centuries (see Figure 8.3). At the beginning of rapid industrialization at the end of the eighteenth century, the mean global $CO_2$ concentration is estimated to have been 280 ppmv (parts per million measured as volumes). In 2011, the mean concentration had increased to 392 ppmv. This increase correlates with a mean global increase in temperature of the earth rising to about 0.8 °C over this time period (see Figure 8.4).[3]

Mean GHG concentrations, particularly $CO_2$, are highly correlated with mean global temperature. Correlation is not necessarily causation, but it does add weight of evidence that GHGs are contributing to climate change (our second question). It is impossible to stop the production of $CO_2$ for 10 years to see if it makes a difference. However, the correlation between the temperature rise and the increase in $CO_2$ concentration is remarkable (especially over the past 100 years) and is supported by the IPCC 2007 and 2011 reports (see Figure 8.4).

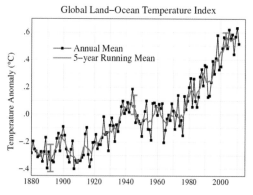

FIGURE 8.3   The $CO_2$ concentration in the atmosphere. *Taken from http://www.our-energy.com/non_renewable_energy_sources.html.*

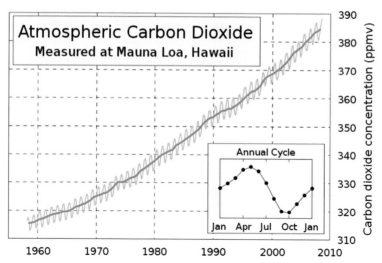

FIGURE 8.4   The correlation of the earth's average temperature and the $CO_2$ concentration. *Taken from http://www.climatechoices.org.uk/pages/cchange3.htm.*

## Radiative Forcing

Radiative forcing is an important feature of GHGs, i.e., the influence that this gas has on the balance of incoming and outgoing energy in the earth-atmosphere system and is an index of the importance of the factor as a potential climate change mechanism.[4] Thus, forcing is the effectiveness of a particular gas to promote global warming (or cooling, as is the case with aerosols). The gases of most importance in forcing are listed in Table 8.1. Climate change results from natural internal processes and from external forcings. Both are affected by persistent changes in the composition of the atmosphere brought about by changes in land use, release of contaminants, and other human activities.

Radiative forcing can be expressed as the change in the net vertical irradiance within the atmosphere. Radiative forcing is often calculated after allowing for stratospheric temperatures to readjust to radiative equilibrium, while holding all tropospheric properties fixed at their unperturbed values. Commonly, radiative forcing is considered to be the extent to which injecting a unit of a GHG into the atmosphere changes global average temperature, but other factors can affect forcing, as shown in Figures 8.5 and 8.6. Note that these radiant

TABLE 8.1   Relative Forcing of Increased Global Temperature

| Gas | Percentage of relative radiative forcing |
| --- | --- |
| Carbon dioxide, $CO_2$ | 64 |
| Methane, $CH_4$ | 19 |
| Halocarbons (predominantly Chlorofluorocarbons, CFCs) | 11 |
| Nitrous oxide, $N_2O$ | 6 |

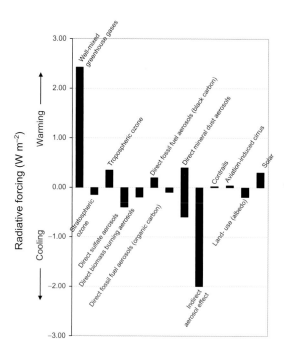

FIGURE 8.5 The global mean radiative forcing (Watts per square meter, W m$^{-2}$) of the climate system for the year 2000, relative to 1750. The International Panel on Climate Change (IPCC) has applied a "level of scientific understanding" (LOSU) index is accorded to each forcing (see Table 8.2). This represents the Panel's subjective judgment about the reliability of the forcing estimate, involving factors such as the assumptions necessary to evaluate the forcing, the degree of knowledge of the physical/chemical mechanisms determining the forcing, and the uncertainties surrounding the quantitative estimate of the forcing. *Data from IPCC. Climate change 2001: the scientific basis. Chapter 6—radiative forcing of climate change; 2001.*

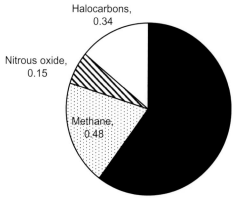

FIGURE 8.6 Relative contribution of well-mixed greenhouse gases to the +2.43 W m$^{-2}$ radiative forcing shown in Figure 8.6. *Data from IPCC. Climate change 2001: the scientific basis. Chapter 6—radiative forcing of climate change; 2001.*

gases include halocarbons, with the CFCs, notorious for their role in another atmospheric problem, i.e., destruction of the stratospheric ozone layer.

There is much uncertainty about the effects of the presence of these radiant gases (see Table 8.2), but the overall effect of the composite of gases is well understood. The effectiveness of $CO_2$ as a global warming gas has been known for over 100 years. However, the

TABLE 8.2    Level of Scientific Understanding (LOSU) of Radiative Forcings

| Forcing phenomenon | LOSU |
|---|---|
| Well-mixed greenhouse gases | High |
| Stratospheric $O_3$ | Medium |
| Tropospheric $O_3$ | Medium |
| Direct sulfate aerosols | Low |
| Direct biomass burning aerosols | Very low |
| Direct fossil fuel aerosols (black carbon) | Very low |
| Direct fossil fuel aerosols (organic carbon | Very low |
| Direct mineral dust aerosols | Very low |
| Indirect aerosol effect | Very low |
| Contrails | Very low |
| Aviation-induced cirrus | Very low |
| Land use (albedo) | Very low |
| Solar | Very low |

*Climate Change 2001: The Scientific Basis. Contribution of Working Group I to the Third Assessment Report of the Intergovernmental Panel on Climate Change, Figure 6.6. Cambridge University Press*

first useful measurements of atmospheric $CO_2$ were not taken until 1957. The data from Mauna Loa show that even in the 1950s, the $CO_2$ concentration had increased from the baseline 280 to 315 ppm; this has continued to climb over the past 50 years at a nearly constant rate of about 1.6 ppm per year. The most serious problem with $CO_2$ is that the effects on global temperature due to its greenhouse effect are delayed. Even in the completely impossible scenario of not emitting any new $CO_2$ into the atmosphere, $CO_2$ concentrations will continue to increase from our present 392 ppm to possibly higher than 600 ppm. The effect of this is discussed below.

Overall, total radiative forcings for $CO_2$, $O_3$, $CH_4$, and $N_2O$ are 1.66, 0.30, 0.48, and 0.16 W m$^{-2}$, respectively. The relative global warming potential for $CO_2$, $CH_4$, and $N_2O$ are 1, 25, and 298, respectively, and the concentrations of $CO_2$, $O_3$, $CH_4$, and $N_2O$ in the atmosphere are 392, 0.034, 1.77, and 0.32 ppmv, respectively. The mean $CH_4$ concentration has more than doubled from 0.72 ppmv (in 1750) to its present value but appears to have stabilized over the past decade.

If it is not GHGs causing climate change and global warming, then what is it? The only contenders are solar radiation changes, volcanic activity, and the earth's orbital characteristics.[5] We have put these questions to world expects in these fields, and the conclusion is that although these are contributing factors to global change, the paramount factor is most likely to be anthropogenic GHGs.[6] What is needed is a sensitivity analysis, i.e., what are the weights of all factors in contributing to the existing condition and how will they conjoin in the future?

# CONSEQUENCES OF GLOBAL WARMING

Global warming is expected to have numerous adverse consequences for human health and wellbeing and the environment, such as:

- increased flooding in coastal areas, with potentially devastating impacts on coastal cities and island nations;
- increased frequency and strength of tropical storms, which produce flooding, property damage, and loss of life;
- flooding in regions at higher altitudes, due to increased precipitation, and droughts in subtropical regions, due to decreased precipitation (National Aeronautics and Space Administration, 2010);
- increased risk of famine and malnutrition in drought-stricken areas (National Aeronautics and Space Administration, 2010);
- decreased availability of clean drinking water in areas affected by droughts (National Aeronautics and Space Administration, 2010);
- increased forest fires as a result of drought and heat;
- higher mortality and morbidity due to heatstroke and heat prostration during the summer months;
- increased prevalence of water-borne and mosquito-borne diseases due to flooding (Interagency Working Group on Climate Change and Health, 2010);
- increased ocean algal blooms, which will have adverse effects on fish population and human health Interagency (Working Group on Climate Change and Health, 2010).

# IS IT A DISASTER?

Scientists must be objective. There is debate about what to do with the information. Weather patterns have not been universally observed to have changed, and there is no clear indication of a major shift in the frequency and magnitude of El Niño events.[7] However, there have been recent changes in the movements of birds as revealed from breeding bird surveys which could have been due to climate change but like many migrations and movements there could well be many other parameters acting as drivers.[8]

The marine pelagic region (open sea zone down to about 11 km depth) is the largest ecological system on the planet and occupies 71% of the earth's surface and a major share of the earth's biosphere. According to M. Edwards of the Marine Institute of the University of Plymouth, UK, there is a large body of observable evidence to suggest that many pelagic ecosystems both physically and biologically are responding to regional climate changes, largely because of warmer air and warmer sea surface temperatures. Some of the strongest evidence comes from plankton surveys. One study showed that over a 50-year period, there was a northerly movement of a key plankton group (calanoid copepods) in the NE Atlantic at a rate of between 200 and 250 km per decade. Also many types of fish in the northern distribution boundaries of the North Sea have shifted northward. One of the largest biogeographical shifts ever observed for fish species is the dramatic increase and subsequent northerly spread of the Snake Pipefish. Once confined to south and west of the UK, it is now found as far north as the Barents Sea and Spitzbergen. Furthermore, some fishes are now moving to deeper water in response to climate change. This is analogous to the shift of some terrestrial species to move to higher altitudes in alpine environments.[9]

Coral reefs are being affected by climate change; in particular, they are being bleached by rising sea temperatures. This loss of habitat is having an effect on associated organisms.[10]

The intertidal region between the high water mark and the lowest level exposed during the low spring tides is particularly sensitive to temperature changes and rising sea levels. The intertidal invertebrates and algae have responded to global warming by moving from the warmer latitudes toward the cooler poles. In general, the rate of advance of the northerly species is not as advanced as the southern species.[11]

Plants are responding to climate change through changing phenology and distribution patterns with species tending to disperse toward cooler areas.[12]

The temperature of the sea is rising and is evident across the top 700 m; this is happening in all oceans. The warming bears no resemblance to a signal forced by solar or volcanic activity. But it does fit closely to modeled anthropogenic forcing signals.[13]

There is no clear evidence that major sea currents have started to decrease. This might be because measurement programs have only recently been set up.[14] The oceans have been absorbing a quarter to a third of the increased $CO_2$ and have been buffering the resultant acid. This is apparent from the measured surface ocean concentrations of $CO_2$, $HCO_3^-$ and $CO_3^-$, and pH.[15]

One last and potentially disastrous result of global warming is the effect on insect species. Changes are occurring both spatially and temporally as a direct result of changing climate. In addition, trophic cascades can occur in a way that changes in the interactions between herbivores and their host plants affect higher trophic levels and changes between predators and herbivorous prey can affect primary producers.[16]

There is also evidence of health effects associated with warming, including:

- increased prevalence of some infectious diseases as a result of changing geographic distributions of species that transmit pathogens to humans (Interagency Working Group on Climate Change and Health, 2010);
- increased respiratory problems due to higher levels of ozone and allergens (Interagency Working Group on Climate Change and Health, 2010).

Again, the key uncertainty in these observation is how much can be attributed to climate change resulting from human activities. Indeed, there is clearly a potential major disaster. Certainly, reducing GHG emissions is one of the important actions that can be taken. The good news is that these reductions would have ecological and public health advantages, notwithstanding climate change. The bad news is that any action, even if taken immediately, will not show profound effects for some time. Our grandchildren will be affected by our actions and, frighteningly, by our failure to act. This supports the argument for a prudent and precautionary approach to address the release GHGs.

# RESPONDING TO CLIMATE CHANGE

There are two basic policy options for responding to the problem of global warming: mitigation and adaptation.[17] Mitigation includes efforts to prevent or minimize climate change, including:

- regulations to control GHG emissions, notably $CO_2$. These include direct controls, such as emission limits at each source, and indirect methods, such as carbon taxes or cap-and-trade systems, in which the total level of $CO_2$ in a nation is capped and large polluters purchase rights to emit $CO_2$, which can be traded;
- tax breaks and other incentives for developing and using alternatives to fossil fuels, such as wind, solar, hydroelectric, geothermal, and nuclear power;
- regulations mandating higher fuel economy standards for automobiles and increased energy efficiency for appliances, heating and cooling systems, and electric lighting[17];
- public support for mass transit, carpooling, biking, and other forms of transportation that save energy;
- telecommuting, teleconferencing, and videoconferencing;
- protection of forests, which remove $CO_2$ from the atmosphere;
- developing trees that are more efficient at removing $CO_2$ from the atmosphere and storing carbon in biomass[18];
- reduction in the consumption of meat, since the livestock industry is a significant source of GHGs (particularly $CO_2$ and methane [$CH_4$]) and contributes to deforestation[19];
- pollution prevention and sustainable design of products, where certain processes (e.g., combustion) are minimized or eliminated[20];
- control of population growth and development.[21]

Adaptation includes steps taken to adjust to or compensate for the effects of global warming, such as making preparations for tropical storms, floods, and heat waves; protecting coastal regions from rising sea levels; developing and growing drought-resistant crops; increasing drinking water supplies; and enhancing infectious diseases surveillance and response.[22]

Thus far, efforts to mitigate global warming have been largely ineffective.[23] Although policymakers and citizens have understood the importance of responding to the problem of climate change for at least two decades, global GHG emissions from human sources have continued to increase at roughly the same rate in the 2000s as they did in the 1990s and show no signs of abating unless some decisive steps are taken.

## Difficulties with Climate Change Mitigation

There are a number of reasons why mitigating global warming has proven to be very difficult. First, most of the mitigation strategies that have been proposed thus far require significant changes in human behavior. Individuals must be willing to drive less, to use fuel efficient cars, to seek alternatives to fossil fuels, to save energy, to eat less meat, and to control population and development. Though some may be willing to do these things, others may not. Taking the steps necessary to mitigate global warming requires sacrifices that they many people are not willing to make. There is a cruel irony here similar to case of the Prisoner's dilemma: by acting according to what they perceive to be in their own interests, individuals may produce an outcome that is actually not in their interests. To produce an outcome that is maximally beneficial to all, individuals must be willing to cooperate, but many are not willing to do this.[24]

The prison's analogy applies to global problems in a number of ways. The population that benefits from a number of the direct impacts of climate change can be distinct from those that must mitigate. For example, rising sea level may not have much meaning for a person living in Kansas, who is asked to eat less meat, but would have a significant impact on islanders who live just above sea level. Ironically, many of the islanders' lifestyles contribute very little to androgenic GHG releases. Another similarity is that the cause and effect are temporally separated.

The second factor diminishing the utility of mitigation is the potential of concomitant adverse social impacts. Proposed policies may have adverse economic impacts that nations are not willing to accept. Cap-and-trade systems or carbon taxes would increase energy costs until alternative sources of energy become economical, which could take decades. Increases in energy costs would affect the price of transportation, manufacturing, food, health care, and many other goods and services. These price increases could contribute to inflation, and undermine economic growth and lead to job losses.[25] According to the Heritage Foundation, a cap-and-trade system for control $CO_2$ emissions would lead to a $4.8 trillion reduction in gross domestic product in the United States and a loss of 3 million manufacturing jobs.[26] Some argue, however, that these adverse economic losses would be offset by gains in new jobs related to alternative energy production as well as the benefits of avoiding a rise in global temperatures.[27] Though it is far from certain that global warming mitigation policies will have the dire economic consequences predicted by some, there may be little political will, especially in these difficult economic times, to embrace policies that could have negative economic impacts.

Third, since climate change is a global problem, effective mitigation requires a high degree of international cooperation, which may be difficult to achieve, especially if countries do not view mitigation as in their collective interests. The Kyoto Protocol is the most significant climate change treaty approved to date. The agreement calls for industrialized nations to reduce their GHG emissions to 5% below 1990 levels through use of a cap-and-trade system for $CO_2$ emissions. Under a cap-and-trade system, $CO_2$ emissions in a country would be capped, and large polluters would purchase emission permits from the government, which they could trade. The working assumption of cap and trade is that a free market in $CO_2$ emissions would encourage investment and innovation concerning $CO_2$ emission control because companies would want to reduce the amount of money they spend on permits. The cap could be gradually lowered over time to reduce overall emissions.[28]

Though 190 nations signed the Kyoto Protocol, the United States did not, due to concerns about its economic impacts and the fact that two other major GHG producers, China and India, also did not sign the treaty.[29] Another key issue has been whether industrialized nations should bear the entire burden of climate change mitigation. Developing nations have argued that they should not have to control their GHG emissions because they contribute a small percentage to the world's total GHG emissions and because they are still trying to develop economically and need to be spared the burden of climate change mitigation rules.

Industrialized nations have argued that all nations, including developing ones, should do their part to mitigate climate change.[30] Though countries are trying to negotiate a new climate change treaty, no new agreement has been reached so far.

Fourth, climate change science has been mired in politics. Global warming skeptics have challenged the scientific consensus concerning climate change. Some have argued that global warming is not really occurring. Others admit that the planet is getting warmer but they argue that human activities are not primarily responsible for global warming.[31] Some admit that global warming is likely occurring and that human activities play a major role and are largely responsible for climate change, but they challenge predictions concerning the impacts of global warming on public health, the economy, and the environment. Much of the skepticism concerning climate change has been fueled by political and economic interests.

## CARBON AND CLIMATE

Living systems both reduce and oxidize carbon. Reduction often takes place in the absence of molecular oxygen ($O_2$), such as in the rumen of cattle, in sludge at the bottom of a lagoon, or in buried detritus on the forest floor. Anaerobic bacteria get their energy by reduction, breaking down organic compounds into methane ($CH_4$) and water.

Conversely, aerobic microbes get their energy from oxidation, forming carbon dioxide ($CO_2$) and water. Plants absorb $CO_2$ for photosynthesis, the process whereby plants convert solar energy into biomass and release $O_2$ as a by-product. Thus, the essential oxygen is actually the waste product of photosynthesis and is derived from carbon-based compounds. Respiration generates carbon dioxide as a waste product of oxidation that takes place in organisms, so there is a balance between green plants' uptake of $CO_2$ and release of $O_2$ in photosynthesis and the uptake of $O_2$ and release of $CO_2$ in respiration by animals, microbes, and other organisms.

Combined with oxygen and hydrogen, carbon forms many biological compounds, including sugars, cellulose, lignin, chitins, alcohols, fats, and esters. Combined with nitrogen, carbon forms alkaloids—naturally occurring amines produced by plants and animals, which combine to form proteins. Combined with sulfur, carbon is the source of antibiotics, proteins, and amino acids. Combined with phosphorus and other elements, carbon forms DNA and RNA, thus creating the chemical codes of life.

Even new technologies are rooted in carbon. For example, nanomaterials are often carbon based, such as carbon-60 ($C_{60}$). Interestingly, these spherical structures consisting of 60 carbon atoms are called fullerenes or Buckyballs, after the famous designer Buckminster Fuller, in honor of his innovative geodesic domes and spheres. Fullerene structures can also include one-atom-thick sheets of carbon, called graphene. These sheets can be rolled into tubes called nanotubes.[32]

Carbon dioxide and methane are two of the most important global GHGs. These are just two of the carbon compounds that are cycled continuously through the environment (see Figure 8.7).

Figure 8.7 demonstrates the importance of sinks and sources of carbon. For example, if carbon can remain sequestered in the soil, roots, sediment, and other compartments, it is not released to the atmosphere. Thus, it cannot have an impact on the greenhouse effect. Even

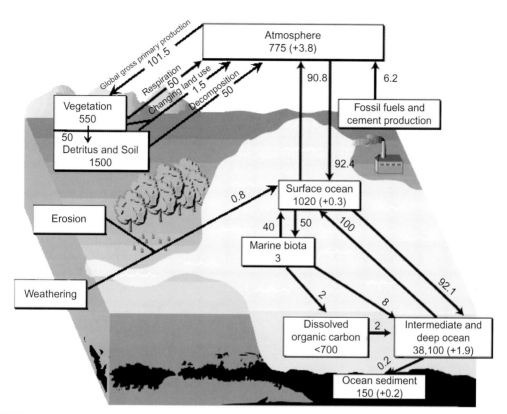

FIGURE 8.7 Global carbon cycle. Carbon pool are boxes, expressed in gigatons (Gt) of carbon (Note: Gt $C = 10^{15}$ g C). Annual increments are expressed in Gt C per year (shown in parentheses). All fluxes indicated by the arrows are expressed in Gt C per year. The inferred net terrestrial uptake of 0.7 Gt C per year considers gross primary production ($\sim$101.5), plant respiration ($\sim$50), decomposition ($\sim$50), and additional removal from the atmosphere directly or indirectly, through vegetation and soil and eventual flow to the ocean through the terrestrial processes of weathering, erosion, and runoff ($\sim$0.8). Net ocean uptake ($\sim$1.6) considers air/sea exchange ($\sim$92.4 gross uptake, $-$90.8 gross release). As the rate of fossil fuel burning increases and $CO_2$ released to the atmosphere, it is expected that the fraction of this C remaining in the atmosphere will increase resulting in a doubling or a tripling of the atmospheric amount in the coming century. *U.S. Department of Energy, Oak Ridge National Laboratory*

relatively small amounts of methane and carbon dioxide can profoundly increase the atmosphere's greenhouse potential.

Since carbon can bond to itself and to other elements in a myriad of ways, it can form single, double, and triple bonds with itself. This makes for millions of possible organic compounds. An organic compound is a compound that includes at least one carbon-to-carbon or carbon-to-hydrogen bond.

Slight changes to an organic molecule can profoundly affect its behavior in the environment. For example, there are large ranges of solubility for organic compounds, depending upon the presence of polar groups in their structure. The addition of an alcohol group to *n*-butane to produce 1-butanol increases the solubility in water several orders of magnitude. This means that an engineer deciding to use an alcohol-based compound in a manufacturing step is making a decision, knowingly or otherwise, that this compound is more likely to end up in the water than if the original, nonhydrolyzed form were used instead. This does not mean that the choice is a bad one. It could be good, since the process also lowers the vapor pressure, the alcohol may be easier to keep from being released from stacks and vents. The key to finding the best approach is to know ahead of time that each choice has distinct consequences. The optimal choice is the one that best fits the problem at hand, in this case, is it better or worse if more of the compound ends up in water.

Organic compounds can be further classified into two basic groups: aliphatics and aromatics. Hydrocarbons are the most fundamental type of organic compound. They contain only the elements carbon and hydrogen. We hear a lot about these compounds in air pollution discussions. In fact, the presence of hydrocarbons is an important part of the formation of smog. For example, places like Los Angeles that have photochemical oxidant smog problems are looking for ways to reduce the amount of hydrocarbons released to the air.

Aliphatic compounds are classified into a few chemical families. Each carbon normally forms four covalent bonds. Alkanes are hydrocarbons that form chains with each link comprised of the carbon. A single link is $CH_4$, methane. The carbon chain length increases with the addition of carbon atoms. For example, ethane's structure is as follows:

$$H-\overset{\overset{\displaystyle H}{|}}{\underset{\underset{\displaystyle H}{|}}{C}}-\overset{\overset{\displaystyle H}{|}}{\underset{\underset{\displaystyle H}{|}}{C}}-H$$

And the protoypical alkane structure is as follows:

$$H-\overset{\overset{\displaystyle H}{|}}{\underset{\underset{\displaystyle H}{|}}{C}} \cdots\cdots \overset{\overset{\displaystyle H}{|}}{\underset{\underset{\displaystyle H}{|}}{C}}-H$$

The alkanes contain a single bond between each carbon atoms and include the simplest organic compound, methane ($CH_4$) and its derivative "chains" such ethane ($C_2H_6$) and butane ($C_4H_{10}$). Alkenes contain at least one double bond between carbon atoms. For example, 1,3-butadiene's structure is $CH_2CHCHCH_2$. The numbers "1" and "3" indicate the position of the double bonds. The alkynes contain triple bonds between carbon atoms, the simplest being ethyne, CHCH, which is commonly known as acetylene (the gas used by welders).

The aromatics are all based upon the six-carbon configuration of benzene ($C_6H_6$). The carbon-carbon bond in this configuration shares more than one electron so that benzene's structure (Figure 8.8) allows for resonance among the double and single bonds, i.e., the actual benzene bonds appear to flip locations. Benzene can be considered as the average of two equally contributing resonance structures.

The term "aromatic" comes from the observation that many compounds derived from benzene were highly fragrant, such as vanilla, wintergreen oil, and sassafras. Aromatic compounds, thus, contain one or more benzene rings. The rings are planar, that is, they

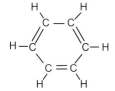

FIGURE 8.8   Benzene structure. The benzene ring is the commonly used condensed form in aromatic compounds.

remain in the same geometric plane as a unit. However, in compounds with more than one ring, such as the highly toxic PCBs, each ring is planar, but the rings may be bound together and may or may not be planar. This is actually a very important property for toxic compounds. It has been shown that some planar aromatic compounds are more toxic than their nonplanar counterparts, possibly because living cells may be more likely to allow planar compounds to bind to them and to produce nucleopeptides that lead to biochemical reactions associated with cellular dysfunctions, such as cancer or endocrine disruption.

Both the aliphatic and aromatic compounds can undergo substitutions of the hydrogen atoms. These substitutions render new properties to the compounds, including changes in solubility, vapor pressure, and toxicity. For example, halogenation (substitution of a hydrogen atom with a halogen) often makes an organic compound much more toxic. For example, trichloroethane is a highly carcinogenic liquid that has been found in drinking water supplies, whereas nonsubstituted ethane is a gas with relatively low toxicity. This is also why one of the means for treating the large number of waste sites contaminated with chlorinated hydrocarbons and aromatic compounds involves dehalogenation techniques.

The important functional groups that are part of many organic compounds are shown in Table 8.3.

Structures of organic compounds can induce very different physical and chemical characteristics as well as changes in the bioaccumulation and toxicity of these compounds. For example, the differences between the estradiol and a testosterone molecule may seem small, but they cause significant differences in the growth and reproduction of animals. The very subtle differences between an estrogen and an androgen, female and male hormones, respectively, can be seen in these structures. Incremental changes to a simple compound, such as ethane, can make for large differences. Replacing two or three hydrogens with chlorine atoms makes for differences in toxicities between the nonhalogenated form and the chlorinated form. The same is true for the simplest aromatic benzene. Substituting a methyl group for one of the hydrogen atoms forms toluene.

Likewise, replacing a hydrogen atom with a hydroxyl group yields another very different molecule, phenol. At standard temperature and pressure, phenol is a solid, whereas benzene is a liquid. Because of the OH group, phenol is more polar than benzene. The $OH^-$ group makes phenol more soluble in water and also reduces its vapor pressure. The group also makes phenol more acidic. Thus, any substitution may yield profound differences in organic compounds.

TABLE 8.3   Structures of Organic Compounds

| Chemical class | Functional group |
|---|---|
| Alkanes | $-\overset{\vert}{\underset{\vert}{C}}-\overset{\vert}{\underset{\vert}{C}}-$ |
| Alkenes | $\overset{}{\underset{}{C}}=\overset{}{\underset{}{C}}$ |
| Alkynes | $-C\equiv C-$ |
| Aromatics | |
| Alcohols | $\cdots\overset{\vert}{\underset{\vert}{C}}-OH$ |
| Amines | $-\overset{\vert}{\underset{\vert}{C}}-N$ |
| Aldehydes | $-\overset{O}{\overset{\Vert}{C}}-H$ |
| Ether | $-\overset{\vert}{\underset{\vert}{C}}-O-\overset{\vert}{\underset{\vert}{C}}-$ |
| Ketones | $-\overset{\vert}{\underset{\vert}{C}}-\overset{O}{\overset{\Vert}{C}}-\overset{\vert}{\underset{\vert}{C}}-$ |
| Carboxylic acids | $-\overset{O}{\overset{\Vert}{C}}-OH$ |
| Alkyl halides[33] | $-\overset{\vert}{\underset{\vert}{C}}-X$ |
| Phenols (aromatic alcohols) | |

SUBSTITUTED AROMATICS (SUBSTITUTED BENZENE DERIVATIVES)

| | |
|---|---|
| Nitrobenzene | $NO_2$ |
| Monosubstituted alkylbenzenes | $C$ |
| Toluene (simplest monosubstituted alky benzene) | $CH_3$ |

TABLE 8.3  Structures of Organic Compounds—Cont'd

| Chemical class | Functional group |
|---|---|
| **POLYSUBSTITUTED ALKYLBENZENES** | |
| 1,2-Alkyl benzene (also known as *ortho* or *o-*…) | |
| 1,2-Xylene or *ortho*-xylene (*o*-xylene) | |
| 1,3-Xylene or *meta*-xylene (*m*-xylene) | |
| 1,4-Xylene or *para*-xylene (*p*-xylene) | |
| **HYDROXYPHENOLS DO NOT FOLLOW GENERAL NOMENCLATURE RULES FOR SUBSTITUTED BENZENES** | |
| Catechol (1,2-hydroxiphenol) | |
| Resorcinol (1,3-hydroxiphenol) | |
| Hydroquinone (1,4-hydroxiphenol) | |

*Source: Vallero DA.* Environmental biotechnology: a biosystems approach. *Amsterdam, NV: Elsevier, Academic Press; 2010.*

## Carbon Biogeochemistry

The GHG receiving the greatest amount of attention for its role in climate is carbon dioxide, an inorganic compound (its carbon atom does not contain a covalent bond with other carbon or hydrogen atoms). Interestingly, warming is not the only climate phenomenon affected by the carbon cycle. Inorganic carbon compounds also play a key role in acid rain. In fact, normal, uncontaminated rain has a pH of about 5.6, owing to its dissolution of carbon dioxide, $CO_2$. As the water droplets fall through the air, the $CO_2$ in the atmosphere becomes dissolved in the water, setting up an equilibrium condition:

$$CO_2(\text{gas in air}) \leftrightarrow CO_2(\text{dissolved in the water}) \tag{8.1}$$

The $CO_2$ in the water reacts to produce hydrogen ions, as

$$CO_2 + H_2O \leftrightarrow H_2CO_3 \leftrightarrow H^+ + HCO_3^- \tag{8.2}$$

$$HCO_3^- \leftrightarrow 2H^+ + CO_3^{2-} \tag{8.3}$$

Given the mean partial pressure $CO_2$ in the air is $3.0 \times 10^{-4}$ atm., it is possible to calculate the pH of water in equilibrium. Such chemistry is always temperature dependent, so let us assume that the air is 25 °C. We can also assume that the mean concentration of $CO_2$ in the troposphere is 390 ppm, but this concentration is rising by some estimates at a rate of 1 ppm per year. The concentration of the water droplet's $CO_2$ in water in equilibrium with air is obtained from the partial pressure of Henry's law constant,[34] which is a function of a substance's solubility in water and its vapor pressure:

$$p_{CO_2} = K_H[CO_2]_{aq} \tag{8.4}$$

The change from carbon dioxide in the atmosphere to carbonate ions in water droplets follows a sequence of equilibrium reactions:

$$CO_{2(g)} \xleftrightarrow{K_H} CO_{2(aq)} \xleftrightarrow{K_r} H_2CO_{3(aq)} \xleftrightarrow{K_{a1}} HCO_{3(aq)}^- \xleftrightarrow{K_{a2}} CO_{3(aq)}^{2-} \tag{8.5}$$

A more precise term for acid rain is acid deposition, which comes in two forms: wet and dry. Wet deposition refers to acidic rain, fog, and snow. The dry deposition fraction consists of acidic gases or particulates. The strength of the effects depends on many factors, especially the strength of the acids and the buffering capacity of the soils. Note that this involves every species in the carbonate equilibrium reactions of Equation (8.5) (see Figure 8.9). The processes that release carbonates increase the buffering capacity of natural soils against the effects of acid rain. Thus, carbonate-rich soils like those central North America are able to withstand even elevated acid deposition compared to the thin soil areas, such as those in the Canadian Shield, the New York Finger Lakes region, and much of Scandinavia.

The concentration of carbon dioxide ($CO_2$) is constant, since the $CO_2$ in solution is in equilibrium with the air that has a constant partial pressure of $CO_2$. And the two reactions and ionization constants for carbonic acid are as follows:

$$H_2CO_3 + H_2O \leftrightarrow HCO_3^- + H_3O^+, \quad K_{a1} = 4.3 \times 10^{-7} \tag{8.6}$$

$$HCO_3^- + H_2O \leftrightarrow CO_3^{2-} + H_3O^+, \quad K_{a2} = 4.7 \times 10^{-11} \tag{8.7}$$

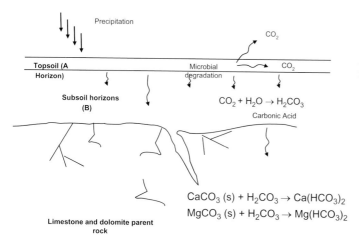

Precipitation

CO$_2$

Topsoil (A Horizon)

Microbial degradation     CO$_2$

Subsoil horizons (B)

CO$_2$ + H$_2$O → H$_2$CO$_3$

Carbonic Acid

CaCO$_3$ (s) + H$_2$CO$_3$ → Ca(HCO$_3$)$_2$

MgCO$_3$ (s) + H$_2$CO$_3$ → Mg(HCO$_3$)$_2$

Limestone and dolomite parent rock

FIGURE 8.9 Biogeochemistry of carbon equilibrium. The processes that release carbonates are responsible for much of the buffering capacity of natural soils against the effects of acid rain.

$K_{a1}$ is four orders of magnitude greater than $K_{a2}$, so the second reaction can be ignored for environmental acid rain considerations. The solubility of gases in liquids can be described quantitatively by Henry's law, so for $CO_2$ in the atmosphere at 25 °C, we can apply the Henry's law constant and the partial pressure to find the equilibrium. The $K_H$ for $CO_2 = 3.4 \times 10^{-2}$ mol L$^{-1}$ atm.$^{-1}$. We can find the partial pressure of $CO_2$ by calculating the fraction of $CO_2$ in the atmosphere. Since the mean concentration of $CO_2$ in the earth's troposphere is 390 ppm by volume in the atmosphere, the fraction of $CO_2$ must be 390 divided by 1,000,000 or 0.000390 atm.

Thus, the carbon dioxide and carbonic acid molar concentration can now be found:

$$[CO_2] = [H_2CO_3] = 3.4 \times 10^{-2}\,\text{mol}\,L^{-1}\,\text{atm}^{-1} \times 0.000390\,\text{atm} = 1.3 \times 10^{-5}\,M$$

The equilibrium is $[H_3O^+] = [HCO^-]$. Taking this and our carbon dioxide molar concentration gives us

$$K_{a1} = 4.3 \times 10^{-7} = \frac{[HCO_3^-][H_3O^+]}{CO_2} = \frac{[H_3O^+]^2}{1.3 \times 10^{-5}}$$

$$[H_3O^+]^2 = 5.2 \times 10^{-12}$$

$$[H_3O^+] = 2.6 \times 10^{-6}\,M$$

Or, the droplet pH is about 5.6.

Carbon dioxide is in the news mainly due to its radiant potential to increase the warming of the troposphere. However, in addition to the radiant effect of carbon dioxide, the discussion so far indicates that increasing $CO_2$ concentrations must also change the acidity of precipitation. For example, if the concentration of $CO_2$ in the atmosphere increases to the very reasonable estimate of 400 ppm, what will happen to the pH of "natural rain"?

The new molar concentration would be $3.4 \times 10^{-2}$ mol L$^{-1}$ atm.$^{-1} \times 0.000400$ atm. $= 1.4 \times 10^{-5}$ M, so $4.3 \times 10^{-7} = [H_3O^+]^2/1.4 \times 10^{-5}$ and $[H_3O^+]^2 = 6.0 \times 10^{-12}$ and $[H_3O^+] = 3.0 \times 10^{-6}$ M. Thus, the droplet pH would be decrease to about 5.5. This means that the incremental increase in atmospheric carbon dioxide can be expected contribute to greater acidity in natural rainfall.

Arguably, other compounds are more important contributors to acid rain than $CO_2$, notably, oxides of sulfur and nitrogen. However, the increase in $CO_2$ means that the pH of rainfall, which is not neutral to begin with, can add marginal acidity that adversely affects the fish and wildlife in and around surface waters. That is, the presence of carbonic acid and other carbon compounds increases soil and water acidity beyond the increases resulting from the sulfur and nitrogen compounds. Thus, as $CO_2$ builds up in the atmosphere, there will also be a concomitant increase in rainfall acidity for a given amount of sulfur and nitrogen compounds in the troposphere.

## POTENTIAL WARMING DISASTER

The average temperature of the earth is difficult to measure, but most measurements show a very small overall change that would not be detectable to humans due to short-term and regional variations. Overall, however, a majority of scientific evidence appears to indicate that the temperature of the Earth is increasing. There have been wide fluctuations in mean global temperatures, such as the ice ages, but on balance, the mean temperature has remained constant, prompting some scientists to speculate some whimsical causes for such consistency. Charles Keeling, an atmospheric scientist, measured $CO_2$ concentrations in the atmosphere using an IR gas analyzer. Since 1958, these data have provided the single most important piece of information on global warming and are now referred to as "Keeling Curve" in honor of the scientist.

The Keeling Curve shows that there has been more than 15% increase in $CO_2$ concentration, which is a substantial rise given that short time that the measurements have been taken. It is likely, if we extrapolate backward, that our present $CO_2$ levels are double what they were in pre-industrial revolution times, providing ample evidence that global warming is indeed occurring.[35]

An explanation for this rise in temperature is that the presence of certain gases in the atmosphere is not allowing the Earth to reflect enough of the heat energy from the sun back into space. The earth acts as a reflector to the sun's rays, receiving the radiation from the sun, reflecting some of it into space (called *albedo*), and adsorbing the rest, only to reradiate this into space as heat (see Figure 8.10). In effect, the earth acts as a wave converter, receiving

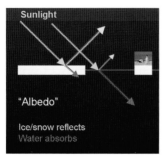

FIGURE 8.10   Various surfaces have differing reflectivity, albedo. Increasing albedo decreases absorption of incoming solar radiation, which means less emitted infrared radiation.

the high-energy high-frequency radiation from the sun and converting most of it into low-energy low-frequency heat to be radiated back into space. In this manner, the earth maintains a balance of temperature.

In order to better understand this balance, the light energy and the heat energy have to be defined in terms of their radiation patterns, as shown in Figure 8.11. The incoming radiation (light) wavelength has a maximum at around 0.5 nm and almost all of it is less than 3 nm. The heat energy spectrum, or that energy reflected back into space, has a maximum at about 10 nm and almost all of it at a wavelength higher than 3 nm.

As both the light and heat energy pass through the earth's atmosphere, they encounter the aerosols and gases surrounding the earth. These can either allow the energy to pass through, or they can interrupt it by scattering or absorption. If the atoms in the gas molecules vibrate at the same frequency as the light energy, they will absorb the energy and not allow it to pass through. Aerosols will scatter the light and provide a "shade" for the earth.

The absorptive potential of several important gases is shown in Figure 8.12 along with the spectra for the incoming light (short wavelength) radiation and the outgoing heat (long wavelength) radiation. The incoming radiation is impeded by water vapor and oxygen and ozone, as discussed in the preceding section. Most of the light energy comes through unimpeded.

The heat energy, however, encounters several potential impediments. As it is trying to reach outer space, it finds that water vapor, $CO_2$, $CH_4$, $O_3$, and nitrous oxide ($N_2O$) all have absorptive wavelengths right in the middle of the heat spectrum. Quiet obviously, an increase in the concentration of any of these will greatly limit the amount of heat transmitted into space. These gases are appropriately called GHGs because their presence will limit the heat escaping into space, much like the glass of a greenhouse or even the glass in your

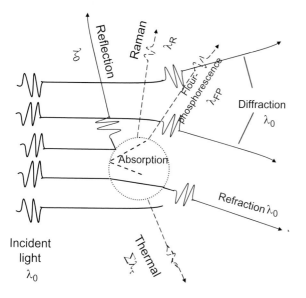

FIGURE 8.11    Patterns for heat and light energy.

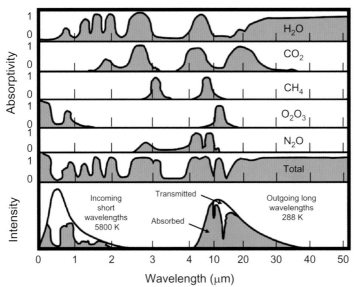

FIGURE 8.12   Adsorptive potential of several important gases in the atmosphere. Also shown are the spectra for the incoming solar energy and the outgoing thermal energy from the earth. Note that the wavelength scale changes at 4 μm. *Masters, Gilbert M., Introduction Environmental Engineering & Science, 2nd Edition, © 1998, p. 468. Reprinted by permission of Pearson Education, Inc., Upper Saddle River, NJ.*

car limits the amount of heat that can escape, thus building up the temperature under the glass cover.

Methane ($CH_4$) is the product of anaerobic decomposition and human food production. Methane also is emitted during the combustion of fossil fuels and cutting and clearing of forests. The concentration of $CH_4$ in the atmosphere has been steady at about 0.75 ppm for over a thousand years and then increased to 0.85 ppm in 1900. Since then, in the space of only a 100 years, the concentration has skyrocketed to 1.7 ppm. Methane is removed from the atmosphere by reaction with the hydroxyl radical (OH) as

$$CH_4 + OH + 9O_2 \rightarrow CO_2 + 0.5H_2 + 2H_2O + 5O_3 \tag{8.8}$$

This indicates that the reaction creates carbon dioxide, water vapor, and ozone, all of which are GHGs, so the effect of one molecule of methane is devastating to the production of the greenhouse effect.

Halocarbons, or the same chemical class linked to the destruction of stratospheric ozone, are also radiant gases. The most effective global warming gases are CFC-11 and CFC-12, both of which are no longer manufactured, and the banning of these substances has shown a leveling off in the stratosphere. Nitrous oxide is also in the atmosphere, mostly as a result of human activities, especially the cutting and clearing of tropical forests. The greatest problem with nitrous oxide is that there appear to be no natural removal processes for this gas and so its residence time in the stratosphere is quite long.

The net effect of these global pollutants is still being debated. Various atmospheric models used to predict temperature change over the next 100 years vary widely. They nevertheless agree that some positive change will occur, even if we do something drastic today (which does not seem likely). By the year 2100, even if we do not increase our production of GHGs and if the United States signs the Kyoto Accord, which encourages the reduction in GHG production, the global temperature is likely to be between 0.5 and 1.5 °C warmer.

# GEOENGINEERING

One of the most frustrating aspects of the global climate change debate is the seeming paucity of proposed solutions. The discussions at present are very polarized. Is there anything that can be done to ameliorate the increase in carbon being released to the atmosphere?

Recently, some engineers and scientists have suggested that it would be prudent to consider engaging in planetary-scale interventions, so-called geoengineering, to mitigate global climate change and global warming, in particular. Geoengineering differs from other methods for mitigating global warming because it involves a deliberate effort to affect the climate at a global scale. Although geoengineering is not a new idea, it has taken on added significance as a result of difficulties with implementing other proposals to mitigate climate change. While proponents of geoengineering admit that these measures can be associated with significant risks to the environment and public health, they maintain that they are well worth pursuing, given the failure of means of mitigating global warming. Conversely, some environmental groups have voiced strong opposition to all forms of geoengineering. In this chapter, we review the arguments for and against geoengineering and discuss some policy options. We argue that geoengineering research should continue, but that specific proposals should not be implemented until we have a better understanding of the risks, costs, and practical and political problems associated with geoengineering.

Carbon sequestration is on type of geoengineering that has received considerable attention. Actually, sequestration is an ongoing, geophysical process. Carbon compounds, especially $CO_2$ and $CH_4$, find their way to the ocean, forests, and other carbon sinks. Like many geobiochemical processes, sequestration is one that can be influenced by human activity. Thus, there is a conservation aspect to protecting these mechanisms that are working to our benefit.

The second approach is one that is most familiar to the engineer, that is, we can apply scientific principles to enhance sequestration. These sequestration technologies include new ways either to sequester carbon or to enhance or expedite processes that already exist.

Conservation is an example of a more "passive" approach. There are currently enormous releases of carbon that, if eliminated, would greatly reduce the loading to the troposphere. For example, anything we can do to protect the loss of forest, woodlands, wetlands, and other ecosystems is a way of preventing future problems. In fact, much of the terrestrial fluxes and sinks of carbon involve the soil. Keeping the soil in place must be part of the overall global strategy to reduce GHGs (see Discussion Box: Soil as a Sink).

## SOIL AS A SINK

Soil is classified into various types. For many decades, soil scientists have struggled with uniformity in the classification and taxonomy of soil. Much of the rich history and foundation of soil scientists have been associated with agricultural productivity. The very essence of a soil's "value" has been its capacity to support plant life, especially crops. Even forest soil knowledge owes much to the agricultural perspective, since much of the reason for investing in forests has been monetary. A stand of trees are seen by many to be a "standing crop." In the United States, for example, the National Forest Service is an agency of the U.S. Department of Agriculture. The engineers have been concerned about the statics and dynamics of soil systems, improving the understanding of soil mechanics so that they may support, literally and figuratively, the built environment. The agricultural and engineering perspectives have provided valuable information about soil that environmental professionals can put to use. The information is certainly necessary, but not completely sufficient, to understand how pollutants move through soils, how the soils themselves are affected by the pollutants (e.g., loss of productivity and diversity of soil microbes), and how the soils and contaminants interact chemically (e.g., changes in soil pH will change the chemical and biochemical transformation of organic compounds). At a minimum, environmental scientists must understand and classify soils according to their texture or grain size (see Table 8.4), ion exchange capacities, ionic strength, pH, microbial populations, and soil organic matter content.

Whereas air and water are fluids, sediment is a lot like soil in that it is a matrix made up of various components, including organic matter and unconsolidated material. And, the matrix contains liquids ("substrate" to the chemist and engineer) within its interstices. Much of the substrate of this matrix is water with varying amounts of solutes. At least for most environmental conditions, air and water are solutions of very dilute amounts of compounds. For example, air's solutes represent small percentages of the solution at the highest (e.g., water vapor), and most of other solutes represent parts per million (a bit more than 390 ppm carbon dioxide). Most "contaminants" in air and water, thankfully, are found in the parts per billion range, if found at all. On the other hand, soil and sediment themselves are conglomerations of all states of matter. Soil is predominantly solid but frequently has large fractions of liquid (soil water) and gas (soil air, methane, carbon dioxide) that make up the matrix. The composition of each fraction is highly variable. For example, soil gas concentrations are different from those in the atmosphere and change profoundly with depth from the surface. Table 8.5 illustrates the inverse relationship between carbon dioxide and molecular oxygen. Sediment is really an underwater soil. It is a collection of particles that have settled on the bottom of water bodies.

Ecosystems are combinations of these media. For example, a wetland system consists of plants that grow in soil, sediment, and water. The water flows through living and nonliving materials. Microbial populations live in the surface water, with aerobic species congregating near the water surface and anaerobic microbes increasing with depth due to the decrease in oxygen levels, due to the reduced conditions. Air is not only important at the water and soil interfaces, but it is a vehicle for nutrients and contaminants delivered to the wetland. The groundwater is fed by the surface water during high water conditions and feeds the wetland during low water.

TABLE 8.4   Commonly Used Soil Texture Classifications[36]

| Name | Size range (mm) |
| --- | --- |
| Gravel | >2.0 |
| Very coarse sand | 1.0-1.999 |
| Coarse sand | 0.500-0.999 |
| Medium sand | 0.250-0.499 |
| Fine sand | 0.100-0.249 |
| Very fine sand | 0.050-0.099 |
| Silt | 0.002-0.049 |
| Clay | <0.002 |

TABLE 8.5 Composition of Two Tropospheric Gases in Soil Air[37]

| Depth from surface (cm) | Silty clay | | Silty clay loam | | Sandy loam | |
|---|---|---|---|---|---|---|
| | $O_2$ (% vol. of air) | $CO_2$ (% vol. of air) | $O_2$ (% vol. of air) | $CO_2$ (% vol. of air) | $O_2$ (% vol. of air) | $CO_2$ (% vol. of air) |
| 30 | 18.2 | 1.7 | 19.8 | 1.0 | 19.9 | 0.8 |
| 61 | 16.7 | 2.8 | 17.9 | 3.2 | 19.4 | 1.3 |
| 91 | 15.6 | 3.7 | 16.8 | 4.6 | 19.1 | 1.5 |
| 122 | 12.3 | 7.9 | 16.0 | 6.2 | 18.3 | 2.1 |
| 152 | 8.8 | 10.6 | 15.3 | 7.1 | 17.9 | 2.7 |
| 183 | 4.6 | 10.3 | 14.8 | 7.0 | 17.5 | 3.0 |

So, another way to think about these environmental media is that they are compartments, each with boundary conditions, kinetics, and partitioning relationships within a compartment or among other compartments. Chemicals, whether nutrients or contaminants, change as a result of the time spent in each compartment. The environmental professional's challenge is to describe, characterize, and predict the behaviors of various chemical species as they move through the media. When something is amiss, the cause and cure lie within the physics, chemistry, and biology of the system. It is up to the professional to properly apply the principles.

## Carbon Sequestration in Soil

When tallying the benefits of soil conservation, a few always come to mind, especially soil's role in sustainable agriculture and food production, keeping soil from becoming a pollutant in the surface waters, and its ability to sieve and filter pollutants that would otherwise end up in drinking water. However, another less obvious benefit is as a sink for carbon. Soil is lost when land is degraded by deforestation and as a result of inadequate land use and management in sensitive soil systems, especially those in the tropics and subtropics, such as slash and burn and other aggressive practices. As is often the case in ecosystems, some of the most valuable ecosystems in terms of the amount of carbon sequestered and oxygen generated are also the most sensitive. Tropical systems, for example, often have some of the thinnest soils due to the rapid oxidation processes that take place in humid, oxidized environments.

Sensitive systems are often societal given value by society for a single purpose. Bauxite, for example, is present in tropical soils due to the physical and chemical conditions of the tropics (aluminum in parent rock material, oxidation, humidity, and ion exchange processes). However, from a life cycle and resource planning perspective, such single mindedness is folly. The decision to extract bauxite, iron, or other materials from sensitive tropical rainforests must be seen in terms of local, regional, and global impacts. With this in mind, international organizations are promoting improved land use systems and land management practices which give both economic and environmental benefits.

Keeping soil intact protects biological diversity, improves ecosystem conditions, and increases carbon sequestration. This last mentioned benefit includes numerous forms of carbon in all physical phases. As discussed and shown in Table 8.5, soil gases include $CO_2$ and $CH_4$. Plant root systems, fungi, and other organisms that comprised amino acids, proteins, carbohydrates, and other organic compounds live in the soil. Even inorganic forms of carbon are held in soil, such as the carbonate, bicarbonate, and carbonic acid chemical species that are in soils as a result of chemical reactions with parent rock material, especially limestone and dolomite.

When the soils are lost, all of these carbon compounds become available to be released to the atmosphere.

# BIOLOGICAL DRIVERS OF CLIMATE CHANGE

It is interesting how connected humans are to trees. Perhaps, it is because trees take many years to mature, so they represent a long-term commitment. Trees are often the tallest and most visible parts of many ecosystems, i.e the climax vegetation. So, they are indicators of ecological well being. Thus, the inordinate loss of trees can be an indicator of ecological disaster.

The principal biological process at work in such ecosystems is photosynthesis, whereby atmospheric $CO_2$ is transformed to molecular oxygen by way of the plant's manufacturing biomass. For example, much of the biomass of a tree is in its root systems (more than half for many species). When the tree is cut down, not only is the harvested biomass releasing carbon, such as in the smoke when the wood is burned, but gradually the underground stores of carbon in the root systems migrate from the soil to the troposphere.

Organic material generated when plants and animals used stored solar energy is known as biomass. Photosynthesis is the process by which green plants absorb the sun's energy, convert it to chemical energy, and store the energy in the bonds of sugar molecules. The process of photosynthesis takes place in the chloroplasts, which are organelles (chloro=-green; plasti=formed, molded), using the green pigment chlorophyll, which has a porphyrin ring with magnesium in the center (chloro=green; phyll=leaf).

The simplest sugars are monosaccharides, which have the molecular formula:

$$(CH_2O)_n \tag{8.9}$$

where $n$ may be any integer from 3 to 8.

Monosaccharides contain hydroxyl groups and either a ketone or an aldehyde group. These functional groups are polar, rendering sugars very soluble in water. Fructose has the same molecular formula as glucose, but the atoms of carbon, hydrogen, and oxygen are arranged a little differently (i.e., they are isomers). Glucose has an aldehyde group; fructose has a ketone group. This structural nuance imparts different physical and chemical properties in the two monosaccharides.

These monosaccharides link by a dehydration synthesis reaction to form disaccharides, forming one water molecule in the process. Maltose is formed by joining two glucose molecules. Sucrose is formed by combining glucose and fructose. Lactose is formed by combining glucose and the monosaccharide galactose. Maltose, sucrose, and lactose have the same molecular formula, $C_{12}H_{22}O_{11}$, but are isomers, each with unique physical and chemical properties.

The energy in the chemical bonds of these sugars moves through the food web, being passed on to animals that consume the plants. Although numerous chemical reactions occur in photosynthesis, the process can be seen as a very simple reaction with water and carbon dioxide reacting in the presence of radiant energy to form sugars (e.g., glucose) and molecular oxygen:

$$6H_2O + 6CO_2(+\text{radiant energy}) \rightarrow C_6H_{12}O_6 + 6O_2 \qquad (8.10)$$

Thus, biomass is a renewable energy source since it will be available so long as green plants can be grown. Biomass energy has been produced from woody plants, herbaceous plants, manure, and solid wastes. When biomass is burned, the process of combustion releases the stored chemical energy as heat. The biomass can be directly combusted in a wood-burning fireplace or in large-scale biomass electricity-generating stations. The industrial sector uses about one-third of primary energy in the United States. Wood as a fuel sources makes up approximately 8% of total industrial primary energy use. Most of this is in the pulp and paper industry, where wood and its by-products are readily available (see Figure 8.13). It must be noted that conservation must be factored into the life cycle assessment for these processes. For example, we are comparing paper and pulp fuel uses; however, if society can find more "paperless" systems such as electronic documentation, the demand for such wood-based products would also drop. This could be accompanied by less tree cutting in the first place, with the advantage of keeping the tree systems intact and preserving the present sequestration of carbon.

Certainly, numerous industrial sectors can put the process of photosynthesis to work to find renewable and sustainable feedstocks. Arguably, those most heavily invested in nonrenewable resources have the most to gain by moving to renewable resources.[38]

Woody plants have connecting systems that link modules together and that connect the modules to the root system. These connecting systems do not rot away after the growing season. In fact, for years a tree thickens these connecting tissues. Actually, most of the mass of a woody tree is dead, with only a thin layer of living tissue below the bark. However, this living stratum regenerates continuously, adding layers after each growing season. This process makes the tree rings. Trees receive nutrients from soil via roots and from air via leaves. The leaves also absorb light energy needed for photosynthesis. So, the tree is a system of living and dead tissue, and each is absolutely necessary for structure and function.

All plants contain cellulose, but woody plants also contain lignin. Both cellulose and lignin are polymers, which are large organic molecules comprising repeated subunits (i.e., monomers). Lignin is the "glue" that binds the cellulose polymers. The monomers that comprise lignin polymers can vary, depending on the sugars from which they are derived. In fact, lignins have so many random couplings that the exact chemical structure is seldom known. One configuration of the lignin molecule is shown in Figure 8.14.

Lignin fills the spaces in a woody plant's cell wall between cellulose and two other compounds, hemicellulose and polysaccharides. Lignin accounts for the rigidity of wood cells and the structural integrity and strength of wood by its covalent bonds to hemicellulose and cross-linking to polysaccharides.

Both herbaceous and woody plants can serve as so-called bioenergy crops, which include annual row crops such as corn, herbaceous perennial grasses (known as herbaceous energy crops, or HECs). One of the most prominently mentioned HECs is switchgrass (*Panicum*

Paper products industries

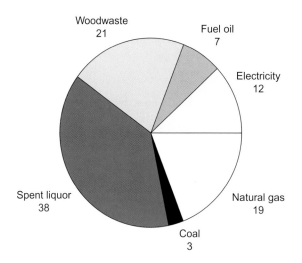

FIGURE 8.13   Fuel sources for the paper and pulp industry. Biomass fuel, represented by wood waste and spent liquor, makes up the majority of end use consumed energy, with 60-75% from biomass. *Source: Energy Information Administration. Estimates of U.S. biofuels consumption 1989. U.S. Department of Energy; April 1991.*

Wood products industries

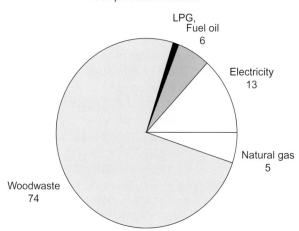

*virgatum*), a hardy, perennial rhizomatous grass that is among the dominant tall grass prairies species in the high plains of North America. Bioenergy crops also include fast-growing shrubs and trees, known as short-rotation woody crops (SRWCs) such as poplar. SRWCs typically consist of a single-genus plantations of closely spaced (2-3 m apart on a grid) trees that are harvested on a 3- to 10-year cycle. Regeneration is an important selection criterion for bioenergy species. HECs must regrow from the remaining stubble, and SRWCs must regrow from the remaining stumps. The harvests can continue for two decades or more. Pesticides, fertilizers, and other soil enhancements may be needed, but the farming does not substantially differ from that typical of growing ordinary crops.

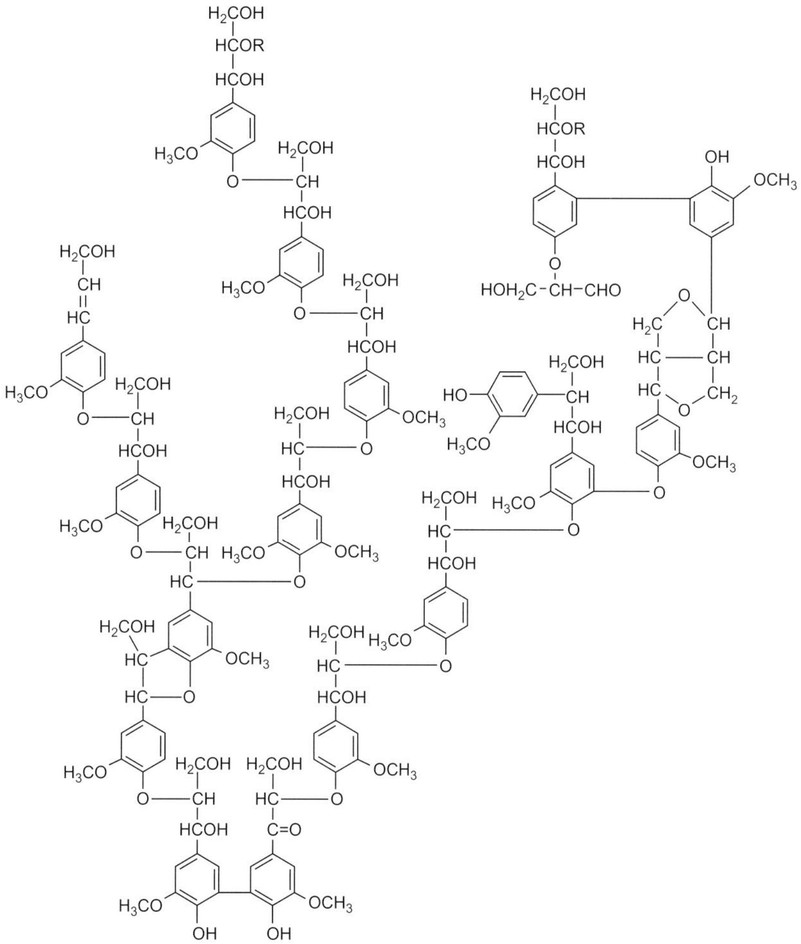

FIGURE 8.14 Configuration of a lignin polymer. *Source: Institute of Biotechnology and Drug Research,* Environmental Biotechnology and Enzymes. *Kaiserslautern: Germany. Adapted from Adler E. Lignin chemistry—past, present and future.* Wood Sci Technol 1977;*11*:169-218.

Both the cellulose and lignin have heat values; thus these crops are known as lignocellulosic energy crops. The feedstocks of HECs and SRWCs may be used directly to generate electricity or can be converted to liquid fuels or combustible gases.

A tree represents a system within a system. It can be part of a forest ecosystem, where it depends on nutrients provided by the air and soil. The soil receives its nutrients through abiotic and biotic processes, such as nitrates from lightning, nitrogen-fixing bacteria in legumes' root nodules, and the breakdown of detritus by aerobes and anaerobes on the forest floor. The nitrogen cycle is quite complex (see Figure 8.15). Basically, there are numerous simultaneous chemical reactions taking place, so the forest ecosystem is a balance of various chemical forms of nitrogen (and phosphorous, sulfur, and carbon, for that matter). The chemical reactions in a nutrient cycle consist of biochemical processes involving organisms

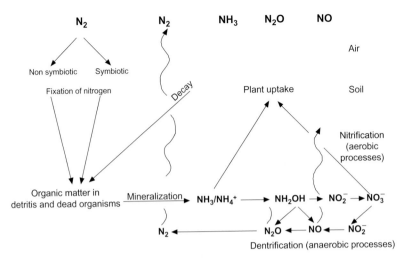

FIGURE 8.15   Nitrogen cycling in a forest ecosystem. *Source: Vallero DA. Environmental contaminants: assessment and control. Burlington, MA: Elsevier, Academic Press; 2004.*

which take the simpler N-compounds from the microbial fixation of molecular nitrogen ($N_2$) from the atmosphere to form the amino acids in the tissues of plants and animals. In the opposite direction, mineralization is the process by which organic matter is reduced or oxidized to mineral forms, such as ammonia, ammonium hydroxide, nitrite, and nitrate. Note that the gases at the top of the figure include those that are important in air pollution. For example, NO is one of the compounds involved in the photochemistry that leads to the formation of the pollutant ozone ($O_3$) in the troposphere. Note also that trees are central in the figure. At their base is the detritus where microbes are breaking down complex molecules. Nutrients in the soil are transported by the roots capillary action to the tree's cells. And gases are transpired through leaves back to the atmosphere.

"Active" approaches include the application of technologies to send carbon to the sinks, including deep rock formations and the oceans. Such technology can be applied directly to sources. For example, fires from China's coal mines presently release about 1 billion tonnes of $CO_2$ to the atmosphere every year. Estimates put India's coal mine fire releases to be about 50 million tonnes. This accounts for as much as 1% of all carbon greenhouse releases. This is about the same as the $CO_2$ released by all of the gasoline-fuel automobiles in the United States. Engineering solutions that reduce these emissions would actively improve the net GHG global flux.

The United States has a checkered history when it comes to coal mine fires. Some have burned for more than a century. Intuitively, putting out such fires may seem straightforward. For example, we know that combustion depends on three components: a fuel, a heat source, and an oxygen. All three are needed, so *all* we have to do to smother a coal fire is to eliminate just one of these essential ingredients. Unfortunately, since the fire is in an underground vein, fuel is plentiful. Actually, the solid-phase coal is less of a factor than the available $CH_4$, which is ubiquitous in coal mines. And like the "whack-a-mole" game, the avenues of access to the fire mean that the heat source is available in different channels. When one is closed off, another appears.

So, that leaves us with depriving the fire of $O_2$. This is much easier said than done. In fact, engineering has been an outright failure in this regard. Flooding the mines has been ineffective, since the fire simply finds alternative pathways in the leaky underground strata. Excavation has to almost be 100% to be effective. Flushing with slurries has the same problems. In fact, miner safety and post-ignition fire suppression can be seen as competing factors in mining. To ensure sufficient oxygen levels and low toxic gas concentrations, the mine's ventilation systems require methane-drainage holes to control methane at the face. In many abandoned mines, cross-measure holes (see Figure 8.16) were the most common types. These systems are one reason that oxygen remains available to the fire.[39]

However, there is promise. Recent studies have shown that certain foams can deprive fires of $O_2$ over extensive areas. For example, a study sanctioned by the U.S. National Institute of Occupational Safety and Health (NIOSH) showed preliminary success in sealing a coal mine from oxygen inflow and suppression of the fire with liquid nitrogen and gas-enhanced foam.[40] The technology needs to be advanced to address the very large fires. The fire studied by NIOSH (see Figure 8.17) was caught in the early stages and suppressed within 2 weeks. But, like many engineering prototypes, showing that it *can* work is the first step to ensure it *will* work.

Another active engineering approach is an enhancement of existing processes. For example, in addition to conserving present levels of carbon sequestration, technologies can be adapted to *increase* the rates of sequestration. The scale of such technology can range from an individual source (see Figure 8.18), such as a fossil fuel burning electricity generation

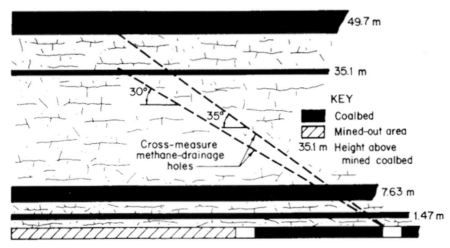

FIGURE 8.16   Section view of cross-measure methane-drainage holes in a coal mine ventilation system. *B.R. McKensey and J. W. Rennie. Longwall ventilation with methane and spontaneous combustion-Pacific Colliery. Paper in Fourth International Mine Ventilation Congress (Brisbane, Australia, July 3-6, 1988). Aust. Inst. Min. and Met., Melbourne, Australia, 1988, pp. 617-624. Reprinted with the permission of The Australasian Institute of Mining and Metallurgy'.*

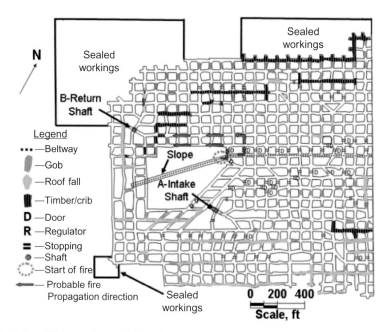

FIGURE 8.17    Map of fire zone in Excel #3 coal mine in eastern Kentucky.

FIGURE 8.18    Carbon dioxide that is produced at the Sleipner natural gas complex off the cost of Norway is removed and pumped into the Utsira Formation, a highly permeable sandstone. In this case, the sequestration cost is less than the Norwegian carbon emission tax. *Photograph is courtesy of Øyvind Hagen, Statoil.*

station that returns its stack gases to an underground rock stratum to an extensive system of collection and injection system, to that which includes a whole network of facilities. The combination of disincentives, like carbon taxes, and application of emerging technologies can decrease the carbon flux to the atmosphere. Thus, green engineering is part of the overall, comprehensive geopolitical strategy.

Even a system as large as the ocean has its limits in GHG sequestration. To begin with most of the $CO_2$ generated by human activities (i.e., anthropogenic) resides in the upper layers of the ocean (see Figure 8.19). Carbon compounds move into and out of oceans predominantly as a function of the solubility of the compound and water temperature. For $CO_2$, this means that more of the compound will remain in the ocean water with decreasing temperature. Ocean mixing is very slow. Thus, the anthropogenic $CO_2$ from the atmosphere is predominantly confined to the very top layers. Virtually half of the anthropogenic $CO_2$ taken up by the ocean for the previous two centuries has stayed in the upper 10% of the ocean. The ocean has removed 48% of the $CO_2$ released to the troposphere from burning fossil fuels and cement manufacturing.[41]

Thus, to keep $CO_2$ sequestered, one factor is to help it find its way to the cooler, deeper parts of the ocean. When it resides near the warmer surface, it is more likely to be released

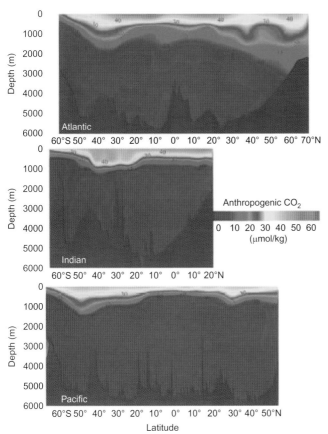

FIGURE 8.19 Anthropogenic carbon concentrations in three ocean systems. Note that most of the $CO_2$ resides above the 1000 m depth. *Source: The Global $CO_2$ survey by National Oceanic and Atmospheric Administration and Feely RA, Sabine CL, Takahashi T, Wanninkhof R. Uptake and storage of carbon dioxide in the ocean: the global $CO_2$ survey. Oceanography 2001;**14**(4):18-32.*

to the atmosphere. The actual mass of carbon can be increased by management. For example, certain species of plankton are often limited in growth by metals, especially iron. Thus, increasing the iron concentrations in certain ocean layers could dramatically increase the ability of these organisms to take up and store carbon. Obviously, any large-scale endeavor like this must be approached with appropriate caution. The best decisions are ones that account for all possible outcomes, certainly not the ones hoped for. Such an approach would likely include tests in laboratories, stepped up to prototypes on as many possible scenarios and species possible, before actual implementation.

The whole area of enhanced carbon sequestration is very promising. Figure 8.20 shows a number of venues where this green engineering approach might be taken. The Intergovernmental Panel on Climate Change has identified four basic systems for capturing $CO_2$ from the use of fossil fuels and/or biomass processes:

1. capture from industrial process streams;
2. post-combustion capture;
3. oxy-fuel combustion capture;
4. pre-combustion capture.[42]

The likely critical paths of these technologies are shown in Figure 8.21. Thus, there are numerous ways of conserving and adding to natural sequestration processes that could significantly decrease the net GHG concentrations in the atmosphere.

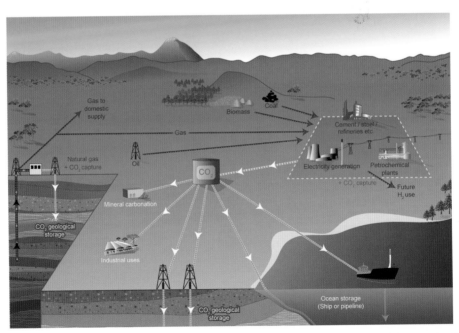

FIGURE 8.20    Potential application of $CO_2$ sequestration technology systems (Courtesy of Cooperative Research Centre for Greenhouse Gas Technologies—CO2CRC).

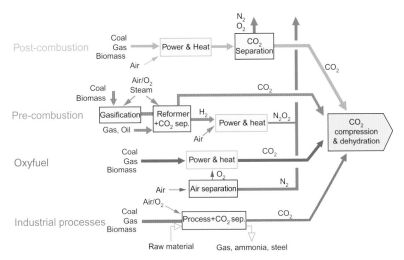

FIGURE 8.21   Schematic diagram of potential means of capturing carbon dioxide. *IPCC 2005: IPCC Special Report on Carbon Dioxide Capture and Storage. Prepared by Working Group III of the Intergovernmental Panel on Climate Change, Figure 3.14. Cambridge University Press.*

# RISING SEA LEVEL: PENDING DISASTER OR UNDUE PRECAUTION?

Rising sea level is one the most indirect effects of anthropogenic climate change. The sea level has been rising at rates of between 3 and 6 mm per year throughout the last century.[13] The rate of sea level rise has increased every decade since 1950. All evidence points to this being due anthropogenic forcing by greenhouse gases which is responsible for rising global temperatures. Some of this evidence comes from the strong correlation between atmospheric $CO_2$ concentrations and sea levels that occurred during the past three glacial-interglacialcycles.

As mentioned, the UN's Inter-Governmental Panel on Climate Change predicts that sea levels associated with increases in global temperature will rise between 0.18 and 0.59 m in the next 100 years. This may be on the low side. Grinsted, et al.[43,44] recently reported that new research indicates that the oceans could rise one meter higher than current sea level within 100 years. This is almost three times higher than the IPCC prediction. The new research attributes the difference to a much a more rapid rate of melting of both Greenland and the West Antarctic ice sheets, due to rising global temperatures.

This rise in sea level would have serious consequences for people living in low lying parts of the world. As expected this has created much interest. The rise in sea level is perplexing from both scientific and policy-setting perspectives. The science is complex because sea level rises due to changes in the hydrological cycle. The amount of water on Earth does not vary, but it changes in form and location. Water is stored in the large and small reservoirs, most being in liquid phase in the oceans and seas; other large reservoirs include freshwater systems (lakes, rivers, and other surface waters), underground (aquifers), in ice (ice caps and glaciers) and the atmosphere. Changes to the hydrological cycle involve many variables. Predicting the effects of a change, such as the melting of ice caps, is not a simple calculation. There are numerous contingencies beyond direct steps from increasing atmospheric temperature to increased melting of polar ice to a rise the global sea level. Among the variables to consider are regional differences.

The global atmosphere is not a homogenous, completely mixed thermal system. Indeed, heat is transferred constantly and varies in time and space. For example, even if mean global temperatures rise, it does not necessarily mean that polar temperatures will rise accordingly. They may rise more or less than the global mean, depending on movements of air masses, changes in albedo and other climatological factors. Similarly, the past may not be a good indicator of future climatic conditions, so straight-line projections will not be accurate if the conditions have changed in recent decades.

The policy-setting standpoint may be more complex and frustrating than the science. Policy makers have to make decisions with incomplete information. The first challenge is to decide whether to believe the models on what will occur several decades hence. Does the seemingly inevitable increase in $CO_2$ atmospheric concentrations necessarily mean a concomitant increase in global temperature? Will other factors also come into play, such as increase vegetative cover, which could attenuate some of the temperature rise? And, even if the sea level were to increase substantially, are there measures that can be taken to adapt to these changes over time?

North Carolina has almost 6000 $km^2$ of land below one-meter elevation, over 500 km of beaches and a shore line of over 7000 km, making it particularly vulnerable to sea level rise. Thus, North Carolina has been at the epicentre of sea level rise debates. Some argue that the scientific consensus about global warming is a logical extension to increase sea level, while others argue that such warming is not occurring. Between these two extreme viewpoints, others argue that warming may occur, but that this would not lead to substantial sea level rise beyond past trends. Still others argue that even if we were to see a one meter rise, humans have a knack for adapting to such changes, so being overly cautious would devastate local economies unnecessarily by placing restrictions on growth and requiring burdensome zoning and land use planning.

A group of businesses from the 20 North Carolina coastal counties is requesting that a law be passed to ensure that planning follows straight-line projections of sea level rise, ignoring the grim projections of a one-meter sea level rise by the end of the century. This led the UK's *Guardian* newspaper to quip in an editorial that "North Carolina is trying to wish away the sea level rise."[45]

Such debate illustrates the complexity and uncertainty that underlies risk tradeoff decisions. There is almost never a unanimous choice. Indeed, some of the biggest losers in the long-run could be those who win the near-term debates. Like the problems associated with decisions to allow developments in hurricane-prone areas, ignoring potential inundations can cause suffering, legal liabilities and monetary costs well beyond any benefits from development.

Even if actions are taken, such as strong land use restriction, other environmental costs from sea level rise may inevitable, such as the increase in salination of groundwater (See Figure 2.6 and discussion of saltwater intrusion in Chapter 2). The increase in salinity threatens drinking water quality of many local coastal communities throughout the world, including the northeast seaboard of the US. This would be disastrous for many coastal communities, especially in rural and unincorporated areas, where well water is the exclusive source of drinking water.[46]

Planning is arguably preferable to engineering solutions brought on by changes in climate. Better stewardship of the earth's resources and conservation can reduce energy demands. Also, wise uses of land can be part of the tool kit in adapting to changes, preventing development in vulnerable areas and ameliorating any indirect effects, such as sea level rise (See Discussion Box: Rising Sea Level: Pending Disaster or Undue Precaution?).

# References and Notes

1. Resnik DB, Vallero DA. Geoengineering: an idea whose time has come? *Earth Sci Clim Change* 2011;**S1**:001 doi:10.4172/2157-7617.S1-001.
2. Intergovernmental Panel on Climate Change. *Climate change 2007: synthesis report;* 2007 May 7 2012. [accessed 30 May 2012].
3. Tans P. *Trends in carbon dioxide.* NOAA/ESRL. http://www.esrl.noaa.gov/gmd/ccgg/trends/[accessed March 2, 2012].
4. IPCC. http://www.ipcc.ch/pdf/assessment-report/ar4/syr/ar4_syr.pdf; 2007 [accessed March 3, 2012].
5. Tuckett RP. The Role of Atmospheric Gases in Global Warming. In: Letcher TM, editor. *Climate change: observed impacts on planet earth.* Oxford: Elsevier; 2009. p. 11.
6. Letcher TM, editor. *Climate change: observed impacts on planet earth.* [chapter 2 by Cohen S. The Role of Widespread Surface Solar radiation Trends in Climate Change: Dimming and Brightening; chapter 3 by Dorman L. The Role of Space Weather and Cosmic Ray Effects in Climate Change; chapter 4 by Stenchikov G. The Role of Volcanic Activity in Climate and Global Change; and chapter 5 by Lourens LJ and Tuenter E]. The Role of Variation of the Earth's Orbital Characteristics in Climate Change. Oxford: Elsevier; 2009. ISBN: 978-0-444-53301-2.
7. Trigo RM, Gimeno L. Weather Pattern Changes in the Tropics and Mid-Latitudes as an Indicator of Global Changes. In: Letcher TM, editor. *Climate change: observed impacts on planet earth.* Oxford: Elsevier; 2009. p. 165.
8. Fiedler W. Bird Ecology as an Indicator of Climate and Global Change. In: Letcher TM, editor. *Climate change: observed impacts on planet earth.* Oxford: Elsevier; 2009. p. 181.
9. Edwards M. Sea Life (Pelagic and Planktonic Ecosystems) as an Indicator of Climate and Global Change. In: Letcher TM, editor. *Climate change: observed impacts on planet earth.* Oxford: Elsevier; 2009. p. 233.
10. Attrill M. Climate Changes in Coral Reef Ecosystems as an Indicator of Climate and Global Change. In: Letcher TM, editor. *Climate change: observed impacts on planet earth.* Oxford: Elsevier; 2009. p. 253.
11. Mieszkowska N. Intertidal Indicators of Climate and Global Change. In: Letcher TM, editor. *Climate change: observed impacts on planet earth.* Oxford: Elsevier; 2009. p. 281.
12. Morecroft MD, Keith SA. Plant Ecology as an Indicator of Climate and Global Change. In: Letcher TM, editor. *Climate change: observed impacts on planet earth.* Oxford: Elsevier; 2009. p. 297.
13. Gehrels R. Rising Sea levels as an Indicator of Global Change. In: Letcher TM, editor. *Climate change: observed impacts on planet earth.* Oxford: Elsevier; 2009. p. 325.
14. Kanzow T, Visbeck M. Ocean Current Changes as an Indicator of Global Change. In: Letcher TM, editor. *Climate change: observed impacts on planet earth.* Oxford: Elsevier; 2009. p. 349.
15. Turley C, Findlay HS. Ocean Acidification as an Indicator of Global Change. In: Letcher TM, editor. *Climate change: observed impacts on planet earth.* Oxford: Elsevier; 2009. p. 367.
16. Pelini S, Prior KM, Parker DJ, Dzurisin JDK, Lindroth R, Hellmann JJ. Climate Change and Temporal and Spatial Mismatches in Insect Communities. In: Letcher TM, editor. *Climate change: observed impacts on planet earth.* Oxford: Elsevier; 2009. p. 215.
17. Patz JA. Climate change. In: Frumkin H, editor. *Environmental health: from global to local.* 2nd ed. New York: John Wiley and Sons; 2010.
18. Mann CC, Plummer ML. Forest biotech edges out of the lab. *Science* 2002;**295**:1626–9.
19. Goodland R, Anhang J. *Livestock and climate change. Worldwatch Institute.* http://www.worldwatch.org/node/6294; 2009 [accessed March 7, 2012].
20. U.S. Environmental Protection Agency. *Opportunities to reduce greenhouse gas emissions through materials and land management practices.* EPA 530-R-09-017; 2009.
21. Hinrichsen D. Population pressure. In: Frumkin H, editor. *Environmental health: from global to local.* 2nd ed. New York: John Wiley and Sons; 2010.
22. Intergovernmental Panel on Climate Change. Climate change 2007: impacts, adaptation, and vulnerability; 2007. Wiley LF, Gostin LO. The international response to climate change: an agenda for global health. *JAMA* 2009;**302**:1218–20.
23. Crutzen P. Albedo enhancement by stratospheric sulfur injections: a contribution to resolve a policy dilemma? *Clim Change* 2006;**77**:211–20.

24. Gardiner S. A perfect moral storm: climate change, intergenerational ethics, and the problem of moral corruption. *Environ Values* 2006;**15**:397–413.
25. Congressional Budget Office. *The economic effects of legislation to reduce greenhouse-gas emissions.*
26. Kreutzer D. The economic impact of cap and trade. *Testimony before the Energy and Commerce Committee U.S House of Representatives.* 2009.
27. Organization for Economic Cooperation and Development. *The economics of climate change mitigation: policies and options for global action beyond 2012.*
28. Environmental Defense Fund. *How cap and trade works. 2011.*
29. Rosenthal E. *Climate change treaty, to go beyond the Kyoto Protocol, is expected by the year's end.* Princeton, NJ: The New York Times Press; 2009.
30. Posner GA, Weisbach D. *Climate change justice.* Princeton: Princeton University; 2010.
31. Spencer RW. *Climate confusion: how global warming hysteria leads to bad science, pandering politicians and misguided policies that hurt the poor.* New York: Encounter Books; 2010.
32. See Wang X, Li Q, Xie J, Jin Z, Wang J, Li Y, et al. Fabrication of ultralong and electrically uniform single-walled carbon nanotubes on clean substrates. *Nano Lett* 2009;**9**(9):3137–41 doi:10.1021/nl901260b.
33. The letter "X" commonly denotes a halogen, e.g., fluorine, chlorine, or bromine, in organic chemistry. However, in this text, since it is an amalgam of many scientific and engineering disciplines, where "x" often means an unknown variable and horizontal distance on coordinate grids, this rule is sometimes violated. Note that when consulting manuals on the physicochemical properties of organic compounds, such as those for pesticides and synthetic chemistry, the "X" usually denotes a halogen.
34. For a complete explanation of the Henry's law constant, including how it is calculated and example problems [see chapter 5, Movement of Contaminants in the Environment].
35. The major source for this discussion is: Vallero DA, Vesilind PA. *Socially responsible engineering: justice in risk management.* Hoboken, NJ: John Wiley & Sons; 2005; 2006.
36. Loxnachar T, Brown K, Cooper T, Milford M. *Sustaining our soils and society.* Washington, DC: American Geological Institute, Soil Science Society of America, USDA Natural Resource Conservation Service; 1999.
37. Evangelou VP. *Environmental soil and water chemistry: principles and applications.* New York: John Wiley and Sons, Inc; 1998.
38. U.S. Congress, Office of Technology Assessment. *Potential environmental impacts of bioenergy crop production-background paper, OTA-BP-E-118.* Washington, DC: U.S. Government Printing Office; September 1993.
39. Smith AC, Diamond WP, Organiscak JA. *Bleederless ventilation systems as a spontaneous combustion control measure in U.S. coal mines.* U.S. Department of the Interior, Bureau of Mines; 1994; Information Circular 9377, NTIS PB94-152816.
40. Trevits MA, Smith AC, Ozment A, Walsh JB, Thibou MR. Application of gas-enhanced foam at the Excel No. 3 mine fire, In: *Proceedings of the national coal show, Pittsburgh, Pennsylvania, June 7-9,* Denver, CO: Mining Media, Inc; 2005.
41. Sabine C. *NOAA Pacific Marine Environmental Laboratory, Seattle, Washington.* Quoted in http://www.noaanews.noaa.gov/stories2004/s2261.htm; 2004 [accessed August 26, 2007].
42. Intergovernmental Panel on Climate Change. *United Nations. IPCC special report on carbon dioxide capture and storage. Approved and accepted by IPCC working group III and the 24th session of the IPCC in Montreal, 26 September 2005;* 2005.
43. Grinsted A, Moore JC, Jevrejeva S. *Climate Dynamics.* 2009, http://dx.doi.org/10.1007/s00382-008-0507-2.
44. Ayyub B, Braileaunu HG, Qureshi N. Prediction and impact of sea level rise on properties and infrastructure on Washington, DC. Risk Analysis, http://onlinelibrary.wiley.com/doi/10.1111/j.153-6924.2011.01710.x/pdf.
45. *Guardian Newspaper.* June 1, 2012.
46. Nourse H. Personal communication.

# Nature

In Chapter 8, we encountered the difficulty of attributing cause to effects in climate change. The atmosphere is very complex. Small changes in the mixture of gases in the atmosphere can wreak havoc in terms of climatic conditions, including ambient temperature, precipitation, storms, winds, currents, and seasons.

It should be noted that there are a few, if any, completely "natural" disasters. Human activities sometimes worsen natural events that allow them to become disastrous. Recent examples include the completely natural occurrence of the earthquake in the Sea of Japan. This was entirely the result of Japan's tectonic situation. The main island, Honshu Island, is located where the Eurasian, Pacific, and Philippine Sea tectonic plates meet and push against each other. The seismic pressure is huge, so one would expect a high frequency of earthquakes. Indeed, about one-fifth of world's earthquakes greater than or equal to magnitude 6 on the Richter scale occur in Japan. The tsunami that occurred was also to be expected, as the first two laws of motion dictate that the release of this seismic energy had to be displaced. The tsunami was merely the result of energy transport via the waves.

What transformed these natural events into human and ecological disasters can be placed squarely on human (anthropogenic) activities. The decision to cite a nuclear power plant within a high-hazard zone, the lack of preparedness for cooling of fuel rods, the weaknesses in evacuation planning, and other planning and engineering failures led to the human and ecological disasters that will continue for decades, at least in terms of unacceptable levels of radioisotopes and other contamination. To some extent, this is true for every disaster discussed in this chapter. Certainly, the natural events trigger and exacerbate disasters, but they all have an anthropogenic component.

The hydrologic cycle plays a huge role in disasters. The obvious examples are meteorological events, such as hurricanes, tornados, and floods. However, disasters are often a mix of atmospheric and terrestrial phenomena. For example, a levee or dam breach, such as the recent catastrophic failures in New Orleans during and in the wake of Hurricane Katrina, experienced failure when flow rates reached cubic meters per second. Conversely, a hazardous waste landfill failure may be reached when flow across a barrier exceeds a few cubic centimeters per decade.

Both of these disasters were determined by the loading of water into a system. In the case of the hurricane, the loading occurs rapidly over a period of a few days, whereas the loading of the landfill occurs over decades. Both systems were also affected by terrestrial phenomena, such as the water-holding capacity of soils and subsurface materials. Once the ground becomes saturated, the water runs overland, leading to pressure on levees and swelling streams. Thus, the damage incurred from or worsened by precipitation and other hydrological factors have temporal dimensions. If the outcome (e.g., polluting a drinking water supply) occurs in a day, it may well be deemed a disaster, but it it the same level of pollution is reached in a decade, it may be deemed an environmental problem, but not a disaster. Of course, if this is one's only water supply, as soon as the problem is uncovered, it becomes a disaster to that person. In fact, it could be deemed worse than a sudden-onset disaster, as one realizes he or she has been exposed for a long time. This was the case for some of the infamous toxic disasters of the 1970s, notably the Love Canal incident (see Chapter 5).

## HURRICANES

Large storms are often associated with large costs in terms of life and property. In addition, they can damage ecosystems and sensitive habitats. Hurricanes, in particular, have uncovered some major weaknesses in protecting areas near the coasts. Interestingly, hurricanes are not all that rare. Approximately 100 hurricanes, typhoons, and tropical storms occur globally every year (see Figure 9.1), but the frequency appears to have been increasing since 1995. The increase in Atlantic hurricane activity could be the result of natural climatic cycles and increasing ocean temperatures in the North Atlantic.[1]

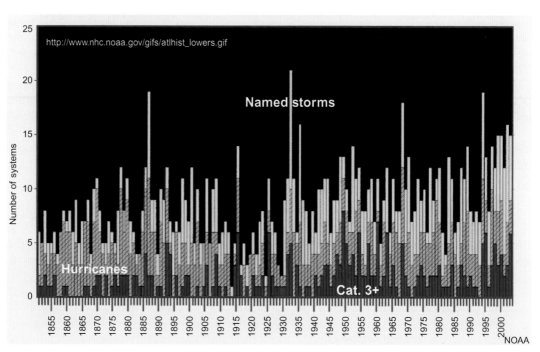

FIGURE 9.1   Recorded storm systems since 1855. *Image courtesy of NOAA/NWS National Hurricane Center.*

Every major storm affects ecosystem conditions to varying degrees. We discuss two examples in this chapter, the very large Hurricane Katrina and the comparatively small Hurricane Andrew. These indicate that ecological damage depends not only on the intensity and severity of the storm but also on the vulnerability of the ecosystem.

## Hurricane Katrina

The strong category 3 (sometimes classified as category 4) Hurricane Katrina made landfall in the Gulf Coast of Louisiana, Mississippi, and Alabama on August 29, 2005. In several ways, this was literally and metaphorically a "perfect storm." That is, all of the conditions for a disaster occurred simultaneously. With winds at 201 km h$^{-1}$ and storm wave surges over 3 m, hundreds of kilometers of shoreline were pummeled. An area greater than 200,000 km$^2$ was impacted. More than 1800 people perished.[2] The damage from the storm resulted from the combination of the sustained intensity of the storm as well as the hydrologic and physiographic conditions in the Delta region. For example, the Mississippi River is less than 1 m above sea level as it traverses New Orleans. Much of the land, developed and undeveloped, is at or below sea level (see Figure 9.2).

Tragically, failures preceded, co-occurred, and followed the storm. The vulnerability of New Orleans was no surprise to many scientists and engineers. For example, long before the hurricane, earth scientist Timothy Kusky[3] warned that "If a Category 4 hurricane ever hits New Orleans directly, the dikes will be breached and destroyed, and thousands will perish." In fact, the cities on the delta of the Mississippi River (or any river system for that matter) are engaged in a constant struggle against nature.

The "perfect storm" required the confluence of meteorological events (high-intensity hurricane, 100-year flood), sociological conditions (traditionally poor and mistrusting populace), and political mistakes (botched evacuation planning, delayed response due to red tape and

FIGURE 9.2   Simulated view of the potential effects of storm surge flooding on Lake Pontchartrain and the New Orleans area, depicting flooding in 1-m increments. Bright areas show regions of high radar reflectivity, such from urban areas, and elevations have been coded in color using height data also from the mission. Dark green colors indicate low elevations, rising through yellow and tan to white at the highest elevations. *Image credit: National Aeronautics and Space Administration (2000). Jet Propulsion Laboratory.*

bureaucracy, corruption, and lack of coordination among responding agencies). In addition to the immediate loss of life and property, the immediate and long-term environmental effects have slowly begun to be fully understood.

The ecosystem damage included washed-away barrier islands, hundreds of millions of killed trees, and submergence of marshlands, which are now actually lakes. These were the basis of habitats for many terrestrial, aquatic, and bird species.

Indeed, the Delta region was already in trouble. Possibly the best characterization was by a nonscientist, New Orleans native singer Aaron Neville. In an appearance on the *Tonight Show* a week after the storm, Neville described the scenario as a "toxic gumbo." The flood waters contain the typical pathogens and vectors (e.g., rats) following flooding. In addition, due to the industries and commercial enterprises in the region, numerous petroleum refineries and pipelines, pesticide manufacturers, chemical plants, and other sources of toxic pollutants were added to the exposures. Again, this is no surprise, as the gulf has some of the highest exposures to toxic contaminants in the nation. Further exacerbating the contamination, is the amount of time it took to pump out the water. The longer the water remained in the New Orleans basin, the greater would be the number of pipe breaks, line failures, and chemical releases. Fires started and gases were released in the days following the hurricane so that thousands of first responders from around the nation had to be called in to suppress fires and repair lines all this while trying to evacuate people and begin recovery.

We are reminded of the old adage, "When you are up to your neck in alligators, it is too late to think about draining the swamp." Conversely in this case, we would have to restate the adage as "When you are up to your neck in toxic gumbo, it is too late to think about saving the wetlands." Wetlands are a natural part of hydrologic systems, especially in deltas and backwater areas. Humans had to make a cognizant (using the advisedly) decision to destroy these natural systems and replace them with structures like buildings and roads. This is doubly bad for the hydrology as the systems now have vulnerable land uses (and the people using the land) and the ability to infiltrate and remove water is exponentially decreased (due to the great increase in impervious surfaces, the loss of plant life, and elimination of the integration of surface and ground water systems). Before the development, the streams were connected to each other and to the aquifers, allowing for efficient water removal. So, the engineers and planners who allowed and even designed these new land uses were key players in the disaster.

Another aspect of the perfect storm was cultural, i.e. the inappropriate city and regional planning. In fact, the New Orleans disaster shares some common elements with one of the worst industrial disasters in Bhopal, India. First, engineers and planners seem to adopt a "one size fits all" mentality. Like Bhopal, where the U.S. company transplanted a western type pesticide plant in a completely different culture, with little regard for the social differences, the design and siting of industrial facilities in the Mississippi delta were little different from that in an upland. Second, land use planning failed in not considering the possible impact on people living next to a facility. The discontinuity should have been obvious. In Bhopal, squatters lived right at the company property line. In New Orleans, whole neighborhoods were in the shadow of heavy industry. Third, the adjacent residents had little voice in decisions made that directly affects their health. This would have been the case even without Katrina, although in a less acute manner, as they were being exposed to contaminants every day. Fourth, the agencies that were supposed to be protecting public health and the environment were actually collaborating with those who were presenting the threat. In Bhopal, the local and national Indian governmental agencies were more concerned about encouraging industry than about protecting the most vulnerable. Unfortunately, it appears that this may also have been the case in New Orleans.

The major similarity between the aftermaths of Bhopal (Chapter 3) and Hurricane Katrina is the disproportionate effect on those who were already at a cultural and social disadvantage. One interesting observation is the disproportionate impact on women and children in New Orleans (some preliminary estimates were that four times more women than men were among the "refugees" and those who lost their lives). This may well be the result of socioeconomic conditions, such as the unstable conditions of lower socioeconomic status families, such as higher percentages of single heads of households. Characterizing such vulnerabilities *in any community* must be part of emergency and contingency planning.

## Hurricane Andrew

Mangroves are marine-based forests that colonize and persist in saline, intertidal waters. In the United States, black mangrove (*Avicennia germinans*), white mangrove (*Laguncularia racemosa*), and red mangrove (*Rhizophora mangle*) are the principal species. These ecosystems provide habitat for aquatic organisms and birds.[4]

In August of 1992, the relatively small but strong Hurricane Andrew cut a path of destruction through south-central Louisiana and southern Florida (see Figure 9.3), with much rain and sustained winds greater than 140 km h$^{-1}$. Rainfall associated with Andrew was light for a hurricane because of the small size and rapid forward movement of the storm. However, rainfall totals of more than 180 mm (7 inches) were recorded for the storm period in southeastern Florida and Louisiana; a high of 302 mm (11.9 inches) was recorded in Hammond, LA.[5] Maximum sustained wind speeds of 227 km h$^{-1}$ and gusts of 272 km h$^{-1}$ were measured on August 24, just before landfall.[5] The storm surge was about 6 m above sea level at Biscayne Bay, FL and about 3 m near Terrebonne Bay in south-central Louisiana.

FIGURE 9.3   Satellite imagery of Hurricane Andrew on August 26, 1992. *Data from National Oceanic and Atmospheric Administration, National Weather Service. Landsat images from U.S. Geological Survey, EROS Data Center.*

FIGURE 9.4    Hammock destruction in Everglades National Park, Florida, after Hurricane Andrew, September 1992. *Photo credit: B.F. McPherson, U.S. Geological Survey.*

The hurricane passed through the Florida Everglades, the largest wetland system in the United States. The tree damage was substantial, severely damaging mangrove trees on 283.3 km$^2$ of wetlands. The storm defoliated nearly all mature trees (mainly hardwood) on islands of dense, tropical undergrowth, with about one-fourth of the trees severely damaged (see Figure 9.4). About the same percentage of the royal palms and one-third of the pine trees in Everglades National Park were severely damaged (see Figure 9.5).

Hardwood trees have a better likelihood of recovery than most conifers when the limbs are damaged, as deciduous hardwood trees generally regrow limbs and even trunks; whereas conifers, like the loblolly pine, do not survive such an insult. This is an important distinction for carbon sequestration, for example, as the root system of a surviving tree stays intact. Root systems of trees often have greater biomass than that above the ground surface, so if the tree stays alive, the rate of carbon released to the atmosphere does not increase. Whereas, if the tree dies, the rate of carbon release increases rapidly as the dead tree's biomass is degraded by microbes (fungi and bacteria). This feature can have profound effects on climate change. For example, it may be prudent to harvest wood from certain hardwoods periodically, rather than to grow whole conifers. Each time a pine or fir tree is harvested, the carbon from its roots is released to the atmosphere, but each time wood is taken from a living hardwood that survives, the carbon remains underground, rather than emitted as carbon dioxide ($CO_2$), methane ($CH_4$) and other greenhouse gases.

# FLOODS

Certainly, floods are a major source of destruction from a hurricane, but they may occur as the result of other meteorological events, such as severe thunderstorms, snow melt, and seasonal precipitation. As disasters go, floods can be counted among the worst. Other than

FIGURE 9.5 Killed and damaged pine trees in Everglades National Park, Florida, after Hurricane Andrew, September 1992. *Photo credit: B.F. McPherson, U.S. Geological Survey.*

pandemics and starvation, the 1931 Central China floods of the Yangtze River and its tributaries comprise the worst natural disaster in recorded history in terms of loss of human lives, estimated to be as high as 4 million.[6]

The likelihood and severity of flooding increases as a result of human activities. These activities include building in and near flood plains and the destruction of wetlands. Floods cause the loss of thousands of lives each year, along with billions of dollars of property loss. They also cause ecological damage. Levee and reservoir construction have partially addressed the need to reduce flooding frequency and severity. However, there have been numerous levee breaches.[7] High water that exceeded design is the principal cause of failure.

The environmental effects of flow control structures are dwarfed by the need to protect human development. In this case, human activities and ecological condition are conflicting values. Flood control systems like levee systems and flood control reservoirs alter a stream's natural disturbance and stimulation. This leads to a separation of the main channel from its natural floodplain, as well as excessive drying and destruction of wetland areas, and changes to the riverine hydrology. Moreover, channel/floodplain separation is directly linked to changes in the hydrologic regime and wetland loss.[8] Many aquatic organisms rely primarily or exclusively on floodplain habitat.[9] Additional species depend on flooded areas to spawn and forage.[10]

In addition to damage caused by a flood, measures taken to prevent floods actually can harm ecosystems. As mentioned, one of the principal causes of wetland loss and destruction is segregating the channel of a stream from its larger flood plain. By design, engineered levees bound the river at its banks. This confinement increases the height of the flood stage and stream velocity. The same amount of energy is confined to within the banks. Eventually, the river will reclaim pre-levee boundaries, usually violently, as we saw in the aftermath of Hurricane Katrina (Figure 9.2).

# DROUGHT

Ecosystems exist within an optimal range of hydrological conditions. As we discussed in the previous sections, too much water in the wrong place at the wrong time can be highly destructive. Conversely, not enough water in the wrong place at the wrong time can also devastate cause or contribute to environmental disaster. For example, many would argue that the worst disaster experienced in the United States was the Dust Bowl in the 1930s. The affected area was mainly western Kansas, eastern Colorado and New Mexico, and the panhandles of Texas and Oklahoma.

As has been a common theme in this chapter, the Dust Bowl was a combination of natural and human-caused events. Certainly, the lack of rain led to drought conditions for a decade, which, in turn, contributed to erosion and loss of top soil. However, agricultural practices were an important contributor as well. Farmers had supplanted drought-resistant native prairie grasses with drought-sensitive crops like corn and beans. Thus, when the crops died, the top soil was easily eroded and lost. Thus, the Dust Bowl's dust that caused respiratory problems and "black blizzards" was actually the invaluable commodity of top soil that took millennia to produce.

# ECOSYSTEM RESILIENCE

The loss of top soil is almost irreversible, as it takes so long to produce. Likewise, wetlands are difficult or impossible to recover when they are lost. Other systems tend to be more elastic. For example, the good news is in less than 1 month after Hurricane Andrew, the surviving trees and shrubs had sprouted new growth.[11] Unfortunately, however, the actual recovery of the mangrove communities, like other ecosystems, is highly complex. An ecosystem's stability and ability to recover after disturbance is a measure of its resilience.[12] This depends on relationships among physicochemical and biological conditions. After a major disruptive event like a hurricane, these are in a state of disarray.

Resilience, then, is reflected at all levels of biological organization. For example, the recovery of a wetland system, no matter the size, involves a complete food chain, including the sustained health of the top carnivore or other indicator species. Matter and energy must be accounted for when evaluating the health of biosystems, whether it is the kinetics and dynamics within an organism (i.e., physiologically based, pharmacokinetics and dynamics) or a multispecies ecosystem (structural and functional ecology).

Indeed, the food web structure will influence its resilience and its return to equilibrium. This is analogous to the concept of hysteresis, i.e., the condition of a system depends not only on its current environment but also on its past environment. Ecosystem hysteresis occurs when changes in the state of an ecosystem are path dependent, that is, the hysteresis is generated by various mechanisms of reinforcement that keep the system in a given state. This dependence arises because the system can be in more than one internal state. To predict its future development, either its internal state or its history must be known. For example, a biological community may be seen to be a functioning relationship among plants, animals, microbes, and the abiotic environment.[13] Thus, ecosystem recovery is complex and sensitive to nuance.

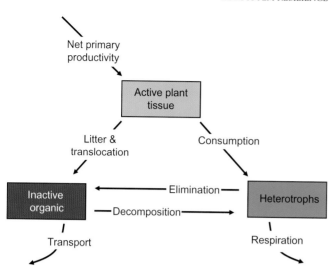

FIGURE 9.6    Transfer of matter and energy within a biological community. *Adapted from Ref. 15.*

Microbial populations comprise key compartments of the food web, including bacterial, fungal, and algal communities (see Figure 9.6). For example, in a six-compartment food web model for sea bass (*Dicentrarchus labrax*),[14] three of these compartments are dominated by microbial populations, i.e., the two plankton compartments and the detritus (see Figure 9.7). The exchange between the environment and the organism is usually observed empirically, e.g., water samples. Similar systematic relationships exist in other media.

The kinetics of this community is interdependent among living and nonliving components. The rate of change of active plant growth and metabolism depends on the input of energy, represented by *net primary productivity* in Figure 9.6. The active plant compartment leads to two outputs consumption of matter (e.g., nutrients) and loss of matter (litter). The rates of change of energy and matter further down the food web depend on subsequent inputs and outputs. The heterotrophs consume living plant biomass and dead organic matter and then release their own elimination products.[15]

Biologists input these energy and matter kinetics into a system resilience index to estimate potential implications, especially irreversible impacts, of ecosystem damage. For example, resilience of various types of ecosystems has been compared according to the energy needed per unit of active plant tissue (e.g., standing crop). The index would likely indicate that a system with low total amount of active tissue and a high amount of biomass turnover would be best able to adapt to perturbations. Thus, in Figure 9.8, the pond would be expected to have much greater resilience (i.e., four orders of magnitude) than a tundra system or a tropical forest (three orders of magnitude).[16] Based on their relatively low energy fluxes, damage to the mangroves (expected to be similar to tropical forests) may take considerably longer to recover than damage to surface waters and have a higher likelihood of irreversibility.

An often overlooked aspect of ecological damage is the damage incurred against microbial populations. Flooding, scouring, and other physical changes can be profound. For example, microbes often exist within finite ranges of oxidation. Scouring of sediments may expose

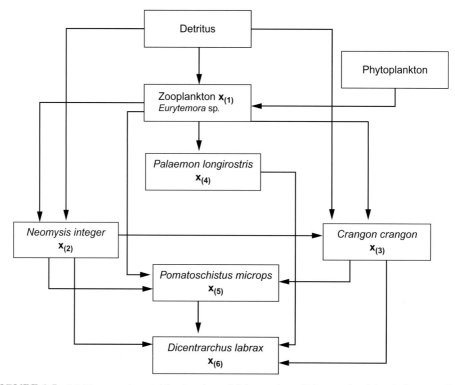

FIGURE 9.7    Multicompartmental food web model for sea bass (*Dicentrarchus labrax*). *Source: Ref. 14.*

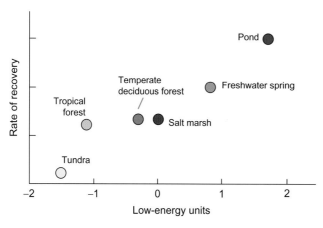

FIGURE 9.8    System resilience index calculated from bioenergetics for six community types. Rate of recovery units are arbitrary; energy units=energy input per unit standing vegetation. *Sources of data: Refs. 15, 16.*

anaerobic bacteria to molecular oxygen, completely altering the microbial ecology. Conversely, aerobic bacteria may be submerged and exposed to anoxic conditions. Either (or both, as is the case in flooding) can upset ecological processes, such as decomposition. Most bacterial growth models have been concerned with the microbial population's response to various physical conditions, especially varying water temperatures, pH, or concentrations of chemical substances.[17] In fact, fish food models have attempted to predict quality and shelf life of the organisms after harvest.[18] Conversely, environmental indices may apply the same parameters, but are interested in the fish as indicators of environmental and ecosystem condition, rather than their value as food commodities. The bottom line is that small things (literally, in the case of microbes) greatly influence ecosystem wellbeing.

Ecosystems are in many ways similar to the energy and mass budgets of the chemical reactors. Ecologists attempt to understand the complex interrelationships and consider humans too among the exchanges and conversions of energy and mass. Scientists try to optimize the intended products and to preserve (limit the effects) on the energy and mass balances. This helps in decisions as to whether potential downstream costs are either acceptable or unacceptable and to highlight the uncertainties, especially the extent to which possible unintended, unacceptable outcomes may occur. Often, this optimization involves more than two variables (e.g., species diversity, productivity and sustainability, costs and feasibility, and efficiencies). The challenge is to discover the extent to which the optimization represents the real world as the variables change in time and space. This is a profound challenge for planners making decisions regarding the development of coastal and other sensitive areas. The temptation may be to exaggerate the short-term benefits (housing, tax base, etc.) and to discount long-term costs (flood damage, habitat destruction, etc.).

This systematic view is also valuable for interventions and recovery measures needed to address disturbed ecosystems. It provides for an assessment of feasibility. That is, in addition to identifying options, it gives planners and engineers an idea of the degree of difficulty in implementing the option (Figure 9.9).

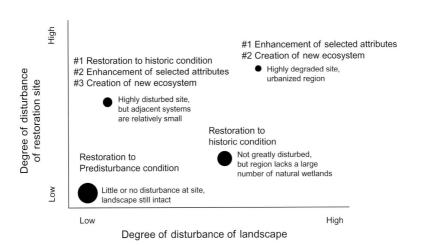

FIGURE 9.9   Restoration strategies applied to Columbia River Estuary ecosystems based on the amount of damage and likelihood of success (size of dot is proportional to relative chance of success). *Source: U.S. Department of Energy (2003). An ecosystem-based approach to habitat restoration projects with emphasis on Salmonids in the Columbia River Estuary. Final report (PNNL-14412). Washington, DC.*

# LESSONS TO BE LEARNED

Throughout this chapter, we have matched natural phenomena with human activities, with reminders that disasters are a function of both. Plans must include measures to complement the natural and cultural environment and to avoid destruction or adverse alteration of the land. This means that approaches to minimize impacts of construction and development must always consider the vulnerability of adjacent and nearby ecosystems.

For example, land use planning must directly address habitat destruction by recommending ways that any development conserve land that serves as habitat for native flora and fauna, both on and off site and directly and indirectly. An example of indirect destruction or secondary impacts from access created by infrastructure, including the siting of new sewer lines or roads in previously undeveloped or low-density land, as well augmenting existing facilities (e.g., road widening, bridge upgrades, port renovations, parking systems, and landfill expansions). Access invites secondary development, which, in turn, calls for more roads, structures, and impervious surfaces. These changes then lead to changes in the physical characteristics of an area, including decreased soil infiltration, with concomitantly increased risks of flooding onsite and downstream, as the holding capacity for water during rain events decreases. Another special consideration for land development is the presence of threatened or endangered species, and the potential that their habitats may be affected by developing a site.

Post-disaster response and planning is a time that is susceptible to potential mistakes. Planners and engineers might be tempted to respond to a disaster by what they do best, that is, "design and build." However, designing and building must be the outgrowth of good planning and a thoughtful consideration of the events that led to the disaster. The thought process should be aimed at what can prevent such disasters in the future, rather than simply restoration to pre-disaster conditions. Indeed, if that is the goal, there is a strong likelihood that the disaster will be repeated. For example, "hardening" the levees and dams after the Hurricane Katrina flooding is not the solution, at least it is not the entire solution. Hindsight does approach "20/20." It seems obvious now that those engineers and planners who called for stronger levees deserve credit, but this is but a small part of the solution. Such engineering projects are only "successful" when they are integrated into an overall plan. There are positive signs in this regard. Numerous engineering experts have called for the construction of wetlands in flood-prone and otherwise environmental sensitive areas. And, many are calling for aggressive and well-enforced land use controls to prevent disasters of all sorts.

The United States has a checkered past when it comes to planning. Some have feared that land use planning is too much like a Soviet-style centralized planning program. As such, the U.S. has often forgone strong land use controls, even in vulnerable settings like wetlands, coast lines, and sensitive habitat, in the interest of unfettered uses by land owners. This is understandable, and some would argue that it is guaranteed by the Constitution, at least to the extent that such interventions are considered "takings" not justified by eminent domain for the public welfare. Indeed, land use controls are *de facto* takings as eminent domain, which must only be for the public good and for which the land owner is justly compensated. The New Orleans and other gulf disasters demonstrate that wise land use planning would have certainly provided for the public good. But, the sticky issue is just how the land owners should be compensated. Actually, zoning and other ordinances have stood the tests of legal challenges for several decades, so it seems that a major reason for the lack of strong planning is a mix of politics and economics. Unfortunately, to get elected often requires immediacy. It takes much courage to run on long-term issues like wetland protection, especially when others are offering short-term benefits (e.g., attracting industry, which, in turn, reduces taxes and offers jobs). The good news for engineers and other environmental professionals is that we are called to make the right decisions irrespective of politics. In reality, however, engineers all too often are beholden in some way to politics and economics (e.g., as line and staff employees in governmental agencies, as contractors to the city, and as beneficiaries of the short-term decisions). However, a glance at our first professional canon trumps these influences. We must hold paramount the health, safety, and welfare of the *public*, not the politicians and our bosses.

One could argue that engineering is becoming increasingly "green" and directed toward sustainable solutions. Actually, the concept of prevention is built into many engineering systems. For example, public impoundments usually proscribe any residential and most commercial buildings in the 100-year floodplain. The "100-year flood" is a purely statistical concept. The Federal Emergency Management Agency characterizes a 100-year flood as one with a magnitude expected to be equaled or exceeded once on the average during any 100-year period. Thus, it is not a flood that will occur once every 100 years, but it is the flood elevation that has a 1% chance of being equaled or exceeded each year. It is less a temporal concept than a hydrological phenomenon. Thus, the 100-year flood could occur more than once in a relatively short period of time, even several times in a single year. The 100-year flood is the standard applied by most Federal and state agencies, for example, it is used by the National Flood Insurance Program as the benchmark for floodplain management and to determine the need for flood insurance. It is used by the U.S. Army Corps of Engineers and the Bureau of Reclamation to prevent encroachment near impoundments and lakes. It is also a common standard for local, regional, and state land use planning. The challenge is that people become used to artificial "100-year" floods. Had the dikes and levees not existed in New Orleans, for example, much of the area would be in a "zero-year" floodplain (i.e., under water).

This begs the question as to whether it is wise engineering practice to build another better dike and levee system. Or, as Benjamin Franklin would suggest, should we apply an ounce of prevention (land use proscriptions) instead of a future pound of cure (repairing and rebuilding again in the vulnerable delta)? Although most engineers and planners may well agree that the answer to both questions is "yes," they will not all agree on how to go about it. They will disagree about space and time. Prevention comes in various forms and scales. The largest scale is planetary; the smallest scale is molecular.

As we discussed in the previous chapter, the intensity of the storm calls to mind the question of what is the role of global climate change, if any, in breeding large hurricanes and other extreme meteorological events. From a purely thermodynamic perspective, one would suspect the answer to be "yes." If the buildup of greenhouse gases has led to greater amounts of stored energy (i.e., infrared— heat—converted from incoming solar radiation), then there is more energy that needs to be released. Hurricanes are simply the result of two energy systems on earth, heat and motion. The heat is almost completely derived from the sun and is converted and transferred through complex systems in the atmosphere. Motion is the result of the earth's rotation (i.e., the Coriolis effect) where the air is deflected so that cyclones (low-pressure systems) and anticyclones (high-pressure systems) are formed. When greater amounts of heat are formed, then the mechanical and thermodynamic systems must become more intense and, if this logic is correct, the storms that result will likely become increasingly violent. Of course, there is much debate about the grounding assumption, that is, does the buildup of carbon dioxide, methane, and other gases in the earth's atmosphere *really* increase global temperatures? Like many uncertainties in science, this is *important if true.*

No matter what is decided, planners and engineers will have plenty to design and build, such as constructed wetlands and hardened facilities within the floodplain. The key is finding the proper balance of knowing what to build and what to avoid building. There is always a need to optimize among science and feasibility. Often, the important consideration in addressing natural disasters is not so much whether we can afford to address them as whether we can afford not to address them. Perhaps the biggest lesson to learn is the need to approach everything we do from a perspective of sustainability. When we design, plan, and build, how does this fit with and how does this affect other parts of the systems within which our projects will exist. We must do complete life cycle analyses and design with the ends in mind. Otherwise, our work will merely be a patchwork, or worse yet, natural conditions will combine with human error to become a "toxic gumbo."

# References and Notes

1. Locke WW. *Teaching with Hurricane Katrina: the physiology climate, storm and impact.* http://serc.carleton.edu/research_education/katrina/understanding.html; 2005 [accessed March 7, 2012].
2. Isreal B. *5 years after Katrina, Gulf ecosystems on the ropes.* Our Amazing Planet. http://www.ouramazingplanet.com/294-hurricane-katrina-gulf-coast-ecological-damage.html; 2010 [accessed March 7, 2012].
3. Kusky T. *Geological hazards.* Westwood, Connecticut: Greenwood Press; 2003 ISBN: 1573564699.
4. U.S. Geological Survey. *Modeling Hurricane Effects on Mangrove Ecosystems.* Report No. USGS FS-095-97; http://www.nwrc.usgs.gov/factshts/fs95_97.pdf; 1997 [accessed March 7, 2012].
5. Rappaport E. *Preliminary report, Hurricane Andrew, 16-28 August 1992.* Coral Gables, FL: National Oceanic and Atmospheric Administration, National Weather Service, National Hurricane Center; 1992.
6. National Oceanic and Atmospheric Administration . *NOAA's top global weather, water and climate events of the 20th century.* http://www.noaanews.noaa.gov/stories/s334b.htm; 2012 [accessed March 8, 2012].
7. Jacobsen RB, Oberg KA. *Geomorphic changes in the Mississippi River floodplain at Miller City, IL as a result of the flood of 1993.* Washington D.C: U.S. Geological Survey circular 1120-J, U.S. Government Printing Office; 1993.
8. Hickey JT, Salas JD. Environmental effects of extreme floods, In: *U.S.-Italy research workshop on the hydrometeorology, impacts, and management of extreme floods, Perugia, Italy, November*; 1995.
9. Leitman HM, Darst MR, Nordhaus JJ. *Floodplain of the Ochlockonee River, Florida, during flood and drought conditions.* Tallahassee, Florida: U.S. Geological Survey, Water-Resources Investigations (90-4202); 1991.
10. Copp GH, Penaz M. Ecology of flood spawning and nursery zones in the flood plain, using a new sampling approach. *Hydrobiologia* 1988;**169**(2):209–24.
11. Alper J. Everglades rebound from Andrew. *Science* 1992;**257**:1852–4.
12. Sustainable Development Commission. London: http://www.sd-commission.org.uk/pages/resilience.html; 2009 [accessed August 14, 2009].
13. Scheffer M, Carpenter S, Foley JA, Folke C, Walker B. Catastrophic shifts in ecosystems. *Nature* 2001;**413**:591–6.
14. Loizeau VR, Abarnou A, Nesguen AM. A steady-state model of PCB bioaccumulation in the sea bass (Dicentrarchus labrax) food web from the Seine Estuary, France. *Estuaries* 2001;**24**(6):1074–87.
15. Begon M, Harper JL, Townsend CR. *Ecology.* 3rd ed. Oxford, United Kingdom: Blackwell Science, Ltd; 1996.
16. O'Neill RV. Ecosystem persistence and heterotrophic regulation. *Ecology* 1976;**57**:1244–53.
17. Iliopoulou-Georgudaki J, Theodoropoulos C, Venieri D, Lagkadinou M. A model predicting the microbiological quality of aquacultured sea bream (*Sparus aurata*) according to physicochemical data: an application in western Greece fish aquaculture. *World Acad Sci Eng Technol* 2009;**49**:1–8.
18. This section is based on: Koutsoumanis K, Stamatiou A, Skandamis P, Nychas GJE. Development of a microbial model for the combined effect of temperature and pH on spoilage of ground meat, and validation of the model under dynamic temperature conditions. *Appl Environ Microbiol* 2006;**72**:124–34; Ross T, McMeeking TA. Modeling microbial growth within food safety risk assessments. *Risk Anal* 2003;**23**:182–97; Koutsoumanis K, Nychas GJE. Application of a systematic experimental procedure to develop a microbial model for rapid fish shelf-life prediction. *Int J Food Microbiol* 2000;**60**:171–84; Taoukis PS, Koutsoumanis K, Nychas GJE. Use of time temperature integrators and predictive modelling for shelf life control of chilled fish under dynamic storage conditions. *Int J Food Microbiol* 1999;**53**:21–31; Augustin JC, Carlier V. Mathematical modelling of the growth rate and lag time for *Listeria monocytogenes*. *Int J Food Microbiol* 2000;**56**:29–51; Gonzalez-Acosta B, Bashan Y, Hernadez-Saavedra N, Ascencio F, De la Cruz-Aguero G. Seasonal seawater temperature as the major determinant for populations of culturable bacteria in the sediments of an intact mangrove in an arid region. *FEMS Microbiol Ecol* 2006;**55**:311–21.

# Minerals

One interesting distinction between scientists and engineers is the way they approach living things. For example, when geologists consider mineralization, they may include many manners of how an earth stratum has reached its current form. A biologist may consider mineralization to be the process whereby large organic molecules become smaller inorganic compounds, such as the process of reducing proteins to ammonia and other simpler molecules.

The collection of all types of science forms the basis for applications. They underpin engineering, which is simply the application of these sciences to meet certain societal needs. Thus, scientific distinctions often become melded into systematic solutions. The distinctions in this chapter are with substances that are extracted from the earth and the problems and disasters that have resulted or could result as these substances are mined, processed, stored, and transported. Any and all of these processes can lead and have led to human and environmental disasters.

## INORGANIC SUBSTANCES

Inorganic compounds include all those that do not contain a carbon-to-carbon or carbon-to-hydrogen bond, i.e., those that are not organic compounds. When considering how such chemicals move and change in the environment and especially when deciding their hazards and risks to humans and ecosystems, quite a few areas of inorganic chemistry are important. First, toxic metals and metalloids and their compounds are foremost among the inorganic substances of concern. A number of metals have received much attention as environmental contaminants. Certain metals are known to harm the central and peripheral nervous systems. Two neurotoxic metals in particular have been involved in public health disasters, i.e., lead (Pb) and mercury (Hg). Other metals, such as manganese (Mn) have also been associated with chronic, neurological disorders.

Metal and inorganic compounds are well known for major contamination events and exposures to large numbers of susceptible populations, such as small children. Mercury is particularly difficult to address since its mobility in the environment and its toxicity to humans and animals is determined by its chemical form. For example, dimethylmercury is highly toxic, accumulates in the food chain, and has high affinity for organic tissues, but elemental mercury is much less toxic and is slower to bioaccumulate. Numerous nonmetals have also caused human health problems, such as nitrates eliciting methemoglobinemia in infants and cyanide compounds which has been responsible for major mass poisonings from releases into the environment.

Many elements exist in the environment in a number of oxidation or valence states. Unlike organic compounds, which can treated by destruction (actually conversion to simpler compounds, and finally to carbon dioxide and water), metals are not treated by destruction, but by changing valence. Each form of metal has its own toxicity and dictates its fate in the environment. Chromium, for example, in its trivalent ($Cr^{3+}$) is an essential form of the metal. Although toxic at higher level, $Cr^{3+}$ is much less toxic than the hexavalent $Cr^{6+}$, which is highly toxic to aquatic fauna and is a suspected human carcinogen. Toxicity, persistence, and fate are also determined by the metal's equilibrium chemistry, especially the amount in ionic forms and the amount that forms salts with nonmetals.

Engineers look as these systems with some endpoint in mind. For example, the same mineralization process that break down proteins are used in wastewater treatment plants. Rather than referring to the more general "reduction," however, the engineer refers to this as "denitrification," as the intent is to mineralize the compounds. This same logic applies to treating water and soil contaminated by metals. The engineer cannot "destroy" the metal, as it is an element, but can change it to less toxic forms. If this involves breaking it down to simpler and safer compounds, one could say call this engineered mineralization. Thus, in this chapter, we consider disasters that have involved extraction processes (with drilling and oil extraction addressed in Chapter 6).

Extracting valuable substances from the earth has been associated with three types of disasters. First, disasters have occurred because of the mining itself, including cave-ins, trapped miners in underground shafts, rapid releases of slurries and large amounts of toxic materials, and long-term contamination of water, sediment, soil, air, and the biosphere. Second, after extraction, the processes used to refine and manufacture products from the ores exposes workers and others to harmful contaminants. Third, more subtle disasters involve the substances themselves that end up in products or otherwise come into contact with people and the environment. This chapter addresses these three types of disasters.

## TOXIC METALS

So-called heavy metals dominate the list of "toxic metals." Indeed, the designation of "heavy" is any metal with the atomic mass greater than or equal to that of iron. These include the transition metals, lanthanides, and actinides.[1] This section addresses the more notorious of the metals, with the most notorious metalloid, arsenic, discussed later in this chapter.

Most toxic metals do exist naturally in very small concentrations but for some, the toxic levels can be just above the background concentration. In many cases, small amounts are very beneficial and are often referred to as trace metals. In most parts of the world, metal toxicity is a relatively uncommon medical condition. In general, it really only becomes important in and near specialized industrial environments.

### Mercury

The metal mercury (Hg) has recently been of particular interest to scientists and the general public. For example, there has been much concern as to whether a preservative used in vaccines might be part of the cause for the apparent increase in autism in recent decades. The metal has also been central to the debate about the safety of seafood and tradeoffs of hazards to unborn and nursing babies and the benefits of breast feeding. Actually, mercury is a natural component of the earth, with an average abundance of approximately 0.05 mg kg$^{-1}$ in the earth's crust, with significant local variations.

It is an unusual metal in that it is a liquid at room temperature (it melts at 38.9 °C and boils at 303 °C) and is very heavy with a density of 13.5 g cm$^{-3}$ at 25 °C. Studies have indicated that mercury can be a toxic substance and that one of its compounds, methylmercury chloride is a highly toxic substance. Measurements have shown that because mercury persists in the environment and methylmercury biomagnifies up the food chain, a wide variety of species and ecosystems may be exposed to excessive levels of mercury in the environment.[2]

Mercury ores that are mined generally contain about 1% mercury but at the Almaden mine in Spain they are mining an ore which contains about 12% mercury. Although about 25 mercury minerals are known, virtually the only deposits that are being mined contain cinnabar (HgS), a bright red substance which is also used to produce the color vermillion. Despite a decline in global mercury consumption, competing sources of mercury and low prices, the mining of mercury continues in a number of countries. Spain, China, Kyrgyzstan, and Algeria have dominated this activity in recent years. The last U.S. mine closed in 1982. There are reports of small mines in China, Russia (Siberia), Outer Mongolia, Peru, and Mexico. In the early 1980s, the annual production from mining (cinnabar) was 7000 tonnes, today it is less than half of that and is about 2000 tonnes.[3]

Mercury is also obtained as a by-product of mining or refining of other metals (such as zinc, gold, silver) or minerals and even from natural gas, from recycling spent products, and reprocessing mine tailings containing mercury. In the United States, this recovery of mercury as a by-product of other metal mining (primarily gold) from recycling and from the decommissioning of chlor-alkali plants, amounts to about 250 tonnes per year.[3]

Concentrations of total mercury in the atmosphere of the northern hemisphere have recently been estimated at 2 ng m$^{-3}$, those in the southern hemisphere being half this value. Values in urban areas are usually higher (e.g., 10 ng m$^{-3}$). Mercury has an appreciable vapor pressure ($2 \times 10^{-3}$ mm Hg or 0.3 Pa at 25 °C) which is the reason for it being in the atmosphere.[4,5] It has been estimated that each year 2000-3000 tonnes[6] enter the atmosphere from natural and anthropogenic sources. Natural sources, such as volcanoes, are responsible for approximately half of atmospheric mercury emissions. The anthropogenic half can be divided into the following estimated percentages which excludes biomass burning, an important source in some regions.[7,8]

- 65% from stationary combustion, of which coal-fired power plants are the largest aggregate source (40% of U.S. mercury emissions in 1999). This includes power plants fueled with gas where the mercury has not been removed. Emissions from coal combustion are between one and two orders of magnitude higher than emissions from oil combustion, depending on the country.[9]
- 11% from gold production. The three largest point sources for mercury emissions in the United States are the three largest gold mines. Hydrogeochemical release of mercury from gold-mine tailings has been accounted as a significant source of atmospheric mercury in eastern Canada.
- 6.8% from nonferrous metal production, typically smelters.
- 6.4% from cement production.

- 3.0% from waste disposal, including municipal and hazardous waste, crematoria, and sewage sludge incineration. This is a significant underestimate.
- 3.0% from caustic soda production.
- 1.4% from pig iron and steel production.
- 1.1% from mercury production, mainly for batteries.
- 2.0% from other sources.

Mercury vapor in laboratories can be a problem especially in laboratories that are heated. One way of reducing the evaporation (mercury has small vapor pressure) is to cover the pool of mercury in a beaker with a layer of water. The diffusion of mercury through water is very slow and it effectively seals off the evaporation process (the diffusion coefficient of mercury in water is $6.3 \times 10^{-10}$ m$^2$ s$^{-1}$).[10,11]

Minamata, a small factory town on Japan's Shiranui Sea, was the site of one of the most tragic industrial disasters. Minamata is "nitrogen" in Japanese, owing to the town's production of commercial fertilizer by the Chisso Corporation for decades, beginning in 1907.[12] Beginning in 1932, the company produced pharmaceutical products, perfumes, and plastics and processed petrochemicals. Chisso became highly profitable, notably because it became the only Japanese source of a high-demand primary chemical, D.O.P. (dioctyl phthalate), a plasticizing agent. These processes needed the reactive organic compound, acetaldehyde, which is produced using mercury. The residents of Minamata played a huge price for this industrial heritage. Records indicate that from 1932 to 1968, the company released approximately 27 tonnes of mercury compounds into the adjacent Minamata Bay. This directly affected the dietary intake for fisherman, farmers, and their families in Kumamoto, a small village about 900 km from Tokyo. The consumed fish contained extremely elevated concentrations of a number of mercury compounds, including the highly toxic methylated forms (i.e., monomethyl mercury and dimethyl mercury), leading to classic symptoms of methyl mercury poisoning. In fact, the symptoms were so pronounced the syndrome of these effects came to be known as the "Minamata Disease."

In the middle of the 1950s residents began to report what they called the "strange disease," including the classic form of mercury toxicity, i.e., disorders of the central and peripheral nervous systems (CNS and PNS, respectively). Diagnoses included numbness in lips and limbs, slurred speech, and constrict vision. A number of people engaged in uncontrollable shouting. Pets and domestic animals also demonstrated mercury toxicity, including cat suicides and birds dying in flight. These events met with panic by the townspeople.

The physician from the Chisso Corporation Hospital, reported in 1956 that, "an unclarified disease of the central nervous system has broken out." The physician correctly associated the fish dietary exposure to the health effects. Soon after this initial public health declaration, government investigators linked the dietary exposures to the bay water. Chisso denied the linkages and continued the chemical production, but within 2 years, they moved their chemical releases upstream from Minamata Bay to the Minamata River, with the intent of reducing the public outcry. The mercury pollution became more widespread. For example, towns along the Minamata River were also contaminated. Hachimon residents also showed symptoms of the "strange disease" within a few months. This led to a partial ban by the Kumamoto Prefecture government responded allowing fisherman to catch, but not to sell, fish from Minamata Bay. The ban did not reduce the local people's primary exposure, as they depended on the bay's fish for sustenance. The ban did acquit the government from further liability, however.

Some 3 years after the initial public health declaration, in 1959, Kumamoto University researchers determined that the organic forms of mercury were the cause of the "Minamata Disease". A number of panels and committees, which included Chisso Corporation membership, studied the problem. They rejected the scientific findings and any direct linkages between the symptoms and the mercury-tainted water. After the company physician performed cat experiments that dramatically demonstrated the effects of mercury poisoning for Chisso managers, he was no longer allowed to conduct such research and his findings were concealed from the public.[13] Realizing the links were true, the Chisso Corporation began to settle with the victims. The desperate and relatively illiterate residents signed agreements with the company for payment, but which released the company from any responsibility. The agreement included the exclusion: "... if Chisso Corporation were later proven guilty, the company would not be liable for further compensation." However, Minamata also represents one of the first cases of environmental activism. Residents began protests in 1959, demanding monetary compensation. These protests led to threats and intimation by Chisso, however, so victims settled for fear of losing even the limited compensation.

Chisso installed a mercury removal device on the outfall, known as a "cyclator," but the omitted a key production phase, so the removal was not effective. Finally, in 1968, the Chisso Corporation stopped releasing mercury compounds into the Minamata River and Bay. Ironically, the decision was not an environmental one, nor even an engineering solution. The decision was made because the old mercury production method had become antiquated. Subsequently, the courts found the Chisso Corporation repeatedly and persistently contaminated Minamata Bay from 1932 to 1968.

Victim compensation has been slow. About 4000 people have either been officially recognized as having "Minamata Disease" or are in the queue for verification from the board of physicians in Kumamoto Prefecture. Fish consumption from the bay has never stopped, but mercury levels appear to have dropped, since cases of severe poisoning are no longer reported.

## Cadmium

The miners of central Japan, near the Toyama Prefecture, have been removing metals from the surrounding mountains from as early as 710. Gold was the first metal to be mined from the area, followed by silver in 1589, and shortly thereafter, lead, copper, and zinc. At the start of the twentieth century, the Mitsui Mining and Smelting Co., Ltd controlled the production of these mines. As a result of the Russo-Japanese War, World War I, and World War II, a surge in the demand for metals in the use of weapons caused mass increases in the mines' production aided with the advent of new European technologies in mining.[14]

Along with the huge increase in mining production, came a significant increase in pollution produced from the mines. Liquid and solid wastes were dumped into the surrounding waters, including the Jinzu River which flows into the Sea of Japan, and the five major tributaries that flow into the Jinzu River. The Jinzu River water system supplies the water to the surrounding city of Toyama, 30 km downstream from the main mining operations. This water was primarily used by the surrounding areas in irrigation for the rice paddies. In addition, the water provided a source of water used for drinking, washing, and fishing.

In addition, large amounts of cadmium were released into the Jinzu River Basin from 1910 to 1945. Cadmium was extracted from the earth's crust during the production of other metals like zinc, lead, and copper that were being mined near the Toyama area. Cadmium is a naturally occurring element that does not corrode easily, enters the air during mining, can travel long distances, and then falls into the ground or water only to be taken up by fish, plants, animals, or humans from the environment.[15] The cadmium from the mines deposited in the river and land of the Jinzu River Basin were absorbed by surrounding plants and animals causing fish to die and the rice to grow poorly. Furthermore, humans living in the area consumed the poisoned water and rice.

As a result of the ingestion of cadmium, a new disease specific to the Toyama Prefecture appeared in 1912. Initially, the disease was not well understood and was suspected to be either a regional or bacterial disease or the result of lead poisoning. However, in 1955, Ogino and his colleagues suspected cadmium as the cause of the disease and named the disease *Itai Itai*. In 1961, the Kamioka Mining Station of Mitsui Mining and Smelting company was linked as the direct source of the cadmium poisoning, and the Toyama Prefecture, 30 km downstream, was designated the worst cadmium contaminated area (see Figure 10.1). The concentrations of cadmium in this prefecture were orders of magnitude higher than that found in background levels and were well above even other industrialized locations (see Table 10.1).

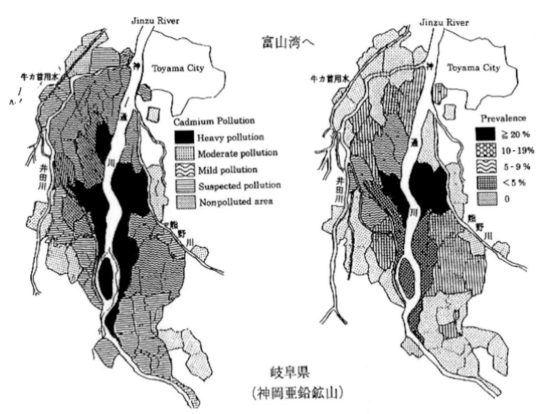

FIGURE 10.1    The co-occurrence of cadmium contamination with the prevalence of *Itai Itai* disease in woman over age 50 in Toyama Prefecture (~1961). *Source: ICETT Itai-itai disease (1998) Preventative Measures Against Water Pollution Jinzu River, Toyama Prefecture. http://icett.or.jp/lpca_jp.nsf/a21a0d8b94740fbd492567ca000d5879/b30e2e489f4b4ff1492567ca0011ff90? OpenDocument [accessed 02 July 2012].*

TABLE 10.1   Estimates of Average Daily Dietary Intake of Cadmium Based on Food Analysis in Various Countries

| Country | Estimates ($\mu$g Cd day$^{-1}$) |
|---|---|
| Areas of normal exposure | |
| Belgium | 15 |
| Finland | 13 |
| Japan | 31 |
| Japan | 48 |
| Japan | 49 |
| Japan | 35 |
| Japan | 49 |
| Japan 5 | 9 |
| Japan | 43.9 (males) 37.0 (females) |
| New Zealand | 21 |
| Sweden | 10 |
| Sweden | 17 |
| United Kingdom | 10-20 |
| USA | 41 |
| Areas of elevated exposure | |
| Japan | 211-245 |
| Japan | 180-391 |
| Japan | 136 |
| United Kingdom | 36 |
| United Kingdom | 29 |
| USA | 33 |

*Source: International Programme on Chemical Safety, 1992, Environmental health criteria: 134 (Cadmium), World Health Organization, Geneva, Switzerland.*

Cadmium exposure results in two major health-related problems of *Itai Itai* disease, irreversible kidney damage and bone disease (*Itai Itai* is Japanese for "Ouch Ouch"). After exposure to high levels of cadmium, the kidneys decrease their ability to remove acids from the blood due to proximal tubular dysfunction resulting in hypophosphatemia (low phosphate blood levels), gout (arthritic disease), hyperuricemia (elevated uric acid levels in the blood), hyperchloremia (elevated chloride blood levels), and kidney atrophy (as much as 30%). Following kidney dysfunction, victims of the disease develop osteomalacia (soft bones), loss of bone mass, and osteoporosis leading to severe joint and back pains and increase risk of fractures.

## Lead

The U.S. ATSDR (Agency for Toxic Substances and Disease Registry) in 1999, ranked lead second in the list of prioritized hazardous substances. The noxious effects of lead have been known for a long time—we are aware of the Romans inadvertently poisoning themselves by drinking and eating out of lead vessels. The World Health Organization has guidelines for lead in the air and in water of 0.5 $\mu g\,m^{-3}$ and 0.1 $mg\,L^{-1}$, respectively. The Centers for Disease Control and Prevention in the U.S. state that a blood level of 10 $\mu g\,dL^{-1}$ (100 $\mu g\,L^{-1}$ or 0.48 $\mu mol\,L^{-1}$) in children is a cause for concern. Lead poisoning occurs through ingestion, inhalation, and dermal contact, with inhalation perhaps, the most common exposure route. Factory workers dealing with lead and lead products and people living near such factories are the most likely to be affected. In countries where lead tetraethyl is still added to gasoline, the general public is exposed to significant lead levels through vehicles exhausts and even lead containing dust in the air.[16]

Exposures to lead can result in anemia; nervous system dysfunction; impaired cognitive, motor, and language skills; learning difficulties; nervousness and emotional instability; insomnia; nausea; lethargy; weakness, hypertension, kidney problems, decreased fertility and increased level of miscarriages, low birth weight and premature deliveries. Children exposed to high levels of lead show neurological impairment, growth retardation, delayed sexual maturation, and impaired vitamin D metabolism. Children are very much more susceptible to damage from lead than adults, and neurological impairment can occur in children with blood lead levels <10 $\mu g\,dL^{-1}$.[17]

Even at present, lead poisoning in children is related to lead paint and continues to be a major disaster since it adversely affects the quality of people's lives into the future. Many toys have in the past been painted with lead-based paints and when children suck, chew, and eat bits of this paint they can be exposed to dangerous levels of lead. Furthermore wood painted with lead-based paints which are now deteriorating can produce dangerous levels of lead through chips and dust formation which can be taken up by crawling babies. Another source of lead is from sanding or torching old paint from dwellings. Before the banning of lead-based pottery glazes eating and drinking out of such vessels was another way of ingesting lead. People who eat animals hunted with lead bullets may be exposed via ingestion.

In the United State, lead poisoning in areas not linked to mining or industry is still an issue as many people (estimated to be 25% of Americans) live in housing with lead-based paint. This is in spite of the fact that lead in paint was banned in the United States in 1950.[18] Lead carbonate (white lead) is the basis of the white paint and is not banned in all countries including Australia. Lead is mined and exported from Australia. In 2006, this led to an environmental tragedy when lead carbonate which was being loaded into a ship, showering the port town of Esperance in Western Australia, with dust, poisoning seven children, killing thousands of birds, and contaminating water tanks.[19] Although lead is not nearly as common in the environment as it used to be (largely due to the ban on lead tetraethyl in gasoline and lead in paint), it is still rated by the Centers for Disease Control (CDC) as the most common preventable poisonings of childhood. Their data shows that in the United States, 6% of all children ages 1-2 years and 11% of black (non-Hispanic) children ages 1-5 years have blood lead levels in the toxic range. Children with developing bodies are especially vulnerable because their rapidly developing nervous systems are particularly sensitive to the effects of lead.[20]

Today the most likely source of lead is from deteriorating lead-based paint, lead-contaminated dust, and from contaminated soil.

## Lead Mining Disasters

The worst lead disaster in U.S. history occurred at Picher, Oklahoma, a town which once had 14,000 residents and was once the most productive lead and zinc mine in the Unite States. Mining ceased in 1967 after the contaminated water from the mines had turned the local creek red. An investigation showed high levels of lead in the blood and tissues of the residents; high cancer levels, well above the average; and three quarters of the elementary school children were reading below grade level. The EPA called it the most toxic place in the America. The children were particularly vulnerable as they played and tobogganed down the mountains of mining waste which were laced with lead.

The area was declared a Superfund site in 1981, but most residents did not leave until 2006 and in 2009 the municipality ceased operating and the town became a ghost town. It was deemed too toxic to clean up and a federal buyout program paid people to leave.[21]

Many countries in the third world do not have the infrastructure or the restrictions to warn against lead poisoning and one can expect future disaster to occur there rather than in the West. One of the worst disasters from lead poisoning in recent years was uncovered in 2010 in Nigeria. Over 170 children died from lead poisoning in an area where digging for gold was the main occupation of the women from the nearby village. Lead was associated with gold in the ore body, a not uncommon occurrence. The mined ore was brought in sacks to the village for processing and at this stage the children played in the lead-contaminated and toxic ore. Over 400 people were tested and all but two had blood levels $>65\,\mathrm{mg\,L^{-1}}$. This is 650 times the danger level. The result was mental retardation, loss of motor skills, and even blindness in many of the women. Again it was the children that suffered most and many died as a result.[22]

## Mechanism of Toxicity in Humans

The toxicity of lead is largely due to its capacity to mimic calcium in the body and substitute it in many of the cellular processes that depend on calcium. However, the chemical basis for lead mimicking calcium is not obvious; neither the electronic structures nor the ionic radii of the two elements are similar. Lead coordination chemistry is broader than that of calcium and will complex with ligands such as the sulfhydryl group, and forms complex ions with $OH^-$, $Cl^-$, $NO_3^-$, and $CO_3^{2-}$.

Lead in the blood stream (inside the red blood cells and mostly linked to hemoglobin) is the cause of anemia which is a common but delayed sign of lead poisoning. Through the blood, lead reaches all other tissues and becomes stored in bones through its capacity to mimic calcium. Lead forms a very stable presence in bones and this makes recovery from lead poisoning extremely slow. Lead does cross the brain-blood barrier, leading to mental retardation and cognitive impairment.[23]

## Arsenic: The Toxic Metalloid

Arsenic has been known for centuries and its compounds have been used in all sorts of preparations, including: cosmetics; paints; artist's colors and dyes; alloys of lead, copper, and brass; pesticides; wood preservatives; tonics; glass production (it removes the green tint from the iron impurities); and even medicines. There is a theory that the once-popular arsenic-based wallpaper pigment, Paris green [copper (II) acetoarsenite], was the cause of Napoleon's mysterious death in 1821. In the late nineteenth century, arsenic compounds were linked to the deaths of more than 1000 children through inhaling arsenic vapors from moldy green wallpaper—probably the Paris green type. About the same time arsenic-based medications for syphilis, asthma, and psoriasis were considered the cause of skin cancer. Paris green is a highly toxic emerald-green crystalline powder that has been used as a rodenticide and insecticide, and also as a pigment, despite its toxicity. It is has also used as a blue colorant in fireworks. The color is apparently vivid, blue green when very finely ground and a deeper true green when coarsely ground.[24–26]

Today, in the United States the main use of arsenic is wood preservatives for outdoor and industrial environments. The use of arsenic compounds have dropped dramatically over the past 10 years, In 2001, the United States imported 25,000 tonnes of arsenic compounds but in 2009 only 3600 tonnes was imported.[27] Almost 90% of the imports are being used in chromated copper arsenate (CCA) wood preservative for "pressure-treated" decking, landscaping, walkways, and industrial usage. The rest is used in semiconductors, specialized metal, a few remaining pesticides, and treatments for acute leukemia and other cancers.

Arsenic and many of its compounds are very toxic to humans and arsenic powder has been the poisoner's choice since Nero's day. It disrupts the ATP reactions in the body and is very toxic to all animal life. Arsenic and its compounds, As(III) in particular, have in the past been used in the production of pesticides (treated wood products), herbicides, and insecticides. In 1980, the U.S. National Toxicology Program's first Report on Carcinogens listed inorganic arsenic compounds as known human carcinogen and soon afterwards in 1981, inorganic arsenic-based pesticides were banned and by 1985 the United States had stopped producing arsenic. The applications of arsenic have declined considerably since that time but in many parts of the world arsenic compounds are used in wood preservatives for industrial applications. The Unite States still imports arsenic for this and other specialized purposes.

Arsenic ores (arsenic sulfides, orpiment, and realgar) have been mined and used since ancient times. It is very probable that its toxic nature has been known for a very long time. Its potency and its discreetness (until the Marsh test for arsenic became known in the nineteenth century) had led to it being used over centuries for murder, and as a result has been called the *Poison of Kings* and the *King of Poisons*.[28]

It was used in the Bronze Age to harden bronze and to lighten the color of bronze and was discovered, as a distinct substance in the thirteenth century.[29,30]

There have probably been many disasters linked to the compounds of arsenic, going back over the centuries, but the Bradford sweet poisoning of 1858, which involved at least 20 deaths, is one of the first well documented disasters.[31]

The main route for human poisoning by arsenic is from drinking ground water that contaives high concentrations of arsenic. This has been the cause of a number of tragic disasters around the world (see later in this section). A 2007 study found that over 137 million people in more than 70 countries are probably affected by arsenic poisoning of drinking water.[32] Arsenic is toxic to aquatic life, birds and land animals and in soils, where arsenic content is high, plant growth and crop yields may be poor. Aquatic life is particularly sensitive to arsenic compounds and moderately toxic to birds and land animals. Arsenic is very persistent in the environment and is expected to bioaccumulate in fish and shellfish. In spite of this, there are some microorganisms that have evolved to tolerate relatively high concentrations of arsenic and some even thrive on it and use arsenic as an energy source. The energy generation is based on the redox chemistry of arsenic. Arsenic has four main oxidation states: $-3, 0, +3$, and $+5$ with the predominant inorganic forms being arsenates $(+5)$ and arsenites $(+3)$. Under aerobic conditions some microorganisms obtain energy by the oxidation of $As^{3+}$ to $As^{5+}$, with the resultant electrons being transferred to electron acceptors such as nitrate ions or oxygen and the ATP pump. Under anaerobic conditions, energy for growth is obtained by the microbial reduction of $As^{5+}$ to $As^{3+}$ coupled to the oxidation of organic matter or inorganic electron donors such as hydrogen or sulfide ions. These microbial processes together with inorganic and physical processes make up the global arsenic cycle.[33,34]

Because arsenic is in the same column of the periodic table as is phosphorus its compounds resembles those of phosphorus. The trivalent form is the most common; and is the basis for the arsenites and most organoarsenic compounds. Both $As_2S_3$ (Orpiment) and $As_4S_4$ (Realgar) are composed of trivalent arsenic. This might not seem possible for $As_4S_4$ but it is true as there are As-As bonds in the molecule.

An advocacy nongovernmental organization in 2001 in the United States, wanting to ban arsenic in all consumer products, found that pressure-treated wood leached more than 1 mg of arsenic onto a moistened hand wipe the size of a 4-year-old's hand. This is 100 times the U.S. Environmental Protection Agency's 10 µg $L^{-1}$ "allowable daily exposure level" for drinking water, assuming the child has a liter a day. Likely because of these findings, the wood processing industry agreed to stop using arsenic-based wood preservatives for household use as of December 2003.

However organic arsenic herbicides (not as toxic as their inorganic compounds) herbicides are still in use on cotton and turf, including golf courses, lawns, school yards, athletic fields, and rights-of-way.

In Europe, the Directive 2003/2/EC[35] restricts the marketing and use of arsenic, including CCA wood treatment. Treated CCA wood is not permitted to be used in residential or domestic constructions but is permitted for use in various industrial and public works, such as bridges, highway safety fencing, electric power transmission and telecommunications poles. This directive is not unlike the ruling in the United States.

In many other parts of the world the same type of ruling exists: in Australia, the use of CCA preservative for treatment of timber was restricted to certain applications from March 2006 and CCA may no longer be used to treat wood used in "intimate human contact" applications and that includes children's play equipment, furniture, residential decking and hand railing. Use for low contact residential, commercial, and industrial applications remains unrestricted, as does its use in all other situations. Similarly to the U.S. EPA regulations, the Australian authorities did not recommend dismantling or the removal of existing CCA treated wood structures.

In many parts of the world (parts of SE Asia, Chile, Argentine, parts of Western United States, Taiwan, Thailand, Mainland China, Bangladesh, and West Bengal) the arsenic concentration in groundwater is high enough to cause serious arsenic poisoning to people drinking the water. However nowhere in the world is the problem greater than in the Ganges delta (Bangladesh and to a lesser extent West Bengal).[36,37]

Bangladesh, in the 1970s, had one of the highest infant mortality rates in the world. This was largely due to ineffective water purification and sewage systems. Most drinking water used to be collected from open dug wells and ponds with little or no arsenic, but contaminated with water transmitting diseases such as diarrhea, dysentery, typhoid, cholera, and hepatitis. At that time the UNICEF and the World Bank aid workers worked out a solution; they decided to drill tube wells (boreholes) deep underground to tap into the groundwater.[38]

As a result 8 million tube wells (boreholes) were constructed to provide "safe" drinking water and in a short time the infant mortality and diarrheal illness were reduced by 50%. Most of the wells were augered to depths between 20 and 100 m. Unfortunately one in five of these wells was contaminated with arsenic which was above the government's drinking water standard set at 0.05 mg $L^{-1}$; this being five times the World Health Organization's acceptable maximum concentrations of arsenic in safe drinking water which was 0.01 mg $L^{-1}$. The crisis came to the attention of international organizations in 1995 and the resultant study involved the analysis of thousands of water samples as well as hair, nail, and urine samples.[39–41]

They found 61 out of 64 provinces in Bangladesh (900 villages) and in West Bengal 17 provinces, with arsenic water levels above the government limit. Results showed that many of wells which had been dug more than 20 m and less than 100 m were contaminated, whereas ground water and well water from depths greater than 100 m were free of arsenic. The explanation was that groundwater closer to the surface had spent a shorter time in the ground, therefore had not dissolved significant amounts of arsenic from the soil, and furthermore, the water from the wells deeper than 100 m was exposed to older sediments which had already been depleted of arsenic.[42] The total number of people using arsenic rich water (levels greater than 0.1 mg $L^{-1}$) was 1.4 million in West Bengal and a staggering 46-57 million in Bangladesh.[43,44] The crisis is still raging as many of the remedial programs have not worked.

## ASBESTOS

Asbestos could have been discussed in almost every chapter thus far. It has been released in the air and water, it has contaminated soil, and it is naturally occurring. The major concern with asbestos is when it is breathed in as a fiber. The size and shape of any aerosol, including a fiber, greatly influences its toxicity. Smaller particles (diameter <2.5 μm) can infiltrate the lungs more deeply and deposit with greater efficiency than larger particles. Particulate matter (PM) is measured using instruments that draw air through filters that collect particles. These instruments usually have size selection components to segregate the mass of each size fraction (i.e., "dichotomous" samplers). This allows for separation of fine particles with aerodynamic diameters <2.5 μm ($PM_{2.5}$) from coarse particles with aerodynamic diameters >2.5 μm, but <10 μm ($PM_{10}$).

A fiber is simply a particles that is elongated (see Figure 10.2). Such elongation is expressed as a particle's aspect ratio, i.e., the ratio of the length to width. Fibers are defined by regulatory agencies like the U.S. Environmental Protection Agency[45] and Occupational Safety and Health Administration[46] to have aspect ratios equal to or greater than 3:1. Asbestos comprises a group of highly fibrous minerals with separable, long, and thin fibers.

Asbestos exists in nature in two forms, *amphibole* and *serpentine*. Chrysotile is the only asbestos member of serpentine group. Some studies (Davis 1989) show that amphibole fibers stay in the lungs longer than chrysotile, and this tendency may account for their increased toxicity.

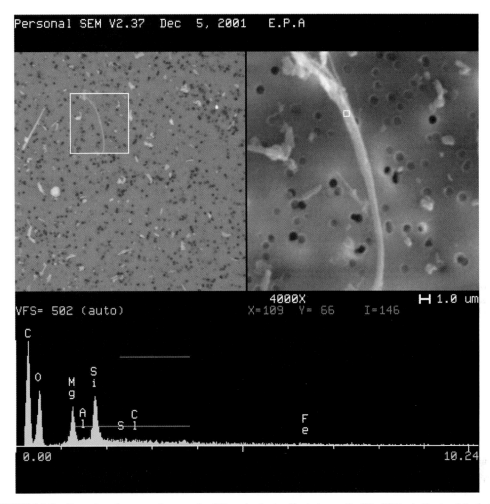

FIGURE 10.2    Scanning electron micrograph of fibers in dust collected near the World Trade Center, Manhattan, NY, in September 2001. The bottom of the micrograph represents the elemental composition of the highlighted 15-μm long fiber by energy dispersive spectroscopy (EDS). This composition (i.e., O, Si, Al, and Mg) and the morphology of the fibers indicate they are probably asbestos. The EDS carbon peak results from the dust being scanned on a polycarbonate filter. *Photo credit: U.S. Environmental Protection Agency; T. Conner.*

Generally, health regulations classify asbestos into six mineral types: chrysotile, which has long and flexible fibers; and five amphiboles, which have brittle crystalline fibers. The amphiboles include actinolite asbestos, tremolite asbestos, anthophyllite asbestos, crocidolite asbestos, and amosite asbestos. Note that each of the amphiboles includes the term "asbestos." This is because, to geologists, amphiboles can also have non-asbestiform habits (i.e., the host rock is an amphibole which may contain a mixture of nonfibrous particles, fibers, and cleavage fragments).

The most important risk factors for asbestos-related diseases are length of exposure, air concentration of asbestos during the exposure, and smoking.[47] Cigarette smoking and

TABLE 10.2   Estimated Lifetime Excess Risks Due to Continuous Exposure to Asbestos (Cases Per Million Population), Calculated with a Confidence Interval = 0.01

| Exposure group | Asbestos Dose (fibers m$^{-3}$) | | | | |
|---|---|---|---|---|---|
| | 8 | 50 | 80 | 500 | 2000 |
| Male smokers | 1 (0-9) | 6 (0-55) | 9 (0-88) | 55 (0-550) | 221 (0-2210) |
| Female smokers | 1 (0-5) | 2 (0-25) | 5 (0-41) | 25 (0-250) | 101 (0-1010) |
| Male nonsmokers | 1 (0-1) | 1 (0-8) | 1 (0-11) | 8 (0-75) | 29 (0-290) |
| Female nonsmokers | 1 (0-1) | 1 (0-3) | 1 (0-5) | 3 (0-28) | 11 (0-110) |

Numbers in parentheses are the estimated ranges with a lower limit = 0 and upper limit calculated from a confidence interval = 0.1 (California Air Resources Board, 1986).

asbestos exposure are synergistic (i.e., the risk of disease is multiplied if a person is both exposed to asbestos and cigarette smoke; see Table 10.2).

There is an ongoing scientific debate about the differences in the extent of disease caused by different fiber types and sizes. Some may be attributed to the physical and chemical properties of the different fiber types. Several studies suggest that amphibole asbestos types (tremolite, amosite, and especially crocidolite) may be more harmful than chrysotile, particularly for mesothelioma.[48] The dimensions (length and diameter) are also important factors for cancer-causing potential, with indications that fibers with lengths greater than 5.0 μm are more likely to cause injury than fibers with lengths less than 2.5 μm. Conversely, other data indicate that short fibers can contribute to injury.[49] This appears to be true for mesothelioma, lung cancer, and asbestosis. However, fibers thicker than 3.0 μm are of lesser concern, since they are less likely to penetrate into the lower regions of the lung.

Asbestos fiber exposure can also occur from drinking water. Studies have indicated high-end exposure groups to have elevated death rates from cancer of the esophagus, stomach, and intestines. This causality for this association has not been established scientifically since all studies include a number of confounding risk factors.

Human exposure to concentrations much higher than $10^{-4}$ fibers mL$^{-1}$ is suspected of causing adverse health effects. Asbestos fibers are very persistent and resist chemical degradation (i.e., they are inert under most environmental conditions) so their vapor pressures are nearly zero, meaning they do not evaporate. Furthermore they do not dissolve in water. However, segments of fibers do enter the air and water when asbestos-containing rocks and minerals are weathered naturally or when extracted during mining operations. One of the most important exposures occurs when manufactured products (e.g., pipe wrapping and fire-resistant materials) begin to wear down or are improperly maintained or removed. Small diameter asbestos fibers may remain suspended in the air for a long time and be transported advectively by wind or water before sedimentation. As is the case for spherical particles, heavier fibers settle more quickly.[50]

Most asbestos is highly persistent. However, chrysotile, the most commonly encountered form, may break down slowly in acidic environments.[51] Asbestos fibers may break into shorter strands and, therefore, increased number of fibers, by mechanical processes (e.g., grinding and pulverization). Inhaled fibers may get trapped in the lungs and with chronic exposures build up over time. Some fibers, especially chrysotile, can be removed from or degraded in the lung with time.[52]

Because of its toxicity, it is necessary to have effective monitoring techniques and analytical methods to detect, quantify, and control asbestos in the environment. A number of techniques and methods have been developed to detect and quantify asbestos in bulk samples, air, water, settled dust, and soil.

## Asbestos Disasters

Many homes and commercial buildings, especially those built prior to the 1980s, were constructed with asbestos products. Those products are safe so long as they are contained. Once ripped, broken and burned, blown or washed away, the products become a possible health hazard and earthquakes, hurricanes, tornados, floods, and fires can expose human beings to asbestos and asbestos-containing products.

Some of the most recent natural disasters that generated concerns about potential asbestos exposure were Hurricane Katrina, the deadly 2011 tornadoes in Tuscaloosa, Alabama, and in Joplin, Missouri, and the devastating earthquake and tsunami in Japan in 2011. In all three cases, homes and buildings were destroyed, some of them turned to rubble. In those cases, asbestos insulation, asbestos-containing drywall and electrical wire and other products were exposed for anyone, including homeowners scouring for belongings, to touch.[53]

Similar concerns were raised following floods in Minot, North Dakota and after wide-sweeping fires in Southern California. Fires present a more difficult challenge in terms of asbestos contamination in that they can put asbestos fibers into the air where anyone can in-hale them. First-responders are aware of this potential. Residents in nearby neighborhoods are not always aware, but should be put on alert to get out of the smoke drift. Smoke can carry microscopic asbestos particles. Once inhaled, they rarely leave the human body.[54]

Since the early 1940s, millions of American workers have been exposed to asbestos. Health hazards from asbestos fibers have been recognized in workers exposed in the shipbuilding trades, asbestos mining and milling, manufacturing of asbestos textiles and other asbestos products, insulation work in the construction and building trades, and a variety of other trades. Demolition workers, drywall removers, asbestos removal workers, firefighters, and automobile workers also may be exposed to asbestos fibers. Studies evaluating the cancer risk experienced by automobile mechanics exposed to asbestos through brake repair are limited, but the overall evidence suggests there is no safe level of asbestos exposure. As a result of Government regulations and improved work practices, today's workers (those without previous exposure) are likely to face smaller risks than did those exposed in the past.[55]

Individuals involved in the rescue, recovery, and cleanup at the site of the September 11, 2001, attacks on the World Trade Center (WTC) in New York city are another group at risk of developing an asbestos-related disease. Because asbestos was used in the construction of the North Tower of the WTC, when the building was attacked, hundreds of tonnes of asbestos were released into the atmosphere. Those at greatest risk include firefighters, police officers, paramedics, construction workers, and volunteers who worked in the rubble at Ground Zero. Others at risk include residents in close proximity to the WTC towers and those who attended schools nearby. These individuals will need to be followed to determine the long-term health consequences of their exposure.[56]

One study found that nearly 70% of WTC rescue and recovery workers suffered new or worsened respiratory symptoms while performing work at the WTC site. The study describes the results of the WTC Worker and Volunteer Medical Screening Program, which was established to identify and characterize possible WTC-related health effects in responders. The study found that about 28% of those tested had abnormal lung function tests, and 61% of those without previous health problems developed respiratory symptoms. However, it is important to note that these symptoms may be related to exposure to debris components other than asbestos.[56]

Although it is clear that the health risks from asbestos exposure increase with heavier exposure and longer exposure time, investigators have found asbestos-related diseases in individuals with only brief exposures. Generally, those who develop asbestos-related diseases show no signs of illness for a long time after their first exposure. It can take from 10 to 40 years or more for symptoms of an asbestos-related condition to appear.[57]

There is some evidence that family members of workers heavily exposed to asbestos face an increased risk of developing mesothelioma.[45] This risk is thought to result from exposure to asbestos fibers brought into the home on the shoes, clothing, skin, and hair of workers. To decrease these exposures, Federal law regulates workplace practices to limit the possibility of asbestos being brought home in this way. Some employees may be required to shower and change their clothes before they leave work, store their street clothes in a separate area of the workplace, or wash their work clothes at home separately from other clothes.[57]

Cases of mesothelioma have also been seen in individuals without occupational asbestos exposure who live close to asbestos mines.[57]

It is important to note that asbestos-containing building materials were not as widely used in residences as it was in larger institutional and commercial buildings. Most products manufactured today do not contain asbestos, but until the 1970s many building materials used in homes contained asbestos. Asbestos-containing building materials in residences includes a variety of products like thermal system insulation around hot or cold water lines, asbestos paper wrap around heating ducts, cement board around furnaces/wood-burning appliances, cement board roofing materials and so on. Other sources of asbestos-containing materials include deteriorating, damaged, or disturbed insulation, fireproofing, acoustical materials, and floor tiles.[58]

## Naturally Occurring Asbestos[59]

Asbestos from natural geologic deposits is known as "naturally occurring asbestos" (NOA). Some would rightly argue that all asbestos occurs naturally in rock strata. However, NOA denotes the type of exposure. People may be exposed to asbestos without using a manufactured product. Health risks associated with exposure to NOA are not yet fully understood, and current U.S. federal regulations do not address exposure from NOA. Many populated areas are in proximity to shallow, natural deposits which occur in 50 of 58 California counties and in 19 other U.S. states. In one study, data was collected from 3000 mesothelioma patients in California and 890 men with prostate cancer, a malignancy not known to be related to asbestos. The study found a correlation between the incidence of mesotheliomas and the distance a patient lived from known deposits of rock likely to include asbestos; the correlation was not present when the incidence of prostate cancer was compared with the same distances. According to the study, risk of mesothelioma declined by 6% for every 10 km that an individual had lived away from a likely asbestos source.

Portions of El Dorado County, California are known to contain natural amphibole asbestos formations at the surface. The USGS studied amphiboles in rock and soil in the area in response to an EPA sampling study and subsequent criticism of the EPA study. The EPA study was refuted by its own peer reviewers and never completed or published. The study found that many amphibole particles in the area meet the counting rule criteria used by the EPA for chemical and morphological limits, but do not meet morphological requirements for commercial-grade-asbestos. The executive summary pointed out that even particles that do not meet requirements for commercial-grade-asbestos may be a health threat and suggested a collaborative research effort to assess health risks associated with NOA.

However, the main criticism pointed at EPA was that their testing was conducted in small isolated areas of El Dorado where there were no amphibole asbestos deposits, thus the language regarding amphibole, nonfibrous particles. Actual surface amphibole deposits in residential areas were ignored for testing purposes.

Fairfax County, Virginia soil was also found to be underlain with tremolite. The county monitored air quality at construction sites, controlled soil taken from affected areas, and required freshly developed sites to lay 6 in. (150 mm) of clean, stable material over the ground.

Globally, collected samples from Antarctic ice indicate chrysotile asbestos has been a ubiquitous contaminant of the environment for at least 10,000 years. Snow samples in Japan have shown ambient background levels are one to two orders of magnitude higher in urban than in rural areas. Higher concentrations of airborne asbestos fibers are reported in urban areas where there are more asbestos-containing materials and mechanisms of release (vehicles braking and weathering of asbestos cement materials); concentrations in the range of 1-20 ng m$^{-3}$ have been reported. Fibers longer than 5 μm are rarely found in rural areas.

## Libby, Montana[60]

A vermiculite mining and milling operation 6 miles north of the town of Libby, Montana is the site of arguably the worst asbestos-related disaster. The vermiculite contained naturally occurring amphibole asbestos, tremolite, which like most asbestos compounds, is particularly toxic to human beings. It also contained richterite and winchite, two other toxic amphibole asbestos compounds. The vermiculite was mined there for over 70 years; first by the Zonolite Corporation from 1919 to 1963 and then by W.R. Grace from 1963 until the mine closed in 1990.

There have been over 200 deaths and a thousand people have, and still are, suffering from illnesses directly related to the inhalation of the asbestos dust in Libby over the past 70 years. The asbestos exposure has been identified as the largest environmental and public health disaster in the nation and this has made Libby one of the highest priority superfund sites in the United States.

Over this time, the asbestos contaminated vermiculite was used in the town of Libby, for cover material for school tracks, baseball fields, public parks, in many other public places, and as insulation in public building including schools. The waste piles of vermiculite were also popular places for children to play. As a result it was not only the miners and mill workers that were exposed but also the local residents, including children.

In December 2001, the U.S. EPA released its risk assessment that concluded that amphibole mineral fibers in source materials in residential and commercial areas of Libby pose an imminent and substantial endangerment to public health. Specifically, the assessment found that:

1. Amphibole asbestos occurs in ore and processed vermiculite from the Libby mine.
2. Asbestos fibers of this type are hazardous to humans when inhaled.
3. Asbestos fibers characteristic of those from the mine are present in many sources locally. Outdoor sources include yard and garden soil, driveway material and mine waste materials. Indoor sources include dust and vermiculite insulation.
4. Disturbance of contaminated source materials through common activities by residents or workers can result in exposure to breathable asbestos fibers in air.
5. Concentrations of fibers in air generated by disturbance of source materials may exceed OSHA occupational exposure standards.
6. Estimated excess cancer risks caused by airborne fibers from disturbance of the material exceed EPA's acceptable risk range.[61]

EPA concluded that source materials, e.g., soil and soil-like media, dust and vermiculite that contain asbestos are a likely source of ongoing release of hazardous fibers to air in Libby. In light of evidence of human asbestos exposure and the associated increase in human risk, it was recommended that EPA take appropriate steps to reduce or eliminate exposure pathways to these materials to protect area residents and workers. In January 2005, the EPA stated that "Since November 1999, EPA has cleaned up the major source areas around town." However, there are still many private properties in the Libby area that are still being cleared and decontaminated; that includes insulation in attics and walls of homes and businesses, and contaminated soil in gardens, yards, driveways, and sandboxes.

It was recently announced by the Environmental Protection Agency that 200 people from Libby will get more than $130 million in cleanup and medical assistance from the U.S. government.

The disaster is actually extends beyond Libby, as these findings suggest that the products using the vermiculite spread the risk to those who come into contact with them. These exposures are difficult to predict. For example, if vermiculite were installed as insulation materials in an attic, the exposure would occur each time the person visited the attic (inhalation), as well as after the visit by carrying fibers from the attic to the living areas (inhalation, dermal, and ingestion). In other words, even after a complete cleanup, the exposure and risk will continue, albeit at a much lower dose than the miners, mill workers, and their families received.

# CYANIDE

By far, most carbon-based compounds are organic, but a number of inorganic compounds exist. In fact, the one that is getting the most attention for its role in climate, carbon dioxide, is an inorganic compound because its carbon atom does not contain a covalent bond with other carbon or hydrogen atoms. Inorganic compounds also include inorganic acids, such as carbonic acid ($H_2CO_3$) and cyanic acid (HCNO) and compounds derived from reactions with the anions carbonate ($CO_3^{2-}$) and bicarbonate ($HCO_3^-$). Other important inorganic carbon compounds include the toxic gas carbon monoxide (CO), sodium cyanide (NaCN) and potassium cyanide (KCN), which are the active ingredient in certain pesticides.

Cyanide has played an important role in the awareness of the need for environmental regulations, especially those targeted at toxic substances. As evidence, the finding in 1971 of a number of metal drums of cyanide that had been dumped at a disused brick kiln at Nuneaton, United Kingdom led to a huge public outcry. As a result, the Royal Commission on Toxic Wastes issued a report which became the impetus for the first ever legislation on the control of hazardous waste. The U.K. Parliament drafted the Deposit of Poisonous Waste Act of 1972 in ten days and passed it the following month.

Many industries use cyanide in various manufacturing processes. It is even found in automobile exhaust.[62] Cyanide is extremely toxic to humans. Acute (short term) inhalation exposure to 100 milligrams per cubic meter ($mg\ m^{-3}$) or more of hydrogen cyanide will cause death in humans.[63] Acute exposure to lower concentrations (6-49 $mg\ m^{-3}$) of hydrogen cyanide will cause a variety of effects in humans, such as weakness, headache, nausea, increased rate of respiration, and eye and skin irritation[64] Chronic (long term) inhalation exposure of humans to cyanide results primarily in effects on the CNS. Other effects in humans include cardiovascular and respiratory effects, an enlarged thyroid gland, and irritation to the eyes and skin.

The Reference Concentration (RfC) for hydrogen cyanide is 0.003 $mg\ m^{-3}$ based on CNS symptoms and thyroid effects in humans (see sidebar discussion on "Reference Concentration and Dose"). Due to their toxicity, cyanide compounds are heavily regulated (see Table 10.3).

TABLE 10.3    Regulations and Guidelines Applicable to Cynanide and Cyanide Compounds
note: 1 pound = 0.454 kg.

| Agency | Description | Information | Reference |
|---|---|---|---|
| International | | | |
| Guidelines: | | | |
| IARC | Carcinogenicity classification | No data | IARC (2004) |
| WHO | Air quality guideline value | No data | WHO (2000) |
| | Drinking water guideline value | | WHO (2004) |
| | Cyanide | 0.07 mg L$^{-1}$ | |
| | Cyanogen chloride (for cyanide as total cyanogenic compounds) | 0.07 mg L$^{-1}$ | |
| National | | | |
| Regulations and Guidelines: | | | |
| a. Air | | | ACGIH (2003) |
| ACGIH | TLV (8-h TWA) | | |
| | Cyanogen | 10 ppm | |
| | Cyanogen chloride (ceiling limit) | 0.3 ppm | |
| | Cyanogen chloride (ceiling limit)[a] | 4.7 ppm | |

*Continued*

TABLE 10.3   Regulations and Guidelines Applicable to Cynanide and Cyanide Compounds
note: 1 pound = 0.454 kg.—Cont'd

| Agency | Description | Information | Reference |
|--------|-------------|-------------|-----------|
| EPA | Hazardous air pollutant | | EPA (2004j) |
| | Cyanide compounds | | 42USC7412 |
| | Regulated toxic and flammable substances and threshold quantities for accidental release prevention | | EPA (2005a) 40CFR68.130 |
| | Cyanogen (toxic) | 10,000 pounds | |
| | Cyanogen chloride (flammable) | 10,000 pounds | |
| NIOSH | REL (10-h TWA) | | NIOSH (2005) |
| | Cyanogen | 10 ppm | |
| | Cyanogen chloride (10-min ceiling limit) | 0.3 ppm | |
| | Hydrogen cyanide (short-term limit)[a] | 4.7 ppm | |
| | Potassium cyanide (10-min ceiling limit) | 4.7 ppm | |
| | Sodium cyanide (10-min ceiling limit) | 4.7 ppm | |
| | IDLH | | |
| | Cyanogen | No data | |
| | Cyanogen chloride | No data | |
| | Hydrogen cyanide | 50 ppm | |
| | Potassium cyanide (as cyanide) | $25 \text{ mg m}^{-3}$ | |
| | Sodium cyanide (as cyanide) | $25 \text{ mg m}^{-3}$ | |
| OSHA | PEL (8-h TWA) for general industry | | OSHA (2004d) |
| | Hydrogen cyanide[a] | 10 ppm | 29CFR1910.1000, Table Z-1 |
| | PEL (8-h TWA) for construction industry | | OSHA (2004c) |
| | Cyanogen | 10 ppm | 29CFR1926.55, Appendix A |
| | Hydrogen cyanide[a] | 10 ppm | |
| | PEL (8-h TWA) for shipyard industry | | OSHA (2004a) |
| | Cyanogen | 10 ppm | 29CFR1915.1000, Table Z |
| | Hydrogen cyanide[a] | 10 ppm | |
| OSHA | Highly hazardous chemicals which present a potential for a catastrophic event at or above the threshold quantity listed. | | OSHA (2004b) 29CFR 1910.119, Appendix A |
| | Cyanogen | 2500 pounds | |
| | Cyanogen chloride | 500 pounds | |
| | Hydrogen cyanide, anhydrous | 1000 pounds | |

**TABLE 10.3** Regulations and Guidelines Applicable to Cynanide and Cyanide Compounds
note: 1 pound = 0.454 kg.—Cont'd

| Agency | Description | Information | Reference |
|---|---|---|---|
| b. Water | | | |
| EPA | Drinking water standards and health advisories | | EPA (2004a) |
| | Cyanide | | |
| | 1-Day HA for a 10-kg child | 0.2 mg $L^{-1}$ | |
| | 10-Day HA for a 10-kg child | 0.2 mg $L^{-1}$ | |
| | DWEL | 0.8 mg $L^{-1}$ | |
| | Lifetime HA (70-kg adult) | 0.2 mg $L^{-1}$ | |
| | Cyanogen chloride | | |
| | 1-Day HA for a 10-kg child | 0.05 mg $L^{-1}$ | |
| | 10-Day HA for a 10-kg child | 0.05 mg $L^{-1}$ | |
| | DWEL | 2.0 mg $L^{-1}$ | |
| | Designated as a hazardous substances pursuant to Section 311(b) of the Clean water Act | | EPA (2004t) 40CFR116.4 |
| | Ammonium thiocyanate | Yes | |
| | Calcium cyanide | | |
| | Cyanogen chloride | | |
| | Hydrogen cyanide | | |
| | Potassium cyanide | | |
| | Sodium cyanide | | |
| | National primary drinking water standards and public notification | | EPA (2004h) 40CFR141.32 |
| | Cyanide[b] | 0.2 ppm | |
| | Reportable quantities of hazardous substances designated pursuant to Section 311(b) of the Clean Water Act | | EPA (2004k) 40CFR117.3 |
| | Ammonium thiocyanate | 5000 pounds | |
| | Calcium cyanide | 10 pounds | |
| | Cyanogen chloride | 10 pounds | |
| | Hydrogen cyanide | 10 pounds | |
| | Potassium cyanide | 10 pounds | |
| | Sodium cyanide | 10 pounds | |
| | National primary drinking water regulations (MCL) | | EPA (2004g) 40CFR141.62 |
| | Cyanide | 0.2 mg $L^{-1}$ | |

*Continued*

TABLE 10.3    Regulations and Guidelines Applicable to Cynanide and Cyanide Compounds
note: 1 pound = 0.454 kg.—Cont'd

| Agency | Description | Information | Reference |
|--------|-------------|-------------|-----------|
| FDA | Bottled water | | FDA (2003) 21CFR165.110 |
| | Cyanide | 0.2 mg L$^{-1}$ | |
| **c. Food** | | | |
| EPA | Tolerance for residues of hydrogen cyanide from postharvest fumigation as a result of application of sodium cyanide on citrus fruits | 50 ppm | EPA (2004m) 40CFR180.130 |
| | Exemptions from the requirement of a tolerance when used in accordance with good agricultural practices in pesticide formulations applied to growing crops; and when used as an adjuvant or intensifier for defoliation and weed control on cotton and soybeans | Ammonium thiocyanate | EPA (2004n) 40CFR180.920 |
| FDA | Indirect food additive for use only as a component of adhesives | Ammonium thiocyanate | FDA (2003) 21CFR175.105 |
| **d. Other** | | | |
| EPA | Carcinogenicity classification | | IRIS (2004) |
| | Calcium cyanide | No data | |
| | Chlorine cyanide | No data | |
| | Copper (I) cyanide | No data | |
| | Cyanide | Group D[c] | |
| | Cyanogen | No data | |
| | Hydrogen cyanide | No data | |
| | Potassium cyanide | No data | |
| | Potassium silver cyanide | No data | |
| | Sodium cyanide | No data | |
| | RfC[d] | | |
| | Calcium cyanide | No data | |
| | Chlorine cyanide | No data | |
| | Copper (I) cyanide | No data | |
| | Cyanide | No data | |
| | Cyanogen | No data | |
| | Hydrogen cyanide | $3 \times 10^{-3}$ mg m$^{-3}$ | |
| | Potassium cyanide | No data | |
| | Potassium silver cyanide | No data | |
| | Sodium cyanide | No data | |

TABLE 10.3 Regulations and Guidelines Applicable to Cynanide and Cyanide Compounds
note: 1 pound = 0.454 kg.—Cont'd

| Agency | Description | Information | Reference |
|---|---|---|---|
| | RfD[e] | | |
| | Calcium cyanide | $4 \times 10^{-2}$ mg$^{-1}$ kg$^{-1}$ day | |
| | Chlorine chloride | $5 \times 10^{-2}$ mg$^{-1}$ kg$^{-1}$ day | |
| | Copper (I) cyanide | $5 \times 10^{-3}$ mg$^{-1}$ kg$^{-1}$ day | |
| | Cyanide | $2 \times 10^{-2}$ mg$^{-1}$ kg$^{-1}$ day | |
| | Cyanogen | $4 \times 10^{-2}$ mg$^{-1}$ kg$^{-1}$ day | |
| | Hydrogen cyanide | $2 \times 10^{-2}$ mg$^{-1}$ kg$^{-1}$ day | |
| | Potassium cyanide | $5 \times 10^{-2}$ mg$^{-1}$ kg$^{-1}$ day | |
| | Potassium silver cyanide | $2 \times 10^{-1}$ mg$^{-1}$ kg$^{-1}$ day | |
| | Sodium cyanide | $4 \times 10^{-2}$ mg$^{-1}$ kg$^{-1}$ day | |
| EPA | Hazardous waste identification | | EPA (2004f) 40CFR261, Appendix VIII |
| | Calcium cyanide | P021 | |
| | Copper (I) cyanide | P029 | |
| | Cyanides (soluble salts and complexes) | P030 | |
| | Cyanogen | P031 | |
| | Cyanogen chloride | P033 | |
| | Hydrogen cyanide | P063 | |
| | Potassium cyanide | P098 | |
| | Potassium silver cyanide | P099 | |
| | Sodium cyanide | P106 | |
| | Pesticide (sodium cyanide) classified as restricted use and limited to use by or under the direct supervision of a certified applicator | All capsules and all ball formulations for all uses[f] | EPA (2004i) 40CFR152.175 |
| | Superfund; emergency planning and notification of extremely hazardous substances and their threshold quantities | | EPA (2004e) 40CFR355, Appendix A |
| | Hydrogen cyanide | 100 pounds | |
| | Potassium cyanide | 100 pounds | |
| | Potassium silver cyanide | 500 pounds | |
| | Sodium cyanide | 100 pounds | |
| | Superfund; designation of hazardous substances and their reportable quantities | | EPA (2004d) 40CFR302.4 |

*Continued*

TABLE 10.3 Regulations and Guidelines Applicable to Cynanide and Cyanide Compounds note: 1 pound = 0.454 kg.—Cont'd

| Agency | Description | Information | Reference |
|---|---|---|---|
| | Ammonium thiocyanate[g] | 5000 pounds | |
| | Calcium cyanide[h] | 10 pounds | |
| | Copper cyanide[i] | 10 pounds | |
| | Cyanides (soluble salts and complexes) | 10 pounds | |
| | Cyanogen | 100 pounds | |
| | Cyanogen chloride[h] | 10 pounds | |
| | Hydrogen cyanide[h] | 10 pounds | |
| | Potassium cyanide[h] | 10 pounds | |
| | Potassium silver cyanide[i] | 1 pounds | |
| | Sodium cyanide[h] | 10 pounds | |
| | Tolerances for pesticide chemicals in food; when calcium cyanide and hydrogen cyanide are on the same agricultural commodity, the total amount shall not yield more residue than the larger of the two tolerances, calculated as hydrogen cyanide | | EPA (2004o) 40CFR180.3 |
| | Toxic chemical release reporting, community right to know, and effective date for hydrogen cyanide | 01/01/1987 | EPA (2004p) 40CFR372.65 |
| | TSCA chemical information rules; manufacturers reporting period for sodium cyanide | | EPA (2004r) 40CFR712.30 |
| | Effective date | 10/29/1990 | |
| | Reporting date | 12/27/1990 | |
| EPA | TSCA health and safety data reporting for sodium cyanide | | EPA (2004s) 40CFR716.120 |
| | Effective date | 10/29/1990 | |
| | Sunset date | 12/19/1995 | |
| State | | | |
| a. Air | | | |
| | No data | | |
| b. Water | | | |
| | Drinking water standards and guidelines | | HSDB (2004) |
| Arizona | Calcium cyanide | $220\ \mu g\ L^{-1}$ | |
| | Copper (I) cyanide | $1300\ \mu g\ L^{-1}$ | |
| | Potassium cyanide | $220\ \mu g\ L^{-1}$ | |
| | Potassium silver cyanide | $50\ \mu g\ L^{-1}$ | |
| | Sodium cyanide | $220\ \mu g\ L^{-1}$ | |

TABLE 10.3   Regulations and Guidelines Applicable to Cynanide and Cyanide Compounds
note: 1 pound = 0.454 kg.—Cont'd

| Agency | Description | Information | Reference |
|---|---|---|---|
| Connecticut | Potassium silver cyanide | 50 µg L$^{-1}$ | |
| Florida | Cyanogen | 10,000 µg L$^{-1}$ | |
| | Cyanogen chloride | 350 µg L$^{-1}$ | |
| | Hydrogen cyanide | 10,000 µg L$^{-1}$ | |
| Maine | Potassium cyanide | 154 µg L$^{-1}$ | |
| | Potassium silver cyanide | 50 µg L$^{-1}$ | |
| | Sodium cyanide | 154 µg L$^{-1}$ | |
| Minnesota | Potassium cyanide | 100 µg L$^{-1}$ | |
| | Potassium silver cyanide | 30 µg L$^{-1}$ | |
| | Sodium cyanide | 100 µg L$^{-1}$ | |
| Wisconsin | Potassium silver cyanide | 50 µg L$^{-1}$ | |
| c. Food | | | |
| | No data | | |
| d. Other | | | |
| | No data | | |

ACGIH, American Conference of Governmental Industrial Hygienists; CFR, Code of Federal Regulations; DWEL, drinking water equivalent level; EPA, Environmental Protection Agency; FDA, Food and Drug Administration; HA, health advisory; HSDB, Hazardous Substances Data Bank; IARC, International Agency for Research on Cancer; IDLH, immediately dangerous to life or health; IRIS, Integrated Risk Information System; MCL, maximum contaminant level; NIOSH, National Institute for Occupational Safety and Health; OSHA, Occupational Safety and Health Administration; PEL, permissible exposure limit; RCRA, Resource Conversation and Recovery Act; REL, recommended exposure limit; Rfc, reference concentration; RfD, reference dose; TLV, threshold limit values; TSCA, Toxic Substances Control Act; TWA, time-weighted average; USC, United States Codes; WHO, World Health Organization.

[a]Skin designation: Potential significant contribution to the overall exposure by the cutaneous route, including membranes and the eyes, either by contact with vapors or of probable greater significance, by direct skin contact with the substance.

[b]EPA sets drinking water standards and has determined that cyanide is a health concern at certain levels of exposure. This inorganic chemical is used in electroplating, steel processing, plastics, synthetic fabrics, and fertilizer products; it usually gets into water as a result of improper waste disposal. This chemical has been shown to damage the spleen, brain, and liver of humans fatally poisoned with cyanide. EPA has set the drinking water standard for cyanide at 0.2ppm to protect against the risk of these adverse health effects. Drinking water that meets the EPA standard is associated with little to none of this risk and should be considered safe with respect to cyanide (EPA, 2004h).

[c]Group D: Not classifiable as a human carcinogen.

[d]An estimate (with uncertainty spanning an order of magnitude) of a daily inhalation exposure concentration that is likely to be without significant risk of adverse effects during a lifetime (chronic exposure).

[e]An estimate (with uncertainty spanning an order of magnitude) of a daily oral exposure dose that is likely to be without significant risk of adverse effects during a lifetime (chronic exposure).

[f]The criteria influencing the restriction of sodium cyanide is based on the inhalation hazard to humans. Also, sodium cyanide capsules may only be used by certified applicators who have also taken the required additional training.

[g]Designated as a hazardous substance pursuant to Section 311(b)(2) of the Clean Water Act.

[h]Designated as a hazardous substance pursuant to Section 311(b)(2) of the Clean Water Act and Section 3001 of RCRA.

[i]Designated as a hazardous substance pursuant to Section 3001 of RCRA.

Source: Agency for Toxic Substances and Disease Registry (2006). Cyanide. U.S. Public Health Service. Atlanta, GA.

# REFERENCE CONCENTRATION AND DOSE

One of the aspects of disasters discussed in this chapter and elsewhere in the book is the inherent hazardous nature of the substances involved. There needs to be a way to differentiate exposures. What level of an exposure to a substance is safe and what level is dangerous?

Reference concentrations (RfCs) and doses (RfDs) are developed by regulatory agencies to add a factor of safety to observational data. That is, when using *in vivo* (animal) studies and *in vitro* (test tube) studies to estimate actual risks to humans, uncertainties must be taken into account. The RfCs and RfDs address such uncertainties The RfC is an estimate of a continuous inhalation exposure to the human population (including sensitive subgroups) at which the population is likely to be without an appreciable risk of deleterious effects during a lifetime. Similarly, the RfD is an estimate of a daily oral exposure to the human population that is likely to be without an appreciable risk of deleterious effects during a lifetime. They can be derived from a threshold below which there is no observed effect [e.g., the no observable adverse effect concentration (NOAEC) or level (NOAEL)] or the lowest concentration (LOAEC) or level (LOAEL) observed in studies. They may also be derived from a benchmark concentration or dose (i.e., that which produces some predetermined change in response rate of an adverse effect compared to background).[65]

The uncertainty factors (UFs) are applied to reflect limitations of the data used. The uncertainties of RfCs and RfDs may span an order of magnitude. They are generally restricted to non-cancer health assessments.

The factors underlying the uncertainties are quantified as specific UFs. The uncertainties in the RfD are largely due to the differences between results found in animal testing and expected outcomes in human population. As in other bioengineering operations, a factor of safety must be added to calculations to account for UFs. So, for environmental risk analyses and assessments, the safe level is expressed in the RfD, or in air the RfC. This is the dose or concentration below which regulatory agencies do not expect a specific unacceptable outcome. Thus, all the UFs adjust the actual measured levels of no effect (i.e., the threshold values, e.g., NOAELs and LOAELs) in the direction of a zero concentration. This is calculated as

$$RfD = \frac{NOAEL}{UF_{inter} \times UF_{intra} \times UF_{other}}. \tag{10.1}$$

The first of the three types of uncertainty are those resulting from the difference in the species tested and that of *Homo sapiens* ($UF_{inter}$). Humans may be more or less sensitive than the tested species to a particular compound. The second UF is associated with the fact that certain human subpopulations are more sensitive to the effects of a compound than the general human population. These are known as intraspecies uncertainty factors ($UF_{intra}$). The third type of uncertainties ($UF_{other}$) results when the available data and science is lacking, such as when a LOAEL is used rather than a NOAEL. That is, data show a dose at which an effect is observed, but the "no effect" threshold has to be extrapolated. Since the UFs are in the denominator, the greater the uncertainties, the closer the safe level (i.e., the RfD) is to zero, i.e., the threshold is divided by these factors. The UFs are usually multiples of 10, although the $UF_{other}$ can range from 2 to 10.

A particularly sensitive sub-population is children, since they are growing and tissue development is much more prolific than in older years. To address these sensitivities, the Food Quality Protection Act (FQPA) now includes what is known as the "10X" rule. This rule requires that the RfD for products regulated under FQPS, e.g., pesticides, must include an additional factor of

10 of protection of infants, children, and females between the ages of 13 and 50 years old. This factor is included in the RfD denominator along with the other three UF values. The RfD that includes the UFs and the 10X protection is known as the population adjusted dose (PAD). A risk estimate that is less than 100% of the acute or chronic PAD does not exceed the Agency's risk concern.[66]

An example of the use of an RfD as a factor of safety can be demonstrated by the U.S. Environmental Protection Agency's decision making regarding the re-registration of the organophosphate pesticide, chlorpyrifos. The acute dietary scenario had a NOAEL of 0.5 mg kg$^{-1}$day$^{-1}$ and the three UF values equaled 100. Thus, the acute RfD$=5 \times 10^{-3}$ mg kg$^{-1}$ day$^{-1}$ but the more protective acute PAD$=5 \times 10^{-4}$ mg kg$^{-1}$ day$^{-1}$. The chronic dietary scenario is even more protective, since the exposure is long term. The chronic NOAEL was found to be 0.03 mg kg$^{-1}$ day$^{-1}$. Thus, the chronic RfD for chlorpyrifos$=3 \times 10^{-4}$ mg kg$^{-1}$ day$^{-1}$ and the more protective acute PAD $5 \times 10^{-5}$ mg kg$^{-1}$ day$^{-1}$. Therefore, had the NOAEL threshold been used alone without the safety adjustment of the RfD, the allowable exposure would have been three orders of magnitude higher.

Factors of safety are important tools to decisions before and after a disaster. For example, they may be needed to design containment structures, monitoring networks, and other preventive measures in hazardous substance contingency plans. They are also important following a disaster wherein hazardous substances have been released, e.g., as a tool for deciding the level of cleanup. In both ways, they will need to be part of the information conveyed about the severity and extent of a disaster. They will also need to be used in communicating to the public about remediation progress and preventative measures that are needed in the future.

Sodium, potassium, or calcium cyanide are all very toxic[67] chemicals and their aqueous solutions are used mainly to extract gold from its ores. Gold occurs as the native metal in a matrix of rock and there are two basic ways to extract the gold: one is to amalgamate the gold with mercury and then distill off the mercury; the other is to dissolve the gold in a cyanide solution and then to use various methods (zinc cementation, carbon in pulp, or ion exchange) to extract the gold. The more common method is to use cyanide and the MacArthur-Forrest *cyanide process*. In this process finely ground high-grade ore is mixed with the cyanide (concentration of about 2 kg NaCN per tonne); low-grade ores are stacked into heaps and sprayed with a cyanide solution (concentration of about 1 kg NaCN per tonne). The gold complexes with cyanide ions to form soluble a derivative $[Au(CN)_2]^-$:

$$4\,Au + 8\,NaCN + O_2 + 2\,H_2O \rightarrow 4\,Na[Au(CN)_2] + 4\,NaOH \qquad (10.2)$$

All cyanide compounds are toxic and rapidly acting. Exposure to high levels of cyanide harms the brain and heart, and may cause coma and death. Exposure to lower levels may result in breathing difficulties, heart pains, vomiting, blood changes, headaches, and enlargement of the thyroid gland. Cyanide binds to key iron-containing enzymes and hemoglobin required for cells to use oxygen and as a result tissues are unable to take up oxygen from the blood.[68]

The low-grade ores extraction process is called "heap leaching." The ore containing the gold is crushed, piled into heaps, and sprayed with cyanide, which trickles down through the ore dissolving gold and forming a solution of gold cyanide. The resulting gold cyanide solution is collected at the base of the heap and pumped to a mill, where the gold is extracted. The cyanide is then stored in dams for possible reuse. Each bout of leaching takes a few months. Usually the scale of the operation is vast and pollution of the surrounding environment with cyanide is almost inevitable. The exhausted ore or tailings are then finally stored in tailings dams which have been the cause of many disasters.

Perhaps the worst disaster took place in 2000 in Romania when 400,000 L of cyanide containing mine waste spilled into the Tisza river killing 1000 tonnes of fish and contaminating the drinking water of 2.5 million people. The incident is described as Europe's worst river pollution disaster in a decade. The upper Tisza was one of Europe's cleanest rivers and was home to at least 20 species of protected fish. Rare Osprey, river otters, fox, many other birds, mammals, and wildlife are known to have died from ingesting poisoned fish. Biologists estimated that at least 5 years was needed to restock fish there, and 10-20 years for most river life to return. The process used in the Romanian disaster is known as the "cyanide leaching gold recovery" process and involves spraying heaps of ore with a weak cyanide solution. These dams store not only cyanide solution but also solutions of heavy metals that are formed from the gold extraction process. The formation of HCN gas formed in these dams is a major cause of concern. Furthermore, if this type of mining is allowed to continue, then at least a double walled dam should be included in the design.[69]

Managing cyanide to minimize risks to human and environmental health is an important issue for the mining industry and Codes of Practice have been drawn up to assist the global mining industry to improve its management of cyanide.[70]

In spite of the increasing level of knowledge about cyanide and the codes of practice significant environmental incidents—most involving water bodies—have continued to occur globally. Over the past 10 years there have been at least 30 reported cases of cyanide spillages, tailings dams overflowing or bursting and polluting of rivers and ground water. It has led to a few human deaths and large scale illnesses, largely through drinking the polluted waters or eating polluted fish. Furthermore it has led to the death of countless fish and marine life. Among the countries affected include: Ghana (2001, 2002, 2003, 2004, 2005, 2006); Romania (2000, 2005); USA (2002, 2003); China (2001, 2004); Australia (2002, 2004); Taiwan (2003); Papua New Guinea (2000, 2004); Guyana (1995, 2000); Nicaragua (2003); and the Philippines (2005). These incidents attract concern from regulators and the public and have led to calls for cyanide use in mining to be banned.

Considering the toxicity of cyanide it is surprising that there have been very few documented accidental human deaths due to cyanide poisoning and in the Australian and North American mining industries over the past 100 years no deaths have been recorded.[71]

# SURFACE MINING

Surface mining is used worldwide to expose and mine ores, which are relatively close to the surface. It involves the removal of the soil and rocks and has caused environmental problems and sometimes loss of life. Surface mining comes in many forms.

Mining a seam of mineral by first removing a long strip of overburden is called strip mining and is often used in coal mining. It is also being used to extract the tar and oil from the sand at Athabasca in Alberta resulting in severe damage to the ecology and posing a threat to Alberta's boreal forest ecosystem. It is also threatening acid rain on Western Canada and is a blot on the local landscape; its toxic tailing lakes are so large they are apparently visible from space. Open pit mining refers to mining from a huge open pit which can be very deep and large. Typical examples include the largest open pit mine in the world at Bingham Canyon

Utah, which covers 8 km$^2$ and is 1.2 km deep and is mined for copper. The second largest is Nchanga mine at Chingola, Zambia which covers 30 km$^2$ and is 400 m deep. Other very large open pit mines are in Australia (gold, uranium, copper), Germany (lignite), Chile (copper), Colombia (coal), USA (copper, iron gold), Russia, to mention a few.[72,73]

Another form of strip mining is sand dune mining for the extraction of rutile and ilmenite which contains titanium and zirconium (e.g., South Africa, India) and even iron (New Zealand). Dune mining is also used for low cost sand excavation for concrete and building purposes. It impact on coastline erosion and also on wildlife can be extremely serious examples include turtles and crocodiles in India; sensitive corals in Australian waters; fishing; destruction and disturbance of ecologically sensitive dune forests in Zululand, South Africa; and beach erosion in New Zealand, to mention just a few.

Mountaintop mining has apparently only been used for coal mining. It involves removing the overburden from the top of a mountain to expose the coal and dumping the waste material in nearby valleys. It has been used in West Virginia, Kentucky and Tennessee Appalachian coal fields (see Figure 10.3). It seriously disturbs the ecosystem and changes the topography and even the flow of rivers and streams. The EPA, together with the U.S. Army Corps of Engineers, the U.S. Department of the Interior's Office of Surface Mining and Fish & Wildlife Service, and the West Virginia Department of Environmental Protection, prepared an environmental impact statement on the environmental impacts of mountaintop mining and valley fills in the Appalachian region of eastern Kentucky, southern West Virginia, western Virginia, and scattered areas of eastern Tennessee. One of the major problems with mountaintop mining is that head water streams are often buried with the resultant loss of ecosystems. This technique leads to forest destruction, loss of biodiversity and affects many species (see Figure 10.4)

FIGURE 10.3    Mountain top mining in West Virginia. *Source: U.S. Environmental Protection Agency (2012). http://www.epa.gov/region03/mtntop/index.htm [accessed 16 March 2012].*

**Step 1.** Layers of rock and soil above the coal (called overburden) are removed

**Step 2.** The upper seams of coal are removed with spoils placed in an adjacent valley

**Step 3.** Draglines excavate lower layers of coal with spoils placed in spoil piles

**Step 4.** Regrading begins as coal excavation continues

**Step 5.** Once coal removal is complete, final regrading takes place and the area is revegetated

FIGURE 10.4   Coal and overburden removal methods used in mountain top mining. *Source: U.S. Environmental Protection Agency (2012). http://www.epa.gov/region03/mtntop/index.htm [accessed 16 March 2012].*

From a study of over 1200 stream segments they found:

- an increase of minerals in the water, for example, zinc, sodium, selenium, and sulfate which could have an impact on the fish, macroinvertebrates, and other streams in watersheds below valley fills tend to have greater base flow
- streams were sometimes covered up

- wetlands which had been created as a result of the mining were generally not of high quality
- some forests were broken into sections
- the regrowth of trees and woody plants on re-graded land was probably slowed down as a result of compacted soils
- grassland birds and snakes were found to be more common on reclaimed mine and amphibians such as salamanders, were less likely.

Most of the above concerns also relate to all types of surface mining. Other impacts of surface mines, include esthetics, ground water and surface water runoff contamination, noise, air quality (dust and mining pollutants), vibration, subsidence, as well as a devastating effect on the flora and fauna of the region.[74]

Plans for reclamation, after mining has ceased, should include: rehabilitation of the top soil, erosion control, reduction of dust from open scars before vegetation has been established, drainage control, water analysis and purification of both surface and underground water.

Mining in general has been responsible for thousands of lives throughout history and especially over the past 100 years, through explosions, subsidence, slurry spills, chemical pollution both above ground and through ground water.

# VALUE

The extraction, processing, and use of minerals illustrate an important lesson for engineers. Selecting a technology to meet a need is complex. For example, the word "precious" in precious metals conveys value. The ratio of amount of precious metal produced compared to the other material from which it is extracted is very small. For example, the cyanide leaching gold recovery process is the technology used to extract gold from ore. The juxtaposition of "cyanide leaching" and "gold" in this process should give one pause for thought.

About 1.1 million tons (1.0 million tonnes) of hydrogen cyanide are produced annually worldwide, with approximately 6% used to produce mainly sodium cyanide for gold processing. The remaining 94% is used in the manufacturing of plastics, adhesives, fire retardants, and pharmaceuticals.[75] Gold is found in nature as the native metal, Au(0), usually as minute particles in a rock matrix. It is one of the rarest metals on earth and requires a significant amount of energy to extract it. Even gold bearing ore contains only small amount of gold—usually less that 10 grams per tonne (0.001% or 10 ppm). In order to extract the gold, it is complexed in a solution of sodium cyanide and then extracted from solution. Sodium cyanide, although highly toxic and dangerous is almost universally used to dissolve the gold. Gold being a noble metal is difficult to get into solution. There are a few other anions that will complex with gold (chloride, bromide, thiourea, or thiosulfate) but they are difficult to handle, not as effective or more expensive than cyanide. The gold is recovered by means of either heap leaching or agitated pulp leaching. Heaped leaching is use for low-grade ores ($2\text{-}5 \text{ g t}^{-1}$, where t refers to tonne) and agitated pulp for the higher grades ($5\text{-}10 \text{ g t}^{-1}$).

The first step in gold extraction, by the agitated pulp method, is to crush, grind and mill the gold bearing rock (to a size of less than 0.1 mm) in order to expose the gold particles for dissolution in aqueous cyanide solution. If the ore contains large gold particles, it is usually gravity separated in large "cyclones." In the agitated pulp leaching process, the cyanide solution, at a pH greater that 11 (to inhibit the formation of deadly HCN gas), is added to the milled gold bearing rock and left for a time (months) in great big tanks for the leaching process to take place. To speed up process oxygen is often added by bubbling in air. The gold complexes with cyanide ions to form a soluble derivative $[Au(CN)_2]^-$; the overall reaction is repeated here:

$$4\,Au + 8\,NaCN + O_2 + 2\,H_2O \rightarrow 4\,Na[Au(CN)_2] + 4\,NaOH \tag{10.3}$$

Typical cyanide concentrations used in practice range from 300 to 500 mg L$^{-1}$ (0.03-0.05% as NaCN) depending on the mineralogy of the ore. Once the gold is in solution it is recovered by one of a number of processes: zinc cementation, carbon in leach, carbon in pulp, or ion exchange. The carbon in leach is perhaps the most common method used today. Small pieces of activated charcoal (>1 mm) are added to the leached slurry solution. The gold is adsorbed onto the charcoal pieces which are then separated by screening. The fine ore particles slip through the sive while the bigger carbon pieces are retained. To ensure that the carbon charcoal does not fracture or break into very small pieces and slip through the sive, hard activated carbon, preferably coconut shell carbon, is used. The carbon is then subjected to further treatment to recover the adsorbed gold, usually by elution in a strong NaOH solution followed by electrolysis in which the gold is plated onto steel electrodes.

In the heap leaching process, the ore or milled fine ore is stacked in heaps on a pad lined with an impermeable membrane. The cyanide solution sprinkled onto the heap and the solution percolates and complexes the gold. The gold bearing solution is then collected for the next step which is most likely treatment with activated charcoal. Heap leaching is the most common method used today because of the low capital cost involved. It is however a slow process and relatively inefficient (extraction efficiency is about 50-75%).[76]

The major lesson learned is that engineers and engineering managers usually select the optimal approach from among various alternatives. They may not even be aware that they are doing this based on tradeoffs. Such tradeoffs are evaluated based on values. Environmental disaster planning and response often do not completely apply a rational, scientific decision framework. Disaster prevention has costs, monetary, and otherwise.

Choices among response and cleanup also involve costs. In a sense, the cultural norms dictate how much is done to prevent and respond to a disaster. That is, few disaster decisions are entirely *amoral.* More often, they involve decisions on whether a cascade of technical and social decisions is morally permissible or impermissible. Elected officials, bureaucrats, scientific advisors, and everyone involved in emergency prepared and response apply unique sets of morals to gauge the value derived from each action being proposed. These actions are determined to be right and wrong, depending on the values placed by these people individually and collectively. A few major ethical viewpoints dominate environmental ethics literature, notably anthropocentrism, biocentrism, ecocentrism, and sentientism (see Figure 10.5).

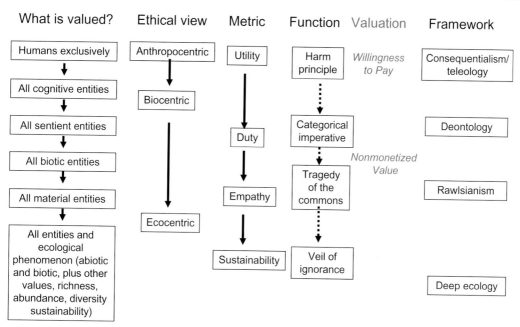

FIGURE 10.5    Continuum of ethical viewpoints. *Adapted from: D.A. Vallero (2007). Biomedical Ethics for Engineers: Ethics and Decision Making in Biomedical and Biosystem Engineering. Elsevier Academic Press, Burlington, MA.; some information from: R.B. Meyers (2003). Environmental Values, Ethics and Support for Environmental Policy: A Heuristic, and Psychometric Instruments to Measure their Prevalence and Relationships. International Conference on Civic Education Research. November 16-18, 2003 New Orleans, Louisiana.*

Anthropocentrism is the philosophy or decision framework entailing that all and only humans have moral value. Non-human species and ecological resources have value only in respect to that associated with human values (known as instrumental value). In this view, the value of protecting or addressing anything actually or potentially damaged by a disaster is ascertained entirely from the utility that it provides to humans. These living and nonliving parts of the environment must have instrumental value rather than intrinsic value of their own. The arguments within anthropocentrism are about the focus of a disaster plan. For example, which subgroups of a society deserve more or less protection? Which humans will benefit and who will be at risk?

Conversely, biocentrism is a systematic and comprehensive account of the value of both humans and other living things. The biocentric view requires an acceptance that all living things have inherent value, so that respect for nature is the ultimate moral attitude. It is encapsulated by Albert Schweitzer's "reverence for life."[77] Here, arguments about the extent and degree of measures to prevent and fully respond to a disaster would consider non-human species. Here, the debate how to dispense value among the various species. For example, should a flooded area be reclaimed for human activities or would it be better to pay attention to nature and allow natural habitats to recolonize?

Actually, the foregoing discussion is an example of integrated intrinsic and instrumental values. Allowing a wetland, for example, to be reclaimed after a flood not only addresses the intrinsic need of threatened species and biodiversity, it could very well prevent human losses in the future. Clearly, this has great potential value for human safety and health, i.e., it provides an anthropocentric utility (e.g., less loss of human life and destruction of property), In addition, from the biocentric perspective, this utility would be weighed against the effects this action has on other nonhuman species.

By extension of the biocentric view, ecocentrism is based on the notion that the whole ecosystem, rather than just single species, has instrinsic value. In the ecocentric view, the actions are only acceptable if viewed from the perspective of the entire system. Thus, even if an action (e.g., building a massive dike) provides some benefit to humans (e.g., allows homes and businesses to be constructed), and it may well not seem to adversely affect any particular organism that produces the benefit (e.g., birds may find alternate habitats), the tradeoffs may still be unacceptable from a systematic perspective (e.g., the change in population ecology by introducing the altered species somehow affects the function or structure of the ecosystem).

It is important to note that it can be problematic to apply a single ethical perspective in every circumstance. For example, extreme anthropocentrism can lead to animal cruelty and destruction of habitat since it ignores the critical interdependence among myriad organisms, including humans, and the environment. In fact, anthropocentrism is always utilitarian, since humans are the only organisms making decisions about the usefulness of an action. In other words, the only utility is the extent to which the action is good for humans. Thus, the only value placed on the technology is instrumental, i.e., how does it serve a certain human need.

Ecologists and others have argued that even an anthropocentric view requires a systematic perspective. That is, even if one only cares about humans, the human support systems of clean air, water, soil, sediment, biota, and even social issues like animal welfare all must be protected. Without these systems, the human population would suffer. Thus, in our role as stewards of the environment, we cannot neglect the intricacies and interconnections and interrelationships that exist between humans and their environment.

Recently, the systematic, anthropocentric view has manifested itself in the form of *ecosystem services*. Prevention of environmental disasters is indeed an ecosystem service. That is, the value of an ecosystem is in the form of processes by which the environment provides resources, often not fully appreciated, such as modulating water flow and protecting water quality. This means that disaster planners should not simply view ecosystems as inherently valuable, but instrumentally valuable to humans. A specific example of an ecosystem service, contructing upstream wetlands, is shown in Figure 10.6.

Disaster planning must integrate a number of decision frameworks. Many worthy projects address areas that could greatly benefit society, but may lead to unforeseen costs. Planners must consider possible contingencies, often where involving *risk tradeoffs* must be considered. Disaster planning calls for a solution that optimizes outcomes; that is, not too much risk and not too much cost. This is done using a number of tools, such as benefit-cost ratios, best practice guidelines, and transparency in terms of possible downstream impacts, costs, side effects and interactions.

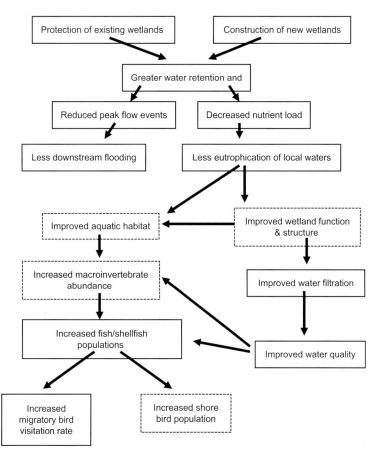

FIGURE 10.6   Ecosystem service flow chart showing need to retain water and to control nutrient loads to local surface and ground water, by protecting and constructing wetlands. This results in ecosystem improvements, in this case indicated by improved aquatic life and bird diversity and abundance. However, the protection is justified, not from the need to protect the wetlands' inherent, ecological value (dashed boxes), but their anthropocentric utility provides instrumental value (bolded boxes provide both anthropogenic and biogenic value). In this case, the instrumental value is preventing a flooding disaster. *Based on information from: D.A. Vallero (2009).* Environmental Biotechnology: A Biosystems Approach. *Elsevier Academic Press, Amsterdam, NV.*

# References and Notes

1. John H. Duffus "Heavy metals" a meaningless term? *Pure Appl Chem* 2002;**74**:793–807. doi:10.1351/pac200274050793 [IUPAC Technical Report].

2. Senese F. *Why is mercury a liquid at STP?* General Chemistry Online at Frostburg State University; *http://antoine.frostburg.edu/chem/senese/101/inorganic/faq/why-is-mercury-liquid.shtml*; 2007 [accessed 1 May 2007].

3. United States Environmental Protection Agency. *Background paper for stakeholder panel to address options for managing U.S. non-federal supplies of commodity-grade mercury.* http://www.epa.gov/mercury/stocks/backgroundpaper.pdf; 2007 [accesses 13 January 2012].

4. The Northeast Waste Management Officials' Association. http://www.newmoa.org/prevention/mercury/Mer curyIndoor.pdf; 2012 [accessed 14 January 2012].

5. Lindqvist O, Jernelov A, Johansson K, Rodhe H. *Mercury in the Swedish environment, global and local sources.* SNV PM 1816, Swedish Environmental Protection Agency, S-171 85, Solna, Sweden; 1984.

6. United States Environmental Protection Agency. *Mercury study report to congress—volume III: fate and transport of mercury in the environment.* EPA-452/R-97-003; December 1997.

7. United States Environmental Protection Agency. *What is EPA doing about mercury air emissions?* http://www.epa. gov/mercury/; 2012 [accessed 13 January 2012].

8. Solnit R. *Winged mercury and the golden calf.* Orion Magazine. September/October http://www.orionmagazine. org/index.php/articles/article/176/; 2006 [accessed 15 January 2012].

9. Pacyna EG, Pacyna JM, Steenhuisen F, Wilson S. Global anthropogenic mercury emission inventory for 2000. *Atmos Environ* 2006;**40**(22):4048–63. doi:10.1016/j.atmosenv.2006.03.041.

10. Martin I, Cowie C. Supplementary Information for mercury Science Report, SC 05002, Environment Agency, Almondsbury, Bristol, BS32 4UD, www.environment-agency.gov.uk. ISBN: 978-1-84911-009-9.

11. Letcher TM. Mercury pollution. *South Afr J Sci* 1979;**75**:80.

12. A principal source for the Minamata case is the Trade & Environment Database, developed by James R. Lee, American University, The School of International Service: http://www.american.edu/TED/ [accessed on April 19, 2005].

13. This is an all too common professional ethics problem, i.e. lack of full disclosure. It is often, in retrospect, a very costly decision to withhold information about a product, even if the consequences of releasing the information would adversely affect the "bottom line." Ultimately, as has been seen in numerous ethical case studies, the costs of not disclosing are severe, such as bankruptcy and massive class action lawsuits, let alone the fact that a company's decision may have led to the death and disease of the very people they claim to be serving, i.e. their customers and workers.

14. Almeida P, Stearns L. Political opportunities and local grassroots environmental movement: the case of Minamata. *Soc Probl* 1998;**45**(1):37–60. doi:10.1525/sp.1998.45.1.03x0156z.

15. Agency for Toxic Substances and Disease Registry. *Toxicological profile for cadmium.* http://www.atsdr.cdc.gov/ toxprofiles/tp.asp?id=48&tid=15; 2008 [accessed 9 March 2010].

16. Center for Disease Control and Prevention. *Documentation for immediately dangerous to life or health concentrations (IDLHs): lead (as Pb).* http://www.cdc.gov/niosh/idlh/7439921.html; 1994 [accessed 8 March 2012].

17. Vella V, O'Brien E, Idris E, et al. *Health impacts of lead poisoning: a preliminary listing of the health effects & symptoms of lead poisoning. Lead Action News* 1998;1324-6011**6**(2). http://www.lead.org.au/fs/fst7.html [accessed 8 March 2012].

18. http://aappolicy.aappublications.org/cgi/content/full/pediatrics;116/4/1036.

19. http://www.watoday.com.au/wa-news/barnett-esperance-lead-pollution-still-a-major-concern-20081110-5lg9. html#ixzz1l2RSOdjM.

20. http://www.aacap.org/cs/root/facts_for_families/lead_exposure_in_children_affects_brain_and_behavior.

21. http://www.mnn.com/earth-matters/wilderness-resources/photos/americas-10-worst-man-made-environ mental-disasters/picher-.

22. http://www.theworld.org/2010/06/lead-poisoning-disaster-in-nigeria/.

23. http://www.brain.oxfordjournals.org/content/126/1/5.full.

24. Health & Safety in the Arts—Painting & Drawing Pigments. Environmental management division, city of Tucson AZ. http://www.tucsonaz.gov/arthazards/paint1.html [accessed 9 February 2012].

25. "Hazardous Substance Fact Sheet". NJ Dept. of Health and Senior Services.

26. http://www.nj.gov/health/eoh/rtkweb/documents/fs/0529.pdf [accessed 7 February 2012].

27. USGS 2010. http://www.minerals.usgs.gov/minerals/pubs/commodity/arsenic/mcs-2011-arsenic.pdf.

28. Vahidnia A, Van Der Voet GB, De Wolff FA. Arsenic neurotoxicity—a review. *Hum Exp Toxicol* 2007;**26**(10):823–32 doi:10.1177/0960327107084539. [PMID 18025055].

29. Lechtman H. Arsenic bronze: dirty copper or chosen alloy? A view from the Americas. *J Field Archaeol* 1996;**23** (4):477–514. doi:10.2307/530550. [JSTOR 530550].

30. Emsley J. *Nature's building blocks: an A-Z guide to the elements.* Oxford: Oxford University Press; 2001 pp. 43,513,529. 0-19-850341-5.

31. Turner A. Viewpoint: the story so far: an overview of developments in UK food regulation and associated advisory committees. *Br Food J* 1999;**101**(4):274–83. doi:10.1108/00070709910272141.

32. Smedley PL, Kinniburgh DG. A review of the source, behaviour and distribution of arsenic in natural waters. *Appl Geochem* 2002;**17**(5):517–68. doi:10.1016/S0883-2927(02)00018-5.

33. http://ww.elements.geoscienceworld.org/content/2/2/85.abstract [accessed 10 February 2012].

34. Klaassen C, Watkins J. *Casarett and Doull's essentials of toxicology.* McGraw-Hill; 2003 p. 512. ISBN 978-0-07-138914-3.

35. Eur-Lex. http://www.eur-lex.europa.eu/LexUriServ/LexUriServ.do?uri=CELEX:32003L0002:en:NOT; 2012 [accessed 6 February 2012].

36. Mukherjee A, Sengupta MK, Hossain MA. *Arsenic contamination in groundwater: a global perspective with emphasis on the Asian scenario. J Health Popul Nutr* 2006;**24**(2):142–63. http://www.202.136.7.26/images/jhpn242_Arsenic-con tamination.pdf.

37. Chowdhury UK, Biswas BK, Chowdhury TR. *Groundwater arsenic contamination in Bangladesh and West Bengal, India. Environ Health Perspect* 2000;**108**(4):393–7. doi:10.2307/3454378 [Brogan &#38] http://www.ehponline. org/members/2000/108p393-397chowdhury/chowdhury-full.html [JSTOR 3454378; accessed 9 February 2012].

38. www.wateraid.org/uk/what_we_do/sustainable_technologies/technology_notes/243.asp [accessed 10 February 2012].

39. Chatterjee A, Das D, Mandal BK, Chowdhury TR, Samanta G, Chakraborti D. Arsenic in ground water in six districts of West Bengal, India: the biggest arsenic calamity in the world. Part I. Arsenic species in drinking water and urine of the affected people. *Analyst* 1995;**120**(3):643–51. doi:10.1039/AN9952000643.

40. Das D, Chatterjee A, Mandal BK, Samanta G, Chakraborti D, Chanda B. Arsenic in ground water in six districts of West Bengal, India: the biggest arsenic calamity in the world. Part 2. Arsenic concentration in drinking water, hair, nails, urine, skin-scale and liver tissue (biopsy) of the affected people. *Analyst* 1995;**120**(3):917–25. doi:10.1039/ AN9952000917 [PMID 7741255].

41. Bradley D. *Drinking the water of death. The Guardian;* 5 January 1995.

42. Singh AK. *Chemistry of arsenic in groundwater of Ganges-Brahmaputra river basin. Curr Sci* 2006;**91**(5):599–606. http:// www.ias.ac.in/currsci/sep102006/599.pdf [accessed 10 February 2012].

43. British Geological Society. http://www.csa.com/discoveryguides/arsenic/reviewf.php; 2000 [accessed 6 February 2012].

44. World Health Organization. Arsenic in drinking water. http://www.who.int/water_sanitation_health/dwq/ chemicals/arsenic.pdf [accessed 5 February 2012].

45. United States Environmental Protection Agency. *Interim method for the determination of asbestos in bulk insulation samples.* EPA-600/M4-82-020; December 1982.

46. Occupational Safety and Health Administration. U. S. Department of Labor. Polarized light microscopy of asbestos. Method Number ID-191; 1992.

47. Berry G, Newhouse ML, Antonis P. Combined effect of asbestos and smoking on mortality from lung cancer and mesothelioma in factory workers. *Br J Ind Med* 1985;**42**:12–8; Hammond EC, Selikoff IJ, Seidman H. Asbestos exposure, cigarette smoking and death rates. *Ann N Y Acad Sci* 1979;**330**:473–90; Selikoff IJ, Seidman H, Hammond EC. Mortality effects of cigarette smoking among amosite asbestos factory workers. *J Natl Cancer Inst* 1980;**65**:507–13.

48. For example, see: Brown SK. *Assessment and remediation of asbestos wastes at Islington rail disposal site.* Highett, Victoria, Australia: CSIRO Division of Building, Construction, and Engineering; 1995; Berry G, Newhouse ML. Mortality of workers manufacturing friction materials using asbestos. *Br J Med* 1983;**40**:1–7; Churg A. Lung asbestos content in long-term residents of a Chrysotile mining town. *Am Rev Respir Dis* 1986;**134**:125–7; Churg A, Wright JL. Fibre content of lung in amphibole- and Chrysotile-induced Mesothelioma: implications for environmental exposure. *Int Agency Res Cancer Scient Publ* 1989;**90**:314–8; Henderson VL, Enterline PE. Asbestos exposure: factors associated with excess cancer and respiratory disease mortality. *Ann N Y Acad Sci* 1979;**330**:17–126; Hodgson JT, Darnton A. The quantitative risks of mesothelioma and lung cancer in relation to asbestos exposure. *Ann Occup Hyg* 2000;**44**(8):565–601; Hughes JM, Weill H, Hammad YY. Mortality of workers employed in two asbestos cement manufacturing plants. *Br J Ind Med* 1987;**44**:161–74; Jones JS, Smith PG, Pooley FD, Berry G, Sawle GW, Madeley RJ, Wignall BK, Aggarwal A. The consequences of exposure to asbestos dust in a wartime gas-mask factory. *Int Agency Res Cancer Scient Publ* 1980;**30**:637–53; McDonald JC, McDonald AD. Chrysotile, tremolite and carcinogenicity. *Ann Occup Hyg* 1997;**41**:699–705; McDonald JC, Armstrong B, Case B, Doell D, McCaughey WTE, McDonald AD, Sebastien P. Mesothelioma and asbestos fiber type. Evidence from lung tissue analysis. *Cancer* 1989;**63**:1544–7; Newhouse ML, Sullivan KR. A mortality study of workers manufacturing friction materials: 1941-86. *Br J Ind Med* 1989;**46**:176–9; Rödelsperger K, Woitowitz H-J,

Brückel B, Arhelger R, Polhbeln H, Jöckel K-H. Dose-response relationship between amphibole fiber lung burden and mesothelioma. *Cancer Detect Prev* 1999;**23**(3):183–93; Rogers AJ, Leigh J, Berry G, Ferguson DA, Mulder HB, Ackad M. Relationship between lung asbestos fiber type and concentration and relative risk of mesothelioma. *Cancer* 1991;**67**:1912–20; Sluis-Cremer GK, Liddell FDK, Logan WPD, Bezuidenhout BN. The mortality of amphibole miners in South Africa 1946-80. *Br J Ind Med* 1992;**49**:66–575; Weill H, Hughes J, Waggenspack C. Influence of dose and fiber type on respiratory malignancy risk in asbestos cement manufacturing. *Am Rev Respir Dis* 1979;**120**:345–54.

49. See, for example: Cunningham HM, Moodie CA, Lawrence GA, Ponterfract RD. Chronic effects of ingested asbestos in rats. *Arch Environ Contam Toxicol* 1977;**6**:507–13; Patel-Mandlik KJ, Millette JR. Chrysotile asbestos in kidney cortex of chronically gavaged rats. *Arch Environ Contam Toxicol* 1983;**12**:247–55; Weinzweig M, Richards RJ. Quantitative assessment of chrysotile fibrils in the bloodstream of rats which have ingested the mineral under dietary conditions. *Environ Res* 1983;**31**:245–55.

50. Vallero DA, Beard ME. Selecting appropriate analytical methods to characterize asbestos in various media. *Pract Period Hazard Toxic Radioact Waste Manage* 2009;**13**(4):249–60.

51. For example, see: Chissick SS. Asbestos. In: Gerhartz W, Yamamoto YS, Campbell FT, Pfefferkorn R, Rounsaville JF, editors. *Ullmann's encyclopedia of industrial chemistry.* Weinheim: VCH; 1985. p. 151–67; Choi I, Smith RW. Kinetic study of dissolution of asbestos fibers in water. *J Collo Interf Sci* 1972;**40**:253–62; World Health Organization. *Chrysotile asbestos: environmental health criteria.* Geneva, Switzerland: World Health Organization; 1998.

52. Langer AM, Nolan RP, Addison J. Physico-chemical properties of asbestos as determinants of biological potential. In: Liddell D, Miller K, editors. *Mineral fibers and health.* Boca Raton, FL: CRC Press; 1991. p. 211–28.

53. Mesothelioma and Asbestos Awareness Center. http://www.maacenter.org/jobsites/katrina/contamination.php; 2012 [accessed 15 January 2012].

54. Santa Barbara County Air Pollution Control District. *Asbestos.* http://www.sbcapcd.org/biz/asbestos.htm; 2011 [accessed 15 January 2012].

55. International Agency for Research on Cancer. *Asbestos.* IARC monographs on the evaluation of carcinogenic risks to humans, vol. 14. Lyon, France http://www.monographs.iarc.fr/ENG/Monographs/vol14/volume14.pdf; 1988 [accessed 23 January 2012].

56. Landrigan PJ, Lioy PJ, Thurston G. Health and environmental consequences of the World Trade Center disaster. *Environ Health Perspect* 2004;**112**:731–9.

57. Agency for Toxic Substances and Disease Registry. *What is asbestos?* http://www.atsdr.cdc.gov/asbestos/more_about_asbestos/what_is_asbestos; 2012 [accessed 16 January 2012].

58. U.S. Environmental Protection Agency. *Basic information: asbestos.* http://www.epa.gov/asbestos/pubs/help.html#health; 2012 [accessed 8 March 2012].

59. Based on: Raloff J. *Dirty little secret. Sci News* 2006;**170**:26–8. doi:10.2307/4017077 http://www.onlinelibrary.wiley.com/doi/10.2307/4017077/abstract; 2006 [accessed 16 January 2012]; Meeker GP, Lowers HA, Swayze GA, Van Gosen BS, Stutley SJ, Brownfield IK. *Mineralogy and morphology of amphiboles observed in soils and rocks in El Dorado Hills, California.* United States Geological Survey; 2006. *http://www.pubs.usgs.gov/of/2006/1362/ [accessed 15 January 2012].*

60. Center for Asbestos Related Disease. http://www.libbyasbestos.org/libby/libby.cfm; 2012 [accessed 24 January 2012].

61. U.S. Environmental Protection Agency. *Memorandum: "risk assessment—amphibole mineral fibers in source materials in residential and commercial areas of Libby Pose an imminent and substantial endangerment to public health"* From C.P. Weis to P. Peronard. December 20, 2001.

62. U.S. Environmental Protection Agency. *Cyanide compounds. Technology Transfer Network Air Toxics.* Web Site; http://www.epa.gov/ttn/atw/hlthef/cyanide.html; 2000 [accessed 27 January 2012].

63. Agency for Toxic Substances and Disease Registry. *Toxicological profile for cyanide (update).* Atlanta, GA: Public Health Service, U.S. Department of Health and Human Services; 1997.

64. Calabrese EJ, Kenyon EM. *Air toxics and risk assessment.* Chelsea, MI: Lewis Publishers; 1991.

65. U.S. Environmental Protection Agency. *Integrated Risk Information System. IRIS Glossary.* http://www.epa.gov/iris/help_gloss.htm#a; 2012 [accessed 27 January 2012].

66. U.S. Environmental Protection Agency. *Interim reregistration eligibility decision for chlorpyrifos.* Report No. EPA 738-R-01-007. Washington, DC; 2002.

67. In small doses, however, they are essential. This is common for many metals. Above a certain dose, they are toxic. Below a certain dose, an organism is deficient. Therefore, there is an optimal range for specific compounds of these metals that are essential. Other compounds of these metals are toxic at any level, that is, the metal's valence and chemical form determines its toxicity.

68. Richardson ML, editor. *The dictionary of substances and their effects.* UK: Royal Society of Chemistry; 1992. p. 716–8.

69. Rainforest Information Centre. http://www.rainforestinfo.org.au/gold/spills.htm; 2012 [accessed 26 January 2012].

70. http://www.ret.gov.au/resources/documents.psdp.psdp-cyanidehandbook.pdf [accessed 26 January 2012].

71. http://www.commdev.org/files/1183_file_28_Cyanide_Mgmt_Gold_Extraction.pdf [accessed 26 January 2012].

72. U.S. Environmental Protection Agency. *Mid-atlantic mountaintop mining.* http://www.epa.gov/region03/mtntop/index.htm; 2011 [accessed 16 March 2012].

73. U.S. Environmental Protection Agency. *Mountaintop mining/valley fill process.* http://www.epa.gov/region03/mtntop/process.htm; 2011 [accessed 16 March 2012].

74. Mine-Engineer.Com. *Open pit surface mining.* http://www.mine-engineer.com/mining/open_pit.htm; 2012 [accessed 16 March 2012].

75. http://www.cyanidecode.org/cyanide_use.php.

76. http://www.goldminded.com/carbon_in_pulp.html.

77. Schweitzer A. *Out of my life and thought.* New York, NY: Henry Holt & Co; 1933 [translated by A.B. Lemke, 1990 edition].

# 11

# Recalcitrance

We now return to disasters involving chemical contamination. No matter how they are released, as spills or leaks, immediately or continuously, into the air, water, or soil, a most important characteristic of chemicals is their persistence. The extent and duration of a chemical disaster depends on the characteristics of the chemical agents being released along with the conditions of the environment. That is, the persistence is a function of both the inherent properties of the chemical and the characteristics of the environment in which that chemical resides. The inherent properties of a chemical agent make each chemical unique. Together, these properties are known as chemical inherency.

Chemical compounds are formulated to have particular inherencies. Some are formed to be highly toxic and to break down readily, such as highly reactive pesticides that kill living organisms (e.g., plants, animals, and microbes) but leave no residue on the treated material after a few day. Other chemicals are formulated to resist breaking down. These properties describe the compound's persistence. The reactive pesticide has low environmental persistence. The long-lived compound has high environmental persistence. As we have seen in earlier chapters, each of these types of compounds has been involved in disasters. For example, the methyl isocyanate released in Bhopal has relatively low persistence compared to the tetrachlorodibenzo-*para*-dioxin (TCDD) released in Seveso.

Environmental persistence is often expressed as a substance's chemical *half-life* ($t_{1/2}$) of a contaminant. As mentioned, in addition to a substance's inherent properties, many other variables determine the actual persistence of a compound after its release. For example, benzene and chloroform have nearly identical Henry's Law coefficients ($K_H$), which indicate the expected movement into the air, and octanol-water coefficients ($K_{ow}$) indicating the expected affinity to move from water to tissue. However, benzene is far less persistent in the environment than in chloroform. Indeed, the presence of chlorine atoms in chloroform does lend persistence to the molecule, but the $t_{1/2}$ is also affected by its bioavailability and other environmental factors.

Certainly, the relative affinity for a substance to reside in air and water relates to its potential to partition not only between water and air but also more generally between the atmosphere and biosphere, especially when considering the long-range transport of contaminants (e.g., across continents and oceans).[1] Such long-range transport estimates make use of both atmospheric $t_{1/2}$ and $K_H$ values. Also, the relationship between octanol-water and air-water coefficients can also be an important part of predicting a contaminants transport.

275

Thus, chemical disasters are not only affected by a substance's health hazards and toxicity but also on its likelihood to remain in the environment long after the disaster event. Environmental scientists and engineers refer to this as "recalcitrance."

## THE DIRTY DOZEN

The concept of persistence came into prominence when certain toxic substances were found in the sediment, water, and biota long after they had been released. Scientists observed that these compounds all shared one characteristic, i.e., every compound contained substituted halogens, especially chlorine (Cl). The first effort to address these compounds was a listing by environmental agencies. The so-called Dirty Dozen is a list of the 12 most notorious persistent organic pollutants (POPs), which includes 9 organochlorine pesticides. The United States, member states of the EU, and numerous other countries signed a United Nations treaty in Stockholm, Sweden in May 2001 (i.e., the Stockholm Convention) agreeing to reduce or eliminate the production, use, and/or release of these POPs (see Table 11.1). The chemicals were found far and wide across the planet, often far from where they had been used, presenting a new kind of disaster, one where the cause for isolated in time and space from the effect.

The presence of these chemicals has presented a disaster in terms of the food chain, finding their way to infants through breast milk. In fact, this is a prominent trade-off

TABLE 11.1   Persistent Organic Pollutants Known as the Dirty Dozen

| Pollutant | Global historical use/source | Overview of U.S. status |
|---|---|---|
| Aldrin and dieldrin | Insecticides used on crops such as corn and cotton; also used for termite control | Under FIFRA: No U.S. registrations; most uses canceled in 1969; all uses by 1987 All tolerances on food crops revoked in 1986 No production, import, or export |
| Chlordane | Insecticide used on crops, including vegetables, small grains, potatoes, sugarcane, sugar beets, fruits, nuts, citrus, and cotton. Used on home lawn and garden pests. Also used extensively to control termites | Under FIFRA: No US registrations; most uses canceled in 1978; all uses by 1988 All tolerances on food crops revoked in 1986 No production (stopped in 1997), import, or export. Regulated as a hazardous air pollutant (CAA) |
| DDT | Insecticide used on agricultural crops, primarily cotton, and insects that carry diseases such as malaria and typhus | Under FIFRA: No US registrations; most uses canceled in 1972; all uses by 1989 Tolerances on food crops revoked in 1986 No US production, import, or export. DDE (a metabolite of DDT) regulated as a hazardous air pollutant (CAA). Priority toxic pollutant (CWA) |
| Endrin | Insecticide used on crops such as cotton and grains; also used to control rodents | Under FIFRA, no US registrations; most uses canceled in 1979; all uses by 1984. No production, import, or export. Priority toxic pollutant (CWA) |

TABLE 11.1  Persistent Organic Pollutants Known as the Dirty Dozen—Cont'd

| Pollutant | Global historical use/source | Overview of U.S. status |
|---|---|---|
| Mirex | Insecticide used to combat fire ants, termites, and mealybugs. Also used as a fire retardant in plastics, rubber, and electrical products | Under FIFRA, no US registrations; all uses canceled in 1977. No production, import, or export |
| Heptachlor | Insecticide used primarily against soil insects and termites. Also used against some crop pests and to combat malaria | Under FIFRA: Most uses canceled by 1978; registrant voluntarily canceled use to control fire ants in underground cable boxes in early 2000<br>All pesticide tolerances on food crops revoked in 1989. No production, import, or export |
| Hexachlorobenzene | Fungicide used for seed treatment. Also an industrial chemical used to make fireworks, ammunition, synthetic rubber, and other substances. Also unintentionally produced during combustion and the manufacture of certain chemicals. Also an impurity in certain pesticides | Under FIFRA, no US registrations; all uses canceled by 1985. No production, import, or export as a pesticide. Manufacture and use for chemical intermediate (as allowed under the Convention). Regulated as a hazardous air pollutant (CAA). Priority toxic pollutant (CWA) |
| Polychlorinated biphenyls (PCBs) | Used for a variety of industrial processes and purposes, including in electrical transformers and capacitors, as heat exchange fluids, as paint additives, in carbonless copy paper, and in plastics. Also unintentionally produced during combustion | Manufacture and new use prohibited in 1978 (TSCA). Regulated as a hazardous air pollutant (CAA). Priority toxic pollutant (CWA) |
| Toxaphene | Insecticide used to control pests on crops and livestock, and to kill unwanted fish in lakes | Under FIFRA: No US registrations; most uses canceled in 1982; all uses by 1990<br>All tolerances on food crops revoked in 1993. No production, import, or export. Regulated as a hazardous air pollutant (CAA) |
| Dioxins and furans | Unintentionally produced during most forms of combustion, including burning of municipal and medical wastes, backyard burning of trash, and industrial processes. Also can be found as trace contaminants in certain herbicides, wood preservatives, and in PCB mixtures | Regulated as hazardous air pollutants (CAA). Dioxin in the form of 2,3,7,8-TCDD is a priority toxic pollutant (CWA) |

*Source: US Environmental Protection Agency. Persistent organic pollutants: a global issue, a global response; 2002. http://www.epa.gov/oia/toxics/pop.htm#thedirtydozen [accessed 10 June 2009].*

with profound implications. Since POPs were found in many populations around the world, is it sound public policy to advise mothers not to breast feed, in spite of the many benefits of mother's milk? Usually, the answer has been "no," but it is truly tragic and disastrous that families and communities have been place on the horns of this dilemma.

# AGENT ORANGE

Another type of disaster in which chemical persistence has been a major concern is the long-term effects of chemicals used in combat. Arguably the most infamous example to date is that of "Agent Orange," which was used extensively as a defoliant during the Vietnam War between 1961 and 1970. Similar to low-level radiation exposures and even some of the leaks and spills discussed in earlier chapters, Agent Orange is a disaster with a protracted "latency period," i.e., the possible effects are not manifested until years or decades after exposure.

As is the case for most persistent substances, the chemicals in Agent Orange provided a function. The U.S. military decided that chemicals would be an efficient means of clearing vegetation, both weeds and leaves on trees to eliminate or to reduce sites for enemy troops to hide. Agent Orange was applied by airplanes, helicopters, trucks, and backpack sprayers. In the 1970s, years after the tours of duty in Vietnam, some veterans became concerned that exposure to Agent Orange might cause delayed health effects.

Given that the mixture was designed to be toxic (to plants), it was somewhat unexpected that the chemical compound linked to the health effects was neither an active or inert ingredient of Agent Orange; it was an unintended chemical byproduct. In fact, it was the same chemical central to the disasters at Love Canal, Times Beach, and Seveso, Italy. Agent Orange contained minute amounts of the highly toxic compound TCDD. However, as mentioned in Chapter 4, TCDD has a very steep cancer slope factor; meaning is a very potent carcinogen.

TCDD has been associated with various other ailments, including increased levels of thyroid-stimulating hormone (TSH) in newborns exposed to TCDD *in utero*, decreased sperm concentrations and decreased motile sperm counts in men who were 1-9 years of age at the time of the Seveso accident (initial TCDD exposure event) in 1976, female reproductive effects, subtle changes in immune system components, development dental defects, and diabetes.[2] Also, the U.S. Department of Veteran Affairs has listed a number of diseases which could have resulted from exposure to herbicides like Agent Orange. The law requires that some of these diseases be at least 10% disabling under VA's rating regulations within a deadline that began to run the day you left Vietnam. If there is a deadline, it is listed in parentheses after the name of the disease:

- Chloracne or other acne form disease consistent with chloracne. (Must occur within 1 year of exposure to Agent Orange.)
- Chronic Lymphocytic Leukemia.
- Diabetes Mellitus, Type II.
- Hodgkin's disease.
- Multiple myeloma.
- Non-Hodgkin's lymphoma.
- Acute and subacute peripheral neuropathy. (For purposes of this section, the term acute and subacute peripheral neuropathy means temporary peripheral neuropathy that appears within weeks or months of exposure to an herbicide agent and resolves within 2 years of the date of onset.)
- Porphyria cutanea tarda. (Must occur within 1 year of exposure to Agent Orange.)
- Prostate cancer.
- Respiratory cancers (cancer of the lung, bronchus, larynx, or trachea).
- Soft-tissue sarcoma (other than osteosarcoma, chondrosarcoma, Kaposi's sarcoma, or mesothelioma).

The issue is international. After all, if indeed U.S. military personnel exposed to Agent Orange express symptoms often associated with dioxin exposure, residual dioxin contamination in the treated areas of Vietnam is also likely. Dioxin is highly persistent, as we learned in Times Beach and other hazardous waste sites. However, exogenous processes, like photolysis and microbial degradation are quite different from endogenous processes, like absorption, distribution, metabolism, and excretion. So, the existence or nonexistence of dioxin in the soil and water in Vietnam is not completely affirmative.

Scientists from Vietnam, the United States, and 11 other countries have discussed the state-of-the-science of research into the health effects of dioxin. In March of 2002, senior scientists from the Vietnamese Ministry of Science, Technology and the Environment, the Vietnamese Ministry of Health, the U.S. National Institute of Environmental Health Sciences, the U.S. Environmental Protection Agency, and the U.S. Centers for Disease Control and Prevention met in Hanoi to establish an agreement for future research activities using the findings from the 3-day conference and 1-day workshop as a guide. The Vietnamese and U.S. Government Agencies agreed to the following joint research plan addressing the need for direct research on human health outcomes from exposure to dioxin and research on the environmental and ecological effects of dioxin and Agent Orange. The participants identified the highest priority areas.

The primary concerns in Vietnam from prolonged exposure to dioxin are for reproductive and developmental disorders that may be occurring in the general population. Chlorinated dioxins have 75 different forms and there are 135 different chlorinated furans, depending how the number and arrangement of chlorine atoms on the molecules. The compounds can be separated into groups that have the same number of chlorine atoms attached to the furan or dioxin ring. Each form varies in its chemical, physical, and toxicological characteristics (see Figure 11.1).

Dioxins are only created unintentionally during combustion processes, i.e., they have never been synthesized for any other reason than for scientific investigation, e.g., to make analytical standards for testing. As mentioned, the most highly toxic form is the 2,3,7,8 configuration of TCDD. This particular isomer remains in the environment after certain pesticides are produced, such as those used in the Vietnam defoliants. Other isomers which may have been present in the formulations along with the 2,3,7,8 configuration are also considered to be more highly toxic than the dioxins and furans with different chlorine atom arrangements.

The key areas for research in Vietnam include miscarriage, premature birth, congenital malformations, endocrine disorders, neurological disorders, immunodeficiency, cancer, genetic damage, and diabetes mellitus. Note that a number of these conditions are transgenerational, that is, the effect is not expressed in the progeny, as opposed to the person who has actually been exposed to the dioxin. Preliminary discussions have suggested two areas of research that should be further developed; research on existing populations with high exposures to dioxin relative to populations with low exposures (for example, people living near hotspots) and research on therapies to reduce dioxin body burdens in humans (such as some herbal therapies being proposed in Vietnam).

Dioxin contaminants of Agent Orange have persisted in the environment in Vietnam for over 30 years. In addition to a better understanding of outcomes of exposure, an improved understanding of residue levels and rates of migration of dioxin and other chemicals in the environment is needed. "Hot spots" containing high levels of dioxin in soil have been identified and others are presumed to exist but have yet to be located.

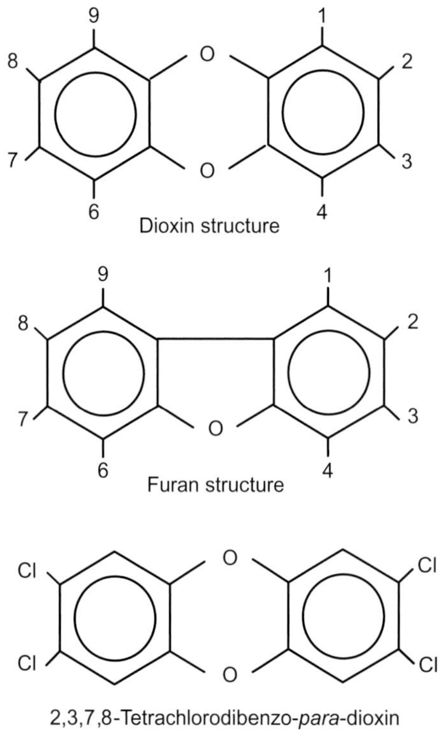

FIGURE 11.1 Molecular structures of dioxins and furans. Bottom structure is of the most toxic dioxin congener, tetrachlorodibenzo-*para*-dioxin (TCDD), formed by the substitution of chlorine for hydrogen atoms at positions 2, 3, 7, and 8 on the molecule.

Dioxin structure

Furan structure

2,3,7,8-Tetrachlorodibenzo-*para*-dioxin

Dioxin has migrated through soil and has been transported through natural processes such as wind-blown dust and erosion into the aquatic environment. Contamination of soil and sediments provides a reservoir source of dioxin for direct and indirect exposure pathways for humans and wildlife. Movement of dioxin through the food web results in bioconcentration and biomagnification with potential ecological impacts and continuing human exposure. Research is needed to develop approaches for more rapid and less expensive screening of dioxin residue levels in soil, sediment, and biological samples which can be applied in Vietnam.

Sampling and analytical methods need to be enhanced in order to be used to more readily determine locations of highly contaminated areas, monitor remediation, and understand migration of dioxin in the natural environment. Monitoring efforts need to be linked to modeling efforts to understand fate and transport of dioxin in the environment. Innovative and cost-effective approaches to environmental remediation for application in Vietnam need to be developed, tested, and applied.

Preliminary discussions have suggested two areas of research that should be further developed: ecological and restoration research on a degraded upland forest (such as the Ma Da forest) and research on the identification, characterization, and remediation of hot spots (such as Da Nang Airport).

Agent Orange was actually one of a number of defoliating agents used in Vietnam (see Table 11.2). Most of the formulations included the two herbicides 2,4-D and 2,4,5-T. The

TABLE 11.2   Formulations of Defoliants Used in the Vietnam War

| Agent | Formulation |
|-------|-------------|
| Purple | 2,4,-D and 2,4,5,-T used between 1962 and 1964. |
| Green | Contained 2,4,5-T and was used 1962-1964. |
| Pink | Contained 2,4,5-T and was used 1962-1964. |
| Orange | A formulation of 2,4,-D and 2,4,5-T used between 1965 and 1970. |
| White | A formulation of Picloram and 2,4,-D. |
| Blue | Contained cacodylic acid. |
| Orange II | 2,4,-D and 2,4,5-T used in 1968 and 1969 (also sometimes referred to as "Super Orange") |
| Dinoxol | 2,4,-D and 2,4,5-T. Small quantities were tested in Vietnam between 1962 and 1964. |
| Trinoxol | 2,4,5-T. Small quantities tested in Vietnam 1962-1964. |

Source: Agent Orange Website: http://www.lewispublishing.com/orange.htm [accessed 22 April 2005].

combined product was mixed with kerosene or diesel fuel and dispersed by aircraft, vehicle, and hand spraying. An estimated 80 million liters of the formulation was applied in South Vietnam during the war.[3]

The Agent Orange tragedy illustrates the problem of uncertainty in characterizing and enumerating effects. There is little consensus on whether the symptoms and disorders suggested to be linked to Agent Orange are sufficiently strong and well documented, i.e., provide weight of evidence, to support cause and effect. Scientists know, for example, that even very strong weight of evidence is merely a part in cause-to-effect linkages. Medical researchers and epidemiologists employ a number of steps in determining causation. For example, the strength of an association between an effect and a potential cause requires sound technical judgment. In the case of cancer, characterizing the weight of evidence for carcinogenicity in humans consists of three major steps[4]:

1. Characterization of the evidence from human studies and from animal studies individually;
2. Combination of the characterizations of these two types of data to show the overall weight of evidence for human carcinogenicity; and
3. Evaluation of all supporting information to determine if the overall weight of evidence should be changed.

None of these steps is completely certain. All require a dose of technical judgment. For instance, an observed cluster of cancers in town may have nothing to do with the green gunk that is flowing out of the abandoned building's outfall. But in their minds, the linkage is obvious.

The challenge is to present information in a meaningful way without violating and over extending the interpretation of the data. If we assign causality when none really exists, we may suggest erroneous solutions. But, if all we can say is that the variables are associated, the public is going to want to know more about what may be contributing an adverse effect (e.g., TCDD exposure and diabetes). This was particularly problematic in early cancer research. Possible causes of cancer were being explored and major research efforts were being directed at a myriad of physical, chemical, and biological agents. So, there needed to be some manner of sorting through findings to see what might be causal and what is more likely to be spurious results. Sir Austin Bradford Hill is credited with articulating key criteria that need to be satisfied to attribute cause and effect in medical research.[5] The factors to be considered in determining whether exposure to a chemical elicits an effect include:

- Criterion 1: Strength of Association
- Criterion 2: Consistency
- Criterion 3: Specificity
- Criterion 4: Temporality
- Criterion 5: Biologic Gradient
- Criterion 6: Plausibility
- Criterion 7: Coherence
- Criterion 8: Experimentation
- Criterion 9: Analogy

In assessing risks, some of Hill's criteria are more important than others. Risk assessments rely heavily on strength of association, e.g. to establish dose-response relationships. Coherence is also very important. Animal and human data should not be extensions of one another and should not disagree. Biological gradient is crucial, as this is the basis for dose-response (the larger the dose, the greater the biological response).

Temporality is crucial to all scientific research, i.e. the cause must precede the effect. However, this is sometimes difficult to see in some instances, such as when the exposures to suspected agents have been continuous for decades and the health data are only recently available.

The Agent Orange debate is still raging. The data themselves will never be sufficient to convince all sides. Sound technical and scientific judgment based on the best available and most reliable data is also needed for reliable risk assessments. Linking cause and effect in the aftermath of environmental disasters is often difficult. Sometimes, the best we can do is to be upfront and clear about the uncertainties and the approaches we use.

## LAKE APOPKA

The Agent Orange disaster is mainly about the health of former military personnel, although there certainly is an ecological component involving contaminated systems in Southeast Asia. However, recalcitrant compounds have presented ecological problems as well. The Lake Apopka spill presents an example of the problem of persistent organic compounds long after the release.

Can alligator penis size be an indication of a disaster? Yes, if this is an indication of widespread endocrine disruption in an ecosystem. In animals and plants, the endocrine system is actually a chemical messaging network. Hormones interact with ligands to initiate biochemical processes. Endocrine disrupting chemicals (EDCs) provide a unique challenge for environmental biotechnology, as EDCs can mimic hormones, antagonize normal hormones, alter the pattern of synthesis and metabolism of natural hormones, or modify hormone receptor levels.[6] Anthropogenic EDCs that are of concern in water and wastewater include pesticide residues (e.g., DDT, endosulfan, and methoxychlor), PCBs, dioxin, alkylphenols (e.g., nonylphenol), plastic additives (e.g., bisphenol A, diethyl phthalate), PAHs, and pharmaceutical hormones (e.g., 17b estradiol, ethinyl estradiol).[7] When microbes and plants and higher animals take part in biotechnological endeavors, implications to these chemical messages need to be considered.

Recent research has shown that many EDCs are present in the environment at levels capable of negatively effecting in wildlife. One of the first EDCs to be heavily researched was DDT.[8,9]

Numerous pesticides and chemicals have been associated with endocrine related abnormalities in wildlife, including the inducement of feminine traits, such as secretion of the egg-laying hormone, vitellogenin in males of numerous aquatic species.[10] Birds and terrestrial animals are also affected by EDCs.[11] Recently, these problems have found their way to humans, exposed to halogenated compounds, and pesticides.[12] A recent nationwide survey of pharmaceuticals in U.S. surface water found EDCs at ng $L^{-1}$ levels in 139 stream sites throughout the United States. Several of these EDCs were found at even $\mu$g $L^{-1}$ levels, including nonylphenol (40 $\mu$g $L^{-1}$), bisphenol A (12 $\mu$g $L^{-1}$), and ethinyl estradiol (0.831 $\mu$g $L^{-1}$).[13]

All of these findings are profound given that recently scientists have recorded a sharp decrease in the numbers of male alligators in Lake Apopka, FL, with feminization and loss of fertility found in the remaining males.[14] Throughout the 1980s, exposure to DDT was found to be associated with abnormal sexual differentiation in seagulls, as well as thinning and cracking of bald eagle eggs,[15] along with the feminization and loss of fertility found in reptiles.[16] A profound endocrine disruption natural experiment was that of a large spill of a pesticide mixture into Lake Apopka in central Florida. Studies following the spill have indicated that male alligators, the lake's top predators, showed marked reductions in gonad size.

A hazardous waste site was located about 1.6 km away from Lake Apopka on a stream connected to the lake. The Tower Chemical Company previously produced dicofol, which is a mixture of the pesticide DDT and its degradation product dichlorodiphenylethene (DDE). Although there were a number of small spills, one large accident occurred in 1980 that released dicofol and sulfuric acid, which migrated to the lake.[17] This well-publicized spill was among the first to highlight the suspected ecological link between chemical exposure and endocrine disruption. These alligators exhibited reproductive and hormonal abnormalities; including elevated levels of estrogen, abnormal seminal vesicles, and smaller than normal penises.

Many of these compounds are extremely persistent in the environment, so their removal before entering environmental media is paramount to reducing exposures.[18]

As in many other cases where DDT is involved, there is no unanimity within the scientific community on its link to the problems in the wildlife in Lake Apopka. For example, it has been argued that sexual problems of alligators in Lake Apopka, Florida, may be a manifestation of exposures to already existing endocrine disruptors prior to the spill and the physiological and hormonal problems are simply the result of these remnant exposures.[19] Another potent substance, dibromochloropropane, well known to sterilize factory workers in California, was formulated and wastes containing high concentrations of this compound were stored in unlined ponds near the Florida lake's shores. Thus the dibromochloropropane may well have leached into the lake, giving rise to the endocrine disruptive effects in the alligators.

# JAMES RIVER

The Allied Chemical Company had operated a pesticide formulation facility in Hopewell, Virginia, since 1928. The Hopewell plant had produced many different chemicals over its operational life. Reflecting the nascent growth of petrochemical revolution in the 1940s, the plant began to be used to manufacture organic[1] insecticides which had recently been invented, DDT being the first and most widely used. In 1949, it started to manufacture chlordecone (trade name Kepone), a particularly potent herbicide that was also highly toxic and carcinogenic (see Table 11.3). The company withdrew its request to the Department of Agriculture to sell this chemical to American farmers. It was, however, very effective and cheap to make, and so the company began to market it overseas.

Chlordecone

In the 1970s, the U.S. Congress amended the Federal Water Pollution Control Act to establish the national pollutant discharge elimination permit system (NDPES). One of the NPDES permit requirements was that Allied list all the chemicals it was discharging into the James River. Recognizing the problem with Kepone, Allied decided not to list it as part of their discharge, and a few years later "tolled" the manufacture of Kepone to a small company called Life Science Products Co. The practice of tolling, long standing in chemical manufacture, involves giving all the technical information to another company as well as an exclusive right to manufacture a certain chemical for the payment of certain fees. Life Sciences Products set up a small plant in Hopewell to manufacture Kepone, discharging all of its wastes into the sewerage system.

The operator of the Hopewell wastewater treatment plant soon noted that anaerobic digester was not working and that the bacteria had died. He had no idea what killed these microbes, and tried vainly to restart it by buffering with bases to neutralize the acidity. In 1975, one of the workers at the Life Sciences Products plant visited his physician, complaining of tremors, shakes, and weight loss. The physician drew a sample of the worker's blood and sent it to the Center for Disease Control for analysis. The worker had 8 mg $L^{-1}$ of Kepone in his blood, an extremely elevated concentration. The State of Virginia immediately closed

---

[1] The term "organic" is sometimes unclear when it comes to pesticides. In this usage, the term means that these pesticide compounds contain at least one carbon-to-carbon or carbon-to-hydrogen covalent bond. In contemporary usage, the term *organic* can also mean the opposite of *synthetic* or even *natural*, such as pesticides that are derived from plant extracts, such as pyrethrin from the chrysanthemum flower. This is another example of how even within the scientific community, we are not clear in what we mean, making risk communications difficult.

TABLE 11.3   Properties of Chlordecone (Kepone)

| Formula | Physicochemical properties | Environmental persistence and exposure | Toxicity |
|---|---|---|---|
| 1,2,3,4,5,5,6,7,9,10,10-dodecachloroocta-hydro-1,3,4-metheno-2H-cyclobuta (cd) pentalen-2-one ($C_{10}Cl_{10}O$). | Solubility in water: 7.6 mg $L^{-1}$ at 25 °C; vapor pressure: less than $3 \times 10^{-5}$ mmHg at 25°C; log Kow: 4.50 | Estimated half-life ($t_{1/2}$) in soils between 1 and 2 years, whereas in air is much higher, up to 50 years. Not expected to hydrolyze, biodegrade in the environment. Also, direct photodegradation and vaporization from water and soil is not significant. General population exposure to chlordecone mainly through the consumption of contaminated fish and seafood. | Workers exposed to high levels of chlordecone over a long period (more than one year) have displayed harmful effects on the nervous system, skin, liver, and male reproductive system (likely through dermal exposure to chlordecone, although they may have inhaled or ingested some as well). Animal studies with chlordecone have shown effects similar to those seen in people, as well as harmful kidney effects, developmental effects, and effects on the ability of females to reproduce. There are no studies available on whether chlordecone is carcinogenic in people. However, studies in mice and rats have shown that ingesting chlordecone can cause liver, adrenal gland, and kidney tumors. Very highly toxic for some species such as Atlantic menhaden, sheepshead minnow, or Donaldson trout with $LC_{50}$ between 21.4 and 56.9 mg $L^{-1}$. |

Source: United Nations Environmental Programme. Chemicals: North American regional report. Regionally based assessment of persistent toxic substances, global environment facility; 2002.

the plant and conducted health appraisals of the workers. Over 75 people were found to have Kepone poisoning. It is unknown how many of these people eventually developed cancer. The Kepone that killed the digester in the wastewater treatment plant flowed into the James River and over 100 miles of the river was closed to fishing due to the Kepone contamination. The sewers through which the waste from Life Science flowed was so contaminated that it was abandoned and new sewers built. These sealed sewers are still under the streets of Hopewell and serve as a reminder of corporate avarice.

Decades after the plant closed, detectable concentrations of Kepone have remained in the James River. In fact, Kepone is still detected in the majority of white perch and striped bass sampled from the James River. A fish consumption advisory ruling remains in effect 30 years after the source of contamination was removed.[20] This means that the compound is still in the food cycle, moving from the sediment to the water and from benthic (bottom) organisms to predator fish.

## PERSISTENT WASTES

We addressed hazardous waste sites in Chapter 5, but it is worth mentioning that the presence of recalcitrant contaminants in a wastestream presents major problems. They are difficult to treat. In abandoned and active waste sites, remnant chemical contaminants are particularly menacing. They are either already reaching human populations or ecosystems, or are a threat to be released. A specific chemical constituent of any waste stream can cause particular kinds of harm, as codified in rules and regulations. For the most part, hazardous waste has been considered a subset of solid waste and has been distinguished from municipal wastes and non-hazardous industrial wastes. For example, in the United States, the Resource Conservation and Recovery Act (RCRA)[21] requires proper handling of wastes from their production through their transport to their ultimate disposal, i.e., the so-called cradle to grave manifest system. RCRA divides wastes into two basic types, i.e., non-hazardous solid waste and hazardous waste. Subtitle D of the act covers solid waste and Subtitle C regulates hazardous waste. Therefore, even though it is a subset of "solid" waste, a hazardous waste may be of any physical phase; i.e., solid, liquid, gas, or mixtures.

The hazardous attributes of the waste are usually based on its inherent physicochemical properties, including its likelihood to ignite, explode, and react with water. A waste's hazardous inherent properties can also be biological, such as the infectious nature of medical wastes, or a chemical compound that has been shown to elicit acute effects, e.g., skin irritations and chronic effects, e.g., cancer, harm to the endocrine, immune, or nervous system, interference with tissue development and reproduction, or mutations, birth defects or other toxic endpoints. Persistence is important, because the longer a hazardous substance remains in the environment, the more likely is the exposure and risk. For chemicals, the most important hazard is the potential for disease or death (morbidity and mortality, respectively). The hazards to human health are referred to collectively in the medical and environmental sciences as toxicity. Human toxicology is the study of these health outcomes and their potential causes. Likewise, the study of hazards to ecosystems is known as ecological toxicology or simply ecotoxicology, which is further subdivided by discipline, e.g., aquatic toxicology and mammalian toxicology.

In the United States, as in many countries, the term hazardous waste is a legal term defined by the regulatory agencies. Under the RCRA hazardous waste regulations, The U.S. Environmental Protection Agency (EPA) is principally responsible for the permitting of hazardous waste treatment, storage, and disposal facilities. The EPA, however, has authorizes most states to operate portions or the entire hazardous waste program.[22] Arguably, the most important definition is found in Section 1004(5) of the RCRA, which describes a hazardous waste as a solid waste that may pose a substantial present or potential threat to human health and the environment when improperly treated, stored, transported, or otherwise managed.

The EPA has developed standard approaches and set criteria to determine if substances exhibit hazardous characteristics.[23] Because RCRA defines a hazardous waste as a waste that presents a threat to human health and the environment when it is improperly managed, the government identified a set of assumptions that would allow for a waste to be disposed if it is not subject to the controls mandated by Subtitle C of RCRA. This mismanagement scenario was designed to simulate a plausible worst case, that is, the conditions where a hazardous substance is most likely to migrate.

Thus, if a compound is persistent and it is likely to move then there is a chance for an exposure. When exposed to the myriad contaminants stored in known and unknown waste sites there will be risks to public health and the environment. These risks reflect many small disasters and a worldwide collective disaster.

## THE ARCTIC DISASTER

Indigenous peoples often subsist on traditional food for all or part of their diet. This is certainly true for the Inuit population who live predominantly in the Arctic and sub-Arctic climes. Ironically, these very remote Arctic regions have been chronically exposed to POPs, rending these subpopulations vulnerable to the POP's effects. Since POPs remain in the environment for long periods of time they can be transported over great distances from their sources. The tendency of these compounds to be toxic, to bioaccumulate, and to biomagnify in food chains increases the risk to the Inuit populations.

In addition to the need for many indigenous people in the Arctic to rely on traditional diets for nourishment, the hunting and fishing are also an important part of their cultural identity. Indeed, alternative sources of food often do not exist. Exacerbating the problem, traditional diets are often high in fat. Since most POPs are lipophilic, they tend to accumulate in fatty tissue of the animals that are eaten. Due to these physicochemical properties, POPs can move many hundreds of kilometers away from their sources, either in the gas phase or attached to particles. They are generally moved by advection, i.e., along with the movement of air masses. Some of the routes of long-range transport of POPs are shown in Figure 11.2.

There is also a fairness problem. That is, most northern residents have not used or directly benefited from the activities associated with the production and use of these chemicals, yet indigenous peoples in the Arctic have some of the highest known exposures to these chemicals.

Lactating Inuit mother's breast milk, for example, contains elevated levels of PCBs, DDT, and its metabolites, chlorinated dioxins and furans, and brominated organics, such as residues from fire retardants, i.e., polybrominated diphenyl ethers and heavy metals.[24] Infants are particularly vulnerable to persistent, bioaccumulating toxic compounds (PBTs) which, as mentioned, are lipophilic and find their way to fat reserves in warm-blooded animals. Thus, infants are particularly vulnerable (see Figure 11.3).

Although POPs are found to varying extents among women in both industrially developed and developing nations, the Canadian Inuit have shown some of the highest levels of contaminants to be detected. Their diet consists of seal, whale, and other species high on the marine

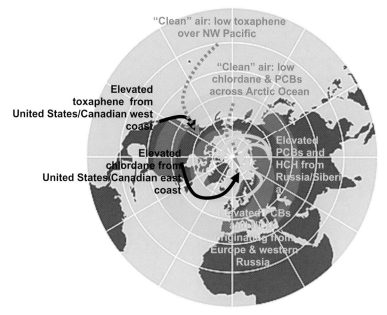

<br/>

FIGURE 11.2   Long-range transport of persistent organic pollutants in the Arctic regions. *Source: Vallero DA. Environmental biotechnology: a biosystems approach. Burlington, MA: Elsevier Academic Press; 2009. Adapted from: Russian Chairmanship of the Arctic Council (2005). Draft Fact Sheet.*

food chain, increasing the Inuit body burden of POPs.[25] These elevated exposures have been associated with reports of health effects similar to the effects of persons exposed to PCBs who also had evidence of other contaminants in body fluids.

A study of Inuit women from Hudson Bay[26] indicated very high levels of PCBs and DDE in breast milk; these results prompted an examination of the health status of Inuit newborns.[27] Correlation analysis revealed a statistically significant negative association between male birth length and levels of hexachlorobenzene, mirex, PCBs, and chlorinated dibenzodioxins (CDDs)/CDFs in the fat of mothers' milk. No significant differences were observed between male and female newborns for birth weight, head circumference, or TSH. Immune system effects have also been detected in Inuit infants suspected of receiving elevated levels of PCBs and dioxins during lactation. These babies had a drop in the ratio of the CD4+ (helper) to CD8+ (cytotoxic) T-cells at ages 6 and 12 months (but not at 3 months).[28]

The Inuit situation demonstrates the critical ties between humans and their environment and the importance of physical properties of contaminants (e.g., persistence, bioaccumulation, and toxicity potentials), the conditions of the environment (e.g., the lower Arctic temperatures increase the persistence of many POPs), and the complexities of human activities (e.g., diet and lifestyle) in order to assess risks and, ultimately, to take actions to reduce exposures. The combination of these factors leaves the Inuit in a tragic dilemma. Since they are subsistence anglers and hunters, they depend almost entirely on a tightly defined portion of the earth for food. Their lifestyle and diet dictate dependence on food sources high in POPs.

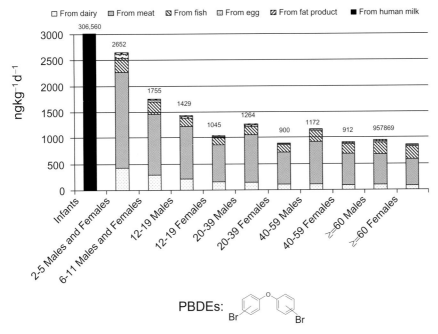

FIGURE 11.3   US population's estimated daily dietary intake of polybrominated diphenyl ethers (PBDE) by age group and food source. Units are picograms per kg (pg kg$^{-1}$) of body weight day$^{-1}$. In all groups older than 1 year of age, total PBDE intake from meat is significantly higher than from any other food sources. The highest dietary intake values of PBDEs were found in nursing infants (307 ng kg$^{-1}$) body weight day$^{-1}$, which compares to 1.0 ng kg$^{-1}$ d$^{-1}$ for men or 0.9 ng kg$^{-1}$ d$^{-1}$ for women at $\geq$ 60 years of age. *Source: Schecter A, Päpke O, Harris TR, Tung KC, Musumba A, Olson J, et al. Polybrominated diphenyl ether (PBDE) levels in an expanded market basket survey of U.S. food and estimated PBDE dietary Intake by age and sex.* Environ Health Perspect 2006;**114**(10):1515-1520.

What makes this disaster even more complex and tragic is that it forces innocent people to make extremely difficult decisions. Pediatricians rightly encourage breast feeding for its many attributes, including enhancing the infant's immune system in the critical first weeks after birth. So, in terms of risk tradeoffs, it is dangerous to discourage breast feeding. This dilemma not only applies to the Inuit, or even just subsistence farmers, hunters, and anglers but also to all of us. The key is to ensure that breast milk everywhere does not contain hazardous levels of PBTs and other contaminants. The only way to do this is to consider the entire life cycle of the pollutants and find ways to prevent their entry into the environment in the first place.

Another lesson is to pay attention to the properties of a compound before its use and to monitor for problems after the product reaches the marketplace (see Chapter 14). For example, the POPs' recalcitrance is greater in the Arctic regions compared to temperate and tropical regions, as a direct result of temperature. Toxicity properties of environmental contaminants are also affected by extrinsic conditions, such as whether the substances are found in the air, water, sediment, or soil, along with the conditions of these media (e.g., oxidation-reduction, pH, and grain size). For example, the metal mercury is usually more toxic in reduced and anaerobic conditions because it is more likely to form alkylated-organometallic compounds, like monomethyl mercury and the extremely toxic dimethyl mercury. These reduced chemical species are likely to form when buried under layers of sediment where dissolved oxygen levels approach zero. Ironically, engineers have unwittingly participated in increasing potential exposures to these toxic compounds. With the good intention of attempting to clean up contaminated lakes in the 1970s, engineers recommended and implemented dredging programs. In the process of removing the sediment, however, the metals and other toxic chemicals that had been relatively inert and encapsulated in buried sediment were released to the lake waters. In turn, the compounds were also more likely to find their way to the atmosphere (see Figure 5.11). This is a lesson to engineers to take care to consider the many physical, chemical, and biological characteristics of a compound and the environment where it exists.

## LESSONS LEARNED

The best and most obvious way to address recalcitrant contaminants is to avoid them in the first place. Green chemistry is advancing, so safer alternatives that meet the same societal needs are slowing growing. Unfortunately, most of the compounds mentioned in this chapter were used and released decades ago. Since they are persistent they would be expected to be around for many more decades without intervention.

### Mimicking Nature

Environmental scientists and engineers have noted that natural systems, such as surface waters and soil, are able to break down organic materials. This is a type of "biomimicry" wherein one can emulate natural processes to achieve desired results. Various genera of microbes were seen to be able to decompose detritus on forest floors, suspended organic material in water, and organic material adsorbed onto soil particles, using these organic compounds as sources of energy need for growth, metabolism, and reproduction. The sanitary engineers in the twentieth century correctly extrapolated from these observations that a more concentrated system could be designed to do the same thing with society's organic wastes. This started with the so-called conventional wastes (human sewage and animal manure). Trickling filters, oxidation ponds, landfills, and other wastewater treatment systems are merely supercharged versions of natural systems, so it was not a major leap in thinking to apply these principles to the more persistent and toxic compounds discussed in this chapter.

Engineers must address recalcitrant compounds contamination in two phases, liquid and solid, which are transported offsite by advection (i.e., moving with the air or water). In quiescent environments like sediment and certain soils, they may also move by molecular diffusion. In North America, landfill regulations call for a system that minimizes liquid infiltration into the solid waste mass by controlling the amount of moisture allowed into these landfills. These so-called dry tomb landfill designs produce strata within the bioreactor system with low moisture content. While this decreases the amount of leachate, it also severely limits biodegradation, since moisture is a limiting factor for biofilm production and microbial metabolism. Thus, the likelihood of incomplete degradation of contaminants increases as does their associated risk since the exposure integration time is protracted. These exposures include emissions from fugitive dust, combustion from the flare, microbial releases and the migration of contaminants through soil, ground, and surface waters. This is the rationale for long-term monitoring around these sites; e.g., current regulations require liquid leachate and gas emissions to be monitored for at least 30 years after closure of a landfill site or even longer if there is reason to believe the risks continue after that time.

A number of small-scale and large-scale projects have demonstrated that the rate of microbial degradation of solid wastes in these landfills can be enhanced, especially by increasing the moisture content of the waste. This can be by increasing the amount of water in the strata and by leachate recirculation[29] (the leachate now is collected and treated; see Figure 11.4).

Waste arrives and is stored in a landfill on an ongoing basis so the age of the waste between and within (e.g., cells within layers) is quite variable. As can be seen in Figure 11.4, the different landfill stabilization phases often overlap and can be viewed systematically. The initial phase results in aerobic decomposition followed by four stages of anaerobic degradation. Thus, the majority of landfill decomposition by volume occurs under anaerobic conditions. Generally, biodegradation follows three basic stages[30]:

1. The organic material in solid phase (represented by chemical oxygen demand, i.e., $COD_S$) decays rapidly as larger organic molecules degrades into smaller molecules.
2. These smaller organic molecules in the solid phase undergo dissolution and move to the liquid phase ($COD_L$), with subsequent hydrolysis of these organic molecules.
3. The smaller molecules are transformed and volatilize as $CO_2$ and $CH_4$ with remaining biomass in solid and liquid phases.

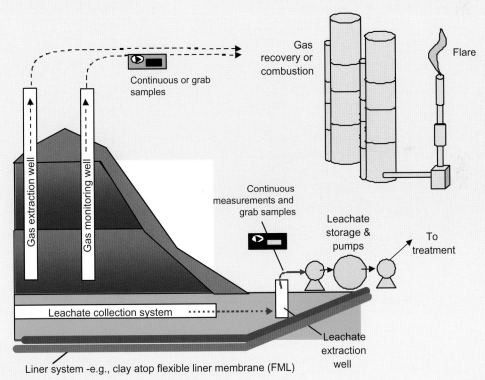

FIGURE 11.4  Schematic of a landfill bioreactor showing gas collection and monitoring wells, leachate collection system, and treatment processes.

During the first two phases, little material volume reaches the leachate. However, the biodegradable organic matter of the waste undergoes rapid reduction. Meanwhile, the leachate COD accumulates as a result of excesses of more recalcitrant compounds compared to the more reactive compounds in the leachate.

These three steps can be further grouped into five phases by which degradation occurs in a landfill bioreactor system, as shown in Figure 11.5. Successful conversion and stabilization of the waste depends on how well microbial populations function in *syntrophy* (i.e., an interaction of different populations that supply each other's nutritional needs.).

### Phase I: Initial Adjustment

In environmental microbiology this phase is referred to as the lag phase. As the waste is placed in the landfill, the void spaces contain high volumes of molecular oxygen ($O_2$). As additional wastes are added and compacted, the $O_2$ content of the landfill bioreactor strata gradually decreases. With increasing moisture, the microbial population density increases, initiating aerobic biodegradation, i.e., the primary electron acceptor is $O_2$.

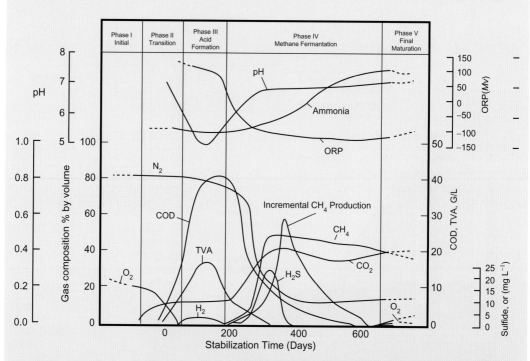

**FIGURE 11.5** Phases of solid waste decomposition in a landfill, showing changes in released compounds and landfill conditions. *Note*: COD, chemical oxygen demand; TVA, total volatile acids; ORP, oxidation-reduction potential. *Source: U.S. Environmental Protection Agency. National risk management research laboratory. Landfill bioreactor performance: second interim report: outer loop recycling & Disposal Facility—Louisville, Kentucky. Report No. EPA/600/R-07/060. Cincinnati, OH; 2007.*

## Phase II: Transition

This phase is short-lived as the $O_2$ is rapidly degraded by the existing microbial populations. The decreasing $O_2$ results in a transition from aerobic to anaerobic conditions in the stratum. The primary electron acceptors during transition are nitrates and sulfates, since $O_2$ is rapidly displaced by $CO_2$ in the effluent gas.

## Phase III: Acid Formation

Hydrolysis of the biodegradable fraction of the solid waste begins in the acid formation phase, which leads to rapid accumulation of volatile fatty acids (VFAs) in the leachate. The increased organic acid content decreases the leachate pH from approximately 7.5 to 5.6.[31] During this phase, the decomposition intermediate compounds like the VFAs contribute much COD. Long-chain volatile organic acids (VOAs) are converted to acetic acid ($C_2H_4O_2$), $CO_2$, and hydrogen gas ($H_2$). High concentrations of VFAs increase both the BOD and VOA concentrations, which initiates $H_2$ production by fermentative bacteria, which stimulates the growth of $H_2$-oxidizing bacteria. The $H_2$ generation phase is relatively short because it is complete by the end of the acid formation phase.

As seen in Figure 11.5, this phase also is accompanied by an increase in the biomass of acidogenic bacteria and rapid degradation of substrates and consumption of nutrients.

Since metals are generally more water soluble at lower pH, metallic compounds may become more mobile during this phase.

## Phase IV: Methane Fermentation

The acid formation phase intermediary products (e.g., acetic, propionic, and butyric acids) are converted to $CH_4$ and $CO_2$ by *methanogenic* microorganisms. As VFAs are metabolized by the methanogens, the landfill water pH returns to neutrality. The organic strength (i.e., oxygen demand) of the leachate decreases at a rapid rate as gas production increases in correspondence with increases in $CH_4$ and $CO_2$ gas production. This is the longest-lived waste decomposition phase.

## Phase V: Final Maturation and Stabilization

The rate of microbiological activity slows in the last phase of waste decomposition in conjunction with nutrient limits, e.g., bioavailable phosphorus. $CH_4$ production almost completely disappears with $O_2$ and oxidized species gradually reappearing in the gas wells as $O_2$ permeates from the troposphere. This moves the oxidation-reduction potential (ORP) in the leachate to oxidative processes. The residual organic materials may incrementally be converted to the gas phase and composting of organic matter to humic-like compounds, although this has not yet been scientifically documented.

On-site degradation, such as that occurs in a landfill, is carried out by different genera of microbes, making the kinetics difficult to predict for any facility. Such microbial populations occur naturally in the landfill (e.g., natural soil bacteria). However, varying temporal and spatial site-specific conditions to achieve optimal performance is often a heuristic process. The kinetics of microorganisms in landfill bioreactors have not been widely investigated, likely because these groups of microorganisms are much more difficult than aerobes to culture. Hopefully, the emergence of molecular-based nonculture techniques will increase this information. To date, landfill bioreactor performance has been evaluated and controlled by indirect evidence, e.g., waste stabilization is characterized by monitoring the outcome of the decomposition process. For example, recirculation of leachate has been shown to shorten the initial lag phase, even though the microbial species responsible for this accelerated decomposition have not been precisely identified.[32]

Bioengineering improvements to a landfill bioreactor requires attention to the sensitivity of variables. To improve efficiency depends on optimizing microbiological metabolic processes. For example, the amount of leachate to be recirculated affects the quantity of organic acids. If VFA concentrations are high, methanogenesis can be inhibited. This is not a direct inhibition of microbial metabolism, but a response of the microbial population to the lower pH induced by the VFAs. Thus, the volume of recirculated leachate must be adjusted to minimize the accumulation of VFAs (see Figure 11.6).

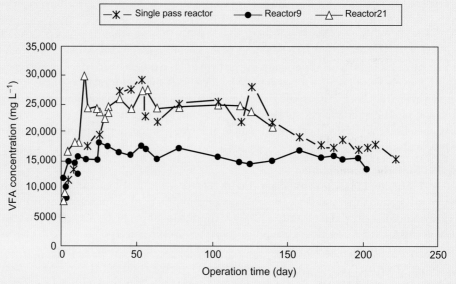

FIGURE 11.6    Effects of leachate recirculation on volatile fatty acid (VFA) accumulation compared with VFA generation under conventional landfill management. The leachate in "Reactor 9" was recirculated at 9 L day$^{-1}$ (2.4 gallons day$^{-1}$; god) = 13% of the reactor volume. The leachate in "Reactor 21" was recirculated at 21 L day$^{-1}$ (5.5 god) = 30% of the reactor volume. The VFA buildup in the reactor with a higher leachate recirculation rate of 21 L day$^{-1}$ (5.5 god) was nearly as high as the VFAs generated in the single-pass (i.e., conventional) reactor. The 21 L day$^{-1}$ (5.5 god), the bioreactor experienced a spike = 30,000 mg VFAL$^{-1}$ within 30 days, which can be detrimental to methanogenic bacteria. *Sources: U.S. Environmental Protection Agency. National risk management research laboratory. Landfill bioreactor performance: second interim report: outer loop recycling & disposal facility— Louisville, Kentucky. Report No. EPA/600/R-07/060. Cincinnati, Ohio; 2007; Sponza D, Agdag O. Impact of leachate re-circulation and re-circulation volume on stabilization of municipal solid wastes in simulated anaerobic bioreactors. Proc Biochem 2004;39(12):2157-2165.*

Thus, effective degradation depends on matching the abiotic and biotic conditions in a bioreactor with the needs of the microbial population. Environmental biotechnologies are designed to enhance and control these relationships.

In such a passive system, the biotechnology makes use of the same microbes that have adapted metabolic processes to degrade an array of organic compounds in natural settings, but they have been allowed to acclimate to the organic material that needs to be broken down. The microbes' inherent or adaptive preference to have more easily and directly derived electron transfer (i.e., energy sources) must be overcome. Environmental biotechnologists have accomplished this by limiting the microbes to an exclusively available carbon and energy source. That is, the bioengineer only permits the microorganism population, under a control setting, to come into contact with the chemicals in the waste. Thus, the microbes adapt their biological processes to use these formerly unfamiliar compounds as their energy sources and, in the process, break them down into less toxic substances. Ultimately the microbes degrade complex organic waste to carbon dioxide and water in the presence of molecular oxygen. In the absence of molecular oxygen, the microbes degrade the organic waste into methane and water. These are known as aerobic and anaerobic digestion, respectively.

Numerous examples of passive systems have been put to use as society has become increasingly complex. Human systems have evolved to support the need for safe food supplies, clean water and air, better shelter and urbanization. For example, passive biotechnologies were needed to allow for large-scale agriculture, including hybrid crops and nutrient cycling in agriculture. Likewise biomedical advances, such as vaccines, have often led to other societal change, e.g., better living standards and disease treatment and prevention.

Very recently, more active systems have been used increasingly to achieve such societal gains, but at an exponentially faster pace. In addition, scientists have developed biotechnologies that produce products that simply would not exist in passive systems.

The relationships between organisms and their environments reveal themselves in cycles of matter and energy into and out of the organism. This means that the organism itself is in a thermodynamic control volume. In turn, the population of organisms is part of the larger control volumes (e.g., microbes in the intestine, the intestine in the animal, the herd as prey in a habitat, the habitat as part of an ecosystem's structure).

Smaller control volumes assimilate into larger ones. Within reactors are smaller scale reactors (e.g., within the fish liver, on a soil particle, or in the pollutant plume or a forest). Thus, scale and complexity can vary by orders of magnitude in environmental systems. For example, the human body is a system, but so is the liver, and so are the collections of tissues through which mass and energy flow as the liver performs its function. Each hepatic cell in the liver is a system. At the other extreme, large biomes that make up large parts of the earth's continents and oceans are systems, both from the standpoint of biological organization and thermodynamics.

The interconnectedness of these systems in crucial to understanding biotechnological implications, since mass and energy relationships between and among systems determine the efficiencies of all living systems. For example, if a toxin adversely affects a cell's energy and mass transfer rates, it could cumulatively affect on the tissue and organs of the organism. And, if the organisms that make up a population are less efficient in survival then the balances needed in the larger systems, e.g., ecosystems and biomes, may be changed, causing problems at the global scale. Viewing this from the other direction, a larger system can be stressed, such as changes in ambient temperature levels or the increased concentrations of contaminants in water bodies and the atmosphere. This results in changes all the way down to the subcellular levels (e.g., higher temperatures or the presence of foreign chemicals at a cell's membrane will change the efficiencies of uptake, metabolism, replication, and survival). Thus, the changes at these submicroscopic scales determines the value of any biotechnology.

# References and Notes

1. See D, Mackay D, Wania F. Transport of contaminants to the arctic: partitioning, processes and models. *Sci Total Environ* 1995;**160/161**:26–38.
2. U.S. Environmental Protection Agency. *2,3,7,8-Tetrachlorodibenzo-p-dioxin (TCDD); CASRN 1746-01-6. Integrated Risk Information System.* http://www.epa.gov/iris/subst/1024.htm; 2012 [accessed 9 March 2012].

3. Agent Orange Website. http://www.lewispublishing.com/orange.htm [accessed 22 April 2005].

4. U.S. Environmental Protection Agency. Guidelines for carcinogen risk assessment, report no. EPA/630/R-00/004, *Federal Register* 1986;**51**(185):33992–4003 Washington, DC.

5. Bradford Hill A. The environment and disease: association or causation? *Proc R Soc Med (Occup Med)* 1965;**58**:295; Bradford-Hill A. The environment and disease: association or causation? President's Address: *Proc R Soc Med* 1965;**9**:295–300.

6. Sonnenschein C, Soto AM. An updated review of environmental estrogen and androgen mimics and antagonists. *J Steroid Biochem Mol Biol* 1998;**65**(1-6):143.

7. United States Environmental Protection Agency. *Removal of endocrine disruptor chemicals using drinking water treatment processes.* EPA/625/R-00/015. Washington, DC.

8. Fry D, Toone C. DDT—induced feminization of gull embryos. *Science* 1981;**213**(4510):922.

9. Weimeyer S, Lamont TG, Bunck CM, Sindelar CR, Gramlich FJ, Fraser JD, et al. Organochlorine, pesticide, polychlorobiphenyl, and mercury residues in bald eagle eggs—1969-79—and their relationships to shell thinning and reproduction. *Arch Environ Contam Toxicol* 1984;**13**(5):529.

10. See, for example: Purdom C, et al. Estrogenic effects from sewage treatment works. *Chem Ecol* 1994;**8**:275; Joblin S, et al. Inhibition of testicular growth in rainbow trout (Oncorhynchus mikiss) exposed to estrogenic alkyphenolic chemicals. *Environ Toxicol Chem* 1996;**15**(2):194.

11. Fox G. Effects of endocrine disrupting chemicals on wildlife in Canada: past, present and future. *Water Qual Res J Can* 2001;**36**(2):233.

12. See, for example: Sheiner EK, et al. Effect of occupational exposures on male fertility: literature review. *Ind Health* 2003;**41**(2):55; Guzelian P. Comparative toxicology of chlordecone (kepone) in humans and experimental—animals. *Ann Rev Pharmacol Toxicol* 1982;**22**:89; Hayes T, et al. Hermaphroditic, demasculinized frogs after exposure to the herbicide atrazine at low ecologically relevant doses. *Proc Natl Acad Sci U S A* 2002;**99**(8):5476.

13. Koplin DW, Furlong ET, Meyer MT, Thurman EM, Zaugg SD, Barber LB, et al. Pharmaceuticals, hormones, and other organic wastewater contaminants in US streams, 1999-2000: a national reconnaissance. *Environ Sci Technol* 2002;**36**(11):1202.

14. Guillette Jr. L, Gross TS, Masson GR, Matter JM, Percival HH, Woodward AR. Developmental abnormalities of the gonad and abnormal sex-hormone concentrations in juvenile alligators from contaminated and control lakes in Florida. *Environ Health Perspect* 1994;**102**(8):680.

15. Weimeyer S, et al. Organochlorine, pesticide, polychlorobiphenyl, and mercury residues in bald eagle eggs—1969-79—and their relationships to shell thinning and reproduction. *Arch Environ Contam Toxicol* 1984;**13**(5):529.

16. Semenza JC, Tolbert PE, Rubin CH, Guillette LJ, Jackson RJ. Reproductive toxins and alligator abnormalities at Lake Apopka, Florida. *Environ Health Perspect* 1997;**105**(10):1030–2.

17. Gills AM. What cautionary tales can Lake Apopka tell? *Zoogoer* 1995. Smithsonian National Zoological Park, July/August 1995. http://nationalzoo.si.edu/Publications/ZooGoer/1995/4/cautionarytales.cfm [accessed 9 March 2012].

18. Koplin DW, Furlong ET, Meyer MT, Thurman EM, Zaugg SD, Barber LB, et al. Pharmaceuticals, hormones and other organic wastewater contaminants in US streams, 1999-2000: a national reconnaissance. *Environ Sci Technol* 2002;**36**(6):1202–11.

19. Risebrough RW. Endocrine disruption: questions for the environmental community. *SETAC News* 1999;**19** (July):16–7.

20. Luellen DR, Vadas GG, Unger MA. *Sci Total Environ* 2005;**358**(1-3):286–97.

21. Resource Conservation and Recovery Act of 1976. Public Law 94-580, 42; United States Code, Sections 901 *et seq*.

22. This differs from Subtitle D, non-hazardous wastes. The U.S. Congress intended that permitting and monitoring of municipal and non-hazardous waste landfills shall be a state responsibility. Information on the permitting process and on individual landfills must be obtained by contacting the state agencies (and in some states the local health departments) and the local municipality. See: Managing Non-Hazardous Municipal and Solid Waste (RCRA); http://yosemite.epa.gov/r10/owcm.nsf/RCRA/nonhaz_waste [accessed 12 June 2010].

23. U.S. Environmental Protection Agency *Test methods for evaluating solid waste, volumes I and II (SW-846)*. 3rd ed. November 1986.

24. Sonawane BR. Chemical contaminants in human milk: an overview. *Environ Health Perspect* 1995;**103** (Suppl. 6):197–205; Hooper K, McDonald TA. The PBDEs: an emerging environmental challenge and another reason for breast-milk monitoring programs. *Environ Health Perspect* 2000;**108**:387–92.

25. Dewailly E, Ayotte P, Bruneau S, Laliberté C, Muir DCG, Norstrom RJ. Inuit exposure to organochlorines through the aquatic food chain in Arctic Quebec. *Environ Health Perspect* 1993;**101**:618–20.

26. Dewailly E, Nantel AJ, Weber JP, Meyer F. High levels of PCBs in breast milk of Inuit women from Arctic Quebec. *Bull Environ Contam Toxicol* 1989;**43**:641–6.

27. Muckle G, Ayotte P, Dewailly E, Jacobson SW, Jacobson JL. Inuit exposure to organochlorines through the aquatic food chain in arctic québec. *Environ Health Perspect* 1993 Dec;**101**(7):618–20.

28. Dewailly E, Bruneau S, Laliberte´ C, et al. Breast milk contamination by PCBs and PCDDs/PCDFs in Arctic Quebec: preliminary results on the immune status of Inuit infants. In: *Dioxin '93: 13th international symposium on chlorinated dioxins and related compounds.* Vienna, Austria: Technical University of Vienna; 1993. p. 403–6.

29. Pohland FG. *Sanitary landfill stabilization with leachate recycle and residual treatment.* Cincinnati, OH: U.S. Environmental Protection Agency; 1975 EPA-600/2-75-043.

30. Long Y, Long Y-Y, Liu H-C, Shen D-S. Degradation of refuse in hybrid bioreactor landfill. *Biomed Environ Sci* 2009;**22**:303–10.

31. Pohland F, Cross W, Gloud J, Reinhart D. *Behavior and assimilation of organic and inorganic priority pollutants co-disposed with municipal refuse.* Cincinnati, OH: Risk Reduction Engineering Laboratory. Office of Research and Development; 1993 Report No. EPA/600/R-93/137a.

32. Amman R, Ludwig W, Schleifer K-H. Phylogenetic identification and in situ detection of individual microbial cells without cultivation. *Microbiol Rev* 1995;**59**:143–69; Hugenholtz P, Goebel B, Pace N. Impact of culture-independent studies on the emerging phylogenetic view of bacterial diversity. *J Bacteriol* 1998;**180**(18):4765–74; Jjemba P. *Environmental microbiology: principles and applications.* Enfield, New Hampshire: Science Publishers; 2004.

# Radiation

Often, environmental scientists and engineers devote most attention to chemical pollutants. Indeed, most of the environmental laws and regulations address chemicals. However, pollutants may also be physical and biological (discussed in the next chapter). In this chapter, we address past, pending, and potential disasters involving various forms of the physical hazard, radiation.

## ELECTROMAGNETIC RADIATION

Electromagnetic radiation (EMR) is energy that can travel through a vacuum and through space. Whenever an electric charge oscillates or is accelerated, an electric and magnetic field propagates outward from it. In a vacuum, EMR travels at the speed of light. EMR exhibits a wave-like behavior as it travels through space and the wavelength and frequency are related through the speed of light:

$$c = v\lambda \qquad (12.1)$$

where $c$ is the speed of light ($3.00 \times 10^8$ m s$^{-1}$), $v$ is the frequency, and $\lambda$ is the wavelength.

The range of EMR is extremely large ranging from gamma radiation ($\lambda$ values of about $10^{-12}$ m), X-rays (about $10^{-10}$ m), far ultra violet (about $10^{-8}$ m), near UV (about $10^{-7}$ m), visible light, near infra-red hot bodies (about $10^{-6}$ m), far infrared hot bodies (about $10^{-4}$ m), microwaves (about $10^{-2}$ m), radar (about $10^{-1}$ m), through to TV, FM, and AM and long radio wavelengths (3-3000 m) and even higher wavelengths for some electronic devices and rotating machinery. The visible region is a small range of EMR from violet (400 nm) through yellow (600 nm) to red (750 nm). Figure 12.1 gives a description of the electromagnetic spectrum.

The energy of the waves is related to the frequency by

$$E = hv = hc/\lambda \qquad (12.2)$$

where $h$ is the Planck's constant, $6.63 \times 10^{-34}$ J s.

EMR can also be considered to have a particle nature and the term used is "photon". A photon of gamma radiation has a greater energy than a photon in the visible region of the electromagnetic spectrum. This will be very important when we discuss nuclear disasters.

    

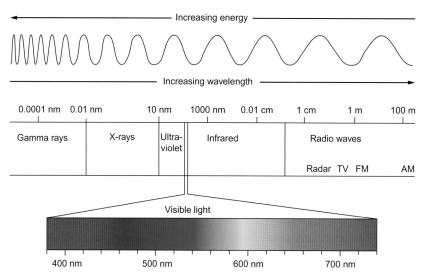

With energy inversely proportional to the wavelength, one can see that the UV has more energy than the IR and that γ radiation has even more energy. The effects of EMR upon living cells, including those in humans, depend upon on this energy. When the radiation is absorbed by the cell, the effect is very small for low-frequency radiation (radio waves to visible light) and most if not all effects involve simple heating. In this range, the frequency dictates the radiation penetration into the organism (for example, microwaves penetrate better than infrared).

At higher frequencies starting with ultraviolet radiation, the effects of individual photons of the radiation begin to become important, and these have enough energy to damage biological molecules. The UV frequencies do more damage to biological systems than do IR heat waves. The far ultraviolet, X-ray, and gamma radiation are referred to as ionizing radiation due to the ability of the photons of this radiation to produce ions in living tissue. It is the gamma radiation we shall meet when discussing nuclear disasters.[1]

## IONIZING AND NON-IONIZING RADIATION

Ionizing radiation refers to the type of radiation that creates ions. It does this by knocking out an electron from an atom, thereby creating a positively charged atom or ion. Such radiation can damages human cells. Ionizing radiation includes high energetic electromagnetic radiation (x-rays, gamma rays and cosmic rays), with wavelengths of less than about 120 nm: that is radiation with wavelengths of less than that of far ultraviolet radiation. As we have seen in this chapter the energy of radiation of frequency $v$ is:

$$E = hv = hc/\lambda$$

Where $h$ is the Planck's constant; $c$ is the velocity of light; and $\lambda$ is the wavelength of the radiation.

From this equation we can see that the shorter the wavelength the larger is the energy. Thus gamma radiation ($\lambda = 0.1{-}1$ picometer [pm]) is more energetic than x-rays ($\lambda = 1$ pm to 10 nm), which in turn are more energetic than radiation in the far ultraviolet ($\lambda \approx 120$ nm).

Ionizing radiation also includes particulate radiation such as alpha particles (helium nuclei, $He^{2+}$), beta particles (high energy electrons, $e^-$), and neutrons.

By contrast, non-ionizing radiation includes ultraviolet radiation ($\lambda$ = 10 to 400 nm), visible light ($\lambda$ = 420 to 700 nm) , microwaves ($\lambda$ = 1 mm to 10 cm), radiowaves ($\lambda$ > 10 cm). Non-ionizing radiation does not have the energy to knock out an electron from atoms so poses little threat to creating mutations and cancer. It does however have the energy to cause molecular excitation which is really a heating effect. This is confined to special chemicals where the incident energy is matched by the energy of the bonds that bind the chemical species. For example the energy of microwave radiation, as found in microwave ovens matches the energy of the bond between the oxygen atom and the hydrogen atom in water. Hence the heating effect experienced when a cup of water is placed in a microwave oven. In general, metals reflect microwaves, glass and ceramics transmits microwaves and water absorbs microwave energies.

The extremely low frequency (ELF) electromagnetic emanations (all non-ionizing radiations) from a cell phones, high voltage current in power transmission lines, and also from some household and industrial electrical equipment, are the least understood types of radiations, arguably making them the most controversial forms of radiation. This is particularly true for the effects of ELF electromagnetic radiation on biological material (especially human cells). The issue of potential biological damage has arisen in recent decades as a result of the introduction of very high voltage electric power transmission lines (> 440 kV), cell phones, television and other electrical and electronic equipment. Many biological studies have been carried out with ELF electromagnetic fields on biological cells (in vitro) and in living animals (in vivo), as well as in humans (epidemiological studies), but the conclusions have been mixed. To date, statistically significant chromosome aberrations have not been observed in this range of radiation suggesting that ELF fields are unlikely to cause cancer or mutations. The most likely effect could be changes to cell membrane activity.

Cell phone ELF electromagnetic radiation has been in the public spotlight over the past few years, triggered by the huge popularity of the phones and the time people spent using them. The amount of radio-frequency energy a cell phone user is exposed to, depends on the type of phone, the distance between the phone's antenna and the user, the extent and type of use, and the user's distance from cell phone towers. So far, most studies have not been able to link cell phone use to cancers of the brain, nerves, or any other tissues of the head or neck. This is really not surprising as ELF electromagnetic radiation is very much a non-ionizing form of radiation, but also because such chronic diseases often have latency periods, i.e. time needed between exposure and effects. With any new technology that introduces a whole new type of exposure, the risk clock only starts running when the technology reaches the marketplace. Indeed, cell phone technology has changed numerous times since its introduction. Each change may introduce a new threat.

In many ways the approach scientists have adopted towards ELF electromagnetic radiation is the reverse of climate change (See Chapter 8). That is, the scientific community seems to want to adopt the precautionary approach to climate (need to take action even with uncertainties in projections), but the same scientific community consensus towards ELF electromagnetic radiation is to abide by an evidence-based risk approach and do nothing until and unless massive amounts of data prove that there is indeed a risk. It could be a big problem, indeed a disaster of global proportions, with many people contracting many different types of effects – neurological, cancer, and other adverse conditions that are presently presymptomatic. Is ELF a pending disaster? At the moment we just do not know!

# NUCLEAR RADIATION

Radioactive decay takes place when an unstable atomic nucleus breaks up by emitting ionizing radiation. This emission is spontaneous and no heat or any interaction is required to make it happen. In a large number of such unstable nuclei, the process is predictable from the known values of the decay constant or from a knowledge of the half-life of the nuclide. It must be remembered that the decay is concerned almost always with the nucleus alone.

Nuclei are only radioactive if there is some instability in the nucleus between the protons (unit positive charge and unit mass) and the neutrons (no charge and unit mass).

For example, there are many known nuclides of oxygen, including $^{15}O$, $^{16}O$, $^{17}O$, $^{18}O$, and $^{19}O$ (being oxygen, they all have eight protons). The number of neutrons here varies from 7 to 11. The $^{15}O$ and $^{19}O$ isotopes are unstable. The former has a half-life of 122 s and decays with a positron $\beta^+$, while the latter has a half-life of 26 s and decays with $\beta^-$ emission. Small nuclei such as oxygen usually decay with beta emissions. Larger nuclei often decay with alpha particle emission. These are helium nuclei with a $2+$ charges ($^4_2He^{2+}$). The alpha particle has two protons and two neutrons. For example,

$$^{235}_{16}U \rightarrow {}^{231}_{90}Th + {}^4_2He \tag{12.3}$$

Radioactive decay takes place by

**(a)** beta emission ($\beta^-$) [this is an electron emission ($^0_{-1}e$)];
**(b)** neutron emission ($^0_1n$);
**(c)** positron emission ($\beta^+$) [this is a positron emission ($^0_1e$)];
**(d)** alpha emission ($\alpha$) [this is an helium nuclei emission ($^4_2He^{2+}$)]; and
**(e)** gamma radiation ($\gamma$), EMR with a very short wavelength.

One radioactive isotope which was very much in the news after the Chernobyl disaster is strontium-90 ($^{90}Sr$). It has a half-life of about 29 years, which makes is very dangerous. It undergoes B$^-$ decay forming yttrium-90.

$$^{90}_{38}Sr \rightarrow {}^{90}_{39}Y + {}^0_{-1}e \tag{12.4}$$

In this process, a neutron in the strontium atom has decayed into a proton (which remained in the nucleus) and an electron is emitted with a certain amount of energy. As a result, the protons have increased from 38 to 39 (producing Y) and the mass number has remained the same at 90.[2]

These decay products, alpha and beta particles, are all charged and can cause serious trouble when striking living material. These particles can damage DNA, for example, and also cause a breakdown of cells that they encounter. A nuclei decaying with a half-life of 20 s is not serious to humans so long as you are not present when the decay starts. After a period of a few minutes, the decay would almost have been complete, and so long as the product or daughter isotope is not radioactive, it would be safe to handle.

Gamma radiation is very much more penetrating than beta or alpha radiation. It is similar to X-rays in that it forms part of the electromagnetic spectrum and has a very short wave length. As such, gamma rays can be considered as being made up of photons. Like all EMR, gamma radiation travels at the speed of light and will pass through the human body very quickly, affecting all organs and tissue. It leaves an ionizing trace which means that exposed body parts can become ionized.[3]

Radiation exposure to the body targets rapidly dividing cells of the gastrointestinal tract and reproductive regions. The effect on humans can be summarized as follows:

1. Hair falls out with dose of 2.00 sievert (Sv) or more.
2. With levels of around 1 Sv, the blood's lymphocyte cell count begins to drop, making the person susceptible to infection. This is mild radiation sickness. This can over many years lead to leukemia and lymphoma.
3. The thyroid is particularly sensitive to radioactive iodine and KI can be used as an antidote to reduce the effect of the exposure.
4. With an exposure of more than 2.00 Sv, the lining of the intestinal tract will cause vomiting and diarrhea.
5. With levels as low as 2.00 Sv, the cells of the reproductive organs can be damaged leading to sterility with long-term exposures.
6. The brain and heart do not involve rapidly dividing cells so are not affected until the levels reach 10-20 Sv.[4]

A sievert is a unit of dose equivalent and has units of $J\,kg^{-1}$.

## NUCLEAR PLANTS

Nuclear power plants are based on the heat released from nuclear reactions. When $^{235}U$ atoms are hit by neutrons, the atom splits into two unequal parts, releasing gamma radiation and two neutrons:

$$^{235}_{92}U + ^{1}_{0}n = ^{142}_{56}Ba + ^{92}_{36}Kr + ^{2}_{0}n + \gamma; \quad \Delta H = 3.1 \times 10^{11}\,J\,mol^{-1} \qquad (12.5)$$

Other pairs of isotopes are also released and they include $^{128}I$, $^{95}Y$, and $^{140}Cs$ with $^{92}Rb$.

The pair of neutrons released reacts with more U atoms and if there is enough U atoms present, the reactions continue as a chain reaction. In a nuclear reactor, the heat of this reaction ($\Delta H$) is used to heat water and the resulting steam is used to turn turbines and hence produce electricity. The energy from this nuclear reactor, per unit mass of fuel, is more than a million times the energy from burning coal (energy from coal is $2.4 \times 10^{7}\,J\,kg^{-1}$ and for the nuclear reaction above, it is $7.3 \times 10^{13}\,J\,kg^{-1}$). The secret to harnessing nuclear power is to control the uranium so that just the right amount of heat is produced. In nuclear plants, the uranium is enriched (by increasing the ratio of the isotope $^{235}U$ to $^{238}U$) but not to the extent that is required for an atomic bomb. In a nuclear reactor, the uranium in the form of pellets is embedded in rods of zirconium which can be lowered or raised into the core of the reactor with other rods. Zirconium metal is chosen because it allows neutrons to pass through. To control the reaction, control rods of metals such as cadmium are used. This metal absorbs neutrons and, like the uranium rods, can be inserted in or withdrawn from the reactor core.

In this way, the rate of the nuclear reaction can be adjusted when required. The reactor core is cooled by various means, and in the Fukushima plant, it was cooled by water. The reactor core is shielded from the outside world by thick steel and concrete walls to prevent the release of radioactive material in the case of an accident or at worst a meltdown.

A meltdown refers to the situation when the cooling fails and the uranium rods and reactors overhead causing them to melt.

## NUCLEAR POWER PLANT FAILURE

Important nuclear events have been extremely influential in our current perception of pollution and threats to public health. Notably, the cases of Three Mile Island in Dauphin County, Pennsylvania (March 28, 1979); the Chernobyl nuclear power-plant disaster in the Ukraine (April 26, 1986); and more recently, the Fukushima nuclear disaster in Japan (beginning March 11, 2011) have had an unquestionable impact on not only nuclear power but also aspects of environmental policy, such as community "right-to-know" and the importance of risk assessment, management, and communication. The Fukushima incident is discussed later in this chapter.

Numerous defense and war-related incidents have also had a major influence on the public's perception of environmental safety. For example, the atomic bombings of Hiroshima and Nagasaki (August 6 and 9, 1945, respectively) were the world's first entrees to the linkage of chronic illness and mortality (e.g., leukemia and radiation disease) that could be directly linked to radiation exposure.

## IS NUCLEAR POWER WORTH THE RISKS?

In the past decade or so, with the increasing links (intellectual, if not necessarily scientific) between anthropogenic sources of greenhouse gases, especially carbon dioxide ($CO_2$) and increasing mean global temperatures, many in the scientific community have argued for curtailing the use of fossil fuels, especially in developed nations. However, to the pronuclear scientists, they see these findings as a requisite to revisit the need for nuclear power, as fission produces no $CO_2$ (there is no combustion, i.e., oxidation of a hydrocarbon). As in the case of the sea turtle taxonomy debate, scientists all too often revert to an "advocacy" position rather than one of objectivity. They know that nuclear power will produce long-lived radioactive byproducts that will need to be stored for thousands of years. They also remember Chernobyl and fear similar accidents. But do these justify a full and open debate on whether nuclear power is a viable means of reducing the emission of greenhouse gases? It is a challenge even to get some scientists to consider the issue, not as a geopolitical decision, but as an engineering, science, or mathematical problem.

An important consideration in making decisions is the amount and type of effects that will result an action. A particularly difficult aspect of a decision or activity is predicting the cascade of events and their future impacts. Manufacturing and commercial decisions about material use can have lasting effects for generations, such as metallic pigments in paint, lead-based fuel additives, and industrial processes that process carcinogenic byproducts. Such decisions are quite complex. A case in point is the comparison of short- and long-term effects of using coal versus nuclear fission to generate electricity. Combusting coal releases particle matter and damaging compounds such as carbon dioxide and sulfur dioxide and toxic substances such as mercury. Nuclear power presents a short-term concern about potential accidental releases of radioactive materials and long-lived (sometimes for hundreds of thousands of years) radioactive wastes.

Similarly, decisions regarding armed conflict must consider not only the tactical warfare but also the geopolitical changes wrought by the conflict. Furthermore, the psychological and medical effects on combatants and noncombatants must be taken into account. Prominent cases of these effects include Agent Orange use in Vietnam and decisions to prescribe drugs and to use chemicals in the Persian Gulf War in the 1990s. The World War II atomic bombings on the Japanese cities of Hiroshima and Nagasaki in August of 1945 not only served the purpose of accelerating the end of the war in the Pacific arena but also ushered in the threat of nuclear war.

## MELTDOWN AT CHERNOBYL[5]

On April 26, 1986, the world's most disastrous nuclear power accident occurred in Chernobyl. Located in northern Ukraine 100 km north of the capital Kiev, the Chernobyl power plant is 7 km from the border of Belarus. The reactor is on the river Pripyat, which joins the Dnieper 12 km away in the town of Chernobyl. The reactor has been inactive since December 12, 2000; however, people are still affected by the spread of radiation. The contaminated territories lie in the north of Ukraine, the south and east of Belarus, and in the western border area between Russia and Belarus. An estimated 125,000-146,000 km$^2$ in Ukraine, Belarus, and Russia are contaminated with high levels of caesium-137. At the time of the explosion, approximately 7 million people lived in the area of contamination, and 5.5 million people continue to live in these territories (see Figure 12.2).

The incident was a combined result of a flawed reactor operated by poorly trained staff without proper regard for safety measures. There was also a lack of communication between the personnel operating the facility and the team in charge. First of all, while plant operators and the USSR Committee of State Security were aware of the reactor's design weaknesses (as stated in a memorandum that outlined the plant's inadequate monitoring of safety equipment), they did not make changes or take precautions. Chernobyl's RBMK reactor type was known to suffer from instability at low power (a positive void coefficient), which could result in uncontrollable increases in power. While other plants developed preventative designs, the Chernobyl power plant did not. Hence, the increased power generation led to more heat and steam pockets, resulting in less neutron absorption. Liquid water is used to absorb escaping neutrons, while steam does not have the ability to slow down the reaction.

During a routine maintenance check, the station technicians neglected to follow proper safety procedures. As Reactor 4 was to be shut off and checked, it was decided to also test whether in an event of a shutdown, there would be enough energy to maintain the plant until the diesel power supply came into effect. The standard 30 control rods were neglected, and instead, the test only used 6-8 rods. Many were withdrawn due to the buildup of xenon that absorbed neutrons and decreased power. As the flow of coolant water fell, the poor design of the plant caused a large power surge that was 100 times the nominal power output. The slowing turbines and reduced cooling caused a positive void coefficient in the cooling channels. At 1:23 am, the rise in heat caused fuel to rupture which resulted in a steam explosion, destroying the reactor core and instigating a second explosion that cast fragments of burning fuel (see Figures 12.3 and 12.4) into the atmosphere.

FIGURE 12.2    Map of region surrounding the Chernobyl nuclear power facility. *Source: World Nuclear Association. http://www.world-nuclear.org/info/chernobyl/ukr_map.gif; 2005 [accessed April 21, 2005].*[6]

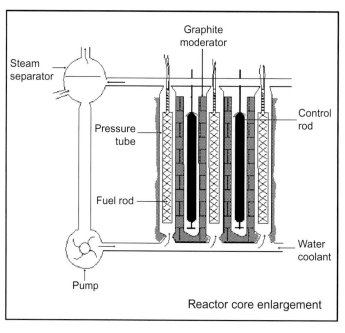

FIGURE 12.3 Reactor core in Chernobyl nuclear power plant. *Source and schematic credit: World Nuclear Association. Chernobyl Appendices. http://www. world-nuclear.org/info/chernobyl/inf07app. htm#sequence; 2001 [accessed April 21, 2005].*

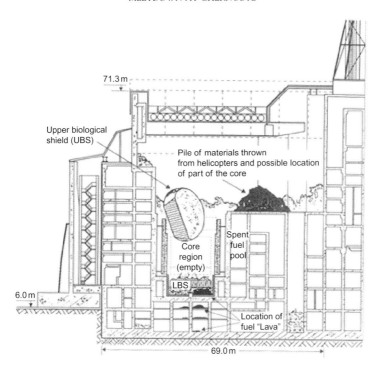

71.3 m

Upper biological
shield (UBS)

Pile of materials thrown
from helicopters and possible location
of part of the core

Spent
fuel
pool

Core
region
(empty)

LBS

6.0 m

Location of
fuel "Lava"

69.0 m

FIGURE 12.4    Schematic of reactor at Chernobyl. *Source and schematic credit: World Nuclear Association. http://www.world-nuclear.org/info/chernobyl/chernowreck2.gif; 2005 [accessed April 21, 2005].*

Firefighters were called in to put out the fire in what remained of the Unit 4 building. A group of 14 firemen first arrived minutes after the explosion, while hundreds more arrived soon after. By 2:30 am, the largest fires on the roof of the reactor were under control and were finally put out by 5:00 am. However, the graphite fire had started at this point, and those firemen who had already suffered from the most radioactive exposure stayed on site. Although the conventional fires were not difficult for the firefighters to handle, there were 31 deaths. The graphite fire posed a much bigger problem for these men as there was little local or international experience controlling that type of fire. The greatest fear was the possibility of a further spread of radionuclides.

It was decided to attack the fire by dumping neutron-absorbing materials onto the site from helicopters. Many of the compounds, however, were not dropped directly onto the target and instead acted as an insulator, raising temperatures and causing a greater dispersion of radionuclides within the next week. The graphite fire was put out on May 9. For the next 3 years, about 800,000 people assisted in the cleanup of Chernobyl, who still suffer from the effects of radiation today, if indeed they are still alive.

The explosion was kept secret from the local population and the world for several days. Life went on as normal in the nearby towns and villages, and it was not until days later with the arrival of military tanks that the explosion and its effects became known. 116,000 people

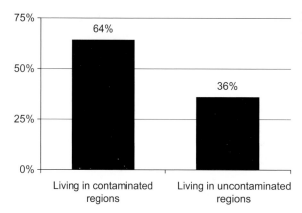

FIGURE 12.5 Percentage of Ukranian thyroid cancer patients aged 15 years of age or younger living.

were ordered to immediately evacuate their homes with minimal possessions. Between 1990 and 1995, 210,000 people resettled in a new town Slavutich that had been built for the personnel of the power plant.

Radioactive particles were carried by wind toward the west and north to prime farm land. Radioactivity was worst in places where it rained the most within the few days after the explosion, and even today particles continue to seep into the ground. People were exposed to both internal and external radiation. "The major routes of human exposure to radiation were from ingestion of cow's milk contaminated with iodine[131] (resulting in internal exposure), contact with gamma/beta radiation from the radioactive cloud, and contact with cesium[137] deposited on the ground (resulting in external exposure)."[7] The water supply, plants, and animals in the area are radioactive. Seventy percent of this type of radiation poisons the body through food and drink, while 30% is breathed into the body as air particles causing thyroid cancer, lymphatic cancer, heart conditions, and poor eyesight. The explosion has also resulted in a decrease in IQ in children, and genetic mutations are twice as likely in families exposed to radiation, causing permanent damage to DNA passed down to their children.

Preceding the explosion, the average rate of thyroid cancer in Ukrainian children was 4-6 per million (Figure 12.5). It rose to an astonishing 45 per million from 1986 to 1997. Sixty-four percent of these children lived in the most contaminated regions (Kiev, Chernigov, Zhitomir, Cherkassy, and Rovno).[8]

Besides the massive physical destruction and health effects, the explosion in Chernobyl's power plant also had serious psychological consequences, along with social, economic, and political effects. The evacuation of the contaminated areas caused a shortage of labor in the area, resulting in serious economic difficulties. People lived in a constant fear of radiation and employees often discriminated against accident survivors. It was a horrific disaster and one that will echo through history.

## THE FUKUSHIMA DAIICHI NUCLEAR DISASTER

On March 11, 2011 at 14.46, the Tōhoku earthquake (magnitude 8.9) struck the NW coast of Japan (see Figure 12.6) destroying the Fukushima Daiichi nuclear plant, owned by TEPCO (Tokyo Electricity Power Company). It came just 25 years after the Chernobyl nuclear

## Japan's Nuclear Energy Plants

FIGURE 12.6    Japan and the position of Fukushima Daiichi nuclear reactors. Map from http://en.wikipedia.org/wiki/Fukushima_Daiichi_nuclear_disaster.

disaster. The Fukushima plant was large, i.e., about 4 GW, consisting of six reactors. On the day of the disaster, three reactors were operating. Reactor 4 had the uranium in place but was not operating and Reactors 5 and 6 had been shut down awaiting maintenance. When the earthquake struck, parts of the reactors were damaged, but not the reactor cores. The emergency diesel generators automatically switched on, and the water pumps were activated to cool the reactor. The generators also switched on the control panels and probes and all systems were working as expected with the control rods inserted, slowing down and controlling the fission reactions and reducing the temperature of the reactor core. The system had been designed by General Electric and was of a similar design to a number of U.S. nuclear plants.

And then the first of the tsunami waves struck about 40 min later, at 15.27. Twenty minutes after that, a massive 14-m wave breached the seawall (it was only 5.7 m high) and flooded the nuclear plant with devastating results. The generators were put out of action together with the water pumps and the plant was left without electricity. There was no electricity supply left on the site and that night the brave workers had to use flashlights to find their way round a plant which was about 350 ha in size.[9]

On reflection, it appears that the fission reaction was slowed down, but because the water used for cooling the reactor core had leaked out, the temperature had increased and the three reactors began to overheat. With seawater everywhere and no power, the plant was isolated and it was very difficult to get near the plant to attempt any rescue mission.

With water everywhere and the core overheating, the zirconium reacted with the steam:

$$Zr + 2H_2O = 2H_2 + ZrO_2 \tag{12.6}$$

This reaction caused two problems. First, the hydrogen gas pressure built up in the reactor concrete housing and second, with the zirconium reacted and melted, the uranium pellets were no longer separated and the reaction rate speeded up, creating higher and higher temperatures. In a nuclear power plant, there is little danger of the core turning into a nuclear bomb because the ratio of $^{235}U$ to $^{238}U$ is not high enough. However, the heat of the reaction at Fukushima was high enough to create a serious nuclear accident.

The hydrogen gas built up inside the concrete housing of the reactors and one after another they exploded over the course of a few days, spewing out radioactive gases. The people within a 20-km radius of the plant were evacuated. The main radioactive fallout was $^{131}I$ (with a half-life of 8 days) and $^{137}Cs$ (with a half-life of 30 years). Due to its volatility, short half-life, and high abundance in fission products, $^{131}I$, along with the short-lived iodine isotope $^{132}I$ from the longer-lived $^{132}Te$ (with a half-life of 3 days), was responsible for the largest part of radioactive contamination during the first week after the nuclear disaster. The radiation was largely gamma rays and $\beta^-$ particles (fast-moving electrons). The $^{137}Cs$ also decays by $\beta^-$ emission and gamma radiation. It is the long half-life that makes this isotope so dangerous. It is the gamma radiation that travels at the speed of light that is very penetrating and causes cell damage to plants and humans. The $\beta$ radiation is less penetrating but still dangerous.

It is possible that the pumping of sea water onto the reactor did more harm than good as it precipitated the reaction with the zirconium which created the pressure that burst the concrete shell of the reactor and allowed the radioactive vapors to escape.

The levels of emitted radioactive iodine and caesium were less than that emitted after the Chernobyl disaster in spite of there being 1760 tonnes of uranium fuel at Fukushima and only 180 tonnes at Chernobyl. An estimated value showed that the levels at Fukushima were 50% of that experienced at Chernobyl. Chernobyl experienced a massive fire which helped to disseminate a wide range of radioactive elements, including fuel particles, in smoke. At Fukushima Daiichi, only the volatile elements, such as iodine and caesium, came bubbling off the damaged fuel and vaporized into the atmosphere through the damaged concrete chamber. Some of these volatile elements were transported by the winds (first easterly winds) and were even detected in the United States. This is not because such large amounts traveled across the Pacific but because of the highly sensitive equipment. Figure 12.7 shows some of the devastation from the earthquake and tsunami. Indeed, even what was thought to be a fortified structure with redundancies and failsafe devices incurred damage that led to the nuclear disaster.

FIGURE 12.7 Aerial view of damage to Sukuiso, Japan, one week after a 9.0 magnitude earthquake and subsequent tsunami devastated the area. *Image Credit: Dylan McCord. U.S. Navy.*

The reason why radioactive iodine and caesium are so dangerous to humans is that nearly all the iodine and caesium inhaled or swallowed crosses into the blood. Caesium is sodium-like in its chemical behavior and is absorbed into the muscles. With a half-life of 30 years, it will stay there emitting gamma and beta radiation, until it is excreted by the body. The half-life of any caesium in the body is somewhere between 10 and 100 days. Iodine on the other hand is absorbed by the thyroid and leaves only after it has decayed (beta and gamma radiation) with a half-life of 8 days. While in the body the beta and gamma emissions cause a significant, amount of damage largely through DNA changes which often results in cancer.

The attempts to save the reactors from exploding were highlighted by many brave Japanese workers. A few workers were severely injured or killed in the disaster as a result of the earthquake, but there were no immediate deaths due to direct radiation exposures. At least six workers exceeded lifetime legal limits for radiation and more than 300 have received significant radiation doses. It has been estimated that between 100 and 1000 people living near Fukushima will suffer cancer deaths due to radiation.

There will always be a comparison between Fukushima and Chernobyl, and the Japanese government has estimated that the total amount of radioactivity released into the atmosphere was approximately one-tenth as much as was released during the Chernobyl disaster.[10]

The amounts of radioactive material (especially caesium) released into ground and ocean waters near Fukushima was high enough for concern, and the Japanese government placed a ban on the sale of food grown in the area 30-50 km from the plant.[11]

The radiation rates on the Fukushima plant site reached levels of 1000 mSv h$^{-1}$ close to the leaking reactor and workers were only allowed to spend a limited time in the danger zone. The levels reached 10 mSv h$^{-1}$ at the gate to the plant at the height of the accident, but there was no health risk outside the area and at Ibaraki, between Tokyo and Fukushima, the levels were 0.109 $\mu$Sv h$^{-1}$ which is a little below the acceptable level. The natural average exposure on earth is between 2 and 10 mSv year$^{-1}$ (which is equivalent to 0.22-1.1 $\mu$Sv h$^{-1}$). The radiation outside the plant, during the accident, was reputed to be one-tenth of the values experienced at Chernobyl.

On December 16, 2011, Japanese authorities declared the plant to be stable, although it would take decades to decontaminate the surrounding areas and to decommission the plant altogether.

As always, there are many lessons to be learnt after such an event:

1. The generators, supply boards, and DC back-up batteries should never have been placed in the basement. When the plant was built, there were many doubts as to the positioning of the mains electricity supply boards and back up electricity. The General Electric design had them in the basement. Had they been higher up, the effect of the tsunami might not have been anywhere near as severe.
2. There were also doubts about the positing of a large nuclear reactor on a coastline which was at the mercy of tsunamis.
3. TEPCO had not prepared for such a devastating accident and had no contingency plans for loss of power. In future, there should be multiple power sources and plants should be able to maintain power during an earthquake. Moreover, even the cell phones at the plant failed with the failure of the mains power (no charging facilities) which led to poor communication with the workers attempting to stop a meltdown and explosion.
4. There were communication problems from the TEPCO officials and from the Government to the people living in the area. For example, the evacuees were not told about the changing wind patterns and they were sent to areas in direct line with the winds blowing from the site. It was reported that in some cases the radioactivity was higher in the area where the evacuees were camping than at the plant itself.[12]

## THREE MILE ISLAND NUCLEAR ACCIDENT

The United States has had its own nuclear accident on March 28, 1979 at the Three Mile Island power plant in Dauphin County, Pennsylvania. It was the worst accident in the U.S. nuclear power plant history. A valve malfunctioned and large volumes of the nuclear reactor's coolant escaped resulting in the release of small amounts of radioactive gases and $^{131}$I into the environment. It led to the release of 150 kL (40,000 gallons) of radioactive waste water into the Susquehanna River. The final report blamed the accident on human factors, including inadequate training, and the interactive computer design was shown to be ambiguous. The cleanup finally ended in December 1993 at a cost of over $1 billion.

The final report stated that as a result of the accident, there were no cancer cases and that in the numbers of possible cancer cases will be so small that it will not be possible to detect them. Follow-up studies support these conclusions. The accident probably had a lasting influence on nuclear energy and certainly influenced the making of the movie *The China Syndrome* which involves a nuclear reactor accident.[13]

# RADIOISOTOPES AND RADIATION POISONING

To recap, different atomic weights of a same element are the result of different numbers of neutrons. The number of electrons and protons of stable atoms must be the same. Elements with differing atomic weights are known as *isotopes*. An element may have numerous isotopes. Stable isotopes do not undergo natural radioactive decay, whereas radioactive isotopes involve spontaneous radioactive decay, as their nuclei disintegrate. Thus, these are known as radioisotopes. This decay leads to the formation of new isotopes or new elements. The stable product of an element's radioactive decay is known as a radiogenic isotope. The toxicity of a radioisotope can be twofold, i.e., chemical toxicity and radioactive toxicity (see Case Study Box: Radiation Poisoning in Goiania, Brazil). For example, Pb is neurotoxic irrespective of the atomic weight, but if people are exposed to its unstable isotopes, they are also threatened by radiation emitted from the nucleus' decay. The energy of the radioactive decay can alter genetic material and lead to mutations, including cancer.

## CASE STUDY BOX: RADIATION POISONING IN GOIANIA, BRAZIL [14]

In the early 1980s, a small cancer clinic was opened in Goiania, but business was not good and the clinic closed 5 years later. Left behind in the abandoned building were a radiation therapy machine and some canisters containing waste radioactive material—1400 curies of Cesium 137, which has a half-life of 30 years. In 1987, the container of Cesium 137 was discovered by local residents and was opened, revealing a luminous blue powder. The material was a local curiosity and children even used it to paint their bodies which caused them to sparkle. One of the little girls went home for lunch and ate a sandwich without first washing her hands. Six days later, she was diagnosed with radiation illness, having received an estimated five to six times the lethal radiation exposure for adults. The ensuing investigation identified the true content of the curious barrel. In all, over 200 persons had been contaminated and 54 were serious enough to be hospitalized, with four people dying from the exposure (including the little girl with the sandwich). Treatment of radiation disease is challenging. The International Atomic Energy Commissions characterized the treatment of the Goianian patients as:

> ... the first task was to attempt to rid their bodies of cesium. For this, they administered Prussian blue, an iron compound that bonds with cesium, aiding its excretion. The problem in this case was the substantial delay—at least a week—from initial exposure to treatment. By that time much of the cesium had moved from the bloodstream into the tissues, where it is far more difficult to remove...the patients were also treated with antibiotics as needed to combat infections and with cell infusions to prevent bleeding.... [15]

By the time the government mobilized to respond to the disaster, the damage was done. A large fraction of the population had received excessive radiation, and the export of produce from Goiania dropped to zero, creating a severe economic crisis. The disaster is now recognized as the second worst radiation accident in the world, second only to the explosion of the nuclear power plant in Chernobyl. [16]

# CARBON DATING

Isotopic tracers can be used to find sources of pollution, e.g., by comparing carbon isotopes. The nucleus of an atom, consisting of protons and neutrons (hydrogen has only a proton in its nucleus), accounts for virtually all of the atomic mass (in units of atomic mass units (amu)). The term nucleon is inclusive of protons and neutrons (i.e., the particles comprising the atom's nucleus). An amu is defined as one-twelfth of the mass of carbon ($C^{12}$) or $1.66 \times 10^{-27}$ kg. The atomic weight of an element listed in most texts and handbooks is the relative atomic mass, which is the total relative mass of a mole of the nucleons that make up the atom. So, for example, oxygen (O) has a relative atomic mass of 16. To recap, the atomic number ($Z$) is the number of protons in the nucleus. The chemical nomenclature for atomic weight $A$ and number of element $E$ is in the form:

$$^{A}_{Z}E$$

However, as an element has only one atomic number, $Z$ is usually not shown. For example, the most stable form of carbon is seldom shown as $^{12}_{6}C$ and is usually indicated as $^{12}C$.

Elements may have different atomic weights if they have different numbers of neutrons (the number of electrons and protons of stable atoms must be the same). The elements with differing atomic weights are known as *isotopes*. All atoms of a given element have the same atomic number, but atoms of a given element may contain different numbers of neutrons in the nucleus. An element may have numerous isotopes. Stable isotopes do not undergo natural radioactive decay, whereas radioactive isotopes involve spontaneous radioactive decay, as their nuclei disintegrate. This decay leads to the formation of new isotopes or new elements. The stable product of an element's radioactive decay is known as a radiogenic isotope. For example, lead (Pb; $Z=82$) has four naturally occurring isotopes of different masses ($^{204}$Pb, $^{206}$Pb, $^{207}$Pb, $^{208}$Pb). Only the isotope $^{204}$Pb is stable. The isotopes $^{206}$Pb and $^{207}$Pb are daughter (or progeny) products from the radioactive decay of uranium (U), while $^{208}$Pb is a product from thorium (Th) decay. Owing to the radioactive decay, the heavier isotopes of lead will increase in abundance compared to $^{204}$Pb.

The kinds of chemical reactions for all isotopes of the same element are the same. However, the rates of reactions may vary. This can be an important factor, for example, in dating material. Such processes have been used to ascertain the sources of pollution (see Note below on using radioactive decay to identify sources of pollution).

Radiogenic isotopes are useful in determining the relative age of materials. The length of time necessary for the original number of atoms of a radioactive element in a rock to be reduced by half (*radioactive half-life*) can range from a few seconds to billions of years. Scientists use these "radioactive clocks" by the following procedure[17]:

1. Extracting and purifying the radioactive parent and daughter from the relevant rock or mineral;
2. Measuring variations in the masses of the parent and daughter isotopes; and
3. Combining the abundances with the known rates of decay to calculate an age.

Radiogenic isotopes are being increasingly used as *tracers* of the movement of substances through the environment. Radiogenic isotope tracer applications using Pb, Sr, and Nd, among others, make use of the fact that these are heavy isotopes, in contrast to lighter isotopes such as hydrogen (H), oxygen (O), and sulfur (S). Heavy isotopes are relatively unaffected by changes in temperature and pressure during transport and accumulation, variations in the rates of chemical reactions, and the coexistence of different chemical species available in the environment. Chemical reactions and processes involving Pb, for example, will not discriminate among the naturally occurring isotopes of this element on the basis of atomic mass differences ($^{204}$Pb, $^{206}$Pb, $^{207}$Pb, $^{208}$Pb).

Long-term monitoring data are frequently not available for environmental systems, so indirect methods, like radiogenic isotope calculations, must be used. For example, in sediments, chronological scales can be determined by the distribution of radioactive isotopes in the sediment, based upon the isotopes' half-lives.[18] The age of the sediment containing a radioactive isotope with a known half-life can be calculated by knowing the original concentration of the isotope and measuring the percentage of the remaining radioactive substance. For this process to work, the chemistry of the isotope must be understood, the half-life known, and the initial amount of the isotope per unit substrate accurately estimated. The only change in concentration of the isotope must be entirely attributable to radioactive decay, with a reliable means for measuring the concentrations. The effective range covers approximately eight half-lives. The four isotopes meeting these criteria ($^{137}$Cs, $^{7}$Be, $^{14}$C, and $^{210}$Pb) are being used to measure the movement (e.g., deposition and lateral transport) over the past 150 years. The following summarizes the uses and potential uses of these four radioisotopes in dating recent sediments.

The process is analogous to an hour glass (see Figure 12.8) where the number of grains of sand in the top reservoir represents the parent isotope and the sand in the bottom reservoir

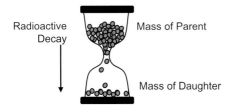

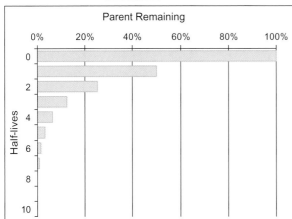

FIGURE 12.8    Radiodating of environmental material, such as sediments, is a function of the radioactive decay of specific isotopes in the environmental compartment. The hourglass analogy holds, where the number of grains of sand in the top reservoir represents the parent isotope and the sand in the bottom reservoir represents the daughter isotopes. A measurement of the ratio of the number of sand grains in the two reservoirs will give the length of time that the sand has been flowing (radioactive decay). *Source: U.S. Geological Survey. FS-073-98. Short-lived isotopic chronometers: a means of measuring decadal sedimentary dynamics; 2003.*

represents the daughter isotopes. A measurement of the ratio of the number of sand grains in the two reservoirs will give the length of time that the sand has been flowing, which represents the process of radioactive decay. For deposited material like sediment, the counting begins when the sediment particle is deposited ($t_0$), and the exchange between the water and particle ceases. As the sediment particles are subsequently buried, the parent isotope decays to the daughter products. The process of radioactive decay can be put to use, e.g., by paleontologists to date materials and environmental scientists to differentiate sources of pollution (see sidebar "Using Radioactive Decay to Identify Sources of Pollution").

## USING RADIOACTIVE DECAY TO IDENTIFY SOURCES OF POLLUTION

When the results of air pollution measurements are interpreted, one of the first questions asked by scientists, engineers, and policy makers is where did it come from? Sorting out the various sources of pollution is known as *source apportionment*. A number of tools are used to try to locate the sources of pollutants. A widely used approach is the "source-receptor model" or as it is more commonly known, the *receptor model*.

Receptor models are often distinguished from the atmospheric and hydrologic dispersion models. For example, dispersion models usually start from the source and estimate where the plume and its contaminants is heading (see Figure 6.2). Conversely, receptor models are based upon measurements taken in the ambient environment and from these observations, make use of algorithms and functions to determine pollution sources. One common approach is the mathematical "back trajectory" model. Often, chemical co-occurrences are applied. So, it may be that a certain fuel is frequently contaminated with a conservative and, hopefully, unique element. Some fuel oils, for example, contain trace amounts of the element vanadium. As there are few other sources of vanadium in most ambient atmospheric environments, its presence is a strong indication that the burning of fuel oil is a most likely source of the plume. The model, if constructed properly, can even quantify the contribution. So, if measurements show that sulfur dioxide ($SO_2$) concentrations are found to be $10~\mu g~m^{-3}$ in an urban area, and vanadium is also found at sufficient levels to indicate that home heating systems are contributing a certain amount of the $SO_2$ to the atmosphere, the model will correlate the amount of $SO_2$ coming from home heating systems. If other combustion sources, e.g., cars and power plants, also have unique trace elements associated with their $SO_2$ emissions, further $SO_2$ source apportionment can occur so that the total may look something like Table 12.1.

Receptor models need tracers that are sufficiently sensitive and specific to identify sources. One very promising development for such tracers is the comparison of carbon isotopes. As combustion involves the oxidation of organic matter, which always contains carbon, it stands to reason that if there was a way to distinguish "old carbon" from "new carbon," we may have a reliable means of differentiating fossil fuels from *biogenic* hydrocarbon sources (e.g., volatile organic carbons released from coniferous trees, including pinene). As the name implies, fossil fuels are made up of carbon deposited long ago and until now, the carbon has been sequestered. During that time, the ratio of the isotopes of carbon has changed. So, the ratios can tell us whether the carbon we are measuring at had been first sequestered a few years ago or many thousands of years ago.

TABLE 12.1   Hypothetical Source Apportionment of Measured Sulfur Dioxide Concentrations

| Source | Distance from measurement (km) | SO$_2$ concentration contributed to ambient measurement ($\mu$g m$^{-3}$) | Percent contribution to measured SO$_2$ |
|---|---|---|---|
| Coal-fired electric generating station | 25 | 3.0 | 30 |
| Coal-fired electric generating station | 5 | 2.0 | 20 |
| Mobile sources (cars, trucks, trains, and planes) | 0-10 | 1.5 | 15 |
| Oil refinery | 30 | 1.5 | 15 |
| Home heating (fuel oil) | 0-1 | 1.0 | 10 |
| Unknown | Not applicable | 1.0 | 10 |
| Total | | 10.0 | 100 |

Naturally occurring radioactive carbon ($^{14}$C) is present at very low concentrations in all biotic (living) matter. The $^{14}$C concentrations result from plants' photosynthesis of atmospheric carbon dioxide (CO$_2$), which contains all of the natural isotopes of carbon. However, no $^{14}$C is found in fossil fuels as all of the carbon has had sufficient time to undergo radioactive decay. Studies have begun to take advantage of this dichotomy in ratios. For example, they have begun to address an elusive contributor to particulate matter (PM), i.e., *biogenic* hydrocarbons. In the summer months, biogenic aerosols are formed from gas-to-particle atmospheric conversions of volatile organic compounds (VOCs) that are emitted by vegetation.[19] New methods for estimating the contribution of biogenic sources of VOCs and PM are needed because current estimates of the importance of biogenic aerosols as contributors to total summertime PM have very large ranges (from negligible to dominant). There are large uncertainties in both the conversion mechanisms and the amount and characteristics of biogenic VOC emissions.

The good news seems to be that direct experimental estimates can be gained by measuring the quantity of $^{14}$C in a PM sample. The method depends on the nearly constant fraction of $^{14}$C relative to ordinary carbon ($^{12}$C) in all living and recently living material, and its absence in fossil fuels. The fine fraction of PM (PM$_{2.5}$) summertime samples are available from numerous locations in the United States, from which $^{14}$C measurements can be conducted. Some recent studies have shown that the carbonaceous biogenic fraction may be contributing as much as one half of the particles formed from VOCs!

The method for measuring and calculating the isotope ratios is straightforward. The percent of modern carbon (pMC) equals the percentage of $^{14}$C in a sample of unknown origin relative to that in a sample of living material, and this pMC is about equal to the percentage of carbon in a sample that originated from nonfossil (i.e., biogenic) sources. So, for sample $x$,[20]

$$\mathrm{pMC}_x = \frac{\left(^{14}C\big/_{13}C\right)_x}{0.95\left(^{14}C\big/_{13}C\right)_{SRM4990B}} \times 100 \qquad (12.7)$$

where, the numerator is the ratio measured in the $PM_{2.5}$ sample, and the denominator is the ratio measured using the method specified by the National Institute of Standards and Testing (NIST) for modern carbon.[21] Further,

$$pMC_{\text{fossil fuel}} = 0 \tag{12.8}$$

Thus, for a sample $x$, the biogenic fraction is

$$\%\text{Biogenic } C_x = \frac{pMC_x}{pMC_{\text{biogenic}}} \times 100 \tag{12.9}$$

The 0.95 correction is needed to address the increase in radiocarbon due to nuclear weapons testing in the 1950s and 1960s (see Figure 12.9) and to calibrate the measurements with the standard used for radiocarbon dating (i.e., wood from 1890).[22] Although the levels have dropped since the 1963 test ban treaty, they are still elevated above the pre-1950s background level.

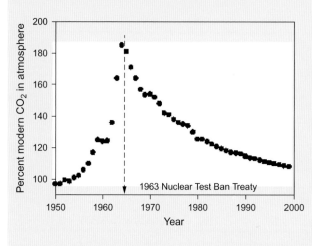

FIGURE 12.9 Biospheric [14]C enhancement of atmospheric modern carbon as a result of radiocarbon additions from nuclear testing and nuclear power generation. Nuclear testing: the plot indicates the time record of [14]C in the biosphere. The [14]C content of northern hemisphere biomass carbon was doubled in 1963, but since the cessation of atmospheric nuclear testing, the excess [14]C is now nearing natural, cosmic ray background levels. Fraction of modern carbon relative standard uncertainties is typically <0.5%. *Sources: National Institute of Standards and Technology. A critical evaluation of interlaboratory data on total, elemental, and isotopic carbon in the carbonaceous particle reference material, NIST SRM 1649a; 2001;107 (3) and Lewis C, Klouda G, Ellenson W. Cars or trees: which contribute more to particulate matter air pollution? Washington, DC: U.S. Environmental Protection Agency, Science Forum; 2003.*

## NUCLEAR WASTE DISPOSAL

Nuclear waste comes from hospitals and nuclear power plants. It is divided into four types:

1. Low-level waste which is made up of clothes, tools medical tubes, etc.
2. Intermediate-level waste refers to waste from reprocessing spent nuclear fuel and from decommissioning nuclear reactors.
3. High-level waste is used as nuclear reactor fuel.
4. Uranium milling tailings which are residues from processing natural ores to extract uranium and thorium.

The low-level waste comes from hospitals, industry, and research labs. It is not dangerous to handle but must be disposed of. It is usually compacted and buried. Worldwide, this makes up 90% of all radioactive waste types.

The intermediate waste (7% of all radioactive waste), so-called radwaste is solidified in concrete and disposed of in deep underground facilities.

High-level waste contains heavy elements with long-lived radioactive fission products. It makes up only 3% of all radwaste but 95% of the radioactivity. It is vitrified by borosilicate (Pyrex) glass and sealed inside stainless steel canisters. The boron atoms are particularly good at absorbing neutrons. This high-level waste is the material that is in dispute and should be disposed of in a deep underground repository. A typical large nuclear reactor produces 24-30 tonnes of high-level waste. [23]

In deciding on the potential danger of an isotope, there are a number of issues to consider. The shorter the half-life, the more radioactive the sample will be. The radio-activity from $^{131}$I ($t_{1/2}=8$ days) is initially high, but after a month or two, the level of radioactivity will be very low. The converse is also true; and the indium isotope, $^{115}$In, is considered benign because of its multi-trillion-year half-life. The picture is further complicated by the fact that many radioisotopes do not decay immediately to a stable state but rather to radioactive daughter elements with its own decay chain before achieving a stable state.

The disposal of high-level radioactive waste is highly contentious. It has been mooted that the waste should be sent into space or buried deep under the oceans. Both options have been strongly vetoed. As a result, the final disposal site must be deep underground in a rocky en-vironment and the waste must be encased in tough materials and the surrounding rock must act as a barrier to prevent radioactive leakage into the environment. France has made a start at building such a repository and so has Sweden and Finland. The UK is debating whether the site should be in Cumbria, and the United States has now withdrawn their plan of burying radwaste in the Yucca Mountain.

There are presently many hundreds of sites around the world where radioactive waste is being stores: Fukushima was one of them.

In debating the use of fossil fuel or nuclear fuel for electricity production, one should con-sider the tradeoff between

(a) 25 tonnes of uranium nuclear fuel producing 24 tonnes of uranium, 200 kg of plutonium, and smaller amounts of other fission products and

(b) 3 megatonnes (3 Mt) of coal producing 7 Mt of $CO_2$, 30 kilotonnes (kt) of $SO_2$, 10 kt of $NO_x$, and 200 kt of ash.

## LESSONS TO BE LEARNED

It is easy in hindsight to criticize decisions, but this is the only way we learn. The basic lessons learned from the nuclear disasters are

1. Human error was much to blame for some of the nuclear accidents that have happened. We need better training for the operators.

2. As nuclear disasters affect everyone on the planet, it is necessary to have an international body of advisors who regularly visit nuclear power stations. In this way, ideas can be networked and safety rules can be defined and carried out.

3. Designers, inspectors, and managers must be very honest and forthcoming about what is happening in a disaster situation.

4. The design and siting of nuclear plants should undergo intensive international scrutiny.

5. Assume worst case scenarios at every step. None of the disasters were unpredictable, given scientific theory, empirical information gathered as fission was first used, and early warnings.

## References and Notes

1. Ebbing DD. *General chemistry*. 5th ed. Boston: Houghton Mifflin Company; 1996 ISBN:0-395-76493-9.

2. Lee JD. *Concise inorganic chemistry*. 4th ed. London: Chapman and Hall; 1991 [chapter 31].

3. http://www.ehow.com/about_5202322_effects-gamma-radiation.html#ixzz1nOX1WvJZ [accessed 24 February 2012].

4. http://en.wikipedia.org/wiki/Radiation_effects_from_Fukushima_I_nuclear_accidents.

5. The principal source for this case was written by Lisa Gerovich, a Duke University undergraduate student, as part of the requirements for the course, Ethics in Professions, EGR 108S.

6. World Nuclear Association. http://www.world-nuclear.org/info/chernobyl/ukr_map.gif; 2005 [accessed on April 21, 2005].

7. U.S. Department of Energy. http://www.eh.doe.gov/health/ihp/chernobyl/chernobyl.html; 2005 [accessed April 21, 2005].

8. U.S. Department of Energy. Ukrainian Cancer Study published on July 1, 1999: http://www.eh.doe.gov/health/ihp/chernobyl/chernobyl.html; 2005 [accessed April 21, 2005].

9. http://en.wikipedia.org/wiki/Fukushima_I_nuclear_accidents accessed 24 February 2012.

10. von Hippel Frank N. *The radiological and psychological consequences of the Fukushima Daiichi accident. Bull At Sci* 2011;**67**(5):27–36. http://bos.sagepub.com/content/67/5/27.full.

11. "Caesium fallout from Fukushima rivals Chernobyl". New Scientist. on 30 March 2011. http://www.webcitation.org/5xZGE47q4. [accessed 22 February 2012].

12. http://www.hse.gov.uk/nuclear/fukushima/ [accessed 25 February 2012].

13. http://www.nrc.gov/reading-rm/doc-collections/fact-sheets/3mile-isle.html [accessed 9 March 2012].

14. General source of information for this case is NBC-Med: http://www.nbc-med.org/SiteContent/MedRef/OnlineRef/CaseStudies/csGoiania.html; [accessed December 3, 2004].

15. Sun M. Radiation accident grips Goiania. *Science* 1987;**238**:1028–31.

16. Source: www.nbc-med.org/sitecontent/medref/onlineref/casestudies/csgiania.html. Other Information Visit: http://environmentalchemistry.com/yogi/hazmat/articles/chernobyl1.html.

17. U.S. Geological Survey. *Radiogenic Isotopes and the Eastern Mineral Resources Program of the U.S. Geological Survey*; 2003.

18. U.S. Geological Survey. *FS-073-98, Short-Lived Isotopic Chronometers: A Means of Measuring Decadal Sedimentary Dynamics*; 2003.

19. Lewis C, Klouda G, Ellenson W. *Cars or trees: which contribute more to particulate matter air pollution?* Washington, DC: U.S. Environmental Protection Agency, Science Forum; 2003.

20. This is the carbon component of a fine particulate sample ($PM_{2.5}$), such as those measured at ambient air monitoring stations. The ratios are calculated according to the National Bureau of Standards, Oxalic Acid Standard Reference Method SRM 4990B.

21. National Bureau of Standards, Oxalic Acid Standard Reference Method SRM 4990B.

22. The defined reference standard for $^{14}C$ is 0.95 times the $^{14}C$ specific activity of the original NBS Oxalic Acid Standard Reference Material (SRM 4990B), adjusted to a $^{13}C$ delta value of $-19.09^0/_{00}$. This is "modern" carbon. It approximates wood grown in 1890 that was relatively free of $CO_2$ from fossil sources. Due to the anthropogenic release of radiocarbon from nuclear weapons testing and nuclear power generation, oxalic acid from plant material grown after World War II that is used currently to standardize $^{14}C$ measurements contains more $^{14}C$ than 1890 wood.

23. http://www.nrc.gov/waste.html.

CHAPTER

# 13

# Invasions

Ecologists consider any organism that is not native to be an "alien species." An alien species that causes harm is an "invasive species." The harm is usually both economic and environmental, but can also be a threat to public health. In fact, the U.S. Department of Agriculture defines an invasive species as one that: (1) is non-native (or alien) to the ecosystem under consideration and (2) whose introduction causes or is likely to cause economic or environmental harm or harm to human health.[1] These may be plants, animals, and other organisms (e.g., bacteria, fungi, or viruses).

In the case of microbes and plants, their seeds, spores, and cysts are ideal for such natural pathways. These may be influenced by changes in climate and other regional and planetary scale changes, such as those discussed in Chapters 3 and 5. Certain species have developed morphological and behavioral characteristics that facilitate such transport, such as stickiness and aerodynamics.[2]

Human activities are usually the means by which these species enter susceptible habitats. Species may be introduced by winds, currents, and other fluid movements. Man-made pathways are those pathways which are enhanced or created by human activity. These are characteristically of two types.

The first type is intentional, which is the result of a deliberate action to translocate an organism. Examples of intentional introductions include the intended movement of living seeds, whole plants, or pets. Intentional introductions as a whole should not be labeled as either good or bad. A specific intentional introduction can only be judged by the positive or negative impacts caused the introduced organisms within the ecosystem to which they are introduced. For example, many of the plants brought to the New World from Europe and Asia since the 17th Century have assimilated well and are even thought of as native. Conversely, some plants introduced in the 20th Century are still wreaking havoc.

The second type of man-made pathways are those pathways which unintentionally move organisms. Examples of unintentional pathways are ballast water discharge (e.g., red-tide organisms), soil associated with the trade of nursery stock (e.g., fire ants), importation of fruits and vegetables (e.g., plant pests), and the international movement of people (e.g., pathogens). In these and countless other unintentional pathways, the movement of species is an indirect by-product of our activities.

TABLE 13.1   Worst Invasive Fish Species as Rated by the Global Invasive Species Database

| Genus and species | Common names |
| --- | --- |
| *Asterias amurensis* | Flatbottom seastar, Japanese Seastar, Japanese starfish, Nordpazifischer Seestern, North Pacific seastar, northern Pacific seastar, purple-orange seastar |
| *Clarias batrachus* | alimudan, cá trê tráng, cá trèn trang, clarias catfish, climbing perch, freshwater catfish, Froschwels, hito, htong batukan, ikan keling, ikan lele, Ito, kawatsi, keli, klarievyi som, koi, konnamonni, kug-ga, leleh, magur, mah-gur, mangri, marpoo, masarai, mungri, nga-khoo, pa douk, paltat, pantat, pla duk, pla duk dam, pla duk dan, pla duk nam jued, pla duk nam juend, Thai hito, Thailand catfish, trey andaing roueng, trey andeng, walking catfish, wanderwels, Yerivahlay |
| *Cyprinus carpio* | carp, carpa, carpat, carpe, carpe, carpe commune, carpeau, carpo, cerpyn, ciortan, ciortanica, ciortocrap, ciuciulean, common carp, crap, crapcean, cyprinos, escarpo, Europäischer Karpfen, European carp, German carp, grass carp, grivadi, ikan mas, kapoor-e-maamoli, kapor, kapr obecný, karp, karp, karp, karp, karp, karp dziki a. sazan, karpa, karpar, karpe, Karpe, karpen, karper, karpfen, karpion, karppi, kerpaille, koi, koi carp, korop, krap, krapi, kyprinos, læderkarpe, lauk mas, leather carp, leekoh, lei ue, mas massan, mirror carp, olocari, pa nai, pba ni, pla nai, ponty, punjabe gad, rata pethiya, saran, Saran, sarmão, sazan, sazan baligi, scale carp, sharan, skælkarpe, soneri masha, spejlkarpe, sulari, suloi, tikure, trey carp samahn, trey kap, ulucari, weißfische, wild carp, wildkarpfen |
| *Gambusia affinis* | Barkaleci, Dai to ue, Gambusia, Gambusie, Gambusino, Gambuzia, Gambuzia pospolita, Gambuzija, guayacon mosquito, Isdang canal, Kadayashi, Koboldkärpfling, Kounoupopsaro, Live-bearing tooth-carp, Mosquito fish, Obyknovennaya gambuziya, pez mosquito, San hang ue, Silberkärpfling, tes, Texaskärpfling, Topminnow, western mosquitofish, Western mosquitofish |
| *Lates niloticus* | chengu, mbuta, nijlbaars, nilabborre, Nilbarsch, nile perch, perca di nilo, perche du nil, persico del nilo, sangara, Victoria perch, victoriabaars, victoriabarsch |
| *Micropterus salmoides* | achigã, achigan, achigan à grande bouche, American black bass, bas dehanbozorg, bas wielkogeby, bass, bass wielkgebowy, biban cu gura mare, black bass, bol'sherotyi chernyi okun', bolsherotnyi amerikanskii tscherny okun, buraku basu, fekete sügér, forelbaars, forellenbarsch, green bass, green trout, großmäuliger Schwarzbarsch, huro, isobassi, khorshid Mahi Baleh Kuchak, lakseabbor, largemouth bass, largemouth black bass, lobina negra, lobina-truche, northern largemouth bass, okounek pstruhový, okuchibasu, Öringsaborre, Ørredaborre, ostracka, ostracka lososovitá, perca americana, perche d'Amérique, perche noire, perche truite, persico trota, stormundet black bass, stormundet ørredaborre, tam suy lo ue, zwarte baars |
| *Oncorhynchus mykiss* | pstrag teczowy, rainbow trout, redband trout, Regenbogenforelle, steelhead trout, trucha arco iris, truite arc-en-ciel |
| *Oreochromis mossambicus* | blou kurper, common tilapia, fai chau chak ue, Java tilapia, kawasuzume, kurper bream, malea, mojarra, mosambik-maulbrüter, Mozambikskaya tilapiya, Mozambique cichlid, Mozambique mouth-breeder, Mozambique mouthbrooder, Mozambique tilapia, mphende, mujair, nkobue, tilapia, tilapia del Mozambique, tilapia du Mozambique, tilapia mossambica, tilapia mozámbica, trey tilapia khmao, weißkehlbarsch, wu-kuo yu |

*Source: The IUCN/SSC Invasive Species Specialist Group. http://www.issg.org/pdf/publications/worst_100/english_100_worst.pdf; 2004 [accessed March 9, 2012].*

# THE WORST 100

The Invasive Species Specialist Group (ISSG) has reluctantly listed the 100 "worst" invasive species in the world (see Table 13.1). In ISSG's own words, the task is difficult:

Species and their interactions with ecosystems are very complex. Some species may have invaded only a restricted region, but have a huge probability of expanding, and causing further great damage (for example, see *Boiga irregularis*, the Brown Tree Snake). Other species may already be globally widespread and causing cumulative but less visible damage. Many biological families or genera contain large numbers of invasive species, often with similar impacts; in these cases one representative species was chosen. The one hundred species aim to collectively illustrate the range of impacts caused by biological invasion.[3]

Invasive species cause damage to habitats by diminishing diversity and otherwise altering biosystems. With few or no predators, these non-native invasive species may consume the food sources much faster than their competitors. In North America, the Great Lakes basin is particularly vulnerable to invasive species. For example, about 170 non-native invasive species have been identified in the Laurentian Great Lakes drainage basin. Lake Erie watershed alone has 132 species, including algae (20 species), submerged plants (8 species), marsh plants (39 species), trees/shrubs (5 species), bacteria (3 species), mollusks (12 species), oligochaetes (9 species), crustaceans (9 species), other invertebrates (4 species), and fishes (23 species). The increase has been attributed for the most part to switching from solid to water ballast in cargo ships, along with the opening of the St Lawrence Seaway in 1959. Among the non-native invasive fish species recently invading Lake Erie is the Chinese bighead carp, *Hypophthalmichthys nobilis*.[4]

# SENSITIVE HABITATS

The introduction of opportunistic species and the loss or destruction of sensitive habitats are closely related. Organisms are often highly selective in where they breed, feed, and live. So, they have finite limits in time and space for survival. Either shrinking the available area or volume of habitat or crowding them out by introducing new species accomplishes the same thing, lower survival rates and loss of biodiversity.

## Everglades

Wetlands protection became a national priority in the United States in the last quarter of the twentieth century, for good reason. Wetlands are being lost at an alarming pace. On average, the loss of wetlands between 1986 and 1997 is estimated to be 270 km$^2$ per year in the conterminous United States. In addition, many of the remaining wetlands have been degraded.[5] Some of the destruction has been obvious, such as intentional draining for agriculture or urban development. Other sources of destruction have been indirect, such as addition of nutrients and sediment flowing into the wetlands, droughts, and floods.

The Florida Everglades cover 16,000 km$^2$ of shallow sawgrass marsh, interspersed with wet grasslands and sloughs interspersed with tree islands. Direct and indirect drainage change the hydrologic and hydraulic character of the system. Also, the Everglades ecosystem evolved under low phosphorus concentrations,[6] so when urbanization and other

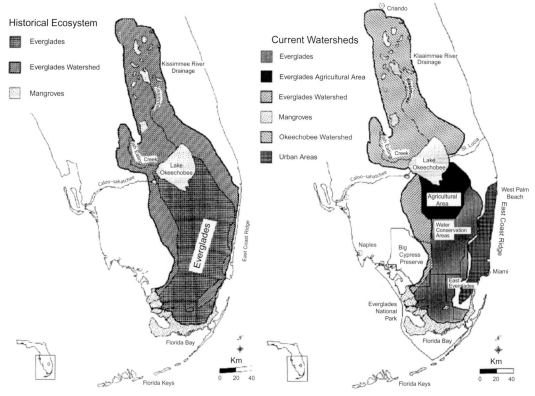

**FIGURE 13.1** Spatial coverage of the Everglades ecosystem prior to agricultural and urban development (left map) and after development (right map). *Source: Bancroft GT. Case study: United States of America, in human population, biodiversity and protected areas: science and policy issues. In: Dompka V, editor.* Report of a workshop, *April 20-21, 1995. Washington, DC: American Association for the Advancement of Science; 1996.*

development added substantial amounts of the nutrient, the ecosystem changed. This led to changes in dominant plant species and biodiversity. Only about half of the original Everglades ecosystem exists today (see Figure 13.1). Indeed, the Everglade plant and animal communities have undergone significant changes, including algal blooms that constrict the amount of sunlight and oxygen available to sea grass species that function as the structural foundation of various habitats.[7]

More than 200 introduced species of plants now live in the Everglades. These include melaleuca (*Melaleuca quinquenervia*), Brazilian pepper (*Schinus terebinthifolius*), Australian pine (*Casuarina equisetifolia*), and Old World Climbing Fern (*Lygodium microphyllum*). They have displaced native species and modified the habitat. Animals have also been introduced, including pythons, boa constrictors, parakeets, and parrots. Non-native fish include the Mayan cichlid (*Cichlasoma urophthalmus*), walking catfish (*Clarias batrachus*), Asian swamp eel (*Monopterus albus*) [see Figure 13.2], black acara (*Cichlasoma bimaculatum*), pike killifish (*Belonesox belizanus*), blue tilapia (*Oreochromis aureus*), spotted tilapia (*Tilapia mariae*), and oscar (*Astronotus ocellatus*).[8]

We have begun our discussion of alien invasions as a U.S. problem, but it is indeed a worldwide vexation, that can only be expected to worsen. The growth of international trade and travel will increase the rate of invasions by species that lack natural predators. The world's biodiversity

FIGURE 13.2 Asian swamp eel (*Monopterus albus*), an invasive species that has entered the Florida Everglades. Photo credit: *U.S. Geological Survey*. USGS and the Everglades ecosystems. *http://fl.biology.usgs. gov/Center_Publications/Fact_Sheets/everglades. pdf; 2012 [accessed March 9, 2012]*.

is at risk, so extensive measures must be taken, including rigorous inspections and controls to prevent entry and to limit the extent of invaders that have already entered new habitats.

## Rainforests

The Earth includes a wide belt of rainforests of magnificent diversity and productivity (see Table 13.2). These are the oxygen factories of the earth. Tropical forests may have extensive species abundance. Other rainforests include seasonally moist forests, where rainfall is

TABLE 13.2   Species Abundance by Ecosystem Type

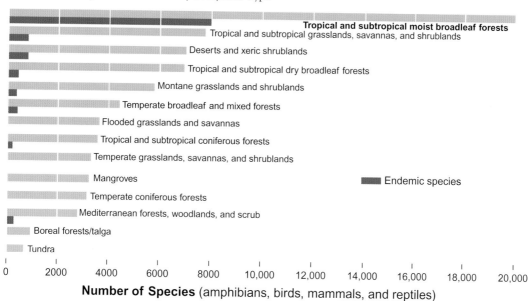

Tropical rainforests contain more species than any other ecosystem, as well as a higher proportion of species unique to a particular ecosystem (endemic).
*Source: Lindsey R. National Aeronautics and Space Administration. Earth Observatory. Tropical deforestation. March 30, 2007; adapted from Simmon R. Millennium ecosystem assessment biodiversity synthesis; 2005.*

abundant for part of the year. These are more open woodlands, yet these two are highly productive. Tropical rainforests are the most threatened of all the forests due to human activities, for example, clearing trees for agricultural products, harvesting whole trees for timber and urbanization, and roads that traverse habitats. These not only supplant habitats, but they truncate migration, foraging, predation, and breeding, i.e., the problem is greater than the areal extent of habitats displaced. The changes interrupt ecosystem dynamics and species activities, such as predator-prey relationships (see Figure 13.3).

Rainforests lose species to extinction at an alarming rate. Scientists estimate that about half of the world's species exist in rainforests, even though they cover only 7% of the Earth's land surface. Rainforest species are particularly vulnerable because they adapted to microhabitats that only exist in the unique conditions under ambient moisture and temperature regimes. Other species are lost to habitat destruction and deforestation. Ecosystem edges are particularly important to species survival. When they change due to climatic and anthropogenic

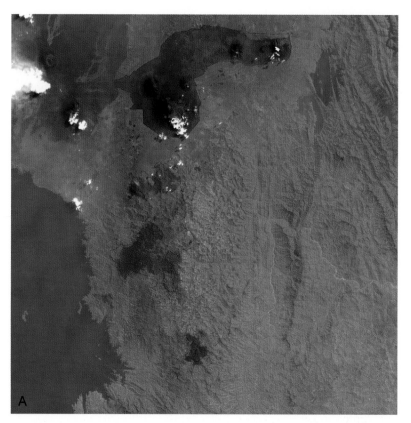

FIGURE 13.3   Decrease in extent and abundance of rainforests in Rwanda, Africa in 1986 (photo A) and 2001 (photo B). The Gishwati Forest, Rwanda has been threatened by environmental and societal influences. The genocide and refugee influxes increased the need for subsistence farming. About 99% of the rainforest vegetation was lost during this 15-year period. *Source: Image of the Day, June 9, 2009. National Aeronautics and Space Administration. Earth Observatory. http://earthobservatory.nasa.gov/IOTD/view.php?id=38644; 2012 [accessed March 10, 2012].*

FIGURE 13.3—CONT'D

stresses, canopy species (larger trees) can no longer survive. This leads to more destruction further within the ecosystem, with rapid decreases in species abundance and biodiversity.[9]

Rainforest destruction is indeed a societal problem. Local cultures have depended on the bounty for centuries. In fact, many of the primitive practices have been highly destructive, notably slash and burn (see Figure 13.4). Farmers have completely deforested areas and other vegetation to make arable land. However, the remaining layer of ash is an indication that many of the soil nutrients have chemically altered and leached from the soil. This exacerbates erosion rates. In a short time, the crops are no longer productive. This is often worsened when the cropped field is converted to pasture, with resulting soil compaction and overgrazing.

In addition to the localized effects, deforestation increases the emissions of carbon dioxide ($CO_2$) and other greenhouse gases to the atmosphere (see Chapter 8). Soil and plants in tropical forests sequester 460-575 billion metric tonnes of carbon worldwide with each square kilometer of tropical forest holding 45,000 tonnes of carbon. From 1850 to 1990, deforestation released 122 billion tonnes of carbon into the atmosphere. Currently, the deforestation carbon emission rate is 1.6 billion tonnes per year.[10]

FIGURE 13.4    Ecosystem destruction following slash and burn activities in rainforests. *Source: Lindsey R. National Aeronautics and Space Administration. Earth Observatory.* Tropical deforestation. *March 30, 2007 [accessed March 10, 2012]. Photo credit: U.S. Forest Service.*

Rainforests are being destroyed by varied and complex factors, so stopping the destruction is equally complicated. Without aggressive interventions, the disaster will only worsen.

## Coral Reefs

Coral reefs are incredibly diverse and productive (see Table 13.3). These so-called "rainforests of the ocean" cover a mere fraction of the ocean floor but are home to millions of organisms and thousands of species (see Figure 13.5). They are threatened by natural and human events, e.g., warm ocean temperatures and high-sea-level overfishing and development. Threats to the function and structure of coral reef ecosystems have been associated with wastewater discharges to major rivers that ultimately drain into oceans, carrying nutrients and microbial populations. More recently, these discharges have been found to contain drugs, personal care products, and antibiotics that are not degraded or incompletely degraded, leading to stresses on aquatic ecosystems. For example, the corals off the coast of Florida, world's third largest barrier reef, have been highly stressed, with half of the live coral off the Florida coast lost in the last few years. An additional indication is that fish feeding on these corals are developing deformities and experience premature mortality.[11]

Disastrous coral reef losses are occurring from physical, chemical, and biological sources. The U.S. Coral Reef Task Force recently identified what it considers to be the most prominent threats that federal agencies and states must address to protect coral reefs in the United States[12]:

TABLE 13.3    Net Primary Productivity of Ecosystems (Grams Dry Organic Matter per Square Meter per Year)

| Ecosystem type | Net primary productivity (g m$^{-2}$ year$^{-1}$) |
|---|---|
| Open ocean water | 100 |
| Coastal seawater | 200 |
| Desert | 200 |
| Tundra | 400 |
| Upwelling area | 600 |
| Rice paddy | 340-1200 |
| Freshwater pond | 950-1500 |
| Temperate deciduous forest | 1200-1600 |
| Cropland (cornfield) | 1000-6000 |
| Temperate grassland | ≤1500 |
| Cattail swamp | 2500 |
| Tropical rain forest | ≤2800 |
| Coral reef | 4900 |
| Sugarcane field | ≤9400 |

*Source: Maier RM, Pepper IL, Gerba CP. Environmental microbiology. 2nd ed. Burlington, MA: Elsevier Academic Press.*

1. Pollution, including eutrophication and sedimentation from poor or overly intensive land use, chemical loading, oil and chemical spills, marine debris, and invasive alien species.
2. Overfishing and exploitation of coral reef species for recreational and commercial purposes, and the collateral damage and degradation to habitats and ecosystems from fishing activities.
3. Habitat destruction and harmful fishing practices, including those fishing techniques that have negative impacts on coral reefs and associated habitats. This can include legal techniques such as traps and trawls used inappropriately, as well as illegal activities such as cyanide and dynamite fishing.
4. Dredging and shoreline modification in connection with coastal navigation or development.
5. Vessel groundings and anchoring that directly destroy corals and reef framework.
6. Disease outbreaks that are increasing in frequency and geographic range are affecting a greater diversity of coral reef species.
7. Global climate change and associated impacts including reduced rates of coral calcification, increased coral bleaching and mortality (associated with variety of stresses including increased sea surface temperatures), increased storm frequency, and sea-level rise.

Microbes appear to be transported long distances in winds aloft. For example, some of the invasive bacteria that threaten coral reef habitats may be coming from Africa in the form of

FIGURE 13.5    Shell of the green sea turtle (*Chelonia mydas*) that forages and breeds in the Great Barrier Reef is one of the thousands of species dependent on healthy coral reefs. *Photo credit: A.C. Randall. Vallero's granddaughter, Chloe Jayne Randall (1 year old) provides a scale reference (used with permission).*

Saharan dust. Deserts commonly contain gravel and bedrock, along with some sand. The Sahara is the exception, with sand covering 20% of the spatial extent of the desert. This means that the Sahara often loses large amounts of dust by winds that advectively transport particles in plumes that can travel across the Atlantic Ocean, depositing dust along the way (see Figure 13.6). Saharan dust carries disease-causing bacteria and fungi that have been associated with the destruction of coral reefs in the Caribbean Sea.

Scientists are investigating these phenomena to evaluate any linkages, threats, and possible interventions. The scientific goals associated with these threats, along with their respective ordinal (high, medium, and low) priorities for scientific research are shown in Table 13.4. Note that invasive species can include numerous organisms, but recently algae and bacteria have been highlighted as a much larger concern than had previously been thought. The bacteria are likely arriving in the coral reef ecosystems by long-range, atmospheric transport. Table 13.5 lists the actions recommended by the National Oceanic and Atmospheric Administration to address these threats that vary by region.

Physical threats include ultraviolet (UV) radiation, which have increased in the twentieth century with the depletion of stratospheric ozone. It can also increase locally when protective screens of organisms die off. UV radiation, therefore, is a ubiquitous stressor that is very likely impacting on human and ecological systems on a global scale. It has been implicated in observed shifts in

FIGURE 13.6   February 9, 2007 deposition of sediment flowing into Princess Charlotte Bay on the east coast of Queensland's Cape York Peninsula in Australia. The plumes merge into a 12-km-wide river of sediment-laden water, moving northwardly and washing over the coral reef. The sediment makes the normally turquoise-colored reef look greenish-brown. The plume veers northeastwardly from the inner reef and eventually reaches the outer reef. *Source: National Aeronautics and Space Administration. MODIS Rapid Response Team, Goddard Space Flight Center; 2007.*

polar plankton community composition, local and global declines in amphibian population abundance and diversity, coral bleaching syndrome, not to mention an increasing incidence of human skin cancer and other diseases. Disruption and loss of coral reef ecosystem communities due to coral bleaching/disease lead to coral mortality, changes in reef persistence, and formation dynamics, as well as cascading reef community interactions.[13]

Chemical contamination threats are many. An example is tributyl tin; a potent endocrine disrupting compound had been used throughout much of the twentieth century as an antifouling agent in coatings applied to watercraft. Since such compounds were added to boat paint for the stated purpose of preventing the growth of marine organisms, when the compounds leach into water, it is likely that they would continue this mode of action. Thus, living aquatic organisms in coral reef habitats could well be negatively impacted by interfering with the reproduction mechanisms in aquatic organisms. This was a major reason for the 2003 ban on this use of tributyl tin in the United States.

Contaminants reach reefs by air and water. For example, streams deposit their loads into reef systems (see Figure 13.6). When a stream reaches standing water, the stream's velocity falls rapidly, so its ability to carry suspended materials decreases. Thus, when large rivers reach the sea, they deposit silt. These loads contain contaminants from upstream sources, both natural (e.g., nutrients) and human activities (e.g., industrial and municipal facilities). Since large areas of coral reefs are adjacent to shorelines, they receive high concentrations

TABLE 13.4  Long-Term Conservation Measures Included in the U.S. Coral Reef Task Force's National Action Plan to Increase Understanding Coral Reef Ecosystem

| Key threats | Understand coral reef ecosystems | | | | Reduce the adverse impacts of human activities on reefs | | | | | | | | |
|---|---|---|---|---|---|---|---|---|---|---|---|---|---|
| | Map all U.S. coral reefs | Assess and monitor reef health | Conduct strategic research | Understand social and economic factors | Improve use of marine protected areas | Reduce impacts of fishing | Reduce impacts of coastal uses | Reduce pollution | Restore damaged reefs | Improve education and outreach | Reduce threats to international reefs | Reduce impacts from international trade | Improve coordination and accountability |
| Global warming/climate change | M | H | H | H | M | L | M | H | L | H | H | L | H |
| Diseases | M | H | H | L | L | M | L | M | L | L | L | L | M |
| Hurricanes/typhoons | L | L | M | L | L | L | L | L | M | L | L | L | L |
| Extreme biotic events | L | M | H | H | L | L | L | L | M | L | M | L | L |
| Overfishing | H | H | H | H | H | H | L | L | L | H | H | H | H |
| Destructive fishing practices | M | H | M | H | H | H | L | L | H | H | H | H | H |
| Habitat destruction | H | H | M | H | H | H | H | L | H | H | H | M | H |

| Threat | | | | | | | | | | | | |
|---|---|---|---|---|---|---|---|---|---|---|---|---|
| Invasive species | L | L | M | L | M | L | H | L | H | M | M | H |
| Coastal development | H | H | H | L | M | M | H | L | H | H | L | H |
| Coastal pollution | H | H | H | L | M | H | H | L | H | H | L | H |
| Sedimentation/ runoff | M | H | H | L | M | H | H | L | H | H | L | H |
| Marine debris | L | M | L | H | L | L | H | L | M | M | L | M |
| Overuse from tourism or recreation | M | H | M | M | H | H | L | L | H | H | M | L |
| Vessel groundings | M | L | L | L | H | H | L | H | H | L | L | H |
| Vessel discharges | L | M | L | M | H | L | H | L | H | H | L | H |

H, high priority action needed to address threat.
M, medium priority action to address threat.
L, low priority action to address threat.
Source: National Oceanic and Atmospheric Administration. National Coral Reef Action Strategy: report to Congress on implementation of the Coral Reef Conservation Act of 2000 and the National Action Plan to conserve coral reefs; 2002.

TABLE 13.5 Relative Importance (H, High; M, Medium; L, Low) of the Objectives Under Each Goal Outlined in the U.S. Strategy and National Action Plan to Address Key Threats to United States Coral Reef Ecosystems by Region

| | | Regions | | | | | | | |
| | | Atlantic/Caribbean | | | Polynesia | | | Micronesia | |
| Goals | Objectives | Florida | Puerto Rico | U.S. Virgin Islands | Main Hawaiian Islands | NW Hawaiian Islands | American Samoa | Guam | N. Mariana Islands |
|---|---|---|---|---|---|---|---|---|---|
| Map U.S. coral reefs | Map all shallow reefs (<30 m) | H | H | H | H | H | H | M | H |
| | Map selected deep reefs (<30 m) + B8 | M | L | H | L | L | M | L | L |
| Assess and monitor reef health | Conduct rapid assessments and inventories | H | M | H | H | H | M | M | H |
| | Monitor coral, fish, and other living resources | H | H | H | H | H | H | H | H |
| | Assess water and substrate quality | H | H | H | M | L | H | H | H |
| | Assess global warming and bleaching | H | M | M | L | L | M | L | M |
| Conduct strategic research | Understand reef processes | H | M | H | M | L | L | M | M |
| | Understand reef diseases and bleaching | H | H | H | L | L | L | L | M |
| | Understand impacts of management actions | M | H | M | H | H | H | M | H |
| Understand social and economic factors | Assess human uses of reefs | H | H | H | H | M | M | H | H |
| | Assess social/economic impacts of reef management | L | H | H | H | M | L | H | M |
| | Assess value of reef resources | M | H | M | H | M | M | H | H |

| Category | Action | | | | | | | | |
|---|---|---|---|---|---|---|---|---|---|
| Improve use of marine protected areas (MPAs) | Strengthen existing MPAs | H | H | H | H | H | H | H | H |
| | Identify gaps in MPA system | M | H | H | H | H | H | L | H |
| Reduce adverse impacts of fishing | Establish new MPAs | L | H | H | H | M | H | L | H |
| | Reduce overfishing | H | H | H | H | M | H | L | H |
| | Reduce habitat destruction and other indirect impacts | M | H | M | H | H | M | M | H |
| Reduce impacts of coastal uses | Reduce dredging and other habitant impacts | H | H | M | L | L | M | L | H |
| | Reduce impacts from ocean recreation | L | H | H | H | L | L | H | H |
| | Improve vessel management | M | H | M | H | H | L | H | M |
| Reduce pollution | Reduce sediment pollution | M | H | H | H | L | H | H | H |
| | Reduce nutrient pollution | H | H | M | H | L | M | H | H |
| | Reduce chemical pollution | M | M | M | M | M | H | H | H |
| | Reduce marine debris | M | M | M | M | H | M | L | L |
| | Prevent and control invasive species | M | L | L | H | H | L | L | L |
| Restore damaged reefs | Improve response capabilities | H | H | M | H | H | M | L | M |
| | Improve restoration techniques | M | H | M | M | L | L | M | M |
| | Restore damaged reefs | M | H | L | L | L | L | L | M |

*Continued*

TABLE 13.5 Relative Importance (H, High; M, Medium; L, Low) of the Objectives Under Each Goal Outlined in the U.S. Strategy and National Action Plan to Address Key Threats to United States Coral Reef Ecosystems by Region—Cont'd

| | | Regions | | | | | | | |
| | | Atlantic/Caribbean | | | Polynesia | | | Micronesia | |
| Goals | Objectives | Florida | Puerto Rico | U.S. Virgin Islands | Main Hawaiian Islands | NW Hawaiian Islands | American Samoa | Guam | N. Mariana Islands |
|---|---|---|---|---|---|---|---|---|---|
| Improve education and outreach | Increase awareness | H | H | H | H | M | H | H | H |
| Reduce international threats to reefs | Increase capability for resource management | L | H | H | H | H | H | L | H |
| | Support international organizations and institutions | L | L | M | L | L | M | H | M |
| | Support project development and implementation | L | L | M | L | L | L | L | H |
| | Provide technical assistance | L | L | M | L | L | L | L | H |
| Reduce impacts from international trade | Reduce destructive fishing practices | L | M | H | L | L | L | L | L |
| | Increase international awareness | L | L | L | L | L | L | L | L |
| Improve coordination and accountability | Improve coordination and accountability | H | M | M | H | H | H | L | H |

H, high priority action needed to address threat.
M, medium priority action to address threat.
L, low priority action to address threat.
Source: National Oceanic and Atmospheric Administration. National Coral Reef Action Strategy: report to Congress on implementation of the Coral Reef Conservation Act of 2000 and the National Action Plan to conserve coral reefs; 2002.

of pollutants before they are diluted. Thus, even though oceans are vast, their pollution varies substantially by location. Unfortunately, coral reefs often exist in the most highly contaminated locations.

Biological agents may be an even greater and more ominous threat to coral reefs. The microbial ecology within a coral reef is complex. For example, some algae are symbiotic and others are parasitic to corals. Fungi are also widely distributed in calcium carbonate, i.e., they have *endolithic* associations with corals.[14] Bacterial diseases are also appearing. Thus, various biological taxa of microorganisms present different, but possibly synergistic threats to coral reef systems.

## Jellyfish Invasion

The Black Sea is the largest enclosed catchment basin in the world, receiving freshwater and sediment inputs from rivers draining half of Europe and parts of Asia. As such, the sea is highly sensitive to eutrophication and has changed numerous times in recent decades. The Danube River receives effluents from eight European countries, flows into the Black Sea, and is the largest source of stream-borne nutrients. In a very short time, the ecology changed from an extremely biodiverse system to one dominated by jellyfish (*Aurelia* and the comb jellyfish *Mnemiopsi*).[15] These invaders were unintentionally introduced in the mid-1980s, culminating in the fisheries almost completely vanishing by the early 1990s. Indeed, fish stock overexploitation and the jellyfish invasion have been major contributors to the collapse of the anchovy fish stocks in the Black Sea and the departure of valuable fish species.[16]

Ballast water from ships has been a very effective means of species invasions, since the water contains a variety of biological organisms. After a ship travels and exchanges cargo, the ballast must be released to decrease the ship's weight. This untreated ballast water introduces organisms and their eggs, spores, and cysts. When they survive and reproduce, they can upset the delicate predator-prey and biodiversity balances of the new environment. The more the ballast water released, the higher the risk of invasion. For example, in the United States, about 200 million tonnes of ballast water is discharged into U.S. waters annually. Of this, approximately 30% is of foreign origin, outside the U.S. Exclusive Economic Zone.

In North America, the zebra mussel (*Dreissena polymorpha*) was probably introduced to the Great Lakes in the 1980s. Since then, zebra mussels have drastically altered ecosystems, mainly by removing suspended material from the habitat. To an environmental engineer, this may seem like a benefit at first sight, since we devote much effort to removing solids from effluent (see Chapter 6). However, the balance of aquatic ecosystems requires optimal ranges of dissolved and suspended solids, which include the planktonic algae that are the primary base of the food web.[17] In Asia, the introduced American Comb Jelly, *Mnemiopsis leidyi* (see Figure 13.7), has fed excessively on zooplankton, which contributed significantly to the collapse of the anchovy and sprat fisheries in the Black and Asov Sea.[18]

Pathogens can also be introduced from ballast waters, such as cholera. In 1991, ballast water containing the bacterium *Vibrio cholera* was released and allowed the microbe to infect a million people in Peru via drinking water. More than 10,000 people died. Later, a South American strain of *V. cholera* was discovered in ballast tanks in the port at Mobile, Alabama.

Once introduced, certain species of algae may form toxic blooms that result in large fish kills and the death of other aquatic organisms when dissolved oxygen is depleted (see Chapter 6) and toxins are released by the algae. Some algal species may contaminate filter-feeding shellfish and contaminate human seafood.[18] Notably, the so-called killer algae

FIGURE 13.7   American comb jelly, *Mnemiopsis leidyi. Source: Smithsonian Institute. http://ocean.si.edu/ocean-photos/seawalnut-mnemiopsis-leidyi; 2012 [accessed March 10, 2012].*

(*Caulerpa taxifolia*), a toxic strain of green seaweed, that has escaped from aquariums and spread in the Mediterranean Sea and along the U.S. Pacific coast habitat.[19]

The Black Sea is illustrative of actual and potential invasion disasters. At least, 41 alien species have entered the ecosystem, with 34% imported for aquaculture and 66% entering as pelagic larvae in ballast waters and/or fouling organisms on ship hulls (see Figure 13.8).[16]

This collapse in the productivity of fisheries was first attributed to unpalatable carnivores that fed on plankton, roe, and larvae. Subsequently, however, the jellyfish takeover was found to result from human perturbations in the coastal ecosystems and in the drainage basins of the rivers, including the changing the hydrologic character of out-flowing rivers. The biggest of these was the damming of the Danube in 1972 by the "Iron Gates," approximately 1000 km upstream from the Black Sea. In addition there was urban and industrial development, heavy use of commercial fertilizers, and over-fishing. These made the Danube particularly vulnerable to the introduction of exotic, invasive organisms, notably Mnemiopsi.

The nutrient concentration changes induced phytoplankton blooms during the warm months in the 1970s and changed the dominance to non-siliceous species. Before this, these were not a first choice as food for zooplankton. The decreased fish stocks further increased the dominance of the jellyfish, since they competed better than the game fish for the same food. Ironically, since the mid-1990s, the ecosystems have begun to improve, mainly due to increased nutrient (phosphorus and nitrogen) loading. In most situations, we are looking to decrease this loading, to prevent eutrophication. But in this system, the added nutrients have allowed certain plankton and benthic (bottom dwelling) organisms to re-colonize. The abundance of jellyfish has also stabilized, with a concomitant increase in anchovy eggs and larvae.

Nutrient limitation occurs when the presence of a chemical, e.g., phosphorus or nitrogen, is insufficient to sustain the growth of a community or species. Usually, marine systems are nitrogen limited whereas freshwater plankton systems are phosphorus limited. Numerous freshwater organisms can fix atmospheric nitrogen but, with minor exceptions, the nitrogen is held in check in high-salinity water, but this differs by species. A disturbance in the ratio of nitrogen, phosphorus, silica, and even iron changes the biotic composition of a particular plankton community. Often, all four nutrients can be considered as limiting in an aquatic system. For instance, the lack of silica-limiting diatoms was observed first in natural blooms off Cape Mendocino in the United States and later in the northwest sector of the Black Sea after closing the Iron Gates dam. Incidentally, ecosystem insults often translate into economic problems, in this case with an actual damage to the economies of Central and Eastern European nations in the 1990s.

The Iron Gate Dam illustrates the importance of small things and a systematic approach. The disaster resulted from what is not ordinarily considered to be limiting factor, i.e., silicates. It clearly represents the huge ecological price that must be paid when biodiversity is destroyed. For example, does the recent migration of comb jellyfish *M. leidyi* from different regions of the Baltic Sea mean that the entire ecosystem in the sea basin has been adversely impacted?

Research has indicated that the species seems to consist mainly of small-size classes with just a few adults. Their food preference appears to be for small and slow swimming prey, predominantly during the low temperature seasons. *Barnacle nauplii* comprise the major cool

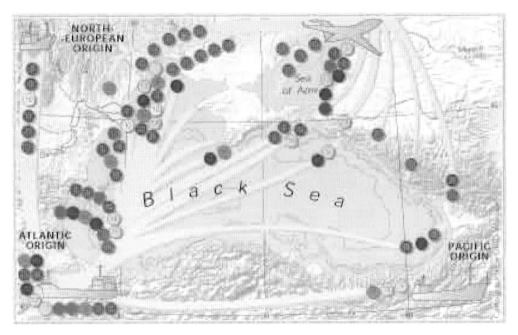

FIGURE 13.8    Alien species in the Black Sea. *Source: European Environmental Agency.* Europe's biodiversity—biogeographical regions and seas: seas around Europe: the Black Sea—an oxygen-poor sea. *http://www.pedz.uni-mann heim.de/daten/edz-bn/eua/02/C__DOKUME~1_ZEFZEI_LOKALE~1_TEMP_plugtmp_BlackSea.pdf; 2002 [accessed March 10, 2012].*

*Continued*

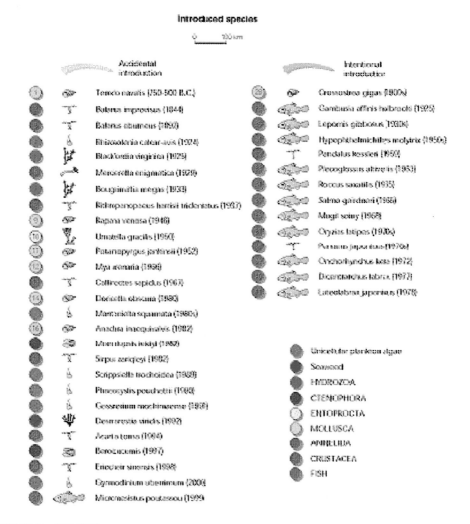

FIGURE 13.8—CONT'D

season carbon source. Also, the highest densities of the species are, not surprisingly, in warm seasons, when the food source is the planula larvae of the jellyfish *Aurelia aurita*. Thus, the species seem to be adapting to their new environment, e.g., reduced size. Some argue that this may mean less damage to the Baltic ecosystem.[20] In addition, the species invasion seems to be kept in check by saline regimes, which limit its expansion to lower salinity waters.[21]

This appears to be good news, but we are still in the midst of the invasion. Biological disasters may take many years, even decades, to play out before their damage can be reasonably assessed.

# Gene Flow

Genetic engineering has many benefits and concerns (see sidebar discussion: Greening Disease and Spinach). One of the concerns is the disaster scenario of genetically modified organisms that become invasive transgenic species. At this time, this is mainly mere conjecture, so the following discussion addresses a hypothetical disaster, not a real one (at least as far as we know).

## GREENING DISEASE AND SPINACH

The Asiatic citrus psyllid, *Diaphorina citri* Kuwayama (see Figure 13.9), is the invasive species vector of the bacterium *Candidatus* Liberibacter spp.,[22] which causes the plant disease Huanglongbing, commonly known as citrus greening disease.[23,24] The psyllids are jumping plant lice that were first discovered in Florida in 1998. The disease was confirmed in the southeastern United States in 2005.[25] The lice carry phloem-inhabiting bacteria that are poised to cause a citrus tree disaster.[26] Of the 13 species of psyllids reported on citrus plants, two species, *D. citri* and *Trioza erytreae* (del Guercio), are spreading the disease.

Citrus greening results from interferences in the distribution of nutrients within the tree. This leads to discoloration, misshapen fruit, and mottled leaves (see Figure 13.10), ultimately cutting

FIGURE 13.9  Leaves (A) and fruit (B) of orange trees showing symptoms of Huanglongbing, commonly known as citrus greening disease. *Source: U.S. Department of Agriculture. Agricultural Research Service. http://www.ars.usda.gov/ Research/docs.htm?docid=18429; 2012 [accessed April 2, 2012].*

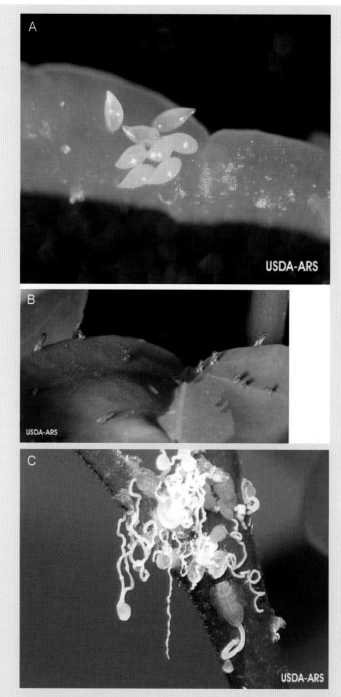

FIGURE 13.10    (A) Eggs of Asiatic citrus psyllid, *Diaphorina citri* Kuwayama. (B) Infestation of *D. citri*. (C) Wax secretions from *D. citri* nymphs. *Source: U.S. Department of Agriculture. Agricultural Research Service. http:// www.ars.usda.gov/Research/docs.htm?docid=18429; 2012 [accessed April 2, 2012].*

the life span of trees to less than 8 years and never allows them to produce usable fruit.[26] In areas where the disease is endemic, citrus trees may live for only 5-8 years and never bear harvestable fruit. In fact, greening is present throughout the subtropical and tropical regions of southern Asia and Africa, on islands in the Indian Ocean, and in the Arabian Peninsula. The pathogenic bacteria are mainly transmitted by psyllids and grafting. The disease has defied control wherever it has colonized.[26]

Some have warned that if the disease is allowed to continue to spread for even a few more years, the U.S. citrus industry will be almost completely destroyed. This caution has led to aggressive searches for solutions.

One potential solution to the problem is genetic engineering. All plants have survival mechanisms. Scientists in this instance are particularly interested in the production of substances that repel or kill fauna (e.g., insects) and pathogens such as bacteria and fungi. Plants that have more of these natural protections are less susceptible to pests than plants that have fewer of them. For example, plants possess proteins that help them resist and fight bacteria. Some plants have more potent proteins than others, so inserting recombinant DNA from such plants into citrus species could allow the genetically modified citrus trees to resist the psyllid-borne pathogens that cause greening. Recently, researchers have identified proteins in spinach that appear to be candidates for genetic insertion into orange trees.

Traditional approaches that are being used are registering pathogen-free nurseries, controlling the vector using pesticides and integrated pest management, and removal of infected trees.[27] In addition to some proven tools that have been limited in addressing the problem, the National Academy of Sciences has identified the need for developing resistant citrus cultivars. However, it has been observed that "there is no clear path by conventional breeding to deliver a robust resistant citrus for many commercial species because these species lack known sources of resistance and a facile breeding system." The Academy also noted, however, that "it is likely that the breeding systems for sweet orange and some other citrus can be greatly enhanced in the long run by capabilities derived from genome sequence analysis and other technologies" and that "genetic engineering, in the form of transgenic citrus or citrus inoculated with a transgene-expressing virus vector, holds the greatest hope for generating citrus cultivars" resistant to the disease.[27]

As mentioned throughout this book, a systematic perspective is needed in disaster prevention and response. For example, the genetic engineering solution is an attempt to manipulate the citrus fruit's genetic material to express certain desired traits, in this instance, to produce particular proteins.

Could solving this problem lead to other unintended consequences? For example, other than making the plants more resistant to pathogens, could the fruit be altered? Could new allergies be introduced? The advocacy group Institute for Responsible Technology suggests this has been the case for a number of crops, associated increases in food allergies in the United States with the insertion of genetic material from bacteria, virus, and other organisms into soy, corn, cottonseed, and canola plants.[28] In addition, transgenes from crops like citrus trees may find their way to other plants, a process known as horizontal gene transfer. Thus, even beneficial agricultural biotechnologies like those proposed to save the citrus crop as well as other industrial, medical, and other biotechnologies must be considered in light of possible and actual environmental risks. In many instances, these risks are difficult to assess, given the lack of reliable data and the lack of precedents.

Perhaps the central lesson from the citrus invasion is the price to be paid for ignoring the need for a diverse and sustainable approach to food. Monocultures are inherently susceptible to the ravages of invaders. Since only one species is grown, if one plant is harmed then all plants can be equally harmed. Thus, the spread can be rapid and damage can approach 100%. This is consistent with Aldo Leopold's advice:

> A thing is right when it tends to preserve the integrity, stability and beauty of the biotic community. It is wrong when it tends otherwise.[29]

Losing Florida's citrus crop would certainly be wrong. Indeed, it would be disastrous.

Estimating and predicting the risks associated with the manufacture and use of biotechnologies are complicated by the diversity and complexity of the types of technologies available and being developed, as well as the seemingly limitless potential uses of these processes. The beginning of risk assessment is a formulation of the problem and the product of the risk assessment is a statement regarding the probability that humans (populations or individuals) or other environmental receptors so exposed will be harmed and to what degree such harm will be manifested (i.e., the overall risk characterization). As more products and by-products are developed using biotechnologies, the potential for environmental exposure has increased. Potential sources of biotechnological risk include direct and/or indirect releases to the environment from the manufacture and processing of biochemicals generated (e.g., proteins), as well the release of the modified organisms themselves and their biological products (e.g., spores and cysts).

The transfer of genetic material between separate populations, i.e., gene flow, is an example of the downstream risks from biotechnologies. Such transfer can be similar to that of chemical compounds in the environment, e.g., by dispersion of matter via advection. It can also take on very different transport mechanisms, such as biological transfer within and between levels of biological organization. An example is the organism-to-organism transport of genetic information via processes that resemble contagion behavior of disease transmission within a species.

Transfer of genetic material from modified strains is not always well understood. Transport models must continue to avail themselves to better science. Hopefully, increasingly improved transport mechanisms will be incorporated into risk assessments so that predictions of damage and risk become more reliable. For instance, the present commercialization of transgenic grasses is raising concerns about the ecological risks associated with future gene flow of modified species from high-use agent contagion centers, such as golf courses adjacent to native and managed plant communities. One particular herbicide-tolerant creeping bentgrass (*Agrostis stolonifera*) has been the center of debate weighing the expected benefits of genetically modified turfgrasses, e.g., less pesticide use and lower labor costs, against potential ecological risks involved in the transfer of the herbicide-resistant trait to ecosystems (e.g., native grasses, introduced grasses, and conventional creeping bentgrass). The transgenic bentgrass populations may alter ecosystem function and structure in nearby ecosystems, e.g., wetlands. Reliable information is currently lacking, e.g., regarding the potential for gene flow to *A. perennans*, a common native perennial bentgrass. Complicating matters further, numerous native or introduced bentgrass species are able to hybridize with the herbicide-tolerant creeping bentgrass. Such genetically modified populations represent a potential environmental hazard in wetlands and other areas where invasive plants and weeds are managed by herbicides.[30]

To date, most agricultural biotechnological products have come from microorganisms. The exact data requirements for each product have been developed on a case-by-case basis. All of the products have been proteins, either related to plant viruses or based on proteins from the common soil bacterium *Bacillus thuringiensis* (Bt). The general data requirements include product characterization, mammalian toxicity, allergenicity potential, effects on nontarget organisms, environmental fate, and for the Bt products, insect resistance management to product from losing use of both the microbial sprays and the Bt plant-incorporated protectants (PIPs). A transgene is an exogenous gene that has been introduced into the genome of another organism, and a transgenic species is one whose genome has been genetically altered. For instance, if a biotechnology is used as a PIP, the movement of transgenes from a host plant into weeds and other crops presents a concern that new types of exposures will occur. Bt corn and potato PIPs that have been registered to date have been expressed in agronomic plant species that, for the most part, do not have a reasonable possibility of passing their traits to wild native plants. Most of the wild species in the United States cannot be pollinated by these crops (corn and potato) due to differences in chromosome number, phenology, and habitat. There is a possibility, however, of gene transfer from Bt cotton to wild or feral cotton relatives in Hawaii, Florida, Puerto Rico, and the U.S. Virgin Islands. Where feral populations of cotton species similar to cultivated cotton exist, regulators have prohibited the sale or distribution of Bt cotton in these areas. These containment measures prevent the movement of the registered Bt endotoxin from Bt cotton to wild or feral cotton relatives.[31]

Researchers have reviewed the potential for gene capture and expression of Bt PIPs (only Cry3A has been introduced into potato) by wild or weedy relatives of cultivated potato in the United States, its possessions or territories.[32] Based on data submitted by the registrant and a review of the scientific literature, regulators have concluded that there is no foreseeable risk of unplanned pesticide production through gene capture and expression of the Colorado potato beetle control protein (Cry3A) in wild potato relatives in the U.S. tuber-bearing *Solanum* species, including *S. tuberosum*. *S. tuberosum* cannot hybridize naturally with the non-tuber-bearing *Solanum* species in the United States. Three species of tuber-bearing wild species of *Solanum* occur in the United States: *Solanum fendleri*, *Solanum jamesii*, and *Solanum pinnatisectum*. But, successful gene introgression into these tuber-bearing *Solanum* species is virtually excluded due to constraints of geographical isolation and other biological barriers to natural hybridization. These barriers include incompatible (unequal) endosperm balance numbers that lead to endosperm failure and embryo abortion, multiple ploidy levels, and incompatibility mechanisms that do not express reciprocal genes to allow fertilization to proceed. No natural hybrids have been observed between these species and cultivated potatoes in the United Species. The extent to which these findings will continue for the potato or will be similar to those of other species depends on the unique genomic characteristics of those species.

The constraints, drivers, and boundary conditions of the control volume wherein gene flow may occur must be understood to predict possible risks of genetically modifying these plant species. A systematic question is the extent to which such transfers present problems in microbial populations (e.g., genetically modified bacteria introduced in oil spills or hazardous waste sites to degrade toxic compounds; industrial applications of microbial reactors to produce pharmaceuticals and other chemicals that are released into the environment), and animal populations (i.e., the animals themselves, e.g., genetically modified fish released into the surface waters) or microbes that undergo transformation (e.g., similar to the recent H1N1 pandemic, but from a genetically modified microbe).

## Threats to Honey Bees

Invertebrates represent 97% of all animal species. They profoundly affect their surroundings. In particular, bees, moths, ants, and other insects are pollinators needed for many plants to survive. If these species are lost to any great degree, it would indeed be catastrophic to ecosystems, as well as the world food supply.

One of the most endangered groups of insects is the honey bees. One of the principal threats is pesticide use, since these chemical are designed to be toxic to insects. They are also unfortunately toxic to birds, mammals, amphibians, or fish.[33]

Agricultural pesticides can adversely affect honey bees either directly from pesticide toxicity or indirectly, e.g., herbicides that reduce the abundance plants that serve as the bees' food sources and habitats. Herbicides and fungicides can change habitats by altering the structure ecosystems (e.g., plant associations and communities), ultimately leading to population decline.[34]

As mentioned in the section "Everglades," food webs are affected by endocrine disruption, so the diversity can be harmed by pesticides, several of which are hormonally active.

Climate change could also affect honey bee habitats. For example, a range shift toward the poles (northward in the Northern Hemisphere) or to higher elevations has occurred among many invertebrates that are considered pests or disease organisms. Butterflies' habitat ranges in North America have shifted northward and in elevation as temperatures increased. In some cases, local butterfly populations have become extinct in the southern portion of their range.[35]

Honey bees are also threatened by other organisms, especially patristic mites and the hive beetle, as well as by invading Africanized bees.[36]

At the risk of sounding sensational, the May 1, 2010 edition of *The (United Kingdom) Observer* ran this headline:

> The world may be on the brink of biological disaster after news that a third of U.S. bee colonies did not survive the winter.[37]

The article reported the phenomenon known as colony collapse disorder (CCD), which is associated with the death of billions of colonies of honey bees.

## Vulnerable Amphibians

Amphibians may well turn out to be the world's "canaries in the coal mine." They are certainly susceptible to the stresses discussed in this chapter, including habitat loss, climate change, overexploitation, and disease.[38]

FIGURE 13.11    Frog with extra legs. *Source: Manuel J. Frog deformities research not leaping to conclusions.* Environ Health Perspect *1997;105(10):1046-47.*

One could add UV radiation and pesticides to the list. Linking cause with effect in terms of decreased amphibian populations is difficult. One indication of the threat is development disorders in amphibians, especially hormonal dysfunction. This has been observed (see Figure 13.11). Some have argued that herbicides like atrazine may be the cause.

Much work needs to be done. Even good science (well designed and adhering to the scientific method) can be confusing. For example, the University of California has stated that concentrations of atrazine as low as 0.1 parts per billion (ppb) caused either multiple or both male and female sex organs in male frogs. Atrazine has been found in surface water at concentrations of 20-40 ppb and is used throughout the United States to control weeds on farms. It is moderately volatile and soluble in water and resists breakdown by microbes in water. Its physicochemical properties and widespread application as an herbicide have led to concerns about possible risks to aquatic organisms.

These findings are uncertain since developmental disorders in frogs have been observed at low doses rather than at high doses. This violates one of the tests for causality, the biological gradient which says that the higher the dose the more the effect. Indeed, the gradient does not always hold, e.g., at very high doses to a carcinogen, tumors may not form because the dose is so high it kills the cell. So there is a strong possibility that some other factors may be causing the problem. The second problem is that atrazine has been applied for decades but only recently has been linked to amphibian endocrine effects. This may be because people had not noticed the problems or began to notice the deformities only recently and felt the need to report them due to the heightened awareness of the problem. It may also be due to the frogs' exposures to chemical transformation products or a synergy of atrazine with newly used products. The white paper gave little credence to these possibilities, but only recently did various government agencies begin to postulate that certain biological mechanisms could trigger the deformities, and so they began to identify possible environmental causes and the need for research.

Other possible explanations for the deformities include chemical contamination, greater exposure to UV radiation as a result of ozone depletion, parasitic infestation, or even combinations of these and other unknown factors.[39] Frogs spend most of their time in surface water, so they may be subjected to chemical contamination. A number of the places where deformed frogs are found are agricultural areas, so pesticides cannot be ruled out, especially when synergies between the chemical exposures and other factors are taken into account.

The amphibians are trying to tell us something. The problem is that the scientific community is yet to reach consensus on what that is.

## LESSONS LEARNED

Most would agree that the Monarch butterfly is a beautiful creature. What if we lost them or one of their species?

Some have argued that genetically engineered material from soil bacterium Bt poses a threat of killing Monarch butterfly larvae.[40] Ironically, this is a so-called organic pesticidal process. The Bt produces a protein that targets insect pests. Scientists "borrow" the genetic material that expresses this protein and insert it into plant species, including corn.

Some studies have indicated that corn pollen normally travels in limited distances and that the pollen has a tendency not to accumulate on the favored Monarch food, i.e., milkweed leaves. Also, pollen production usually does not occur at the same time as the active feeding by Monarch larvae. These factors supported the U.S. EPA decision to continue to approve the planting of Bt corn. The question in such decisions is whether the decision was based on sufficient field studies and the possibility of the combination of rare events.

Phytoremediation utilizes biochemodynamic processes to remove, degrade, transform, or stabilize contaminants that reside in soil and ground water. Subtle changes in any of these processes can make the difference between a successful remediation effort and a failure. Phytoremediation uses plants to capture the water from plumes of contaminated aquifers. The plants take up the water by the capillary action of their roots and transport it upward through the plant until the water is transpired to the atmosphere. The good news is that many of the contaminants have been biochemically transformed or at least sequestered in the plant tissue.

Plants do not metabolize organic contaminants to carbon dioxide and water like microbes do. Rather they transform parent compounds into non-phytotoxic metabolites. After uptake by the plant, the contaminant undergoes a series of reactions to convert, conjugate, and compartmentalize the metabolites. Conversion includes oxidation, reduction, and hydrolysis. Conjugation reactions chemically link these converted products (i.e., phase 1 metabolites) to glutathione, sugars, or amino acids, so that the metabolites (i.e., phase 2 metabolites) have increased aqueous solubility and, hopefully, are less toxic than the parent compound. After this conjugation, the compounds are easier for the plant to eliminate or compartmentalize to other tissues. Compartmentalization (phase 3) causes the chemicals to be segregated into vacuoles or bound to the cell wall material, such as the polymers lignin and hemicellulose. Phase 3 conjugates are considered to be bound residues. This supposition comes from the evidence laboratory extraction methods have difficulty finding the original parent compounds.[41]

Enter the butterfly. It turns out that some of the phytoremediation products of conversion reactions can become more toxic than the parent contaminants when consumed by animals or potentially leached to the environment from fallen leaves. For example, the release of contaminants from conjugated complexes or compartmentalization could occur in the gut of a worm, a snail, or a *butterfly*.[42] This means that there is a distinct possibility of re-introducing the pollutant, by means of the butterfly, into the food chain.

Ironically, the butterfly is also also happens to be a popular metaphor for chaos. Edward Lorenz's Butterfly Effect, which postulates "sensitive dependence upon initial conditions,"[43] as a postulate of chaos theory. In essence, chaos means that a small change for good or bad can reap exponential rewards and costs. The metaphor was introduced by Edward Lorenz who, at a 1963 New York Academy of Sciences meeting, related the comments of a "meteorologist who had remarked that if the theory were correct, one flap of a seagull's wings would be enough to alter the course of the weather forever." Lorenz later revised the seagull example to be that of a butterfly in his 1972 paper, "Predictability: Does the Flap of a Butterfly's Wings in Brazil set off a Tornado in Texas?" meeting of the American Association for the Advancement of Science, Washington, DC. In both instances, Lorenz argued that future outcomes are determined by seemingly small events cascading through time. Engineers and mathematicians struggle with means to explain, let alone predict, such outcomes of so-called ill-posed problems. Engineers generally prefer to design within orderly systems with the certainty and straightforwardness of a well-posed problem, that is, one that is uniquely solvable (i.e., one where a unique solution exists) and one that is dependent upon a continuous application of data. By contrast, an ill-posed problem does not have a unique solution and can only be solved by discontinuous applications of data, meaning that even very small errors or perturbations can lead to large deviations in possible solutions.[44] Unfortunately, predicting the occurrence and magnitude of an environmental disasters usually falls within the province of ill-posed problems.

The importance of seemingly small things within a systematic approach is demonstrated by what happened near the Iron Gate Dam, in the Great Barrier Reef, in tropical rainforests and every sensitive habitat. With ecosystem destruction comes an enormous ecological price that must be paid when biodiversity is destroyed. In many of this chapter's disasters the causes are not necessarily what we scientists may have considered to be a pollutant or even a limiting ecological factor, e.g., silicates or subsistence farming or dust blown bacteria.

So what is the lesson from the butterfly and jellyfish? Small changes for good or bad can produce unexpectedly large effects. Ignoring the biochemodynamic details can lead to big problems down the road. The smallest living systems, the viruses, bacteria, and other microbes, are amazing biochemical factories. For much of human history, we have treated them as marvelous black boxes, wherein mysterious and elegant processes take place. These processes not only keep the microbes alive, but they also provide remarkable proficiencies to adapt to various hostile environments. Some produce spores; many have durability and protracted latency periods; all have the ability to reproduce in large numbers until environmental conditions become more favorable. The various systems that allow for this efficient survival have become increasingly better understood in recent decades, to the point that cellular and subcellular processes of uptake and absorption, nutrient distribution, metabolism, and product elimination have been characterized, at least empirically.

The principal lessons from the disasters discussed in this chapter are that every ecosystem is vulnerable. All are valuable and the loss of some would wreak havoc for the entire planet. The Earth is a complex system of increasingly smaller systems, which means that neglect of the small things is a recipe for disaster.

# References and Notes

1. Executive Order 13112. February 8, *Fed Regist* 1999;**64**(25):6183–6.
2. National Invasive Species Information Center, U.S. Department of Agriculture. *Manager's tool kit*. http://www.invasivespeciesinfo.gov/toolkit/vectors.shtml; 2012 [accessed February 22, 2012].

3. IUCN/SSC Invasive Species Specialist Group. 100 of the world's worst invasive alien species http://www.issg.org/worst100_species.html [accessed February 22, 2012].

4. Environment Canada and US Environmental Protection Agency. *Lake Erie Lakewide Management Plan.* Chicago, IL; 2004.

5. U.S. Environmental Protection Agency. *Wetlands—status and trends.* http://water.epa.gov/type/wetlands/vital_status.cfm; 2012 [accessed March 9, 2012].

6. U.S. Environmental Protection Agency. *Wetland bioassessments in the Florida Everglades.* http://water.epa.gov/type/wetlands/assessment/fl2.cfm; 2012 [accessed March 9, 2012].

7. U.S. Geological Survey. *USGS and the Everglades ecosystems.* http://fl.biology.usgs.gov/Center_Publications/Fact_Sheets/everglades.pdf; 2012 [accessed March 9, 2012].

8. Florida Museum of Natural History. *Everglades: introduced species.* http://www.flmnh.ufl.edu/fish/southflorida/everglades/exoticglades.html#plant; 2012 [accessed March 9, 2012].

9. Lindsey R. *Tropical deforestation.* National Aeronautics and Space Administration: Earth Observatory; March 30, 2007.

10. National Aeronautics and Space Administration. *Earth Observatory Tropical deforestation.* http://earthobservatory.nasa.gov/Features/Deforestation; 1999 [accessed March 10, 2012].

11. Future of corals is going down. *New Scientist* 2002.

12. National Oceanic and Atmospheric Administration. *National Coral Reef Action Strategy: report to Congress on implementation of the Coral Reef Conservation Act of 2000 and the National Action Plan to conserve coral reefs*: 2002.

13. Munns Jr. WR, Kroes R, Veith G, Suter II GW, et al. Approaches for integrated risk assessment. *Hum Ecol Risk Assess* 2003;**9**(1):267–73.

14. Golubic S, Radtke G, Le Campion-Alsumard T. Endolithic fungi in marine ecosystems. *Trends Microbiol* 2005;**13**:229–35.

15. The sources for the Iron Gates discussion are: Global Environmental Facility. *Project brief/Danube regional project—phase 1: ANNEX 11 causes and effects of eutrophication in the Black Sea.* http://www.gefweb.org/Documents/Council_Documents/GEF_C17/Regional_Danube_Annex_II_Part_2.pdf; 2005 [accessed April 27, 2005] and Lancelot C, Staneva J, Van Eeckhout D, Beckers JM, Stanev E. Modelling the Danube-influenced north-western continental shelf of the Black Sea. II: ecosystem response to changes in nutrient delivery by the Danube river after its damming in 1972. *Estuar Coast Shelf Sci* 2002;**54**:473-499.

16. European Environmental Agency. *Europe's biodiversity—biogeographical regions and seas: seas around Europe: the Black Sea—an oxygen-poor sea.* http://www.pedz.uni-mannheim.de/daten/edz-bn/eua/02/C__DOKUME~1_ZEFZEI_LOKALE~1_TEMP_plugtmp_BlackSea.pdf; 2002 [accessed March 10, 2012].

17. NOAA Coastal Services Center. *National Oceanic and Atmospheric Administration. Ballast water: Michigan takes on the law. Coastal Services July/August 2007.* http://www.csc.noaa.gov/magazine/2007/04/article2.html; 2007 [accessed March 10, 2012].

18. NOAA Coastal Services Center, 2007.

19. Smithsonian Institute. *5 Invasive species you should know.* http://ocean.si.edu/ocean-news/5-invasive-species-you-should-know; 2012 [accessed March 10, 2012].

20. Javidpour J, Molinero JC, Lehmann A, Hansen T, Sommer U. Annual assessment of the predation of *Mnemiopsis leidyi* in a new invaded environment, the Kiel Fjord (Western Baltic Sea): a matter of concern? *J Plankton Res* 2009;**31**(7):729–38.

21. Jaspers C, Møller LF, Kiørboe T. Salinity gradient of the Baltic Sea limits the reproduction and population expansion of the newly invaded comb jelly *Mnemiopsis leidyi. PLoS One* 2011;**6**(8):e24065. http://dx.doi.org/10.1371/journal.pone.0024065.

22. Garnier M, Jagoueix-Eveillard S, Cronje PR, LeRoux GF, Bové JM. Genomic characterization of a Liberibacter present in an ornamental rutaceous tree, *Calodendrum* capense, in the Western Cape Province of South Africa. Proposal of 'Candidatus Liberibacter africanus subsp. capensis'. *Int J Syst Evol Microbiol* 2000;**50**:2119–25.

23. Aubert B. Prospects for citriculture in Southeast Asia by the year 2000. *FAO Plant Prot Bull* 1990;**38**:151–73.

24. da Graça JV. Citrus greening disease. *Annu Rev Phytopathol* 1991;**29**:109–39.

25. The Miami Herald. *Spinach could be weapon against citrus scourge.* March 30 http://www.miamiherald.com/2012/03/30/2723053/spinach-could-be-weapon-against.html; 2012 [accessed April 2, 2012].

26. Halbert SE, Manjunath KL. Asian citrus psyllids (Sternorrhyncha: Psyllidae) and greening disease of citrus: a literature review and assessment of risk in Florida. *Fla Entomol* 2004;**87**:330–53.

27. National Academy of Sciences. *Strategic planning for the Florida citrus industry: addressing citrus greening.* Washington, DC: The National Academies Press; 2010.

28. Smith M. *Institute for Responsible Technology. Genetically engineered food may cause rising food allergies Organic Consumers Association.*. http://www.organicconsumers.org/articles/article_5296.cfm; 2007 [accessed August 31, 2009].

29. Leopold A. A sand county almanac: and sketches here and there ISBN:0-19-500777-8. In: Oxford, UK: Oxford University Press; 1949. p. 262.

30. Auer CA. Ecological risk assessment and regulation for genetically-modified ornamental plants. *Crit Rev Plant Sci* 2008;**27**:255–71.

31. Evenson RE, Santaniello V, editors. *The regulation of agricultural biotechnology.* Oxfordshire, UK: CABI, Wallingford; 2004.

32. US Environmental Protection Agency. *Regulating biopesticides.* http://www.epa.gov/pesticides/biopesticides/index.htm; 2009 [accessed July 20, 2009].

33. Isenring R. *Pesticides and the loss of biodiversity: how intensive pesticide use affects wildlife populations and species diversity.* http://www.pan-europe.info/Resources/Briefings/Pesticides_and_the_loss_of_biodiversity.pdf; 2010 [accessed March 9, 2012].

34. Boatman ND, Parry HR, Bishop JD, Cuthbertson AGS. Impacts of agricultural change on farmland biodiversity in the UK. In: Hester RE, Harrison RM, editors. *Biodiversity under threat.* Cambridge, UK: RSC Publishing; 2007.

35. Intergovernmental Panel on Climate Change. Contribution of working group II to the fourth assessment report of the intergovernmental panel on climate change. In: Parry ML, Canziani OF, Palutikof JP, van der Linden PJ, Hanson CE, editors. *Climate change 2007: impacts, adaptation, and vulnerability.* Cambridge, UK: Cambridge University Press; 2007. p. 103.

36. Palmer D. *Honey bees may be threatened by Africanized bees. Impacts Magazine.* Spring 2006: Clemson Public Service Activities; 2007.

37. Benjamin A. A. Fears for crops as shock figures from America show scale of bee catastrophe: the world may be on the brink of biological disaster after news that a third of US bee colonies did not survive the winter. *The Guardian/The Observer Sunday, May 2,* 2010.

38. Sodhi NS, Bickford D, Diesmos AC, Lee TM, Koh LP, Brook BW, et al. Measuring the meltdown: drivers of global amphibian extinction and decline. *PLoS One* 2008;**3**:e1636.

39. *Environ Health Perspect* 1997;**105**(10).

40. Losey OJ, Rainier L, Carter M. Transgenic pollen harms monarch larvae. *Nature* 1999;**399**:214.

41. Kamath R, Rentz JA, Schnoor JL, Alvarez PJJ. Phytoremediation of hydrocarbon-contaminated soils: principles and applications. *Stud Surf Sci Catal* 2004;**151**:447–78.

42. Yoon JM, Oh BT, Just CL, Schnoor JL. Uptake and leaching of octahydro-1,3,5,7-tetranitro-1,3,5,7-tetrazocine by hybrid poplar trees. *Environ Sci Technol* 2002;**36**(21):4649.

43. Hilborn RC. *Chaos and nonlinear dynamics.* Oxford, UK: Oxford University Press; 1994.

44. Hadamard J. *Lectures on the Cauchy problem in linear partial differential equations.* New Haven, CT: Yale University Press; 1923.

# CHAPTER

# 14

# Products

It may not be the first thing that comes to mind when we think about environmental disasters, but what people do in their daily lives largely determines risk. That is to say, the marketplace can play a large role in human health risks ecological problems. Consumer products are regulated as food, cosmetics, and other items that are used intentionally. However, their use and misuse can be very important contributors to public health and the environment. The most obvious products that can cause harm are the pesticides, which are designed to kill things. Other chemical ingredients, however, are also considered in this chapter as to their role in environmental damage.

## PRECAUTION

Product protection approaches vary significantly among nations. For example, the United States applies a *product-oriented approach,* whereas Europe generally employs a *process-oriented approach.*

A product-oriented approach is concerned with the benefits and risks of a particular product. That is, regulators are concerned with making sure that the products meet the criteria for risk and safety, not necessarily how the products are produced. The environmental objective is to produce products that are less harmful. From a green engineering perspective, a product-oriented approach is based on the assumption that the product will be produced, so the bioengineer needs to find ways to make it more sustainable. At this point, all phases of the product's life cycle are optimized, based on systematic thinking. Factors that go into such thinking include environmental and health risks associated with every material in the life cycle. It also considers the services involved in the process rather than the apparatus to generate the product.[1] For example, a sustainable process to generate a solvent would not start with the design of a reactor or other equipment, but how best to produce a good solvent in a sustainable manner (e.g., it may not need a traditional reactor but may be produced using modular components of other nearby plants to cogenerate the solvent or even avoid using organic solvents altogether by using steam from a nearby power plant).

A process-oriented approach to environmental protection considers how products come to market, analyzing the input/output and material flow, ecological and economic factors, and risks. This information helps to identify technical and organizational options to improve a process, including considerations on how to reduce the number of processes needed to bring a product to market. This includes a review of the internal cycles for auxiliary materials and how production wastes are introduced, hazardous substances are replaced and can be used more efficiently and safely, and how to introduce and apply innovative technologies.[2] Of course, biotechnologies comprise an important group of such innovations.

The differences in policies based on these two approaches can have profound impacts on international trade. In fact, the United States, Canada, and Argentina filed a complaint with the World Trade Organization (WTO) that mandates to apply the process-oriented, precautionary principles to genetically modified organisms that constituted a threat to free trade. The precautionary approach relies on anticipatory outcomes of risks in the absence of sufficient evidence, when such risks are deemed to be serious and unreasonable. The distinction between risk and prevention in products has been summarized recently[2]:

> European officials claim that, in the absence of scientific proof of risk, nobody should assume the absence of risk. Therefore, officials should undertake proportionate measures to remove or reduce threats of serious harm. Not knowing what the long-term detriments are of GM seeds/food, the EU position is that we must assume that the product is not safe unless otherwise proven. US trade negotiators believe that this attitude prevents the unwarranted entrance of GMOs into the EU market. To them, this type of reasoning must conceal ulterior motivations. In the US, after all, hardly a debate has occurred on GMO. Yet Americans are very health conscious and are equally obsessed about "risks."

In 2006, a panel of the WTO ruled that the European Union had invoked a *de facto* moratorium on genetically modified food products between June 1999 and August 2003 that led to "undue delay" that violated the WTO Agreement on the Application of Sanitary and Phytosanitary Measures. The panel also struck down some individual nations' bans that were not considered to be based on evidence-based risk assessments. The panel's ruling was quite narrow. So, for example, it has not resolved the differences between the European Union and U.S. perspectives on the safety of genetically modified food trade. Indeed, the panel did not address the safety of genetically modified organisms, nor did it rule on the legality of the precautionary principle, i.e., that a product that could cause substantial and irreversible damage can be banned or severely limited in use, even if the supporting data do not meet traditional risk thresholds.[3]

Certainly, disasters can be prevented by precaution and prospective risk assessment. This involves a balance between what society needs and the risks introduced in supplying that need. This is seldom a single solution. That is, all may agree on the need, but the means of providing the needed benefit can vary. Choosing the right option may well be the difference between success and disaster.

## ENDOCRINE DISRUPTORS AND HORMONALLY ACTIVE AGENTS

The endocrine system is the chemical messaging scheme in organisms used for regulation by secretion of hormones by glands that are sent through the circulatory system to cells where the hormones bind to receptors. Any substance that interferes with the messaging system is considered an endocrine disruptor or an endocrine-disrupting compounds (EDCs). Anthropogenic EDCs include pesticide residues (e.g., DDT, endosulfan, and methoxychlor),

Polychlorobiphenyls (PCBs), dioxin, alkylphenols (e.g., nonylphenol), plastic additives (e.g., bisphenol A (BPA), diethyl phthalate), PAHs, and pharmaceutical hormones (e.g., 17β-estradiol, ethinylestradiol).

Throughout the 1980s, exposure to DDT was associated with abnormal sexual differentiation in seagulls, eggshell thinning and cracking of bald eagle eggs,[4] and a sharp decrease in the numbers of male alligators in Lake Apopka (see Chapter 11) with feminization and loss of fertility found in the remaining males.[5] Since then, other pesticides and chemicals have been associated with endocrine-related abnormalities in wildlife, including the inducement of feminine traits, such as secretion of the egg-laying hormone, vitellogenin, in males of numerous aquatic species downstream for treatment.[6] Birds and terrestrial animals are also affected by EDCs. Recently, these problems have found their way to humans who have been exposed to halogenated compounds and pesticides.[7] A recent nationwide survey of pharmaceuticals in U.S. surface water found EDCs at ng $L^{-1}$ levels in 139 stream sites throughout the United States. Several of these EDCs were found at even μg $L^{-1}$ levels, including nonylphenol (40 μg $L^{-1}$), BPA (12 μg $L^{-1}$), and ethinylestradiol (0.831 μg $L^{-1}$).[8] Many of these compounds are extremely persistent in the environment, so their removal before entering environmental media is paramount to reducing exposures.

The search for the specific chemical structure moiety responsible for inducing the estrogenic response is a key area of endocrine disruption researchers. Phenolic rings appear to be a major chemical structure involved in the estrogenicity of EDC.[9] Figure 14.1 shows how several known EDCs compare structurally with estrogen, the hormone they are thought to mimic. The problem with such structural activity relationships is that they are not always intuitively obvious. A single molecule may have parts that appear to have estrogenic modes of actions and androgenic modes of action.

Biological assays are developed and tested for their ability to predict the likelihood of endocrine disruption by various compounds. These assays work in various ways, but all have the common goal of identifying compounds that will cause responses similar to estrogen in various organisms. Some of these bioassays include the yeast estrogen screen (YES), human

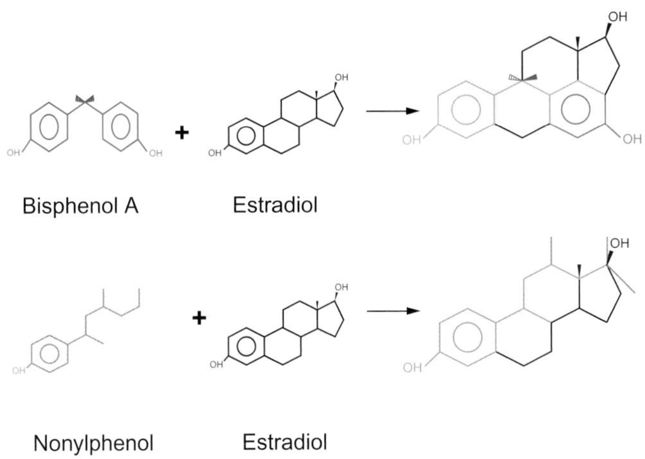

FIGURE 14.1 Comparison of the structure of bisphenol A and nonylphenol with estradiol, showing their overlap in the combined structures.

Bisphenol A          Estradiol

Nonylphenol          Estradiol

cell reporter gene construct (ER-CALUX), MCF-7 cell proliferation (E-Screen), vitellogenin induction in fish, and developmental studies of fish with specific endpoints.

The YES assay, for example, is based on yeast cells modified to harbor the human estrogen receptor. When activated, this receptor binds to the estrogen response element of some plasmid DNA that is engineered to produce S-galactosidase. When estrogens are present, S-galactosidase is excreted by the cells into the culture medium where it reacts and liberates a red dye. The resulting color change is measured with a spectrophotometer, and the responses have been calibrated based on the response of actual estrogen. This method has been widely used to determine the "estrogenicity" (in terms of ability to bind with the estrogen receptor and produce a response) of many compounds as well as mixtures of compounds, of known and unknown composition. Table 14.1 displays the relative binding affinity for several suspected EDCs as compared with estrogen (17β-estradiol).

Examining the properties of suspected EDCs can help to predict the environmental threat from a chemical, hopefully before it is widely used. Table 14.2 provides some physical properties and major uses of three EDCs of particular concern to human health, BPA, 17β-estradiol (E2), and 17β-ethinylestradiol (EE2). These three compounds are xeno-estrogens, natural, or synthetic compounds that act to mimic the effect of estrogens.

Recall from Chapter 11 that the low vapor pressures may mean that these chemical substances would not be likely to be found in high concentrations in the atmosphere unless they

TABLE 14.1   Relative Binding Affinity Compared to Estrogen (YES assay)

| Test compound | Relative estrogenic potency |
|---|---|
| 17β-estradiol (E2) | 1.0 |
| 17β-ethinylestradiol (EE2) | 0.7 |
| Diethylstilbestrol (DES) | 1.1 |
| Nonylphenol (NP) | $7.2 \times 10^{-7}$ |
| Bisphenol A (BPA) | $6.2 \times 10^{-5}$ |

Source: Data from Silva E, Rajapakse N, Kortenkamp A. Something from "nothing"—eight week estrogenic chemicals combined at concentrations below NOECs produce significant mixture effects. Environ Sci Technol 2002;36(8):1751-56; Folmar L, et al. A comparison of the estrogenic potencies of estradiol, ethinylestradiol, diethylstilbestrol, nonylphenol, and methoxychlor in vivo and in vitro. Aquat Toxicol 2002;60: 101-10.

TABLE 14.2   Physical Data for and Major Products Containing BPA, EE2, and E2

| Compound | Melting point (°C) | Vapor pressure (mmHg) | Solubility (mg/L) | Log $K_{ow}$ | Uses |
|---|---|---|---|---|---|
| BPA | 153 | $4 \times 10^{-8}$ | 129 (25 °C) | 3.32 | Plasticizer (adhesives, paints, CDs, baby bottles) |
| EE2 | 183 | NA | 11.3 (27 °C) | 3.67 | Synthetic estrogen (birth control pills) |
| E2 | 178.5 | NA | 3.6 (27 °C) | 4.01 | Natural estrogen |

Source: Physical data from Chemfinder.com.

are sorbed to particles. Similarly, due to their hydrophobic nature (high $K_{ow}$ values), they will more readily associate with organic solvents or particles within a liquid water phase. However, all of these compounds have been found in the environment in the aqueous phase. Furthermore, increasing the water's pH values will increase these water concentrations, especially for BPA. Also, due to the hormonal nature of these compounds, their effects can be felt at extremely low concentrations (of the order of ng $L^{-1}$).

To illustrate, assume that a chemical plant that produces polycarbonate has just spilled 1 ton (907 kg) of BPA into a wastewater stream with an effluent of 1 million gallons per day (3.785 ML $d^{-1}$) that discharges into a major U.S. river. The plant has the capability to feed 10 mg/L of powdered activated carbon (PAC) into the wastewater stream and can hold its wastewater for 4 h of contact time. To remove this PAC and other solids, the plant also can filter solid particles to 1 μm from their wastewater in an emergency. If the spill is evenly dispersed throughout 1 day and equilibrium conditions are achieved in the water stream, what is the final concentration of the water being discharged from the plant into the river? Also, according to the YES assay, how "estrogenic" is the wastewater stream due to the BPA? This can be accomplished in three steps, based on the physical and chemical characteristics given:

1. Find the concentration of BPA in the waste stream before any treatment.
   If 1 ton (907 kg) of solid BPA is spilled into 1 million gallons (3.785 ML) (assuming even dispersion through the waste stream for 1 day), upon unit conversion, a concentration of 239 mg $L^{-1}$ would be achieved if all BPA dissolved in water. However, Table 14.2 indicates that the solubility of BPA in water is only 129 mg $L^{-1}$. This then would be the maximum concentration of BPA in water at 25 °C. The rest of the BPA remains as solid particles in the water (assumed to be greater than 1 μm in diameter because of the emergency filtering).
2. Determine the concentration after PAC addition and filtration.
   For the conditions given (10 mg $L^{-1}$ PAC with a contact time of 4 h removing BPA), approximately 4% of the original concentration of BPA remains in solution. Also, the filtration step will remove all PAC, plus any undissolved BPA, implying that the final concentration in the wastewater stream will be approximately 5.16 mg $L^{-1}$.
3. Calculate the estrogenicity of the effluent in the stream.
   According to the YES data given in Table 14.1, BPA has a relative potency of $6.2 \times 10^{-5}$ in comparison to estrogen (i.e., it is 0.000062 as estrogenic as estradiol). This means the concentration of 5.16 mg $L^{-1}$ would give an estrogenic response of 0.32 μg $L^{-1}$ for 17β-estradiol. This is equivalent to an estrogen concentration capable of inducing estrogenic responses in all of the bioassays.

Note that the wastewater will be substantially diluted when it enters the river. However, in natural riverine systems, effluent released in a larger water body will not disperse completely. That is, there would be pockets of very high concentrations of the contaminant. If the high-concentration area is used by aquatic fauna for feeding and breeding, the ecological insult would be much higher than that indicated by this calculated estrogenicity. In fact, this was a conclusion supported by a U.S. Geological Survey study examining wastewater discharge from Las Vegas, Nevada municipal treatment plant into Lake Meade. The investigators used a vitellogenin bioassay to show elevated levels of EDCs greatly affecting male carp, fish that prefer sheltering near large underwater objects, including wastewater effluent outfall structures.[10]

Vitellogenin is an egg-laying hormone. One of the most troubling aspects of the vitellogenin is that it has been found in male fish downstream for estrogenic effluent releases, including those from municipal wastewater treatment facilities. Some of this induced estrogen agonism is likely attributable to conjugated estrogen in pharmaceuticals, especially contraceptives, that have passed through the treatment processes.[11] This is among a number of problems associated with pharmaceuticals, including antibiotics passing through municipal sewers and released from confined animal feeding operations (this is discussed later in this chapter).

## Screening to Prevent Hormonal Disasters

Acknowledging the wide-ranging environmental impact of EDCs, the 1996 Food Quality Protection Act and the 1996 amendment to the Safe Drinking Water Act directed the EPA to test approximately 87,000 compounds and formulations for their estrogen-modulating capacity (subsequently expanded to include modulators of androgens and thyroid hormones). The Endocrine Disruptor Screening and Testing Advisory Committee adopted a tiered approach that includes a prioritization stage to consider such aspects as potency and likelihood of exposure.[12] Initial sorting involved an evaluation of existing data to classify chemicals into one of four categories: (1) chemicals (primarily polymers) that have sufficient data indicating that they are not likely to interact with the estrogen, androgen, and thyroid systems and therefore require no further analysis; (2) chemicals that have insufficient data and therefore require Tier 1 screening for hormonal activity; (3) chemicals that have sufficient evidence of hormonal interaction and therefore require Tier 2 testing; and (4) chemicals that have sufficient evidence of hormonal interaction and hormone-related effects and therefore require hazard assessment.

The Endocrine Disruptor Screening Program focuses on methods and procedures to detect and characterize the endocrine activity of pesticides and EDCs (see Figure 14.2). The U.S. EPA uses biological assays in a two-tiered screening and testing process. Tier 1 identifies chemicals with the potential to interact with the endocrine system. Tier 2 characterizes the endocrine-related effects caused by each chemical and obtains information about effects at various doses.

The scientific data needed for the estimated 87,000 chemicals in commerce do not exist to conduct adequate assessments of potential risks. The screening program is being used by EPA to collect this information for endocrine disruptors and to decide appropriate regulatory action by first assigning each chemical to an endocrine disruption category:

Chemicals will undergo sorting into four categories according to the available existing, scientifically relevant information:

- Category 1 chemicals have sufficient, scientifically relevant information to determine that they are not likely to interact with the estrogen, androgen, or thyroid systems. This category includes some polymers and certain exempted chemicals.
- Category 2 chemicals have insufficient information to determine whether they are likely to interact with the estrogen, androgen, or thyroid systems, thus will need screening data.
- Category 3 chemicals have sufficient screening data to indicate endocrine activity, but data to characterize actual effects are inadequate and will need testing.
- Category 4 chemicals already have sufficient data for the EPA to perform a hazard assessment.

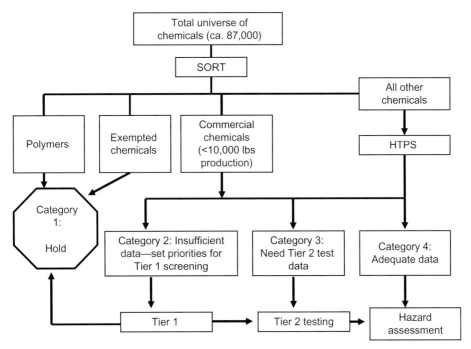

FIGURE 14.2   Endocrine Disruptor Screening Program of the U.S. Environmental Protection Agency. *Note*: HTPS = high-throughput prescreening.

TSCA gives the EPA the authority to track tens of thousands of industrial chemicals currently produced or imported into the United States. This is accomplished through screening of the chemicals and requiring that reporting and testing be done for any substance that presents a hazard to human health or the environment. If a chemical poses a potential or actual risk that is unreasonable, the EPA may ban the manufacture and import of that chemical.

The EPA tracks thousands of new chemicals being developed by industries each year for either unknown or dangerous characteristics. This information is used to determine the type of control that would be needed to protect human health and the environment from these chemicals. Manufacturers and importers of chemical substances first submit information about chemical substances already on the market during an initial inventory. Since the initial inventory was published, commercial manufacturers or importers of substances not on the inventory have been subsequently required to submit notices to the EPA, which has developed guide lines about how to identify chemical substances to assign a unique and unambiguous description of each substance for the inventory. The categories include

- Polymeric substances;
- Certain chemical substances containing varying carbon chain;
- Products containing two or more substances, formulated and statutory mixtures; and
- Chemical substances of unknown or variable composition, complex reaction products, and biological materials (UVCB substance).

Many chemicals can disrupt the endocrine systems of animals in laboratory studies, and there is strong evidence that chemical exposure has been associated with adverse developmental and reproductive effects on fish and wildlife in particular locations.

An example of the possible threat to human physiological development from EDCs is diethylstilbestrol (DES), a synthetic estrogen. Before it was banned in early 1970s, physicians prescribed DES to as many as 5 million pregnant women to block spontaneous abortion and promote fetal growth. The chemical was later found to have transgenerational effects. That is, the children of the treated women had developmental disorders following puberty, including harm to the reproductive system and vaginal cancer.

## ANTIBIOTICS: SUPERBUGS AND CROSS-RESISTANCE

As mentioned in the previous section, an emerging concern, particularly about human and animal pharmaceuticals, is their pass-through into the environment. For example, drugs used in combined animal feeding operations (CAFOs) have been found in waters downstream, even after treatment. This is problematic in at least two ways. First, the drugs and their metabolites (after passing through the animals) may themselves be hormonally active or may suppress immune systems. Second, antibiotics are being introduced to animals in large quantities, giving the targeted pathogens an opportunity to develop resistance and rendering less effective.

Even more troubling is the phenomenon of *cross-resistance*. For example, the U.S. Food and Drug Administration recently proposed withdrawing the approval of enrofloxacin, in the treatment of poultry in CAFOs. Enrofloxacin is one of the antibacterials known as fluoroquinolones, which have been used to treat humans since 1986.[13] Fluoroquinolone drugs keep chickens and turkeys from dying from *Escherichia coli* infection, usually contracted from the animals' own droppings. The pharmaceutical may be an effective prophylactic treatment for *E. coli*, but another genus, *Campylobacter*, appears to be able to build a resistance (see Figure 14.3). Human consumption of poultry products contaminated with fluoroquinolone-resistant *Campylobacter* substantially elevates the risk of infection by a strain of *Campylobacter* and difficult to treat, due to the superbugs' new resistance. This means that an entire class of reliable fluoroquinolone drugs is at risk of losing their efficaciousness, as the cross-resistance can carry over to drugs with similar structures.

Antibiotic resistance results from recombinatorial events, i.e., genetic exchanges among organisms inside populations and communities. The so-called genetic reactors in which antibiotic resistance evolves are shown in Figure 14.4. The level 1 reactor consists of the human and animal microbial populations (>500 species) in which the microbes exert their actions (intentional pharmaceutical actions). The level 2 reactor includes the dense nodes of microbial exposures and exchange, i.e., the aggregation of susceptible subpopulations in hospitals, long-term care facilities, feeding, farming operations, etc. The level 3 reactor consists of the wastes and biological residues, e.g., lagoons, wastewater treatment plants, compost piles, septic tanks, etc., wherein microbes from many different individuals can assimilate and exchange genetic material. The level 4 reactor includes the various environmental media (soil, surface, or groundwater environments) in which the microbes from the levels 1 through 3 reactors mix and counteract with organisms in the environment.[14]

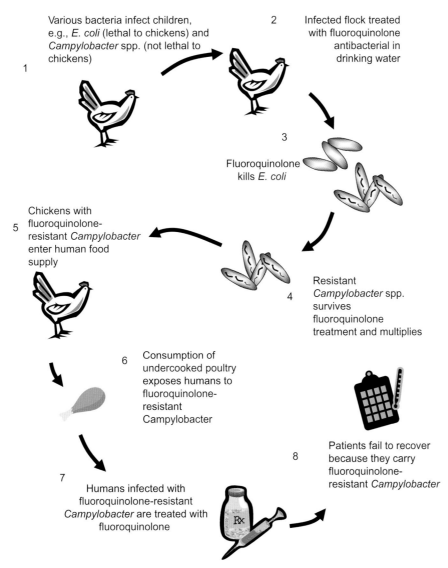

1  Various bacteria infect children,
   e.g., *E. coli* (lethal to chickens) and
   *Campylobacter* spp. (not lethal to
   chickens)

2  Infected flock treated
   with fluoroquinolone
   antibacterial in
   drinking water

3  Fluoroquinolone
   kills *E. coli*

4  Resistant
   *Campylobacter* spp.
   survives
   fluoroquinolone
   treatment and multiplies

5  Chickens with
   fluoroquinolone-
   resistant *Campylobacter*
   enter human food
   supply

6  Consumption of
   undercooked poultry
   exposes humans to
   fluoroquinolone-
   resistant
   Campylobacter

7  Humans infected with
   fluoroquinolone-resistant
   *Campylobacter* are treated with
   fluoroquinolone

8  Patients fail to recover
   because they carry
   fluoroquinolone-
   resistant *Campylobacter*

FIGURE 14.3   Likely cross-resistance process, i.e., how *Campylobacter* become resistant to fluoroquinolone drugs. *Source: Vallero DA. Environmental biotechnology: a biosystems approach. Burlington, MA: Elsevier Academic Press; 2009; adapted from US Food and Drug Administration, Bren L. Antibiotic resistance from down on the farm. FDA Veterinarian 2001;16(1):2-4. Graphic by R. Gordon.*

Carry over and cross-resistance have been observed in numerous classes of drugs, including synthetic penicillin. Exacerbating the problem, the use of drugs is not limited to treating diseases. In fact, large quantities of antibiotics have been used as growth promoters in CAFOs, so the probability of cross-resistance is further increased.

Computational and green chemistry approaches can "tweak" molecules to see what impacts might result down the road. In some cases, the molecule is never actually synthesized

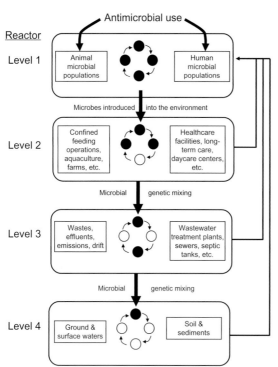

Reactor

Level 1

Level 2

Level 3

Level 4

FIGURE 14.4 Systems within environmental regimes that lead to antibiotic resistance. In the lower
level reactors (1 and 2), human and animal microbial
populations (filled circles) mix with environmental microbial populations (clear circles), which increases genetic variation, allowing new resistance mechanism
in the microbial populations, whereupon these new
strains, with the potential for greater resistance, are
reintroduced to the human and animal environments
(feedback arrows). Therefore, even if the human populations have not yet used an antibiotic, if a similar form
is used in animals, the genetic adaptations may allow
for resistant strains of bacteria to find their way into
human populations, rendering a new antibiotic less efficacious. *Source: Vallero DA. Environmental biotechnology: a biosystems approach. Burlington, MA: Elsevier
Academic Press; 2009; adapted from Baquero F, Martínez JL,
Cantón R. Antibiotics and antibiotic resistance in water
environments.* Biotechnology 2008;19:260-5.

but is a virtual molecule that can be run through various biochemodynamic scenarios as a first
screen on possible hazards. These tools can also help with predicting hazards, exposures,
and risks to humans and other organisms by improving the synthetic chemistry, e.g.,
preventing the formulation of chiral and enantiomer compounds that are resistant to natural
biodegradation (e.g., left-hand chirals may be much more easily broken down than right-
hand chirals of the same compound; also, one chiral may be toxic and the other efficacious).
This may also apply to genetically modified organisms. For example, subtle changes to a
microbe's DNA can foster unexpected changes in ecosystem competition, which might be
predicted using proteomics and other computational tools.

# ORGANOPHOSPHATES

It is not really all that surprising to many that a substance that came into existence as nerve
gases used in war would now be banned for most societal uses. Organophosphates (OPs)
have been used as insecticides since the 1930s but really took off in the 1960s when they were
developed to replace DDT and other organochlorine insecticides. Some are very easy and
cheap to make, which must have been an incentive to develop and use them back in the

1960s. They have become the most commonly used pesticides and are responsible for 70% of pesticidal use in the United States.[15,16]

OP insecticides have been responsible for keeping agricultural productivity high all over the world. They have even been used to control mosquitoes in the United States. In the United Kingdom, they are particularly important in sheep dipping. They have been used in head lice treatments, pet shampoos, and other household products and have been used in many medical trials and experiments investigating cures for dementia and Parkinson's disease.

Over 25,000 brands of pesticides are available in the United States, and their use is monitored by the EPA.

OP compounds are toxic to humans and are responsible for a large number of poisoning. These insecticides are used in thousands of licensed pesticides today.

## Chemistry

Most of the OP insecticides have the general formula:

$$(RR'X)P = O \qquad\qquad 14.1$$

where R and R' are short-chain groups, and X is a group that is readily removed from the molecule after reaction in the body. This is a great advantage from the toxicological point of view. The persistent OPs are mainly thiophosphates with the oxygen replaced by a sulfur atom:

$$(RR'X)P = S \qquad\qquad 14.2$$

OPs form a very large group of compounds with a very wide range of insecticidal and herbicidal activity, persistence, and action. Many are extremely toxic, and compounds such as tabun $\{[(CH_3)_2N](CN)P(O)OC_2H_5\}$ and sarin $\{[(CH_3)_2CHO](CH3)P(O)F\}$, both nerve poisons, have been banned by the Chemical Weapons Convention of 1993. Other OPs include dichlorvos $\{(CH_3O)_2P(O)OC_2HCl_2\}$, malathion $\{(CH_3O)_2P(S)SCH(C_3H_5O_2)(C_4H_7O_2)\}$,[13] parathion, methyl parathion, chlorpyrifos, diazinon, disulfoton, azinphos-methyl, fonofos, diazinondichlorvos, phosmet, fenitrothion, dimethoate, tetraethylpyrophosphate, and tetrachlorvinphos. Many have now been banned or their use restricted. Compounds such as simazine and atrazine, diuron, isoproturon, diazinon, and chlorpyrifos have been phased out largely as a result of them being considered as special risk substances for children.[17]

Malathion is not quite as toxic as some other OPs (oral $LD_{50}$ 1400-1900 mg kg$^{-1}$) and is widely used in agriculture, residential landscaping, public recreation areas, and public health pest control programs such as mosquito eradication.[18] In the United States, malathion is the most commonly used OP insecticide. Forty OP pesticides are registered in the United States.[19]

## Poisoning Action

The main mechanism in poisoning involves the blocking of the enzyme acetylcholinesterase causing nervous and respiratory damages that result in the death of insects and illness or death in humans and animals. This mechanism of poisoning is the same for all OPs. In more detail, they act by inhibiting important enzymes of the nervous system which are vital in the transmission of nerve impulses which travel along neurons (nerve cells). When the impulse reaches a synapse (the junction between two neurons) and when it reaches a neuromuscular junction (between a neuron and a muscle), the impulse is transmitted to a neurotransmitter which is a chemical substance, acetylcholine. Once it has acted, the acetylcholine is broken down and inactivated in milliseconds by the enzyme acetylcholinesterase and is then returned to normal by the enzyme, ready for the next impulse. When exposed to OPs, this enzyme cannot function and there is a buildup of acetylcholine. Muscular spasms in involuntary muscles occur first and this is followed by overactivity of glands. In serious cases, respiratory failure and death can occur.[20]

## Health Risk

The toxic effect of OPs can take place by inhalation through the lungs, by contact through the skin or by ingestion on food. People who are most at risk include farmers and their families and other persons who use chemical pesticides regularly. The danger is spread out to larger areas, as the pesticides are blown by the wind, left as residues on produce or remains within the produce or animals, or are allowed to run off into open water, contaminating public water supply as well as fish and other seafood.

OPs are all highly toxic but some more than others. Minton and Murray[21] have divided OPs into three groups. The first most and toxic group, e.g., chlorfenvinphos [2-chloro-1-(2,4-dichlorophenyl)vinyl diethyl phosphate], has a lethal dose required to kill half the members of a tested population ($LD_{50}$) in the range 1-30 mg kg$^{-1}$. The $LD_{50}$ range for the second group, e.g., dichlorvos, is 30-50 mg kg$^{-1}$, and the least toxic group, e.g., malathion, has a range of 60-1300 mg kg$^{-1}$.[22–24]

OP pesticides degrade rapidly, via cleavage of the X–P bond (see above), as a result of hydrolysis on exposure to sunlight, air, and soil, although small amounts can be detected in food and drinking water. This ability to degrade rapidly made them an attractive alternative to the persistent organochlorine (e.g., DDT, aldrin, and dieldrin) insecticides they replaced. In spite of their rapid degradation in the environment, they are very much more toxic than the organochlorines and do pose a severe risk to farmers and horticulturists who work with these insecticides. OPs have been responsible for a very large number of accidents and fatalities (see later).

It does appear that the scientific understanding of the health effects of OPs and safe exposure levels is limited. This might be a result of their complex chemistry of degradation. Those who are convinced of the dangers continue to campaign for a ban on OP pesticides, putting them into conflict with the agrochemical industry and long-established agricultural practice. Over the years, campaigners have alleged that the expert committees advising governments on pesticide safety have been too close to and dominated by the chemicals industry.

Poisoning symptoms include excessive sweating, salivation and lachrymation, nausea, vomiting, diarrhea, abdominal cramp, general weakness, headache, poor concentration, and tremors. With high doses, respiratory failure and death can occur. Even at relatively low levels, OPs may affect brain development of fetuses and young children. As a result, many OPs have been banned and those that are still being used must be used under strict control and sometimes a permit is required for their use. Some OPs can only be applied to crops by commercially certified aerial applicators and treated crops may not be harvested by hand.

A study in 2010 has found that OP exposure is associated with an increased risk of ADHD in children. Researchers analyzed the levels of OP residues in the urine of more than 1100 children aged 8-15 years old and found that those with the highest urine levels of dialkyl phosphates, which are the breakdown products of OP pesticides, also had the highest incidence of ADHD.[25]

In the Europe and in the UK, the dangers of OP poisoning have mainly been raised in relation to: their use in sheep dips; the Gulf War syndrome; the dangers experienced by farm workers; and the effect on bees.

Because the manufacture of some OPs is cheap and easy, they are often produced in third world countries and often it is the highly toxic compounds that are easier to make and hence produced. Many of these countries do not have the restrictions that are imposed in the first world countries.

There have been investigations into the possibility of OPs being carcinogenic.[26]

## Disasters

It is possible that tabun was used in the 1994 Gulf War. Sarin was the poisonous gas released by a Japanese cult member in the Tokyo subway in 1995. Such OP chemical weapons still pose a very real concern in this age of terrorist activity.

The most common poisoning occurs through inhalation, absorption, and ingestion of food that has been treated with an OP herbicide, and OPs are one of the most common causes of poisoning worldwide. Also, they are frequently used in suicides in agrarian areas. There are around 1 million OP poisonings per year with several hundred thousand resulting in fatalities each year.[27,28]

In the 1930, it was implicated in the toxic oil syndrome disaster in Spain when oil was apparently contaminated with OPs and thousands of people died.[29] Contaminated seed in Paraguay in 1999 was another OP disaster which left many ill and at least one dead.[30]

The evidence for OP poisoning has not always been very clear. This is probably due to lack of experience on the part of the investigating officers. During the 1980s and 1990s, soon after the widespread use of OPs in the UK, hundreds of farm workers began to report symptoms including fatigue, memory loss, weakness, joint and muscle pain, and depression, which they put down to low-level exposure to OPs over long periods of time. The government's position was to deny that there was a clear link, but in 2000 and 2001, it did, however, fund more research into the effects of OP exposure and poisoning. The results of some of these studies provided support for the poisoning hypothesis, but the outbreak of a Foot and Mouth Disease epidemic in 2001 led to the postponement of the completion of Government-funded studies.[31]

In 1998, an outbreak of Mediterranean fruit flies (Medflies) threatened to significantly decrease agricultural yields in Florida. In order to minimize the damage, malathion and diazinon were applied to the areas of concern. Within 5 months of application, 123 people reported symptoms consistent with pesticide exposure, such as respiratory distress, gastrointestinal distress, neurological problems, skin reaction, and eye distress.

There is a great danger in having OP pesticides in the home as they can easily be swallowed by little children. In the United States, 4% of patients admitted to poison control centers report pesticide exposure and of those patients, 34% are children younger than 6 years.[32,33]

## SCIENTIFIC PRINCIPLES AT WORK

The cases in this chapter illustrate that the inherent properties of a chemical ingredient in a product which determines both its toxicity and its persistence after it is released. Thus, the molecular form of compounds is important in disaster prevention and response. This is known as stereochemistry.

### Conformational Isomers

Organic chemicals are three-dimensional structures. The simplest molecule is methane, $CH_4$. It is composed of a carbon atom with four identical hydrogen atoms. To visualize it, consider the C atom in the center of a tetrahedron and the H atoms at the four corners of the tetrahedron (see Figure 14.5).

In space, these atoms vibrate along the bond axis and the degree of vibration is dependent on the temperature. At 0 K, the vibration ceases and at very high temperatures (well above 1000 K), the vibrations are so great that the H atoms fly off and the methane is destroyed and converted into C and H atoms.

In a more complex molecule, ethane ($CH_3CH_3$), there is a further motion within the molecule and the C atoms rotate relative to one another, giving rise to different orientations in space of the H atoms. Figure 14.6 shows two forms of ethane—a staggered conformation and an eclipsed conformation. In the staggered form, the H atoms of two C atoms are as far apart from each other as is possible. In the eclipsed form, the H atoms of the two C atoms are directly in line with one another. These forms have also been drawn in Figure 14.6, in the form of Newman projections where the molecule is viewed down the C-C axis. These two

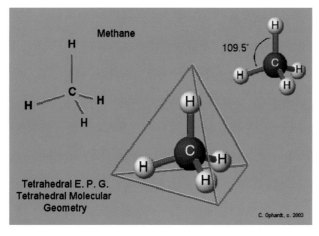

FIGURE 14.5    Carbon at the center of a tetrahedron. *Image Source Page: http://www.elm hurst.edu/~chm/vchembook/204tetrahedral.html; Charles Ophardt, PhD, Professor Emeritus Chemistry, Elmhurst College, Elmurst, IL 60126, USA*

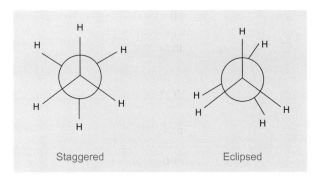

FIGURE 14.6    The staggered and eclipse forms of ethane (Newman projections). *Modified from http://chemistry.tutorvista.com/organic-chemistry/ stereochemistry-of-alkene-compounds.html.*

conformations have different energies, and although there is rotation about the C–C bond, the molecule does spend most of its time in the staggered form.

The word isomer is applied to two or more molecules which have the same chemical formula, but in which the constituent atoms are arranged differently. The conformational forms discussed here are indeed isomers.

Moving onto a more complex molecule, butane ($CH_3CH_2CH_2CH_3$), we see in Figure 14.7 many new conformations when looking at the 3D forms and the Newman projections. Again there is rotation about the C–C bond, but the situation is more complex and there are many

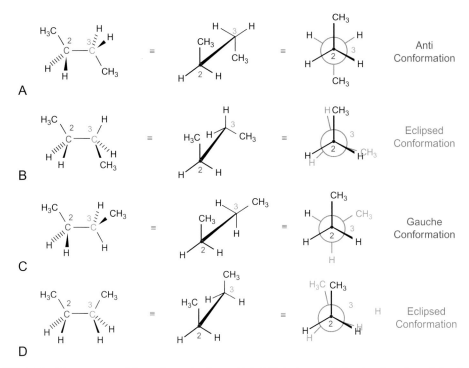

FIGURE 14.7    The many possible conformation forms (A,B,C,D) for butane. *Taken from http://www2.chemistry.msu. edu/faculty/reusch/VirtTxtJml/sterisom.htm.*

possible conformations. This time, at 25 °C, the molecule spends 75% of its time in the anti-staggered or anticonformation form (with the $CH_3$ groups as apart as possible) and 25% of the time in the gauche conformation.

At 0 K, the antistaggered form would be the only form and there would be no motion around the C–C bond and no vibrations of the H atoms. The isomers discussed above are called CONFORMATIONAL isomers and arise only because of rotation about a single bond.

## Configurational Isomers and Chirality

There is another type of stereoisomerism which is also due to the arrangement of the atoms in space. Configurational isomers have the same set of atoms but differ from each other in that they cannot be converted from one to another by rotations about bonds and moreover are mirror images of one another. They cannot be superimposed on one another. An example is 2-chlorobutane as depicted in Figure 14.8. Imagine a mirror between the two molecules A and B.

These two are called enantiomers of each other and have identical physical properties except they rotate plane-polarized light in opposite directions. They are said to be optically active. The concept of not being able to be superimposed can be easily seen by looking at one's hands. Our left and right hands are mirror images of each other and cannot be superimposed (see Figure 14.9). In this figure is a set of chiral molecules.

Looking at the 2-chlorobutane enantiomers in Figure 14.9, one can see that one of the carbon atoms is surrounded by four different groups. This is the clue to the molecule having a mirror image. Such molecules are known as CHIRAL molecules and the atom in the center is

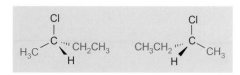

FIGURE 14.8    The two mirror images of 2-chlorobutane. They cannot be superimposed. *Modified from http://mysite.du.edu/_jhornbac/organic2ed/clbutane.html.*

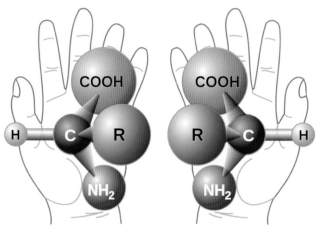

FIGURE    14.9    Nonsuperimposibility. The left hand and right hand cannot be superimposed. The molecules are chiral. *taken from: http://en.wikipedia.org/wiki/chirality.*

the stereocenter. Chirality is particularly important in biological systems and many compounds in living organisms (e.g., proteins) are chiral. To support the idea that our hands are chiral, the word chiral comes from the Greek word for hand which is cheir.

It is often important to distinguish between two enantiomers especially as there is no simple correlation between the sign of rotation of light (+ or −) and the structure. As a result, rules have been drawn up to define the structures. These are the Cahn-Ingold-Prelog rules. In brief and for very simple chiral compounds, a stereocenter is defined as being R (rectus or right) or S (sinister or left) depending on the order in which the groups are arranged around the stereocenter.

Rule 1. Each group at the stereocenter is assigned a priority in order of the atomic number of the atom bonded directly to the stereocenter:
$$Cl > O > N > C > H$$
Rule 2. View the molecule with the group of lowest priority away from the viewer. You are then left with a "steering wheel" of atoms. Trace a path from the highest atomic number group to the next highest and then on to the third group. If the path moves in a clockwise direction, then the stereocenter is assigned an R configuration. If anticlockwise, the assignment is S.

Looking at the two stereoisomers of $CH_3CH(OH)(CHO)$ in Figure 14.10, you can see how the (R)-$CH_3CH(OH)(CHO)$ and (S)-$CH_3CH(OH)(CHO)$ are defined.

It is not only carbon atoms that can be chiral. Any atom that is bonded to other atoms so as to create a possible mirror image molecule can be chiral. For example, the P atom in sarin, the nerve poison, is chiral. One form is the more active enantiomer due to its greater binding to acetylcholinesterase.

Many of the basic molecular building blocks of life are chiral species. For example, serine, the proteinogenic amino acid (2-amino-3-hydroxypropanoic acid), is chiral and only the S form appears naturally in proteins. It is amazing that in life forms there is a unique handedness, and all naturally occurring amino acids are found only in the S form. It is believed that

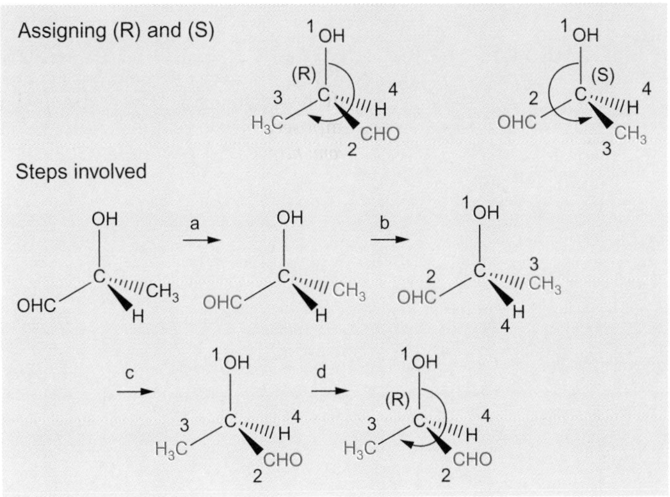

FIGURE 14.10 R and S forms. Look at the molecule and prioritize the groups (step b), then align the molecule so that the smallest group "H" is away from you (step c). You are looking into a steering wheel and the order around the wheel from highest to lowest (1 to 2 to 3) and that in this case is clockwise, i.e., R form. *Modified from http://mcat-review.org/covalent-bond.php.*

this homochirality is a key to the origins of life. Because our basic biochemistry is chirally specific, organisms react differently to different members of a chiral compound. This is true for chiral odor molecules and our noses can differentiate between chiral perfumes.

## Configurational Isomers and Double Bonds

There is another type of configurational isomerism, usually called geometric isomerism, which occurs as a result of double bonds between carbon atoms. Because of the rigidity of double bonds (the carbon atoms making up a double bond cannot rotate as they do in single bonds), the relative positions of groups around the double bond can produce distinctly different molecules with different properties. Consider butene, $C_4H_8$. There are four noncyclic isomers of this compound; two of them are not stereoisomers and the molecules are distinctively different and can be named as such, 1-butene and 2-methylpropene. The other two are difficult to name as there is one methyl group attached to each of the carbon atoms of the double bond. Spatially they are different and their properties are different (e.g., their boiling points). These are defined as *cis*-2-butene and *trans*-2-butene, depending on whether the methyl groups are on the same side of the double bond or on opposite sides of the double bond (see Figure 14.11).

The unsaturated fatty acids found in nature are usually in the *cis* form. These are more asymmetrical than the *trans* form and the molecules will tend to have a pronounced kink or bend in the carbon chain. As a result, the unsaturated fatty acid molecules are unable to pack closely and are mostly liquid at room temperature, while more saturated fats (such as tallow) are straight chained and are usually hard solids.[34]

## Effect of Shape of Molecules

Polychlorinated biphenyls (PCBs) give an excellent example of the effect of molecular shape on toxicity and potential exposures (see Figure 14.12). PCBs are lipophilic (fat soluble) and are notoriously toxic to humans and animal. The parent compound, biphenyl, is made up

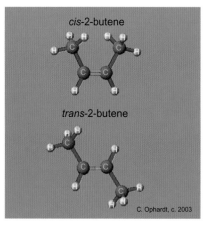

FIGURE 14.11    Carbon at the center of a tetrahedron. *Image Source Page: http://www.elmhurst.edu/~chm/vchembook/204tetrahedral.html; Charles Ophardt, PhD, Professor Emeritus Chemistry, Elmhurst College, Elmurst, IL 60126, USA*

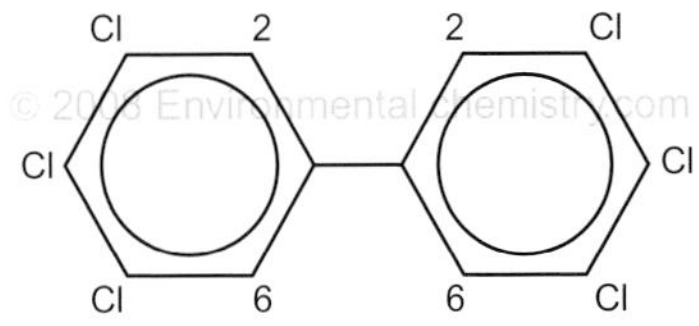

FIGURE 14.12   Polychlorobiphenyl, PCB molecule.

of two flat benzene rings and is flat and planar with the two benzene rings in the same plane. The compounds that make up PCBs involve any chloro-substituted biphenyl molecule with 2-10 chloro groups attached. There are 209 different congeners (separate distinctive molecular types) of PCBs. We shall look at but a few and focus on the simplest of the PCBs, namely, dichlorobiphenyl. The two chloro groups can be in the para-position (position 4 in the benzene rings in Figure 14.12) and would then be furthest away from each other. This molecule, para-dichlorobiphenyl, is planar. So is meta-dichlorobiphenyl (Cl atoms in the 3 or 5 position). But ortho-dichlorobiphenyl with the Cl groups in the 2 or 6 position is not planar because of the steric effects of the Cl groups adjacent to the C–C bond. This results in a partial twist of the C–C bond and the two benzene rings are staggered. It has been reported that the nonplanar ortho-dichlorodiphenyl compound is very much less toxic than the planar dichlorodiphenyls. This example of the planar or flat configuration being more toxic than the nonplanar is also found in the dioxin molecules.[35]

## MILK AND TERRORISM

We have discussed threats to health from indirect contamination, but we would be remiss not to mention intentional contamination. Recently, a study pointed out specific deficiencies in the protection of the milk supply and its vulnerability to widespread contamination by the *botulinum* toxin. The manuscript from the study was submitted to, and ultimately published in, *Proceedings of the National Academy of Sciences*.[36] The U.S. Department of Health and Human Services had strongly opposed the publication on the grounds that it could encourage and instruct would-be bioterrorists.[37] One mediating aspect of this debate is that the authors of the article are not funded by the federal government. Had they received federal assistance, the U.S. government would most likely have had a greater onus and in a stronger position to veto the text.

In fact, the authors and their advocates made two arguments that favored publication. First, the information could be helpful to agricultural and food security decision makers charged with protecting the milk supply (analogous to publishing vulnerabilities with a hope this information will drive homeowners to make the necessary changes to improve home safety). The second argument was that the information had already been made readily available via the Internet and other sources.

Engineering often requires a decision about vulnerabilities. In this instance, the information being shared was indeed readily available and not confidential or secret in any way. However, engineers and scientific investigators are trained "to connect the dots" in ways that many are not, so even if the source information is readily available to anyone interested, we know where to look and how to assimilate the information into new knowledge.

There is an onus on engineers and scientists undertaking endeavors in sensitive subject matter to take care to avoid giving new knowledge to those who intend to use it nefariously. And, engineers must be diligent not to fall victim to our own rationalizations, i.e., that we are doing it for the public good or the advancement of the state of the science, if in fact our real intentions are to improve our own lot (e.g., a gold-standard publication, a happy client, or public recognition). The bottom line is that, when it comes to ingredients in products, very large factors of safety are needed. One cannot assume products will be used safely and as intended. Once the ingredient reaches the marketplace, there likelihood of misuse grows. Also, many negative impacts are uncovered only after the product reaches the user. This means that "average" potential exposure and hazard will not suffice. Something closer to a "worst case" misuse scenario may be needed.

## LESSONS LEARNED

The problems discussed in this chapter involve the commonplace balances that must be found between providing useful products and avoiding public health and ecological disasters. Drugs, food, and other products do not exist in social or environmental vacuums. They must be considered merely parts of larger systems. Single-minded product development and delivery can introduce threats. Providing safe food must include not only the targeted consumer but also the entire system. Producing tons of meat or drugs or other desired commodities is not worth causing health and environmental disasters like ineffective antibiotics and hormonal problems at the population scale.

Scientists and engineers are in a position of trust and must hold paramount the public's safety, health, and welfare. And, as the famous physicist Richard Feynman[38] reminded us:

> Science is a long history of learning how not to fool ourselves.
> And:
> Science is a way of trying not to fool yourself. The first principle is that you must not fool yourself, and you are the easiest person to fool.

Researchers and practitioners engaged in biotechnology need a healthy dose of realism and a critical eye toward our own justifications. Therefore, better technology cannot be the only, or maybe not even a primary, engineering response to the threat of terrorism. Terrorists with money and skill can get around our technology, and they can use our own technology against us. Even if we were good at antiterror research, this would eventually fail to protect us.

The argument is not against the use of antiterrorism technology, but to suggest that such technology is only part of the answer. The safety of food and water supplies is too important to be seen as merely an academic and intellectual enterprise. It is not possible for engineers to prevent all such deeds, just as it is not possible for engineers to make anything 100% safe from other kinds of failure.

One of the most interesting, albeit confusing, typologies of the uncertainties involved in risk management decisions was expounded by the former U.S. Secretary of Defense, Donald Rumsfeld[39]:

> As we know, there are known knowns. There are things we know we know. We also know there are known unknowns. That is to say we know there are some things we do not know. But there are also unknown unknowns, the ones we don't know we don't know.

Acceptable risk includes uncertainties and ambiguity. Prevention of disasters requires that a sufficient action does enough to identify and weigh the factors that can lead to adverse environmental

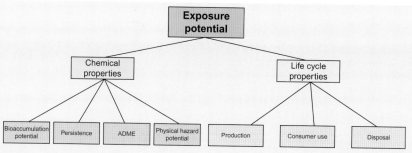

**FIGURE 14.13** Screening approach for potential exposure to chemical ingredients in products, taking into account both inherent properties of a chemical compound and its life cycle. *Source: Personal communication with Linkov I, U.S. Army Corps of Engineers, Mitchell Blackwood J, U.S. Department of Agriculture, 2012.*

hazards and risks, but the risk decision will need to be monitored and reevaluated in light of the chaotic nature of both the products of genetic manipulations and the environmental systems into which they are released. It is worth noting that knowing something about one chemical does not usually allow one to say much about another, even similar, chemical. The tools to do so, such as quantitative structure activity relationships (QSARs) have been improving, but are still highly uncertain. In addition, inherent chemical properties are but one part of potential risk. The formulation of the product, including mixtures of active and inert ingredients, as well as the way the product is used (e.g. direct application to skin, sprayed as aerosol, added to fuel, or used in processed food) largely determines exposure and risk.

The worldwide increasing dependence on synthetic chemicals has not been matched by an adequate increase in our understanding of the threats they may pose to the environment and human health.[40] Several nations have begun to screen product ingredients for risks early in the life cycle. This entails both the potential toxicity of the substances and how they are used. The harm is a function of the inherent properties and how people and ecosystems can be exposed. State-of-the-art tools and advanced models for anticipating the potential toxicity and exposure of new chemicals have advanced in quality and scope.[41] These screening tools make use of physicochemical properties and human factors, such as use scenarios (see Figure 14.13). These tools should continue to be enhanced to prevent dangerous substances from reaching the marketplace and to monitor them after they are used. This could go a long way to avoiding future public health and environmental disasters.

# References and Notes

1. Eionet—European Topic Centre on Sustainable Consumption and Production. *Waste prevention.* http://scp.eionet.europa.eu/themes/waste/prevention/#product [accessed October 12, 2009].
2. Kurzer P. *Working Paper: European Citizens Against Globalization: Public Health and Risk Perceptions.* Pennsylvania: Lehigh University; 2004.
3. Gonzalez CG. Genetically modified organisms and justice: the international environmental justice implications of biotechnology. *Geo Int'l Envtl L Rev* 2007;**19**:584–642.
4. Weimeyer S, Lamont TG, Bunck CM, Sindelar CR, Gramlich FJ, Fraser JD, Byrd MA. Organochlorine, pesticide, polychlorobiphenyl, and mercury residues in bald eagle eggs—1969-79—and their relationships to shell thinning and reproduction. *Arch Environ Contam Toxicol* 1984;**13**(5):529.
5. Guillette Jr. L, Gross TS, Masson GR, Matter JM, Percival HH, Woodward AR. Developmental abnormalities of the gonad and abnormal sex-hormone concentrations in juvenile alligators from contaminated and control lakes in Florida. *Environ Health Perspect* 1994;**102**(8):680–8.

14. PRODUCTS

6. Fox GA. Effects of endocrine disrupting chemicals on wildlife in Canada: past, present and future. *Water Qual Res J Can* 2001;**36**(2):233.

7. See, for example: Purdom C, et al. Estrogenic effects from sewage treatment works. *Chem Ecol* 1994;**8**:275; Joblin S, et al. Inhibition of testicular growth in rainbow trout (*Oncorhynchus mikiss*) exposed to estrogenic alkyphenolic chemicals. *Environ Toxicol Chem* 1996;**15**(2):194.

8. See Sheiner EK, et al. Effect of occupational exposures on male fertility: literature review. *Ind Health* 2003;**41**(2):55; Guzelian P. Comparative toxicology of chlordecone (kepone) in humans and experimental animals. *Annu Rev Pharmacol Toxicol* 1982;**22**:89; Hayes T, et al. Hermaphroditic, demasculinized frogs after exposure to the herbicide atrazine at low ecologically relevant doses. *Proc Natl Acad Sci USA* 2002;**99**(8):5476.

9. Koplin DW, Furlong ET, Meyer MT, Thurman EM, Zaugg SD, Barber LB, Buxton HT. Pharmaceuticals, hormones, and other organic wastewater contaminants in US streams, 1999-2000: a national reconnaissance. *Environ Sci Technol* 2002;**36**(11):1202.

10. Bevans HE, Goodbred SL, Miesner JF, Watkins SA, Gross TS, Denslow ND. *Synthetic organic compounds and carp endocrinology and histology in Las Vegas Wash and Las Vegas and Callville Bays of Lake Mead.* U.S.: Nevada; 1996 Geological Survey Water-Resources Investigations Report 96-4266.

11. Björkblom C, Högfors E, Salste L, Bergelin E, Olsson PE, Katsiadaki I, Wiklund T. Estrogenic and androgenic effects of municipal wastewater effluent on reproductive endpoint biomarkers in three-spined stickleback (Gasterosteusaculeatus). *Environ Toxicol Chem* 2009;**28**:1063–71.

12. Gierthy JF. Testing for endocrine disruption: how much is enough? *Toxicol Sci* 2002;**68**(1):1–3.

13. Selinger B. *Chemistry in the marketplace.* Sydney: Harcourt, Brace and Jovanovich; 1988 p. 127.

14. Basquero F, Martínez J-L, Cantón R. Antibiotics and antibiotic resistance in water environments. *Curr Opin Biotechnol* 2008;**19**:260–5.

15. PANNA. http://www.panna.org/blog/3-new-separate-studies-confirm-common-pesticides-harm-kids-cognition [accessed February 10, 2012].

16. http://toxipedia.org/display/toxipedia/ [accessed 11.02.12].

17. http://www.epa.gov/pesticides/health/children-standards.html [accessed February 10, 2012].

18. U.S. Environmental Protection Agency . *Malathion for mosquito control.* http://www.epa.gov/opp00001/health/mosquitoes/malathion4mosquitoes.htm#malathion; [accessed on March 11, 2012].

19. Bonner MR, Coble J, Blair A, et al. Malathion exposure and the incidence of cancer in the agricultural health study. *Am J Epidemiol* 2007;**166**(9):1023–34. http://dx.doi.org/10.1093/aje/kwm182 DOI:dx.doi.org PMID 17720683.

20. http://emedicine.medscape.com/article/167726-overview [accessed February 14, 2012].

21. Minton NA, Murray VS. *A review of organophosphate poisoning. Med Toxicol Adverse Drug Exp* 1988;**3**(5):350–75. http://www.ncbi.nlm.nih.gov/pubmed/3057326 [accessed February 14, 2012].

22. http://en.wikipedia.org/wiki/Chlorfenvinphos [accessed February 13, 2012].

23. http://en.wikipedia.org/wiki/Dichlorvos [accessed February 13, 2012].

24. http://en.wikipedia.org/wiki/Malathion [accessed February 10, 2012].

25. http://www.medscape.com/viewarticle/721892 [accessed February 15, 2012].

26. http://www.beyondpesticides.org/lawn/factsheets/30health.pdf [accessed February 15, 2012].

27. Pandit V, Seshadri S, Rao SN, Samarasinghe C, Kumar A, Valsalan R. *A case of organophosphate poisoning presenting with seizure and unavailable history of parenteral suicide attempt. J Emerg Trauma Shock* 2011;**4**(1):132–4. http://dx.doi.org/10.4103/0974-2700.76825 DOI:dx.doi.org. PMC 3097564. PMID 21633583 http://www.pubmedcentral.nih.gov/articlerender.fcgi?tool=pmcentrez&artid=3097564 [accessed February 14, 2012].

28. Yurumez Y, Durukan P, Yavuz Y, Ikizceli I, Avsarogullari L, Ozkan S, Akdur O, Ozdemir C. Acute organophosphate poisoning in university hospital emergency room patients. *Intern Med* 2007;**46**(13):965–9 PMID 17603234.

29. http://en.wikipedia.org/wiki/Organophosphate_poisoning [accessed February 12, 2012].

30. http://www.newyouth.com/archives/science/other/pesticide_treated_seeds_cause_di.html [accessed February 12, 2012].

31. http://www.politics.co.uk/reference/organophosphates [accessed February 14, 2012].

32. http://emedicine.medscape.com/article/1175139-overview [accessed February 14, 2012].

33. http://www.amazon.com/Toxicology-Organophosphate-Carbamate-Compounds-Ramesh/dp/0120885239 [accessed February 15, 2012].

34. http://www2.chemistry.msu.edu/faculty/reusch/VirtTxtJml/intro1.htm [accessed February 1, 2012].

35. Ege S. *Organic chemistry.* 3rd ed. Lexington, Massachusetts: D.C. Heath and Company; 1989 chapter 5.

36. Wein LM, Liu Y. Analyzing a bioterror attack on the food supply: the case of Botulinum toxin in milk. *Proc Natl Acad Sci USA* 2005;**102**:9984.

37. Kaiser J. ScienceScope. *Science* 2005;**309**:31; McCook A. PNAS publishes bioterror paper, after all. *The Scientist* 2005; June 29, 2005.
38. Feynman FP, Robbins J. *The pleasure of finding things out*. New York, NY: Perseus Publishing Co; 1999.
39. Rumsfeld D. *Press conference. US Department of Defense, February 12, 2002*; 2002. *This is in some ways similar to Socrates' advice that wisdom begins with knowing what one does not know. Perhaps Rumsfeld was reminded of Henry David Thoreau's similar quote: "To know that we know what we know, and that we do not know what we do not know, that is true knowledge"*. http://www.famousquotesandauthors.com/authors/henry_david_thoreau_quotes.html [accessed August 25, 2009].
40. Dellarco V, Henry T, Sayre P, Seed J, Bradbury S. Meeting the common needs of a more effective and efficient testing and assessment paradigm for chemical risk management. *J Toxicol Environ Health Part B* 2010;**13**(2):347–60.
41. Money CD, Van Hemmen JJ, Vermeire TG. Scientific governance and the process for exposure scenario development in REACH. *J Expo Sci Environ Epidemiol* 2007;**17**:S34–7.

# Unsustainability

Beginning after the Second World War, popular culture was becoming increasingly aware of the concept of "spaceship earth." That is, a general consensus was growing that our planet consisted of a finite life support system and that our air, water, food, soil, and ecosystems were not infinitely elastic in their ability to absorb humanity's willful disregard. The petrochemical industry, the military, and capitalism were all coming under increased scrutiny and skepticism, as were individuals themselves, as being wasteful of the Earth's limited and invaluable resources.

After the tumultuous and contentious 1960s, decision makers in the private and public sectors came to appreciate that environmental quality had become an almost universally accepted expectation of the populace. This did not eliminate major debates that continue today on exactly *how* to achieve a livable environment. When finite resources are mentioned, it is likely that, no matter the extent of one's environmental expertise, the likely topic will be fossil fuels. However, there are many more resources that are being expended with seeming disregard for their limits.

A potential set of disasters that threaten our planet sometime in the next 100 years is a consequence of the currently unsustainable practices of the industrialized and, to a lesser extent, even the less industrialized countries. We are slowing exhausting certain substances derived from our planet; oil, phosphates, helium, platinum metals, zinc, gallium, germanium, arsenic, tellurium, the rare earth elements, and even uranium is becoming scarce.[1] Furthermore, we are polluting the atmosphere with vast amounts of carbon dioxide ($CO_2$) and $CH_4$ which threaten to change our climate, and our agricultural land in being polluted with heavy metals. Our present generation's overzealous exploitation of the planet is in a sense robbing future generations.

## OIL

Oil supplies are about to or have just peaked with new oil and gas fields becoming more and more difficult to find and also to operate. The environmental issues linked to undersea mining are all too clear in our minds after the recent BP Gulf of Mexico Deep Horizon oil leak (see Figure 15.1).

*Unraveling Environmental Disasters*      377     

FIGURE 15.1    The Deepwater Horizon oil rig on fire April 21, 2010, a day after it exploded in the Gulf of Mexico. *Picture from http://en.wikipedia.org/wiki/deepwater_horizon.*

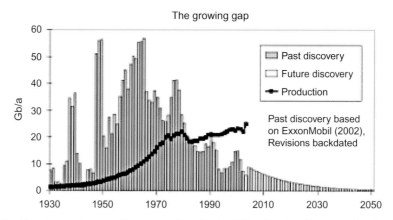

FIGURE 15.2    Growing gap between discovery and production. *Taken from http://www.en.wikipedia.org/wiki/Peak_oil.*

Furthermore, with much of the oil that is pumped out of the ground or from under the sea having to undergo long tanker journeys, the possibility of another major oil leak at sea is not far from our minds. It could be that the environmental impacts of difficult oil exploration and transport will cause a significant reduction in supply, long before we physically run out of the oil. Moreover, there is a growing gap between discovery and production as can be seen in Figure 15.2.

## PHOSPHATES

Phosphate compounds are vital to farmers as a fertilizer and billions of people around the world depend on it for growing their food. The global reserves have recently been estimated at 60 Gt with almost 60% being in the disputed territory between Morocco and Western Sahara.

It has been estimated that phosphorus production will peak sometime between 2050 and 2090, followed by a rapid decline in production. That assumes the reserves are still available for export.[2]

Phosphate rock is sometimes associated with the metal cadmium, and in both parts of the United States and in New Zealand, the yearly top-up of phosphates is causing the levels of cadmium in the soil to rise and in some areas is reaching the limit for pasture and agriculture.

## HELIUM

Helium gas is another strategic element. Its cryogenic properties are unique and for many applications, there are no substitutes. It has a boiling point of $-269\,^\circ$C (4.2 K) and is used extensively in research laboratories and in space launches. It is the only substance that can be used to assist in the pumping of liquid hydrogen and oxygen rocket fuel into the burners. It is found in only a few gas wells around the world, and once these gas wells have been depleted, there will be no helium in significant and winnable quantities on earth. It is possible that this might happen within the next 100 years, assuming that the demand for this noble gas does not increase significantly.[3] The annual demand is about $200 \times 10^6$ m$^3$ (at normal temperature and pressure). A very small percentage is used for party balloons.[4]

## PLATINUM GROUP METALS

Platinum group metals (PGMs) are used by many industries. At the moment, about 50% is used for catalytic converters (mainly platinum and palladium) for exhaust control in transport vehicles and 30% is used in jewelry. The demand for catalytic converters is growing at a rapid rate and has tripled since 1990. There is also a huge potential demand for using platinum in fuel cells. The global reserves (largely in South Africa, Russia, and Zimbabwe) have been estimated at over 90 kilotonnes (kt) with an annual production of 500 t.[5] With each catalytic converter using at least 1.5 g PGM for a small car and 15 g for a large truck, there is just not enough PGM to supply a converter to all the cars presently running on the world's roads today.[6] And moreover, fuel cells could well create a new demand that just cannot be met in the short term.

## LITHIUM

Lithium is another element that could soon be in short supply with a potential massive demand for use in new lithium batteries for vehicles. For example, the production and demand for lithium ion phosphate and lithium–sulfur batteries are rapidly growing, and this type of battery will be a strong contender when it comes to choosing a battery to meet ever increasing safety requirements. Another lithium battery which is at an early stage of development is the lithium titanate battery.[7]

## RARE EARTH METALS

Many of the REEs (there are 14 lanthanides and 14 actinides) have some very important and unique properties. They are used as catalysts in hydrocarbon cracking (La and Ce) and, above all, to make permanent magnets for motors and generators. For example, the Prius hybrid electric vehicle uses 1 kg of Nd and Pr and 150 g Dy. Also, the next generation of wind turbines will be using 200 kg of Nd and Pr and perhaps 30 kg Dy per MW of generating capacity.[8] The world reserves are estimated to be of the order of 100 Mt of REE with China having at least half of the reserves. The annual demand at present is 120 kt and this is predicted to more than double over the next 10 years.[9] Unfortunately, the mining and extracting of rare earth metals (REEs) are difficult, and there are many environmental concerns about the present mining practices.

Like many commodities, the supply of REEs cannot always be guaranteed, and at present, China, by far the largest producer of REEs, has placed an embargo on exporting the metals.

## OTHER METALS

The mining of many metals is becoming more and more difficult and environmental issues are beginning to curb mining and also to increase the costs. China's recent embargo on exporting rare earths is thought to have been prompted by the growing concern within China of the environmental impacts of some mining practices, including those related to rare earth mining. Gold mining is causing concern, especially when it is not under proper control. The cyanide leaching process has often led to cyanide spills and leaks with the accompanying health hazards and sometimes death (see Chapter 10). Zinc mining and the associated tailings from the mining process which can contain dangerous amounts of cadmium is also an area for concern. These cases and many others are some of the environmental impacts that will most likely cause supply constraints long before we physically run out of the metals.

## BIOMASS

One of the problems with the oil industry is that it has been too successful, and oil refineries produce not only fuel but also chemicals for a wide range of products, including the monomers for all the plastics which have become so very important in our society. Total reliance on fossil fuels is potentially disastrous for two main reasons: firstly the supply of oil is being depleted or will soon be too expensive to pump out of the ground and secondly the fuel derived from fossil fuel is causing a buildup of $CO_2$ in the atmosphere which in turn is setting us on the path of climate change (see Chapter 8). One way to reduce our dependency on oil-based chemicals is to use biomass for producing chemicals and especially the precursors to plastic material. This is a very active field of chemical research and industry at the moment. Brazil has led the field with an enormous program of producing ethanol from sugarcane, and in 2009/2010, Brazil produced 30 billion liters of ethanol (see Figure 15.3).[10]

The ethanol from sugarcane represented 17.6% of the country's total energy consumption for transport in 2008 and in Brazil, cars no longer run on pure gasoline. All gasoline is blended with anhydrous ethanol in the range 18–25% (known as E18 and E25) with the remainder

FIGURE 15.3    Growing sugarcane for fuel and chemicals. *Image from http://www.sucrose.com/learn.html.*

being gasoline. The reason for the range is that the amount of ethanol available for blending does depend on the harvest. The United States is however the largest producer of bioethanol in the world, producing $49.2 \times 10^9$ L in 2010 of which 99% was used in gasohol.[11]

There is much research activity into aquatic biomass for the production of chemicals. One great advantage of aquatic biomass is that high concentrations of $CO_2$ can be used to help stimulate growth of seaweeds and algae (see Figure 15.4).

Aquatic biomass has the added advantage of higher (6–8%) solar energy utilization efficiency than terrestrial plants (1.5–2.2%). This is due to their higher photosynthetic efficiency. Another advantage is that $CO_2$ from power plants can be pumped into algae ponds and in that way, these plants can store carbon in the form of useful compounds.

Planting trees is always a good way of reducing the $CO_2$ in the air; in the case of long-lived species like trees, carbon can be sequestered for decades.[12,13]

The types of compounds that can be extracted from biomass include energy chemicals such as methanol, ethanol, and hydrocarbons including diesel; food chemicals such as proteins, oils fats, and sterols; and specialty chemicals such as perfumes, vitamins, and enzymes.

Terrestrial biomass for chemicals is only a sustainable option if the plants and trees are grown in a way which does not lead to depletions of natural flora, and moreover, it must not conflict with food production. Perhaps, the most exciting area is the development of a polymer industry using monomers extracted from plant material. Another area that could yield dividends in the future is lignin chemistry. Lignin is the dark aromatic material that is bonded to the carbohydrate material in trees and some plants and gives them their rigidity. It is composed of very large aromatic polymers made up in complex networks. Many biomass industries (paper, sugar, cellulose) have no use for lignin (it is usually burnt to make energy of one form or another), so there is a vast amount available for possible new and exciting uses.

FIGURE 15.4   Algae production. *Image from http://badger.uvm.edu/xmlui/handle/2051/4812.*

Developing plastics from monomers extracted from biomass is at a very exciting stage with new materials being developed by many groups around the world. Biomass-derived chemicals include oils, waxes, glycerol (and many new compounds derived from this tribasic alcohol) solvents, dibasic esters (paint solvents), surfactants of all types including biodegradable compounds, and of course biodiesel. These compounds are being produced in factories which can be termed biorefineries. Their products are often very different to that found in oil-based refineries and are creating a whole new breed of chemists and chemical engineers.

It will never be possible to produce all the motor transport fuel needed in the world today from biomass. There is just not enough land available to grow the trees or plants, and also, there is the food lobby which makes the point that we should not be using agricultural land to produce fuel for the rich, while the poor starve. However, the amount of biomass for nonfuel chemicals and plastic production is well within the realms of possibility.

## METHANE

There is a surfeit of methane in the world and its concentration in the atmosphere is growing at an alarming rate. It is indeed one of the modern day greenhouse gases which is rapidly pushing the earth into a time of global warming and climate change. Levels of methane have increased from 0.72 to 1.77 ppm over the past 250 years, and moreover, methane is 25 times far effective as a GHG than is carbon dioxide (see Chapter 8).[14]

Much work is being done by engineers and chemists to utilize the methane for useful purposes. It is being used as the feedstock for Fischer–Tropsch synthesis of hydrocarbons, largely to produce transport fuels. It is far superior to the process that uses coal because of methane's high ratio of C to H (1:4). In the coal process, hydrogen has to be supplemented, and moreover, the coal-based process produces a large fraction of oxygenated compounds (alcohols and acids) together with the hydrocarbons. Methane is also used to produce nonfuel chemicals, and the chemical industry will soon find that this is a very profitable route because of the large quantity of methane available. Using $CH_4$ to make fuel is really just putting off the moment when one produces $CO_2$. This is true but the world is still in need of a liquid transport fuel, and it is preferable to send $CO_2$ gas into the atmosphere than to send $CH_4$ gas ($CH_4$ is 25 times more effective as a GHG).

## CARBON DIOXIDE

$CO_2$ is the most important of the GHGs. Its concentration in the atmosphere has been increasing since the start of the Industrial Revolution. It has increased from 280 to 392 ppm in 250 years—an increase of over 35%.[13] It has a very large negative Gibbs energy of formation ($\Delta G_f = -394.4$ kJ mol$^{-1}$) compared to most organic chemicals making it difficult to be used as a starting material for producing new organic chemicals. That has not stopped many researchers from looking into the possibilities of using it as a chemical feedstock in coupled reactions.

As mentioned in Chapter 3, one way to stem the onset of global warming is to sequester the $CO_2$ pouring out of fossil fuel burning power plants or cement factories. This has been the subject of much research and even government plans (see Figure 15.5). One plan is to pump it into exhausted oilfields or even under the sea. Other ideas include dissolving the $CO_2$ in solvents such as amines, calcium carbonate loops, and forming $CO_2$ gas hydrates. $CO_2$ in its critical state is an excellent solvent ($T_C = 31.1\ °C$ and $P_C = 73.9$ bar) and as such it can be put to many good uses. The fact that the critical properties are relatively low gives it a great advantage. It is a very

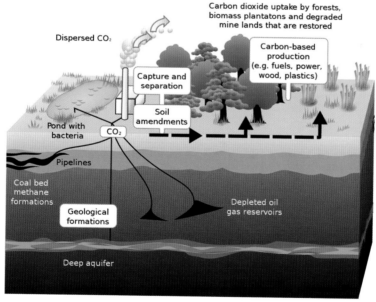

FIGURE 15.5   Carbon capture and separation. *Image from http://en.wikipedia.org/wiki/Carbon_capture_and_storage.*

clean solvent and there is no expensive separation processes required. Once the crit-$CO_2$ has dissolved a compound, it can very easily be separated by simply reducing the pressure. This great advantage is not shared with most other solvents, including $H_2O$, as the critical properties of $H_2O$ are less convenient ($T_C = 374\ °C$ and $P_C = 220.64$ bar). The more recent applications of super critical $CO_2$ include cleaning processes, purification processes, impregnation processes, dyeing, and atomization processes. It has for a long time been used for decaffeinating coffee.

There are many good ideas floating around to improve our sustainability on Earth. Many of these ideas must be tested before it is too late. Alternative energy and reduction of greenhouse gases are but two of the crucial issues. Without enough transport fuel and grid power, the world could be heading for disaster, and furthermore, in a world of rising temperatures and the accompanying climate and weather changes, we could face disasters of gigantic proportions.

At the very least, we can step up efforts to view finite resources from a life cycle perspective. Indeed, the finite limits of natural resources call for systems thinking in at least two ways. First, after a thorough review concluding that a resource is indeed needed, then every step in obtaining that resource must be efficient. This calls for a life cycle assessment of that resource (see Figure 15.6). The second aspect of systems thinking is more preventative. That is, can the same service or need be provided without using this limited, finite resource?

To answer this question, all reasonable options must be explored on how to find alternatives to the finite resource. This can be done using an alternatives assessment, which is a formal technique to characterize the hazards of substances based on a full range of human health and environmental information.[15] Chemical choices made based on these assessments ameliorate potential for unintended consequences *a priori*. However, this approach could advance

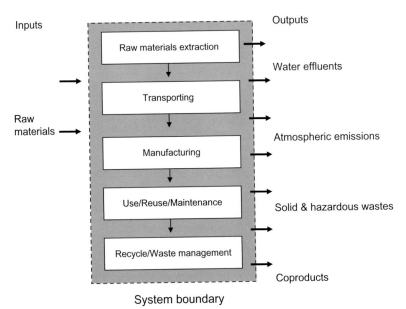

FIGURE 15.6    Life cycle stages of a process must follow the conservation law, with material and energy balances. *Source: U.S. Environmental Protection Agency. Life cycle assessment: inventory guidelines and principles. EPA/600/R-92/245. Office of Research and Development, Cincinnati, Ohio; 1993.*

beyond hazard to address benefits and utility, that is, look at a process that currently calls for helium and find points in the life cycle where the need for helium can be reduced or eliminated. The current approach for alternatives assessment is provided in Table 15.1, along with recommendations of how it might be adapted to address finite resources.

These and other life cycle approaches could supplant many of the single-use, unsustainable solutions with more systematic, sustainable solutions.

TABLE 15.1    Key Steps in Alternatives Assessment

| Process | Action | Application to finite resources |
|---|---|---|
| Step 1: Determine feasibility | Consider whether alternatives are commercially available and cost effective, have the potential for an improved health and environmental profile, and are likely to result in lasting change. Stakeholder interest is also a key consideration | Consider whether the goods and services can be provided with lesser amounts of these resources |
| Step 2: Collect information | Consider how well characterized the possible alternatives are, the chemical manufacturing process, the range of functional uses that the chemical serves, and the feedstock or contaminants and residuals from the production process. Also consider work of other organizations in exploring alternatives for the chemical of concern, similar chemicals, and functional uses. Based on analysis of this information and preliminary stakeholder consultation, develop a proposed project scope and an approach for developing the alternatives assessment | Same, except collect market and production information |
| Step 3: Convene stakeholders | Stakeholders are drawn from entire supply chain and all life cycle stages of the chemical of concern. Involvement throughout the project helps to ensure that stakeholders contribute to, understand, and support the outcome, enhancing credibility and promoting adoption of the safer alternatives. Typical stakeholders include chemical manufacturers, product manufacturers, nongovernmental organizations, government agencies, academics, retailers, consumers, and waste and recycling companies. Chemical and technology innovators are critical members of the group | Same process, but include additional stakeholders, for example, from similar industries |
| Step 4: Identify viable alternatives | Collect information about viability on a range of potential alternatives. The focus is on finding alternatives that are functional with minimum disruption to the manufacturing process. To identify the most likely alternatives, it may be necessary to include viability demonstrations by chemical and product manufacturers | Same |

*Continued*

TABLE 15.1    Key Steps in Alternatives Assessment—Cont'd

| Process | Action | Application to finite resources |
|---|---|---|
| Step 5: Conduct hazard assessment | Based on the best data that are available from the literature or can be modeled, assign descriptor of hazard concern level—high, moderate, or low—for each alternative across a range of end points, including acute and repeated dose toxicity, carcinogenicity and mutagenicity, reproductive and developmental toxicity, neurotoxicity, sensitization and irritation, acute and chronic aquatic toxicity, and persistence and bioaccumulation. In addition, we provide a qualitative description of potential endocrine activity | Rather than an assessment solely of potential hazards, include potential substitutions and utility of these substitutions in terms of providing the same goods and services as current processes |

*Source of two left columns: Ref. 15.*

# References and Notes

1. Materials for our Future. *RSC News*; April 2011. p. 8.
2. Van Kauwenbergh SJ. *World phosphate rock reserves and resources.* Washington, DC: IFDC report; 2010.
3. *RSC News*, April 2011, p. 8–11 and RSC's roadmap chemistry for tomorrow's world in www.rsc.org/sustainablematerials [accessed 20 February 2012].
4. Salazar K, McNutt MK, editors. *Helium: minerals commodity survey.* Reston, Virginia: US Geological Survey; 2011 http://minerals.usgs.gov/minerals/pubs/commodity/helium/ [accessed 20 February 2012].
5. Mudd G. Private Communication, Civil Engineering, Monash University, Melbourne, Australia.
6. http://www.nature.com/news/2007/071114/full/450334a.html [accessed 21 February 2012].
7. Salminen J. Private Communication, European Batteries, Finland.
8. Hatch GP. *How does the use of permanent magnets make wind turbines more reliable?* Carpentersville. Terra Magnetica; 2009. http://www.terramagnetica.com/?p=263 [accessed 21 February 2012].
9. Hatch GP. *A summary overview of the rare-earths market.* Carpentersville: Technology Metals Research; 2011.
10. http://en.wikipedia.org/wiki/Ethanol_fuel_in_Brazil [accessed 19 February 2012].
11. http://www.ethanolrfa.org/pages/statistics# [accessed 21 February 2012].
12. Dibenedetto A. Private Communication, University of Bari, Bari, Italy.
13. Kadam KL. Power plant flue gas as a source of CO2 for microalgae cultivation: Economic impact of different process options. *Energy Convers Manage* 1997;**38**:505.
14. Tuckett RP. The Role of Atmospheric Gases in Global Warming. In: Letcher TM, editor. *Climate change.* Oxford: Elsevier; 2009. p. 3–19 [chapter 1].
15. U.S. Environmental Protection Agency. *Alternatives assessments.* http://www.epa.gov/dfe/alternative_assessments.html [accessed 15 March 2012].

# Society

By far, most of the actual and pending disasters in this book have been generally well documented, with many reaching consensus within most of the scientific community as to whether they are problematic and, to some extent, their causes. They have served as motivation for environmental laws, regulation, and policy. Many perceived problems, however, do not enjoy such a consensus. The hypotheses linking anthropogenic activities to changes in global climate and the threats posed by long-term storage of radioactive wastes (and the whole issue of using fission to produce electricity, for that matter) are examples of major disagreements between policy makers, journalists, and lay people, as well as within the scientific community.

Humans are inextricably tied to the environment. Not only does it provide sustenance and shelter but also to some degree all human enterprises are environmentally constrained. Thus, society and the environment exist as a very complex set of systems. The impact of an environmental disaster goes beyond physiological health and ecosystem condition. It affects the human condition as well.

In this chapter, we consider some perplexing societal issues, most of which have uneven support from either the scientific community or the society at large.

## JUSTICE

Humans breathe from the air in a common troposphere. Water circulates through the hydrological cycle. Plant life stores and converts the solar energy from the sun. Humans make products derived from the same earth's resources. This means that the environment is a "common" shared by humankind. In 1968, biologist Garrett Hardin (1915-2003) wrote an article entitled "The tragedy of the commons," wherein he imagines an English village with a common area where everyone's cow may graze. At first, the common readily sustains the livestock. Village life is stable. However, this begins to change after one of the villagers learns that if he has two cows instead of one, the cost of the extra cow will be shared by everyone, whereas the profit will be his alone. The two cows allow him to prosper in comparison to his neighbors for some time. However, the others take note of his success and correspondingly want two cows. Their logic is extended so that if two are better than one, then three must certainly be better than two. At some point, however, the village common is no longer able to support the large number of cows, the system crashes, and everyone suffers.

This concept can be extended intellectually to the finite resources which drive the carrying capacity of ecosystems. A similar argument can be made for the use of nonrenewable resources. If we treat diminishing resources such as oil and minerals as capital gains, we will soon find ourselves in the "common" difficulty of having too many people and not enough resources.

Environmental resources are not distributed between and among populations evenly in terms of amount and quality. Some breathe cleaner air than others, drink purer water than most, eat food that is less contaminated than the majority of the world's inhabitants, and have better tools and toys than everyone else.

As the distribution of goods and services is so uneven, we may be tempted to assume that systems are fair simply because "most" are satisfied with the current situation. However, the only way to protect public health and the environment is to ensure that *all* persons are adequately protected. In the words of Reverend Martin Luther King, "Injustice anywhere is a threat to justice everywhere."[1] By extension, if any group is disparately exposed to an unhealthy environment, then the whole nation is subjected to inequity and injustice. Put in a more positive way, we can work to provide a safe and livable environment by including everyone, leaving no one behind. The term *environmental justice* (EJ) is usually applied to social issues, especially as they relate to neighborhoods and communities. The so-called *environmental justice communities* possess two basic characteristics:

1. They have experienced historical (usually multigenerational) exposures to disproportionately[2] high doses of potentially harmful substances (the *environmental* part of the definition). These communities are home to numerous pollution sources, including heavy industry and pollution control facilities, which may be obvious by their stacks and outfall structures, or which may be more subtle, such as long-buried wastes with little evidence on the surface of their existence. These sites increase the likelihood of exposure to dangerous substances. Exposure is preferred to *risk*, since risk is a function of the hazard and the exposure to that hazard. Even a substance with a very high toxicity (one type of hazard) that is confined to a laboratory of a manufacturing operation may not pose much of a risk due to the potentially low levels of exposure.
2. EJ communities have certain, specified socioeconomic and demographic characteristics. EJ communities must have a majority representation of low socioeconomic status, racial, ethnic, and historically disadvantaged people (the *justice* part of the definition).

These definitions point to the importance of an integrated response to ensure justice. The first component of this response is a sound scientific and engineering underpinning to decisions. The technical quality of designs and operations is vital to addressing the needs of any group. However, the engineering codes' call that we be "faithful agents" lends an added element of social responsibility to environmental practitioners.[3] For example, we cannot assume a "blank slate" for any design. Historic disenfranchisement and even outright bias may well have put certain neighborhoods at a disadvantage.

Thus, the responsibility of professionals cannot stop at sound science, but should consider the social milieu, especially possible disproportionate impacts. The determination of disproportionate impacts, especially pollution-related diseases and other health endpoints, is a fundamental step in ensuring EJ. But, even this step relies on the application of sound physical science. Like everything else that technical professionals do, we must first assess the situation to determine what needs to be done to improve it. As a first step in assessing environmental insult, epidemiologists look at clusters and other indications of elevated exposures and effects in populations. For example, certain cancers, neurological, hormonal, and other chronic diseases have been found to be significantly higher in minority communities and in socioeconomically depressed areas. Acute diseases, as indicated by hospital admissions, may also be higher in certain segments of society, such as pesticide poisoning in migrant workers.[4] These are examples of *disparate effects*. In addition, each person responds to an environmental insult uniquely and that person is affected differently at various life stages. For example, young children are at higher risk to neurotoxins. This is an example of *disparate susceptibility*. However, subpopulations also can respond differently to the whole population, meaning that genetic differences seem to affect people's susceptibility to contaminant exposure. Scientists are very interested in genetic variation so that genomic techniques[5] (e.g., identifying certain polymorphisms) are a growing area of inquiry.

In a sense, historical characteristics constitute the "environmental" aspects of EJ communities, and socioeconomic characteristics entail the "justice" considerations. The two sets of criteria are mutually inclusive, so for a community to be defined as an EJ community, both of these sets of criteria must be present.

A recent report by the Institute of Medicine[6] found that numerous EJ communities experience a "certain type of double jeopardy." The communities must endure elevated levels of exposure to contaminants, while being ill equipped to deal with these exposures because so little is known about the exposure scenarios in EJ communities. The first problem (i.e., higher concentrations of contaminants) is an example of *disparate exposure*. The latter problem is exacerbated by the disenfranchisement from the political process that is endemic to EJ community members. This is a problem of *disparate opportunity* or even *disparate protection*.[7] The report also found large variability among communities as to the type and amount of exposure to toxic substances. Each contaminant has its own type of toxicity. For example, one of the most common exposures in EJ communities is to the metal lead (Pb) and its compounds. The major health problem associated with Pb is brain, as well as central and peripheral nervous system diseases, including learning and behavioral problems. Another common contaminant in EJ communities is benzene, as well as other organic solvents. These contaminants can also be neurotoxic but also have very different toxicity profiles from neurotoxic metals like Pb. For example, benzene is a potent carcinogen, having been linked to leukemia and lymphatic tumors, as well as severe types of anemia. They also have very different exposure profiles. For example, Pb exposure is often in the home and yard, while benzene exposures often result from breathing air near a source (e.g., at work or near an industry, such as an oil refinery or pesticide manufacturer). The Institute's findings point to the need for improved approaches for characterizing human exposures to toxicants in EJ communities. One of the first places to recognize the disparate exposures was in Warren County, North Carolina, but numerous other communities have experienced uneven, and arguably unjust, disparities in environmental protection. However, there is little consensus on what defines an environmental injustice and whether, in fact, an injustice has occurred in many of these communities.

# SOLID WASTE

Municipal solid waste (MSW),[8] i.e., the trash or garbage collected by towns, cities, and counties, is made up of commonly used and disposed off items like lawn waste and grass clippings, boxes, plastics and other packaging, furniture, clothing, bottles, food scraps, newspapers, appliances, paint, and batteries. In 2001, U.S. residents, businesses, and institutions produced more than 229 million tons (208 tonnes) MSW, which is approximately 4.4 pounds (2.0 kg) of waste per person per day, up from 2.7 pounds (1.2 kg) per person per day (see Figure 16.1).

There is little argument that the amount of solid waste generated in the United States has grown steadily. Indeed, nearly every local authority in North America and Europe, since the 1990s, has implemented management practices to stem the burgeoning amounts of solid waste being generated and needing disposal. These measures have included source reduction, recycling, composting, prevention, or diversion of materials from the waste stream. Source reduction involves altering the design, manufacture, or use of products and materials to reduce the amount and toxicity of what gets thrown away. Recycling averts items from reaching the landfill or incinerator. Such items include paper, glass, plastic, and metals. These materials are sorted, collected, and processed and then manufactured, sold, and bought as new products. Composting is the microbial decomposition of the organic fraction of wastes, e.g., food and yard trimmings. The microbes, mainly bacteria and fungi, produce a substance that is valuable as a soil conditioner and fertilizer, which is sold or given away by the local authorities often at the landfill site itself.

The technology of waste handling has also greatly advanced. For example, landfill must be engineered in a manner in which and in areas where waste is placed into the land (Table 16.1). Landfills usually have liner systems and other safeguards to prevent

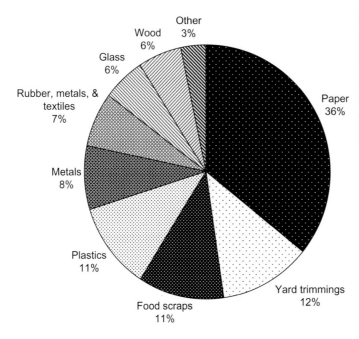

FIGURE 16.1  Composition of waste generated in the United States in 2001. *Source: Vallero DA.* Paradigms lost: learning from environmental mistakes, mishaps and misdeeds. *Amsterdam, NV: Butterworth-Heinemann; 2005; based on data from U.S. Environmental Protection Agency.* Municipal solid waste. *http://www.epa.gov/epaoswer/non-hw/muncpl/facts.htm; 2005 [accessed April 5, 2005].*

TABLE 16.1   Summary of Federal Landfill Standards as Prescribed by the U.S. Environmental Protection Agency

Location restrictions ensure that landfills are built in suitable geological areas away from faults, wetlands, flood plains, or other restricted areas

Liners are geomembrane or plastic sheets reinforced with 2 ft (0.6 m) of clay on the bottom and sides of landfills

Operating practices such as compacting and covering waste frequently with several inches of soil help reduce odor, control litter, insects, and rodents, and protect public health

Groundwater monitoring requires testing groundwater wells to determine whether waste materials have escaped from the landfill

Closure and postclosure care include covering landfills and providing long-term care of closed landfills

Corrective action controls and cleans up landfill releases and achieves groundwater protection standards

Financial assurance provides funding for environmental protection during and after landfill closure (i.e., closure and postclosure care)

*http://www.epa.gov/epaoswer/non-hw/muncpl/landfill; 2005 [accessed April 22, 2005].*

groundwater contamination. Combusting solid waste is another practice that has helped reduce the amount of landfill space needed. Combustion facilities burn solid wastes at high temperatures, reducing waste volume and generating electricity.

This is all well and good and demonstrates great progress in how we think about wastes. However, there is an argument that the original premise on which this progressed is based is in fact flawed. Are we really facing a solid waste crisis? Talk show hosts and a recent Home Box Office show hosted by the comedy team, Penn and Teller, consider the solid waste problem to be a convenient myth. One of their postulations is that the issue is another way that the government interferes with privacy and freedoms. In fact, one of Penn and Teller's conclusions is that the recycling is okay, but the ends should not justify the means. They argue that it is unethical to control people's life based on a flawed premise.

The controversy cuts both ways. Others believe that the progress being made is overstated and that measures to reduce waste, for example, looking at only total volume reduced, are inadequate because pockets of intractable problems exist. Take "disposable" diapers, for instance. A cloth diaper service, with an obvious vested interest, argues:

> An entire generation is growing up believing that the term "disposable diaper" is redundant: There's only one thing you put on babies' bottoms. They're plastic, you get them in huge bags and boxes at the grocery store or the convenience store, and you fold them up; and toss them in the trash when they're dirty. The product name itself is a misnomer, testament to the power of Madison Avenue and to our own Freudian neuroses surrounding our bodies and our wastes. For Huggies and Pampers and Luvs are not "disposable" at all. We throw about 18 billion of them away each year into trash cans and bags, believing they've gone to some magic place where they will safely disappear. The truth is, most of the plastic-lined "disposables" end up in landfills. There they sit, tightly wrapped bundles of urine and feces that partially and slowly decompose only over many decades. What started out as a marketer's dream of drier, happier, more comfortable babies has become a solid-waste nightmare of squandered material resources, skyrocketing economics, and a growing health hazard, set against the backdrop of dwindling landfill capacity in a country driven by consumption.[9]

If the volume of solid waste is not a disaster on a global scale, perhaps the waste streams themselves may be. Recent quantification studies have also looked at household hazardous waste (HHW) disposal pathways. It has been estimated that almost 50% of the HHW stream is likely to be codiscarded with general, nonhazardous household waste in the general household bin so forming part of MSW.[10] Internationally, almost 70% of MSW is disposed of to landfill.[11] The remaining portions are disposed of through incineration, energy-from-waste incineration, recycling, and reuse. Much of the remaining HHW (about 45%) is discarded at household waste reception centers (HWRCs) or collected from homes. Discarding of HHW items at HWRCs or separate collection from households need not imply that the items are separately collected; householders may not necessarily be aware of the operation of oil, paint, and battery collection banks and hazardous waste safes, simply placing the items in the general household waste receptacle. In the European Union, waste electrical and electronic equipment (WEEE) is also separately collected as is equipment containing ozone-depleting substances as required by legislation. Increasingly, however, improved accessibility and signage at HWRCs are making it simpler for householders to identify the alternative disposal options for their waste and hence will make it increasingly likely that those discarding HHW may do so via a separate collection facility. Separate collection means that HHW can be treated as hazardous waste and hence treated appropriately prior to disposal at, for instance, hazardous waste landfills.

Worldwide, it is quite difficult to quantify the amount of HHW being generated, as it is a highly variable waste stream compared to other types of MSW. Each of the HHW subcategories is produced in very different amounts, by mass, due to very variable composition, initial mass, and product usage patterns. Arguably, by mass, WEEE is the greatest component of HHW and hence disguises the true scope of HHW.

It is somewhat ironic that such a high-technology industry is responsible for such a major hazard. While WEEE has been estimated to be produced in quantities ranging from 200,000 to over 900,000 tonnes per year in the United Kingdom and chlorofluorocarbon-containing waste at over 160,000 tonnes per year combined estimates for the remaining HHW categories accounting for hundreds of thousands of tonnes, depending upon the waste types considered.[12] One estimate assumes that each household in developed countries disposes off 3.5 kg of HHW per year.[13] A recent study[14] estimated the amount of nine categories of HHW defined in European Union legislation and found that these nine categories contribute 100,000 tonnes per year to the MSW stream in the United Kingdom; the study notes that some of the categories contain products with negligible hazardous content such as water-based paints (compared to the more hazardous solvent-based paints). Generally as a proportion of MSW, estimates vary from >0% to 4% with inclusion of WEEE or 0% to 1% for all other HHW categories[15]; this value is fairly consistent across North America and Europe. If adequate collection facilities and disposal mechanisms are to be provided, more accurate estimates will be needed.

Unlike other waste types, in many countries, general MSW (including codisposed HHW) sent to landfill is relatively unregulated, with no waste separation or proof of contents. Consequently, hazardous materials can be disposed of alongside nonhazardous waste, in such a way that the presence of hazardous organic contaminants can be identified in MSW landfill leachate (see Figure 16.2).[16] As markets open up, consumers may be exposed to a greater range of products, and manufacturers are likely to produce a wider variety of merchandise to compete effectively. This could result in the utilization of a greater diversity and amount of chemicals, while ongoing assessments throw more and more substances into the domain of "potential hazard," such as phthalates, monosodium glutamate, and antibacterial agents.

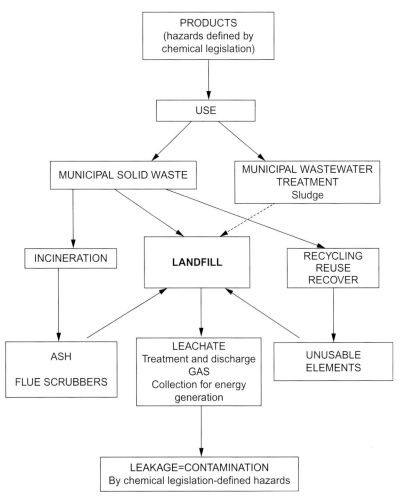

FIGURE 16.2   Hazardous household waste is predominantly disposed off to landfill. Alternative means of disposal, such as to sewer, incineration, or through recycling, all contribute fractions of waste to landfill. *Source: Slack R, Gronow J, Voulvoulis N.* Crit Rev Environ Sci Technol *2004;34:419-445.*

Hence, waste streams are not only constantly growing but are also becoming more varied than at any time in the past. Although HHW represents a small fraction of total household waste, and an even smaller amount of total MSW, the range and types of hazardous substances used in households have the potential to cause problems on disposal, particularly to the aquatic environment. Due to the predominance of landfill disposal around the world, it is therefore through landfill that the environmental consequences of HHW disposal will be most apparent, as indicated in Figure 16.2.

We are still not at the point where many communities and industries are producing zero waste or zero-hazard waste. Most products should not be landfilled. Unfortunately, from recycling to incineration, even alternative disposal practices generate waste that is ultimately landfilled.

# FOOD SUPPLY

Food contamination is a real and vexing problem. In the past decade, the public has been frightened over mad cow disease, tomato, spinach, and cantaloupe bacterial contamination, and pesticide residues.

The U.S. Centers for Disease Control and Prevention estimates that each year about one in six Americans (48 million people) suffer from foodborne illnesses. Further, 128,000 are hospitalized and 3000 die. These ailments fall into two major categories[17]:

- *Known foodborne pathogens*: Thirty-one pathogens are known to cause foodborne illness. Many of these pathogens are tracked by public health systems that track diseases and outbreaks (see Table 16.2).
- *Unspecified agents*: Agents with insufficient data to estimate agent-specific burden; known agents not yet identified as causing foodborne illness; microbes, chemicals, or other substances known to be in food with an unproven ability to cause illness; and agents not yet identified. Because you can not "track" what is not yet identified, estimates for this group of agents started with the health effects or symptoms that they are most likely to cause—acute gastroenteritis.

Actually, only eight known pathogens have accounted for the vast majority of illnesses, hospitalizations, and deaths. Tables 16.3–16.5 show the top five pathogens causing illness, hospitalization, and death.

In addition to the public health costs in terms of death and disease, these disasters are perplexing. How can large populations protect food supplies most efficiently? For example, the United States employs numerous surveillance systems to determine the occurrence of

TABLE 16.2    Estimated Annual Number of Domestically Acquired, Foodborne Illnesses, Hospitalizations, and Deaths Due to 31 Pathogens and Unspecified Agents Transmitted Through Food, United States

| Foodborne agents | Estimated annual number of illnesses (90% credible interval) | Percentage | Estimated annual number of hospitalizations (90% credible interval) | Percentage | Estimated annual number of deaths (90% credible interval) | Percentage |
|---|---|---|---|---|---|---|
| 31 Known pathogens | 9.4 Million (6.6-12.7 million) | 20 | 55,961 (39,534-75,741) | 44 | 1351 (712-2268) | 44 |
| Unspecified agents | 38.4 Million (19.8-61.2 million) | 80 | 71,878 (9924-157,340) | 56 | 1686 (369-3338) | 56 |
| Total | 47.8 Million (28.7-71.1 million) | 100 | 127,839 (62,529-215,562) | 100 | 3037 (1492-4983) | 100 |

*Source: U.S. Centers for Disease Control and Prevention. CDC estimates of foodborne illness in the United States. http://www.cdc.gov/foodborneburden/2011-foodborne-estimates.html; 2012 [accessed March 11, 2012].*

TABLE 16.3   Top Five Pathogens Contributing to Domestically Acquired Foodborne Illnesses

| Pathogen | Estimated number of illnesses | 90% Credible interval | % |
|---|---|---|---|
| Norovirus | 5,461,731 | 3,227,078-8,309,480 | 58 |
| *Salmonella*, nontyphoidal | 1,027,561 | 644,786-1,679,667 | 11 |
| *Clostridium perfringens* | 965,958 | 192,316-2,483,309 | 10 |
| *Campylobacter* spp. | 845,024 | 337,031-1,611,083 | 9 |
| *Staphylococcus aureus* | 241,148 | 72,341-529,417 | 3 |
| Subtotal | | | 91 |

*Source: U.S. Centers for Disease Control and Prevention. CDC estimates of foodborne illness in the United States. http://www.cdc.gov/foodborneburden/2011-foodborne-estimates.html; 2012 [accessed March 11, 2012].*

TABLE 16.4   Top Five Pathogens Contributing to Domestically Acquired Illnesses Resulting in Hospitalization

| Pathogen | Estimated number of hospitalizations | 90% Credible interval | % |
|---|---|---|---|
| *Salmonella*, nontyphoidal | 19,336 | 8545-37,490 | 35 |
| Norovirus | 14,663 | 8097-23,323 | 26 |
| *Campylobacter* spp. | 8463 | 4300-15,227 | 15 |
| *Toxoplasma gondii* | 4428 | 3060-7146 | 8 |
| *Escherichia coli* (STEC) O157 | 2138 | 549-4614 | 4 |
| Subtotal | | | 88 |

*Source: U.S. Centers for Disease Control and Prevention. CDC estimates of foodborne illness in the United States. http://www.cdc.gov/foodborneburden/2011-foodborne-estimates.html; 2012 [accessed March 11, 2012].*

TABLE 16.5   Top Five Pathogens Contributing to Domestically Acquired Foodborne Illnesses Resulting in Death

| Pathogen | Estimated number of deaths | 90% Credible interval | % |
|---|---|---|---|
| *Salmonella*, nontyphoidal | 378 | 0-1011 | 28 |
| *Toxoplasma gondii* | 327 | 200-482 | 24 |
| *Listeria monocytogenes* | 255 | 0-733 | 19 |
| Norovirus | 149 | 84-237 | 11 |
| *Campylobacter* spp. | 76 | 0-332 | 6 |
| Subtotal | | | 88 |

*Source: U.S. Centers for Disease Control and Prevention. CDC estimates of foodborne illness in the United States. http://www.cdc.gov/foodborneburden/2011-foodborne-estimates.html; 2012 [accessed March 11, 2012].*

foodborne disease. However, surveillance only catches a fraction of cases that actually occur. Such underdiagnosis and underreporting of foodborne illnesses are dangerous if it misses or is late in getting outbreak information to the public. Most federal systems rely on data from state and local health agencies. There is an ongoing quest for better and faster surveillance methods that will improve the quality, quantity, and timeliness of data (e.g., sentinel surveillance systems and national laboratory networks).

Obviously, society has high expectations of government agencies at all levels. This includes consumer protection, agricultural, environmental, and medical agencies and institutions. The calling is indeed daunting, but crucial.

One challenge is to improve means of prioritizing risks and distinguishing real from merely perceived threats.

## Alar

Alar may represent a "nondisaster." Or, it may represent a different kind of disaster, one that reminds us that the public's trust in science is tenuous.

From the mid-1960s through the 1980s, most apples grown in U.S. orchards were sprayed with the compound N-(dimethylamino)succinamic acid, also known as daminozide ($C_6H_{12}N_2O_3$) and best known by its trade name Alar. The compound is an amino acid derivative growth retardant that was formulated by the Uniroyal Chemical Company. The chemical was a valuable asset to orchard operations. When sprayed on apples, the growth process can be controlled to allow for nearly simultaneous ripening, allowing orchards to be harvested all at once. Thus, labor, machinery, and other expenses could be minimized. Laboratory testing conducted from 1973 through 1977 began to suggest a linkage between Alar and its degradation product unsymmetrical dimethyl hydrazine (UDMH) to cancer in rodents, especially mice and hamsters (see Table 16.6). This weight of evidence led to the 1984 designation by the National Toxicology Program that UDMH be considered a "probable human carcinogen." It is

TABLE 16.6   Cancer Classifications in the U.S. Carcinogens Fall into the Following Classifications (Strength in Descending Order Based on Type of Weight-of-Evidence)

| Cancer classification | Description |
| --- | --- |
| A | The chemical considered to be a human carcinogen |
| B | The chemical is a probable human carcinogen, with two subclasses |
| B1 | Chemicals that have limited human data from epidemiological studies supporting their carcinogenicity |
| B2 | Chemicals for which there is sufficient evidence from animal studies and for which but inadequate or no evidence from human epidemiological studies |
| C | The chemical is a possible human carcinogen |
| D | The chemical is not classifiable as to human carcinogenicity |
| E | There is evidence that the chemical does not induce cancer in humans |

*Source: U.S. Environmental Protection Agency.* Municipal solid waste. *http://www.epa.gov/epaoswer/non-hw/muncpl/facts.htm; 2005 [accessed April 5, 2005]*

not unusual for a degradation product to be more toxic than the parent compound (see Sidebar: Parent versus Progeny). By extension, due to the widespread exposure to apples and apple products, some preliminary risk assessments predicted as many as 30 million additional cancer deaths from ingesting Alar in products like applesauce. Although this risk was subsequently lowered to 20 million, it was considered an extremely important public health issue, especially in light of the fact that one of the largest demographic groups ingesting apple products is young children. Such information is important if true.

As a precaution, it is generally assumed in cancer risks assessments that there is no safe level of exposure, i.e., there is no "threshold" below which an exposure is acceptable. Since a dose-response curve has response (i.e. cancers) on its y-axis and dose (i.e. concentration) on its x-axis, the cancer dose-response curve must intersect the x-axis at zero. That is, the only dose expected to elicit no cancer is zero. Such thresholds include the "no observed adverse effect level" (NOAEL) or the "lowest observed adverse effect level" (LOAEL), which is the area of the dose-response curve where studies have actually linked a dose to an effect. Thus, the precautionary principle renders the NOAEL and LOAEL irrelevant to cancer risk. Instead, cancer slope factors are used to calculate the estimated probability of increased cancer incidence over a person's lifetime (the so-called excess lifetime cancer risk or ELCR). Like the reference doses, slope factors follow exposure pathways, i.e., they will differ whether they are ingested, inhaled, or come into contact with the skin. Another metric used to compare potential risk is the margin of exposure (MOE), which is the ratio of the NOAEL to the dose at which humans are likely to be exposed (i.e. based on the totality of sources and routes of exposure). This dose is called the estimated exposure dose (EED) or, for inhalation exposure the estimated exposure concentration (EEC).

Uncertainties or an elevated concern for sensitive subpopulations, especially children, are not always sufficiently addressed using uncertainty factors in the reference dose for oral exposure (RfD) and MOE. In the U.S., for example, the Food Quality Protection Act of 1996 (FQPA) defines safety standards and tolerances for pesticides in food. The law requires an additional evaluation of the weight of all relevant evidence. This involves examining the level of concern for how children are particularly sensitive and susceptible to the effects of a chemical and determining whether traditional uncertainty factors already incorporated into the risk assessment adequately protect infants and children. This is accomplished mathematically in the exposure assessment. The U.S. EPA has prepared guidance on how data deficiency uncertainty factors should be used to address the FQPA childrens' safety factor. The default factor of safety was introduced because children are a 10 times more risk from pesticide exposure, so their exposure should be 10 times less than the general population (known as the "10X rule"). The final decision to retain the default 10X FQPA safety factor or to assign a different FQPA safety factor is made during the characterization of risk, and not determined as part of the RfD process. The "weight-of-the-evidence" approach, therefore, includes both hazard and exposure considered together for the chemical being evaluated. The FQPA safety factor for a particular chemical is that it must have the level of confidence in the hazard and exposure assessments and an explicit judgment of the possibility of other residual uncertainties in characterizing the risk to children.

By extension, other sensitive strata of the population also need protection beyond those of the general population.[18] The elderly and asthmatic members of society are more sensitive to airborne particles. Pregnant women are at greater risk from exposure to hormonally active agents, such as phthalates and a number of pesticides. Pubescent females undergo dramatic changes in their endocrine systems and, consequently, sensitive to exposures during this time.

Timing was critical in the Alar case. The National Toxicology Program was established in 1978 by the U.S. Health, Education, and Welfare (today known as the Department of Health and Human Services), right about the time that the Alar data were being released and evaluated. The program was created because the government was being criticized for a lack of coordination of its myriad toxicology testing programs. A central program was seen as a way to strengthen the science base in toxicology, to develop and to validate improved testing methods. The program was also designed to provide more reliable information about potentially toxic chemicals to health, regulatory, and research agencies, scientific and medical communities, and the general public.

The 1970s saw an increasing amount of concern by scientists, politicians, journalists, and activists about the human health effects of chemical agents in our environment. Many human diseases were thought to be directly or indirectly related to chemical exposures; so many argued that decreasing or eliminating human exposures to those chemicals would help prevent some human disease and disability. This sounds almost trite by contemporary standards, where chemical exposure and risks are logical, but such linkages were nascent and risk assessment was still in its formative stages.

While many considered the whole problem of toxic substances to be much ado about nothing, others saw a cancer link to virtually any chemical other than water. The latter was brought home to me in 1977 in a discussion with a regional administrator of the U.S. EPA. She was trying to convince people in a meeting that "everything doesn't cause cancer." She was particularly irritated by some of the local cartoons that showed a rat consuming massive amounts of artificial sweeteners with bylines to the effect that any substance consumed to excess would lead to cancer. Her major point was that if a substance is not carcinogenic, it will not lead to cancer, no matter the dose. Again, through the prism of risk assessment, such a statement seems unnecessary, but in retrospect it was not only needed, but also in many venues it was seen as "prochemical" or even "antienvironmental!" In fact, this EPA official was one of the most "environmental" of any I have met, but her objectivity would not allow her to ignore the dose-response relationships. Vestiges of these concerns are still with us, as we try to have a common understanding of terms like organic, additives, natural, and holistic. Few chemicals, even those where data seem to support their safety, are considered acceptable for certain segments of society.

So, Alar was at the focal point for this controversy. Its structure was perceived to be menacing by many (see Figure 16.3). In February 1989, *60 Minutes* ran a story about a Natural Resources Defense Council (NRDC) report on Alar as a human carcinogen—one that posed particular risks for children. Public protest forced apple growers to stop using it and Uniroyal to pull it off the market. Although Uniroyal voluntarily canceled its use on fruits and vegetables, the chemical is still used for ornamental and bedding plants.

The scientific debate centered around unsymmetrical dimethyl hydrazine (UDMH), a contaminant of commercial daminozide—0.005% (50 mg/L)—and a metabolite of daminozide, formed in the body during food processing or when spray mixes containing daminozide are left standing in the mixing tank.

It appears that Alar's degradation product may indeed be linked to cancer (see Table 16.7).

So then, what are the real effects? The problem with answering this question includes both the adjective and the noun: what is "real" and what is the "effect" in question? In some

N-(dimethylamino)succinamic acid

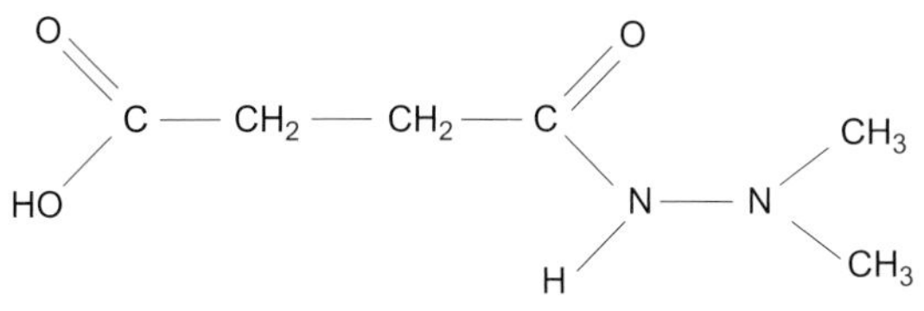

FIGURE 16.3 Alar structure.

TABLE 16.7 Results of Cancer Studies of Alar and Its Degradation Product

| Animal | Substance | Amount | Time (years) | Result |
|--------|-----------|--------|--------------|--------|
| Rats | Daminozide | 5, 25, 250, or 500 mg/kg/day | 2 | No increase in tumor formation |
| Mice | Daminozide | 15, 150, 300, or 500 mg/kg/day | 2 | No increase in tumor formation |
| Rats | UDMH in water | 0, 1, 50, or 100 ppm | 2 | Significant, but slight, dose-related increase in liver tumors in females |
| Rats | UDMH in water | 100 ppm | 2 | Bile duct hyperplasia and inflammation of the liver in males |
| Rats | UDMH in water | 50 and 100 ppm | 2 | Bile duct hyperplasia and inflammation of the liver in females |
| Mice | UDMH in water | 0, 1, 5, or 10 ppm (males) 0, 1, 5, or 20 ppm (females) | 2 | Females exhibited decreased survival at the highest dose tested; also a significantincrease in the incidence of lung tumors |

cases, for example, the answer is partially answered by animal studies, e.g., mammals may experience skin or eye irritation. Also, Alar seems to be very rapidly distributed after mammalian exposure, e.g., 96 h after swine were exposed to a single oral dose ($5$ mg kg$^{-1}$) of daminozide, it was detected in all body tissues at concentrations as high as 73 ppb. The highest levels were found in the liver and the kidney. Urinalysis showed that about 84% of the dose was eliminated in the urine and that 1% of the dose was metabolized to UDMH. The majority of daminozide residues ingested by milk animals is rapidly excreted in the urine and feces.

Science was never "left alone" to do its objective and careful research, however. The NRDC, a nonprofit environmental group, allegedly encouraged CBS's *60 Minutes* into running a story on the dangers of Alar. The broadcast was based largely on the NRDC report "Intolerable Risk: Pesticides in Our Children's Food," which identified 66 potentially carcinogenic pesticides in foods that a child might eat.

The NRDC's public relations firm, Fenton Communications, then convinced other major news organizations to feature the story. Meryl Streep testified before Congress, and on TV talk shows, about the dangers of Alar. The public panicked: school systems removed apples from their cafeterias and supermarkets took them off their shelves. The scare cost apple growers over $100 million. The American Council on Science and Health paid Walter Cronkite $25,000 to narrate a TV documentary on the Alar scare entitled *Big fears, little risks*.

In a previous 2-year period, stocks rose an average 14% for companies negatively profiled on *60 Minutes*. Market insiders, aware of the upcoming story, bought a large number of shares in Uniroyal.

Another important lesson learned from the Alar episode is that of risk perception, especially as it pertains to children. Children are particular sensitive to many environmental pollutants. They are growing, so tissue development is highly prolific. Plus, society has stressed (as it certainly should) special levels of protection for infants and children. For example, regulations under the Food Quality Protection Act mandate special treatment of children, evidenced by the so-called 10 X Rule, which recommends that, after all other considerations, that the exposure calculated for children include 10 times more protection (thus, the exposure is multiplied by 10) when children are exposed to toxic substances. The Federal Food Quality Protection Act[19] requires that risk assessments related to children include a safety factor regarding the potential for prenatal and postnatal effects. Several concepts of risk are introduced in Chapter 2, including the observation that environmental risk is a function of hazard and exposure. The 10 X policy is an effort to ameliorate possible risks to children by addressing the potential exposures, even when the hazard is not completely understood. Frequently, the prenatal and postnatal toxicities are included when trying to establish some level of safety or precaution.

Recall that the concept of risk is expressed as the likelihood (statistical probability) that harm will occur when a receptor (e.g., human or a part of an ecosystem) is exposed to that hazard. So, an example of a toxic hazard is a carcinogen (a cancer-causing chemical), and an example of a toxic risk is the likelihood that a certain population will have an incidence of a particular type of cancer after being exposed to that carcinogen (e.g., the population risk that one person out of a million will develop lung cancer when exposed to a certain dose of a chemical carcinogen for a certain period of time).

## Genetically Modified Food

Food is at the center of the controversy surrounding many positive and negative aspects of biotechnology. That hunger is directly related to poverty in the developing world is more a function of poverty than of food scarcity. Indeed, the world's food production has far outpaced population growth in recent decades. Rural areas account for 75% of the world's poor and undernourished people, in spite of the global urbanization trend. Biological diversity is a requirement for a sustainable and reliable global food supply. As discussed in Chapter 13, short-term methods for providing food (e.g., slash and burn) may lead to long-term costs, including famine and loss of productive habitat.

Food has been genetically modified for millennia. However, in recent decades, the methods of engineering new strains of species have been accelerated by the insertion of recombinant DNA from one species to another in order to transfer a desirable trait (e.g., slower spoilage, frost resistance, and higher yields). There are a number of disaster scenarios being debated, including possible health effects (e.g., increased allergenicity and toxicity) and environmental damage (e.g., gene flow into vulnerable, indigenous habitats).

The law of unintended consequences should be respected when it comes to predicting possible environmental outcomes from genetic manipulation to improve the food supply.

Biological agents elicit myriad effects, for example, molds have intricate mechanisms to ward off predators that may produce substances that are toxic. A slight modification of the transcription could lead to undesirable results. To make matters worse, bioengineered genes "are typically inserted into random positions in the receiving organism's genome."[20] Such lack of precision is unsettling when we are talking about chaotic ecosystems, wherein miniscule differences in initial conditions can lead to startling differences in outcome (i.e. the "butterfly effect" of a slight change in the flap of an insect's wing in the Amazon, could change initial conditions that would otherwise not have led to a hurricane in the Atlantic Ocean). The less the certainty about the location of the desired trait on the DNA molecule, the less the control over outcomes. The location in the genome is not precisely known, but the traits are being selected empirically, as are other traits of which the biotechnologist may or may not be aware. The many previous environmental and health disasters in the past should instill more humility within the scientific community:

> Inserting genes is similar to ecological practices that we thought we understood well, but which held unexpected consequences, such as introducing industrial chemicals to the environment (consider DDT, PCBs), or such as introducing alien species (consider Purple Loosestrife, Kudzu, Starlings).... Regardless of our fundamental ignorance of the genetic mechanisms mentioned above, no one has properly studied the ecological and health ramifications of releasing so many GMOs into farms and grocery stores.[21]

## Fairness

Even before the genetic engineering revolution, crop practices presented threats to sustainable food supply, notably the introduction of monocultures to what were the world's most diverse habitats. Substituting indigenous crop varieties and diverse cultivation systems with monocultures has increased vulnerability to the ravages of pests and plant diseases, loss of soil fertility, and increased application of agrochemicals. As evidence, global food supplies now depend on merely 100 or so species of food crops, rather than the thousands of species and varieties that have been used locally for millennia. This consolidation is inextricably threatening to the individual farmers in developing countries as they cannot sustain this practice, leading to more monocultures, and further diminishing diversity.

Many of the farmers in developing nations and in certain demographic strata of developed nations are poor and susceptible to offers of quick fixes to food supplies. They are unlikely to complain, which is similar to other vulnerable communities. Thus, what may seem to be a scientific issue (e.g., growing crops that produce the most food) in fact can also frequently be an issue of justice. Indeed, it is similar to the need for EJ, as articulated in the U.S. with Executive Order 12898, "Federal Actions to Address Environmental Justice in Minority and Low-Income Populations." This order directs that federal agencies in their day-to-day operation to be sensitive to "disproportionately high and adverse human health and environmental effects of programs, policies and activities on minority populations and low-income populations." Unsustainable food production, then, falls under the rubric of disproportionate harm to vulnerable people.

## VINYL CHLORIDE

The ubiquitous chemical compound vinyl chloride is illustrative of how the majority may gain at the expense of the minority. Society's dependence on plastics grew exponentially in the second half of the 20th Century. The key polymer in this growth was polyvinyl chloride (PVC).

Whereas, PVC has been invaluable in every economic sector, from medicine to building materials to electronics, it has also played a role in disasters. A recent reminder of the downsides of plastics was when a PVC production unit at Formosa Plastics in Illiopolis, Illinois, exploded on April 23, 2004, killing five workers and seriously injuring two others. The explosion followed a release of highly flammable vinyl chloride, which ignited. The explosion forced a community evacuation and ignited fires that burned for several days at the plant.[22] This horrible disaster indicated the immediate threat of vinyl chloride. The compound also has a more insidious and veiled threat when people are exposed over years and decades.

Certainly, such isolated disasters are tragic. However, there is a broader and arguably greater threat from vinyl chloride. Long-term exposure to vinyl chloride through inhalation and oral exposure in humans has resulted in liver damage and cancer. Vinyl chloride is classified in the worst group of carcinogens, Group A, human carcinogen (see Table 16.6).

## Cancer Alley

The industrial corridor along the lower Mississippi River[23] known as "Cancer Alley" is home to a predominantly low-income, minority (African-American and Latino) community who are being exposed to many pollutants.[24] This 80-mile long region, between Baton Rouge and New Orleans, has experienced releases of carcinogens, mutagens, teratogens (birth-defect agents), and endocrine disruptors in the atmosphere, soil, groundwater, and surface water. More than 100 oil refineries and petrochemical facilities are located in this region. It has been reported that per capita release of toxic air pollutants is about 27 kg, nine times greater than the U.S. average of only 3 kg.[25] The U.S. average 260 kg of toxic air pollutants per square mile is dwarfed by the more than 7700 kg per square mile in this industrial corridor.

In the 1970s, cases of liver cancer (hepatic angiosarcoma) began to be reported in workers at polymer production facilities and other industries where vinyl chloride was present. Since then, the compound has been designated as a potent human carcinogen (inhalation slope factor = 0.3 milligrams per kilogram per day).

Vinyl chloride may at first glance appear to be readily broken down by numerous natural processes, including abiotic chemical and microbial degradation (see Figure 16.4); numerous studies have shown that vinyl chloride concentrations can remain elevated over long periods of time. In fact, under environmental conditions, vinyl chloride can be extremely persistent, with an anaerobic $t_{1/2}$ in soil greater than 2 years. It can also be difficult to treat with conventional engineering methods. For example, aerobic degradation in sewage treatment plants and surface water in an isolated bacteria culture with vinyl chloride concentrations of 20-120 mg $L^{-1}$ needs a minimum of 35 days to complete degrade the compound. Nontraditional treatment methods, such as attack by hydroxyl radicals, can significantly reduce the half-life.[26] In heavily polluted areas like Cancer Alley, vinyl chloride repositories can remain intact for decades, serving as a continuous potential source. These repositories can actually be compounds other than vinyl chloride, but which break down to form the compound, e.g., chloroethylene solvents degrade to vinyl chloride. With its high vapor pressure (2300 mmHg at 20 °C) and high aqueous solubility (1100 mg $L^{-1}$), the chances of people being exposed via the air or drinking water once vinyl chloride is formed can be considerable (see Sidebar: Parent versus Progeny).

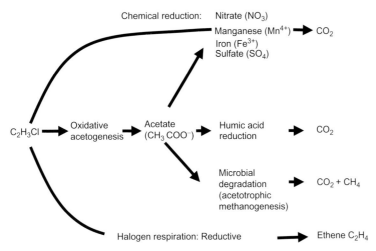

FIGURE 16.4   Biodegradation pathways for vinyl chloride. *Source: U.S. Geological Survey. Microbial degradation of chloroethenes in ground water systems. Toxic substances hydrology program: investigations. http://toxics.usgs.gov/sites/ solvents/chloroethene.html; 2004 [accessed November 29, 2004].*

# PARENT VERSUS PROGENY

Chemical kinetics is the description of the rate of a chemical reaction.[27] This is the rate at which the reactants are transformed into products. In environmental situations, this is the process by which chemicals are synthesized, such as in microbial processes, and degraded. Degradation is both good and bad. It is beneficial in situations where we are able to manufacture substances in a way that they are "biodegradable," meaning that they are relatively easily broken down to simpler compounds, such as by sunlight (photodegradation), by ubiquitous chemicals like carbonic acid (abiotic chemical degradation), or by organisms (biodegradation). It can be very harmful when the substances are changed to become more persistent, more bioaccumulating or more toxic. It is not uncommon, for example, for a compound to become more toxic when it is metabolized, a process known as bioactivation.

Changes to a parent compound, such as a pesticide formulated to kill plants or insects, will lead to the formation of new compounds, known as degradation products or progeny. Depending on the chemical and the conditions surrounding it, these degradation processes occur at specific rates. Because a rate is a change in quantity that occurs with time, the most important environmental change is thus the concentration of our contaminants into new chemical compounds:

$$\text{Reaction rate} = \frac{\text{change in product concentration}}{\text{corresponding change in time}} \qquad (16.1)$$

and,

$$\text{Reaction rate} = \frac{\text{change in reactant concentration}}{\text{corresponding change in time}} \qquad (16.2)$$

In environmental degradation, the change in product concentration will be decreasing proportionately with the reactant concentration, so for when a chemical (X) is being degraded, we can show this differentially as

$$\text{Rate} = -\frac{\Delta(X)}{\Delta t} \qquad (16.3)$$

The negative sign denotes that the mass of the parent chemical is decreasing. Assuming only one the degradation product Y is forming from this reaction, Y must be simultaneously increasing in proportion to the decreasing concentration of the contaminant X, and the reaction rate for Y is

$$\text{Rate} = \frac{\Delta(Y)}{\Delta t} \qquad (16.4)$$

By convention, the concentration of the chemical is shown in parentheses to indicate that the system is not at equilibrium, the slope of mass versus time is not equal to zero. $\Delta(X)$ is calculated as the difference between an initial concentration and a final concentration:

$$\Delta(X) = \Delta(X)_{final} - \Delta(X)_{initial} \qquad (16.5)$$

So, if we were to observe the chemical transformation[28] of an isomer of the compound butane to different isomer over time, this would indicate the kinetics of the system. The rate of reaction at any time is the negative of the slope of the tangent to the concentration curve at that specific time.

The reaction rate is a function of the concentrations of the reacting substances. The mathematical expression of this function is known as the "rate law." The rate law can be determined experimentally for any contaminant. Varying the concentration of each reactant independently and then measuring the result will give a concentration curve. Each reactant has its own rate law. Thus, considering the reaction of parent compounds A and B which yield C (A+B→C), where the reaction rate increases with the increasing concentration of either A or B: quadrupling the mass of A or B in the reaction quadruples the rate of this whole reaction. Thus, the rate law for such a reaction is

$$\text{Rate} = k[A][B] \qquad (16.6)$$

But another reaction, X+Y→Z, has a reaction rate that increases only if the concentration of X is increased (changing the Y concentration has no effect on the rate law). In this reaction, the rate law must be

$$\text{Rate} = k[X] \qquad (16.7)$$

Thus, the concentrations in the rate law are the concentrations of reacting chemical species at any specific point in time during the reaction. The rate is the velocity of the reaction at that time. The constant $k$ in the equations above is the *rate constant*, which is unique for every chemical reaction and is a fundamental physical constant for a reaction, as defined by environmental conditions (e.g., pH, temperature, pressure, and type of substrate or solvent). The rate constant is defined as the rate of the reaction when all reactants are present in a 1 M concentration, so the rate constant $k$ is the rate of reaction under conditions standardized by a unit concentration.

The rate law can be shown by drawing a concentration curve for a contaminant that consists of an infinite number of points at each instant of time, so that an instantaneous rate can be calculated along the concentration curve. At each point on the curve, the rate of reaction is directly proportional to the concentration of the compound at that moment in time. This is a physical demonstration of *kinetic order*. The overall kinetic order is the sum of the exponents (powers) of all the concentrations in the rate law. So for the rate $k[A][B]$, the overall kinetic order is 2. Such a rate describes a second-order reaction because the rate depends on the concentration of the reactant raised to the second power. Other decomposition rates are like $k[X]$ and are first-order reactions because the rate depends on the concentration of the reactant raised to the first power.

The kinetic order of each reactant is the power that its concentration is raised in the rate law. So, $k[A][B]$ is first order for each reactant and $k[X]$ is first order X and zero order for Y. In a zero-order reaction, compounds degrade at a constant rate and are independent of reactant concentration.

Further, plotting the number of moles with respect to time shows the point at which kinetics ends and equilibrium begins. This simple example applies to any chemical kinetics process, but the kinetics is complicated in the "real world" by the ever changing conditions of ecosystems, tissues, and human beings.

This is often described as the change of a "parent compound" into "chemical daughters" or "progeny." Pesticide kinetics often concerns itself with the change of the active ingredient in the pesticide to its "degradation products." Environmental practitioners must understand and explain these processes in most environmental situations, including assessments and cleanup. So, in addition to compounds X, Y, and Z that may have been used, stored, or transferred to a site, the extent to which other toxic degradation products X', X'', and Z' may have formed in the water, soil, sediment, and air at various times must also be determined. Such equilibrium chemistry is complicated for engineers and scientists, let alone those members of the community who may never consider these complex processes. For example, when investigating an abandoned hazardous waste site, monitoring and chemical testing should be conducted to target those contaminants that may have resulted from the breakdown of parent compounds. A general surveillance is needed to identify a broad suite of contaminants, given that decades may have passed since the waste was buried, spilled, or released into the environment. This is particularly important in soil and ground water, as their rates of migration ($Q$) are quite slow compared to the rates usually found in air and surface water transport, so new compounds that are formed before the parents are flushed. Thus, the likelihood of finding remnant parent compounds and their progeny is generally greater in soil, sediment, and groundwater than in surface waters.

Local groups have begun arming themselves with environmental data, such as the emissions and other release information in the Toxic Release Inventory, that show the inordinately high toxic chemical release rates near their communities. Local communities have challenged nearby industries with possible health effects linked to chemical exposures. For example, residents in Mossville, Louisiana, argued that several health problems in their community could be linked to chemical releases by 17 industrial facilities located within 1 km of the community. These confrontations led to a number of advocates writing the 2000 report, *Breathing poison: the toxic costs of industries in Calcasieu Parish, Louisiana*, which called for "pollution reduction, environmental health services, and a fair and just relocation for consenting residents."[29] These efforts have gained the attention of national media and regulatory agencies and have been emblematic of the EJ movement.

Vinyl chloride ($C_2H_3Cl$), usually known as vinyl chloride monomer (VCM), is made in very large quantities and is a known human carcinogen that causes a rare cancer of the liver.[30] Vinyl chloride is used primarily for production of PVC, accounting for 99% of its consumption. It has also been linked to leukemia, neurological damage, birth defects, and brain cancer.[31]

vinyl chloride

The U.S. EPA has defined the reference concentration for inhalation (RfC) as $0.1$ mg m$^{-3}$ (about 1 ppm) and the RfD as $3 \times 10^{-3}$ mg kg$^{-1}$ d$^{-1}$ where d refers to day and the kg refers to a person's mass. These values are also used in the United Kingdom.[32]

Vinyl chloride is a gas under normal conditions of temperature and pressure (boiling point $= -13.4\,°C$). It has a mild sweet odor at a concentration of 3000 ppm and can be tasted at a concentration in water of 3.4 ppm. The odor threshold is at a concentration 10,000 times the RfC value, i.e., well past the danger level. Drinking a liter of water contaminated with 3.4 ppm VCM would be 10 times less than the daily limit for an adult.

Before use, vinyl chloride is stored as a liquid under pressure in high-capacity spheres.

In 2010, 30 million tonnes of VCM was produced worldwide, largely for the production of PVC, which consists of long repeating units of vinyl chloride.[33] At one time, vinyl chloride was used as a coolant, as a propellant in spray cans, and in some cosmetics. However, since the mid-1970s, this has been stopped because of the toxic nature of VCM.

Vinyl chloride does not occur naturally. It is manufactured from the olefin, ethylene, which is obtained from crude oil distillation. There are two commercial routes to its production.

The most common method today involves two reactions: firstly, ethylene is chlorinated using chlorine gas together with an iron chloride catalyst:

$$CH_2 = CH_2 + Cl_2 \xrightarrow{FeCl_3} ClCH_2CH_2Cl \tag{16.8}$$

In a second reaction, the ethylene dichloride vapor is heated to 500 °C at 15-30 atm (1.5-3 MPa) pressure, resulting in the decomposition of the ethylene dichloride to produce vinyl chloride:

$$ClCH_2CH_2Cl \rightarrow CH_2 = CHCl + HCl \tag{16.9}$$

The pre-1950s method for producing VCM was to use acetylene as the carbon-based feedstock:

$$CHCH + HCl \rightarrow CH_2 = CHCl \tag{16.10}$$

This is the method currently used in China. This acetylene route is considered to be highly polluting and energy consuming. However, China uses this method because China has large low-cost coal fields. Otherwise it would have to depend on ethylene derived from crude oil. The future of China's acetylene-based plants will depend upon global crude oil prices.

## THE MANUFACTURING PROCESSES USED IN THE MAKING OF VINYL CHLORIDE

Before the 1950s, much of the chemical industry and the manufacturing of organic chemicals and plastics was based on coal; with acetylene being the main building block and the starting reactant for many useful products, including vinyl chloride. Acetylene was prepared by the hydrolysis of calcium carbide a reaction discovered by Friedrich Wohler in 1862:

$$CaC_2 + 2H_2O \rightarrow Ca(OH)_2 + C_2H_2$$

The calcium carbide was produced in an electric arc furnace from a mixture of lime (CaO) and coke (largely carbon and obtained from coal). This method has not changed since its invention in the 1892 by T. L. Wilson, (North Carolina, USA)

$$CaO + 3C \rightarrow CaC_2 + CO$$

The arc furnace (with graphite electrodes) is necessary because of the high temperature required for this reaction to take place (2000°C). This process is only viable if large amounts of low cost electricity are available to power the arc furnaces.

The coke in turn was made by the pyrolysis (heating in the absence of air) of coal. In this process coal is fed into a series of ovens, which are sealed and heated at high temperatures in the absence of oxygen. The volatile compounds are driven off the coal (and should be collected and processed to recover combustible gases, other by-products, and to remove pollutants.) and the solid carbon remaining in the oven is coke. Volatile pollutants include , benzene and polynuclear aromatic compounds, particulate matter, sulphur oxides, and nitrogen oxides and even hydrogen sulphide and hydrogen cyanide. It has been reported that for every tonne of coke produced: 50–80 g of $H_2S$; between 0.7 and 7 kg of particulate matter; between 0.2 and 6.5 kg of $SO_x$; 3 kg of volatile organic compounds (VOCs) including 2 kg of benzene, are produced. [reference: Pollution Prevention and Abatement Handbook: WORLD BANK GROUP, Effective July 1998: http://www1.ifc.org/wps/wcm/connect/9ecab70048855c048ab4da6a6515bb18/coke_PPAH.pdf] If these pollutants are not collected and treated they will contribute significantly to the pollution of the atmosphere. There are, today, cleaner ways of making acetylene (either by the partial combustion of methane or as a side product in the ethylene stream from the cracking of hydrocarbons from oil refineries, but in China the old fashioned and well tested method of carbide chemistry is still used in the chemical industry and in particular in the manufacture of vinyl chloride:

$$CHCH + HCl = CH_2CHCl$$

In the 1960s the organic chemical industries changed radically when oil supplanted coal as the chief source of carbon for making useful organic chemicals such as plastics. It was found easier to make vinyl chloride from ethylene which was produced in the petrochemical industry by steam cracking gaseous or light liquid hydrocarbons. In this process steam at between 750–950°C reacts with the larger hydrocarbon molecules. These molecules are converted into smaller ones and double bonds (unsaturation) are introduced. The ethylene is then separated by distillation. This is a much cleaner process and ethylene can be considered as a by-product of the petrochemical industry. The more modern method for producing vinyl chloride, in its simplest form, is:

$$CH_2CH_2 + Cl_2 = CH_2CHCl + HCl$$

The earliest report on the toxicity of VCM was as early as 1930 when Patty noted that test animals exposed to VCM suffered liver damage. This was followed by many similar reports and then, in 1963, a Romanian researcher, Suciu, published his findings of liver disease in VC workers.[34] And again, in 1968, Mutchler and Kramer, two Dow researchers, reported their finding that exposures as low as 300 ppm caused liver damage in VCM workers. This confirms earlier animal data in humans.[35] Soon after that cancer was diagnosed in VCM workers, but it was not until 1974 that the Government was informed by B. F. Goodrich company that it was investigating whether the cancer deaths at its PVC plant at their Louisville, Kentucky plant were related to occupational causes. At that time, the RfC for VCM was 500 ppm. Soon after this, the EPA reconsidered the toxicity of VCM and it was reduced 500-fold to its present level.

In the United Kingdom, as in the United States, angiosarcoma liver cancer has been directly linked to VCM exposure, and as a result, rigid rules were implemented to reduce the levels of VCM in the atmosphere of factories.[36–39]

The toxicity of VCM is the focus of many environmental moves to have it outlawed. It suffers also from being linked to PVC which is linked to dioxins which form when PVC is burnt or incinerated. Today, with the stringent levels of VCM allowed in factories, the real problem comes when there is a fire in a VCM or PVC plant. As mentioned at the beginning of this discussion, the 2004 explosion in Illiopolis, Illinois ignited highly flammable vinyl chloride in a PVC plant. The fires burnt for several days and forced the community to evacuate. The danger of dioxins from such explosions and fires are ever present since all of the ingredients for dioxin and furan formations are present, i.e. high temperature, chlorinated precursor compounds and sorbants (e.g. smoke particles).

## Polyvinyl Chloride

As mentioned, PVC is a very common plastic (the third most popular plastic today), and because it is easily worked, durable, and cheap to produce, it is used to make a variety of plastic products including pipes, hosepipes, wire and cable coatings, and packaging materials, automobile and furniture upholstery, wall coverings, doors and windows, housewares, and automotive parts. The worldwide production of PVC is increasing at a rate of 3% annually. Much of the world's production of VCM and PVC is now centered in Asia and China.

In the United States, PVC is manufactured predominantly near low-income communities in Texas and Louisiana. The toxic impact of pollution from these factories on these communities has made them a focus in the EJ movement.[40]

In spite of PVC being such a popular plastic, its combustion products include highly toxic compounds like the halogenated furans and dioxins (see Table 16.8). From a green engineering standpoint, PVC also raises concerns about VCM and numerous other toxic chemicals in its life cycle; PVC has been the focus of many environmental movements calling for its ban.[41]

TABLE 16.8   Balanced Combustion Reactions for Selected Organic Compounds

| | |
|---|---|
| Chlorobenzene | $C_6H_5Cl + 7O_2 \rightarrow 6CO_2 + HCl + 2H_2O$ |
| TCE | $C_2Cl_4 + O_2 + 2H_2O \rightarrow 2CO_2 + HCl$ |
| HCE | $C_2Cl_6 + \frac{1}{2}O_2 + 3H_2O \rightarrow 2CO_2 + 6HCl$ |
| CPVC | $C_4H_5Cl_3 + 4\frac{1}{2}O_2 \rightarrow 4CO_2 = 3HCl + H_2O$ |
| Natural gas fuel (methane) | $CH_4 + 2O_2 \rightarrow CO_2 + 2H_2O$ |
| PTFE Teflon | $C_2F_4 + O_2 \rightarrow CO_2 + 4HF$ |
| Butyl rubber | $C_9H_{16} + 13O_2 \rightarrow 9CO_2 + 8H_2O$ |
| Polyethylene | $C_2H_4 + 3O_2 \rightarrow 2CO_2 + 2H_2O$ |

Wood is considered to have the composition of $C_{6.9}H_{10.6}O_{3.5}$. Therefore, the combustion reactions are simple carbon and hydrogen combustion:

$$C + O_2 \rightarrow CO_2$$
$$H + 0.25O_2 \rightarrow 0.5H_2O$$

TCE, tetrachloroethene; HCE, hexachloroethane; CPVC, postchlorinated polyvinyl chloride; PFTE, polytetrafluoroethylene.
*Source: Vallero DA.* Fundamentals of air pollution. *Burlington, MA: Elsevier Academic Press; 2008; U.S. Environmental Protection Agency.*

# FOOD VERSUS FUEL

The unavailability of food is a growing problem and has been a part of natural and human-induced disasters throughout history. Droughts and other meteorological events have triggered famines. Poor and malicious governmental actions have caused or exacerbated natural disasters, causing massive starvation, particularly in the developing world. However, good shortages have the potential of becoming a geopolitical disaster, especially in light of the shortages and trade-offs among the Earth's finite resources. Emblematic of this potential disaster is the increasing use of grain to produce biofuels, most notably ethanol ($C_2H_5OH$). Ethanol fuel is generally produced by bacterial fermentation:

$$C_6H_{12}O_6 \rightarrow 2C_2H_5OH + 2CO_2 + \text{heat} \tag{16.11}$$

Ethanol has been increasingly touted as an alternative to crude oil-based fuels. This interest has been diverse, with coverage in the national media and in professional and research journals. In his 2007 State of the Union Address, U.S. President George W. Bush[42] set a two-part goal:

- Setting a mandatory standard requiring 35 billion gallons (130 million liters) of renewable and alternative fuels in the year 2017, which is approximately five times the 2012 target called for in current law. Thus, in 2017, alternative fuels will displace 15% of projected annual gasoline use.
- Reforming the corporate average fuel economy standards for cars and extending the present light truck. Thus, in 2017, projected annual gasoline use would be reduced by up to 8.5 billion gallons (32 billion liters), a further 5% reduction that, in combination with increasing the supply of renewable and alternative fuels, will bring the total reduction in projected annual gasoline use to 20%.

These and other alternative fuel standards have met with skepticism and even dissent. During recent elections campaigns, certain politicians in U.S. farm states have supported subsidies to produce fuels using grains, especially corn, that would otherwise be available for human or livestock consumption. This has been in spite of challenges to the viability of ethanol as a fuel from a thermodynamic perspective. Indeed, since the presidential proclamation, dedicated corn crops and ethanol refining facilities in these states have emerged. On the other hand, the geopolitical impacts of food versus fuel dilemmas have increasingly demonstrated that ethanol production from food grains is generally inefficient from a thermodynamic standpoint.

Some have accused advocates of ethanol fuels of using "junk science" to support the "sustainability" of an ethanol fuel system. Notably, certain critics contend that ethanol is not even renewable, as its product life cycle includes a large number of steps that depend on fossil fuels. The metrics of success are often deceptively quantitative. For example, the two goals for increasing ethanol use include firm dates and percentages. However, the means of accountability can be quite subjective. For example, the 2017 target *could* be met, but if overall fossil fuel use were to increase dramatically, the percentage of total alternative use could be quite small, i.e., less than 15%. Thus, *both* absolute and fractional metrics are needed.

On the surface, the choice of whether to pursue a substantial increase in ethanol production is a simple matter of benefits versus costs. Is it more or less costly to generate ethanol than other fuels, especially those derived from crude oil? Engineers make much use of the benefit-to-cost ratio (BCR), owing to a strong affinity for objective measures of successes. Thus, *usefulness* is an engineering measure of success. Such utility is indeed part of any successful engineering enterprise. After all, engineers are expected to provide reasonable and useful products. Two useful engineering definitions of utilitarianism (Latin *utilis*, useful) are imbedded in BCR and life-cycle-analysis (LCA):

1. the belief that the value of a thing or an action is determined by its utility and
2. the ethical theory that all action should be directed toward achieving the greatest happiness for the greatest number of people.

The BCR is an attractive metric because of its simplicity and seeming transparency. To determine whether a project is worthwhile, one need only add up all of the benefits and put them in the numerator and all of the costs (or risks) and put them in the denominator. If the ratio is greater than 1, its benefits exceed its costs. One obvious problem is that some costs and benefits are much easier to quantify than others. Some, such as those associated with quality of life, are nearly impossible to accurately quantify and monetize. Further, the comparison of action versus no-action alternatives cannot always be captured within a BCR. Opportunity costs and risks are associated with taking no action (e.g., loss of an opportunity to apply an emerging technology may mean delay or nonexistent treatment of diseases). Simply comparing the *status quo* to costs and risks associated with a new technology may be biased toward no action. Costs in time and money are not the only reasons for avoiding action. The greater availability of ethanol may introduce unforeseen risks that, if not managed properly, could interfere with quality of life of distant and future populations and could add costs to the public (e.g., air pollutants and topsoil loss) with little net benefit. So it is not simply a matter of benefits versus cost; it is often one risk being traded for another. Often, addressing contravening risk is a matter of optimization, which is a proven analytical tool in engineering. However, the greater the number of contravening risks that are possible, the more complicated such optimization routines become. The product flows, critical paths, and life cycle inventories can become quite complicated for complex issues. Risk trade-off is likely to occur in ethanol and biofuel decisions. For example, if the government mandates more ethanol usage, it will also have to enforce new air pollution laws associated with the fuel. These added regulations can be associated with indirect, countervailing risks. For example, the costs of construction of new facilities and the price of feedstock (especially corn) may increase safety risks via "income" and "stock" effects. The income effect results from pulling money away from other fuel ventures to pay the capital costs associated with ethanol, making it more difficult for a company or backers to invest in other services that would have provided improved fuel efficiency. The stock effect results when the capital costs increase to a point where companies have to wait to purchase new facilities, so they are left with substandard manufacturing. Thus, the engineer is frequently asked to optimize for two or more conflicting variables in many situations. The success of ethanol in displacing fossil fuels depends on the efficiency with which it can be produced and used. Complicating matters, the use of fossil fuels in their production and/or operation is part of ethanol production, as it is for all biofuels. Societal benefits and costs are tied to ethanol's energy balances.

Another accountability challenge is whether losses are included in calculations. From a thermodynamics standpoint, the nation's increased ethanol use could actually increase demands for fossil fuels, such as the need for crude oil-based infrastructures, including farm chemicals derived from oil, farm vehicle and equipment energy use (planting, cultivation, harvesting, and transport to markets) dependent on gasoline and diesel fuels, and even embedded energy needs in the ethanol processing facility (crude oil-derived chemicals needed for catalysis, purification, fuel mixing, and refining). A comprehensive LCA is a vital tool for ascertaining the actual efficiencies.

The questions surrounding alternative fuels and ethanol, specifically, can be addressed using a three-step methodology. First, the efficiency calculations must conform to the physical laws, especially those of thermodynamics and motion. Second, the "greenness," as a metric of sustainability and effectiveness, can be characterized by life cycle analyses. Third, the policy and geopolitical options and outcomes can be evaluated by decision force field analyses. In fact, these three approaches are sequential. The first must be satisfied before moving to the second. Likewise, the third depends on the first two methods. No matter how politically attractive or favorable it is to society, an alternative fuel must comport with the conservation of mass and energy. Further, each step in the life cycle (e.g., extraction of raw materials, value-added manufacturing, use, and disposal) must be considered in any benefit-cost or risk-benefit analysis. Finally, the societal benefits and risks must be viable for an alternative fuel to be accepted. Thus, even a very efficient and effective fuel may be rejected for societal reasons (e.g., religious, cultural, historical, or ethical).

The challenge of the scientist, engineer, and policy maker is to sift through the myriad data and information to ascertain whether ethanol truly presents a viable alternative fuel. Of the misrepresentations being made, some clearly violate the physical laws. Many ignore or do not provide correct weights to certain factors in the life cycle. There is always the risk of mischaracterizing the social good or costs, a common problem with the use of benefit/cost relationships.

## BURNING AS A SOCIETAL ISSUE

All societies depend on fire. Western civilization is often criticized for its disproportionate demand for fuel, especially nonrenewable fossil fuels. The way that a nation addresses burning is an important measure of how advanced it is, not only in dealing with pollution but also in the level of sophistication of its economic systems. As evidence, many poorer nations are confronted with the choice of saving sensitive habitat or allowing large-scale biomass burns. And, the combustion processes in developing countries are usually much less restrictive than those in more developed nations.

Most scientists view pollution predominantly from a perspective akin to that of the most industrialized nations. However, industrial processes can vary significantly between developed and underdeveloped nations. For example, in Canada and the United States, the major sources of dioxins, a chemical group comprising some of the world's most toxic and carcinogenic compounds, range from dispersed activities, such as trash burning, to heavy industry (see Figure 16.5). The major sources of dioxin emissions in Latin America are distributed quite differently to those in Canada and the United States. Actual emission inventories are being developed, but preliminary information indicates that much of the dioxin produced in

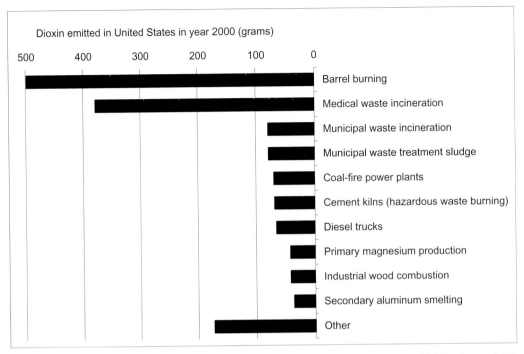

FIGURE 16.5    Industrial categories of dioxin emitters in the United States in 2000. *Source: U.S. Environmental Protection Agency. The inventory of sources of dioxin in the United States (external review draft). http://cfpub.epa.gov/ncea/cfm/recordisplay.cfm?deid=132080; 2005 [accessed June 12, 2006].*

Mexico, for example, is from backyard burning, such as neighborhood scale brick making. Refractory in developing nations are often small-scale, neighborhood operations. Often, the heat sources used to reach refractory temperatures are furnaces with scrap materials as fuel, especially petroleum-derived substances such as automobile tires. This is not only important to the country in which the combustion occurs but can also be an international concern when the burning is near borders. This is the case for the metropolitan area of El Paso, Texas, and Ciudad Juarez, Mexico, with a combined population of 2 million. The cities are located in a deep canyon between two mountain ranges, which can contribute to thermal inversions in the atmosphere (see Figure 4.6). The air is seriously polluted, with brick making on the Mexican side identified as a major source.[43]

In Mexico, workers who make bricks are called *ladrilleros*. Many ladrilleros live in unregulated settlements known as *colonias* on the outskirts of Ciudad Juarez. The kilns, using the same design as those in Egypt thousands of years ago, are located within these neighborhoods, next to the small houses. The *ladrilleros* are not particular about the fuel, burning anything with caloric value, including scrap wood and old tires, as well as more conventional fuels like methane and butane. The dirtier fuels, such as tires, release large black plumes of smoke that contains a myriad of contaminants.

Children face an elevated risk of health problems when exposed to these plumes, as their lungs and other organs are undergoing prolific tissue growth. Thus, the *ladrilleros'* families have particularly elevated risks due to their frequent and high-dose exposures. "The health impact is not only of concern to the worker but also to the entire family, especially pregnant women and children who, because of their socioeconomic status, tend to be undernourished," according to Beatriz Vera, project coordinator for the U.S.-Mexico Border Environment and Health Projects. She adds that "many times the entire family participates in the process. Sometimes children are put directly into the area where the kiln is fired."

The two nations' governments appear to recognize the problem, as do numerous nongovernmental organizations (known as "NGOs"). These have included Environmental Defense, Physicians for Social Responsibility, the Federacion Mexicana de Asociaciones Privadas de Salud y Desarrollo Comunitario (FEMAP), and El Paso Natural Gas (EPNG). For example, FEMAP and EPNG offer courses to the *ladrilleros* from areas throughout the region on ways to use higher quality fuel, including improved safety and business practices as well. Often, however, even if the brick makers know about cleaner fuels, they cannot afford them. For example, they used butane, but in 1994, the Mexican government started to phase out its subsidy and about the same time the peso was devalued, leading to a sharp increase in butane costs. The *ladrilleros* were forced to return to using the cheaper fuels. In the meantime, the Mexican government banned the burning of tires; so much of the more recent tire burning has been surreptitiously done at night.

A number of solutions to the problem have been proposed, including more efficient kilns. However, arguably the best approach is to prevent the combustion in the first place. In fact, many of the traditional villages where bricks are now used had previously constructed with adobe. A return to such a noncombustion approach could hold the key. The lesson here is that often in developing countries the simpler, "low-tech" solutions are the most sustainable.

In the mid-1990s, the U.S. EPA and the Texas Natural Resource Conservation Commission conducted a study in the Rio Grande valley region to address concerns about the potential health impact of local air pollutants, and especially as little air quality information was available at the time. There are numerous "cottage industries," known as *maquiladoras*,[44] along both sides of the Texas-Mexico border as ascribed by the Rio Grande. In particular, the study addressed the potential for air pollution to move across the U.S.-Mexican border into the southern part of Texas. Air pollution and weather data were collected for a year at three fixed sites near the border in and near Brownsville, Texas. The study found overall levels of air pollution to be similar to or even lower than other urban and rural areas in Texas and elsewhere and that transport of air pollution across the border did not appear to adversely impact air quality across the U.S. border.

Many developing countries are evolving into industrialized nations. Not long ago in the United States, the standard means of getting rid of household trash was the daily burn. Each evening, people in rural areas, small towns, and even larger cities made a trip into the backyard, dumped the trash they had accumulated into a barrel,[45] and burned the contents. Also, burning was a standard practice elsewhere, such as intentional fires to remove brush, and even "cottage industries," such as backyard smelters and metal recycling operations. Beginning in the 1960s and 1970s, the public acceptance and tolerance for open burning was waning. Local governments began to restrict and eventually ban many fires. Often, these restrictions had multiple rationales, especially public safety (fires becoming out of control, especially during dry seasons) and public health (increasing awareness of the association between particulate matter in the air and diseases like asthma and even lung cancer).

## RISK TRADE-OFFS

Few decisions about the environment involve a single means of providing a single benefit, about which every scientist, engineer, and planner would agree. They all involve trade-offs in one form or another. These trade-offs may involve the time, place, and manner of providing a benefit or of avoiding a risk. The trade-off decision is unacceptable if it leads to unacceptable risk, however that is defined.

The classic risk trade-off is one where two societal values are in conflict, e.g., acute health benefit versus a chronic health problem, such as using a pesticide to kill an insect that carries a disease, but the pesticide is cancer causing. It may also involve a trade-off between food versus fuel for transportation, as in the case of ethanol derived from food crops.

Other trade-offs may involve the manner in which a need is provided, such as how ethical, feasible, or worthwhile it is to modify genes to respond to what seems to be an anthropogenic problem. For example, if it is likely that certain adverse outcomes will be on the increase as in the case of climate change, e.g., malaria and other tropical diseases or increases in fungal infestations of crops, should we be trying to "improve" the genetic structures of plant life to deal with these changes? Here the trade-off is twofold, should we allow climate change to occur (maintain *status quo* for economic reasons), and if so, what is the best way to adapt to what we have allowed to occur? Sometimes, this is ameliorated, for example, when most agree that more drought-resistant species are preferable, no matter if the climate is changing. Other times, it involves risk shifting, often at the expense of developing nations. For example, tropical and island nations may disproportionately suffer from warming compared to temperate nations. The latter generally are much wealthier and able to adapt than the former.

The persistent organic pollutants have involved risk trade-offs from the outset. They have all helped to meet society's needs, such as protection and enhancement of the food supply (aldrin, dieldrin, hexachlorobenzene), disease control (1,1,1-trichloro-2,2-bis-(4-chlorophenyl)-ethane, DDT), and expansion of services by increasing access to electricity (polychlorinated biphenyls, PCBs).

All of these benefits were accompanied by contravening risks. For decades, DDT was seen as bad or good, depending on perceptions about its environmental and public health risks versus its commercial, agricultural, and public health benefits. Most of these substances, including DDT, are now banned in Canada and the United States, although people may still be exposed by importing food that has been grown where these pesticides are not banned. So, in the long run, the pesticide comes back in the imported products treated with the domestically banned pesticide. This is known as the "circle of poisons."

Risks versus risks decisions are not simply a matter of taking an action, e.g., banning worldwide use of DDT, which leads to many benefits, e.g., less eggshell thinning of endangered birds and less cases of cancer. Rather, it sometimes comes down to trading off one risk for another. As there are yet to be reliable substitutes for DDT in treating disease bearing insects, policy makers must decide between ecological and wildlife risks and human disease risk. These decisions are complicated by chronic effects like cancer and endocrine disruption, which must be balanced against expected increases in deaths and morbidity from malaria and other tropical diseases where DDT is part of the strategy for reducing outbreaks.

Arguably, it may not be appropriate for economically developed nations to push developing nations to restrict products that can cause major problems to the health of people living in developing countries. This can be seen as Western nations foisting temperate climate solutions onto tropical, developing countries. It looks like they are exporting measures based upon one set of values (anticancer, ecological) that are incongruent to another set of values. Tropical nations may consider acute, infectious diseases to be more important public health threats than chronic effects, given the thousands of cases of malaria in their country versus a few additional cases of cancer and that threats to the eggshell thinning in birds. Conversely, this can be seen as a need for a more systematic mosquito control program where pesticides are not the primary solution (e.g., eliminating breeding in standing water).

It can be very difficult to find substitutes for chemicals proven to provide a crucial function, like pest control. This has been the case for DDT. In fact, the chemicals that have been formulated to replace have been found to be either more dangerous, e.g., aldrin and dieldrin (which have also been subsequently banned), or much less effective in the developing world (e.g., pyrethroids). For example, spraying DDT in huts in tropical and subtropical environments, fewer mosquitoes are found compared to untreated huts. This likely has much to do with the persistence of DDT in mud structures compared to the higher chemical reactivity of pyrethroid pesticides.

## Cross-Media Transfer

Regulatory and policy decisions must account for potential risk trade-offs. This is illustrated by the call for fuel additives to reduce the emission of certain air pollutants. Gasoline is the principal fuel source for most cars. The exhaust from automobiles is a major source of air pollution, especially in densely populated urban areas. To improve fuel efficiency and to provide a higher octane rating (for antiknocking), most gasoline formulations have relied on additives. Up to relatively recently, the most common fuel additive to gasoline was tetraethyl-lead. But with the growing awareness of lead's neurotoxicity and other health effects, tetraethyl-lead has been banned in most parts of the world, so suitable substitutes were needed.

$$(CH_3)_3COCH_3$$

Methyl tertiary-butyl ether (MTBE) was one of the first replacement additives, first used to replace the lead additives in 1979. It is manufactured by reacting methanol and isobutylene and has been produced in very large quantities (more than 200,000 barrels per day (32 million liters per day) in the United States in 1999). MTBE is a member of the chemical class of oxygenates. MTBE is a quite volatile (vapor pressure $= 27$ kPa at $20\,^{\circ}C$), so that it is likely to evaporate readily. It also readily dissolves in water (aqueous solubility at $20\,^{\circ}C = 42$ g $L^{-1}$) and is very flammable (flash point $= -30\,^{\circ}C$). In 1992, MTBE began to be used at higher concentrations in some gasoline to fulfill the oxygenate requirements set the 1990 Clean Air Act Amendments. In addition, some cities, notably Denver, used MTBE at higher concentrations during the wintertime in the late 1980s.

In the United States, the Clean Air Act of 1990 called for greater use of oxygenates in an attempt to help reduce the emissions of carbon monoxide (CO), one of the most important air pollutants. CO toxicity results by interfering with the protein hemoglobin's ability to carry oxygen. Hemoglobin absorbs CO about 200 times faster than its absorption rate for oxygen. The CO-carrying protein is known as carboxyhemoglobin and when sufficiently high it can lead to acute and chronic effects. This is why smoking cigarettes leads to cardiovascular problems, i.e., the body has to work much harder because the normal concentration of oxygen in hemoglobin has been displaced by CO. CO is also a contributing factor in the photochemistry that leads to elevated levels of ozone ($O_3$) in the troposphere. In addition, oxygenates decrease the emissions of volatile organic compounds, which along with oxides of nitrogen are major precursors to the formation of tropospheric $O_3$. This is one of the most important roles of oxygenates, as unburned hydrocarbons can largely be emitted before catalytic converters start to work.

Looking at it from one perspective, the use of MTBE was a success by providing oxygen and helping gasoline burn more completely, resulting in less harmful exhaust from motor vehicles. The oxygen also dilutes or displaces compounds such as benzene and its derivatives (e.g., toluene, ethylbenzene, and xylene), as well as sulfur. The oxygen in the MTBE molecule also enhances combustion (recall that combustion is oxidation in the presence of heat). MTBE was not the only oxygenate, but it has very attractive blending characteristics and is relatively cheap compared to other available compounds. Another widely used oxygenate is ethanol.

The problem with MTBE is its suspected links to certain health effects, including cancer in some animal studies. In addition, MTBE has subsequently been found to pollute water, especially groundwater in aquifers. Some of the pollution comes from unburned MTBE emitted from tailpipes, some from fueling, but a large source is underground storage tanks at gasoline stations or other fuel operations (see Figure 16.6). A number of these tanks have leaked into the surrounding soil and unconsolidated media and have allowed the MTBE to migrate into the groundwater. As it has such a high aqueous solubility, the MTBE is easily dissolved in the water.

When a pollutant moves from one environmental compartment (e.g., air) to another (e.g., water) as it has for MTBE, this is known as cross-media transfer. The problem has not really been eliminated, just relocated. It is also an example of a risk trade-off. The risks posed by the air pollution have been traded by the new risks from exposure to MTBE-contaminated waters.

Every risk trade-off decision must be based on sound science. Often, sound science can be eclipsed by economics, politics, and public perception. Indeed, environmental protection efforts are never entirely risk free. To some extent, they always represent risk shifting in time and space. The mathematics of benefits and costs are inexact. Finding the option is seldom captured with a benefit/cost ratio. Opportunity costs and risks are associated with taking no action. The Hurricane Katrina disaster has offered planners an opportunity to save valuable wetlands and to enhance a shoreline by not developing and not rebuilding major portions of the Gulf Region, but this has been resisted by land use inertia; i.e., it can be difficult to change to more ecologically acceptable land uses, even those that are costly, once they have been established. Even sound ecological decision making can be met with secondary and indirect impacts. For example, the costs in time and money are not the only reasons for avoiding constructing a new wetland or nourishing a shoreline. The protections could inadvertently attract tourists and other users who could end up presenting new and greater environmental threats.

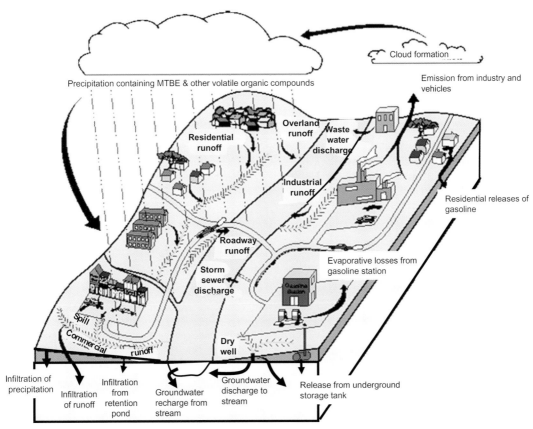

FIGURE 16.6 Migration of MTBE in the environment. *Source: Delzer GC, Zogorski JS, Lopes TJ, Bosshart RL. Occurrence of the gasoline oxygenate MTBE and BTEX in urban stormwater in the United States, 1991-95.* Water resources investigation report 96-4145. *Washington, DC: U.S. Geological Survey; 1996.*

## References and Notes

1. Letter from Birmingham Jail in King ML. *Why we can't wait.* New York, NY: HarperCollins; 1963.
2. Presidential Executive Order 12898. *Federal actions to address environmental justice in minority populations and low-income populations;* 1994 (February 11, 1994).
3. For example, this is the fourth canon of the American Society of Civil Engineers, 1996, Code of Ethics, Adopted 1914 and most recently amended November 10, 1996, Washington, DC. This canon reads: "Engineers shall act in professional matters for each employer or client as faithful agents or trustees, and shall avoid conflicts of interest."
4. Even this is a challenge for environmental justice communities, as certain sectors of society are less likely to visit hospitals or otherwise receive early healthcare attention. This is not only a problem of assessment but also can lead to more serious, long-term problems compared to those of the general population.
5. Burke W, Atkins D, Gwinn M, Guttmacher A, Haddow J, Lau J, et al. Genetic test evaluation: information needs of clinicians, policy makers, and the public. *Am J Epidemiol* 2002;**156**:311–8.
6. Institute of Medicine. *Toward environmental justice: research, education, and health policy needs.* Washington, DC: National Academy Press; 1999.
7. This harkens back to the Constitution's requirement of equal protection.

8. The source of background information in this section is U.S. Environmental Protection Agency. *Municipal solid waste*. http://www.epa.gov/epaoswer/non-hw/muncpl/facts.htm; 2005 [accessed April 5, 2005].

9. *Dy-Dee Diaper Service*. Household hazardous waste data for the UK by direct sampling. http://www.dy-dee.com/; 2005 [accessed April 22, 2005].

10. Slack RJ, Bonin M, Gronow JR, Van Santen A, Voulvoulis N. *Environ Sci Technol* 2007;**41**:2566–71; Slack RJ, Zerva P, Gronow JR, Voulvoulis N. *Environ Sci Technol* 2005;**39**:1912–9.

11. Organization for Economic Cooperation and Development. Household energy and water consumption and waste generation: trends, environmental impacts and policy responses. Report: ENV/EPOC/WPNEP(2001)15/FINAL, Sector Case Studies Series. *Programme on Sustainable Development 1999-2001*. Paris: Organization for Economic Co-operation and Development Environment Directorate; 2001. Zacarias-Farah A, Geyer-Allely E. *J Clean Prod* 2003;**11**:819–27.

12. Department for Environment, Food and Rural Affairs. *Waste strategy 2000: England & Wales (Part 2)*. London: Her Majesty's Stationary Office; 2000; Gendebien A, Leavens A, Blackmore K, Godley A, Lewin K, Franke B, et al. *Study on hazardous household waste (HHW) with a main emphasis on hazardous household chemicals (HHC)*. Brussels: European Commission-General Environment Directorate; 2002; Pendle W, Poll AJ. *Common household products: a review of their potential environmental impacts and waste management options*. Stevenage: Warren Spring Laboratory: Warren Spring Laboratory and Dept. of Enterprise report LR927 (RAU).; 1993; Poll AJ. *The composition of municipal solid waste in Wales*. Cardiff: Welsh Assembly Government and AEA Technology; 2003; Stevens P. *Priority waste stream project—household hazardous waste: stage 1*. Leeds: Save Waste & Prosper Ltd (SWAP) and Recycling Advisory Group Scotland (RAGS); 2003 62pp.

13. Otoniel BD, Liliana M-B, Francelia PG. Consumption patterns and household hazardous solid waste generation in an urban settlement in México. *Waste Manag* 2008;**28**:S2–S6.

14. Slack. RJ, et al.

15. Burnley SJ, Ellis JC, Flowerdew R, Poll AJ, Prosser H. Assessing the composition of municipal solid waste in Wales. *Resour Conser Recycl* 2007;**49**:264–83; Poll AJ. *Variations in the composition of household collected waste*. Didcot: AEAT for EB Nationwide; 2004; Reinhart DR. A review of recent studies on the sources of hazardous compounds emitted from solid waste landfills: a US experience. *Waste Manag Res* 1993;**11**:257–68; Stanek EJ, Tuthill RW, Willis C, Moore GS. Household Hazardous Waste in Massachusetts. *Arch Environ Health* 1987;**42**:83–6; Letcher TM, Schutte R. The cost effectiveness of exploiting landfill gas in South Africa. *J Energy Res Dev South Afr* 1992;**3**:26–8.

16. Zacarias-Farah A, Geyer-Allely E. Household consumption patterns in OECD countries: trends and figures. *J Clean Prod* 2003;**11**:819–27.

17. U.S. Centers for Disease Control and Prevention. *CDC estimates of foodborne illness in the United States*. http://www.cdc.gov/foodborneburden/2011-foodborne-estimates.html; 2012 [accessed March 11, 2012].

18. A very interesting development over the past decade has been the increasing awareness that health research has often ignored a number of polymorphs or subpopulations, such as women and children, and is plagued by the so-called healthy worker effect. Much occupational epidemiology has been based upon a tightly defined population of relatively young and healthy, adult, white males who had already been screened and selected by management and economic systems in place during the twentieth century. Also, health studies have tended to be biased toward adult, white males even when the contaminant or disease of concern was distributed throughout the general U.S. population. For example, much of the cardiac and cancer risk factors for women and children have been extrapolated from studies of adult, white males. Pharmaceutical efficacy studies have also been targeted more frequently toward adult males. This has been changing recently, but the residual uncertainties are still problematic.

19. The FQPA was enacted on August 3, 1996, to amend the Federal Insecticide, Fungicide, and Rodenticide Act (FIFRA) and the Federal Food, Drug and Cosmetics Act (FFDCA). Especially important to risk assessment, the FQPA established a health-based standard to provide a reasonable certainty of no harm for pesticide residues in foods. This new provision was enacted to assure protection from unacceptable pesticide exposure and to strengthen the health protection measures for infants and children from pesticide risks.

20. See Ref. 19 and also Anonymous. *Unpalatable truths. New Scientist*. April 17, 1999. Ronald PC. Making rice disease-resistant. *Sci Am* 1997;**277**:100–5.

21. Picone, et al. 1999.

22. U.S. Chemical Safety Board. *Formosa plastics vinyl chloride explosion.* http://www.csb.gov/investigations/detail. aspx?SID=22; 2004 [accessed March 11, 2012].

23. The source of this discussion is the U.S. Commission on Civil Rights report. *Not in my backyard.*

24. Chatham College. *Leaders of Cancer Alley.* http://www.chatham.edu/rci/well/women21-30/canceralley.html; 2003 [accessed April 10, 2003].

25. Elizabeth Teel, deputy director, Environmental Law Clinic, Tulane Law School, testimony before the U.S. Commission on Civil Rights, hearing, Washington, DC, January 11, 2002, official transcript, p. 117.

26. German Federal Ministry for Economic Cooperation and Development. *Environmental handbook: documentation on monitoring and evaluating environmental impacts: compendium of environmental standards vol. III.* http://www.gtz. de/uvp/publika/English/vol369.htm; 2004 [accessed November 29, 2004].

27. Although kinetics in the physical sense arguably can be shown to share many common attributes with kinetics in the chemical sense, for the purposes of this discussion, it is probably best to treat them as two separate entities. Physical kinetics, as discussed in previous sections, is concerned with the dynamics of material bodies and the energy in a body owing to its motions. Chemical kinetics address rates of chemical reactions. The former is more concerned with mechanical dynamics, the latter with thermodynamics.

28. This example is taken from Spencer J, Bodner G, Rickard L. *Chemistry: structure and dynamics.* 2nd ed. New York, NY: John Wiley & Sons; 2003.

29. Mossville Environmental Action Network. *Breathing poison: the toxic costs of industries in Calcasieu Parish, Louisiana.* http://www.mapCruzin.com/mossville/reportondioxin.htm; 2000.

30. Patty FA, et al. Acute response of guinea pigs to vapors of some commercial organic compounds. *Public Health Rep* 1930;**45**(24) 22 August.

31. http://www.lawyershop.com/practice-areas/personal-injury/product-liability/toxic-chemical-exposure/vi nyl-chloride [accessed January 26, 2012].

32. http://www.ncbi.nlm.nih.gov/pmc/articles/PMC1128629/pdf/oenvmed00085-0021.pdf [accessed January 27, 2012]

33. http://www.marketwire.com/press-release/vinyl-chloride-monomer-production-expected-to-grow-27-annu ally-through-2020-1364433.htm [accessed January 26, 2012].

34. http://en.wikipedia.org/wiki/Vinyl_chloride [accessed January 28, 2012].

35. http://www.pvcinformation.org/links/index.php?catid=3 [accessed January 29, 2012].

36. http://www.ncbi.nlm.nih.gov/pubmed/3393850 [accessed January 28, 2012].

37. Boffetta P, et al. Meta-analysis of studies of occupational exposure to vinyl chloride in relation to cancer mortality. *Scand J Work Environ Health* 2003;**29**(3):220–9.

38. Jones RD, Smith DM, Thomas PG. *Scand J Work Environ Health* 1988;**14**:153–60.

39. http://www.ncbi.nlm.nih.gov/pmc/articles/PMC1569348/ [accessed January 26, 2012].

40. Chanda M, Salil RK. Plastics technology handbook. In: Boca Raton, Florida, USA: CRC Press; 2006. p. 1–6 ISBN 9780849370397.

41. http://www.chemicalindustryarchives.org/dirtysecrets/vinyl/1.asp [accessed January 29, 2012].

42. Bush GW. *President's State of the Union Address.* January 23, 2007.

43. The major source of information about Rio Grande brick making is *Environ Health Perspect* 1996;104(5).

44. The Coalition for Justice in the Maquiladoras, a cross-border group that organizes maquiladora workers, traces the term maquiladora to *maquilar,* a popular form of the verb maquinar that roughly means "to submit something to the action of a machine, as when rural Mexicans speak of maquilar with regard to the grain that is transported to a mill for processing. The farmer owns the grain; yet someone else owns the mill who keeps a portion of the value of the grain for milling. So, the origin of maquiladora can be found in this division of labor. The term has more recently been applied to the small factories opened by U.S. companies that to conduct labor-intensive jobs on the Mexican side of the border. Thus, maquilar has changed to include this process of labor, especially assembling parts from various sources, and the maquiladoras are those small assembling operations along the border. While the maquiladoras have provided opportunities to entrepreneurs along the Mexico-U.S. border, they have also given opportunity for the workers and their families to be exploited in the interests of profit and economic gain.

45. Often, these barrels were the 55-gallon drum variety, so the first burning likely volatilized some very toxic compounds, depending on the residues remaining in the drum. These contents could have been solvents (including halogenated compounds like chlorinated aliphatics and aromatics), plastic residues (like phthalates), and

petroleum distillates. They may even have contained substances with elevated concentrations of heavy metals, such as mercury, lead, cadmium, and chromium. The barrels (drums) themselves were often perforated to allow for higher rates of oxidation (combustion) and to take advantage of the smokestack effect (i.e., driving the flame upward and pushing the products of incomplete combustion out of the barrel and into the plume). Vallero recalls the neighbors not being happy about burning trash while their wash was drying on the clothes line. They would complain of ash (aerosols) blackening their clothes and the odor from the incomplete combustion products on their newly washed laundry. Both of these complaints are evidence that the plume leaving the barrel contained harmful contaminants.

# Future

Every environmental disaster results from failure. Even a so-called natural disaster can be traced back to decisions or nondecisions that increased the incurred damage. If a nuclear plant were not allowed to be built in a tsunami risk zone, many of the problems that have resulted from the damage incurred would not have existed. However, this does not mean that another decision would have been entirely acceptable. Few are.

Human populations and ecosystems are complex. They are threatened by complicated and multifaceted hazards. Thus, they must be viewed systematically. Every hazard exists within a milieu of life cycles. Every substance released into the environment has a life cycle. It is during this life cycle that the substance became a threat or contributed to a weakness that, among other contributors in the environment, led to the disaster. Every unit of mass or energy exists within a mass or energy balance, respectively.

It is within the systems perspective that we will find solutions. Disasters can be prevented and the harm from them much abated by considering life cycles.

The events and steps that lead to a disaster vary in their influence on the outcome. Some may not initiate the disaster's event cascade but may make it worse or better; i.e., they merely modify the outcome but are not responsible for. For example, for the Bhopal disaster occur, there had to be several essential steps leading to the explosion, e.g., critical mass of MIC, over-filled tank, etc. The damage incurred by the disaster was exacerbated by other actions, but they were not in the causal chain of the chemical reaction, e.g., proximity of people to the factory increased the magnitude and duration of their exposure to MIC. In other words, the reaction would have occurred, but its the injuries and loss of life would have been much less or even avoided completely. In deconstructing the disaster, all of these factors and their weights in terms of causes and outcomes must be evaluated.

The process can be likened to a sensitivity analysis, i.e., identifying and giving weights to the factors that lead to an outcome, i.e., greater weighted factors will change the outcome more dramatically than will lesser weighted factors. For example, if one particular species of plant is eliminated from a habitat, the weight of the loss of that species would be very high if it were the exclusive prey of a predator. Its weight would be lower if all the consumers in the niche were not selective in their prey. Such sensitivies can be documented for any habitat and be part of any vulnerability assessment prior to stresses and certainly before these stresses reach disaster thresholds. Likewise, human safety, health and welfare is affected differently, depending on the type of stress, e.g., the aftermath of flooding may lead to diseases that differentially impact sensitive subpopulations, such as newborns' susceptibility to contagious diseases while their immune systems are not yet mature.

Unfortunately, there will undoubtedly be future disasters. Preventing or ameliorating them when they happen is an exercise in prediction. Models are used to predict an event or series of events. The processes that lead to environmental disasters are difficult enough to identify, but predicting how contributing factors will interrelate is impossible to predict with much accuracy.

Retrospective analysis is also difficult. Identifying the factors that have led to a disaster is complicated. Few credible information sources are available about what was occurring at any given period of time. Almost always, actual measurement data are not available to characterize the movement and change of materials and energy in the environment. Models then must extrapolate from currently available information that very likely was collected for reasons other than the disaster at hand. Figure 17.1 illustrates the steps that should be taken to develop an environmental model. Note that this approach is designed for problems that have been documented, whereas disaster planners may not even be aware of some of the vulnerabilities that could lead to a disaster. For example, even in the rare instance when data are of high quality, there is little or no precedent on how to combine and integrate these data. We have the "dots," but we do not know how to connect them to prevent a disaster.

The model generators are to the left in Figure 17.1, and the users (stakeholders) are to the right. This illustrates the need for both scientific and societal factors in environmental decision making. Each arrow indicates the connection between processes; each factor and process introduces information to the model but simultaneously adds uncertainty.

Perhaps, identifying and weighting societal factors are even more difficult than doing the same for physical and biological scientific factors. For example, the uncertain, yet looming threat of global climate change can be attributed in part to technological and industrial progress. But using straight-line trends or even sophisticated climatological models will be insufficient to predict the extent and degree of damage. The number of variables necessary to define climate is so large and the interrelationships among them so complex, even the highly advanced computational methods and climatological models have large uncertainties when used to predict climate change. But we must press on and continue digging away at the problem. It is that important. The good news is that emergent technologies will likely help assuage some of the contributing factors, e.g., improvements to alternative sources of energy, such as wind and solar, which in turn could lead to less global demand for fossil fuels. Conversely, these same factors could lead to complacencies or even lead to other environmental problems (e.g., changes in migratory patterns if wind turbines interfere with bird habitats).

Much of society promotes urbanization, industrial output, and other stressors that have contributed to disasters. Ironically, society also demands the control of the consequences caused by these same endeavors. These seemingly conflicting demands are often quite rational. For example, advances in radioisotope technology are part of the arsenal to treat cancer, but radioactive wastes from hospitals can increase the risk of contracting cancer, if these wastes are not properly disposed of and handled safely. Likewise, cleanup of polluted waters and sediments can benefit from combustion and incineration to break down some very persistent contaminants, but combustion in general is problematic in its release of products of complete combustion (carbon dioxide) or incomplete combustion (e.g., dioxins, furans, polycyclic aromatic hydrocarbons, and carbon monoxide). In almost every discussion in this book, the environmental problems have emerged as a by-product of an enterprise that is deemed useful and is in demand, at least for some period of time, by large sectors of the population.

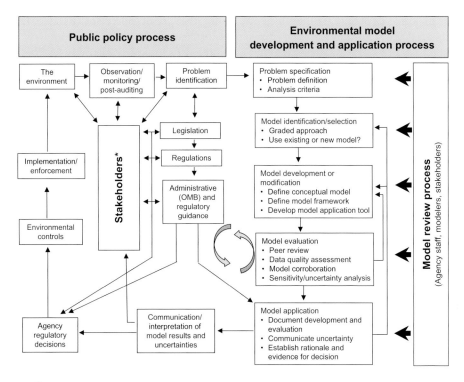

*Stakeholders include
• Source facility owners or responsible parties
• Directly affected neighboring property owners and public
• Courts and interested government entities (e.g, agencies)
• Advocacy groups (e.g., environmental, industry, and trade organizations

FIGURE 17.1    Steps needed to develop and implement an environmental decision model from inception to completion. These include problem specification, model identification and selection (a site-specific model may be generated *de novo* or based on an existing model framework), model development (including problem- and site-specific model conceptualization, model formulation and design, and model calibration), model evaluation (e.g., based on peer review, data quality assessment, model code verification, model confirmation/corroboration, sensitivity analysis, and uncertainty analysis), model use (diagnostic analysis, solution, and application support for decision making), and review after use. *Source: U.S. Environmental Protection Agency. Science Advisory Board, Regulatory Environmental Modeling, Guidance Review Panel.* Review of agency draft guidance on the development, evaluation, and application of regulatory environmental models *and* models knowledge base. *EPA-SAB-06-009. Letter to Administrator Stephen L. Johnson; August 22, 2006.*

This is a succint apparent dichotomy between the requirement that "modern science and technology have enormous potential for harm" and that science and technology also be "bounteous sources of social benefits." Thus, science and technology is called on to address disasters, including the man-made catastrophes that technology itself enables or exacerbates.[1]

Another example of this dichotomy involves genetically modified organisms (GMOs) to produce food mentioned in Chapter 16. There is a fear that the new organisms will carry with them unforeseen ruin, such as in some way affecting living cell's natural regulatory systems. An extreme viewpoint, as articulated by the renowned cosmologist and astrophysicist Martin Rees, is the growing apprehension about nanotechnology, particularly its current trend toward producing "nanomachines." Biological systems, at the subcellular and molecular levels, could very efficiently produce proteins, as they already do for their own purposes. By tweaking some genetic material at a scale of a few angstroms, parts of the cell (e.g., the ribosome) that manufacture molecules could start producing myriad molecules designed by scientists, such as pharmaceuticals and nanoprocessors for computing. However, Rees is concerned that such assemblers could start self-replicating (like they always have), but without any "shut-off." Some have called this the "gray goo" scenario, i.e., accidentally creating an "extinction technology" from the cell's unchecked ability to exponentially replicate itself if part of the cell design is to be completely "omnivorous," using all matter as food! No other "life" on earth would exist if this "doomsday" scenario were to occur.[2] Certainly, this is the stuff of science fiction, but it calls attention to the need for vigilance, especially since our track record for becoming aware of the dangers of technologies is so frequently tardy. In environmental situations, messing with genetic materials may harm biodiversity, i.e., the delicate balance among species, including trophic states (producer-consumer-decomposer) and predator-prey relationships. Engineers and scientists are expected to push the envelopes of knowledge. We are rewarded for our eagerness and boldness. The Nobel Prize, for example, is not given to the chemist or physicist who has aptly calculated and safely applied important scientific phenomena, with no new paradigms. It would be rare indeed for engineering societies to bestow awards only to the engineer who for an entire career used only proven technologies to design and build structures. This begins with our general approach to contemporary scientific research. We are rugged individualists in a quest to add new knowledge. For example, aspirants seeking PhDs must endeavor to add knowledge to their specific scientific discipline. Scientific journals are unlikely to publish articles that do not at least contain some modicum of originality and newly found information.[3] We award and reward innovation. Unfortunately, there is not a lot of natural incentive for the innovators to stop what they are doing to "think about" possible ethical dilemmas propagated by their discoveries.[4]

Products that contain dangerous materials like asbestos, lead, mercury, polybrominated compounds and polychlorinated biphenyls were once considered acceptable and were even required by law or policy to protect the public safety and health, such as: asbestos-containing and polybrominated materials to prevent fires; DDT, and other persistent pesticides to kill mosquitoes in an effort to prevent disease; and methyl *tert*-butyl ether as a fuel additive to reduce air pollution from vehicles. Subsequently, these products were all found to cause adverse environmental and health problems, although there is still much disagreement within the scientific community about the extent and severity of these and other contaminants. We must also consider the cases that are yet to be resolved and those where there is incomplete or nonexistent unanimity of thought as to their importance or even whether indeed they are problems, such as global climate change, acid rain, and depletion of the stratospheric ozone layer.

## RECOMMENDATIONS

The complexity and differing scales of environmental disasters obviate "one size fits all" recommendations. However, there are enough common factors that have led to many of these disasters that a few recommendations are in order. Numerous mechanisms have been employed to help prevent and prepare for disasters, including:

1. regulatory measures, e.g., zoning and land-use controls designed and enforced by public agencies;

2. economic incentives, e.g., taxation schemes and subsidies that can orient location of activities;
3. property rights, which provide land tenure security to promote long-term investment in land-use improvement by landowners and/or users. This measure is particularly important for squatter communities in urban and rural areas that are not located on hazard-prone land, as well as sprawl allowing neighborhoods to encroach into vulnerable zones;
4. infrastructure installment sited and design according to technical and environmental criteria to manage risk in hazard-prone areas, including properly sited and maintained flood control systems;
5. public education and information, which can encourage voluntary conservation and participation from the private sector and from the general public. Increasing public awareness of environmentally sensitive or hazard-prone areas can improve decisions by individuals and groups, e.g., avoiding certain structures and activities in high hazard areas, increasing conservation measures and avoiding short-term actions that may lead to long-term problems[5];
6. international inspection system for industrial plants that could involve an international disaster (e.g., nuclear); and
7. more international cooperation on industrial planning and designs.[6]

## Thoughtful Land-Use Decisions

Much of the damage caused by environmental disasters results from previous decisions, or lack thereof, about where to site structures and operations. A common feature of the disasters in Bhopal, the U.S. Gulf Coast, and Japan is poor planning. Most failure assessments point to a combination of technological and sociological problems, but had the land-use planning decisions been matched to the obvious hazards, much of the loss of life, damage to property and ecological resources would have been avoided.

In addition to the technological failures at the chemical plant, Bhopal was an example of ignoring cultural differences. One of these was the societal tolerance of squatting and allowing makeshift housing on or near company property. Planning and zoning authorities in most Western nations would likely have enforced codes more rigorously. This is not to say that planning in the United States and Europe is perfect; it is far from it. However, developing nations often lack the resources for long-term and less obvious needs since they are so busy trying to meet basic human needs.

This is akin to Maslow's[7] hierarchy of needs, where he differentiated between two classes of needs: basic and growth (see Figure 17.2). The basic needs must first be satisfied before a person can progress toward higher-level growth needs. Within the basic needs' classification, Maslow separated the most basic physiological needs, such as water, food, and oxygen, from the need for safety. Therefore, one must first avoid starvation and thirst, satisfying minimum caloric and water intake, before being concerned about the quality of the air, food, and water. The latter is the province of environmental protection, but as we saw with rainforest destruction (Chapter 13), local communities often ignore long-term costs (complete loss of rainforest habitats) to meet immediate, basic needs (slash and burn agriculture).

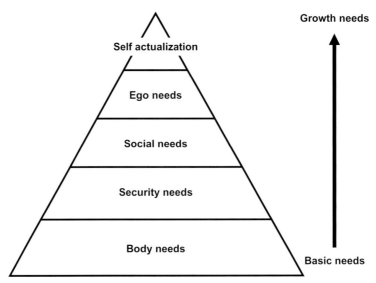

FIGURE 17.2    Maslow's hierarchy of needs. The lower part of the hierarchy (i.e., basic needs) must first be satisfied before a person can advance to the next growth levels.

Providing food requires ranges of soil and water quality for agriculture. Thus, any person and any culture that is unable to satisfy these most basic needs cannot be expected to "advance" toward higher-order values, such as free markets and peaceful societies. In fact, the inability to provide basic needs militates against disaster prevention. People will do what they can to survive, and groups of people will behave in ways that they perceive to be in their own, often short-term, interests. Building a house near a beach serves this purpose for the individual, and building several houses near a beach serves this purpose for the developer. They seem to devalue the longer term costs of the damage that will inevitably occur a few years down the road. And, the damage is not limited to the individual and the developer, but is also borne by the larger society, e.g., higher taxes and insurance premiums for an entire state to pay for the damage.

Some of this seemingly willful ignorance is actually perpetuated by society. For example, insurance companies may pass the greater part of costs on to other policyholders who have a little or no coastal risks. Or, disaster relief systems may compensate hazard-prone disasters at the expense of taxpayers. Viewed systematically, this makes no sense, since we are encouraging actions that the majority of people would oppose. This was driven home some years back when one of Vallero's colleagues was complaining that a recent storm had not destroyed his beach home. The colleague was waiting for the property to be declared a total loss so that he would be compensated and *build a larger home on the same property.* Most frustratingly, however, this colleague was an environmental scientist!

In many cases, governments attempt to take some steps to address hazards before they occur, but these are often abandoned or not fully released. This is a vicious cycle wherein any progress is undone by episodes of scarcity.

Actually, land-use planning failures have occurred without respect to a nation's economic development. Indeed, it has led to disasters in more highly developed countries, often with much greater economic losses than in less developed nations. Consider the destruction caused by Hurricane Katrina and many other storms along the coasts of Gulf of Mexico and Atlantic Ocean over the past half century and the earthquake and tsunami in Japan in 2010. The disasters were amplified geometrically by the failure to recognize and prioritize hazards and to match land-use restrictions to abate these hazards.

This is doubly frustrating in that we are not fully using the technologies that have greatly advanced in recent decades to assist in siting facilities. Understanding environmental disasters depends on constraints and drivers, which adhere to the laws of thermodynamics and motion. Designs and development must be done in ways that heed nature, i.e., we must "design with nature." In engineering and planning, small details matter. To wit, the preposition "with" in "design with nature" means that nature should not be overcome, but should inform designs by planners, engineers, and developers.

This is not new advice. Ian McHarg's groundbreaking 1969 book was indeed entitled *Design with Nature* (John Wiley & Sons). In it, McHarg urged planners to conform to ecology, rather than to compete with it. Vallero recalls in the mid-1970s using the book in his urban planning and design graduate courses and being particularly struck by the profound yet simple use of overlays (stacked Mylar maps). A transparency was prepared for each attribute, such as wetlands, littoral vulnerability, urbanization, sensitive forests, or water supplies. By overlaying different attributes (transparencies) atop each other, patterns would become obvious, such as areas that needed special protection from development.

We now have much more sophisticated technologies, but they are based on the same premise, i.e., there must be a characterization of hazards before allowing development in sensitive settings. We cannot be reductionist when considering hazards that may lead to disaster. Hazards can be compounded. The effect of combining individual hazards may be more than additive. Indeed, even intrinsically nonhazardous factors may become hazardous when combined with other nonhazardous factors. A collective set of factors may act synergistically to magnify problems to the point of disaster. For example, the combination of a large storm, aging levees, weak soils, urbanization below sea level, poor construction quality of structures, and ineffective zoning individually would be problematic. Experienced together, these and other factors led to the Hurricane Katrina disaster.

Information technology has certainly improved the timeliness and quality of McHarg's concept. Geographic information systems (GIS) have become more readily available and reliable in recent years, e.g., availability of a GIS in a Windows operating system environment, availability of low-cost computer hardware, and the development and implementation of user-friendly GIS applications. An example of the use of GIS as a decision support tool is its use for siting a warehouse built on 5-m stilts. Typical data layers that are required are the location of suitable soils, wells, surface water sources, residential areas, schools, airports, roads, and other infrastructure. From these data layers, queries are formulated to provide the most suitable site(s). For example, the warehouse would not itself be expected to suffer flood damage since the tidal and wave data layers indicate that the highest water levels would be predicted to be lower than the floor of the building. However, the infrastructures would be predicted to change the pattern of development, eliminate wetlands, and increase paved surfaces (parking lots and roads). Other GIS layers, e.g., soil permeability and tidal river stream flow, would indicate that the remaining unpaved surfaces would not allow sufficient infiltration, so more water would run overland. Further, if an agency has jurisdiction over a larger area, e.g., an entire state, the GIS tools could determine the additive effects of similar development across the entire ecosystem (e.g., the state's entire coast line). Typically, quantitative weighting criteria are associated with the siting criteria as well as elements of the data layers (e.g., certain types of soils would be more suitable than others and thus would have applicable quantitative values).[8]

Some of the tools currently available to support land-use and siting decisions are provided in Table 17.1. Note that these rely on high-quality data and reliable models. This is the case not only for land-use controls and planning but also for every aspect of disaster assessment and prevention, including information technologies, sensors, and early warning devices.

TABLE 17.1    Available Measures for Environmental Hazard and Vulnerability Assessments

| Tools and measures | Explanation, advantages, and constraints |
|---|---|
| Meteorological forecast | • Based on data, geophysical and oceanic factors, statistical techniques, and climate variability. Meteorological forecast is possible on a seasonal, monthly, weekly, and daily basis.<br>• Forecast can be utilized for weather-related disaster prediction, which can provide warnings and information to prevent damage and permit escape during hazard events.<br>• Accurate and timely warnings and forecasts are expected, but uncertainty should always be taken into account. |
| Geographic information systems (GIS) | • Computer systems capable of combining layers of digital data from different sources, including satellite images, to create maps and data sources.<br>• Maps and data can support land-use planning, risk and vulnerability assessment, disaster forecasting, and hazard management.<br>• Cost, specialized expertise, and commitment of updating data may be constraints in using this system. |
| Environmental assessment (EA) | • EA is a framework of environmental analysis and includes strategic assessment, impact assessment, management program, and auditing.<br>• At project level, EA helps in avoiding or mitigating negative impacts, or finding alternatives, and improving project design.<br>• There are checklists and guidelines available for assessment, but evaluation is subjective, and predicting all negative impacts is difficult. |
| Social assessment (SA) | • SA is a framework of social analysis, which investigates sociocultural and social variables systematically.<br>• Indigenous population, gender, and involuntary resettlement are key issues of SA. |
| Institutional building for collaboration and coordination | • Networking and coordination provides diversity of skills, knowledge, and resources, and collaboration between public, private, NGOs, international organizations, and local community to ensure maximum results of development efforts.<br>• Each stakeholder has different needs and interests, and the bureaucratic organization has an inflexible and paternalistic nature, which makes it difficult to collaborate with other stakeholders. |

*Source: Inter-American Development Bank.* Consultative group for the reconstruction and transformation of Central America reducing vulnerability to natural hazards: lessons learned from hurricane Mitch: a strategy paper on environmental management. *http://www.iadb.org/regions/re2/consultative_group/groups/ecology_workshop_1.htm#2; 2000 [accessed March 13, 2012].*

When a reliable hazard assessment indicates vulnerabilities that could lead to environmental problems, a number of approaches are available to protect vulnerable areas and to prevent direct or indirect problems introduced or exacerbated by development. One approach is eminent domain, which allows land to be taken with just compensation for the public good. Easements are another means of land-use protection. An easement is an agreement by a person who owns the property to relinquish a particular property right, while still owning property, for example, a 100-m right-of-way for a highway project that converts any existing land use (e.g., farming, housing, or commercial enterprises) to a transportation use. Sometimes, the government or conservation groups are able to buy sensitive properties, i.e., fee simple.

Often, however, huge areas are vulnerable to natural events, so land-use decisions must not be limited to direct threats but also to those that may result indirectly. These include secondary effects of a project that extend, in time and space, the influence of a project. For example, if one is only concerned about treating municipal waste, the design and construction of a wastewater treatment plant may seem a prudent course of action, especially if care is taken to site the plant. However, the very existence of the plant and its connected sewer lines will create accessibility which spawns suburban growth.[9] Many residents are unaware that their building lots were once farmland or open space. Had it not been for expenditure of public funds (e.g., millions of dollars in grants to construct wastewater treatment plants and sewers in the U.S. during the 1970s and 1980s) and the use of public powers like eminent domain, there would be no subdivision.

Land-use plans must aim to protect the quality of neighborhoods and simultaneously address the potential for collective effects of the approval of uses. The 1968 *Science* article entitled "The Tragedy of the Commons"[10] imagines an English village with a common area where everyone's cow may graze. The common is able to sustain the cows and village life is stable, until one of the villagers figures out that if he gets two cows instead of one, the cost of the extra cow will be shared by everyone, while the profit will be his alone. So he gets two cows and prospers, but others see this and similarly want two cows. If two, why not three—and so on—until the village common is no longer able to support the large number of cows, the systems crashes, and everyone suffers. So, even though the individual homeowner or even a few developments succeed, the entire ecosystem can be stressed so that all end up suffering.

## Information Technology

Computational and informatics tools are also evolving and should become increasingly useful for land-use and siting decisions. Disaster informatics is the study of the use of information and technology in the preparation, mitigation, response, and recovery phases of disasters and other emergencies.[11]

Following Hurricane Katrina, people began blogging to share and to disseminate emergency information. This was an impetus for Indiana University to develop Web-based applications that integrate alerts and blog entries in a combined map-enabled tool designed to assist in emerging situations and to share information in a meaningful way. The system is being prototyped, emphasizing weather-related emergencies, with the intent to release an independent, mobile kit that is available in disaster areas, to allow logging of alerts and reports of dangers and losses of service. Another project is designing real-time integrated geospatial monitoring of sensors (e.g., earthquake, tsunamis, and storms) and simulations.[11] By extension, these same approaches could be used to prevent development in areas where informatics indicate past vulnerabilities, e.g., similar to the blogging and social network communications about outages, but retrospective.

Improving interoperability of information systems may also assist in disaster prevention. The ease with which information connections and dependencies occur is known as interoperability. From the Haiti and Chile earthquakes to the volcanic ashes in Scandinavia, to the BP rig explosion and the oil spill in the Gulf of Mexico, the consequences and ripple effects of these interdependencies induce unintended consequences. A key aspect of interoperability is to examine events holistically and systematically by incorporating the perspectives of multiple scientific, engineering, and other disciplines. As such, it offers ways to model systems and predict their behavior.

The current challenge is that

- the factors that lead up to a disaster often seem unrelated, so the information that appears unrelated is frequently very much related;
- health-care, environmental, and public health information is connected, and yet functionally, it is disconnected;
- a "systems approach" is crucial, as is the need to take a "holistic view" of the problem; to be able to see the whole and not just discrete pieces, and help determine, for example, unintended consequences; and
- it is necessary to integrate multidisciplinary and interdisciplinary orientations and activities when trying to understand the problem, and moving toward generating potential solutions; yet, present approaches are grossly insufficient.[12]

An example of where interoperability can be used to address a disaster is that of the foodborne illness, ciguatera. A large-scale exposure to the toxin occurred in several U.S. cities in the winter of 2008, with a particularly severe outbreak in Washington, DC. One potential source of the toxin was frequent occurrences of dust storms throughout the world. Linking multiple sets of information related to individual health and public health, particularly global food sustainability and global security, researchers were able to arrive at plausible causes and responses. Such a shift in "interoperability" is needed not only to achieve information sharing and a common operational picture but also to build cost-effective and efficient systems. In this example, the world's population increases exponentially without sustainable environmental resources and strains food supplying systems and other natural resources (e.g., supplies of drinking water and reliable sources of energy). Worsening contamination strains already vulnerable nations. Thus, the environmental conditions have a direct effect on public health and security.[12]

Interoperability can also be used to investigate threats to global climate and ecosystems. Threats to the function and structure of coral reef ecosystems have been associated with wastewater discharges to major rivers that ultimately drain into oceans, carrying nutrients and microbial populations. More recently, these discharges have been found to contain pharmaceuticals, personal care products, and antibiotics that are not degraded or incompletely degrade, leading to stresses on aquatic ecosystems. For example, the corals off the coast of Florida, world's third largest barrier reef, have been highly stressed, with half of the live coral off the Florida coast lost in the past few years. An additional indication is that fish feeding on these corals are developing deformities and experience premature mortality.

Interdisciplinary communications are rare among public health and environmental professionals. For example, medical practitioners commonly do not access environmental databases as part of standard of care, even though these are often rich in information needed for proper diagnosis, treatment, and prevention of diseases. Contaminants have been measured and modeled in many communities, so health-care providers could glean information about exposures and risk. This could be a key part of disaster preparedness. If a child shows symptoms of neurotoxicity, for instance, the provider would be wise in determining the proximity of a child's home to possible sources of lead and mercury. In immediate postdisaster situations, the same type of data search may reveal acutely toxic substances that may have been released. Such information could be readily loaded into GISs and other tools to improve medical care and prevent future exposures. Food and water scarcity, either short term (following a disaster) or long term (famines and droughts), can also benefit from improved interoperability.

Spatially relevant health information is scarcely available to a clinician at the time of a medical diagnostic encounter, and certainly, it is not a typical part of a comprehensive electronic medical record. Leveraged by a GIS, information on patients' potential environmental exposures can be delivered into the hands of clinicians while the patient is in the examination room, and influence future outcomes by modifying behaviors to reduce or avoid future exposures, for example. Using modern information technology in this way can go a long way to help both the physician and the patients they serve.

## Systems Thinking

Mechanical engineers may not be the first group of scientists that one associates with environmental disasters, given that they are mainly concerned about nonliving things. However, they have an appreciation for systems thinking that is needed to prevent or lessen the impacts of disasters. In fact, the American Society of Mechanical Engineers draws a systematic example from ecology that can be applied to every disaster mentioned in this book.

To an engineer, a sustainable system is one that is in equilibrium or changing at a tolerably slow rate. In the food chain, for example, plants are fed by sunlight, moisture, and nutrients and then become food themselves for insects and herbivores, which in turn act as food for larger animals. The waste from these animals replenishes the soil, which nourishes plants, and the cycle begins again.[13]

Sustainability is, therefore, as systematic phenomenon, so it is not surprising that engineers have embraced the concept of "sustainable design." At the largest scale, manufacturing, transportation, commerce, and other human activities that promote high consumption and wastefulness of finite resources cannot be sustained. At the individual designer scale, the products and processes that engineers design must be considered for their entire lifetimes and beyond.

A common way for engineers to approach disasters, or any problem for that matter, is to describe the problem and then solve it. Consider the problem of polluting a river. Not too long ago, paper and pulp processors had a problem. Or, stated more accurately, people and other organisms coming into contact with streams near the processors had a problem. The chlorinated bleaching process was generating detectable levels of highly toxic dioxins that were polluting the streams. The typical approach to the problem was to measure the concentrations of each dioxin and decide the best way to treat the water to remove the compounds. The choices included abiotic and biotic treatment methods, with different microbes and oxidation-reduction techniques. Numerous treatment approaches were tried, with varying degrees of success.

This is an example of well-organized, yet reductionist thinking. Eventually, chemists, engineers, and others asked what should have been an obvious question. How is the dioxin being generated? And, specifically, why is chlorinated bleach being used? Part of the answer was intellectual inertia, i.e., this is how it had been done as long as we can remember. This is actually a fairly common perspective in almost every scientific and engineering enterprise. We tend to approach things more as "onions" onto which we add a layer or two, rather than "apples" where now and then we find a whole new one that works better.

In this case, an altogether different bleaching process was found, one that did not use halogenated chemicals. Hence, the dioxin was not created in the first place so did not have to be treated. This is systems thinking.

To extend our example further to demonstrate systems thinking, let us engage in a thought experiment. What if our hypothetical chemists in the pulp and paper processing industry adopted a systems approach to the point that they started talking with the botanists and plant physiologists at the company? And, what if these tree experts were well versed in biotechnology and recommended a genetically modified tree that, in essence, would lose all of its pigmentation after being harvested (recall that this is a thought experiment, so we can assume that this is a reasonable process, e.g., the pigments photodegrade easily after the bark is removed). So, now the company would have no need to bleach whatsoever.

The thing about systems thinking is that it really never ends. So, our thought experiment must continue. Systems thinking requires that we consider all possible outcomes. So, does our story end with the new tree and the new pigment-free pulp? No, we also have to ask if there are now some new event pathways. For example, what if in the process of manipulating the tree's DNA, the tree became a threat to the biodiversity of nearby ecosystems? For example, what if the tree's pollen were toxic to insects and pollination was greatly reduced? Or, what if the pollen were so desirable to insects that they no longer pollinated native strains and the natural strains of the tree died out?

Again, this is systems thinking. The entire critical paths of any action must be considered. These paths extend not only into the future but also into the past. For example, in the bleaching example, what if the synthesis of the chlorine-free bleach releases toxic substances? We now have traded off one pollutant early in the process to avoid producing another later in the process.

Disasters have occurred as the result of lots of well-intended and even well-designed operations. For example, the damage from hurricanes is in part due to the levee systems that themselves may have been well designed in terms of materials and integrity. However, the very process of installing levees has changed the hydrology and biology of complex riverine systems. Not only that, but the reduced risk of flooding may well induce greater development and urbanization; thus, putting greater numbers of people at risk. As such, these actions can contribute to the disaster.

Sometimes, the concept is correct, but the choice is wrong. For example, levees may have been a good idea to protect urbanized areas, not necessarily those that constrict flow into channels, but those that allow flow above a certain level to be diverted. Well-placed agricultural levees can allow flows to be diverted over farmland rather than urbanized areas. However, this requires even more systems thinking with regard to crop selection (ability to withstand periodic inundation), water quality (diverted stream water will contain toxic substances, so plants that translocate these pollutants should be avoided), and other factors (natural wetlands and other habitats can be destroyed by too much or too little water during diversions).

Every disaster in this book could have been avoided or greatly lessened in scope and intensity if systems thinking had been more prominent. Of course, we have the convenience of hindsight. However, we can now apply systems thinking from the ones that have occurred to those that are pending. For example, the Japanese nuclear disaster has emphasized the need to avoid siting any nuclear power plant within similar hazard zones. Further, earthquake and tsunami likelihood are not the only hazards of concern, so storms, terrorism, and other threats should be considered, even if their likelihood is very low.

Nuclear power siting should also consider availability of cooling water, alternative means of pumping water to the core, likelihood of exposure to radiation, chemical hazards and damage to ecosystems.

Systems thinking is also needed in policy making and regulatory decisions. That is, the decisions to protect one aspect of the environment must consider the effect this will have on the rest of society (see discussion of cross-media transfer in Chapter 16).

Applying systems thinking to the oil and other spills includes consideration of vulnerable habitats, e.g., ecosystems damage isopleths could be drawn around rigs and along routes of tankers. Also, the mistakes and breaches in contingency plans during some of the spills call for more rigorous and frequent inspections, drills, and challenges to preventive measures. Mechanical integrity testing of casings, strengths of rigs, explosion and fire hazards, and efficiency of dynamic positioning systems should meet scientifically sound specifications. This calls for improved oversight by governmental agencies, which means they will need well-credentialed engineering and scientific expertise. The use of government and nongovernmental trustees onboard and elsewhere could both enhance compliance with environmental and safety criteria and engender more trust with the general public. These could prevent similar disasters in the near future.

## Some Good News

It may not be readily apparent, but both authors consider themselves to be technological optimists. We believe that scientists and engineers not only compete on society's playing field, but they also reshape it. There is no greater example than the green revolution of food productivity in the twentieth century. The Neo-Malthusians[14] expected food production to hit an impenetrable limit in the latter part of the last century. But, the scientific advancements in agriculture and food science more than kept up with population growth.

Disasters have been avoided and moderated by technological advances. For example, a straight-line project of oil spills seemed in order in the past half century, given the increases in crude oil extracted and shipped around the work. However, the opposite occurred and in spite of the increasing seaborne oil trade, the oil spills in the oceans have decreased enormously (see Figure 17.3). We do learn from our mistakes and that is what this book is about. We have highlighted some of the past major disasters and touched on some impending disasters and we hope we have unraveled them in the reader's eyes.

## Less Hubris, More Humility

To paraphrase Socrates, it seems the more we learn, the less we know about disasters. Scientists must be objective. It is difficult to separate policy from scientific perspective, but we must if we are to retain credibility. It is unsettling when scientists engage in politics, as

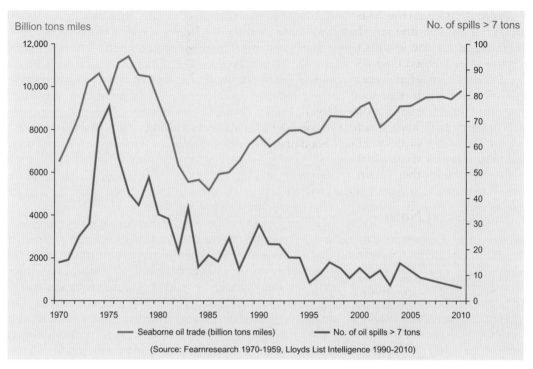

FIGURE 17.3　Seaborne crude oil and oil product trade and number of tanker spills over 7 tons, 1970-2010. *Source: International Tanker Oil Owners Pollution Federation, Limited. Statistics. http://www.itopf.com/information-services/data-and-statistics/statistics; 2012 [accessed March 14, 2012]. Note: 1 ton = 0.907 tonne.*

has been the case when credible scientists are labeled "global warming deniers" and criticized by fellow scientists for any skepticism of a particular point of view regarding climate change or fossil fuels or any other societal problem. These issues are too complex and important to require blind adherence to any scientific postulation at this time. That said, scientific credentials must also not be used by either side of a debate other than to provide objective and credible evidence.

We have attempted in this book to maintain objectivity, although it has been difficult at times not to become didactic, especially when we have witnessed ignorance and forgetfulness. Unfortunately, few of the disasters in this book came without precedents. Indeed, some were so bad that we had never seen anything like them, but all had at least been preceded by smaller problems that should have been sufficient warning.

Decades before Hurricane Katrina, there were warnings that the region was at great risk of flooding and other damage due to the hydrologic conditions and the type of urbanization allowed. Vulnerabilities were documented in ecosystems prior to most of the spills and leaks. Air pollution episodes had been experienced prior to disasters in Donora and London. These episodes suffered by U.S. and Europe should have been instructive in how they can be avoided, but it appears there are all too many repeats in China, India and other rapidly developing nations. Even the early hazardous waste disaster at Love Canal came after red flags from the military and industry, albeit without the needed urgency.

We recognize that the disasters in this book are merely a subset of those already documented. We drew the line on which to discuss, not so much because of their magnitude and severity, but on the lessons they have provided. We are aware that there are many more lessons to be learned than what we have shared here.

Most of the disasters were not so-called black swan events, i.e., those that result from such low probable confluences of events that one could not have expected them. In most cases, current state of the science did indeed expect such events to occur, although not necessarily within predictable and circumscribed boundaries in space and time. We will consider our efforts to have been successful if this work encourages others to find ways to prevent or reduce the likelihood of environmental disasters in the future and to discover better ways to address these insults after they occur.

## References and Notes

1. Posner RA. *Catastrophe: risk and response.* New York, NY: Oxford University Press; 2004.
2. Rees M. *Our final hour: a scientist's warning: how terror, error, and environmental disaster threaten humankind's future in this century—on earth and beyond.* 387 Park Avenue, South, New York, NY: Basic Books; 2003.
3. Depending on the journal, this can contradict another tenet of scientific research, i.e., the research should be able to be conducted by other researchers, following the methodology described in the article, and derive the same results. However, there is little incentive to replicate research if the likelihood of publication is low. That is, the research is no longer "new" because it was conducted by the original researcher, so the journal may well reject the second, replicate research.
4. The engineering profession is improving in this area, for example, in emergent "macroethical" areas like nanotechnology, neurotechnology, and even sustainable design approaches. For example, see: National Academy of Engineering. *Emerging technologies and ethical issues in engineering.* Washington, DC: The National Academies Press; 2004.
5. Inter-American Development Bank. *Consultative group for the reconstruction and transformation of Central America reducing vulnerability to natural hazards: lessons learned from hurricane Mitch: a strategy paper on environmental management.* http://www.iadb.org/regions/re2/consultative_group/groups/ecology_workshop_1.htm#2;2000 [accessed March 13, 2012].
6. The authors added these two mechanisms to the five recommended by Inter-American Development Bank; 2000.
7. Maslow Abraham. *Motivation and personality.* 2nd ed. New York, NY: Harper & Row; 1970.
8. ESRI. *Understanding GIS: the Arc/Info method.* 3rd ed. California: Redlands; 1995.
9. Marriott BB. *Environmental impact assessment: a practical guide.* New York, NY: McGraw-Hill; 1997, [chapter 5, Land Use and Development].
10. Hardin G. The tragedy of the commons. *Science* 1968;**162**(3859):1243–8. DOI: 10.1126/science.162.3859.1243.
11. Indiana University. *School of Informatics. Disaster Informatics.* http://www.informatics.indiana.edu/djwild/disaster [accessed March 13, 2012].
12. Vallero DA, Kun LG. *Health and environmental interoperability.* New York, NY: McGraw-Hill; 2012. Yearbook of Science & Technology; AccessScience. http://accessscience.com/content/Health-and-environmental-interoperability/YB110168; 2012 [accessed 13.03.12].
13. American Society of Mechanical Engineers. *Professional practice curriculum: sustainability.* http://www.professionalpractice.asme.org/communications/sustainability/index.htm; 2004 [accessed November 2, 2004].
14. Thomas Malthus (*Essay on the Principle of Population*, 1798) argued that when a fixed input is combined in production with a variable input, using a given technology, increases in the quantity of the variable input will eventually depress the productivity of the variable input. Malthus proposed this as a law from his pessimistic idea that population growth would force incomes down to the subsistence level. Based on this concept of diminishing returns, he predicted that starvation would result as projected population growth exceeded the rate of increase in the food supply. This is due to his forecast that the population would grow at an exponential rate, whereas the food supply grows at a linear rate. Apparently, Malthus did not realize that technology could increase food supply. For example, consider the NeoMalthusian P.R. Ehrlich's predictions in his book,

*Population Bomb* (Ballantine Books: New York, 1968). Ehrlich—often referred to as the modern Malthus—gives an exceedingly grim prognosis for the future: "Each year food production in underdeveloped countries falls a bit further behind burgeoning population growth, and people go to bed a little hungrier. While there are temporary or local reversals of this trend, it now seems inevitable that it will continue to its logical conclusion: *mass starvation.*" Not only does Ehrlich state that the world is headed toward calamity, he is also convinced that there is nothing anyone can really do that will provide anything more than temporary abatement. If one were to focus on Ehrlich's attitude toward technology as part of the solution to the impending problem, he would see Ehrlich's *technological pessimism*, so to speak. Ehrlich's lack of confidence in technology to deal with the problems plaguing the future is perhaps seen most explicitly on page 20: "But, you say, surely Science (with a capital 'S') will find a way for us to occupy the other planets of our solar system and eventually of other stars before we get all that crowded." Ehrlich was sure that "the battle to feed humanity is over." He insisted that India would be unable to provide sustenance for the 200 million person influx in its population by 1980. He was wrong—thanks to the *green revolution* and Norman Borlaug. Borlaug and his team engaged in a program that developed a special breed of dwarf wheat that was resistant to a wide spectrum of plant pests and diseases and that produced two or three more grains than the traditional varieties. His team then taught local farmers in both India and Pakistan how to cultivate the new strain of wheat. This astonishing increase in the production of wheat within a few years has come to be called the green revolution, its inception credited to Norman Borlaug. Since 1968, when Ehrlich published his frightful predictions, "India's population has more than doubled, its wheat production has more than tripled, and its economy has grown nine-fold." Pakistan has progressed from harvesting 3.4 million tons of wheat each year to around 18 million, and India has made similar impressive movement from 11 million tons to 60 million [Singh S. *Norman Borlaug: a billion lives saved.* AgBioWorld. http://www.agbioworld.org/biotech-info/topics/borlaug/special.html; 2011 [accessed March 15, 2012].

# Glossary of Terms[1]

**Abiotic**  Description of chemical and physical processes occurring without the involvement of living organisms. In some cases, such processes do not involve microorganisms or plants at all, whereas in other cases, biological and abiotic processes occur simultaneously and/or serve to enhance each other.

**Absorbed dose**  1. Amount of a substance that enters the body of an organism, e.g., through the eyes, skin, stomach, intestines, or lungs. 2. Amount of active ingredient crossing exchange boundaries of a test organism or human (same as "internal dose").

**Absorption**  1. Process wherein a substance permeates another substance; a fluid is sorbed into a particle. 2. After uptake, the process by which a substance moves to tissues in an organism, e.g., absorption of a substance into the bloodstream. 3. Process by which incident radiated energy is retained in a medium, e.g., shortwave radiation from the sun is absorbed by soil and reradiated as longer wave radiation, e.g., infrared radiation (see *greenhouse effect*). Compare to *adsorption*.

**Acceptable daily intake (ADI)**  The amount of a chemical a person can be exposed to on a daily basis over an extended period of time (usually a lifetime) without suffering deleterious effects.

---

[1] These terms are the authors' operational definitions. The sources are numerous, and many terms have been modified from their original definitions. However, here are the resources used to augment this glossary:

1. The Interstate Technology & Regulatory Council. *Enhanced attenuation: chlorinated organics*. EACO-1. Washington, DC: Interstate Technology & Regulatory Council; 2008.
2. Enhanced Attenuation: Chlorinated Organics Team. The Risk Assessment Information System Glossary. http://rais.ornl.gov/homepage/glossary.shtml#Committed%20effective%20dose%20equivalent.
3. U.S. Environmental Protection Agency. *Integrated Risk Information System Glossary*. http://www.epa.gov/NCEA/iris/help_gloss.htm.
4. U.S. Environmental Protection Agency, Argonne National Laboratory and U.S. Army Corps of Engineers. The Brownfields and Land Revitalizaiton Support Center. Glossary. http://www.brownfieldstsc.org/glossary.cfm; 2009 [accessed September 9, 2009].
5. L. M. Hinman's "Ethics Update—Glossary." http://ethics.sandiego.edu/Glossary.html.
6. R. N. Johnson's "A Glossary of Standard Meanings of Common Terms in Ethical Theory." http://web.missouri.edu/~philrnj/eterms.html.
7. U.S. Department of Health and Human Services, Office of Research Integrity. http://ori.dhhs.gov/education/products/rcradmin/glossary.shtml.
8. U.S. Department of Health and Human Services, Agency for Toxic Substances and Disease Registry. http://www.atsdr.cdc.gov/glossary.html.
9. U.S. Environmental Protection Agency. Terms of Environment: Glossary, Abbreviations and Acronyms. http://www.epa.gov/OCEPAterms/.
10. U.S. Environmental Protection Agency. Glossary of IRIS Terms. http://www.epa.gov/iris/gloss8.htm.
11. Fox Chase Cancer Center. Glossary of Ethics Terms. http://www.fccc.edu/ethics/Glossary_of_Ethics_Terms.html.
12. Inter-American Development Bank. *Consultative group for the reconstruction and transformation of Central America reducing vulnerability to natural hazards: lessons learned from Hurricane Mitch: a strategy paper on environmental management.* http://www.iadb.org/regions/re2/consultative_group/groups/ecology_workshop_1.htm#2; 2000.

In addition, the sources cited in the Notes and Commentary following each chapter of this book contain useful definitions of terms used in these specific instances.

---

**Acclimation** Adapting a microbe to food sources for carbon and energy in an attempt to enhance biodegradation (e.g., in wastewater treatment).

**Accuracy** Degree of agreement between a measured value and the true value; usually expressed as ±% of full scale. Compare to *precision.*

**Acid rain** Precipitation with depressed pH due to increases in concentrations of acid-forming compounds, such as oxides of sulfur and oxides of nitrogen, in the atmosphere. Term is usually limited to atmospheric deposition with $pH < 5.6$, which about the mean value for natural water (mainly due to carbonic acid content).

**Action level** 1. Concentration threshold above which actions must be taken, e.g., remediation, removal, treatment, or use restrictions and closures (e.g., beaches). 2. Regulatory level recommended by the U.S. Environmental Protection Agency for enforcement by Food and Drug Administration and U.S. Department of Agriculture when pesticide residues occur in food or feed commodities for reasons other than the direct application of the pesticide. Set for inadvertent residues resulting from previous legal use or accidental contamination. Compare to *tolerance.*

**Activated carbon** Carbon with a very high ratio of surface area to mass, rendering it a strong *adsorbent.* In granulated form, known as granulated activated carbon (GAC).

**Activation energy** Energy needed to bring all molecules in 1 mol of a substance to their reactive state at a given temperature.

**Active ingredient** Compound in a pesticide formulation that provides the biocidal mechanism of action. All other components are known as *inerts.*

**Acute** Describing exposures, diseases, or responses with short durations.

**Acute exposure** A single exposure to a substance that results in severe biological harm or death. Acute exposures are usually characterized as lasting no longer than a day, as compared to longer, continuing *exposure* over a period of time.

**Acute toxicity** Any adverse effect that occurs within a short period of time following *exposure*, usually up to 24-96 h, resulting in biological harm and often death.

**Adaptive management (AM)** Also known as "adaptive resource management" (ARM), a structured, iterative process of optimal decision making in the face of uncertainty, with an aim to reducing uncertainty over time via system monitoring. In this way, decision making simultaneously maximizes one or more resource objectives and, either passively or actively, accrues information needed to improve future management. AM is often characterized as "learning by doing."

**Additive effect** Response to exposure to multiple substances that equals the sum of responses of all the individual substances added together (compare with *antagonism* and *synergism*).

**Adenosine 5′-triphosphate (ATP)** The triphosphate of the nucleoside adenosine, which is a high energy molecule or has high phosphate group transfer potential and serves as the cell's major form of energy currency (see *photosynthesis*).

**Adenosine diphosphate (ADP)** The nucleoside diphosphate usually formed upon the breakdown of ATP when it provides energy for work (see *photosynthesis*).

**Adsorption** Process wherein a substance permeates another substance; a fluid is sorbed onto the surface of a particle. Compare to *absorption* (1).

**Advanced waste treatment** Physical, chemical, or biological treatment beyond that achieved by secondary treatment (e.g., additional removal of nutrients and solids). Synonymous with and preferred over *tertiary treatment.*

**Advection** Transport of a solute by the bulk motion of flowing groundwater.

**Adverse effect** A biochemical change, functional impairment, or pathologic lesion that affects the performance of the whole organism or reduces an organism's ability to respond to an additional environmental challenge.

**Aerobe** 1. Microorganism that can survive in the presence of molecular oxygen ($O_2$). 2. Microorganism that requires sufficient concentrations of $O_2$ to survive.

**Aerobic** Conditions for growth or metabolism in which the organism is sufficiently supplied with molecular oxygen.

**Aerobic respiration** Metabolic process whereby microorganisms use oxygen as the final *electron acceptor* to generate energy.

**Aerobic treatment** Process by which microbes decompose complex organic compounds in the presence of oxygen and use the liberated energy for reproduction and growth.

**Aerodynamic diameter** The diameter of a sphere with unit density that has aerodynamic behavior identical to that of the particle in question; an expression of aerodynamic behavior of an irregularly shaped particle in terms of the diameter of an idealized particle. Particles having the same aerodynamic diameter may have different dimensions and shapes (see also *Stokes diameter*).

**Aerosol** A suspension of liquid or solid particles in air.

**Affinity** Attraction, e.g., between an antigen and an antibody, or for a polar compound to the aqueous compartments of the environment.

**Agar** Polysaccharide complex gel derived from marine algae used to grow microbiological cultures. Gelling temperature usually ranges between 40 and 50 °C.

**Agonist** Substance that binds to a cell's receptor, often mimicking the actions of a normally occurring substance. Compare to *antagonist.*

**Agonist** Substance that blocks a cell's receptor, interfering with normal cellular response. Compare to *agonist.*

**ALARP** As low as reasonably possible.

**Albedo** Reflectivity of light; inverse of light absorption.

**Algae** Phototrophic *eukaryotic* microbes that can be either unicellular or multicellular. Plural of alga.

**Algal bloom** Masses of *algae*, plants, and other organisms that form scum at the top of surface waters; usually attributed to large inputs of nutrients to the waters.

**Aliphatic compounds** Acyclic or cyclic, saturated or unsaturated carbon compounds, excluding aromatic compounds.

**Alkane** Single-bonded carbon chains or branched structures.

**Alkene** Carbon chains or branched structures that contain at least one double bond.

**Alkyne** Carbon chains or branched structures that contain at least one triple bond.

**Allele** One of several alternative forms of a gene that occupies a given locus on a chromosome.

**Allergen** Substance that causes an allergic reaction.

**Allergenicity** Capacity or potential that a substance will elicit and allergic reaction.

**Alum** 1. *Flocculant*, $K_2SO_4Al_2(SO_4)_3 \cdot 2H_2O$. 2. Aluminum sulfate alum, used to precipitate hydroxides for coagulation.

**Ambient** 1. Outdoor (e.g., ambient air). 2. Describing general environmental conditions, as contrasted with effluent or emission, e.g., ambient measurements versus effluent measurements. 3. Surrounding conditions.

**Amendment** Substrate introduced to stimulate the *in situ* microbial processes (vegetable oils, sugars, alcohols, etc.).

**Amino acid** Any of 20 basic building blocks of proteins with a free amino ($NH_2$) and a free carboxyl (COOH) group, and having the basic formula $NH_2C_RCOOH$. According to the side group R, they are subdivided into polar or hydrophilic (serine, threonine, tyrosine, asparagine, and glutamine), nonpolar or hydrophobic (glycine, alanine, valine, leucine, isoleucine, proline, phenylalanine, tryptophan, and cysteine), acidic (aspartic acid and glutamic acid), and basics (lysine, arginine, and histidine). The sequence of amino acids determines the shape, properties, and the biological role of a protein.

**Amino group** $NH_2$ attached to carbon structures (e.g., in amines and amino acids).

**Amoral** Lacking any moral characteristics. An amoral act is neither morally good nor morally bad; it simply exists. Contrast with *moral* or *immoral.*

**Amphibole** Inosilicate minerals, composed of double chain $SiO_4$ tetrahedra, linked at the vertices and generally containing iron and/or magnesium. Amphibole asbestos is a mixture of different fibers. For example, Libby, Montana amphiboles comprise 85% winchite, 10% richerite, and 5% tremolite. Most toxic form of asbestos.

**Amphiphilic** Describing a chemical compound that has both *hydrophilic* and *lipophilic* properties.

**Amphoteric** Able to react as either a weak acid or a weak base.

**Amplification** 1. Treatment (e.g., use of chloramphenicol) designed to increase the proportion of plasmid DNA relative to that of bacterial (host) DNA. 2. Replicating a gene library in bulk. 3. Duplication of genes within a chromosomal segment. 4. Creation of numerous copies of a segment of DNA by the *polymerase chain reaction.*

**Anabolism** Synthesis of complex molecules from simpler molecules with the input of energy.

**Anaerobe** 1. Microorganism that cannot survive in the presence of molecular oxygen ($O_2$). 2. Microorganism that requires electron acceptors other than $O_2$ to survive.

**Anaerobic respiration** Process whereby microorganisms use a chemical other than oxygen as an electron acceptor. Common substitutes for oxygen are nitrate, sulfate, iron, carbon dioxide, and other organic compounds (fermentation).

**Analogy** Comparison of similarities between two things to a conclusion about an additional attribute common to both things. This is a type of inductive reasoning (see *inductive reasoning*). One of *Hill's criteria.*

**Analyte** 1. Substance measured in a scientific study. 2. Chemical for which a sample (e.g., water, air, or blood) is tested in a laboratory, e.g., to determine the amount of cadmium in soil, the specified amount of soil to be collected and analyzed in the laboratory.

**Analytic epidemiology** Evaluation of associations between exposure to physical, chemical and biological agents and disease by testing scientific hypotheses.

**Anion** Negatively charged ion, e.g., chloride ($Cl^-$).

**Anion exchange capacity (AEC)** Total of exchangeable anions that can be sorbed by a soil (units = centimoles of negative charge per kg soil).

**Anisotropy** Conditions under which one or more hydraulic properties of an aquifer vary with direction.

**Anoxic** An environment where there is no free oxygen and where microbial and chemical reactions use other chemicals in the environment to accept electrons.

**Antagonism** 1. Effect from a combination of two agents is less than the sum of the individual effects from each agent ($1 + 1 < 2$). Contrast with *synergism* and *additive effect*. 2. *Amensalism*.

**Anthropocentrism** Philosophy- or decision framework-based human beings. View that all and only humans have moral value. Nonhuman species and abiotic resources have value only in respect to that associated with human values. Contrast with *biocentrism* and *ecocentrism*.

**Anthropogenic** 1. Made, caused, or influenced by human activities. Contrast with *biogenic*. 2. Derived from human activities, as opposed to those occurring in natural environments without human influences.

**Antibody** Protein, e.g., immunoglobulin, manufactured by lymphocytes (a type of white blood cell) to neutralize an *antigen* or foreign protein. Microbes, pollens, dust mites, molds, foods, and other substances contain antigens which will trigger antibodies.

**Antigen** Foreign substance (e.g., protein, nucleoprotein, polysaccharide) to which lymphocytes respond. When immune system responds, it is known as an immunogen.

**Antinutritional** Factor, when present, stifles metabolism and growth of an organism (especially humans in the context of food biotechnologies). One of the three major risks associated with food biotechnology, along with toxicity and *allergenicity*.

**Apoptosis** Programmed cell death.

**Applied mathematics** Mathematical techniques typically used in the application of mathematical knowledge to domains beyond mathematics itself.

**Aquifer** A porous underground bed or layer of earth, sand, gravel, or porous stone that contains water. Geologic formation, group of formations, or part of a formation containing saturated permeable material that yields sufficient, economical quantities of groundwater.

**Association** Relationship, not necessarily causal, between two variables. The antecedent variable comes before and is associated with an outcome; however, it may or may not be the cause of the outcome. For example, mean birth weight of minority babies is less than that of babies of the general population. Ethnicity is an antecedent of low birth weight, but not the cause. Other factors, e.g., nutrition, smoking status, and alcohol consumption, may be the causal agents.

**Attenuation** The process by which a chemical compound's concentration decreases with time, through sorption, *degradation*, *dilution*, and/or *transformation*. The term applies to both destructive and nondestructive contaminant removal.

**Attenuation rate** The rate at which a contaminant is removed. This is not a rate constant but a rate, with typical units of $\mu g\ L^{-1}\ year^{-1}$.

**Attributable risk** The rate of a disease in exposed individuals that can be attributed to the *exposure*. This measure is derived by difference between the rate (usually *incidence* or *mortality*) of the disease among persons not exposed to the suspected agent and the corresponding rate among exposed individuals.

**Autotroph** Organisms feeding on inorganic minerals, producing complex organic compounds from simple inorganic molecules using energy by *photosynthesis* or by inorganic chemical reactions.

**Average daily dose (ADD)** Dose rate averaged over a pathway-specific period of exposure expressed as a daily dose on a per-unit-body-weight basis. The ADD is usually expressed as $mg\ kg^{-1}\ day^{-1}$ or other mass-time units.

*Bacillus* Rod-shaped bacterium.

*Bacillus thuringiensis* **(Bt)** Bacterium that repels or kills insects; a major component of the microbial pesticide industry.

**Bacteria** Unicellular microorganisms that exist either as free-living organisms or as parasites, ranging from beneficial to harmful to humans.

**Bacteriophage** Virus (phage) that infects a bacterium.

**Bayesian** Statistical approach that addresses probability inference, named after Thomas Bayes (*An essay towards solving a problem in the doctrine of chances*, 1763), to decision making and inferential statistics that deals with probability inference (i.e., using knowledge of prior events to predict future events). In a Bayesian network, priors are updated by additional data that yield posterior probabilities that are often more robust than classical probabilities.

**Bayesian belief network**  Cause-and-effect tool represented by a probabilistic graphic model of a set of random variables and their conditional independencies.

**Benefit-cost analysis (or cost-benefit analysis)**  Method designed to determine the feasibility or utility of a proposed or existing project. Yields a benefit-cost ratio (see *benefit-cost ratio (BCR)*).

**Benefit-cost ratio (BCR)**  Weighted benefits divided by weighted costs; used to compare and differentiate among project alternatives. Gross $BCR < 1$ is undesirable. The greater the BCR, the more acceptable the alternative.

**Benthic**  Pertaining to the bottom of a body of water. Often used to distinction bottom organisms from those that swim and float.

**Best available control technology**  An *emission* limitation (including a visible emission standard) based on the maximum degree of reduction for each pollutant subject to regulation under the Clean Air Act which would be emitted from any proposed major stationary source or major modification which the Administrator, on a case-by-case basis, taking into account energy, environmental, and economic impacts and other costs, determines is achievable for such source or modification through application of production processes or available methods, systems, and techniques, including fuel cleaning or treatment or innovative fuel combustion techniques for control of such pollutant.

**Best management practice (BMP)**  Methods that have been determined to be the most effective, practical means of preventing or reducing pollution from *nonpoint sources*.

**Best practice**  1. Optimal service to the client. 2. Treatment is appropriate, accepted, and widely used according to expert consensus; embodies an integrated, comprehensive, and continuously improving approach to care (medicine). It is morally obligatory that health-care practitioners provide patients with the best practice (also known as standard therapy or standard of care).

**Bias**  1. Systematic error in one direction, such as the positive bias of a scale that reads 1 mg too high (instrument error) or the negative bias in interpretations of lesions reported by a physician performing the procedure (operator bias) that consistently miss some lesions. Bias makes the reported values less accurate. 2. Any difference between the true value and that measured due to all causes other than sampling variability.

**Binding site**  Location on cellular DNA to which a can bind. Typically, binding sites may be in the vicinity of genes and involved in activating *transcription* of that gene (i.e., promoter elements), in enhancing transcription of that gene (enhancer elements), or in reducing transcription of that gene (silencers).

**Bio-**  Prefix indicating "life" (Greek).

**Bioaccumulation**  The process whereby certain substances build up in living tissues.

**Bioaccumulation factor (BAF)**  Ratio of a tissue concentration of substance in an organism to its concentration in the environment (usually water) where the organism lives. BAF indicates a compound's potential to accumulate in tissue through exposure to both food and water. Compare to *biomagnification* and *bioconcentration factor*.

**Bioassay**  Test to assess the effects of certain substances on animals. Often used to estimate *acute toxicity*.

**Bioaugmentation**  Addition of beneficial microorganisms into groundwater to increase the rate and extent of *biodegradation*. Part of a *bioremediation* strategy.

**Bioavailability**  The degree to which a substance becomes available to the target tissue after administration or exposure.

**Biocatalysis**  Mediation of chemical reactions by biological systems, e.g., microbial communities, whole organisms or cells, cell-free extracts, or purified enzymes.

**Biocentrism**  View that all life has moral value. Contrast with *anthropomorphism*.

**Biochemical oxygen demand (BOD)**  A standard test to assess wastewater pollution due to organic substances. $BOD_5$ is based on the measurement of the oxygen used under controlled conditions of temperature ($20\,^{\circ}C$) and time (5 days). Compare to *chemical oxygen demand*.

**Biochemodynamics**  The physical, chemical, and biological processes that transport and transform substances.

**Bioconcentration factor (BCF)**  Ratio of the concentration of substance in an organism's tissue versus its concentration in the environment (usually water) in situations where the organism is exposed exclusively to water. BCF measures the compound's potential to accumulate in tissue through direct uptake from water (excludes uptake from food). Compare to *bioaccumulation factor*.

**Biodegradation**  Breakdown of a contaminant, usually catalyzed by enzymes produced by organisms. Term usually applies only to microorganisms. Compare to *phytodegradation*.

**Biodiversity**  Number and variety of organisms in a given system (e.g., wetland or forest). Usually, lower biodiversity indicates that the system is stressed and in a poor condition.

**Bioenergetics** Energy flow and transformation through living systems. Can be within an organism, e.g., cellular energetics, or within and between levels of *biological organization*, e.g., *trophic states* (energy transfer from producers to first-order consumers, to second-order consumers, to and from decomposers, etc.)

**Bioengineering** See *biological engineering.*

**Bioethics** 1. Inquiry into ethical implications of biological research and applications. 2. Ethical inquiry into matters of life, especially biomedical and environmental ethics.

**Biofilm** Organized microbial system consisting of layers of microbial cells associated with surfaces, often with complex structural and functional characteristics. Influence microbial metabolic processes. Site where chemical degradation occurs both via extracellular enzymatic activity and by intracellular microbial processes. *Pseudomonas* and *Nitrosomonas* strains are notable for their ability to form a strong biofilm.

**Biogenic** Made, caused, or influenced by natural processes. Contrast with *anthropogenic.*

**Biogeochemistry** 1. Study of the fluxes, cycles, and other chemical and biological processes at various scales on earth. 2. Study of microbially mediated chemical transformations, especially with regard to nutrient cycling (N, P, S, and K, for example).

**Bioinformatics** Management and analysis of data using advanced computing techniques applied to biological research and inquiry.

**Biolistic gun (particle gun)** Method used to modify genes by directly shooting genetic information into a cell. DNA is bound to tiny particles of gold or tungsten and subsequently inserted into tissue or single cells under high pressure. The accelerated particles penetrate both the cell wall and membranes, slowing down upon impact. The DNA separates from the metal and can be integrated into the genetic material inside the nucleus.

**Biolitic** Formed by living organisms or their remains (e.g., sedimentary rocks).

**Biological control** Method of addressing problematic organisms by using a biochemical product or bioengineered or naturally occurring organism, e.g., introducing the European beetle (*Nanophyes marmoratus*) that feeds exclusively on the highly invasive purple loosestrife (*Lythrum salicaria*).

**Biological criteria** Measures of the condition of an environment, e.g., incidence of cancer in benthic fish species.

**Biological engineering** Combination of biomedical and biosystem engineering (see *biomedical engineering* and *biosystem engineering*) to develop useful biology-based technologies that can be applied across a wide spectrum of societal needs, including diagnosis, treatment, and prevention of disease; design and fabrication of materials, devices, and processes; and enhancement and sustainability of environmental quality.

**Biological half-life** The time required for a biological system (such as a human or animal) to eliminate, by natural processes, half the amount of a substance (such as a radioactive material) that has been absorbed into that system.

**Biological magnification** See *biomagnification.*

**Biological organization** Levels of living things, from *biomolecules* to planetary. The levels generally representing biological systems are molecule, cell, tissue, organ, organ system, organism, population, community, ecosystem, and biosphere.

**Biological response** Manner and type of effect in an organism (e.g., disease, change in metabolism, and homeostasis).

**Biologically based dose-response (BBDR) model** Predictive model that describes biological processes at the cellular and molecular level linking the target organ dose to the adverse effect.

**Biomagnification (biological magnification)** Process whereby certain substances, such as substances that move up the *food chain*, work their way into rivers or lakes and are eaten by aquatic organisms such as fish, which, in turn, are eaten by large birds, animals, or humans. The substances become increasingly concentrated in tissues or internal organs as they move up the chain.

**Biomarker** 1. Chemical, physical, or biological measurement that indicates biological condition. The biomarker may be a chemical to which an organism is exposed (e.g., lead in blood), a metabolite of the chemical (e.g., cotinine in blood as an indication of exposure to nicotine), or a biological response (e.g., an increase in body temperature as a result of exposure to a pathogen). 2. In geochemistry, organic compounds that are remnants of former living creatures (e.g., the suite of compounds that indicate the processes by which coal or petroleum has formed).

**Biomass** Material produced by the growth of microorganisms.

**Biomedical engineering** Application of engineering principles to medicine, including drug delivery systems, therapeutic systems, and medical devices.

**Biomedical testing** Investigations to determine whether a change in a body function might have occurred because of exposure to a hazardous substance.

**Biomolecule** Building block compounds of life that perform essential functions in living organisms, e.g., amino acids, carbohydrates, lipids, polysaccharides, proteins, and nucleic acids.

**Biophile** An element, arranged in myriad ways, that provides the structure for all living systems, e.g., oxygen, carbon, hydrogen, and nitrogen.

**Bioprospecting** Search for novel products from organisms in the natural habitats, usually plants and microbes. In its negative connotation, known as biopiracy.

**Bioremediation** Treatment processes that use microorganisms such as bacteria, yeast, or fungi to break down hazardous substances into less toxic or nontoxic substances. Bioremediation can be used to clean up contaminated soil and water. *In situ* bioremediation treats contaminated soil or groundwater in the location in which it is found. For *ex situ* bioremediation processes, contaminated soil is excavated or groundwater is pumped to the surface before they can be treated.

**Biosecurity** Measures to control the transmission of microorganisms into or out of a specified area or population (see *physical containment*).

**Biosensor** A portable device that uses living organisms, such as microbes, or parts and products of living organisms, such as enzymes, tissues, and antibodies, to produce reactions to specific chemical contaminants.

**Biosolids** 1. See *sludge.* 2. Organic product of wastewater treatment that can be beneficially used.

**Biosphere** Earth's zone that includes *biota*, extending from ocean sediment to mountaintops.

**Biostatistics** Application of statistical tools to interpret biological and medical data.

**Biostimulation** Adding chemical amendments, such as nutrients or electron donors, to soil or groundwater to support bioremediation.

**Biosystem** Living organism or a system of living organisms that are able to interact with other organisms directly or indirectly.

**Biosystem or biosystems engineering (bioengineering)** 1. Application of biological sciences to achieve practical ends. 2. Integration of physical, chemical, or mathematical sciences and engineering principles for the study of biology, medicine, behavior, or health to advance fundamental concepts; to create knowledge for the molecular to the organ systems levels; and to develop innovative biologics, materials, processes, implants, devices, and informatics approaches for the prevention, diagnosis, and treatment of disease; for patient rehabilitation; and for improving health.

**Biota** 1. Any living creature, plant (flora), animal (fauna), or microbial. 2. Total of the living organisms of any designated area.

**Biotechnology** Use of living creatures to produce things of value to humans (e.g., hazardous waste cleanup, production of drugs, and improving agriculture and food supplies).

**Bioterrorism** Use of living agents to cause intentional harm to people (e.g., anthrax spores or pathogenic viruses) and society (e.g., agricultural pests).

**Biotic** Related to living systems.

**Biotransformation** Biologically catalyzed transformation of a chemical to some other product.

**Bio-uptake** 1. Process by which a compound enters an organism. 2. Amount of a substance that enters an organism.

**Bioventing** An *in situ* remediation technology that stimulates the natural biodegradation of aerobically degradable compounds in soil by the injection of oxygen into the subsurface. Bioventing has been used to remediate releases of petroleum products, such as gasoline, jet fuels, kerosene, and diesel fuel. Bioventing stimulates the aerobic bioremediation of hydrocarbon-contaminated soils and vacuum-enhanced free-product recovery extracts light nonaqueous-phase liquids (LNAPL) from the capillary fringe and the water table.

**Black swan even** An outcome that would not have been predicted from past evidence due to the low probability of a possible confluence of events, but the event in fact occurred.

**Blackbody radiator** Idealized object that absorbs all electromagnetic radiation that reaches it. The earth behaves like a blackbody radiator when it absorbs incoming solar radiation (e.g., shortwave and visible light) and reemits it at longer wavelengths (e.g., infrared heat). See *greenhouse effect.*

**Blastocyst** Early stage embryo that consists of cells enclosing a fluid-filled cavity.

**Body burden** Total amount of a specific substance in an organism, including the amount stored, the amount that is mobile, and the amount *absorbed.*

**Bottom-up** View where fundamental components are first considered, working upward to larger perspectives. Contrast with *top-down.*

**Brownfield** Abandoned, idled, or underused industrial and commercial site where expansion or redevelopment is complicated by real or perceived environmental contamination. Generally applied to such sites that have been or are expected to be reused.

**BTEX** Term used for benzene, toluene, ethylbenzene, and xylene, which are volatile aromatic compounds typically found in petroleum products such as gasoline and diesel fuel.

**Bulk density** The mass of a soil per unit bulk volume of soil; mass is measured after all water has been extracted, and the volume includes the volume of the soil particles and pores.

**Butterfly effect** Sensitive dependence on initial conditions. Metaphor for the extreme sensitivity of chaotic systems (see Chaos), in which small changes or perturbations lead to drastically different outcomes. The phrase is derived from a butterfly flapping its wings in California, thereby initiating a change in weather patterns that results in the formation of a thunderstorm in Nebraska (from Edward Lorenz in his 1963 article, "Deterministic nonperiodic flow," *J Atmos Sci* **20**:130-41; although in his presentation to the New York Academy, it was not a butterfly but a seagull's flapping of the wing that posited as the initial condition. Later in 1972, Lorenz used the butterfly in the example).

**Calvin cycle** Dominant pathway for the fixation (or reduction and incorporation) of $CO_2$ into organic material by *photoautotrophs* during photosynthesis. Also is found in *chemolithoautotrophs*.

**Cancer** Disease of heritable, somatic mutations affecting cell growth and differentiation, characterized by an abnormal, uncontrolled growth of cells.

**Capillary force** Interfacial force between immiscible fluid phases, resulting in pressure differences between the two phases. Force due to capillary action that "pulls" water and/or waterborne contaminants toward a substance that attracts them, leading to the production of thin trails of contamination and the incorporation of contamination into the inner windings of a soil particle.

**Carbonaceous biochemical oxygen demand (CBOD)** Measure of the dissolved oxygen used for biological oxidation of C-containing compounds in a sample. See *biochemical oxygen demand*.

**Carcinogen** Physical, chemical, or biological agent that induces cancer.

**Carcinogenesis** Origin or production of a benign or malignant tumor. The carcinogenic event modifies the genome and/or other molecular control mechanisms of the target cells, giving rise to a population of altered cells.

**CAS registration number** An organization from Columbus, Ohio, which indexes information published in Chemical Abstracts by the American Chemical Society and provides index guides by which information about particular substances may be located in the Abstracts when needed. CAS numbers identify specific chemicals.

**Case study** Evaluation of an actual occurrence of events to describe specific environmental and health conditions and past exposures.

**Case-control study** An epidemiologic study contrasting those with the disease of interest (cases) to those without the disease (controls). The groups are then compared with respect to exposure history, to ascertain whether they differ in the proportion exposed to the chemical(s) under investigation.

**Catabolism** Metabolism in which larger, more complex molecules are broken down into smaller, simpler molecules with the release of energy. Compare to *anabolism*.

**Cation** Positively charged ion.

**Cation exchange capacity (CEC)** Ability of soil, sediment, or other solid matrix to exchange *cations* with a fluid. Very important measure of soil productivity and root behavior.

**Causation (causality)** Relationship between causes and effects. Contrast with association.

**Cell** Basic unit of life; autonomous, self-replicating unit that either constitutes a unicellular organism or is a subunit of a multicellular organism; the lowest denomination of life.

**Central nervous system** Portion of the nervous system that consists of the brain and the spinal cord.

**Chaos theory** Exposition of the apparent lack of order in a system that nonetheless obeys specific rules. Condition discovered by the physicist Henri Poincaré around the year 1900 that refers to an inherent lack of predictability in some physical systems (i.e., Poincaré's concept of dynamical instability).

**Chemical oxygen demand (COD)** Measure of the amount of oxygen required for the chemical oxidation of carbonaceous (organic) material in a waste, using inorganic dichromate or permanganate salts as oxidants in a 2-h test. Compare to *biochemical oxygen demand*.

**Chemisorption** Type of *adsorption* process wherein an adsorbate is held on the surface of an adsorbent by chemical bonds.

**Chemotroph** Organism that derives energy from inorganic reactions.

**Chimera** Organism, usually animal, that is a mixture of cells from two different embryonic sources.

**Chlorinated ethene** Chemical substances, such as trichloroethene and tetrachloroethene that have been used in industry as solvents.

**Chlorinated solvent** Organic compounds with chlorine substituents that commonly are used for industrial degreasing and cleaning, dry cleaning, and other processes.

**Chloromethanes** Chemical substances, such as carbon tetrachloride and chloroform that have been used in industry as solvents.

**Chloroplast** Organelle containing chlorophyll, which carries out photosynthesis in plants and green algae.

**Chromosome** Structure within a cell's nucleus consisting of strands of deoxyribonucleic acid (DNA) coated with specialized cell proteins and duplicated at each mitotic cell division. Chromosomes transmit the genes of the organism from one generation to the next.

**Chronic** Having a persistent, recurring, or long-term nature. Contrast with *acute*.

**Chronic effect** An adverse effect on a human or animal in which symptoms recur frequently or develop slowly over a long period of time.

**Chronic exposure** Multiple exposures occurring over an extended period of time, or a significant fraction of the animal's or the individual's lifetime.

**Chronic toxicity** Capacity of a substance to cause long-term adverse effects (usually applied to humans and human populations).

**Chrysotile** Most common type of asbestos; a soft, fibrous silicate mineral in the serpentine group of phyllosilicates. Compare to *amphibole*.

**Ciliate** Class of protozoans distinguished by short hairs on all or part of their bodies.

**Cinnabar** Bright red sulfide compound of mercury, HgS.

**Cisgenesis** Process by which genes are artificially transferred between organisms that could be conventionally bred (i.e., close related). Compare to *transgenesis*.

**Citrus greening disease** Huanglongbing; destructive plant disease in citrus trees caused by the phloem-limited bacterium *Candidatus* spp. and transmitted by *psyllids*, especially *Diaphorina citri* Kuwayama and *Trioza erytreae* (del Guercio).

**Clarification** Removal of suspended solids. Preferred terms are *sedimentation* or *settling*.

**Clay** Soil particle <0.002 mm in diameter. Compare to *silt* and *sand*.

**Cleanup** Actions taken to address a release or threat of release of a pollutant. Often used synonymously with *remediation* but also can consist of pollutant removals and other corrective actions that do not necessarily require *degradation* and *detoxification*.

**Clone** Line of cells genetically identical to the originating stem cell; group of genetically identical cells or organisms derived by asexual reproduction from a single parent. Act of generating these organisms is known as cloning.

**Closure** Procedure following a *remediation* project or the useful life of a landfill, e.g., installing a permanent cap.

**Coccus** Bacterial cell that is roughly spherical.

**Code of ethics** Established set of moral expectations of a group, especially of professional societies.

**Coefficient of determination ($r^2$)** Proportion of the variance of one variable predictable from another variable. The ratio of the explained variation to the total variation, which represents the percentage of the data nearest to the line of best fit. For example, if $r = 0.90$, then $r^2 = 0.81$, meaning that 81% of the total variation in one variable ($y$) can be explained by the linear relationship between the two variables ($x$ and $y$) as described by the regression equation. Thus, the remaining 19% of the total variation is unexplained.

**Coenzyme** Loosely bound nonprotein component of an enzyme required for catalytic activity that often dissociates from the enzyme active site after product has been formed.

**Coherence** Criterion for causality (i.e., *Hill's criteria*) based on the amount and degree of agreement among studies linking cause to effect; especially among various types of studies (e.g., animal testing, human epidemiological investigations, and *in vitro* studies).

**Cohort study** Epidemiologic study comparing those with an exposure of interest to those without the exposure. These two cohorts are then followed over time to determine the differences in the rates of disease between the exposure subjects. Also called a prospective study.

**Coliform** Gram-negative, nonsporing, facultative rod that ferments lactose with gas formation within 48 h at 35 °C.

**Colloid** Fine solid (<0.002 mm and >0.000001 mm) that does not readily settle; intermediate between true solutions and suspensions.

**Combinational biology** Introduction of genes from one microorganism into another microorganism to synthesize a new product or a modified product, especially in relation to antibiotic synthesis.

**Combustion** Sequence of rapid exothermic oxidation reactions that release heat and generate products.

**Cometabolism** A reaction in which microorganisms transform a contaminant even though the contaminant cannot serve as an energy source for growth, requiring the presence of other compounds (primary substrates) to support growth.

**Commensalism** Symbiosis where an organism lives on or within another organism with neither a positive nor a negative effect on the other organism.

**Comparative risk** An expression of the risks associated with two (or more) actions leading to the same goal; may be expressed quantitatively (e.g., ratio of 1.5) or qualitatively (one risk greater than another risk). Any comparison among the risks of two or more hazards with respect to a common scale.

**Compartmental model** Model that predicts or characterizes the transport and fate of a compound within an organism (e.g., moving from blood to tissues, transformed by metabolism, and detoxified or bioactivated during the path to elimination).

**Compartmentalization** Viewing a system by its individual components. This can be problematic when an engineer does not consider the system as a whole (e.g., when the structural engineer and soil engineer do not collaborate on selecting the best and safest combination of materials and structures suited to a soil type, or when a biomedical engineer does not work closely with various specialized health-care professionals in a clinical setting to adapt a realistic device to the comprehensive needs of the patient). Compartmentalization can be good when it allows the engineer to focus adequate attention on the components (see *bottom-up*), so long as the design is properly built into a system.

**Competence** 1. Skill in practice. For professionals, competence is requisite to ethical practice. 2. Sufficient velocity for a fluid to carry a load (especially a stream's ability to carry solids).

**Complementary DNA (cDNA)** DNA copy of an RNA molecule.

**Complexity** Relative measure of uncertainty in achieving functional requirements or objectives. Designers are frequently expected to reduce the complexity of engineered systems.

**Compliance monitoring** Collection of data needed to evaluate the condition of the contaminated media against standards such as soil and/or water quality regulatory standards, risk-based standards of remedial action objectives.

**Composite sample** 1. Series of samples taken over a given period of time and weighted by flow rate or by other means to represent a concentration integrated with respect to time. 2. Soil sample that consists of soil taken from various depths or various locations.

**Composite sample** Combined individual environmental samples collected at preselected intervals to minimize the effect of the variability of the individual sample. Individual samples may be of equal volume or may be proportional to flow.

**Compost** Organic material produced from microbial degradation that is useful as soil conditioners and fertilizers. Process to produce such matter is known as composting.

**Concentration** 1. Quantity of substance per unit volume (fluid) or per unit weight (solid matrix, e.g., soil, sediment, tissue). 2. Method of increasing the dissolved solids per unit volume of solution, e.g., via evaporation of the liquid. 3. Increasing suspended solids per unit volume of *sludge* via sedimentation or dewatering.

**Conceptual site model (CSM)** A hypothesis about how releases occurred, the current state of the source zone, and current plume characteristics (plume stability).

**Confidence level** 1. Client's trust in a professional. 2. Amount of certainty that a statistical prediction is accurate. Physical sciences may differ from social sciences in what is considered acceptable confidence; e.g., the former may require 99%, while social scientific research may consider 95% to be acceptable. Depending on the application, engineering research ranges in acceptable confidence level (e.g., structural fatigue research may require higher confidence levels than environmental research).

**Conflagration** Destructive fire.

**Confounder** Factor that distorts or masks the true effect of risk factors in an epidemiologic study. A condition or variable that is a risk factor for disease and is associated with an exposure of interest. This association between the exposure of interest and the confounder (a true risk factor for disease) may make it falsely appear that the exposure of interest is associated with disease. For example, a study of low birth weight children in low-income families must first address the confounding effects of tobacco smoking before ascribing the actual risk associated with income.

**Confounding factor** Variable that may introduce differences between cases and controls, which do not reflect differences in the variables of primary interest. Factors that must be considered in *epidemiological* studies to ensure that the experimental variables are indeed the cause of an outcome (e.g., smoking can be a confounder in most cancer studies).

**Conjugation**  In *genetic engineering*, transferring genetic material between bacteria through direct cell-to-cell contact, or through a bridge between the two cells.

**Constitutive**  Quality of enzyme meaning that it always synthesized and ready.

**Contact stabilization**  Enhanced *activated-sludge* process by adding a period of contact between waste water and *sludge* for rapid removal of soluble *biochemical oxygen demand* by adsorption, followed by a longer period of aeration in a separate tank so that the sludge is oxidized and new biosolids are synthesized.

**Contamination**  Contact with an admixture of an unnatural agent, with the implication that the amount is measurable. Increase in harmful or otherwise unwanted material in the environment. Often used synonymously with pollution.

**Contingency plan**  Document setting out an organized, planned, and coordinated course of action to be followed in case of an emergency or episodic event that threatens public health or the environment (e.g., an oil spill, toxic release, or natural disaster).

**Contingent probability**  Probability that an event will occur as a result of one or more previous events. Also known as conditional probability.

**Continuous culture**  Microbial growth that is limited, and the effect of limiting the substrate or nutrients can be described by *Monod equation*.

**Continuous sample**  A flow of water from a particular place in a plant to the location where samples are collected for testing; may be used to obtain grab or composite samples.

**Control group**  Group used as the baseline for comparison in epidemiologic studies or laboratory studies. This group is selected because it either lacks the disease of interest (case-control group) or lacks the exposure of concern (cohort study). Also known as a reference group.

**Control volume**  Arbitrary volume in which the mass of the fluid remains constant at steady state so that as a fluid moves through, the mass entering the control volume is equal to the mass leaving the control volume.

**Correlation coefficient (*r*)**  Statistical measurement of the strength and the direction of a linear relationship (association) between two variables.

**Cost-benefit analysis**  A formal quantitative procedure comparing costs and benefits of a proposed project or act under a set of preestablished rules. To determine a rank ordering of projects to maximize the rate of return when available funds are unlimited, the quotient of benefits divided by costs is the appropriate form; to maximize absolute return given limited resources, benefits-costs is the appropriate form.

**Criteria**  Descriptive factors in setting standards for various pollutants. These factors are used to determine limits on allowable concentration levels and to limit the number of violations per year (plural of criterion).

**Critical path**  Systems engineering of activities, decisions, and actions that must be completed on schedule and at a sufficient level of quality for the entire project to be successful.

**Cross-resistance**  Mutation of a microbe that has mutated in such a way that it loses its susceptibility to more than one antibiotic simultaneously, not just the one to which it has been directly exposed.

**Cross-sectional study**  Epidemiological study of observations representing a particular point in time. Contrast with *longitudinal study*.

**Culture**  Intentional organic growth.

**Cyanobacteria**  Large group of bacteria that carry out oxygenic photosynthesis using a system similar to that of photosynthetic *eukaryotes*.

**Cyst**  Specialized microbial cell enclosed in a wall; formed by protozoa and a few bacteria. They may be dormant, resistant structures formed in response to adverse conditions or reproductive cysts that are a normal stage in the life cycle.

**Cytochrome**  Heme protein that carries electrons, usually as members of electron-transport chains.

**Cytochrome P450 (CYP)**  Enzymes that use iron to oxidize substances, often as part of the body's strategy to dispose of potentially harmful substances by making them more water soluble. Varying versions of CYP are used to identify different enzymatic activities so are important in *toxicodynamics* and *toxicokinetics modeling*.

**Cytokine**  Nonantibody protein released by a cell in response to inducing stimuli, which are mediators that influence other cells. Produced by lymphocytes, monocytes, macrophages, and other cells.

**Dalton's law**  Total pressure exerted by a mixture of gases is equal to the sum of the pressures that would be exerted if each of the individual gases were to occupy the same volume by itself.

**Damage**  Economical, social, and environmental loss or level of destruction caused by an event.

**Darcy's law** An empirically derived equation for the flow of fluids through porous media; it is based on assumptions that flow is laminar and inertia can be neglected. It states that the specific discharge, $q$, is directly proportional to the hydraulic conductivity and the hydraulic gradient.

**Dark field** Microscope's optical system that makes small, clear, and colorless particles (e.g., many microbes) visible, by illuminating the object at an angle such that no light enters the microscope system except that which is diffracted by particles.

**Data** Plural of datum. Gathered facts from which conclusions can be drawn.

**Decision tree** Diagram indicating various steps to different outcomes. Supports the optimal course of action in situations where several possible alternatives have uncertain outcomes.

**Declining growth phase** Period of time in microbial population dynamics between the *log-growth phase* and the *endogenous phase*, where the amount of food is in short supply, leading to incrementally slowing growth rates.

**Decomposer** Organism that degrades complex materials into simpler ones.

**Deductive reasoning** A conclusion is necessitated by previously known facts. If the premises are true, the conclusion must be true. Starting from general knowledge and moving to specifics (e.g., from cause to effects). Contrast with inductive reasoning.

**Deep ecology** Environmental movement initiated in 1972 by Norwegian philosopher, Arnie Naess, that advocates radical measures to protect the natural environment irrespective of their effect on the welfare of humans (opposite of *anthropocentrism*).

**Dehydrohalogenation** A process by which a halogenated alkane loses a halogen from one carbon atom and a hydrogen from the adjacent carbon atom, producing the alkene and an acid (e.g., 1,1,2,2-tetrachloroethane dehydrohalogenates to produce trichloroethene and HCl).

**Demand** Quantity of a good or service that society chooses to buy at a given price.

**Denitrification** Reduction of nitrate to gas products, primarily nitrogen gas ($N_2$), during anaerobic respiration.

**Dense, nonaqueous-phase liquid (DNAPL)** An immiscible organic liquid that is denser than water (e.g., tetrachloroethene).

**Deontology or deontological ethics (Greek: *deon* meaning obligation)** Ethical theory basing right and wrong on duty.

**Deoxygenation constant** Expression of the rate of the biochemical oxidation of organic matter under aerobic conditions. Value depends on the time unit involved (often 1 day) and varies with temperature and other environmental conditions.

**Deoxyribonucleic acid (DNA)** Double-stranded nucleic acid containing genetic information; polynucleotide composed of deoxyribonucleotides connected by phosphodiester bonds.

**Depuration** Cleansing of a previously dosed organism by ending the dosing completely.

**Dermal exposure** Contact between a chemical and the skin.

**Dermal toxicity** The ability of a pesticide or toxic chemical to poison people or animals by contact with the skin.

**Descriptive epidemiology** Study of the amount and distribution of a disease in a specified population by person, place, and time. Compare to *analytic epidemiology.*

**Desorption** The converse of sorption, i.e., when a compound slowly releases from a surface(s) that it has previously accumulated upon or within.

**Destruction and removal efficiency (DRE)** Percentage of compound removed or destroyed by a process, usually thermal. Calculated as *efficiency*, where *I* equals the mass of compound to be treated and *E* equals the amount remaining after treatment; thus DRE does not account for new compounds created during the treatment process. See *efficiency* and *treatment.*

**Detection limit** See *limit of detection.*

**Detritus** Dead biota matter, usually at varying degrees of *decomposition* by microbes.

**Developmental toxicity** Adverse effects on developing organism that may result from exposure prior to conception (either parent), during prenatal development, or postnatally until the time of sexual maturation. The major manifestations of developmental toxicity include death of the developing organism, structural abnormality, altered growth, and functional deficiency.

**Dewater** 1. Remove or separate a portion of the water in a sludge or slurry to dry the sludge, so it can be handled and disposed. 2. Remove or drain the water from a tank or trench.

**Diatom** Algal protist with siliceous cell wall (frustule); constitute a substantial group of phytoplankton.

**Dichlorodiphenyltrichloroethane (DDT)** Organochlorine pesticide, banned in many parts of the world due to associations with eggshell thinning, endocrine effects, and human effects. Still used to control mosquitoes and other disease *vectors.*

**Diethylstilbestrol (DES)** Synthetic nonsteroidal estrogenic *endocrine-disrupting compound* that caused cancer to children exposed *in utero*.

**Diffused aeration** Injection of air through submerged porous plates, perforated pipes, or other devices to form small air bubbles from which oxygen is transferred to the liquid as the bubbles rise to the water surface.

**Diffusion** 1. Process of net transport of solute molecules from a region of high concentration to a region of low concentration caused by their molecular motion and not by turbulent mixing. Graham's law of diffusion states that a gas diffuses at a rate inversely proportional to its density. Liquids also diffuse as a result of net spontaneous and random movement of molecules or particles from a region in which they are at a high concentration to a region of lower concentration. Diffusion will continue for a fluid until an uniform concentration is achieved throughout the region of the system. Diffusion is not a major mechanism of mass transport in rapidly flowing systems, such as air and surface waters, but is quite important in more quiescent systems, such as across cellular *membranes*, and in slow-moving regions of the environment, e.g., covered *sediment* and groundwater. 2. Synonym for *dispersion*.

**Digestion** 1. In environmental biotechnology, the process of decomposing organic matter by microbial growth and metabolism. As such, organic matter is transformed and transferred to *sludge*, resulting in partial liquefaction, mineralization, and volume reduction. 2. Actions that occur in a *digester*.

**Dilution** A reduction in solute concentration caused by mixing with water at a lower solute concentration.

**Dimer** Molecule that consists of two identical simpler molecules: e.g., $NO_2$ can form the molecule $NO_2O_2N$ or simply $N_2O_4$ that consists of two identical simpler $NO_2$ molecules.

**Dinoflagellate** Algal protist characterized by two flagella used in swimming in a spinning pattern; many are bioluminescent and an important group of marine phytoplankton. A few species are important marine pathogens.

**Dioxin** Highly *toxic*, *recalcitrant*, and *bioaccumulating* product of incomplete combustion and chlorination processes with a structure of two phenyl rings bonded by two oxygen atoms, with chlorine substitution. Most toxic form is *2,3,7,8-tetrachlorodibenzo-para-dioxin*.

**Diploid** Cell with normal amount of DNA per cell, i.e., two sets of chromosomes or twice the *haploid* number.

**Direct effects** Effects that have a direct cause relationship with the occurrence of an event, most often represented as physical damage to people, goods, services, and/or the environment or by the immediate impact of social and economical activities.

**Direct filtration** A method of treating water that consists of the addition of coagulant chemicals, flash mixing, coagulation, minimal flocculation, and filtration. Sedimentation is not used.

**Direct runoff** Water that flows over the ground surface or through the ground directly into streams, rivers, and lakes.

**Disaster** A relative term meaning a catastrophic event that wreaks great destruction. However, the term is not exclusive to large-scale events, such as hurricanes or earthquakes, but can also include small-scale events with highly negative consequences, such as an engineering or medical failure where one or a few people are impacted but that has other implications (malpractice, bad publicity, blame, etc.).

**Disaster** Situation caused by a natural, technological, or human-induced phenomena, resulting in intense alterations for the people, goods, services, and/or the environment.

**Discharge** 1. Flow ($Q$) in a stream or canal or the outflow of a fluid from a source. Used in calculating liquid effluent from a facility or particulate or gaseous emissions into the air through designated venting mechanisms. 2. Any flow in an open or closed conveyance.

**Disease** Abnormal and adverse condition in an organism.

**Disparate effect** Health outcome, usually negative, that is disproportionately high in certain members of a population, such as an increased incidence of certain cancers in minority groups.

**Disparate exposure** *Exposure* to a physical, chemical, or biological agent that is disproportionately high in certain members in a population, such as the higher than average exposure of minority children to lead.

**Disparate susceptibility** Elevated risk of certain members of a population (e.g., genetically predisposed) to the effects of a physical, chemical, or biological agent; can lead to disparate effects (see *disparate effect*).

**Dispersion** Spreading material in time and space.

**Dispersion** The spreading of a solute from the expected groundwater flow path as a result of mixing of groundwater.

**Dispersion model** Prediction tool of how a substance will behave after release.

**Dissolution** Act of going into solution; dissolving.

**Dissolved oxygen (DO)** Concentration of molecular $O_2$ in water.

**DNA ligase** Enzyme that joins two DNA fragments together through the formation of a new phosphodiester bond.

**DNA marker** Cloned chromosomal locus with allelic variation that can be followed directly by a DNA-based assay such as Southern blotting or *PCR*.

**Dose**  Amount of a substance available for interactions with metabolic processes or biologically significant receptors after crossing the outer boundary of an organism. Potential dose is the amount ingested, inhaled, or applied to the skin. Applied dose is the amount presented to an absorption barrier and available for absorption (although not necessarily having yet crossed the outer boundary of the organism). Absorbed dose is the amount crossing a specific absorption barrier (e.g., the exchange boundaries of the skin, lung, and digestive tract) through uptake processes. Internal dose is a more general term, denoting the amount absorbed without respect to specific absorption barriers or exchange boundaries. The amount of the chemical available for interaction by any particular organ or cell is termed the delivered or biologically effective dose for that organ or cell.

**Dose-effect**  The relationship between dose (usually an estimate of dose) and the gradation of the effect in a population, that, is a biological change measured on a graded scale of severity, although at other times one may only be able to describe a qualitative effect that occurs within some range of exposure levels.

**Dose-response**  1. Relationship between a quantified exposure (*dose*) and the proportion of subjects demonstrating specific biologically significant changes in incidence and/or in degree of change (response). 2. Correlation between a quantified exposure (*dose*) and the proportion of a population that demonstrates a specific *effect* (response).

**Dose-response assessment**  Process of characterizing the relationship between dose of an agent and the effect elicited by that dose.

**Doubling time**  Time required for a population, e.g., bacterial, or cells to double in number or biomass.

**Downgradient**  The direction that groundwater flows; analogous to "downstream" for surface waters.

**Drawdown**  Lowering of water table of an unconfined aquifer or the potentiometric surface of a confined aquifer caused by pumping of groundwater from wells. Vertical distance between the original water level and the new water level. See *cone of depression*.

**Drug**  Substance intended for use in the diagnosis, cure, mitigation, treatment, or prevention of disease, which is regulated by the U.S. Food and Drug Administration. Contrast with device and nutritional supplement.

**Dry lab**  1. *In silico* research (contrast with wet lab). 2. Walkthrough prior to actual laboratory work (step preceding wet lab). 3. Unethical practice of forging (making up) data.

**Dual use**  1. Science, engineering, and technology designed to provide both military and civilian benefits. 2. Research and technology that simultaneously benefit and place society at risk (e.g., biotechnological advances that improve vaccines but also increase the risks of bioterrorism).

**Dynamical instability**  See *chaos theory*.

*E. Coli*  *Escherichia coli*, a Gram-negative, rod-shaped bacterium, often found in the intestine of warm-blooded animals.

**Ecocentrism**  Perspective based on the whole ecosystem rather than a single species. Contrast with *anthropocentrism*.

**Ecological impact**  Total effect of an environmental change, natural or of human origin, on the community of living things.

**Ecological indicator**  A characteristic of the environment that, when measured, quantifies magnitude of stress, habitat characteristics, degree of exposure to a stressor, or ecological response to exposure. The term is a collective term for response, exposure, habitat, and stressor indicators.

**Ecological risk assessment**  The application of a formal framework, analytical process, or model to estimate effects of human action(s) on a natural resource and to interpret the significance of those effects in light of the uncertainties identified in each component of the assessment process.

**Ecology**  Science dealing with the relationship of all living things with each other and with their environment.

**Ecosystem**  The interacting system of a biological community and its nonliving surroundings.

**Ecosystem function**  Processes and interactions that operate within an ecosystem, including energy flow, nutrient cycling, filtering and buffering of contaminants, and regulation of populations.

**Ecosystem service**  Benefit to humans derived from ecosystems. *Anthropocentric* and *instrumental* value provided by natural ecosystems.

**Ecosystem services**  Anthropocentric benefits of ecosystems, e.g., flood control, fisheries, and pharmaceutical sources.

**Ecosystem structure**  Attributes related to instantaneous physical state of an ecosystem; examples include species population density, species richness or evenness, and standing crop biomass.

**Ecotone**  A habitat created by the juxtaposition of distinctly different habitats; an edge habitat; or an ecological zone or boundary where two or more ecosystems meet.

**Effect** A biological change caused by an exposure.

**Effectiveness** Measure of the extent and degree to which a design achieves a goal.

**Efficacy** A measure of the probability and intensity of beneficial effects.

**Efficiency** Ratio of total energy or mass output to total energy or mass input, expressed as a percentage. Treatment or removal efficiency is the product of the contaminant mass prior to treatment ($I$) times the contaminant mass after treatment ($E$) divided by $I$. To express efficiency as a percentage, these values are multiplied 100 times: $\frac{I \times E}{I} \times 100$.

**Effluent** Waste material discharged into the environment, treated or untreated. Generally refers to surface water pollution (analogous to *emission* in air pollution).

**Effusion** Escape of fluid into a body space or tissue. Effusion of a gas is inversely proportional to the square root of either the density or molecular weight of the gas. Compare to *diffusion*.

**Electron** A negatively charged subatomic particle that may be transferred between chemical species in chemical reactions.

**Electron acceptor** 1. Oxidant. 2. Chemical substance, such as oxygen, nitrate, sulfate, and iron, which receives the electrons during microbial and chemical reactions. Microorganisms need these compounds to obtain energy. For MNA and EA, these electron acceptors often compete with chlorinated solvents and reduce the attenuation rates.

**Electron donor** 1. Reductant. 2. Chemical substance, such as molecular hydrogen or organic substrate, which yields an electron as they are oxidized, producing energy to sustain life and for the subsequent degradation of other chemicals, in this case, chlorinated solvents.

**Electron-transport chain** Final steps of reactions occur in biological oxidation; composed of series of oxidizing agent (i.e., *electron acceptors*) arranged in sequence by increasing strength and terminating with oxygen (the strongest oxidizer).

**Electrophoresis** See *gel electrophoresis*.

**Emission** Release of a pollutant or other substance to the atmosphere (analogous to *effluent* in water pollution).

**Endergonic** Describing a reaction that does not spontaneously go to completion as written; the standard free-energy change is positive, and the equilibrium constant is less than 1.

**Endocrine system** Chemical messaging system in organisms used for regulation by secretion of hormones by glands that are sent through the circulatory system to cells where the hormones bind to receptors.

**Endocrine-disrupting compound (EDC) or endocrine disruptor** Chemical substance that interferes with endocrine system, as either an *agonist* or an *antagonist*.

**Endogenous phase** Microbial population growth period dominated by endogenous respiration.

**Endoplasmic reticulum** Organelle consisting of a network of membranes within the cytoplasm of cells, where proteins and lipids are synthesized.

**Endospore** Seed-like structure, formed by a microbe to survive during hostile conditions.

**Endothermic** Chemical reaction that absorbs energy from surroundings.

**Endotoxin** Heat-stable lipopolysaccharide in the outer membrane of the cell wall of Gram-negative bacteria that is released when the bacterium lyses, or during growth, and is toxic to the host.

**Endpoint** Observable or measurable biological event or chemical concentration (e.g., metabolite concentration in a target tissue) used as an index of an effect of a chemical.

**Energy** Capacity of a physical system to perform work.

**Engineering** 1. Application of scientific and mathematical principles to practical ends, especially design; manufacture; and operation of structures, machines, processes, and systems. 2. The profession that implements these applications.

**Enhanced attenuation** Any type of intervention that might be implemented in a source-plume system to increase the magnitude of attenuation by natural processes beyond that which occurs without intervention. Enhanced attenuation is the result of applying an enhancement that manipulates a *natural attenuation* process, leading to an increased reduction in mass of contaminants.

**Enhanced bioremediation** An engineered approach to increasing biodegradation rates in the subsurface.

**Enteric bacteria** 1. Members of the family Enterobacteriaceae, i.e., Gram-negative, peritrichous, or nonmotile, facultatively anaerobic, straight rods with simple nutritional requirements. 2. Bacteria that live in the intestinal tract.

**Enthalpy of formation** Standard enthalpy of formation of a substance is the enthalpy change for the formation of 1 mol of the substance from its elements, all in their standard states.

**Enthalpy of reaction** Heat of a reaction at constant pressure, usually 1 bar.

**Entropy** Entropy is a measure of disorder and can be determined by $\Delta S = k \ln W$, where $k$ is the Boltzmann constant and $W$ is the number of possible arrangements of the molecule having the same energy.

**Entropy, standard** The standard entropy of a substance or ion (also called the absolute entropy) is the entropy value for the standard state of the species, $S°$.

**Environmental assessment (EA)** Investigation whether a proposed action will adversely affect the environment. If so, in the United States, such action is usually followed by a formal *environmental impact statement*. If not, the agency will issue a "finding of no significant impacts" document.

**Environmental engineering** Subdiscipline of engineering (usually civil engineering) concerned with applications of scientific principles and mathematics to improve the condition of the environment.

**Environmental impact statement (EIS)** Document prepared by a government agency detailing the potential effects resulting from a major action being considered by that agency. In the United States, the EIS is required under the National Environmental Policy Act and is usually preceded by an *environmental assessment*.

**Environmental science** Systematic study of the environment and its components and processes (e.g., nutrient cycling, pollutant transport, and adverse effects).

**Environmentalism** 1. Advocacy in the protection of the environment. 2. Philosophy underpinning this advocacy. Such advocacy may or may not be scientifically based (i.e., differs from environmental science and environmental engineering).

**Enzyme** Protein catalyst with specificity for both the reaction catalyzed and its substrates.

**Enzyme-linked immunosorbent assay (ELISA)** A technique used for detecting and quantifying specific antibodies and antigens.

**Epidemic** Disease outbreak that occurs simultaneously or nearly simultaneously in a large area or in large percentage of a population.

**Epidemiology** 1. Study of the causes, distribution, and control of disease in populations. 2. The study of the distribution and determinants of health-related states or events in specified populations.

**Epigenetics** Concern with mechanisms that regulate gene activity.

**Equilibrium** Condition in which a reaction is occurring at equal rates in its forward and reverse directions so that the concentrations of the reacting substances do not change with time.

**Equilibrium constant** Value representing relationship between a compound in a system that has reached equilibrium. Related to *partitioning coefficient*, e.g., *octanol-water coefficient*, *bioconcentration factor*, and *Henry's law constant*.

**Error** 1. Mistake. 2. In statistics, the difference between a reported value and the actual value (see Bias).

**Estimated exposure dose (EED)** The measured or calculated dose to which humans are likely to be exposed considering all sources and routes of exposure.

**Ethics** 1. Set of moral principles. 2. Study of morality and moral decision making.

**Ethylenediaminetetraacetic acid (EDTA)** Chelating agent that binds to and makes unavailable metal ions in a solution; because certain cations are essential for many enzymes to function, EDTA is applied to halt enzymatic and cellular activity (as such, is a common preservative).

**Eukaryote** Organism whose cell contains a distinct, membrane-bound nucleus.

**Eutrophication** Process by which water bodies receive excess nutrients, primarily nitrogen and phosphorus, which stimulate excessive algal and plant growth.

**Event** Natural, technological, or human-induced phenomena, in terms of its characteristics, severity, location, and area of influence. It is the registration in time and space of a phenomena that characterizes a threat.

**Event** Set of outcomes that are preceded and linked to an earlier set of outcomes (probability theory).

**Event tree** Diagram of the flow of events following an initial event, showing subsequent possible events toward different outcomes. Each event has its own possible outcomes so that the critical path chosen will result in numerous potential outcomes.

**Ex situ** Moved off-site (e.g., contaminated soil transported to an incinerator for treatment).

**Ex vivo** Outside the body, frequently the equivalent of *in vitro* (see *in vitro*).

**Exergonic** Describing a reaction that spontaneously goes to completion as written; the standard free-energy change is negative, and the equilibrium constant is greater than one.

**Exothermic** Chemical reaction that releases energy, usually heat.

**Exotoxin** Heat-labile, toxic protein produced by a bacterium as a result of its normal metabolism or because of the acquisition of a plasmid or prophage that redirects its metabolism, usually released into the bacterium's surroundings.

**Experiment** Investigation to support or reject a hypothesis or to increase knowledge about a phenomenon.

**Exponential growth phase** Microbial growth at a constant percentage per unit time, i.e., log phase growth.

**Exposure** Contact made between a chemical, physical, or biological agent and the outer boundary of an organism. Exposure is quantified as the amount of an agent available at the exchange boundaries of the organism (e.g., skin, lungs, gut).

**Exposure assessment** Identification and evaluation of the human population exposed to a toxic agent, describing its composition and size, as well as the type, magnitude, frequency, route, and duration of exposure.

**Exposure scenario** Set of facts, assumptions, and inferences regarding how exposure occurs to support risk assessors in evaluating, estimating, or quantifying exposures.

**Expression (genetic expression)** Effect on cell resulting from the gene's instructions in *transcription*.

**Extended aeration** Enhancement of activated-sludge process using long aeration periods to promote aerobic digestion of the biological mass by endogenous respiration; includes stabilization of organic matter under aerobic conditions and disposal of the gaseous end products into the air. Effluent contains both dissolved and fine, suspended matter.

**Extrapolation** 1. Estimate of the extent of conditions from measured data. 2. Estimate of the response at a point above or below the range of the experimental data, generally through the use of a mathematical model. Compare to *interpolation*.

**Fact** That which can be shown to be true, to exist, or to have occurred.

**Facultative anaerobe** Microorganism, usually a bacterium, which grows equally well under *aerobic* and *anaerobic* conditions.

**Facultative pond** Most common type of treatment pond in current use. The upper portion (*supernatant*) is *aerobic* and the bottom layer is *anaerobic*. *Algae* supply most of the oxygen to the supernatant.

**Failure** Lack of success as indicated by design specifications and measures of success.

**False negative** Finding of the absence of a condition (e.g., disease) in a test when, in fact, the disease is present (e.g., a lung cancer screen shows that the patient has no cancer, but, at a level of detection below the screen, the cancer has cancer cells in the lung). See *type II error*.

**False positive** Positive finding of a test when, in fact, the true result was negative (e.g., a drug screen shows that a person has used opiates, even though the person has not). See *type I error*.

**Fault tree analysis (FTA)** Failure analysis in which an undesired state of a system is analyzed by combining a series of lower level events. Mainly used in the field of safety engineering to find probability of a safety hazard.

**Fecal coliform** Coliform with the intestinal tract as its normal habitat and that can grow at 44.5 °C.

**Feedstock** Material entering a *reactor*.

**Fermentation** Energy-yielding process in microbes oxidize an energy substrate without an exogenous electron acceptor. Usually, organic molecules serve as both electron donors and acceptors.

**Finding of no significant impact (FONSI)** Statement by an agency after completing an *environmental assessment* that a proposed action will not lead to significant impacts, so an *environmental impact statement* would not be required for this action.

**Fire** Exothermic process wherein matter is oxidized by rapid combustion, releasing heat, light, and reaction products.

**Fishbone diagram** See *Ishikawa diagram*.

**Fixed phase reactor** System in which solid-phase particles are fixed in position as the fluid phase passes through.

**Flagellum** Threadlike appendage on numerous prokaryotic and eukaryotic cells responsible for their motility.

**Flare** Device that combusts gaseous materials exiting a system; e.g., a landfill flare burns methane and a chemical processing facility includes a flare backup system in the event of unplanned releases of otherwise toxic substances.

**Floc** Particles, including cells, which adhere to one another loosely to form clusters.

**Flocculation** Process by which *flocs* are formed; often enhanced in water treatment processes by addition of flocculant, e.g., alum—aluminum sulfate [$Al_2(SO_4)_3$].

**Flow cytometer** Instrument with a laser detector and a very small orifice through which particles (including microbes) flow through one at a time. As they pass through a laser beam, biochemicals may be determined on a per-cell basis.

**Fluidized bed reactor** System that suspends small solid particles in an upwardly flowing stream of fluid. Fluid velocity must be sufficient to suspend the particles, but not so high as to transport them out of the vessel. Mixing occurs as the solid particles swirl around the bed rapidly. The material fluidized is nearly always solid, and the fluidizing medium can be either a liquid or a gas.

**Flux** Rate of flow of fluid, particles, or energy through a given two-dimensional surface.

**Food chain** A biological system in which individuals at a trophic level feed on organisms in the trophic level below theirs. As such, energy is transferred from level to level.

**Food web** Complex of interrelated *food chains* in an ecological community.

**Force** Capacity to do work. Interaction between two physical bodies, e.g. an object and its environment. Proportional to acceleration and the derivative of momentum with respect to time.

**Free energy (ΔG)** Intrinsic energy in a substance available to do work, especially to drive chemical transformations. Also known as Gibbs free energy.

**Free energy, standard** The standard free energy or standard Gibbs free energy is the standard free energy of reaction per mole of compound when it is formed from its elements, all in their standard states.

**Freundlich sorption isotherm** See *sorption isotherm.*

**Fugacity** Tendency of a substance to prefer one phase over another, and tendency to flee or escape one compartment (e.g., water) to join another (e.g., atmosphere).

**Functional ecology** Ecology, with an emphasis on the roles and behavior of species in ecosystems. Compare to *structural ecology.*

**Fungus** Achlorophyllous, heterotrophic, spore-bearing eukaryotes with absorptive nutrition, often with a walled thallus.

**Fuzzy logic** System dealing with the partial truths, assigning with values ranging from completely true to completely false.

**Game theory** Decision making under conditions of uncertainty and interdependence; taking into account, the characteristics of players, strategies, actions, payoffs, outcomes at equilibrium.

**Gamete** Reproductive cell (i.e., an egg or a sperm).

**Gene** Ordered sequence of nucleotides located in a particular position on a particular chromosome, representing the fundamental unit of heredity. DNA segment or sequence that codes for a polypeptide, *rRNA* or *tRNA.*

**Gene flow** Movement of genes from one population to another.

**Generation time** See *doubling time.*

**Genetic engineering (GE)** Modification of the structure of genetic material in a living organism, involving the production and use of *recombinant DNA.*

**Genetic material** *Deoxyribonucleic acid* and *ribonucleic acid.*

**Genetically modified microbe (GMM)** Subdivision of *genetically modified organisms* that includes bacteria, fungi, algae, and other microbes whose genetic material has been altered.

**Genetically modified microbial pesticide** Bacteria, fungi, viruses, protozoa, or algae, whose DNA has been modified to express pesticidal properties. The modified microorganism generally performs as a pesticide's active ingredient. For example, certain fungi can control the growth of specific types of weeds, while other types of fungi can kill certain insects.

**Genetically modified organism (GMO)** Organism whose genetic material has been changed in a way that does not occur under natural conditions through cross-breeding or natural recombination.

**Genetics** Scientific investigation of heredity.

**Genome** Entire genetic complement, i.e., all of the hereditary material possessed by an organism.

**Genomics** 1. Study of genes, including their functions. 2. Study of the molecular organization of genomes, their information content, and the gene products they encode.

**Genotype** Combination of alleles, situated on corresponding chromosomes, that determine a specific trait of an individual.

**Geographic information system (GIS)** Mapping system that uses computers to collect, store, manipulate, analyze, and display data. For example, GIS can show the concentration of a contaminant in an ecosystem with respect to land cover, water depth, and potential sources of the contaminant.

**Germ theory** Paradigm that diseases are caused by singular, proximate, pathogenic microbes. Displaced miasma theory (see Miasma) in late nineteenth century.

***Gestalt* theory (German: Form)** View that perception and other psychological phenomena must be understood for their overall patterns and forms, as opposed to the individual components.

**Gestation** Time from fertilization of the ovum to birth. Also known as uterogestation.

**Gibbs free energy** See *free energy.*

**Glycolysis** Anaerobic conversion of glucose to lactic acid via the *Embden-Meyerhof-Parnas pathway.*

**Glyoxylate cycle** Modification of Kreb's cycle in certain bacteria wherein *acteyl coenzyme A* is generated directly by oxidization of light lipids (e.g., *fatty acids*).

**Grab sample** Single sample of environmental material collected without regard to flow or time.

**Gram negative** Describing a bacterial cell that retains crystal violet during staining processes and is then colored by a counterstain, e.g., *Thiobacillus* and *Pseudomonas*.

**Gram positive** Describing a bacterial cell that loses crystal violet during staining processes, e.g., *Bacillus*.

**Gram stain** Differential staining procedure that divides bacteria into Gram-positive and Gram-negative groups based on their ability to retain crystal violet when decolorized with an organic solvent such as ethanol.

**Gray goo scenario** Doomsday scenario related to *nanotechnology* in which an "extinction technology" is created from the cell's unchecked ability to exponentially replicate itself if part of their design is to be completely "omnivorous," using all organic matter as food. No other "life" on earth would exist if this "doomsday" scenario were to occur.

**Green engineering** Design, commercialization, and use of processes and products, which are feasible and economical while minimizing the generation of pollution at the source and the risk to human health and the environment.

**Greenhouse effect** Physical process by which incoming solar radiation is reradiated as infrared wavelengths from the earth's surfaces. In turn, the heat is retained by radiant gases (i.e., *greenhouse gases*) so that the earth stays warm. Without these gases, virtually all of the heat would be returned to space so that the diurnal heat variations would range from extremely hot during the day and extremely cold at night. Thus, the greenhouse effect is absolutely essential to life on earth. However, the increase in greenhouse gas concentrations in the troposphere is causing concern within the scientific community, with fears of global warming and other changes in global climate.

**Greenhouse gas (GHG)** Gas released to the atmosphere that in turn retains heat that has been radiated from the earth.

**Guanine** Purine derivative, 2-amino-6-oxypurine, found in nucleosides, nucleotides, and nucleic acids.

**Half-life ($t_{1/2}$)** Time needed for half the quantity of a substance taken up by a living organism to be metabolized and eliminated by normal biological processes. Also called biological half-life. Also applicable to any chemical reaction.

**Haploid** Cell with only one complete set of chromosomes.

**Harm** Damage to another person or creature.

**Harm principle** John Stuart Mill's recommendation that utilitarianism's (see Utilitarianism) premise of greatest good is restricted (e.g., by law) when others are harmed.

**Hazard** 1. Underlying danger associated with physical phenomena of natural, technological, or anthropogenic origin that can occur at a specific site and at a defined time, producing severe effects to the people, goods, services, and/or the environment; based on the probability that an event of a certain magnitude will occur, at a specific site and determined time. 2. Potential source of harm. Term is often formally defined and distinguished from nonhazards by regulatory agencies, e.g., hazardous and nonhazardous wastes.

**Hazard assessment** Process by which the probability that an event will occur is determined for a specific site and time.

**Hazard assessment** 1. The process of determining whether exposure to an agent can cause an increase in the incidence of a particular adverse health effect (e.g., cancer, birth defect) and whether the adverse health effect is likely to occur in humans. 2. Process by which the probability that an event will occur is determined for a specific site and time.

**Hazard characterization** A description of the potential adverse health effects attributable to a specific environmental agent; the mechanisms by which agents exert their toxic effects; and the associated dose, route, duration, and timing of exposure.

**Henry's Law** Relationship between the partial pressure of a compound and its equilibrium concentration in a dilute aqueous solution through a constant of proportionality, i.e., Henry's law constant. Expression of *fugacity*.

**Herbicide-tolerant crop** Crop that contains new genes that allow the plant to tolerate herbicides. The most common herbicide-tolerant crops (cotton, corn, soybeans, and canola) are those that are resistant to glyphosate, an effective herbicide used on many species of grasses, broadleaf weeds, and sedges.

**Heterocyst** Specialized cell produced by cyanobacteria; sites of nitrogen fixation.

**Heterologous encapsidation (transcapsidation)** Generation of "new" viruses by surrounding one virus with the envelope protein of another virus; a natural process that can occur when plants are coinfected by different strains of viruses.

**Heterotroph** Organism needs carbon-energy compounds.

**Heterozygous** Having different alleles at a genetic locus.

**Hill's criteria** Minimal conditions necessary to establish causal relationship between two items; presented by British medical statistician Sir Austin Bradford Hill (1897-1991) as a means of finding causal links between a specific factor (e.g., exposure to air pollution) and specific adverse effects (e.g., asthma). These criteria, originally recommended for occupation setting but now applied to numerous health and environmental problems, are meant to be guidelines rather than inviolable rules of *epidemiology*.

**Homeostasis** Ability of an organism to self-regulate functions; inherent trend toward stability.

**Homozygous** Having two identical alleles of a gene.

**Horizontal gene transfer** Process by which an organism incorporates genetic material from another organism without being the offspring of that organism.

**Hormonally active agent** Substances that possess hormone-like activity, regardless of mechanism. Synonymous with *endocrine disruptor*.

**Hormone** Chemical released by glands of the endocrine system (see *endocrine system*).

**Host** Organism that harbors another organism; microenvironment that shelters and supports the growth and multiplication of a parasitic organism.

**Hours of retention (HRT)** Common unit of time that a substance is held in a *bioreactor*.

**Household hazardous waste (HHW)** Discarded household products that contain corrosive, toxic, ignitable, or reactive ingredients.

**Huanglongbing** See *citrus greening disease*.

**Humus** Dark-colored organic material in soil and sediment that is a product of plant material decomposition.

**Hybrid** Offspring of genetically dissimilar parents or stock.

**Hybridization** 1. Act of mixing different species or varieties of organisms to produce *hybrids*. 2. Reaction by which pairing of complementary strands of nucleic acid occurs. Usually double stranded, when the strands of DNA are separated, they will rehybridize under appropriate conditions. Hybrids can form between DNA-DNA, DNA-RNA, or RNA-RNA.

**Hydraulic conductivity** A measure of the capability of a medium to transmit water.

**Hydraulic gradient** The change in hydraulic head (per unit distance in a given direction) typically in the principal flow direction.

**Hydrolysis** Decomposition or change of a chemical compound by reaction with water, such as the dissociation of a dissolved salt or the catalytic conversion of starch to glucose.

**Hydrophilic** Describing a polar substance with a strong affinity for water (i.e., high aqueous solubility).

**Hydrophobicity** Tendency of a substance to repel water or to be incapable of completely dissolving in water. Hydrophobic substances are readily soluble in many nonpolar solvents, such as octanol, but only sparingly soluble in water, a polar solvent. That is, most hydrophobic compounds are also *lipophilic*. The hydrophobicity of an organic contaminant influences the fate of the contaminant in the environment. In general, the more hydrophobic a contaminant is, the greater the likelihood it will be associated with nonpolar organic matter such as humic substances and lipids (fats). Can be predicted fairly well by the *octanol-water coefficient*.

**Hypothetico-deductive method** Method of logical deduction, attributed to Karl Popper (*The Logic of Scientific Discovery*, 1934), limiting scientific discovery to that which is testable; requiring an approach that formulates hypotheses, *a priori*, with the intent of rejecting these hypotheses. The method assumes that a hypothesis can never truly be proved but at best can be corroborated.

**Hysteresis** 1. Changes that occur depending on the direction taken in a pathway; e.g., a material may behave differently in the same temperature range when cooled than when heated in that same range. In mechanics, the changes of a body as it returns to its original shape after being stressed. 2. Failure to return to previous condition, such as due to an energy loss that always occurs under cyclical loading and unloading of a spring, proportional to the area between the loading and unloading load-deflection curves within the elastic range of a spring (engineering), or the failure of a variable to return to its initial equilibrium after a temporary shock (economics).

**Ideal gas law** The product of pressure and volume of a gas is equal to the product of amount of gas and temperature: $n/V = P^0/RT$, where $V$ is the volume of the container, $n$ is the number of moles of chemical, $R$ is the molar gas constant, and $n/V$ is the gas phase concentration (mol L$^{-1}$) of the chemical.

**Imhoff tank** Two-story vessel for both settling and *digestion* occurs in a waste treatment system, with one compartment below the other. This allows for a stepped and separate *aerobic* and *anaerobic* treatment.

**In silico** Based on information, usually using computational methods, rather than using actual materials being studied. To some extent, *in silico* research is an alternative to *in vivo* and *in vitro* research (see *in vivo* and *in vitro*), which is desirable in the case of limiting animal research and in reducing risks in humans who undergo *in vivo* procedures.

**In situ** Taking place where it is found (e.g., bioremediation of a hazardous waste site where it exists, rather than moving the materials off-site).

**In utero** In the womb (e.g., fetal alcohol syndrome results from the unborn child's exposure to alcohol and its metabolites during gestation (see *gestation*)).

**In vitro** Outside the organism (literally: "in glass," i.e., in a test tube).

*In vivo* Inside the organism (e.g., experiments within a rat to observe biochemical responses to a chemical dose).

**Incidence or incidence rate** Number of new cases in a defined population within a period of time (compare to *prevalence*).

**Index of biological integrity (IBI)** Method of indicating the quality of aquatic systems. Usually, the total number of organisms and the number of different species present are inventoried, followed by the application of an index, or scale, that lists organisms according to their sensitivity to pollution.

**Indicator organism** Organism whose abundance indicates the condition of a substance or environment. For example, the potential presence of pathogens in fecal pollution is indicated by *coliforms*.

**Indirect effects** Effects that indirectly influence the social and economic activities of the population as well as the environment.

**Inductive reasoning** Starting from a specific experience and drawing inferences from the specific set of facts or instances to a larger number of instances (generalization). Conclusions are drawn from the perspective that all individuals of a kind have a certain character on the basis that some individuals of the kind have that character. Contrast with *deductive reasoning*.

**Industrial ecology** Study of industrial system that focuses on material cycling, energy flow, and the ecological impacts of such systems.

**Inert ingredient (inert)** 1. Nonreactive ingredient. 2. Any ingredient in a pesticide formulation other than the ones that provide the mechanisms of biocidal action. An inert ingredient may or may not be reactive or may or may not be toxic. See *active ingredient*.

**Inference** Reasoning that one statement (the conclusion) is derived from one or more other statements (the premises). See *syllogism*.

**Informatics** Application of computational and other technologies to access and to enhance information; one means of turning data into information (see *data* and *information*).

**Information** Processed and organized *data*. Value-added data as a step toward knowledge.

**Initiation** The first stage of carcinogenesis.

**Inoculum** Microbial culture used to initiate growth and introduced to a container.

**Inorganic compound** A compound that is not based on covalent carbon bonds, including most minerals, nitrate, phosphate, sulfate, and carbon dioxide.

**Instrumental value** Worth based on usefulness. In biomedical ethics, the perspective of whether a human life has value that depends on usefulness (Will the baby be loved? Will the elderly person continue to enjoy life?) is an instrumental viewpoint. In environmental ethics, the use of the term environmental resource implies that ecological value is based on the utility of the ecosystem (e.g., wetlands as breeding area for game fish, as retention areas to prevent floods, and as sinks for carbon to prevent global warming). Contrast with *intrinsic value*.

**Integrated pest management (IPM)** Combination of various strategies to reduce pests, rather than simply relying on the application of pesticides, including use of natural predators, physical removal of breeding areas (e.g., standing water for mosquitoes), and introduction of organisms that lead to sterile offspring, i.e., interruption of a pest or vector's life cycle.

**Integrated Risk Information System (IRIS)** Internet-based system that provides information related to the human health risk of hundreds of specific chemical compounds and classes of compounds.

**Intensity** Qualitative and quantitative measure of the severity of a phenomena at a specific site.

**Interspecies dose conversion** The process of extrapolating from animal doses to human equivalent doses.

**Intervention** Direct involvement of corrective action to change existing condition for the better.

**Intrinsic value** Worth based on existence, not usefulness. All humans have intrinsic value in contemporary morality. In biomedical ethics, however, there is no unanimity of thought about the intrinsic value of an embryo or a fetus, or a person nearing end of life. Those subscribing to sanctity of life viewpoints see intrinsic value of any human being (beginning with the human zygote and ending in natural death). In environmental ethics, there is no unanimity of thought about nonhuman species. For example, the loss of a species is morally wrong based on the value of the existence of the species, not its actual or potential value (e.g., as a cure for cancer or as a food source for a food species). Contrast with instrumental value.

**Intuition** Direct perception of meaning without conscious reasoning. Compare to deductive and inductive reasoning.

**Ion exchange** Transfer of ions between two electrolytes or between an electrolyte solution and a complex. Physicochemical process in which ions held electrostatically on the surface of a solid phase are exchanged with ions of similar charge in a solution (e.g., drinking water).

**Ionic strength** Related to solution's total concentration and valences of ions.

**Irreversible sorption** A hysteresis effect in which a chemical species becomes more strongly bound over time. The term sometimes appears to be used to describe a situation where, once sorbed, the contaminant is removed from the plume and remains associated with the soil.

**Ishikawa diagram** Graphical technique for identifying cause-and-effect relationships among factors in a given situation or problem (also known as a fishbone diagram).

**Isolation** Separation of specific microorganisms from cultures.

**Isotope** One of the two or more atoms having the same atomic number but different mass numbers.

**Kinetics** Rates of reactions and processes.

**Knock-in** Targeted mutation in which an alteration in gene function other than a loss-of-function allele is produced.

**Knock-out** Targeted mutation in which a loss of function (often a null allele) is produced.

**Knowledge** Familiarity, awareness, or understanding gained through experience or study. A necessary step toward wisdom.

**Kreb's cycle** Oxidative pathway in respiration by which pyruvate, via *acetyl coenzyme A*, is decarboxylated to form $CO_2$.

**Lag phase** In microbial growth, period after inoculation and before exponential (log) growth.

**Lagoon** Shallow surface water system used for wastewater treatment; often aerated mechanically to increase *aerobic* decomposition of waste material.

**Laminar** Describing flow of a viscous fluid in which particles of the fluid move in parallel layers, each of which has a constant velocity but is in motion relative to its neighboring layers. Also called streamline or viscous flow.

**Land farming** Addition of waste material, e.g., organic compound-laden waste, to the soil surface for *biodegradation*. The soil may be moistened or mixed to stimulate the desired degradation process.

**Latency** Period of time between disease occurrence and detection, sometimes used interchangeably with induction.

**Latency period** The time between first exposure to an agent and manifestation or detection of a health effect of interest. Period of time between disease occurrence and detection, sometimes used interchangeably with induction.

**Law of diminishing returns** Economic principle espoused by Thomas Malthus (*Essay on the Principle of Population*, 1798) stating that when a fixed input is combined in production with a variable input, using a given technology, increases in the quantity of the variable input will eventually depress the productivity of the variable input. Malthus proposed this as a law from his pessimistic idea that population growth would force incomes down to the subsistence level.

**Law of supply and demand** Economic principle stating that, in equilibrium, prices are determined so that demand equals supply; thus changes in prices reflect shifts in the demand or supply curves.

**Leachate** 1. Percolated liquid through solid waste or other permeable material. 2. Extracted materials from this liquid.

**Lethal concentration ($LC_X$)** Concentration of a substance in air in which $X\%$ of test animals die, e.g., the median lethal concentration is $LC_{50}$: a common measure of *acute toxicity*.

**Lethal dose ($LD_X$)** Amount of a substance delivered to a test animal in a single dose that kills $X\%$, e.g., the median lethal dose is $LC_{50}$: a common measure of *acute toxicity*.

**Lichen** Organism composed of a fungus and either green algae or cyanobacteria in a symbiotic association.

**Life** Period from onset (i.e., conception) to end (i.e., death) of a unique organism. Antonym can be either death or nonliving.

**Lifetime average daily dose (LADD)** Estimated dose to an individual averaged over a lifetime of 70 years; used in assessments of *carcinogenic risk*.

**Ligand** Molecule that travel through the bloodstream as chemical messengers that will bind to a target cell's *receptor*.

**Lignin** Organic polymer stored in plant cell walls of woody plants; an aromatic hydrocarbon compound forming a three-dimensional structural matrix.

**Limit of detection (LOD)** Lowest concentration of a chemical that can reliably be distinguished from a zero concentration (also known as detection limit).

**Linearity** Following the mathematical equation for a line ($y = mx + b$, where $m$ is the slope and $b$ is the $y$ intercept). Also used to describe the degree to which data points approximate the line of best fit (linear regression).

**Liner** Clay or manufactured material that serves as a barrier against the movement of *leachate*. Liners have very low *hydraulic conductivity*.

**Lipophilicity** Tendency of a chemical compound to dissolve in fats, oils, lipids, and nonpolar solvents. See *hydrophilicity.*

**Log-growth phase** Also known as trophophase, portion of a population's life cycle when the number of organisms is increasing at logarithmic rate.

**Logic** Branch of philosophy addressing inference (e.g., using a syllogism (see *syllogism*) to determine the validity of an ethical argument).

**Longitudinal study** Epidemiological study using data gathered at more than one point in time, e.g., after an exposure or a medical intervention. Contrast with cross-sectional study.

**Loss** Any economic, social, or environmental value lost by a variable during a specific exposure time.

**Lowest observed adverse effect level (LOAEL)** Lowest exposure level at which there are biologically significant increases in frequency or severity of adverse effects between the exposed population and its appropriate control group. Compare to *NOAEL.*

**Malaria** Serious infectious disease caused by the parasitic protozoan *Plasmodium.* Characterized by bouts of high chills and fever that occur at regular intervals.

**Mass balance** Assessment includes a quantitative estimation of the mass loading to the dissolved plume from various sources, as well as the mass attenuation capacity for the dissolved plume.

**Mass loading** Contaminant released to the environment from the source material.

**Mass transfer** The irreversible transport of solute mass from the nonaqueous phase (i.e., DNAPL) into the aqueous phase, the rate of which is proportional to the difference in concentration.

**Mechanism of action** Specific biochemical interaction through which a substance produces its intended effect in the case of a pesticide or drug, or toxic reaction in the case of a toxic substance. The mechanism is usually characterized by specific molecular targets to which the substance binds, such as to an enzyme or to a receptor. For example, numerous pesticides' mechanism of action is by inhibition of neurotransmitters, e.g., acetylcholine. Organochlorine pesticides often alter the movement of ions across the nerve cell membranes, changing the ability of the nerve to fire. Organophosphate and carbamate pesticides act primarily at the synapses, altering the regulation of the transmission of signal between neurons.

**Medium** 1. Substance in which organisms are grown. 2. Material in a bioreactor, e.g., *trickling filter*, on which microbes grow and produce *biofilm*. 3. Environmental compartment (e.g., air, water, soil, sediment, or biota).

**Meiosis** Process by which diploid germ cell precursors segregate their chromosomes into haploid nuclei within eggs and sperm.

**Meltdown, nuclear** Severe damage to a nuclear power plant's core, resulting in overheating to the point that it "melts" the materials (floor, soil) allowing the core to sink.

**Membrane** 1. Film with pores. 2. Cellular amphiphilic layer that encloses the cell or separates parts within a cell.

**Membrane bioreactor (MBR)** System that combines suspended growth with solids separation using ultrafine porous membranes; often follows aeration step in *activated-sludge* treatment.

**Mendelism** Heredity theory underlying classical genetics, proposed by Roman Catholic monk and scientist Gregor Mendel in 1866.

**Messenger RNA (mRNA)** RNA containing sequences coding for a protein.

**Metabolism** Act of a living organism converting and degrading a substance from one form to another (known as a metabolite). Chemical reactions in living cells that convert food sources to energy and new cell mass. See *catabolism* and *anabolism.*

**Metabonomics** Study of total metabolite pool (especially using computational methods).

**Methanogen** Strictly anaerobic Archaebacteria able to use only a very limited substrate spectrum (e.g., molecular hydrogen, formate, methanol, carbon monoxide, or acetate) as substrates for the reduction of carbon dioxide to methane.

**Michaelis constant** Kinetic constant for an enzyme reaction equal to the substrate concentration required for the enzyme to operate at half -maximal velocity.

**Microarray** A multifaceted tray or array of DNA material. Microarrays are expected to revolutionize medicine by helping pinpoint a very specific disease or the susceptibility to it. Sometimes called "biochips," microarrays are commonly known as "gene chips."

**Microbe** Microorganism.

**Microbial ecology**  Study of microorganisms in their natural environments, with a major emphasis on physical conditions, processes, and interactions that occur on the scale of individual microbial cells.

**Microbiology**  Study of *microorganisms* (those too small to be seen with the naked eye). Special techniques are required to isolate and grow such organisms.

**Microcosm**  A batch reactor used in a bench-scale experiment designed to resemble the conditions present in the groundwater environment.

**Microenvironment**  Location of a potential or actual exposure in which an activity occurs, e.g. a garage is an indoor microenvironment; the interior of an automobile is a mobile microenvironment.

**Microethics**  Expectations of the individual professional practitioner or researcher. Compare to *macroethics*.

**Microinjection**  Process by which DNA or other materials are injected into fertilized eggs or blastocysts.

**Microorganism**  An organism of microscopic or submicroscopic size, including bacteria.

**Mineralization**  The complete degradation of an organic compound to carbon dioxide and other inorganic compounds, such as water and chloride ions.

**Minimal risk level (MRL)**  Estimate of daily human exposure to a hazardous substance at or below which that substance is unlikely to pose a measurable risk of harmful, noncancerous effects. Calculated for a route of exposure (inhalation or oral) over a specified time period (*acute*, intermediate, or *chronic*). Not recommended as predictors of adverse health effects.

**Minimax theorem**  Key convention of game theory holding that lowest maximum expected loss in a two-person zero-sum game equals the highest minimum expected gain. It is a useful technique to address uncertainties in decision making.

**Miscibility**  Chemical property where two or more liquids or phases readily dissolve in one another, such as ethanol and water.

**Mitigation**  Definition of intervention measures directed to reduce or decrease a risk. Mitigation is the result of a political decision of the level of acceptable risk, obtained by an extensive analysis and based on the criteria that the risk is not totally preventable.

**Mitochondrion**  Eukaryotic organelle that is the site of electron transport, oxidative phosphorylation, and pathways such as the Krebs cycle; it provides most of a nonphotosynthetic cell's energy under aerobic conditions. Constructed of an outer membrane and an inner membrane, which contains the electron-transport chain.

**Mitosis**  Process in the nucleus of a eukaryotic cell that results in the formation of two new nuclei, each with the same number of chromosomes as the parent.

**Mixed acid fermentation**  Process carried out by members of the family Enterobacteriaceae in which ethanol and a complex mixture of organic acids are produced.

**Mixed liquor**  Activated sludge and water containing organic matter undergoing *activated-sludge* treatment in aeration tank.

**Mixed liquor suspended solids (MLSS)**  Volume of *suspended solids* in *mixed liquor.*

**Mixed liquor volatile suspended solids (MLVSS)**  Volume of organic solids from *mixed liquor* that will evaporate at relatively low temperatures (e.g., $55\,°C$); MLVSS is an indicator that microbial populations are active.

**Mixotrophic**  Characteristic of microorganisms that combine autotrophic and heterotrophic metabolic processes (i.e., use both inorganic electron sources and organic carbon sources).

**Mode of action**  Overall manner in which a substance acts, e.g., the way a pesticide kills an insect at the tissue or cellular level, or the way that a drug works at the cellular level.

**Model**  A mathematical function with parameters that can be adjusted, so the function closely describes a set of empirical data. A mechanistic model usually reflects observed or hypothesized biological or physical mechanisms and has model parameters with real world interpretation. In contrast, statistical or empirical models selected for particular numerical properties are fitted to data; model parameters may or may not have real world interpretation. When data quality is otherwise equivalent, extrapolation from mechanistic models (e.g., biologically based dose-response models) often carries higher confidence than extrapolation using empirical models (e.g., logistic model).

**Modifying factor (MF)**  A factor used in the derivation of a reference dose or reference concentration. The magnitude of the MF reflects the scientific uncertainties of the study and database not explicitly treated with standard uncertainty factors (e.g., the completeness of the overall database). An MF is greater than zero and less than or equal to 10, and the default value for the MF is 1. Use of a modifying factor was generally discontinued in 2004. Compare to *uncertainty factor (UF).*

**Molecular pharming** Use of *genetically modified organisms* to produce pharmaceuticals. Application of genetic engineering that introduces genes, primarily of human and animal origin, into plants or farm animals to produce medicinal substances. Premise is using plants as efficient chemical factories for producing antibodies, vaccines, blood proteins, and other therapeutically valuable proteins.

**Monod equation** Empirically derived expression of the rate of microbial biomass: $\mu = \frac{\mu_{\max} S}{K_s + S}$, where $\mu$ is the specific growth rate of the microbe, $\mu_{\max}$ is the maximum specific growth rate, and $K_s$ is the Monod growth rate coefficient representing the substrate concentration at which the growth rate is half the maximum rate. The $\mu_{\max}$ is reached at the higher ranges of substrate concentrations. $K_s$ is an expression of the affinity of the microbe for a nutrient, i.e., as $K_s$ decreases the more affinity that microbe has for that particular nutrient (as expressed by the concomitantly increasing $\mu$). Named in honor of French researcher, Jacques Monod.

**Monte Carlo technique** Repeated random sampling from the distribution of values for each of the parameters in a calculation (e.g., lifetime average daily exposure), to derive a distribution of estimates (e.g., of exposures) in the population.

**Moral** 1. Pertaining to the judgment of goodness or evil of human action and character. 2. Often, an adjective for goodness or ethically acceptable actions (opposite of immoral).

**Morality** Distinction between what is right and wrong.

**Morbidity** State of disease.

**Mortality rate** Proportion of a population that dies during a specified time period. Also called death rate.

\**Mosaic** Individual consisting of cells of two or more *genotypes*.

**Most probable number (MPN)** Estimation of the probable population in a liquid by diluting and determining endpoints for microbial growth and conducting statistical tests.

**Motile** Capable of movement, e.g., used to characterize microorganisms.

**Municipal solid waste (MSW)** Garbage and trash.

**Mutagen** Substance that can induce an alteration in the structure of DNA.

**Mutagenesis** Generation of mutations; breeding whereby random mutations are induced in cell's DNA using chemicals or ionizing radiation.

**Mutualism** Symbiosis in which both partners gain from the association and are unable to survive without it. The mutualist and the host are metabolically dependent on each other.

**Mycelium** Branching hyphae found in fungi and some bacteria.

**Mycoplasma** Bacteria that are members of the class Mollicutes and order Mycoplasmatales, lacking cell walls and unable to synthesize peptidoglycan precursors; most require sterols for growth, smallest organisms capable of independent reproduction.

**Myxobacteria** Gram-negative, aerobic soil bacteria characterized by gliding motility, a complex life cycle with the production of fruiting bodies, and the formation of myxospores.

**Nanoscale** Having at least one dimension $< 100$ nm.

**Nanotechnology** Emergent technologies at the *nanoscale*.

**Nanotechnology** Science and engineering addressing the design and production of extremely small ($< 100$ nm diameter) devices and systems fabricated from individual atoms and molecules.

**Natural attenuation** Naturally occurring processes in soil and groundwater environments that act without human intervention to reduce the mass, toxicity, mobility, volume, or concentration of contaminants in those media. When analyzing data from a natural attenuation site, a key question often is whether the mechanisms that destroy or immobilize contaminants are sustainable for as long as the source area releases them to the groundwater. More specifically, whether the rates of the protecting mechanisms will continue to equal the rate at which the contaminants enter the groundwater may be a concern. Sustainability is affected by the rate at which the contaminants are transferred from the source area and whether or not the protecting mechanisms are renewable.

**Natural disaster** A disaster that is initiated by a natural event, e.g., volcano, earthquake or hurricane. Although the trigger may have been natural, the damage is always determined by human activities.

**Navier-Stokes equations** Equations that explain motion of fluids, usually nonlinear partial differential equations.

**Negative paradigm** Most unacceptable or unethical action or case possible. In line drawing, the negative paradigm is the polar opposite of the positive paradigm (compare to *positive paradigm*).

**Nephelometry** Measurement of turbidity using light scattered at an angle to the incident beam; particularly sensitive at low turbidity.

**Nerve** Enclosed, cable-like bundle of nerve fibers or axons.

**Net primary productivity** Organisms' generation of organic compounds from carbon dioxide. Rate at which an ecosystem accumulates biomass and energy, but excluding the energy used for respirartion.

**Niche** Function of an organism in a complex system, including place of the organism, the resources used in a given location, and the time of use.

**Nicotinamide adenine dinucleotide (NAD)** Coenzyme for dehydrogenases; reduced form is *nicotinamide adenine dinucleotide phosphate*. Formerly called DPN (diphosphopyridine nucleotide) and Coenzyme I.

**Nicotinamide adenine dinucleotide phosphate (NADP)** Coenzyme for dehydrogenases; reduced form is NADPH. Formerly called TPN (triphosphopyridine nucleotide) and Coenzyme II.

**Nitrification** Oxidation of reduced forms of nitrogen, e.g., ammonia to nitrate.

**Nitrifying bacteria** *Chemolithotrophic*, Gram-negative members of the family Nitrobacteriaceae that convert ammonia to nitrate and nitrite to nitrate.

**Nitrogen fixation** Metabolic process by which atmospheric molecular nitrogen is reduced to ammonia; carried out by cyanobacteria, Rhizobium, and other nitrogen-fixing bacteria.

**Nitrogen oxygen demand (NOD)** Demand for oxygen in sewage treatment, caused by nitrifying microorganisms.

**Nitrogenase** Enzyme that catalyzes biological *nitrogen fixation*.

**Nongovernmental organization (NGO)** Entity that advocates or represents positions, including scientific, legal, and medical perspectives, without a governmental mandate. Examples include Doctors without Borders, Resources for the Future, and Engineers without Borders.

**No-observed-adverse-effect level (NOAEL)** Highest exposure level where there are no biologically significant increases in the frequency or severity of adverse effect between the exposed population and its appropriate control. Compare to *LOEAL*.

**Nosocomial** Describing infection acquired in a medical facility.

**Nuclear transfer cloning** Transfer of a nucleus into an enucleated egg cell.

**Nuclease** An enzyme which degrades nucleic acids.

**Nucleotide** Combination of ribose or deoxyribose with phosphate and a purine or pyrimidine base; a nucleoside plus one or more phosphates.

**Nucleus** Eukaryotic organelle enclosed by a double-membrane envelope that contains the cell's chromosomes.

**Null mutation** The complete elimination of the function of a gene.

**Nutritional supplement** A dietary supplement intended to be ingested in pill, capsule, tablet, or liquid form, not represented for use as a conventional food or as the sole item of a meal or diet, and labeled accordingly. It is regulated by the U.S. Food and Drug Administration as a food and not as a drug.

**Nymph** Form of insects during metamorphosis after larvae and before adult stage.

**Obligate** Absolutely required, e.g., an obligate *aerobe* can live only in the presence of molecular oxygen and an obligate *anaerobe* can live only in the absence of molecular oxygen.

**Ockham's razor** Principle espoused by medieval nominalist William of Ockham that entities are not to be multiplied beyond necessity. The principle encourages asking whether any proposed kind of entity is necessary.

**Octanol-water coefficient ($K_{ow}$)** Ratio of the concentration of a chemical in octanol and in water at equilibrium and at a specified temperature. Octanol is used as a surrogate for natural organic matter. $K_{ow}$ is used to help determine the fate of chemicals in the environment, e.g., to predict the extent a contaminant will *bioaccumulate* in aquatic biota.

**Odds ratio** Ratio of the odds of disease among the exposed compared with the odds of disease among the unexposed. For rare diseases, such as cancer, the odds ratio can provide an estimate of relative risk.

**Offsetting behavior** Inadvertent attenuation or reversal of a risk management action due to a reduction of care by those targeted for risk reduction. For example, if actions are taken to reduce bacterial growth in food supplies, and consumers consider the foods to be safer to the extent that they are less careful in food preparation, this behavior offsets at least some of the safety margin of the risk reduction efforts.

**Oligonucleotide** Short DNA sequence of up to 1000 nucleotides.

**Omics** Shorthand term for computational, biological subfields for describing very large-scale data collection and analysis, all with the suffix "omics" (e.g., genomics, proteomics, and metabonomics).

**Onus** Burden of responsibility.

**Opportunity risk** Likelihood that a better opportunity will present itself after an irreversible decision has been made (e.g., prohibiting research in an emerging technology may prevent exposure to a toxic substance to a few, but, in the process, the cure for a disease may be lost).

**Optimal range**  Range of success, below and above which are unacceptable (e.g., trivalent chromium must be taken within the optimal range because intake at too low a dosage leads to a nutritional deficiency and too high a dosage leads to toxicity).

**Optimization**  Selecting the best design for the conditions. The "best" is determined by the designer based on one or more variables (e.g., a heart valve may have three key variables: flow rate, reliability, and durability: the engineer would design the valve by optimizing these three variables to achieve the best performance).

**Oral slope factor**  Upper bound, approximating a 95% confidence limit, on the increased cancer risk from a lifetime oral exposure to an agent. This estimate, usually expressed in units of proportion of a population affected per $mg\,kg^{-1}\,day^{-1}$, is generally reserved for use in the low-dose region of the dose-response relationship, that is, for exposures corresponding to risks less than 1 in 100.

**Organ**  Completely differentiated unit of an organism that provides a certain, specialized function.

**Organelle**  Structure within or on a cell that performs specific functions.

**Organism**  Living entity; consisting of one or more cells (unicellular and multicellular organisms, respectively).

**Organophosphate (OP)**  Phosphorous-containing synthetic pesticide active ingredient that acts on the nervous system by inhibiting acetylcholinesterase. Irreversible inhibition is characteristic of many OPs. Azamethiphos, chlorpyrifos, diazinon, dichlorvos, and malathion are OPs.

**Organotroph**  Organism that uses reduced organic compounds as its electron source.

**Orpiment**  $As_2S_3$, yellow, sulfur compound of arsenic.

**Osmosis**  Movement of fluid through a partially (selectively) permeable membrane separating solutions of different concentrations. Movement of a fluid across a selectively permeable membrane from a dilute solution to a more concentrated solution. Cellular *membranes* and root systems, for example, take advantage of the separation by osmosis for nutrient transport.

**Outlier**  Value that is markedly smaller or larger than other values in a data set. Can be problematic for researchers since it decreases the coefficient of determination (i.e., $r^2$).

**Oxidation**  Loss of electrons from a compound.

**Oxidation-reduction potential (ORP)**  Degree of completion of chemical reaction expressed as the ratio of reduced ions to oxidized ions.

**Oxidation-reduction reaction**  Reaction involving electron transfer; the reductant donates electrons to an oxidant. Also called redox reaction.

**Ozonation**  Addition of ozone ($O_3$) to water and other *media* for disinfection and other oxidative processes.

**PAH**  See *polycyclic aromatic hydrocarbon.*

**Pandora's box**  Metaphor for a prolific source of problems (Greek: All gifted; from mythology of a box given to Pandora by Zeus who ordered that she not open it; Pandora succumbed to her curiosity and opened it; all the miseries and evils flew out to afflict humankind).

**Paradox**  Argument appearing to justify a self-contradictory conclusion by using valid deductions from acceptable premises.

**Parametrics**  Descriptors of an entire population, without the need of inference. Compare to *statistics.*

**Pareto efficiency**  Resource allocation wherein there is no rearrangement that can make anyone better off without making someone else worse off.

**Partial pressure**  Pressure exerted by a single gas in a mixture of gases.

**Particulate matter (PM)**  Complex mixture of small solid particles and liquid droplets, consisting of numerous components, e.g. acids (such as nitrates and sulfates), organic chemicals, metals, and soil or dust particle. Compare to *aerosol.*

**Partitioning**  Chemical equilibrium condition where a chemical's concentration is apportioned between two different phases according to the partition coefficient, which is the ratio of a chemical's concentration in one phase to its concentration in the other phase, e.g., *octanol-water coefficient.*

**Pathogen**  Microbe capable of producing disease.

**PBT**  Chemical that is persistent, bioaccumulates, and is toxic.

**PCB**  See *polychlorinated biphenyl.*

**PCR**  See *polymerase chain reaction.*

**Pedagogy**  Instruction techniques used to promote learning.

**Peptide**  1. Chain formed by two or more *amino acids* linked through *peptide bonds*: dipeptide, two *amino acids*; oligopeptide, small number of *amino acids*. 2. Molecule formed by peptide bonds covalently linking two or more *amino acids*. Larger peptides (i.e., *polypeptides*) are usually *expressed* from recombinant DNA.

**Peptide bond** Covalent bond between two *amino acids*, in which the carboxyl group of one amino acid ($X_1COOH$) and the amino group of an adjacent amino acid ($NH_2X_2$) react to form $X_1CONHX_2$ plus $H_2O$.

**Perception** Information and knowledge gained through the senses.

**Performance monitoring** The collection of information which, when analyzed, evaluates the performance of the system on the environmental contamination.

**Permeability** Ease at which a fluid moves through a substance.

**Permeable reactive barriers** Subsurface walls composed of reactive materials that will either degrade or alter the state of a contaminant when that contaminant in a groundwater plume passes through the wall.

**Permissible exposure level (PEL)** Occupational limit for a contaminant.

**Persistence** Resistance to degradation in the environment.

**Persistent organic compound (POP)** Recalcitrant organic compounds, most of which are semi-voltile and lipophilic.

**Pesticide** Substance used to control pesticide by using its toxic properties.

**pH** Negative logarithmic measure of the hydrogen ion concentration in water, ranging from 0 to 14 (acidic to basic).

**Pharmacodynamics** Manner in which a substance exerts its effects on living organisms (compare to *toxicodynamics*).

**Pharmacokinetics** Behavior of substances within an organism, especially by absorption, distribution, biotransformation, storage, and excretion (compare to *toxicokinetics*).

**Phenotype** Physical manifestation of the *genotype*.

**Phosphorylation** Addition of phosphate monoester to macromolecule, catalyzed by a specific *kinase enzyme*.

**Phosphotase, alkaline** Enzyme that catalyzes the hydrolysis of phosphomonoesters of the $5'$ nucleotides.

**Photolithotrophic autotroph** Organism that uses light energy, an inorganic electron source (e.g., $H_2O$, $H_2$, $H_2S$), and $CO_2$ as a carbon source.

**Photoorganotrophic heterotroph** Microbe that uses light energy and organic electron donors, and simple organic molecules rather than $CO_2$ as their carbon source.

**Photoreactivation** Increase in survival rate or reduction in the frequency of mutation of a microbial population previously irradiated with ultraviolet light by exposure to light of 300-450 nm wavelength.

**Photosensitization** Increased sensitivity of microbes to oxygen and light by applying certain stains to cells (e.g., acridine orange, methylene blue).

**Phototaxis** Microbial movement (especially photosynthetic bacteria) toward light.

**Phototroph** Organism that can use light as an energy source. Green algae (and higher plants produce) oxygen. Photosynthetic bacteria produce sulfur (for instance). Blue-green algae are sometimes considered algae (Cyanophyta) and sometimes bacteria (Cyanobacteria).

**Phycology** Study of algae.

**Physical containment** Stopping the migration of an entity, e.g., a microbe being kept in a sealed containment system.

**Physiologically based pharmacokinetic (PBPK) model** Model used to characterize pharmacokinetic behavior of a chemical. Available data on blood flow rates and on metabolic and other processes that the chemical undergoes within each compartment are used to construct a mass-balance framework for the PBPK model.

**Phytodegradation** Process by which plants metabolically degrade a contaminant to a nontoxic form in roots, stems, or leaves.

**Phytoextraction** Removal of a substance from soils and groundwater surrounding the roots of a plant through that plant's vascular system.

**Phytoplankton** *Flora* in the *plankton community*.

**Phytoremediation** Use of plants to clean up contamination.

**Phytovolatilization** Plants translocate contaminants into the atmosphere via normal transpiration.

**Plankton** Small, mainly microscopic, members of animal, and plant communities in aquatic system. See *phytoplankton* and *zooplankton*.

**Plant-incorporated protectants (PIPs)** Proteins and other chemicals introduced to plants either through the conventional breeding of sexually compatible plants or through techniques of modern biotechnology, e.g., transferring specific genetic material from a bacterium to a plant to induce the plant to produce pesticidal proteins or other chemicals that the plant could not previously produce.

**Plasmid** Extrachromosomal DNA molecule separated from the chromosomal DNA capable of replicating independently of the chromosomal DNA; found in bacteria and protozoa. Since it is capable of replicating autonomously, it is often used for the insertion of genetic material.

**Plasmolysis** Water loss with concomitant shrinkage of the cell contents and cytoplasmic membrane resulting from high osmotic pressure in a medium.

**Pleiotropy** Phenomenon in which one gene can influence two or more independent characteristics.

**Ploidy** Number of complete sets of chromosomes in a cell.

**Plume** A zone of dissolved contaminants, originating from a source and extending in the direction of flow. Volume of a substance moving from its source away from the source.

**PM** See *particulate matter*.

**$PM_{2.5}$** Particulate matter with aerodynamic diameters less than 2.5 microns. Also known as fine particulates.

**$PM_{10}$** Particulate matter with aerodynamic diameters less than 10 microns. Also known as coarse particulates.

**Point of departure** The dose-response (see *dose-response*) point that marks the beginning of a low-dose extrapolation. This point is most often the upper bound on an observed incidence or on an estimated incidence from a dose-response model.

**Polychlorinated biphenyl (PCB)** Highly toxic molecule of two benzene rings bonded to each other with chlorine substituents (209 structural variations, known as congeners); presently banned but manufactured by Monsanto for much of the twentieth century.

**Polycyclic aromatic hydrocarbon (PAH)** Class of products of incomplete combustion consisting of fused aromatic rings. A number of them are suspected carcinogens (e.g., benzo(*a*)pyrene).

**Polymerase** Enzyme that links individual nucleotides together into a long strand, using another strand as a template.

**Polymerase chain reaction (PCR)** Technique that enables the *in vitro* amplification of target DNA sequences.

**Pool** An accumulation of DNAPL above a capillary barrier.

**Porosity** Percentage of void space in a solid matrix (e.g., soil, sediment, or gravel).

**Positive paradigm** Most acceptable or ethical action or case possible. In line drawing, the positive paradigm is the polar opposite of the negative paradigm (see *negative paradigm*).

**Precautionary principle** Position that if the suspected health or environmental risk of an action is sufficiently widespread or irreversible, in the absence of scientific consensus that the action or policy is harmful, the burden of proof that it is *not* harmful falls on those taking the action.

**Precautionary principle** Risk management approach taken when scientific knowledge is incomplete and the possible consequences could be substantial and irreversible (e.g., global climate change). The principle holds that scientific uncertainty must not be accepted as an excuse to postpone cost-effective measures to prevent a significant problem.

**Precision** Exactness and reproducibility. Usually represented by the number of significant figures.

**Prevalence** Proportion of cases that exist within a population at a specific point in time, relative to the number of individuals within that population at the same point in time.

**Prevention** Intentional modification of the characteristics of a phenomena with the purpose of reducing risk and the intrinsic characteristics of an element with the purpose of reducing vulnerability. The intervention has the purpose of modifying the risk factors. Examples of measures to reduce a threat include, control, or affect the actual physical path of an event or reduce the magnitude and frequency of phenomena. The reduction to a minimal possible level of the material damages through the modification of the impact resistance of the exposed elements is an example of structural measures related to the intervention of the physical vulnerability. Aspects related to the planification and regulation of land/soil use, insurances, emergency measures, and public education are examples of nonstructural measures related to the physical or functional vulnerability.

**Primary treatment** Clarification of wastewater influent (i.e., removal of suspended solids) by *sedimentation*.

**Probability** Measurement of the likelihood that an event will occur; ranging from 0 (no likelihood whatsoever) to 1 (absolute certainty).

**Process monitoring** The collection of information documenting the operation of a system's engineered components.

**Profession** Group (e.g., physicians or engineers) with a common mission, requiring substantial education and training, self-determination of professional requirements to enter, organized into an identifiable professional body, and requiring the adherence to standards of conduct.

**Progenitor strain** Original strain prior to *hybridization* or genetic modification. Unmodified strain.

**Program evaluation review technique (PERT) chart** Diagram depicting project tasks and their interrelationships.

**Prokaryote** Organism lacking a true nucleus and other membrane-bound cellular compartments, and containing a single loop of stable chromosomal DNA in the nucleoid region and cytoplasmic structures.

**Promoter**  An agent that is not carcinogenic itself, but when administered after an initiator of carcinogenesis, stimulates the clonal expansion of the initiated cell to produce a neoplasm.

**Proteobacteria**  Bacteria, primarily Gram-negative, that 16S *rRNA* sequence comparisons show to be phylogenetically related; proteobacteria contain the purple photosynthetic bacteria and their relatives and are composed of *a, b, g, d*, and *e* subgroups.

**Proteome**  Complete collection of proteins that an organism produces.

**Proteomics**  Study of proteins in the body, especially the protein complement of the genome *omics*).

**Protist**  Eukaryote with unicellular organization, in the form of either solitary cells or colonies of cells lacking true tissues.

**Protoplast**  Cell bounded by cytoplasmic membrane, yet lacking rigid layer. Protozoa: Microscopic animals.

**Protozoa**  *Motile* microbes that consume bacteria as a carbon and energy sources.

**Psychrophilic**  Describing a microbe with optimal temperatures between 0 and 20 °C.

**Psyllid**  Jumping plant louse; usually host specific. See *citrus greening disease*.

**Public, the**  Whole collection of people comprising a society.

**Pure culture**  Cell population with all members identical because they arise from a single cell.

**Purine**  Basic, heterocyclic, nitrogen-containing molecule with two joined rings that occurs in nucleic acids and other cell constituents; most purines are oxy- or amino-derivatives of the purine skeleton. The most important purines are adenine and guanine.

**Pyrethroid**  Natural (from the chrysanthemum family) or synthetic pesticide, of varying chemical structure, which acts on the nervous system by interfering with nerve conduction. Permethrin and D-phenothrin are synthetic pyrethroids.

**Quantitative polymerase chain reaction (qPCR)**  Determination of a polynucleotide by including a known amount of readily distinguished template as an internal standard to compensate for variation in efficiency of amplification.

**Quantitative structure activity relationship (QSAR)**  Understanding and application of chemical structure to estimate the behavior of a compound, e.g., *toxicity* or *persistence*.

**Quantum yield**  Number of photons required per molecule of carbon dioxide converted to sugar (or per oxygen molecule produced).

**Radioactive half-life**  Time taken for half the initial number of nuclei to disintegrate, $t_{1/2}$.

**Rainforest**  Forest with mean rainfall greater than 1750 mm per year.

**Raoult's law**  A dissolved substance will lower the partial pressure of the solvent proportionally to the mole fraction of the dissolved substance.

**Reactor**  System where physical, chemical, and biological reactions occur. Traditionally, these have been thought of vessels or other engineered systems, but reactors can be quite large and occur in natural systems (e.g., a wetland is a reactor in which *aerobic, anaerobic*, and mixed reactions occur). At the other end of the scale, any living cell is a reactor.

**Realgar**  $As_4S_4$, red-orange, sulfur compound of arsenic

**Reasonable person standard**  Position (legal, engineering, etc.) expected to be held by a hypothetical person in society who exercises average care, skill, and judgment in conduct.

**Reasoning**  Derivation of a conclusion from premises.

**Rebound**  After contaminant concentrations in groundwater have been reduced through *in situ* treatment and the treatment is terminated or reduced, concentrations return to elevated levels from the continued release of mass from a source zone beyond the natural attenuation capacity of the groundwater system.

**Recalcitrance**  1. Resistance of a compound to degradation. 2. Inverse of degradability.

**Receptor**  1. Molecule in a cell or on its surface that binds to a specific substance and causes a specific physiologic effect in the cell. 2. The potentially or actually affected entity exposed to a physical, chemical, or biological agent.

**Recombinant**  Describing material produced by *genetic engineering*.

**Recombinant DNA (rDNA)**  Genetically engineered DNA prepared by transplanting or splicing genes from one individual to another, including from the cells of one species into the cells of a host organism of a different species. Thereafter, the rDNA becomes part of the host's genetic makeup and is replicated.

**Redictable**  Ridiculously predictable (coined by Vallero DJ and Randall ACV). For example, if a microbe that has been genetically modified to degrade crude oil spilled from a tanker, the likelihood that the same microbe will degrade asphalt in adjacent roads is redictable.

**Reductionism** 1. Understanding complex phenomenon by reducing them to the interactions of their parts, or to simpler or more fundamental processes and components. 2. Perspective that a complex system is merely the sum of its parts, and that an account of it can be reduced to accounts of individual constituents. Compare reductionist to *systematic*.

**Reductive dechlorination** The removal of chlorine from an organic compound and its replacement with hydrogen. Often, part of a two-step degradation process for *recalcitrant* halogenated compounds, i.e., the anaerobic step to remove halogens and the aerobic step to break aromatic rings and otherwise reach *ultimate degradation*.

**Reference concentration (RfC)** An estimate (with uncertainty spanning perhaps an order of magnitude) of a continuous inhalation exposure to the human population (including sensitive subgroups) that is likely to be without an appreciable risk of deleterious effects during a lifetime. It can be derived from an NOAEL, LOAEL, or benchmark concentration, with uncertainty factors generally applied to reflect limitations of the data used. Generally used in noncancer health assessments. Durations include *acute*, *short-term*, *subchronic*, and *chronic*.

**Reference dose (RfD)** An estimate (with uncertainty spanning perhaps an order of magnitude) of a daily oral exposure to the human population (including sensitive subgroups) that is likely to be without an appreciable risk of deleterious effects during a lifetime. It can be derived from an NOAEL, LOAEL, or benchmark dose, with uncertainty factors generally applied to reflect limitations of the data used. Generally used in noncancer health assessments. Durations include *acute*, *short-term*, *subchronic*, and *chronic*.

**Relative risk** Ratio of the risk of disease or death among the exposed segment of the population to the risk among the unexposed. The relative measure of the difference in risk between the exposed and unexposed populations in a cohort study. The relative risk is calculated as the rate of an outcome in an exposed divided by the rate of the disease among the unexposed; e.g., a relative risk of two means that the exposed group has twice the disease risk as the unexposed group. Also known as *relative risk*.

**Reliability** Probability that a device or system will perform its specified function, without failure under stated environmental conditions, over a required lifetime.

**Replicase** DNA-duplication catalyzing enzyme.

**Resilience** Attribute of ecosystem stability, expressing the systems ability to recover after disturbance.

**Respiration** Energy-yielding process in which the energy substrate is oxidized by means of an exogenous or externally derived electron acceptor.

**Response boundary (control plane)** A location within the source area, or immediately downgradient of the source area, where changes in the plume configuration are anticipated due to the implementation of the *in situ* bioremediation DNAPL source zone treatment.

**Restriction enzyme** Enzyme that cleaves DNA molecules at a precisely defined site; provides ubiquitous defense proteins in bacteria that cut DNA strands at specifically defined sequences.

**Reverse osmosis** High-pressure filtration to separate extremely fine particle and ions.

**Reverse transcriptase** Enzyme that synthesizes a strand of DNA complementary to the base sequence of an RNA template.

**Reynolds number** Dimensionless number associated with fluid flow that determines the transition point from laminar to turbulent flow. It represents the ratio of the momentum forces to the viscous forces in the fluid flow.

**Rhizodegradation** Plants promote a soil environment suitable for microbes that can degrade or sequester contaminants.

**Rhizosphere** Narrow region of soil directly influenced by soil microbes and plant root secretions.

**Ribonucleic acid (RNA)** Nucleic acid molecule similar to *deoxyribonucleic acid*, but containing ribose rather than deoxyribose.

**Ribosomal RNA (rRNA)** Any of several RNAs that become part of the ribosome and thus are involved in translating *mRNA* and synthesizing proteins.

**Risk** 1. Likelihood of an adverse outcome. 2. Probability of adverse effects resulting from exposure to an environmental agent or mixture of agents.

**Risk assessment** The evaluation of scientific information on the hazardous properties of environmental agents (hazard characterization), the dose-response relationship (dose-response assessment), and the extent of human exposure to those agents (exposure assessment). The product of the risk assessment is a statement regarding the probability that populations or individuals so exposed will be harmed and to what degree (risk characterization).

**Risk characterization** The integration of information on hazard, exposure, and dose-response to provide an estimate of the likelihood that any of the identified adverse effects will occur in exposed people.

**Risk homeostasis** Defeat of built-in factors of safety by asserting new way to use the products.

**Risk management** Decision-making process that accounts for political, social, economic, and engineering implications together with risk-related information in order to develop, analyze, and compare management options and select the appropriate managerial response to a hazard.

**Risk ratio (RR)** See *relative risk.*

**Risk shifting** Taking an action that changes and reduces the risk of one population but increases the risk in a different population (e.g., banning DDT reduces the risk of cancer in developed nations but increases the risk of malaria in tropical and subtropical developing countries).

**Risk tradeoff** Eliminating or reducing one risk, but introducing or increasing a countervailing risk (e.g., reducing the pain of a headache by taking aspirin, but increasing the risk of Reye's syndrome; or removing mold in buildings may increase worker exposure to asbestos).

**Risk-benefit analysis** Comparison of risks of various options to their benefits (e.g., health and wildlife risks of applying a pesticide compared to the benefits of crop protection).

**Runoff** Water running overland, often carrying solids and other pollutants to surface waters; important vehicle in *nonpoint* pollution.

**Sanctity of life** View that human life is precious from conception to natural death, since it is created in the image of the Creator.

**Sand** Soil particle between 0.05 and 2.0 mm in diameter.

**Saprophyte** Organism that derives its nutrients from decomposing organic matter.

**Saturated zone** See *zone of saturation.*

**Saturation** Ratio of the volume of a single fluid in the pores to pore volume expressed as a percentage or a fraction.

**Scale** Spatial extent from very small (molecular) to very large (planetary).

**Science** Systematic investigation, through experiment, observation, and deduction, in an attempt to produce reliable explanations of the physical world and its processes.

**Scientific method** Progression of inquiry (1) to identify a problem you would like to solve, (2) to formulate a hypothesis, (3) to test the hypothesis, (4) to collect and to analyze the data, and (5) to draw valid conclusions.

**Secondary treatment** Clarification followed by a biological process with separate sludge collection and handling.

**Sedimentation** Process in surface waters or in engineered systems wherein particles fall in direct proportion to a particle's mass and indirect proportion to flow. Most particle mass in a wastewater treatment facility is collected during *primary treatment.*

**Senescence** Organism's aging process.

**Sensitivity** 1. Ability of a test to detect a condition when it is truly present. 2. Smallest change in a physical quantity or parameter that can be detected by a measuring system. Determined by signal to noise ratio, system amplification, or quantizing limit. Compare to *specificity.*

**Sewage** Untreated, predominantly liquid, waste in need of treatment; the fluid being transported to a wastewater treatment plant. Preferred term is wastewater.

**Silage** Fermented plant material with increased palatability and nutritional value for animals; often can be stored for extended periods.

**Silt** Soil particle with a diameter between 0.002 and 0.05 mm. Compare to *clay* and *sand.*

**Sink** Site where matter or energy is lost in a system; e.g., a wetland can be a sink for $CO_2$, but it may not be a net sink for carbon, for example, if it releases $CH_4$ from *anaerobic decomposition*, i.e., it would be a net carbon sink only if more is lost and stored than is released. If it releases more carbon than it takes up and stores it is a net *source.*

**Slash and burn** Cutting and using fire to clear land for agriculture.

**Slime mold** Organism that produces spores but moves with amoeba-like gliding motility; phenotypically similar to fungi and protozoa. Phylogenetically, slime molds are more closely related to amoeboid protozoa than to fungi. Cellular slime molds are composed of single amoeboid cells during their vegetative stage. Vegetative acellular slime molds are made up of plasmodia, amorphous masses of protoplasm.

**Slope factor, cancer** Dose-response curve for a substance, indicating cancer potency (units = mass per body mass per time, e.g., $mg\ kg^{-1}\ day^{-1}$). An upper bound, approximating a 95% confidence limit, on the increased cancer risk from a lifetime exposure to an agent. This estimate, usually expressed in units of proportion of a population affected per $mg\ kg^{-1}\ day^{-1}$, is generally reserved for use in the low-dose region of the dose-response relationship, that is, for exposures corresponding to risks less than 1 in 100.

**Sludge** Muddy aggregate at the bottom of tanks generated as particles settle. Also known as biosolids when a sludge contains large amounts of organic materials, e.g., microbes and their remnants.

**Slurry** Liquid mixture of aqueously insoluble matter, e.g., a lime ($CaO$, $CaCO_3$) slurry.

**Social ecology** View that environmental problems are firmly rooted in human social interactions. Social ecologists believe that an ecologically sustainable society can still be socially exploitative.

**Society** Collection of human beings that is distinguished from other groups by shared institutions and a common culture.

**Solids retention time (SRT)** Average time of retention of suspended solids in a treatment system, equal to the total weight of suspended solids exiting the system, per unit time.

**Solubility** The amount of substance that will dissolve in a given quantity of solvent, at a given temperature, to form a saturated solution.

**Sorption** The uptake of a solute by a solid. General term that embodies *absorption, adsorption, chemisorption*, and *ion exchange.*

**Sorption isotherm** Curves based on properties of both the chemical and the soil (or other matrix) that determine how and at what rates the molecules partition into the solid and liquid phases. Examples are the Freundlich sorption isotherms.

**Source** Site from which matter or energy originates. Contrast with *sink.*

**Source loading** The flux of a substance leaving the original disposal location and entering the water migrating through the soil and aquifer.

**Source zone** The subsurface zone containing a contaminant reservoir sustaining a plume in groundwater. The subsurface zone is or was in contact with DNAPL. Source zone mass can include sorbed and aqueous-phase contaminant mass as well as DNAPL.

**Spatial scale** Geographic extent of a resource or problem. Global scale examples include pandemics, changes in climate, or nuclear threats. Continental scale examples are shifting biomes and border control between nations. Regional scale examples include the contamination of rivers or polluting the air. Local scale examples include crime, job loss, hazardous waste sites, and landfills.

**Specialization** Degree to which an individual professional concentrates his or her practice into a narrow range of expertise and activities.

**Species** Subdivision of a genus having members differing from other members of the same genus in minor details.

**Species abundance** How common a species is in an ecological community. Compare to *biodiversity.*

**Specific gravity** Ratio of the mass of a body to the mass of an equal volume of water at a specific temperature, typically 20 °C.

**Specificity** Ability of a test to exclude the presence of a condition when it is truly not present. Compare to *sensitivity.*

**Spirochete** Spiral-shaped bacterium with periplasmic flagella.

**Spore** Differentiated, specialized form that can be used for dissemination, for survival of hostile conditions because of its heat and desiccation resistance or for reproduction. Highly variable and usually unicellular. May develop into vegetative organisms or gametes and can be produced asexually or sexually.

**Stakeholder** A person other than regulators, owners, or technical personnel involved in the environmental activity of concern, who has a vested interest in decisions related to those particular activities.

**Standard deviation** Measure of the spread in a data set; wider spread means larger standard deviation.

**Standard mortality ratio (SMR)** Ratio of the number of deaths observed in the study group to the number of deaths expected based on rates in a comparison population, multiplied by 100.

**Stationary phase** Microbial growth period after rapid growth, in which cell multiplication is balanced by cell death.

**Statistical significance** The probability that a result is not likely to be due to chance alone. By convention, a difference between two groups is usually considered statistically significant if chance could explain it only 5% of the time or less. Study design considerations may influence the *a priori* choice of a different level of statistical significance.

**Statistics** Mathematics concerned with collecting and interpreting quantitative data and applying probability theory to estimate conditions of a universe or population from a sample.

**Stoichiometric** Related to chemical proportions exactly needed in a reaction.

**Stokes diameter** Diameter of a spherical particle with the same density and settling velocity as the particle of interest.

**Stokes law** At low velocities, frictional force on a spherical body moving through a fluid at constant velocity equals $6\pi$ times the product of the velocity, the fluid viscosity, and the radius of the sphere.

**Strain** 1. Geometrical expression of deformation caused by the action of stress (see *stress*) on a physical body. 2. In biological taxonomy, group of organisms bred within a closed colony to maintain certain defining characteristics.

**Stratified random sample** Separation of a sample into several groups and randomly assigning subjects to those groups.

**Stratospheric ozone** Layer just above the troposphere in the earth's atmosphere with high concentrations of ozone ($O_3$) that absorbs much of the incoming ultraviolet light.

**Stress** 1. Applied force or system of forces that are apt to strain (see Strain) or deform a physical body. 2. The internal resistance of a physical body to such applied force or system of forces.

**Structural ecology** Ecology, with an emphasis on the components (e.g., niches, associations, canopies) of ecosystems. Compare to *functional ecology*.

**Subchronic exposure** Repeated exposure by the oral, dermal, or inhalation route for more than 30 days, up to approximately 10% of the life span in humans (more than 30 days up to approximately 90 days in typically used laboratory animal species) (see also longer-term exposure).

**Substrate** Molecule that can transfer an electron to another molecule. Substance upon which an enzyme or microorganism acts. For example, organic compounds, such as lactate, ethanol, or glucose, are commonly used as substrates for bioremediation of chlorinated ethenes.

**Sulfate reducer** A microorganism that exists in anaerobic environments and reduces sulfate to sulfide.

**Supernatant** 1. Liquid stratum in a bioreactor, e.g., a sludge digester. 2. Layer of liquid above a precipitate (e.g., sediment) after settling.

**Supply** Quantity of a good or service that a seller would like to sell at a particular price.

**Supply curve** Relationship between a good's quantity supplied and the good's price.

**Surfactant** Surface-active agent that concentrates at interfaces, forms micelles, increases solution, lowers surface tension, increases adsorption, and disperses otherwise sorbed substances into the aqueous phase. All have common chemical structure, i.e., a *hydrophobic* and a *hydrophilic* moiety. The hydrophobic part usually consists of an alkyl chain, which is then linked to a hydrophilic group. Each part of the surfactant molecule interacts differently with water. The hydrophilic group is surrounded by water molecules, leading to enhanced aqueous solubility. Simultaneously, the hydrophobic moieties are repulsed by strong interactions between the water molecules. This combination allows for otherwise insoluble substances to be desorbed from soil and sediment.

**Susceptibility** 1. Extent to which an individual is prone to the effects of an agent. 2. Increased likelihood of an adverse effect, often discussed in terms of relationship to a factor that can be used to describe a human subpopulation (e.g., life stage, demographic feature, or genetic characteristic).

**Susceptible subgroups** May refer to life stages, for example, children or the elderly, or to other segments of the population, for example, asthmatics or the immune-compromised, but are likely to be somewhat chemical specific and may not be consistently defined in all cases.

**Suspended solids (SS)** 1. Floating solids with low aqueous solubility. Common measure of water pollution and treatment efficiency, e.g., 20 mg SS $L^{-2}$ prior to treatment and 1 mg SS $L^{-1}$ after treatment.

**Sustainability** 1. Processes and activities that are currently useful and that do not diminish these same functions for future generations. 2. The ability of a system to maintain the important attenuation mechanisms through time. In the case of reductive dechlorination, sustainability might be limited by the amount of electron donor, which might be used up before remedial goals are achieved.

**Sustainable design** Application of principles of sustainability (see *sustainability*) to structures, products, and system; an aspect of green engineering.

**Sustainable enhancement** An intervention action that continues until such time that the enhancement is no longer required to reduce contaminant concentrations or fluxes.

**Symbiosis** Two dissimilar organisms living together or in close association.

**Synergism** Effect from a combination of two agents is greater than the sum of the additive effects from both agents ($1+1>2$). Contrast with *antagonism*.

**System** 1. Combination of organized elements comprising a unified whole. 2. In thermodynamics, a defined physical entity containing boundaries in space, which can be open (i.e., energy and matter can be exchanged with the environment) or closed (no energy or matter exchange).

**Systematic** Perspective that includes relationships of numerous factors simultaneously. Compare to *reductionist*.

**Systemic effect** Toxic effect as a result of absorption and distribution of a toxicant to a site distant from its entry point. Also known as systemic toxicity.

**Systems biology** 1. Discipline that seeks to study the relationships and interactions between various parts of a biological system (e.g., metabolic pathways, organelles, cells, and organisms) and to integrate this information to understand how biological systems function. 2. Treatment of biological entities as systems composed of defined elements interacting in distinct ways to enable the observed function and behavior of that system. Properties of such systems are embedded in a quantitative model that guides further tests of systems behavior.

**Target organ** The biological organ(s) most adversely affected by exposure to a chemical, physical, or biological agent.

**Taxonomy** Classification system.

**Technology** 1. Application of scientific knowledge. 2. The apparatus that results from such applications.

**Temporal scale** Range of complexity associated with time. Extremely short temporal scale may be measured in nanoseconds, e.g., nuclear reactions, whereas long-temporal scales may be measured in millions of years, e.g., fossilization of plants to coal.

**Temporality** Criterion for causality requiring that the cause (e.g., exposure to an infectious agent) precedes the effect (e.g., disease). One of *Hill's criteria.*

**Teratogen** Substance that causes defects in development between conception and birth. A teratogen is a substance that causes a structural or functional birth defect.

**Teratogenic** Structural developmental defects due to exposure to a chemical agent during formation of individual organs.

**Terrorism** Unlawful use of, or threatened use of, force or violence against individuals or property to coerce or intimidate governments or societies, often to achieve political, religious, or ideological objectives.

**Tertiary treatment** Removal of nutrients, especially phosphorus and nitrogen, along with most suspended solids; generally synonymous with *advanced waste treatment*, which is becoming the preferred term.

**Tetrachlorodibenzo-*para*-dioxin (TCDD)** Most toxic *dioxin* form, especially when 2,3,7,8-TCDD.

**Texture** Particle size classification of soil in terms of the U.S. Department of Agriculture system, which uses the term loam for a soil having equal properties of *sand*, *silt*, and *clay*. The basic textural classes, in order of their increasing proportions of fine particles, are sand, loamy sand, sandy loam, loam, silt loam, silt, sandy clay loam, clay loam, silty clay loam, sand clay, silty clay, and clay. The sand, loamy sand, and sandy loam classes may be further divided by decreasing size, i.e., coarse, fine, or very fine.

**Thallus** Body devoid of root, stem, or leaf; characteristic of certain algae, many fungi, and lichens.

**Thermodynamics** Principles addressing the physical relationships between energy and matter, especially those concerned with the conversion of different forms of energy.

**Thermophilic** Describing microbes that thrive in temperatures $>45\,^\circ$C, e.g., *Bacillus licheniformis*.

**Threshold** The dose or exposure below which no deleterious effect is expected to occur. An example is the *no observable adverse effect level.*

**Threshold limit value (TLV)** Occupational standard of the concentration of airborne substances to which a healthy person may be exposed during a 40-h workweek with adverse effects.

**Tissue** Collection of interconnected cells that carry out a similar function in an organism.

**Tolerance** Established concentration of a substance (e.g., in pesticide residues) occurring as a direct result of proper usage. Compare to *action level.*

**Top-down** Starting at the upper levels of organization and working downward to the details. Contrast with *bottom-up.*

**Total dissolved solids (TDS)** Common measure of the aqueously soluble content in water or wastewater, estimated from electrical conductivity, since pure water is a poor conductor and the solids are often electrolytes and other conducting substances.

**Total maximum daily load (TMDL)** Maximum amount of a pollutant that a water body can receive and still meet water quality standards, and an allocation of that amount to the pollutant's sources; varies according to specific watersheds. Sum of the allowable loads of a single pollutant from all contributing point and nonpoint sources. Must include a margin of safety to ensure that the water body can be used for the purposes the State has designated. Calculation must also account for seasonal variation in water quality.

**Total suspended particulate (TSP)** Entire quantity of particulate matter in the air; i.e. all PM. Compare to $PM_{2.5}$ and $PM_{10}$.

**Total suspended solids (TSS)** Fraction of *suspended solids* collected by a filter in water.

**Toxic Release Inventory (TRI)** Database of annual releases from specified manufacturers in the United States, which includes almost 400 chemicals, as part of the Community Right to Know regulations. Data are self-reported by the manufacturers annually.

**Toxic substance** A chemical, physical, or biological agent that may cause an adverse effect or effects to biological systems.

**Toxicity** 1. Deleterious or adverse biological effects elicited by a chemical, physical, or biological agent. 2. Extent and degree of biological harm of a chemical, physical, or biological agent, ranging from *acute* to *chronic*.

**Toxicodynamics** The determination and quantification of the sequence of events at the cellular and molecular levels, leading to a toxic response to an environmental agent. Often used synonymously with the broader term *pharmacodynamics*, but toxicodynamics is exclusively applied to adverse agents rather than the efficacy of substance.

**Toxicokinetics** The determination and quantification of the time course of absorption, distribution, biotransformation, and excretion of chemicals. Often used synonymously with the broader term *pharmacokinetics*, but toxicokinetics is exclusively applied to adverse agents rather than the efficacy of substance.

**Toxicology** Study of harmful interactions between chemical, physical, or biological agents and biological systems.

**Tragedy of the Commons** Term coined by Garrett Hardin [*Science* (1968), volume 162] characterizing the degradation of commonly held resources as a result to selfish self-interest in maximizing utility of each individual using the resource.

**Transcapsidation** See *heterologous encapsidation*.

**Transcription** Transfer of information in DNA sequences to produce complementary *messenger RNA* (*mRNA*) sequences. It is the beginning of the process by which the genetic information is translated to functional peptides and proteins.

**Transduction** Gene transfer between bacteria by bacteriophages.

**Transect** 1. Cross-section through which groundwater flows. 2. Straight line placed on a surface along which measurements are taken.

**Transfection** Method by which experimental DNA is inserted into a cultured mammalian cell.

**Transfer RNA (tRNA)** Small RNA that binds an amino acid and delivers it to the ribosome for incorporation into a polypeptide chain during protein synthesis, using an mRNA as a guide.

**Transformation** 1. Chemical change to a substance. 2. Process by which bacterium acquires a plasmid and gains antibiotic resistance. Commonly refers to bench procedure that introduces experimental plasmids into bacteria. 3. Change in cell morphology and behavior, especially related to carcinogenesis. Transformed cell sometimes referred to as transformed phenotype.

**Transgenic** Referring to cells or organisms containing integrated sequences of cloned DNA transferred using techniques of *genetic engineering*.

**Translation** Decoding of *messenger RNA* (*mRNA*) occurs after transcription to produce a specific polypeptide according to the rules specified by the genetic code.

**Translocation** 1. Transfer, usually in plants, of compounds from the *rhizosphere* by *capillarity* to roots, and ultimately to other tissue, especially leaves. 2. Chromosome rearrangement in which two nonhomologous chromosomes are each broken and then repaired in such a way that the resulting chromosomes each contain material from the other chromosome (a reciprocal translocation).

**Transmissivity** Rate at which a fluid of the prevailing kinematic *viscosity* is transmitted through a unit width of the aquifer under a unit hydraulic gradient.

**Transpiration** Process by which water is released to the atmosphere by plants, usually through leaves.

**Treatment** In environmental engineering, the general term for any process that removes or detoxifies a substance.

**Tricarboxylic acid cycle (TAC)** Cycle of the oxidation of *acetyl coenzyme A* to $CO_2$, and the generation of NADH and FADH2 for oxidation in the electron-transport chain; the cycle also supplies carbon skeletons for biosynthesis.

**Trickling filter** Beds of rock and other media covered *biofilm* that aerobically degrades organic waste during secondary sewage treatment.

**Trophic state** *Level of biological organization*.

**Truth** Conformity to fact.

**Turbidity** Scattering and adsorption of light in a fluid, usually caused by suspended matter.

**Turbulence (turbulent flow)** 1. Fluid property characterized by irregular variation in the speed and direction of movement of individual particles or elements of the flow. 2. State of flow of which the fluid is agitated by cross-currents and eddies, as contrasted with *laminar* flow.

**Two-film model** Resistance model in which dissolved compound moves from the bulk fluid through a liquid film to the evaporating surface and then diffuses through a stagnant air film to well-mixed atmosphere above; assumes that chemical is well mixed in the bulk solution below the liquid film and that mass transfer across each film is proportional to the concentration difference.

**Type I error** Error of rejecting a true null hypothesis. Contrast with *type II error*.

**Type II error** Error of accepting (not rejecting) a false null hypothesis. Contrast with *type I error*.

**Ultimate biochemical oxygen demand (BOD$_u$)** 1. Total quantity of oxygen needed for complete degradation of organic material in the first stage of biochemical oxygen demand. 2. Quantity of oxygen required to completely degrade all biodegradable material in a wastewater.

**Ultimate degradation** The final breakdown products of reactions of contaminants; usually carbon dioxide and water but also methane and water for anaerobic systems.

**Ultrafines or ultrafine particulate** Very small particles that are able to infiltrate deeply into lung tissues. Smaller than $PM_{2.5}$.

**Uncertainty** Difference between what is known and what is actually the truth. Scientific uncertainty includes error and unknowns, such as those resulting for selecting variables, undocumented variability, and limitations in measurements and models. In science, there is almost always uncertainty. The goal is to decrease uncertainty and to document known uncertainties.

**Uncertainty factor (UF)** One of several, generally 10-fold, default factors used in operationally deriving the *RfD* and *RfC* from experimental data. The factors are intended to account for (1) variation in *susceptibility* among the members of the human population (i.e., interindividual or intraspecies *variability*); (2) uncertainty in extrapolating animal data to humans (i.e., interspecies uncertainty); (3) uncertainty in extrapolating from data obtained in a study with less-than-lifetime exposure (i.e., extrapolating from subchronic to chronic exposure); (4) uncertainty in extrapolating from a *lowest observed adverse effect level* rather than from a *no-observed-adverse-effect level*; and (5) uncertainty associated with extrapolation when the database is incomplete.

**Unicellular** Describing an organism that consists of a single cell.

**Unit risk** The upper-bound excess lifetime cancer risk estimated to result from continuous exposure to an agent at a concentration of 1 μg L$^{-1}$ in water or 1 μg m$^{-3}$ in air. The interpretation of unit risk would be as follows: if unit risk $= 2 \times 10^{-6}$ per μg L$^{-1}$, two excess cancer cases (upper bound estimate) are expected to develop per 1,000,000 people if exposed daily for a lifetime to 1 μg of the chemical per liter of drinking water.

**Upper bound** A plausible upper limit to the true value of a quantity. This is usually not a true statistical confidence limit.

**Utilitarianism** Theory proposed by Jeremy Bentham (*Principles of Morals and Legislation*, 1789) and James Mill (*Utilitarianism*, 1863) that action should be directed toward achieving the greatest happiness for the greatest number of people (if applied to nonhuman species, this is referred to merely as "greatest number").

**Utility** 1. Useful outcome. 2. Level of enjoyment an individual attains from choosing a certain combination of goods.

**Vadose zone** Unsaturated zone of soil or other unconsolidated material above the water table (i.e., above the *zone of saturation*). Includes root zone, intermediate zone, and capillary fringe. Pore spaces contain water, as well as air and other gases at less than atmospheric pressure. Saturated bodies, such as perched groundwater, may exist in the unsaturated zone, and water pressure within these may be greater than atmospheric. Also known as unsaturated zone.

**Valuation** Quantifying or otherwise placing value on goods and services. Monetized valuation uses monetary currency (e.g., gross domestic product), whereas many environmental and quality of life resources are not readily conducive to monetized valuation, e.g., old growth forests have nonmonetized value (e.g., habitat, ecological diversity) but little monetized value since they are not used for timber.

**Value** 1. Principle, standard, or quality that is good for a person to hold. 2. Worth.

**Value engineering (VE)** Systematic application of recognized techniques by a multidisciplinary team to identify the function of a product or service, establish a worth for that function, generate alternatives through the use of creative thinking, and provide the needed functions to accomplish the original purpose of the project, reliably, and at the lowest life cycle cost without sacrificing safety, necessary quality, and environmental attributes of the project.

**Valve** Device in a pipe that controls the magnitude and direction of flow.

**Vapor** 1. Gas. 2. Gas phase of compound that under standard conditions would not be a gas.

**Vapor pressure** Pressure exerted by a vapor in a confined space.

**Vaporization** Change of a liquid or solid to the vapor phase.

**Variability** 1. True heterogeneity or diversity. For example, among a population that is exposed to airborne pollution from the same source and with the same contaminant concentration, the risks to each person as a result of breathing the polluted air will vary; among a population that drinks water from the same source and with the same contaminant concentration, the risks from consuming the water may vary, i.e., different people drinking different amounts of water and having different body weights, different exposure frequencies, and different exposure durations. Variability exists in every aspect of environmental data, e.g., in transport, fate, exposures, and effects. Overall variability may be due to differences in exposure (i.e., different people drinking different amounts of water and having different body weights, different exposure frequencies, and different exposure durations) as well as differences in response (e.g., genetic differences in resistance to a chemical dose). Differences among individuals in a population are referred to as interindividual variability, and differences for one individual over time are referred to as intraindividual variability. 2. In modeling, the differences in responses and other factors among species, i.e., *interspecies variability*, and within the same species, i.e., *intraspecies variability*, are part of the *uncertainty factors*, important to calculating *reference dose and concentrations.*

**Variety** Distinct population within a species with distinguishing, heritable traits.

**Vector** 1. Vehicle by which genetic material is inserted into a cell (usually a *plasmid* or *virus*). 2. Agent that carries *pathogens* among hosts (e.g., mosquito). 3. In physics, straight line segment with length representing magnitude and orientation in space representing direction.

**Vegetative** In a growth mode, e.g., a vegetative bacterial cell is one that is growing and feeding, in contrast with its *spore.*

**Vertical gene transfer** Crossing of organisms sexually and passing their genes on to following generations (usually called "crossing"). For example, gene transfer via pollen between plants of the same or related species takes place in the wild, so the transfer of disease and pest resistance from cultivated plants to related wild species and vice versa takes place irrespectively to the resistance genes that were initially acquired.

**Vesicle** Arbuscular mycorrhizal fungi's intracellular structures, usually spherical in shape.

*Vibrio* 1. *Anaerobes* of the genus *Vibrio.* 2. Rod-shaped, curved bacterial cell.

**Virology** Branch of microbiology that is concerned with viruses and viral diseases.

**Virulence** Degree of pathogenicity, i.e., the greater the virulence, the more pathogenic the microbe is.

**Virus** Submicroscopic organism typically containing a protein coat surrounding a nucleic acid core, only able to grow in a living cell.

**Viscosity** Molecular attractions with a fluid that evokes a tendency to deform under applied force. Internal friction within a fluid that causes it to resist flow. Absolute or dynamic viscosity is a measure of a fluid's resistance to tangential or shear stress (typical units are centipoises). Kinematic viscosity is the ratio of dynamic viscosity to mass density, obtained by dividing dynamic viscosity by the fluid density (typical units are centistokes).

**Volatile** Capacity to change to the vapor phase, often expressed as *vapor pressure.*

**Volatile acid** Fatty acid containing $\leq 6$ carbon atoms, with relatively high *aqueous solubility.* Often produced by *anaerobes.*

**Volatile organic compound (VOC)** Organic compound that readily evaporates, e.g., benzene, methylene chloride.

**Volatile solids (VS)** Materials, generally organic, that can be driven off from a sample by heating, usually to $550\,°C$ ($1022\,°F$); nonvolatile inorganic solids (ash) remain.

**Volatilization** The transfer of a chemical from its liquid phase to the gas phase.

**Vulnerability** 1. Condition of an individual or population determined by physical, social, economic, and environmental variables, wherein susceptibility to a hazard increases (e.g., asthmatics are more vulnerable to the effects of some pollutants than is the average person). 2. Recently, the term has been a combination of *susceptibility* and high end exposure; i.e., vulnerable subpopulations are those that are both susceptible and receive sufficient levels of exposure for an adverse outcome.

**Vulnerability assessment** The process by which the level of exposure is determined.

**Vulnerability elements** Social, material, or environmental context represented by the people and the resources and services that can be affected during an event. This corresponds to human activities, the systems created by humans, such as houses, roads, infrastructure, production centers, services, the people that use these systems, as well as the environment.

**Waste-activated sludge** Solids taken from the activated-sludge systems to prevent accumulation and an in sludge return to add microbes to increase waste degradation.

**Watershed** Topographic area drained by surface water, wherein all outflows are discharged through a single outlet.

**Weight-of-evidence** Strength of data and information supporting a conclusion. When little reliable data are available, the weight of evidence is lacking, whereas when numerous studies provide reliable information to support a particular position (e.g., exposure to a chemical associated with a health effect), the weight of evidence is strong. Used by regulatory Agencies to characterize the extent to which the available data support a hypothesis, e.g., whether a specific agent causes cancer in humans. Under the U.S. EPA's 1986 risk assessment guidelines, the WOE was described by categories "A through E," i.e., Group A for known human carcinogens through Group E for agents with evidence of noncarcinogenicity. The approach outlined in EPA's guidelines for carcinogen risk assessment (2005) considers all scientific information in determining whether and under what conditions an agent may cause cancer in humans and provides a narrative approach to characterize carcinogenicity rather than categories. Five standard weight-of-evidence descriptors are used as part of the narrative.

**Wetland**  Lands inundated by water at least part of the year, indicated by plants that require or at least tolerate saturated soil conditions for substantial time periods.

**Wilderness**  A large, natural (or nearly natural) region, not controlled by humans.

**Willingness to pay**  Economic concept meaning the most money that people will give for a good or service; depicted by the total area under a demand curve.

**Wisdom**  Insight, erudition, and enlightenment resulting from the accumulation of knowledge and the ability to discern what is meaningful from what is not.

**Work**  Product of a force times the distance through which the force acts.

**Xenobiotic**  1. Compound that is not normally found in natural systems. 2. A general term for an *anthropogenic* substance that is not easily degraded (see *recalcitrant*) by native microbial populations.

**Xenotransplantation**  Transplantation of cells, tissue, and organs between nonrelated species.

**Xerophile**  Organism adapted to dry conditions.

**Yeast**  Unicellular fungus with a single nucleus that reproduces either asexually by budding or fission, or sexually through spore formation.

**Zone of saturation**  Underground layers below the water table where to void space is filled with water. See *aquifer*. Compare to *vadose zone*.

**Zooplankton**  *Fauna* in the *plankton community*.

**Zygote**  *Diploid* cell that results from the fertilization of an egg cell by a sperm cell.

# Index

Note: Page numbers followed by *b* indicate boxes, *f* indicate figures and *t* indicate tables and *np* indicate footnotes.